Export-Oriented Industrialization in Developing Countries

Export-Oriented Industrialization in Developing Countries

HANS LINNEMANN (Editor)
PITOU VAN DIJCK
HARMEN VERBRUGGEN
Free University, Amsterdam

Published for Council for
Asian Manpower Studies, Manila
by Singapore University Press

HC
59.7
.D517
1987

© 1987 Council for Asian Manpower Studies, Manila

ISBN 9971-69-112-4 (Paper)

Typeset by International Typesetters
Printed by Vetak Services

CALIFORNIA STATE UNIVERSITY, HAYWARD
LIBRARY

Contents

PREFACE	xi
1. SETTING AND OBJECT OF THE STUDY	1

Part I. Causes and Characteristics of Export-Oriented Industrialization, by Pitou van Dijck — 7

2. THE CHANGING INTERNATIONAL DIVISION OF LABOUR — 9
 2.1 Introduction — 9
 2.2 The Growth of World Industry since 1960 — 9
  2.2.1 Major Changes in the Location of World Industry — 9
  2.2.2 Growth of Manufacturing Production in Developed Countries — 15
  2.2.3 Growth of Manufacturing Production in Developing Countries — 16
 2.3 The Manufacturing Sector as a Basis for Exports — 18
  2.3.1 Industrial Transformation of Production and Exports — 18
  2.3.2 Industrial Transformation of Production and Exports: A Presentation of Time Series — 20
  2.3.3 Manufactured Export Performance of Developing Countries — 26
 2.4 Summary and Conclusions — 32
  Appendix — 33

3. THE EXPORT ORIENTATION OF THE MANUFACTURING SECTOR — 36
 3.1 Industrialization and Economic Development — 36
 3.2 Export Performance and Patterns of Development — 37
 3.3 Survey of Empirical Studies — 39
 3.4 Hypotheses — 45
  3.4.1 Level of Economic Development — 45
  3.4.2 Level of Industrialization — 46
  3.4.3 Size of the Domestic Market — 47
  3.4.4 Availability of Natural Resources and Population Density — 48
  3.4.5 Export-Stimulation Policies — 49
 3.5 Cross-Country Analysis — 50
  3.5.1 Introduction to the Analysis — 50
  3.5.2 Analysis 1: Three Groups of Countries — 53
  3.5.3 Analyses 2 and 3: The Structural Variables — 54

		3.5.4 Analysis 4: The Role of Population Density Once Again	56
		3.5.5 Analysis 5: Introducing Trade Policy	58
	3.6	Summary and Conclusions	61
		Appendix	63

4. EXPORT STRATEGIES — 65

4.1 Introduction — 65
4.2 Government Intervention and the Trade Regime — 66
4.3 First-Best and Next-Best Systems of Intervention — 74
    4.3.1 The Infant-Industry Argument — 75
    4.3.2 Correcting for Market Imperfections — 76
    4.3.3 Non-Economic Arguments for Intervention — 76
    4.3.4 The Preference for Protection — 78
4.4 Effects of Protection — 80
4.5 Regime Transformation: Reducing the Anti-Trade Bias — 85
    4.5.1 Some General Observations on Regime Transformation — 85
    4.5.2 An Inventory of World Bank Recommendations on Regime Transformation — 86
    4.5.3 The Role of Economic Atmosphere in Regime Transformation — 97
4.6 Processing before Export of Primary Products — 98
4.7 Export-Processing Free Zones — 101
    4.7.1 Characteristics of EPFZs — 101
    4.7.2 The Spread of EPFZs — 102
    4.7.3 The Rationale for Establishing EPFZs — 102
    4.7.4 Types of Activity in EPFZs — 104
    4.7.5 The Contribution of EPFZs to Development — 105
4.8 Foreign Firms in the Export Sector — 106
    4.8.1 The Role of TNCs in Export Production — 106
    4.8.2 The Role of International Trading Houses in the Export Drive — 110
4.9 Summary and Conclusions — 112

5. THE COMPOSITION OF THE EXPORT SECTOR — 114

5.1 Introduction — 114
5.2 Comparative Advantages of Developing Countries: A Review of Trade Theories — 115
    5.2.1 The Neo-Classical Theory of Specialization — 115
    5.2.2 Linder's Theory — 117
    5.2.3 The Product-Cycle Theory — 118
5.3 Challenges to the Explanation of Trade Flows — 119

5.4	Factor Intensities of Manufacturing Sectors	122
	5.4.1 Intersectoral Differences in Factor Inputs	122
	5.4.2 Intersectoral Differences in Wages and Skills	125
	5.4.3 Comparison of Total-, Physical-, and Human-Capital Intensity of Manufacturing Sectors	126
5.5	Classification of Sectors according to Factor Intensities	127
	5.5.1 The Strong Factor-Intensity Assumption	127
	5.5.2 The Order of Ranking of Sectors	130
	5.5.3 A Classification of Manufacturing Sectors	132
5.6	Specialization in Production and Trade	135
	5.6.1 Scope of the Analysis	135
	5.6.2 Variation in the Composition of Production and Exports of Manufactures	137
	5.6.3 Labour-intensive Sectors in Production and Exports of Manufactures	141
	5.6.4 Specialization in Exports to OECD Countries	143
	5.6.5 Skills, Wages and Labour Conditions in Export Industries	149
5.7	The Composition of Manufactured Exports to OECD Countries: Time Series	153
5.8	Summary and Conclusions	161
	Appendix	164
6.	**SUMMARY AND CONCLUSIONS**	170
6.1	The Study	170
6.2	The Changing International Division of Labour	171
6.3	The Export Orientation of the Manufacturing Sector	172
6.4	Export Strategies	173
6.5	The Composition of the Export Sector	175

Part II. Gains from Export-Oriented Industrialization — With Special Reference to South-East Asia, by Harmen Verbruggen 178

7.	**THE IMPACT OF MANUFACTURED EXPORT EXPANSION ON ECONOMIC DEVELOPMENT**	180
7.1	Gains from Trade	180
7.2	Uneven Distribution of Gains from Trade	182
7.3	The Spread Effects of Manufactured Export Expansion	185
7.4	Production and Employment-Reducing Leakages	187
7.5	Linkages to the Primary Sector	189
7.6	Negative Effects on Production and Employment	190
7.7	Balanced versus Unbalanced Growth of Manufactured Exports	192

8. THE MEASUREMENT OF SPREAD EFFECTS OF MANUFACTURED EXPORT EXPANSION 198
- 8.1 Introduction 198
- 8.2 The Input-Output Method 198
- 8.3 Treatment of Imports in Input-Output Tables 200
- 8.4 Some Limitations of the Input-Output Approach 207
- 8.5 Measures of Sectoral Interdependence and Spread Effects 212
  - 8.5.1 Measures in Terms of Production 212
  - 8.5.2 Measures in Terms of Employment 215
  - 8.5.3 Measures of Secondary Production and Employment Effects 219

9. THE PATTERN OF INTERDEPENDENCE AMONG ECONOMIC SECTORS 223
- 9.1 Introduction 223
- 9.2 The Development of the Structure of Production 224
- 9.3 The Hierarchy of Sectors 230
- 9.4 The "Normal" Pattern of Sectoral Interdependence 232
- 9.5 The Pattern of Sectoral Interdependence in Developing Countries 235
- 9.6 The Spread Effects of Manufactured Exports in Developing Countries — A Survey of Empirical Evidence 238

10. FRAMEWORK OF THE INDIVIDUAL COUNTRY STUDIES 244
- 10.1 Introduction 244
- 10.2 Selection of Countries 244
- 10.3 Coverage of the Country Studies 246
- 10.4 Definition of Concepts 248
- 10.5 Description of the Data 251
- Appendix 254

11. THE CASE OF INDONESIA 255
- 11.1 Introductory Remarks 255
- 11.2 Industrialization and Trade Strategies in Indonesia 256
- 11.3 Structural Features of the Indonesian Economy 259
- 11.4 Development and Structure of Indonesian Manufactured Exports 261
- 11.5 Spread Effects of Indonesian Manufactured Exports 267
- 11.6 Summary 269
- Appendix 272

12. THE CASE OF THE PHILIPPINES 274
- 12.1 Introductory Remarks 274

	12.2	Industrialization and Trade Strategies in the Philippines	274
	12.3	Structural Features of the Philippine Economy	277
	12.4	Development and Structure of Philippine Manufactured Exports	280
	12.5	Spread Effects of Philippine Manufactured Exports	285
	12.6	Summary	290
		Appendix	292
13.	THE CASE OF THAILAND		296
	13.1	Introductory Remarks	296
	13.2	Industrialization and Trade Strategies in Thailand	296
	13.3	Structural Features of the Thai Economy	299
	13.4	Development and Structure of Thai Manufactured Exports	302
	13.5	Spread Effects of Thai Manufactured Exports	308
	13.6	Summary	312
		Appendix	313
14.	THE CASE OF SOUTH KOREA		318
	14.1	Introductory Remarks	318
	14.2	Industrialization and Trade Strategies in South Korea	319
	14.3	Structural Features of the Korean Economy	323
	14.4	Development and Structure of Korean Manufactured Exports	326
	14.5	Spread Effects of Korean Manufactured Exports	331
	14.6	Summary	335
		Appendix	337
15.	THE CASE OF TAIWAN		340
	15.1	Introductory Remarks	340
	15.2	Industrialization and Trade Strategies in Taiwan	341
	15.3	Structural Features of the Taiwanese Economy	344
	15.4	Development and Structure of Taiwanese Manufactured Exports	348
	15.5	Spread Effects of Taiwanese Manufactured Exports	354
	15.6	Summary	358
		Appendix	360
16.	THE CASE OF MALAYSIA		363
	16.1	Introductory Remarks	363
	16.2	Industrialization and Trade Strategies in Malaysia	364
	16.3	Structural Features of the Malaysian Economy	367
	16.4	Development and Structure of Malaysian Manufactured Exports	369
	16.5	Spread Effects of Malaysian Manufactured Exports	373

	16.6	Summary	377
		Appendix	378
17.	THE CASE OF SINGAPORE		381
	17.1	Introductory Remarks	381
	17.2	Industrialization and Trade Strategies in Singapore	382
	17.3	Structural Features of the Singapore Economy	387
	17.4	Development and Structure of Singapore's Manufactured Exports	391
	17.5	Spread Effects of Singapore's Manufactured Exports	400
	17.6	Summary	406
		Appendix	408
18.	CROSS-COUNTRY SUMMARY OF FINDINGS AND CONCLUSIONS		416
	18.1	Introduction	416
	18.2	Trade Strategy and the Structure of the Economy	417
	18.3	Trade Strategy and the Structure of Manufactured Exports	419
	18.4	Production Spread Effects of Manufactured Exports	423
	18.5	Employment Spread Effects of Manufactured Exports	428
	18.6	Lessons from South-East Asia's Experience	434

NOTES	438
BIBLIOGRAPHY	450
SUBJECT INDEX	465

Preface

During the years 1981-1985 a research project *Export-Oriented Industrialization and Economic Development in Developing Countries* was undertaken jointly by the Department of Development Economics and Agricultural Economics of the Faculty of Economics, Free University, Amsterdam, and the Council for Asian Manpower Studies (CAMS), Manila. The project received financial support from the special research fund of the Free University and from the Minister for Development Cooperation of the Government of the Netherlands. This support is gratefully acknowledged.

The two institutions cooperating in the project each organized a research team. The CAMS team undertook four in-depth country studies on export-oriented industrialization; the core of this team was formed by Florian A. Alburo (Philippines), Mohamed Ariff (Malaysia), Chia Siow Yue (Singapore) and Somsak Tambunlertchai (Thailand), while Narongchai Akrasanee acted as coordinator. Their research results are reported in a companion volume edited by Chia Siow Yue entitled *Export Incentives and Manufactures in ASEAN Countries*.

The Free University research team was composed of Pitou van Dijck, Els Hoogteijling and Harmen Verbruggen, with Hans Linnemann as project director. The present volume is the result of their efforts. The two principal research economists Pitou van Dijck and Harmen Verbruggen are now on the staff of the Economic and Social Institute of the same university.

For various forms of assistance, the Free University team is indebted to P. Berenst-de Bruijn, F.G. van Dijck, J. Kasow, M. Lindeboom, R.J. Langhammer, W. Niesing, H.P. Smit, Suparman, A.M. Teppema, S.E. Teppema, and S.H. Tjoa. A special word of acknowledgement is due to Wouter Tims whose comments on earlier drafts led to substantial improvements.

Parts of the present volume have been brought out earlier in various forms for limited circulation only. Precursors of (parts of) the final text were:

— P. van Dijck and H. Verbruggen (eds.), *Export-Oriented Industrialization and Employment: Policies and Responses — With Special Reference to ASEAN Countries* (Manila, 1984)
— Harmen Verbruggen, *Gains from Export-Oriented Industrialization in Developing Countries — With Special Reference to South-East Asia* (Amsterdam, 1985)
— Pitou van Dijck, *Causes and Characteristics of Export-Oriented Industrialization in Developing Countries* (Amsterdam, 1986).

Finally, the members of the Amsterdam-based research team would like to express their sincere gratitude towards their colleagues in South-East Asia for the stimulating cooperation in this joint project.

Amsterdam, June 1987

1
Setting and Object of the Study

Export-oriented industrialization is a recent phenomenon in developing countries. It reflects a new stage in their development process and brings about changes in the international division of labour. During the 1950s and early 1960s industrialization already resulted in a transformation of the production structure of developing countries. At that time, however, this transformation was hardly reflected in the structure of exports. In most countries manufacturing production was almost exclusively oriented towards the domestic market while production for exports was heavily concentrated in primary sectors. Increasingly, however, the manufacturing sector in developing countries is becoming a new basis for exports.

This study deals with factors underlying the increasing export orientation of the manufacturing sector in developing countries and with the economic characteristics of export-oriented industrialization. In particular, the study focuses on structural variables that have an impact on the export orientation of the manufacturing sector at large, on the role of trade and industrialization regimes, on the product composition and factor intensities of manufactured exports, and on the spread effects of manufactured exports production in the national economies of developing countries.

The increasing export orientation of the manufacturing sector and the rising share of manufactures in total exports are not merely the inherent outcomes of a "normal" process of growth and transformation. They result as well from shifts in pursued industrialization and trade regimes. There are wide differences between countries in industrialization and trade regimes adopted and such differences are at least in part related to differences in structural characteristics of the economies. Nevertheless, most of the more recently formulated and implemented industrial development strategies emphasize the contribution of the manufacturing sector to export production and include specific instruments to promote export-oriented industries.

This revision in strategies was called for to abolish some of the inherent limitations of more inward-oriented industrialization strategies, as pursued in the past, and to reduce disadvantages of foreign-exchange dependence on primary commodities. Central arguments in favour of export-stimulation policies are the creation of foreign-exchange earnings and of employment opportunities.

For many traditional export commodities of developing countries, market prospects are poor, as compared to market prospects for manufactured exports. As export earnings are a major source for the financing of imports of goods and services which are vital for the continuation and acceleration of growth, policies are required to stimulate non-traditional exports. The recent aggravation of debt-servicing problems has further stressed the need for broadening the export sector.

A good export performance will stimulate growth, but high growth of production does not automatically result in improved living conditions for low-income groups. Experience suggests that, rather than relying merely on the trickle-down effects of growth, policies should be geared directly to reducing poverty. The key to income growth and basic-needs satisfaction for low-income groups is the creation of productive employment opportunities. The contribution of the modern industrial sector to employment creation has, however, been limited due to the unappropriateness of industrial policies. Revising industrial policies to bring the structure of production and the actual choice of techniques more in line with factor availabilities would increase the employment-generating capacity of the industrial sector in labour-surplus economies. The stimulation of labour-intensive industries to produce for world markets may thus contribute to the creation of employment and income opportunities for low-income groups in developing countries.

Revision of the industrialization strategies for the goals stated above — stimulation of foreign-exchange earnings and employment opportunities — is by now widely advocated in the economic literature on industrialization policies, supported by international agencies involved in policy formulation, and increasingly reflected in more recent approaches to industrial development of many governments in developing countries. To a certain degree, export-promotion policies are even imposed upon countries as part of the restructuring programmes to be implemented as a condition for external balance-of-payments support by the IMF and the World Bank.

At the same time, however, this approach to industrial development, which centres around the liberalization of the trade and industrialization regime, the stimulation of labour-intensive export-oriented industries and the attraction of foreign capital in the export sector, has been criticized in the literature for its inherent weaknesses and drawbacks that may frustrate the achievements of the stated goals and may ultimately undermine the capacity of developing countries to sustain development. These conceived weaknesses and drawbacks are not so much related to export production as such but to open and export-oriented development strategies in countries which have a weak domestic economic and technological basis and a high degree of dependence on external factors. The theoretical roots of the criticism are in the *dependencia* model, the centre-periphery model and Marxian and neo-Marxian models of accumulation on a world scale. These models have in common the notion that integration of developing countries in the world economy is the root cause of their underdevelopment. Further integration will not result in the abolition but in the prolongation or even aggravation of underdevelopment. The criticism focuses on (1) the economic and political implications of the policies needed to stimulate manufactured exports; (2) the technological characteristics of the production processes in the export sector and the quality of employment generated in this sector; (3) the limited effects of such a strategy on the creation of foreign exchange and employment.[1] The main points of criticism may be summarized as follows.

First, it is argued that manufactured exports can be generated in low-wage economies only by pursuing specific policies, i.e. by liberalizing the trade and investment regime or by creating separate export enclaves that are specifically designed to attract foreign investment, such as Export-Processing Free Zones (henceforth EPFZs). Consequently, either the economy is integrated more strongly in the world economy or a new export enclave, to a high degree dominated by transnational corporations (henceforth TNCs), is grafted onto the already existing inward-oriented manufacturing sector. TNCs are conceived as the driving forces behind the process of international relocation of industrial production and the manufactured export performance of developing countries. Thus, an increased export orientation of the manufacturing sector is not so much the expression of a mature domestic industry, grown out of its infant stage, but results from particular locational factors that attract foreign firms. Such locational factors are a sufficient supply of disciplined unskilled labour at low wages, an adequate infrastructure, and stimulating government policies. By inviting foreign firms to take part in export-oriented industrialization, developing countries are forced to offer a favourable investment climate, which turns out to be unfavourable for the government budget and for labour conditions. Incentive schemes reduce possible government receipts, whereas the imposition of low-wage regimes results in the curtailment of labour unionism and in political oppression.

Also, export-oriented industrialization policies result in further dependence on foreign firms, external markets and externally designed trade and investment policies. Essentially, the structure and volume of production are highly determined by factors beyond the control of domestic decision makers.

At the same time, such policies reduce the possibilities of a more self-reliant growth path, based on the growth of the domestic market and the development of indigenous and appropriate techniques.

Furthermore, so the argument goes, the pattern of specialization that results from an export-oriented industrialization strategy is at the lower end of the technology spectrum. Comparative advantage is based on an unlimited supply of unskilled and low-wage labour. Specialization is in labour-intensive and/or standardized production processes. The contribution to the creation of a skilled labour force and to technological development is limited since such production is mainly a kind of non-complex assembly activity that is process-specific and routine-like. Possibilities for upgrading and shifting the comparative advantage towards more skill- and capital-intensive sectors are considered to be limited.

Finally, the open trade regime or export-enclave regime, specifically designed to stimulate manufactured exports, results in footloose export activities, dependent on imports of capital goods and intermediate inputs to be processed or assembled. Such an export sector has very few linkages with other manufacturing sectors as well as with the rest of the economy. Indirect production and income effects are limited. The major contribution to income and foreign-exchange creation would be wage income in the export sector itself, which is characterized by low-wage levels.

Surveying the literature on issues related to export-oriented industrialization in developing countries, a dichotomy may be observed as regards the way in which the subject matter is approached. On the one hand, a great deal of the literature on patterns of industrial development, trade policies and comparative advantage bypasses almost entirely the widespread existence of export enclaves such as EPFZs — although over 60 of those were already in operation in developing countries at the beginning of the 1980s — and the important role of TNCs and international trading houses in shaping comparative advantage and export performance. On the other hand, in many studies that focus on the drawbacks of export-oriented industrialization in developing countries, the latter phenomenon is virtually identified with the activities of TNCs and trading houses operating in export enclaves, bypassing almost entirely the internal dynamics in technological development and international competitiveness of the domestic industrial sectors in developing countries.

The ongoing debate on the potential merits and demerits of export-oriented industrialization forms the background of the present study. The study is an attempt to shed light on the issues at stake on the basis of empirical evidence mainly. It is divided into two parts, with roughly speaking Part I concentrating on the international context and using predominantly cross-country analyses, and Part II focusing on the domestic setting and the spread effects of manufactured export production in a number of individual developing countries.[2]

Specifically, Part I examines three related questions. First, it is analyzed what developing countries in particular opt for an export-oriented industrialization strategy. To put it differently: what are the specific structural characteristics of economies with a relatively strong export orientation of the manufacturing sector? In addition to certain common structural characteristics such as the size of the domestic market and the relative endowment with natural resources, it is most likely that national economic policies matter as well. Hence, the second question to be studied is what policies are in fact pursued to stimulate export of manufactures. Here (as in Part II) three different avenues to encourage and increase manufactured exports are distinguished: reduction of the home-market bias in the trade and industrialization regime leading to a change-over from import substitution to manufactured export expansion, stimulation of industrial processing of products from primary sectors before export, and the establishment of new export-oriented industries. Moreover, the role of external economic actors in such policies has to be dealt with. Once the principal causes of export-oriented industrialization have been identified, the third question comes to the fore: what are the characteristics of manufactured export production in terms of labour and skill intensities and relative wage levels? This raises the important issue whether or not the order of ranking of manufacturing sectors according to their factor intensities is stable across countries. As this turns out not to be the case, a "representative" classification for the countries involved has to be established before it can be analyzed to what degree manufactured exports are concentrated in products that are at the lower end of the technology spectrum. As observed already, cross-section analysis over countries figures prominently in the empirical investigations in Part I; the number of countries included varies according to the availability of data.

In Part II the focus shifts to the role played by manufactured exports in the development of the national economy, i.e. to the question of the linkage effects and the actual or potential gains from export production in terms of total spread effects throughout the economy. The impact of manufactured export expansion on economic development can only be properly assessed if the relations between the export sector and the rest of the economy are taken into account. In analyzing the gains that can be realized with exports of manufactures, four sets of effects within the national economy are estimated:

(1) the extent of production stimuli passed on to other sectors of the economy;
(2) the extent of employment effects — direct as well as indirect through interindustry or linkage effects — and the spending of wage incomes on the domestic market;

(3) the degree to which foreign exchange is earned or saved;
(4) the contribution to the integration of the economy.

Based on a quantitative assessment of these spread effects, alternative industrialization strategies can be compared and "evaluated". This requires, of course, that also the specific country characteristics and the actually pursued industrialization and trade strategies have to be an integral part of the analysis.

The empirical analysis of Part II is based on the experience of seven South-East Asian countries, covering Indonesia, Malaysia, the Philippines, Singapore, Thailand — together constituting the ASEAN[3], South Korea and Taiwan. The individual country studies are carried out within a common analytical framework, so that the country findings are sufficiently comparable to have some general validity. The essential features of this framework are determined by the use of the input-output method, which is thought to be an appropriate analytical tool to study the spread effects of economic activities empirically.

The opening paragraphs of each of the two parts give a more detailed overview of the setup of the analysis and the chapter contents. The main findings are summarized in Chapters 6 and 18, respectively.

PART I
CAUSES AND CHARACTERISTICS OF EXPORT-ORIENTED INDUSTRIALIZATION

Pitou van Dijck

Part I analyzes the principal factors underlying the increasing export orientation of the manufacturing sector in developing countries, and the economic characteristics of export-oriented industrialization. The attempt here is to answer three main questions:
(1) What developing countries in particular opt for an export-oriented industrialization strategy, and what factors underly the increased export orientation of industry in developing countries?
(2) What policies are pursued to stimulate export of manufactures, and to what extent is export production a process externally generated by TNCs and international trading houses?
(3) What are the characteristics of the export sector in terms of labour and skill intensities and relative wage levels?

The analysis proceeds as indicated below.

In Chapter 2 we describe the changing position of developing countries in the international division of labour. First we trace changes in the location of manufacturing production since 1960 and the coming into being of new industrial workshops in the world economy. Next we highlight changes in the structure of exports of developing countries and we identify a small but increasing number of countries that play a new role in the world economy as suppliers of manufactures for world markets. Special attention is paid to the process of industrial growth and transformation in East and South-East Asia, which is the most dynamic area in this respect.

In Chapter 3 we analyze the factors underlying the variation across countries in export orientation of the manufacturing sector. The export orientation of the manufacturing sector at large is seen as the outcome of specific structural characteristics of economies and of the trade and industrialization regimes implemented. In other words, it is seen as the outcome of the "normal" pattern of development in countries that have specific structural characteristics in common — provided that their economic policies do not bias the market orientation of the manufacturing sector.

In Chapter 4 we discuss in more detail the role of government intervention in the process of industrialization, and its impact on the market orientation of manufacturing industry. Here we distinguish three avenues that may be pursued to stimulate exports of manufactures: reduction of the anti-trade bias in the trade and industrialization regime, stimulation of processing of natural resources before export, and the creation of a new export-enclave sector. Conflicting views on the merits and demerits of export-oriented industrialization may partly be due to the fact that (implicit) points of reference differ. In the final section of this chapter we discuss the actual role in the export sector of such external economic actors as TNCs and international trading houses.

In Chapter 5 we examine the product composition and factor intensities of manufactured exports. First we review hypotheses of trade theories regarding the factor intensities of manufactures exported by developing countries. Next we analyze differences in capital and skill intensities between manufacturing sectors, and the order of ranking of sectors according to factor intensities in a sample of countries. Stability in this order of ranking is a necessary prerequisite for a universally applicable classification of manufacturing sectors according to factor intensities. Since the outcome of our investigation is that this order of ranking is not stable across countries, we construct a classification of sectors in such a way that it is representative for the classification of manufacturing sectors in the countries in our study. This classification is applied to examine patterns of specialization in manufacturing production and in exports and to relate factor intensities in export production to the level of development of the exporting economy. This analysis shows to what degree exports are concentrated in products that are at the lower end of the spectrum of technology. Finally we examine to what extent such manufactured exports have been upgraded in the course of time.

In Chapter 6 we use the summary of our findings in an attempt to provide answers to the questions formulated earlier on the causes and characteristics of export-oriented industrialization in developing countries.

2
The Changing International Division of Labour

2.1 INTRODUCTION

The position of many developing countries in the international division of labour has been changing significantly for the last 25 years or so. Developing countries can no longer — if ever possible — be adequately characterized as a fairly homogeneous group of countries with relatively low levels of income *per capita* and a strong specialization in the production and exports of primary products. Increasingly, a differentiation is taking place between groups of developing countries, as reflected in wide differences in the level of industrialization, the degree of export orientation of the manufacturing sector, and the contribution of manufactures to total exports.[1]

In this chapter we show in a stylized fashion the changes in the position of developing countries in the world economy and the process of industrial growth and transformation in these economies. Changes in the location of manufacturing production and the coming into being of new industrial centres in the world economy are indicated. The main purpose is to show to what extent the ongoing process of industrialization in developing countries is reflected in the structure of their exports. Our findings indicate that in a small but increasing number of developing countries the manufacturing sector is becoming a new basis for exports, particularly so since the 1970s.

2.2 THE GROWTH OF WORLD INDUSTRY SINCE 1960

2.2.1 Major Changes in the Location of World Industry

Historically, the first steps of an emerging industrialization process in developing countries can be traced back to the end of the 19th century in some countries with a large domestic market such as Argentina, Brazil, Chile, India and Mexico. This process was stimulated in the first half of the 20th century during both World Wars and the great depression in the *interbellum*. Obstacles to international trade during both World Wars and import-restrictive policies because of balance-of-payments problems during the years of depression resulted in decreasing imports of manufactures from traditional suppliers in developed countries, and offered import-substitution possibilities for domestic firms in these developing countries. After World War II, a large number of newly independent developing countries implemented policies that favoured domestic production of manufactures over imports. Import-substitution industrialization policies laid the basis for a widespread and major change in the traditional division of labour between developed and developing countries.

Focusing now on the period 1960–1980, we may distinguish five major changes in the location of world industry. First, the shares of developing countries and centrally-planned economies in world manufacturing production increased substantially. Second, within the "triad" of developed regions, North America, OECD Europe and Japan, the role of Japan rose rapidly. Third, within the "triad" of developing regions, Latin America, Africa and Asia, the countries at the East and South-East Asian edge showed the greatest dynamism. East Asia became a new industrial centre in the world economy. Next, within Latin America manufacturing production was increasingly concentrated, in relative terms, in two traditional regional industrial centres, Brazil and Mexico. Finally, industrialization in Asia was becoming more diffused with the declining role of the traditional industrial centre, India, and the increasing importance of countries in the Middle East and at the East and South-East Asian edge.

Industrial growth in developed and developing countries during the period 1960–1980 is illustrated in Figure 2.1, and the shares of these two groups of countries and of the centrally-planned economies in world manufacturing production are shown in Figure 2.2. Seen at this aggregated level, the shift in the location of world manufacturing industry from developed to developing countries was only limited during the 1960s. Comparison of annual average compound growth rates of manufacturing production in constant prices shows that the growth rate in developed countries (6.3 per cent) was only less than one percentage point below the growth rate in developing countries (7.1 per cent) during this decade (see Table 2.1). However, during the 1970s differences became more pronounced. While developing countries managed to sustain growth of manufacturing production at a rate of 7.1 per cent, notwithstanding the decline in growth at the end of the decade, growth in developed countries in the 1970s was considerably lower than in the previous decade and dropped to only 3.3 per cent.

Figure 2.1
Growth Rates of Manufacturing Production in Developed and Developing Market Economies in Constant Prices, 1961–1980

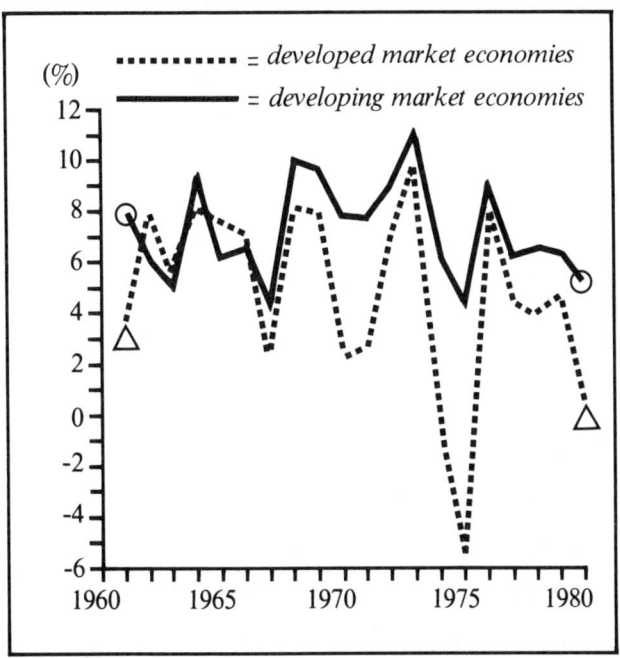

Sources: Growth rates for the period 1961–1970 taken from United Nations, *Yearbook of National Accounts Statistics 1975*, Volume III, New York, 1976, Table 4A. Growth rates for the period 1970–1980 taken from United Nations, *National Accounts Statistics: Analysis of Main Aggregates, 1982*, New York, 1985, Table 7.

According to UNIDO, the share of 94 developing countries in world manufacturing production increased from 8.2 per cent in 1960 to 8.8 per cent in 1970 and 10.9 per cent in 1980. During the same period, the share of 26 developed market economies decreased from 77.8 per cent in 1960 to 72.6 per cent in 1970 and 65.3 per cent in 1980. The contribution of the centrally-planned economies to world manufacturing production increased substantially, from 14.0 per cent in 1960 to 18.6 per cent in 1970 and 23.8 per cent in 1980.[2]

These percentage shares refer to world manufacturing production excluding China, as the latter country's output of manufactures could not accurately be determined. A few comments on this problem are in place.

Figure 2.2
Share of Developed and Developing Market Economies and of Centrally-Planned Economies in World Manufacturing Production (excluding China), 1960–1980

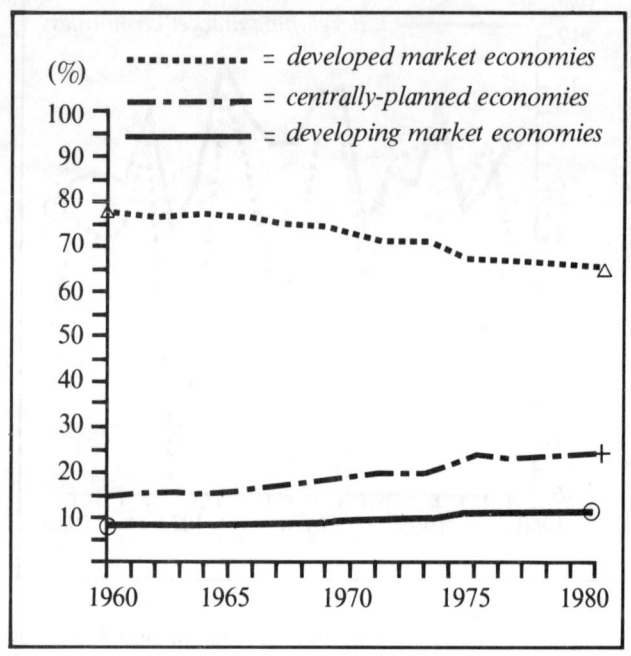

Source : UNIDO, *World Industry in 1980, Regular Issue of the Biennial Industrial Development Survey*, United Nations, New York, 1981, Figure 1, p. 29.

In the UNIDO study *World Industry in 1980*, published in 1981, it was estimated that China's share in world manufacturing value added in 1979 was 7.0 per cent.[3] This is a remarkably high percentage since the share of all other (94) developing countries in the UNIDO sample in 1979 was 9.9 per cent. The UNIDO estimate of the value of manufacturing production in China was made when the findings of the World Bank mission to China in 1980 were not yet published. In the World Bank country study *China: Socialist Economic Development*, published in 1983, *net* output of industry (in the broader sense) including production in brigade industry in 1979 was valued at yuan 160.9 billion. The contribution of industry to gross domestic production (GDP) was estimated at yuan 170.8 billion, which is 43.7 per cent of GDP. The value

TABLE 2.1
GROWTH RATES OF MANUFACTURING PRODUCTION IN THE
1960s AND 1970s
(Annual average percentage growth rates in constant prices)

	1960–1970	1970–1980
Market economies	6.4	3.7
Developed market economies	6.3	3.3
North America	5.4	3.1
Canada	6.0[1]	3.5
USA	5.3	3.1
Japan	..	6.5
Europe	5.8	2.5
European Community	5.6	2.5
France	6.6	3.6
Germany (Fed. Rep.)	5.4	2.2
Italy	7.3	3.8
United Kingdom	3.4	0.1
Developing market economies	7.1	7.1
Caribbean and Latin America	6.7	6.5
Argentina	5.7	1.3
Brazil[2]	9.7	8.7
Chile	5.5	–0.8
Colombia	5.7	5.8
Mexico	9.4	7.0
Venezuela	6.7	5.7
Asia — Middle East	10.4	7.7
Asia — East and South-East (excl. China)	6.8	8.5
China[3]	10.0	9.2
Hong Kong[4]	13.6	10.2
India	4.7	4.7
Indonesia	2.4	14.1
South Korea	17.6	16.6
Philippines	5.8	7.1
Taiwan[5]	20.1	11.8
Thailand	11.0	10.6
Africa	7.3	5.7
Egypt	3.3	6.8[6]

(*cont'd overleaf*)

Symbol: . . = no data available.
Notes and Sources:
[1] relates to the period 1963–1970.
[2] taken from The World Bank, *World Tables, The Third Edition*, Volume I, The Johns Hopkins University Press, Baltimore and London, 1984.
[3] first growth rate relates to the growth of gross output of heavy and light industry in constant prices during the period 1957–1970; second growth rate relates to the period 1970–1979. Data taken from The World Bank, *China: Socialist Economic Development*, Volume II, Washington DC, 1983, p. 110.
[4] taken from The World Bank, *World Tables, The Third Edition*, Volume I.
[5] first growth rate relates to the period 1963–1972; second growth rate relates to the period 1973–1980. Data taken from *Taiwan Statistical Data Book 1981*, Council for Economic Planning and Development, Executive Yuan, Republic of China, 1981, Table 5-2b.
[6] relates to the period 1970–1979.
Unless otherwise indicated, growth rates for the period 1960–1970 taken from United Nations, *Yearbook of National Accounts Statistics, 1979*, Volume II, New York, 1980, Table 6A. Growth rates for the period 1970–1980 taken from United Nations, *National Accounts Statistics: Analysis of Main Aggregates, 1982*, New York, 1985, Table 7.

generated in the manufacturing sector only was estimated at about 35 per cent of GDP, or nearly yuan 137 billion. At the official exchange rate in 1979 (1 US$ = yuan 1.541) this is the equivalent of nearly US$88.9 billion. If we assume a continuation in 1980 of the annual average rate of growth of net industrial output during the period 1970–1979 — 8.3 per cent in current prices — this would result in a value of manufacturing production in China in 1980 of over yuan 148 billion. At the official exchange rate in 1980 (1 US$ = yuan 1.498), this is nearly US$99 billion.[4]

Data on the value of manufacturing production in developed and developing countries in 1980 are presented in Table A.2.1 in the appendix to this chapter. According to those calculations, mainly based on World Bank data, the value of manufacturing production of 26 developed countries was nearly US$2000 billion, while the value of manufacturing production in 98 developing countries, excluding China, was about US$331 billion. The latter figure rises to about US$430 billion when China is included. It can be seen that the UNIDO estimates of the share of developed and developing countries excluding China in world manufacturing production are in line with the results of our calculation. In 1980, the value of manufacturing production in developing countries excluding China was 16.7 per cent of the value of production in developed countries according to UNIDO and our calculations. However, if China is included, UNIDO finds that in 1979 the value of manufacturing production in developing countries was 27.5 per cent of the value of production in developed countries, while we find this to be only 21.7 per cent in 1980.

Returning to the main line of discussion, we note that a more disaggregated view of the process of industrialization during the twenty-year period reveals some significant changes in the location of manufacturing industry within the groups of developed and developing countries. Traditional industrial workshops decline and new industrial centres come into being as is shown in Table 2.1. The table shows annual average growth rates of manufacturing production in constant prices in major regions in the world economy and in selected countries during the decades of the 1960s and 1970s. The 15 developing countries included in the table are the major producers of manufactures in the group of developing countries in 1980. First we focus on growth and transformation in the developed market economies.

2.2.2 Growth of Manufacturing Production in Developed Countries

The fact that manufacturing production in the world economy shifts from the group of developed market economies to the group of developing market economies and centrally-planned economies implies by no means that developed countries have reached a stage of de-industrialization and post-industrial development. It is true that manufacturing in developed countries during the period 1960–1980 was not the most dynamic sector in terms of growth rates. Growth in the sector of transportation and communications exceeded growth in the manufacturing sector, particularly during the 1970s, but such a pattern of growth and transformation was not typical of developed countries since it occurred in middle-income countries as well. De-industrialization, defined as a declining share of manufacturing in GDP, was not a general phenomenon in developed countries up to 1980, but it did take place in OECD Europe during the 1970s. This was mainly due to the relatively low rates of growth of manufacturing production in Germany (Fed. Rep.) and particularly in the United Kingdom. In North America, the contribution of the manufacturing sector to GDP stabilized while in Japan the industrial basis of the economy continued to increase during the era.

Comparison of growth rates of manufacturing production in the major developed areas, North America, OECD Europe and Japan, shows the rise of Japan as a new industrial superpower in the world economy. During the 1970s growth of manufacturing production in Japan proceeded at a pace 2.5 times faster than in OECD Europe and over twice as fast as in the USA (see Table 2.1). The consistently high growth rate in Japan, as compared to other developed countries, has resulted in a significant shift of manufacturing production within the "triad" of developed regions. In 1960, the size of Japan's manufacturing sector, measured in US dollars, was only 10 per cent of that in the USA; in 1970 it was already 29 per cent and in 1980 it was 53 per cent of that in the USA. By that time, Japan had surpassed Germany (Fed. Rep.) as a producer of manufactures and was the second largest industrial power among the developed market economies. Thus, while on balance the size of the manufacturing sectors of North America and OECD Europe *vis-à-vis* each other did not change much during the two decades, the relative size of both regions *vis-à-vis* Japan declined substantially.

2.2.3 Growth of Manufacturing Production in Developing Countries

The two major industrial areas in the group of developing countries are Latin America and East and South-East Asia. Manufacturing production in Africa (excluding South Africa) is still at a very low level. The major producers of manufactures among developing countries are listed in Table 2.2. Historically, Latin America was by far the more developed and industrialized region in the developing world. As early as the beginning of the

TABLE 2.2
MAJOR PRODUCERS OF MANUFACTURES AMONG
DEVELOPING COUNTRIES, 1980

Country	Value of production (million US$)	Share in developing countries' production (percentage)	Cumulative share (percentage)	Share in world production excl. CMEA countries (percentage)
China[1]	98 998	23.01	23.01	4.10
Brazil	55 998	13.02	36.03	2.32
Mexico	42 918	9.98	46.01	1.78
Argentina	38 760	9.01	55.02	1.61
India	24 958	5.80	60.82	1.03
South Korea	16 283	3.78	64.60	0.68
Taiwan	10 695	2.49	67.09	0.44
Venezuela	9 647	2.24	69.33	0.40
Philippines	8 786	2.04	71.37	0.36
Indonesia	8 434	1.96	73.33	0.35
Egypt	7 093	1.65	74.98	0.29
Thailand	6 569	1.53	76.51	0.27
Colombia	6 558	1.52	78.03	0.27
Chile	5 991	1.39	79.42	0.25
Hong Kong	5 908	1.37	80.79	0.24

Note : [1] value is estimated.
Sources : The World Bank, *World Tables, The Third Edition*, Volume I, The Johns Hopkins University Press, Baltimore and London, 1984. Data on China taken from The World Bank, *China: Socialist Economic Development*, Washington DC, 1983, Volume I, Appendix Table A.10; Volume II, pp. 115–119. Data on Taiwan taken from *Taiwan Statistical Data Book 1981*, Council for Economic Planning and Development, Executive Yuan, 1981, Republic of Taiwan, 1981, Table 3–7a.

1960s, the manufacturing sector contributed 18 to 23 per cent to total production in Brazil, Mexico and Chile, and even up to 29 per cent in Argentina, far more than in any other region in the developing world. Due to the upsurge of manufacturing industry in some more recently industrializing areas as the Middle East and the East and South-East Asian countries, the relative share of Latin America in total manufacturing production in developing countries decreased somewhat during the past two decades. Nevertheless, total manufacturing production in Latin America, which amounted to about US$181 billion in 1980, still was 55 per cent of total manufacturing production in developing countries excluding China, and 42 per cent if China is included. As follows from Table 2.1, growth of manufacturing production during the past two decades was particularly high in the two largest Latin-American economies, Brazil and Mexico. Almost all other countries in the region, such as Argentina, Chile, Colombia, Peru and Venezuela, show markedly lower rates of growth throughout the period. This implies that, at least in relative terms, manufacturing production in Latin America became increasingly concentrated in the two regional industrial superpowers Brazil and Mexico.

In contrast to the Latin-American experience, development in Asia shows a relative decline of the traditional regional industrial centre, India, which experienced low growth of its total as well as of its manufacturing production, and a slow industrial transformation of its economy during the two decades under review. The annual average growth rate of manufacturing production in India was only 4.7 per cent, far below the average of all developing countries. It is true that growth of manufacturing production was high in Pakistan during the 1960s and in Bangladesh during the 1970s, but the manufacturing sectors of these two countries of the South-Asian subcontinent have only limited weight in total manufacturing production in developing countries.

The most dynamic developing area in the world economy in terms of growth and transformation during the period under review was East and South-East Asia. While at the beginning of this period the industrial base of the economies in this region was small, they transformed into semi-industrialized countries within a twenty-year timespan and are now as industrialized as the major economies in Latin America, or even more so. Growth rates of manufacturing production in China, Hong Kong, South Korea, Taiwan, Thailand, Malaysia and Singapore (and in Indonesia during the 1970s only) were higher or even much higher than in other developing areas. Growth rates in the Philippines were somewhat lower, but during the 1970s the growth rate of manufacturing production in this country was equal to the average growth rate for all developing countries during the decade.

It follows clearly from the patterns discerned here that a new industrial centre in the world economy is coming into being at the East and South-East Asian edge. Manufacturing production in the developing economies in this area, excluding China, amounted to US$65 billion in 1980, or nearly 20 per cent of total manufacturing production in developing countries. If we include China — with its major industrial centres located at the Pacific border — the share increases to over 38 per cent. Together with Japan, the second industrial workshop among the market economies, this area produced by 1980 nearly 20 per cent of the total value of manufacturing production in the world economy excluding the CMEA countries.

2.3 THE MANUFACTURING SECTOR AS A BASIS FOR EXPORTS

In the previous section we described summarily the diffusion of manufacturing production in the world economy and the industrialization of developing countries during the period 1960–1980. In this section we study the contribution of the manufacturing sector in developing countries to exports and the changing position of developing countries in world trade in manufactures.

2.3.1 Industrial Transformation of Production and Exports

In the initial stage of industrialization, production was predominantly oriented towards the domestic market. This was due to inherent difficulties in entering foreign markets and to the industrialization and trade strategies pursued in most countries during the infant stage of industrialization which favoured import substitution over export production. An import-substitution strategy results in a fairly rapid industrial transformation of the domestic economy in the initial stage of industrialization. Three causes of industrial growth may be distinguished in this stage: (1) growth of domestic demand for manufactures, which is relatively high because of the high elasticity of demand for manufactures at low levels of income *per capita*; (2) substitution for products initially produced by the domestic handicraft sector; (3) substitution for imports, which is stimulated by import barriers. The first two are "natural" causes, inherent in the process of growth and transformation, while the third brings in the government as a lever. When measured in domestic market prices (as is the case in national accounts statistics) instead of world market prices, the industrial transformation of the economy appears to proceed even more rapidly since protection of manufacturing activities causes domestic market prices to exceed world market prices of manufactures. Consequently, the share of manufacturing value added in GDP is artificially raised. However, the industrial transformation of the economy was initially hardly reflected in the export structure for the two reasons mentioned earlier. In this particular sense manufactured export was a rather late and sometimes unduly delayed phenomenon in the transformation process of the economy. During this initial industrialization stage, the export structure reflected the economy's comparative advantage in primary production. Exports are in many countries still dominated by only a few export crops or mining products. Adaptations in industrialization strategies to stimulate manufactured exports were implemented in countries at quite different stages of development and industrialization, depending on the available options for alternative strategies, as will be discussed in Chapters 3 and 4. Growth of industry out of its infant stage and policy adaptations to stimulate manufactured exports resulted in a more industrialized and diversified export structure in some developing countries in the 1960s and more generally in the 1970s.

In low-income countries production is strongly concentrated in the primary sector and the industrial base of the economy is still small. According to World Bank estimates, the weighted-average contribution of the manufacturing sector to GDP in low-income countries (excluding China and India) was only 8 per cent in 1960 and 10 per cent in 1980.[5] The contribution of this group of countries to world manufacturing production or to manufacturing production in developing countries is negligible. This goes as well for their role in world trade in manufactures. In most of these countries, industry is still in its infant stage, inefficient, highly protected and hardly able to contribute to exports. This is particularly true of low-income countries in sub-Saharan Africa where exports still consist almost entirely of unprocessed and some semi-processed primary products.

In the group of low-income countries, China and India are two exceptional cases because of their high degree of industrial transformation in production and exports, and the major role they play as producers and exporters of manufactured products in the group of developing countries. Apart from China and India there are some more low-income countries where the contribution of the manufacturing sector to foreign-exchange earnings is substantial, such as Bangladesh, Pakistan, Nepal and Sri Lanka on the South-Asian subcontinent, as well as Sierra Leone and Haiti. This, however, is not necessarily an indication of overall industrial maturity, as manufactured exports in most of these countries are highly concentrated in only a few product groups and/or are generated in an export enclave.

In the group of middle-income countries the industrial transformation of production and exports proceeded at a much higher rate. According to World Bank estimates, the annual average growth rate of manufacturing production in constant prices in this group of countries was 6.8 per cent in the period 1960–1970 and 6.4 per cent in the period 1970–1980. By 1980, the weighted-average share of the manufacturing sector in GDP in oil-importing middle-income countries was 23 per cent and in oil-exporting countries 16 per cent.[6]

Although for many of these countries it still holds that the contribution of the manufacturing sector to exports is relatively small as compared to its contribution to production, it is also true that the share of manufactures in total exports has been increasing substantially in this group of countries, particularly so since the 1970s, as will be shown later. An extremely high dependence on manufactured exports for foreign-exchange earnings is found in some middle-income countries in East Asia that play a major role in overall manufactured export performance of developing countries, as well as in a series of small island economies in the Caribbean — even though these small countries are only marginal suppliers of manufactures to the world market.

2.3.2 Industrial Transformation of Production and Exports: A Presentation of Time Series

The process of industrial transformation of production and exports in the 15 countries that are the most important producers of manufactures in the group of developing countries (apart from China) is shown graphically in Figure 2.3. The share of these 15 countries in total manufacturing production in developing countries in 1980 was over 80 per cent while their contribution to total manufactured exports of developing countries was 70 per cent. Apart from China and India, all of these countries are middle-income countries. No time series could be constructed for China, the largest industrial workshop in the group of developing countries, but data on the period 1976–1980 are presented below.

Figure 2.3 shows that even at the beginning of the period under review the manufacturing sector was already sizeable in some of the economies such as Argentina, Chile, Mexico, Hong Kong and Taiwan. Typically, in 1960 some Latin-American countries were at a much higher level of development and income *per capita* than the Asian countries. In Venezuela, income *per capita* at the time was over US$1000, in Argentina about US$600 and in Chile about US$500. At the other extreme were Indonesia, Thailand and India with levels of income *per capita* below US$100. Strikingly, the level of industrialization is not reflected in the structure of exports in the Latin-American countries, except Mexico, and in Indonesia, the Philippines and Thailand. In these countries the manufacturing sector hardly contributed to foreign-exchange earnings at the beginning of the 1960s. Exports of manufactures are a rather late phenomenon in the industrial transformation in these countries. The opposite goes for Hong Kong, India, South Korea, Taiwan, Egypt and Mexico, where the manufacturing sector already contributed to exports at an early stage in the process of development.

During the twenty-year period, and particularly in the 1970s, the structure of exports changed substantially in many of the sample countries. In Brazil,

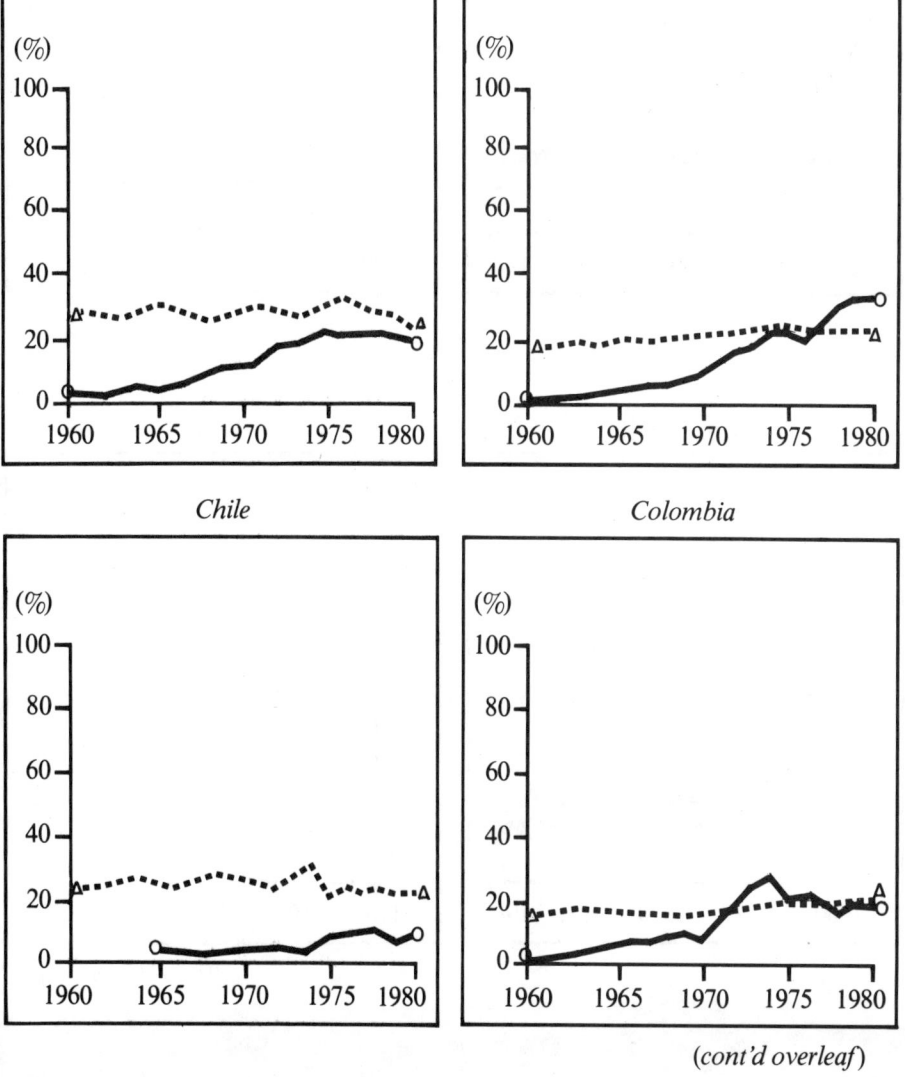

Figure 2.3
Industrial Transformation in 14 Developing Countries, 1960–1980

— = manufactured exports in total exports of goods
····· = manufacturing value added in GDP

(cont'd overleaf)

Figure 2.3 (cont'd)

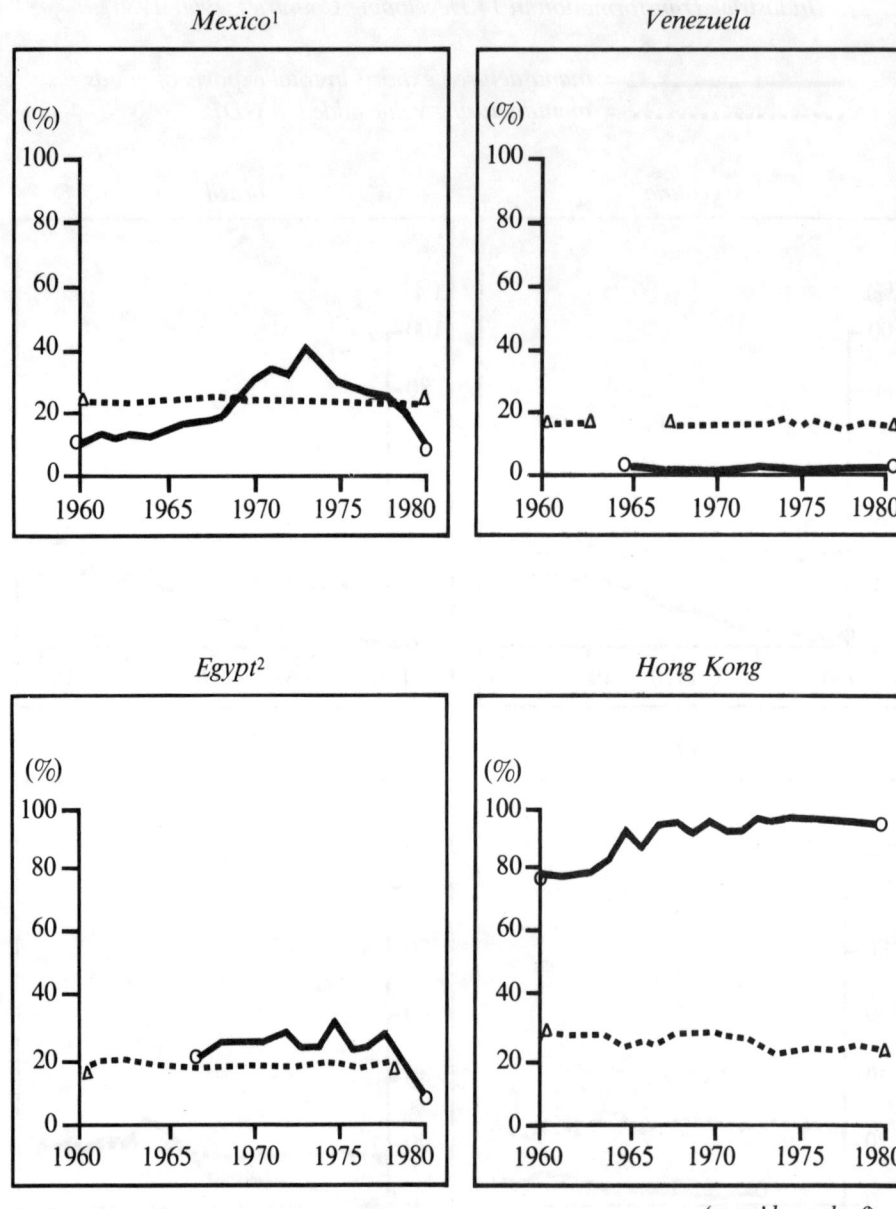

(*cont'd overleaf*)

Figure 2.3 (cont'd)

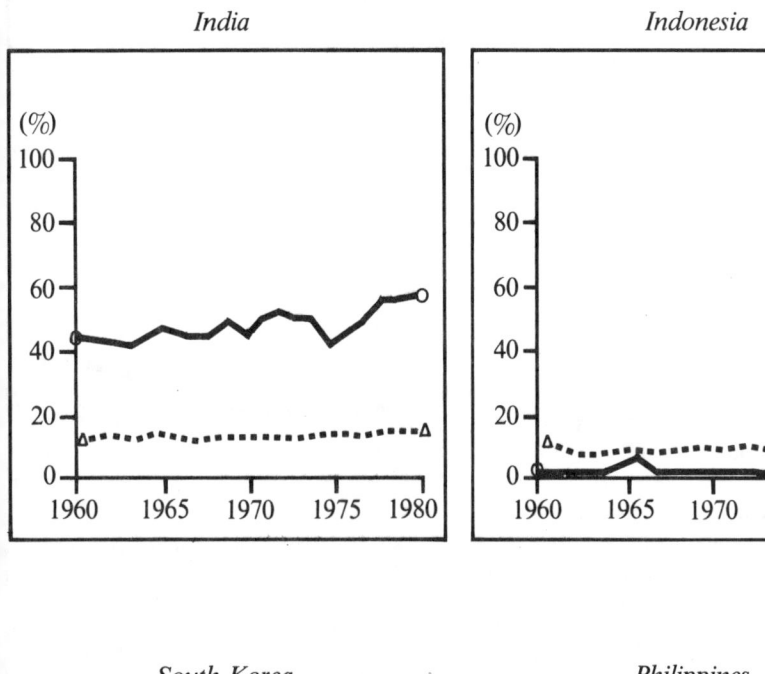

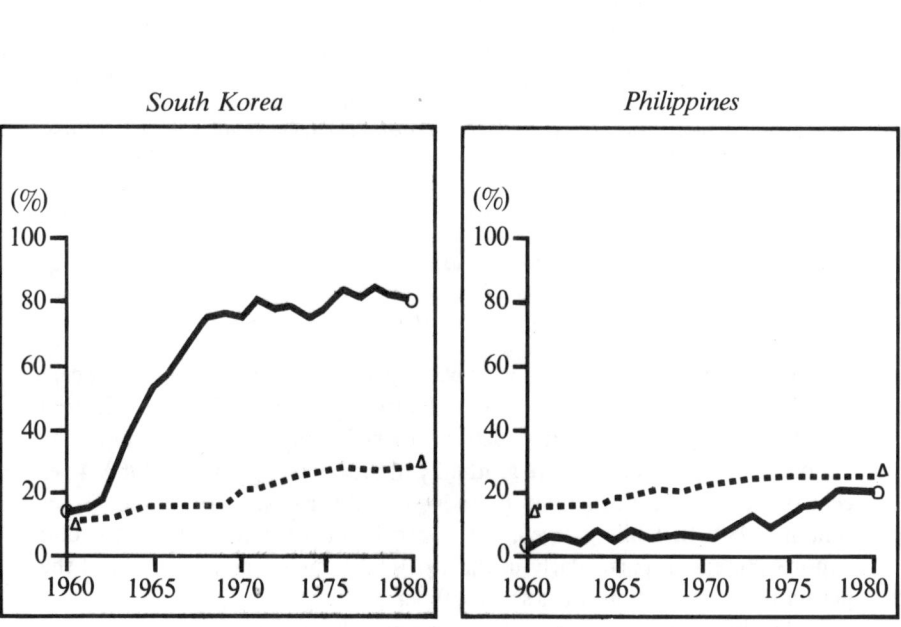

Figure 2.3 (cont'd)

Taiwan

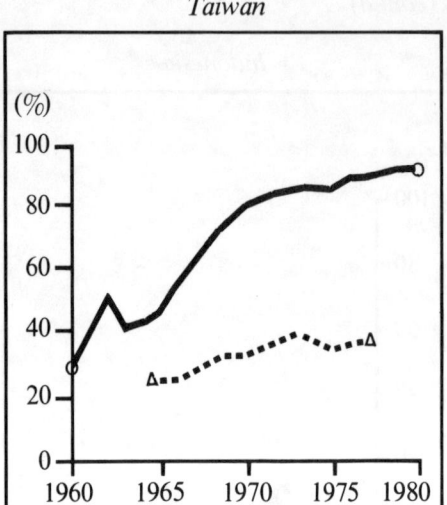

Thailand

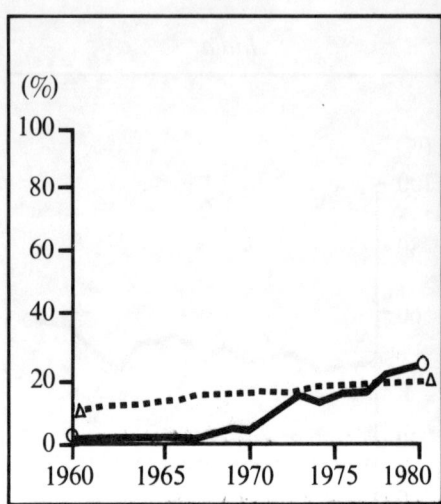

Notes and Sources:
¹ share of manufacturing production in GDP in 1980 taken from United Nations, *National Accounts Statistics: Main Aggregates and Detailed Tables, 1982*, New York, 1985.
² manufacturing includes mining.
Unless otherwise indicated, data on the share of manufacturing production in GDP in the period 1960-1964 taken from The World Bank, *World Tables 1976*, The Johns Hopkins University Press, Baltimore and London, 1976. Data on the period 1965-1969 taken from The World Bank, *World Tables, The Second Edition (1980)*, The Johns Hopkins University Press, Baltimore and London, 1980. Data on the period 1970-1980 taken from The World Bank, *World Tables, The Third Edition*, Volume I, The Johns Hopkins University Press, Baltimore and London, 1984. In the case of Taiwan, all data on the years 1960, 1965-1977 taken from The World Bank, *World Tables, The Second Edition (1980)*.

Data on the share of manufactures in exports taken from UNCTAD, *Handbook of International Trade and Development Statistics*, United Nations, New York, various issues, and United Nations, *Yearbook of International Trade Statistics*, New York, various issues.

the share of manufactures in exports was 2 per cent in 1960, nearly 10 per cent in 1970 and 33 per cent in 1980. Especially after 1973 the industrial transformation of the export structure proceeded rapidly. In Argentina, the export structure changed more gradually in the course of time. In 1960, 4 per cent of exports were generated by industry, 12 per cent in 1970, and 21 per cent in 1980. In Chile as well, the contribution of manufactures to total exports increased, particularly in the 1970s, although even at the end of the period this contribution was less than 9 per cent.

Colombia, too, shows a steadily increasing share of manufactures in total exports. In 1960 this share was only 1 per cent, in 1970 it was 8 per cent and in 1980 nearly 20 per cent. Mexico and Venezuela are two oil-exporting countries that show a different pattern of transition. In Mexico the contribution of the manufacturing sector to exports was 11 per cent in 1960, which is unusually high compared to other countries on the continent. The contribution of manufacturing industry to exports increased remarkably to 41 per cent in 1973. As a consequence of the enormous expansion of the value of oil exports, this share declined to 11 per cent in 1980. However, excluding oil exports, the share of manufactures in total exports was as high as 34 per cent. In Venezuela, oil dominated the export sector completely and manufactures continued to be of marginal importance in exports throughout the period under review.

In the Asian continent, Indonesia is another case of an oil-exporting economy with a low dependence on non-oil products for its export revenue. As compared to the other countries in our sample, the industrial base of this economy is exceptionally small. The sector is heavily protected and not yet capable of exploiting export opportunities. Thailand and the Philippines are two cases in which the transformation of the export sector proceeded at an increasing rate in the 1970s. In the Philippines only 3 per cent of exports were manufactures in 1960; in 1970 this share was 6 per cent and by 1980 it was 20 per cent. In Thailand the initial contribution of manufacturing industry to exports was even smaller: 1 per cent. This share rose slowly to 4 per cent in 1970, but in the next decade it increased to 24 per cent. Hong Kong, India, South Korea and Taiwan all are heavily dependent on manufactures as a source of foreign-exchange earnings and in all four countries this was the case throughout the period 1960–1980, particularly so in Hong Kong. South Korea and Taiwan are two cases *par excellence* of an early and rapid transformation of the export structure. India, being one of the older industrial workshops among the developing countries, has a long industrial tradition and the industrial sector's contribution to the country's export performance was significant throughout the 1960s and 1970s. In 1960, 44 per cent of total exports were manufactured products. At that time the country ranked as one of the major exporters of manufactures among the developing countries, a position that has by now been overtaken by some East-Asian economies.

The only African country in our sample of most industrialized developing countries is Egypt. No data on the structure of exports are available for the period before 1965. During the period 1965–1978 the share of manufactures in exports fluctuated between 22 and 32 per cent. Here again, oil changed the structure of exports abruptly in the 1970s. While in 1970 oil contributed less than 5 per cent to export earnings, this share increased to 64 per cent in 1980. Excluding oil, 29 per cent of exports were manufactured products in 1980.

No consistent set of data is available on the contribution of the manufacturing sector to production and exports in China during the period 1960–1980. In Table 2.3 we present data for the period 1976–1980.

TABLE 2.3
PRODUCTION AND EXPORTS OF MANUFACTURES IN CHINA, 1976-1980

Year	Share of manufacturing production in GDP (percentage)	Share of manufactures[1] in total exports (percentage)
1976	..	45.4
1977	..	46.4
1978	44.2	46.3
1979	43.5	46.4
1980	44.1	43.6[2]

Symbol: .. = no data available.
Notes : [1] SITC sections 5-8.
[2] estimated share.
Sources: data on the share of manufacturing production in GDP taken from The World Bank, *World Tables, The Third Edition*, The Johns Hopkins University Press, Baltimore and London, 1984. Data on the share of manufactures in total exports taken from The World Bank, *China: Socialist Economic Development*, Volume II, Washington DC, 1983, pp. 152, 424, 425.

For a discussion on the value of manufacturing production in China, see Section 2.2 of this Chapter.

The contribution of the manufacturing sector to GDP is remarkably large in proportion to the low level of income *per capita* in China, which was only US$290 in 1980. Transformation of the structure of exports in China appears to be a rather recent phenomenon. According to the World Bank, 82 per cent of total exports in 1953, and 72 per cent in 1957, were unprocessed and processed agricultural products.[7] By 1976, the share of primary products in exports was only 55 per cent. Here again oil exports, increasing rapidly since the end of the 1970s, change the export structure.

2.3.3 Manufactured Export Performance of Developing Countries

Reviewing the export structure of the entire list of nearly 140 developing countries included in the international trade statistics of the UN, we find the following 23 countries that are to a high degree — over 40 per cent — dependent on manufactured exports for their commodity-export earnings. The percentage shares of manufactures in total exports of goods in 1980 are presented within brackets.

Low-income Asia: Bangladesh (67.7), India (57.7), Pakistan (48.2) and China (46.4).
Low-income Africa: Sierra Leone (63.4 in 1976).

Low-income Latin America: Haiti (48.0 in 1979).
Middle-income Asia: Macao (96.6), Hong Kong (95.6), Taiwan (90.8), South Korea (80.1) and Singapore (45.6).
Middle-income Latin America: Antigua and Barbuda (76.6 in 1978), Montserrat (41.5 in 1978), Jamaica (62.1), Barbados (51.5), Bermuda (45.4 and 83.3 in 1982), Cayman Islands (42.7), Saint Lucia (42.3) and Puerto Rico (no recent data available).
Middle-income Middle East and the Mediterranean area: Malta (93.5), Lebanon (72.5 in 1977), Cyprus (55.0) and Yemen (42.6 and 73.0 in 1981). Another case is Israel (81.3), but this country is not always classified as a developing country. However, out of this fairly large number of countries —many of them small (island) economies — only a few play a major role in overall manufactured export performance of developing countries.

Total manufactured export performance of developing countries is dominated by a relatively small group of countries. Table 2.4 shows that over 50 per cent of total manufactured exports of developing countries are generated by four extremely export-oriented East-Asian economies: Taiwan, South Korea, Hong Kong and Singapore. Including China, we find that over 65 per cent of all manufactured exports of developing countries are from East and South-East Asia.

The value of manufactured exports from China increased rapidly in the recent past. Its growth rate in current domestic prices was 13 per cent in 1977, 28 per cent in 1978, 41 per cent in 1979 and 28 per cent in 1980. According to the World Bank, the value of manufactured exports in 1979 was US$6.3 billion.[8] Manufactured exports are promoted as part of the policy to finance import of modern technology. For that purpose, special export zones are created at the Pacific border.

In Latin America, Brazil is by far the most important exporting economy. At the end of the 1970s manufactured exports were specially stimulated to cope with debt-servicing problems. During the period 1977–1980 the growth of the value of manufactured exports in current US dollars exceeded 30 per cent each year.

The role of India in the manufactured export performance of developing countries declined substantially. While its share in 1960 was 23.7 per cent, it was only 9.9 per cent in 1970 and dropped further to only 4.2 per cent in 1980. However, as is reflected in more recent government plans, some attempts are currently undertaken to stimulate export production.

Malaysia, Thailand and the Philippines pursue policies to diversify their export structure and to stimulate the growth of export-oriented industry. Manufactured export performance and export-oriented industrialization policies in these countries as well as in Indonesia, South Korea, Taiwan and Singapore are analyzed in Part II, Chapters 11–17 of this volume. Industrial

TABLE 2.4
MAJOR EXPORTERS OF MANUFACTURES AMONG DEVELOPING COUNTRIES, 1980

Country	Value of manufactured exports (million US$)	Share in developing countries' exports of manufactures (percentage)	Cumulative share (percentage)	Share in world exports of manufactures (percentage)
Taiwan	17 990	17.33	17.33	1.77
South Korea	13 972	13.46	30.79	1.38
Hong Kong	13 069	12.59	43.38	1.29
Singapore	8 835	8.51	51.89	0.87
China[1]	8 119	7.82	59.71	0.80
Brazil	6 609	6.37	66.08	0.65
India	4 319	4.16	70.24	0.43
Malaysia	2 411	2.32	72.56	0.24
Kuwait	2 080	2.00	74.56	0.20
Argentina	1 713	1.65	76.21	0.17
Mexico	1 679	1.62	77.83	0.17
Thailand	1 554	1.50	79.33	0.15
Pakistan	1 247	1.20	80.53	0.12
Philippines	1 165	1.12	81.65	0.11

Note : [1] value is estimated.
Sources: UNCTAD, *Handbook of International Trade and Development Statistics, Supplement 1984,* United Nations, New York, 1984, Table 4.1. Data on Taiwan taken from *Taiwan Statistical Data Book 1981,* Council for Economic Planning and Development, Executive Yuan, Republic of Taiwan, 1981, Table 10-8. Data on China taken from The World Bank, *China: Socialist Economic Development,* Volume II, Washington DC, 1983, pp. 152, 424, 425.

transformation in Thailand and the Philippines is depicted in Figure. 2.3. In Malaysia, the current US dollar value of manufactured exports increased by 28.8 per cent annually during the 1970s. Much of the growth and transformation of exports is attributable to the special export zones that have been established since 1972. By 1980, 18.6 per cent of total exports consisted of manufactures.

Together, the 14 developing countries included in Table 2.4 produced nearly 82 per cent of the total value of manufactured exports of developing countries. The value of manufactured exports in all other countries was less than one billion US dollars in 1980 and each of them contributed less than 1 per cent to total manufactured exports of developing countries. All the previously mentioned small Mediterranean and Caribbean countries that are highly dependent on manufactured exports for commodity-export earnings are marginal suppliers.

The substantial transformation of the structure of exports of developing countries, taken as a group, during the period 1960–1980, and the increasing importance of the manufacturing sector as a source of foreign-exchange earnings are shown in Figure 2.4. The share of manufactures in total exports almost doubled from nearly 9 per cent in 1960 to over 17 per cent in 1980. The upward-moving trend in this share was uninterrupted during the period 1960–1973. In 1973, the share of manufactures was 20.2 per cent of total exports. The upsurge in oil prices in October and December of 1973 caused a threefold increase in the value of oil exports from 1973 to 1974, and a reduction in the share of all other product groups in total exports of developing countries. The share of oil in the export value of developing countries increased from 39.5 per cent in 1973 to 60.3 per cent in 1974 while

Figure 2.4
Share of Manufactures in Total Exports of Developing Countries (excluding China), 1960–1980

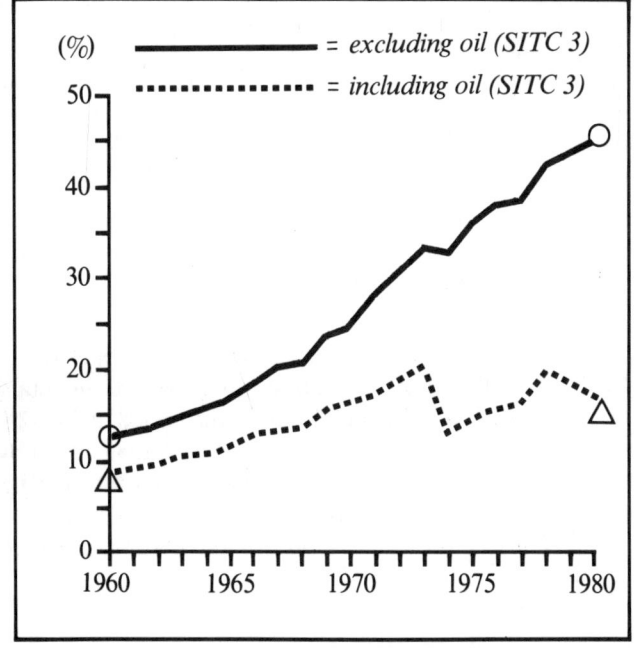

Sources: UNCTAD, *Handbook of International Trade and Development Statistics*, United Nations, New York, various issues.

the share of manufactures dropped from 20.2 per cent to 13.1 per cent. In subsequent years the latter share increased gradually to 20.1 per cent in 1978. A new upsurge in oil prices in that year caused the value of oil exports to increase by 48 per cent. By 1980 total exports of developing countries consisted of the following main categories: oil and related products (62.0 per cent), all other non-processed and semi-processed primary products (20.0 per cent), manufactured products (17.1 per cent). A more detailed breakdown is given in Table 2.5.

TABLE 2.5
COMPOSITION OF EXPORTS OF DEVELOPING COUNTRIES
(EXCLUDING CHINA), 1980

Product category	SITC code	Export value (million US$)	Share in exports (percentage)
Food items	0+1+22+4	63 269	11.33
Agricultural raw materials	2−(22+27+28)	20 105	3.60
Crude fertilizers, crude minerals, metalliferous ores and metal scrap	27+28	13 036	2.23
Mineral fuels, lubricants and related materials	3	346 465	62.03
Iron and steel and non-ferrous metals	67+68	15 275	2.73
Manufactures	5+6+7+8−(67+68)	95 704	17.13
All products	0−9	558 579	100.00

Sources: UNCTAD, *Handbook of International Trade and Development Statistics, Supplement 1984*, New York, 1984, Tables A.1–A.10.

To neutralize the impact of changes in prices and export values of oil, Figure 2.4 also gives the share of manufactured exports in total exports exclusive of products in SITC group 3 during the period 1960–1980. From 1960 to 1970 the share of manufactures in exports excluding oil doubled from 12.4 per cent to 24.9 per cent. From 1970 to 1980 it increased to 45.1 per cent.

The data presented here do not include exports of China. From data presented in the World Bank China report of 1983, we made the following estimates of China's exports in 1980.[9]

	(million US$)
Total exports	18 635
Fuels	3 333
Manufactures	8 119

Whether or not China is included, the contribution of developing countries to world trade in manufactures is still limited. This is not surprising in view of the size of the markets of developing countries as compared to developed countries. Large domestic markets, liberal trade regimes and, in the case of OECD Europe, small distances stimulate trade among developed countries, which was 57.6 per cent of world trade in manufactures in 1980. The share of developing countries in world trade in manufactures increased substantially during the period 1960–1980, and particularly so during the 1970s, as is shown in Figure 2.5. In 1960 the contribution of all developing countries to world trade in manufactures was no more than 4.2 per cent and in 1970 only slightly higher: 5.3 per cent. During the 1970s this share increased to 9.4 per cent in 1980. If China is included the share is 10.2 per cent in 1980.

Figure 2.5
Share of Developing Countries (excluding China) in World Trade in Manufactures, 1960–1980

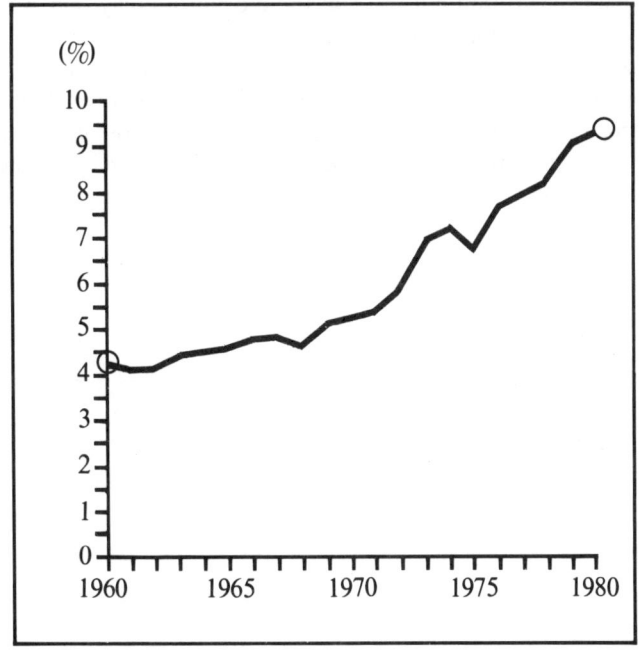

Sources: UNCTAD, *Handbook of International Trade and Development Statistics*, United Nations, New York, various issues.

2.4 SUMMARY AND CONCLUSIONS

In this chapter we have described the industrial transformation of the structure of production and exports in developing countries. We have shown that new industrial centres in the world economy are coming into being, most notably in Latin America and in South-East and East Asia. The growth of manufacturing production and exports is particularly high in the latter region.

In the initial stages of industrialization production was almost exclusively oriented towards the domestic market. Even at the beginning of the 1980s it was still true that many developing countries, particularly low-income countries, were almost entirely dependent on primary production for their foreign-exchange earnings. The manufacturing sector in these economies is still small and not capable of penetrating world markets. However, in an increasing number of countries, most of which are middle-income countries, the manufacturing sector is becoming a new basis for exports as is reflected by an increasing share of manufactures in exports. By 1980, the contribution of the manufacturing sector to the value of non-oil exports of goods of developing countries was over 45 per cent. A fairly large number of developing countries is to a high degree dependent on manufactures for their foreign-exchange earnings but most of these countries play only a marginal role in world trade in manufactures.

The next two chapters will deal with the causes of the increasing export orientation of the manufacturing sector in developing countries. In Chapter 3 we shall analyze the factors underlying the variation across countries in the export orientation of the manufacturing sector at large, while Chapter 4 will focus in more detail on the impact of economic policy on export performance.

APPENDIX TABLE A. 2.1
PRODUCTION AND EXPORTS OF MANUFACTURES IN DEVELOPING COUNTRIES, 1980

Country	Value of manufacturing production (million US$)	Share of manufacturing production in GDP (percentage)	Value of manufacturing exports (million US$)	Share of manufactures in exports (percentage)
China[1]	98 998	35.0	8 119	43.6
Brazil	55 998	22.0	6 609	32.8
Mexico	42 918	23.1	1 679	11.0
Argentina	38 760	25.3	1 713	21.4
India	24 958	15.4	4 319	57.5
South Korea	16 283	28.0	13 972	80.1
Taiwan	10 695	34.3	17 990	90.8
Venezuela	9 647	16.2	216	1.1
Philippines	8 786	24.8	1 165	20.3
Indonesia	8 434	11.6	482	2.2
Egypt	7 093	31.0	317	10.4
Thailand	6 569	19.6	1 554	24.4
Colombia	6 558	19.6	774	19.6
Chile	5 991	21.5	397	8.7
Hong Kong	5 908	26.0	13 069	95.6
Saudi Arabia	5 763	5.0	698	0.6
Iran	5 688	6.5	213[2]	0.8[2]
Peru	5 430	28.0	530	16.2
Malaysia	5 205	21.9	2 411	18.6
Puerto Rico	5 377	35.0	..	..
Algeria	4 476	11.1	27	0.2
Nigeria	4 304	..	49[4]	0.3[4]
Pakistan	3 545	14.8	1 247	48.2
Singapore	3 340	29.5	8 835	45.6
Iraq	3 199	6.5	53[3]	0.5[3]
Morocco	3 051	17.1	565	23.5
Syrian Arab Rep.	2 557	18.9	124[4]	7.5[4]
Uruguay	2 522	24.6	394	37.2
Ivory Coast	1 252	11.9	193[4]	7.7[4]
Zimbabwe	1 313	23.9	133[4]	12.5[4]
Uganda	1 166	3.5	..	..
United Arab Emirates	1 131	3.8	311[3]	3.4[3]

(cont'd overleaf)

APPENDIX TABLE A.2.1 (cont'd)

Country	Value of manufacturing production (million US$)	Share of manufacturing production in GDP (percentage)	Value of manufacturing exports (million US$)	Share of manufactures in exports (percentage)
Ghana	1 072	7.2	11[4]	1.3[4]
Tunisia	1 026	11.8	796	35.6
Dominican Rep.	1 006	15.1	64	9.1
Ecuador	1 004	8.8	74	3.0
Other developing countries[5]	19 189			
All developing countries excluding China	331 214		95 704	17.1
All developing countries	430 212		103 823	18.0
Developed market economies	1 981 479[6]		837 933	66.5

Symbol: .. = no data available.

Notes:
[1] values of manufacturing production and exports estimated.
[2] relates to 1977.
[3] relates to 1978.
[4] relates to 1979.
[5] other developing countries (63): Angola, Bangladesh, Barbados, Belize, Benin, Bolivia, Botswana, Burma, Burundi, UR of Cameroon, Cape Verde, Central African Rep., Chad, Congo People's Rep., Costa Rica, Cyprus, El Salvador, Ethiopia, Fiji, Gabon, Gambia, Grenada, Guatemala, Guinea, Guinea-Bissau, Guyana, Haiti, Honduras, Jamaica, Jordan, Kenya, Lesotho, Liberia, Madagascar, Malawi, Mali, Malta, Mauritania, Mauritius, Mozambique, Nepal, Nicaragua, Niger, Panama, Papua New Guinea, Paraguay, Rwanda, Sao Tome and Principe, Senegal, Sierra Leone, Sri Lanka, Sudan, UR of Tanzania, Togo, Trinidad and Tobago, Upper Volta (Burkina Faso), Yemen Arab Rep., Zaire, Zambia, Bahrain, Kuwait, Libyan Arab Rep., Oman.
[6] developed countries (26): Australia, Austria, Belgium, Canada, Denmark, Finland, France, Germany (Fed. Rep.), Greece, Ireland, Israel, Italy, Japan, Luxembourg, Netherlands, New Zealand, Norway, Portugal, South Africa, Spain, Sweden, Switzerland, Turkey, United Kingdom, USA, Yugoslavia.

Sources: the main source of data on the value of manufacturing production, the share of manufacturing production in GDP and exchange rates is The World Bank, *World Tables, The Third Edition*, Volume I, The Johns Hopkins University Press, Baltimore and London, 1984. Additional sources: United Nations, *National Accounts Statistics: Main Aggregates and Detailed Tables, 1982*, New York, 1985; UNCTAD, *Handbook of International Trade and Development Statistics, 1984 Supplement*, United Nations, New York, 1984, Table 6.4; OECD, *Industrial Structure Statistics 1982*, Paris, 1984. Data on China taken from The World Bank,

China: Socialist Economic Development, Washington DC, 1983, Volume I, Appendix Table A.10, p. 290; Volume II, pp. 115-119. Data on Taiwan taken from *Taiwan Statistical Data Book 1981,* Council for Economic Planning and Development, Executive Yuan, Republic of Taiwan, 1981, Table 3-7a.

Data on value of manufactured exports and the share of manufactures in exports taken from UNCTAD, *Handbook of International Trade and Development Statistics, 1984 Supplement,* Tables 4.1, A.1, A.6, A.9, A.10, except for data on China and Taiwan. Data on China taken from The World Bank, *China: Socialist Economic Development,* Volume II, pp. 152, 424, 425. Data on Taiwan taken from *Taiwan Statistical Data Book 1981,* Table 10-8.

3
The Export Orientation of the Manufacturing Sector

3.1 INDUSTRIALIZATION AND ECONOMIC DEVELOPMENT

The process of transformation of an economy oriented towards production and exports of primary products into an economy oriented towards production and exports of manufactures is the outcome of a set of changes that is closely interrelated with the change in the level of income *per capita* in the economy. In that sense the level of income *per capita* is a general indicator of the overall level of development of an economy and of its comparative advantage. Many dimensions of the transformation of an economy during the process of development, i.e. with rising levels of income *per capita*, have been studied by Kuznets, Maizels, Chenery and others.[1] On the demand side, growth of income *per capita* is accompanied by a shift in demand from primary products to manufactured products and services. On the supply side, accumulation of physical and human capital is accompanied by a shift in comparative advantage from labour-intensive, agricultural activities towards more capital- and skill-intensive industrial production processes. Consequently, up to a certain point there is a strong positive correlation between the level of income *per capita* and the level of industrialization of the economy.

Given the level of income *per capita* of an economy, differences between countries with respect to the share of the manufacturing sector in GDP may result from differences in structural variables such as population size and natural-resource endowment, in policy-related variables such as the trade and industrialization regime, and access to foreign capital.[2] The size factor has a positive impact on the level of industrialization of the economy since it facilitates the rise of industries that require a relatively large (domestic) market in order to operate efficiently. An economy well endowed with natural resources or with considerable areas of arable land *per capita* tends to be relatively specialized in the production and exports of primary products as compared to an economy poorly endowed with natural resources at the same level of income *per capita*. Stimulation of manufacturing industry has been a priority in almost all developing countries for economic and non-economic reasons. Modernization and growth have virtually been identified with industrialization. Government policies have usually been biased in favour of industrial development, often at the expense of the agricultural sector. This is reflected in the setting of priorities in investment plans, price policies and the trade regimes. While the (net) effective rate of protection for manufacturing industry is substantial, it is negative for agricultural activities in many countries.[3] This bias against agricultural activities intensifies the dual character of the economy, increases income disparities between urban and rural areas and stimulates urbanization.[4] Above all, these policies have an impact on the size, structure and market orientation of the manufacturing sector. Finally, net capital inflow may have a positive impact on industrialization since it adds to the domestic accumulation of resources. Size and allocation of capital inflow are not independent of the other factors mentioned above that underly the industrialization of the economy. The main locational factor for foreign investment oriented towards the domestic market of the host country is the size of the (protected) domestic market. For export-oriented foreign investment, the availability of a "suitable" labour force is the major locational factor. For processing of primary resources, a rich natural-resource endowment is the major locational factor. Government policies with respect to investment, industrialization and trade determine to what extent this potential to attract foreign investment turns into actual capital inflow.

The variables introduced above are central to our analysis throughout this study of the transformation of the production and export structure of developing countries. They offer a framework to distinguish countries according to their comparative advantage, options for inward-oriented and export-oriented industrialization, the selection of trade and industrialization strategy and the potential or need to attract foreign capital.

3.2 EXPORT PERFORMANCE AND PATTERNS OF DEVELOPMENT

An increasing export orientation of the manufacturing sector, accompanied by a rising share of manufactures in total exports, is part of the "normal" pattern of structural change in the growth process of developing countries. Up to a certain point, growth of income *per capita* is "normally" accompanied by an increasing share of the manufacturing sector in total domestic production. The industrial transformation of the structure of production is reflected in the structure of exports with a time lag that may vary considerably among countries, as was shown in the previous chapter.[5] In general, export of manufactures is a relatively late phenomenon. In the initial phase of industrialization, production is oriented towards the domestic market and the growth of manufactured output is determined by import-substitution possibilities and the growth rate of domestic demand. After a certain period, the contribution of import substitution to growth decreases and, once a number of preconditions are fulfilled, exports can create a new momentum for the process of industrialization. Although this sequence of events appears to be a "normal" pattern of development, there are significant differences in the export orientation of the manufacturing sector between countries that are at similar levels of income *per capita*. To a large extent, these differences can be explained by two major structural characteristics of the economy, i.e. the size of the domestic market and natural-resource endowment. These factors influence the economy's pattern of specialization and have an impact on the relative value and the composition of exports.

Apart from these structural variables affecting the viability of industrialization strategies, still other factors may influence the outward orientation of the manufacturing sector and its capability of penetrating world markets; this holds in particular for the economic policies pursued. In the next chapter we shall discuss in more detail several strategies that countries may pursue to stimulate exports of manufactured products. Countries have the option to revise or abandon an anti-trade biased protectionist industrialization strategy. Also, they may create an export enclave unrelated to the manufacturing sector already in existence. Gradual dismantling of the traditional protectionist industrialization regime may be a hard and time-consuming process towards the end of an initial stage of inward-oriented industrial development. Export stimulation through the creation of an export enclave, however, may take place irrespective of the stage of development of domestic industry. Within this range of options some countries, particularly but not exclusively countries well endowed with natural resources, may focus on the processing of primary products before exporting. This diversity in the choice of strategies complicates the explanation of the export performance of countries.

The process of footloose export production gained momentum in the 1970s with a rapidly increasing number of developing countries setting up EPFZs or comparable facilities to stimulate export production. This may finally thwart any systematic relationship between a country's overall level of development, indicated by its level of income *per capita*, and its export performance. Indeed, as Chenery and Hughes put it, "countries are becoming industrial exporters at different stages in their development and with widely varying factor endowments and technological skills".[6] Successful early industrial specialization and export orientation may, according to Chenery, result from "rather special social and political characteristics" which are hard to identify accurately such as entrepreneurship, the quality of the labour force, and the wage regime.[7] Hofheinz and Calder refer to a host of social and cultural factors to explain the export success of the countries at East Asia's edge.[8] This implies that an explanation of a country's export performance may not be fully adequate when confined to purely "economic" factors only.

3.3 SURVEY OF EMPIRICAL STUDIES

A first attempt to identify factors that explain differences in manufactured export performance between developing countries was made in an UNCTAD study of 1969.[9] The study suggests that manufactured exports *per capita*, which is the variable to be explained, are likely to be affected by four variables. The first variable is a structural country characteristic, namely the availability of natural resources for primary production, measured by the variable hectares of arable land *per capita*. The underlying assumption is that countries that are amply endowed with natural resources and that have a low population pressure on arable land will tend to specialize in primary exports. On the other hand, a country with a poor endowment of natural resources and a high population pressure on arable land may tend to export manufactures. The second variable indicates that a certain level of manufacturing production for the domestic market is a necessary precondition for entering world markets successfully. The importance of technical and managerial know-how for a country's international competitiveness, which results from learning-by-doing, is approximated by the percentage share of the population employed in manufacturing. The third variable takes into consideration that a developing country may stimulate its manufacturing capacity by attracting foreign direct investment and foreign aid. It is expected that the variable inflow of official aid *per capita*, which is a proxy for the total inflow of private capital as well, will be positively related to a country's manufactured export performance. In addition to these three variables on the supply side, a fourth variable on the demand side is introduced. This variable suggests that membership of a preferential trade area will increase the level of manufactured exports *per capita*.

Estimation of the impact of these variables on manufactured exports *per capita* is based on data from 53 developing countries and refers to exports of manufactures from these countries to the major developed countries only.[10] Manufactured exports comprise products in SITC sections 5-8 as well as some semi-processed and processed primary products from SITC sections 0–4.[11] The result of the estimation is the following:

$$X = -1.95 - 2.51\ H + 1.41\ L + 0.22\ F + 3.39\ P_c + 5.61\ P_f \qquad \bar{R}^2 : 0.41$$
$$(0.87)\ \ \ (0.27)\ \ \ (0.07)\ \ (1.27)\ \ \ (1.72)$$

where

- X = manufactured exports *per capita* in US dollars, 1966
- H = hectares of arable land *per capita*, base year 1961
- L = percentage share of total population employed in manufacturing, base year 1961
- F = annual average official foreign aid *per capita* in US dollars, 1961–1965
- P_c = membership of the Commonwealth preference system, dummy variable
- P_f = membership of the French and Belgian preference systems, dummy variable
- $\bar{R}^2$ is the adjusted coefficient of determination. Figures in parentheses are standard errors.

The explanatory variables are all statistically significant and have the expected sign: the availability of arable land *per capita* is negatively associated with developing countries' manufactured export performance; the level of industrialization, the inflow of official aid in the recent past, and membership in a preference system have a positive impact on a country's manufactured export performance.

Another inquiry into the determining factors of the manufactured export performance of developing countries was undertaken by Mahfuzur Rahman, who assumed that these factors are to be found on the supply side only.[12] Protection in developed countries against competition from developing countries may indeed be a serious impediment to export expansion. However, so Mahfuzur Rahman's argument goes, as no systematic discrimination against specific individual developing countries exists, it follows that protection as such does not explain why some countries are more successful than others in penetrating world markets. This clearly contradicts the findings of the UNCTAD study, discussed above, in which it was found that membership in a preferential trade system has a significant positive impact on a country's export performance. On the supply side, Mahfuzur Rahman distinguishes six variables that might explain the value of manufactured exports of a country. First, the absolute size of a country's manufacturing sector is expected to affect the value of manufactured exports positively. Second, it is expected that there is a positive relationship between a country's level of industrialization, expressed as the share of manufacturing in GDP, and the value of manufactured exports. Both factors are based on the assumption that an economy should at least be industrialized up to a certain level before it can penetrate world markets successfully. Third, a positive relationship is expected between the value of manufactured exports and the degree of diversification of these exports. Diversification is expressed by a Gini coefficient. Fourth, a positive relationship is expected between the value of exports and the number of export markets: the more market outlets, the larger the value of exports. Here again, a Gini coefficient measures diversification in export flows. However, this measure does not take into account the widely different sizes of the markets and the geographical distances between trade partners. Therefore, the fourth explanatory variable is standardized to abstract from such influences. The corrected Gini coefficient for market concentration is the fifth explanatory variable. Finally, a proxy for the market orientation of the economy is constructed. It is suggested that the number of export flows, defined as the export of any one manufactured product to any one foreign market, reflects the degree of outward orientation of the economy. The index of the foreign-market orientation of the exporting economy i, N_i, represents the number of X_{ij}^h, which is the export flow of product h from country i to country j. So, the greater the number of flows of manufactures to foreign countries, the more the economy is outward-oriented, which will have a positive impact on the value of manufactured exports. The hypothesis is that the industrialization and trade policies behind this orientation influence the value of exports.

The six explanatory variables above are regressed separately against the value of manufactured exports as the dependent variable. The analysis is based on data on export flows from 37 developing countries to 11 developed countries. Manufactured exports comprise SITC sections 5-8 less natural-resource-based products. The results of the regression analyses are unsatisfactory for all but one explanatory variable. The explanatory power of the first five variables appears to be very small. Only the index of the market orientation yields a highly significant result, as follows from the results below.

$log\ X = -0.51 + 1.43\ log\ N$ $R^2 : 0.81$
             (0.12)

where
X = value of manufactured exports in millions of US dollars
N = number of flows at the three digits SITC level.
Figures in parentheses are standard errors.

When the size of the manufacturing sector or the share of manufacturing in GDP is regressed in combination with the index of foreign-market orientation against the value of manufactured exports, the first two variables fail to be statistically significant, while the index of foreign-market orientation remains highly significant. The results of these multiple regressions are as follows:

$$\log X = -0.54 + 0.02 \log Ym + 1.41 \log N \qquad R^2 : 0.81$$
$$\qquad\qquad\quad (0.13) \qquad\quad (0.16)$$

$$\log X = -0.17 - 0.36 \log Ym/Y + 1.50 \log N \qquad R^2 : 0.81$$
$$\qquad\qquad\quad (0.37) \qquad\qquad (0.14)$$

where
Ym = value of manufacturing production in millions of US dollars
Ym/Y = percentage share of manufacturing in GDP.

The variables Ym and Ym/Y are not significant and Ym/Y has the wrong sign. Apparently neither the absolute size of the manufacturing sector nor its share in GDP is a necessary precondition for successful export performance. From the results, Mahfuzur Rahman concludes that "(i)n so far as the number of flows is an appropriate index of foreign-market orientation, the result strongly supports our hypothesis that it is such orientation of the economy that principally determines the volume of its export of manufactures".[13]

Mahfuzur Rahman's regression analyses were repeated in a UNIDO study for the years 1965 and 1971.[14] The same variables are used to analyze the export performance of ten developing countries. The results of the UNIDO study strongly support the above findings: the index of foreign-market orientation again is the only significant variable.

Next we shall discuss Morrison's study on the determinants of developing countries' export performance.[15] Like Mahfuzur Rahman's, Morrison's analysis includes supply factors only. Trade liberalization in developed countries may favour export growth of developing countries but the realization of increased export opportunities depends on the ability of developing countries to produce for world markets. From various trade theories Morrison selects four country characteristics that may affect a country's export performance. The first explanatory variable is the size of the domestic market. A large domestic market may favour export performance as it enables a country to realize economies of scale in the domestic market, which may result in a comparative advantage in products, the production process of which is characterized by increasing returns to scale. However, a large domestic market need not be a necessary precondition for successful export performance. According to Morrison, countries may specialize in exports of products that do not require large-scale production in order to be produced efficiently, such as assembly and processing operations that are subcontracted. Additionally, a large domestic market may result in a rather poor export performance as it may favour an import-substitution policy. With such a policy, production for the home market is favoured over export production. Thus, on balance, the impact of a large domestic market on a country's export performance is not self-evident. Second, analyses of patterns of development suggest that there is a positive relationship between the level of economic development and the export orientation of the manufacturing sector. However, Morrison argues that a relatively high level of economic development is not a necessary precondition for successful export performance. Not unlikely, the higher the level of economic development of a country, the more sophisticated its manufactured exports will be. But there is no reason why countries at low levels of development should not be successful in exporting traditional or standardized products. The experience of a number of developing countries shows that the handicaps of a small domestic market and a low level of industrial development are surmountable. However, it seems likely that the range of products in which small economies at low levels of development may have a comparative advantage is narrow. A third country characteristic, dealt with in Morrison's study, is a country's natural endowment. It is assumed that there is an inverse relationship between the availability of natural resources and the ability, or necessity, to export manufactures. Finally, the availability of a skilled labour force is assumed to have a positive impact on the diversity of a country's manufactured exports and is therefore positively related to a country's export performance.

The four factors mentioned above are called structural country characteristics as they are fixed in the short run. Apart from these structural characteristics, Morrison investigates the impact of some factors that are not fixed but that depend on economic policy, such as the level of protection, the rate of inflation and government's commitment to export stimulation. A high level of protection, an overvalued exchange rate and relatively high levels of inflation have often accompanied import-substitution policies and have reduced a country's ability to compete in world markets. On the other hand, specific export-stimulation schemes may compensate for the negative impact of import-substitution policies on the export performance and are therefore expected to result in a higher level of manufactured exports.

In a cross-country analysis Morrison tests the impact of the abovementioned variables on export performance. Export performance is approximated by two separate variables: manufactured exports *per capita* and manufactured exports as a share of manufacturing production. Manufactured exports are defined as SITC sections 5-8 less all marginally processed primary products. Export data relate to exports to OECD countries only. From the set of regressions, based on different sets of variables and countries, we select two equations, related to the export flows from 45 developing countries.[16] The results of the estimations are the following:[17]

$$\ln Xc = -15 + 0.41 \ln N + 2.2 \ln Y + 0.72 \ln D + 1.1 \ln O - 0.05 \ln P -$$
$$\quad\quad\quad\quad (2.3)\quad\quad (5.9)\quad\quad (4.3)\quad\quad (2.3)\quad\quad (0.16)$$

$$\quad - 0.42 \ln L \quad\quad\quad\quad R^2 : 0.64$$
$$\quad\quad (1.6)$$

$$\ln Xs = -7 + 0.37 \ln N + 1.0 \ln Y + 0.44 \ln D + 1.3 \ln O - 0.62 \ln P -$$
$$\quad\quad\quad\quad (2.1)\quad\quad (2.7)\quad\quad (2.6)\quad\quad (2.6)\quad\quad (1.7)$$

$$\quad - 0.48 \ln L \quad\quad\quad\quad R^2 : 0.44$$
$$\quad\quad (1.8)$$

where
Xc = annual average manufactured exports *per capita* in US dollars, 1968–1970
Xs = annual average share of manufactured exports in manufacturing value added, 1968–1970
N = total population, 1969
Y = GDP *per capita* in US dollars, 1969
D = population divided by total land area, 1969
O = share of imported goods in the increase of consumption of finished manufactured goods in the period 1963–1969
P = consumer price index for 1970 (1963 = 100)
L = per cent of population that is literate.
Figures in parentheses are t-statistics.

The explanatory variables approximate the factors domestic market size (N), level of economic development (Y), natural-resource endowment (inverse) (D), level of protection (inverse)(O), rate of inflation (P) and labour skills (L). A proxy for export-stimulation schemes could not be constructed. The results of the regression analysis show that manufactured export performance is positively and significantly related to the size of the domestic market, the level of development, population density and the degree of openness. The impact of the level of inflation and of the availability of skilled labour on a country's export performance is not significant.

According to Morrison, none of the factors is a necessary precondition for successful export performance. The impact of the size factor remains uncertain. The factor loses its significance in regressions based on both larger and smaller samples than the sample used for the regressions presented here. In another study, in which Morrison regresses the value of manufactured exports *per capita* on GNP *per capita*, population size and population density, the variable population size has a significant negative impact.[18] Next, although the level of development appears to have a significant impact on the export performance, Morrison does not wish to conclude that a certain minimal level of development is a precondition for export of manufactures in view of the countries that appear to be successful exporters at low income levels, such as Haiti, India and Pakistan.[19] His findings show countries with a successful export performance to have a relatively poor natural-resource endowment. It is true that countries well endowed with natural resources might start processing such primary exports but these processed primary products are excluded from the analysis. Morrison finally concludes that there is not one type of developing country that is successful in exporting manufactures, and that implementation of export-stimulation policies is most likely the decisive factor for a country's manufactured export performance. This factor is partly reflected in the openness index, but its full impact could not be tested empirically.

3.4 HYPOTHESES

In the previous section we discussed structural variables as well as policy-related variables that are likely to be relevant to the explanation of the export performance of developing countries. However, the results of the studies discussed above do not appear to be conclusive, and the causes of recent changes in the international division of labour and in the export performance of developing countries have not yet been adequately revealed. From the mid-1960s onwards, more and more developing countries have been changing their industrialization strategy more or less comprehensively from a basically inward-oriented towards a more export-oriented strategy. Export production has gained momentum since the 1970s as was shown in Chapter 2. This is the very reason why the empirical reality of the 1950s and 1960s differs from that of the 1970s. The studies discussed above are mainly based on observations from the import-substitution era and from the period during which at most a gradual transition towards export-oriented strategies was implemented in only a few countries. In order to set up a framework for a new investigation into the determining factors of the export performance of developing countries during the 1970s, we shall summarize the findings of some other studies and formulate hypotheses for our analyses.

3.4.1 Level of Economic Development

In studies on development patterns, as those by Chenery, an increasing level of income *per capita* is associated with an increasing share of manufacturing production and of manufactured exports in GDP. These patterns are based on cross-country data on developing and developed countries. However, if the wide range of levels of income *per capita* is reduced by excluding the group of developed countries from the analysis, the variable income *per capita* may cease to be statistically significant. This is shown by Balassa, who introduces a dummy variable in Chenery-style equations in order to differentiate between developed and developing countries.[20] From the studies that specifically focus on the manufactured export performance of developing countries, only in Morrison's study does income *per capita* have a significant impact on manufactured exports *per capita*. The variable of income *per capita* does not appear in the UNCTAD study nor in Mahfuzur Rahman's study and the subsequent UNIDO analysis.

We assume that a certain level of economic development is not a necessary precondition for successful export performance when a country specializes in the production and export of unskilled labour-intensive and standardized products for which no sophisticated production techniques are required. The same holds if manufactured exports are concentrated in assembly activities or in the processing of imported components in foreign-owned or foreign-controlled firms. One can even imagine that — as far as a low level of economic development results in low average wage levels — low-income countries may have a cost advantage in these lines of production compared to developing countries at higher income levels. This will be discussed in more detail in Chapter 5 where we deal with comparative advantages of developing countries at different levels of income *per capita*. Therefore, we hypothesize that income *per capita* has no significant effect on the export orientation of the manufacturing sector.

3.4.2 Level of Industrialization

This variable can be conceived of as an alternative proxy for the level of economic development as there is a strong correlation between the level of income *per capita* and the share of the manufacturing sector in the economy. The level of industrial development can also be expressed as the share of the industrial labour force in the total labour force, or in total population. Presumably, in all developing countries, manufacturing production is almost completely oriented towards the domestic market at the very beginning of the process of industrialization. We expect that the industrialization level has an impact on the composition of manufactured exports. Countries that have reached a relatively high level of industrialization will have a more diversified manufacturing sector — and hence more diversified manufactured exports —than countries at relatively low levels of industrialization. But countries at low levels of industrialization may well specialize in unsophisticated and standardized manufactured exports. Our hypothesis may therefore be that there is no significant relationship between the level of industrialization of an economy and the export orientation of its manufacturing sector.

3.4.3 Size of the Domestic Market

Chenery's studies on development patterns show that at the same level of income *per capita* the level of industrialization is systematically higher in large countries than in small countries. These studies also show that small countries are relatively more involved in international trade than large countries. In analyzing the impact of the domestic market size on a country's export performance, we should distinguish between the volume and the composition of manufactured exports. According to Linder's theory, which will be discussed in Chapter 5, the range of a country's potential exports is determined by the level of domestic "representative demand", as production for domestic demand precedes production for foreign demand. Because of economies of scale, the size of the domestic market does have an impact on the range of exportable manufactures: at a given level of income *per capita*, the range of exportables will be smaller in small countries than in large countries.

Keesing investigates the relationship between country size and the volume of trade by using population size alongside of income *per capita* as an explanatory variable for manufactured exports *per capita*. His hypothesis is that small countries find their comparative advantage outside the manufacturing sector and thus have a relatively low level of manufactured exports *per capita*.[21] This is analyzed at a disaggregated level for 40 groups of manufactured products. From Keesing's results it follows that the variable population size is significant, but it is more often so in the small sample ($n = 18$) that includes developed countries only, than in the extended sample ($n = 31$) that includes developed and developing countries. In the latter sample, the income effect becomes more predominant in the explanation, and for 21 of 40 product groups the size effect is not significant. This tunes down a bit Keesing's rigorous conclusion that "(s)mall countries appeared to experience a comparative disadvantage in most of the important manufacturing industries, uncompensated by a comparative advantage in others".[22] However, it appears that the size effect is of significant importance in the manufacturing sectors of machinery and transport equipment (SITC section 7). This supports the thesis that small countries have a comparative disadvantage in industries where economies of scale are of importance.

Keesing and Sherk experiment with Chenery-style equations using income *per capita*, population size and population density as variables to explain manufactured exports *per capita* and the share of manufactures in total exports. Their hypothesis with respect to the size effect is "that large countries enjoy a comparative advantage in manufactures, compared to small countries, even after taking into account differences in natural resources".[23] The regression analyses aim at explaining the export performance of developed and developing countries in separate equations. Regressions based on data for 26 developing countries show that (1) there is a positive and significant relationship between population size and the share of total manufactured exports in total exports; (2) there is a positive relationship between population size and the value of total manufactured exports *per capita* but this relationship is not statistically significant; (3) a special equation, based on data from SITC section 7 only, is unrevealing with respect to the size effect. Keesing and Sherk conclude that "large countries enjoy major advantages over small countries in manufacturing".[24]

Balassa calls in question the relevance of the results of Keesing's 1968 study, which is based on disaggregated data. Indeed, there may be a size effect for specific products or product groups but this does not imply that the value of total manufactured exports *per capita* is positively associated with the size of the domestic market. Small developing countries may be highly specialized and very successful in the exports of only a few manufactures for which scale economies are not of great importance. By doing so, they may reach high levels of manufactured exports *per capita*. From Balassa's regression analysis it follows that the size effect is not significant for the explanation of total manufactured exports *per capita*, but size has a positive and significant effect on the overall share of manufactures in total exports. From this, Balassa concludes that "small countries are at some disadvantage in the international trade of manufactured goods although the size effect explains only a relatively small part of intercountry variations in trade patterns".[25]

We hypothesize that small countries will be more export-oriented than large countries and that manufactured exports in small countries will be relatively more concentrated in sectors of production that do not require large-scale production in order to be efficient.

3.4.4 Availability of Natural Resources and Population Density

The impact of the availability of natural resources on the primary or industrial orientation of production, and consequently on the pattern of trade, stands all empirical tests, in any case with respect to small countries. Countries poorly endowed with natural resources are "forced" to an industrial orientation in production and export. Keesing and Sherk postulate a negative correlation between population density and "the combined availability of mineral wealth, arable land, and other economically useful endowments from nature" on a *per capita* basis.[26] The variable population density may then be a proxy for (the inverse of) the availability of natural resources *per capita*. The variable population density as such stands for the number of people per unit of land area. In developing countries, a high population density in rural areas may result in low levels of labour productivity and the existence of surplus labour. The existence of a surplus labour force, i.e. an elastic supply of labour to manufacturing industry, may be a favourable condition for the expansion of labour-intensive manufacturing (export) industries.

We hypothesize that there will be a positive relationship between population density and the export orientation of the manufacturing sector. If densely populated developing countries are characterized by a poor natural-resource endowment and an abundant supply of (unskilled) labour, there will be only limited opportunities to finance imports with exports of natural resources and consequently there will be a tendency to stimulate labour-intensive manufactured exports to finance the required imports.

3.4.5 Export-Stimulation Policies

The hypotheses formulated so far are all related to the impact of structural variables on the export orientation of industry. The underlying assumption is that, to a high degree, structural country characteristics determine the market orientation of manufacturing industry. This, however, does not imply that government policies are insignificant. Although the options from which policy makers have to choose may be limited by structural characteristics of the economy, there are internal and external factors, independent of these characteristics, that may influence the actual choice of economic policies. Deliberate and consistent policies do affect the market orientation of the manufacturing sector and seeing the process of industrial development as exclusively the outcome of the working of structural variables would be too mechanistic an approach.

In the previous section we reviewed some regression analyses of the export performance of developing countries that included policy variables. In Mahzufur Rahman's study, an index for outward orientation is used that is supposed to reflect the trade and industrialization regime. Morrison also applies several variables to show the impact of policies, such as a proxy for the openness of the economy to foreign supply of manufactures and a proxy for inflation. Donges and Riedel estimate the impact of a policy change from import substitution towards export promotion in a time series analysis by means of a dummy variable. They conclude, despite some exceptions, that "the strong association between policy reorientation and improved export performance does suggest that the government has leverage".[27]

The need to focus on export-stimulation policies may occur at different moments during the development process, because of differences in the economic structure between countries. Small countries may feel the need of a re-orientation in production at an earlier moment during the growth process of the industrial sector than large countries, as the latter group of countries has more opportunities for import substitution in sectors where economies of scale are important. Resource-rich countries may postpone a re-orientation in industrialization policy as they continue to finance imports with exports of primary products. Consequently, policies are to be analyzed within the framework of a country's possibilities and necessities. However, within this framework there are still degrees of freedom. A country amply endowed with natural resources may nevertheless decide to generate manufactured exports if its export earnings from primary products are stagnating or fluctuating too strongly. The implementation of an industrial export policy can also be part of a strategy to diminish a heavy dependence on only a small number of primary export products, which makes the economy vulnerable to the effects of policies by importing countries.

The need of foreign exchange has been a factor influencing policies in almost all developing countries, particularly so since the 1970s. Many developing countries suffer from balance-of-payments problems and problems of servicing debts. In order to finance imports that are required to maintain relatively high rates of growth, countries are forced to increase their export efforts. Additionally, in order to obtain access to foreign loans, countries are required to improve their trade balance by implementing changes in the trade regime. This may lead to devaluations, import controls and export-stimulation policies.

Our hypothesis is that this need of foreign exchange has stimulated countries to adopt policies that favour manufactured export production. The relationship between trade and industrialization policies and the export orientation of the manufacturing sector will be investigated by introducing a trade-policy variable into the analysis. As will be discussed in more detail in Chapter 4, countries can stimulate exports of the manufacturing sector by reducing protection. It is true that this relationship between protection and export performance may be rather weak. Countries can continue to foster domestic-market-oriented industrialization through import barriers while at the same time promoting manufactured exports through compensating facilities or by concentrating the manufactured export activities in an enclave such as an EPFZ. Despite these complications, we may hypothesize that there will be a negative relationship between the level of protection and the export orientation of the manufacturing sector.

3.5 CROSS-COUNTRY ANALYSIS

3.5.1 Introduction to the Analysis

On the basis of the various hypotheses formulated in the previous sections, a number of empirical cross-country analyses have been made. For the purpose of these analyses, manufactured exports are defined as SITC sections 5–8 less 67 and 68. Deliberately, a number of processed products from SITC sections 0–4 and resource-based semi-manufactures from SITC sections 67 and 68 are excluded. Manufactured exports are defined narrowly because of the specific relationship between the availability of natural resources in an economy and the manufactured export performance that is to be investigated. In contrast to some studies, manufactured exports relate to the total flow of these products to all countries.

As follows from the review of studies presented earlier, various measures that represent a country's manufactured export performance are in use. These measures differ in scope and are not interchangeable. For the analysis of intercountry differences in export performance a relative measure is used. Absolute measures are inadequate because of large differences in the size of countries. To analyze intercountry differences in the outward orientation of the manufacturing sector, i.e. differences in countries' capacity or necessity to export part of their manufacturing production, we use the export-output ratio in manufacturing industry as the dependent variable in the regression analysis. All developing and developed countries for which this ratio could be constructed are included. The study of developing countries' manufactured export performance is subdivided into five successive steps.

The following variables are used.

Dependent variable:
E_m/O_m = ratio of the value of manufactured exports (E_m) to the value of manufacturing production (O_m), expressed as a percentage

Independent variables:
GNP/P = Gross National Production *per capita* in US dollars
P = size of population in thousands of inhabitants
D = density of population, i.e. the number of inhabitants per km² of land area
Da = density of population on arable land, i.e. the number of inhabitants per km² of arable land area
T^m = average tariff rate, i.e. the ratio of total import duty revenue (T^m) to the value of total imports (M), expressed as a percentage
T^m/M_m = average tariff rate on manufactures, i.e. the ratio of total import duty revenue (T^m) to the value of imports of manufactures (M_m), expressed as a percentage.

Sources of data and lists of countries included in the analyses with base years 1973, 1977 and 1980 are presented in the appendix to this chapter. All equations presented in this chapter are in semi *ln*-form. The t-statistics are in parentheses. An asterisk (*) indicates that the variable is statistically significant at a 95 per cent confidence interval.

In the previous chapter we indicated that the manufacturing sector has become a new basis for exports that increasingly contributes to the total export performance of many a developing country. Comparison of export-output ratios in the three years used in our analyses indicates that in many countries indeed a slowly increasing share of manufacturing production was exported during the 1970s. Before we discuss the results of our investigations of the factors underlying the export orientation of the manufacturing sector, we show the actual export-output ratios for a sample of 50 developed and developing countries in 1980 in Table 3.1. There is a wide variation in export-output ratios of the manufacturing sector among the sample countries,

TABLE 3.1
EXPORT-OUTPUT RATIOS
IN THE MANUFACTURING SECTOR, 1980

	(percentage)		(percentage)
Australia	6.20	Jordan	13.68
Austria	26.17	South Korea	23.39
Barbados*	40.14	Malaysia*	17.03
Bolivia*	1.70	Malta	57.17
Brazil*	3.15	Mauritius	18.18
Canada	17.10	Mexico	1.65
Chile	2.88	Netherlands	28.58
Colombia*	4.59	Nicaragua	6.11
Costa Rica	9.70	Niger	13.25
Cyprus	26.75	Norway	16.11
Dominican Rep.	2.70	Panama*	2.36
Ecuador	1.99	Peru	4.19
El Salvador	22.20	Philippines	6.36
Fiji	0.75	Portugal	17.70
Finland	22.83	Singapore	57.83
France	17.21	Sri Lanka	17.10
Germany (Fed. Rep.)	23.91	Sweden	29.62
Ghana	0.46	Syrian Arab Rep.	3.40
Greece	10.22	Tunisia	22.24
Guatemala	17.87	Turkey	2.78
Hong Kong	58.10	United States	7.35
India*	6.56	Uruguay	7.08
Indonesia	4.43	Venezuela*	0.73
Italy	24.45	Yugoslavia	8.78
Japan	11.05	Zimbabwe*	5.10

Note : ratios for countries marked by an asterisk (*) refer to 1979.
Sources : see Appendix to Chapter 3.

ranging from less than one per cent to over 50 per cent. However, in most developing countries in the sample, the contribution of exports to manufacturing production is below ten per cent and only in very few cases does it exceed 25 per cent.

3.5.2 Analysis 1: Three Groups of Countries

The cross-country regressions of analysis 1 are closely akin to those used in Chenery's studies on development patterns. Income *per capita* and the size of the domestic market are used as variables to explain the export-output ratio in the manufacturing sector. The sample of countries is subdivided into three relatively homogeneous subgroups according to population size and natural resource endowment:

country group L : large developed and developing countries; the dividing line between large and small countries is a population size of 20 million in 1970.
country group S-1 : small developed and developing countries with a modest natural-resource endowment.
country group S-2 : small developed and developing countries with ample natural resources.

Country groups L, S-1 and S-2 are based on a stratification of countries as applied in a UNIDO study on industrialization patterns.[28] In this UNIDO study, country group S-2 is subdivided into two groups: small countries with ample natural resources and a primary orientation, and small countries with ample resources and an industrial orientation. These groups have been pooled together here.

The base year of the analysis is 1973. In Table 3.2 the results of the regression analysis are presented. As follows from regressions 1-3 in this table, the effect of GNP *per capita* is statistically significant in country group S-2 only. The size variable P is not significant in any of the three country groups, but the negative sign is in line with our hypothesis of a negative relationship between population size and the share of manufactured exports in output. The overall level of explanation of this specification is poor.

Keesing and Sherk show that by inclusion of the variable population density alongside of the variables income *per capita* and population size, the size effect can be separated from the resource-endowment effect.[29] Population density is added as an independent variable in the regressions for the three country groups to find out whether inclusion of this variable improves the explanatory power of the variables income *per capita* and population size. As follows from Table 3.2, regressions 4-6, the overall level of explanation increases substantially when population density is included. However, apart

TABLE 3.2
THE EXPORT ORIENTATION OF THE
MANUFACTURING SECTOR — ANALYSIS 1, 1973

No.	Country group	Dependent variable	Constant term	GNP/P	P	D	n	R^2
1.	L	E_m/O_m	11.2	2.1	− 1.5		19	0.18
			(0.45)	(1.70)	(0.72)			
2.	S-1	E_m/O_m	29.3	6.3	− 6.1		14	0.50
			(0.66)	(1.93)	(1.58)			
3.	S-2	E_m/O_m	2.2	5.5*	− 3.4		33	0.31
			(0.12)	(3.10)	(2.02)			
4.	L	E_m/O_m	15.8	2.1	− 3.1	3.3*	19	0.47
			(0.77)	(2.07)	(1.73)	(2.87)		
5.	S-1	E_m/O_m	61.8	2.0	− 8.2*	3.0	14	0.64
			(1.44)	(0.54)	(2.27)	(1.95)		
6.	S-2	E_m/O_m	−27.5	5.8*	− 2.2	4.6*	33	0.57
			(1.62)	(4.03)	(1.54)	(4.13)		

from P in regression 5 and GNP/P in regression 6, the income and size variables are not significant.

It should be noted that the independent variables population size and natural-resource endowment have both been used to subdivide the original sample into three groups of countries. With respect to population size, it has often been stated that this may not be too serious as the intra-group variation of this variable remains large. It may be that this line of reasoning is also applicable to population density. Nevertheless, the poor regression results may be due to this classification problem. Therefore, the subdivision into more or less homogeneous country groups, as has been used in patternlike studies, is abandoned in the next analysis.

3.5.3 Analyses 2 and 3: The Structural Variables

Subsequent analyses are based on the complete sample of countries (sample A) as well as on data on developing countries only (sample B). Again, the effect of income *per capita*, population size and population density on the export-output ratio is tested. The regression analyses are done for 1973 and 1977. The results are presented in Table 3.3.

As expected, abandoning the country classification according to population size and resource endowment enhances the explanatory power of the variables P and D. The sign of variable P is in accordance with our hypothesis and is statistically significant in seven out of eight regressions. As expected, the variable D is positively associated with the dependent variable

TABLE 3.3
THE EXPORT ORIENTATION OF THE MANUFACTURING SECTOR — ANALYSIS 2, 1973 AND 1977

No.	Country group	Year	Dependent variable	Constant term	GNP/P	P	D	n	R^2
1.	A	1973	E_m/O_m	12.0 (1.00)	3.7* (3.20)	-2.7* (2.77)		70	0.21
2.	B	1973	E_m/O_m	11.1 (0.6)	3.7 (2.00)	-2.6* (2.13)		56	0.19
3.	A	1973	E_m/O_m	0.4 (0.04)	2.7* (2.93)	-2.7* (3.60)	5.0* (6.66)	70	0.53
4.	B	1973	E_m/O_m	8.6 (0.66)	0.5 (0.34)	-2.7* (3.11)	6.3* (7.09)	56	0.59
5.	A	1977	E_m/O_m	9.3 (0.66)	3.5* (2.72)	-2.2* (2.05)		60	0.19
6.	B	1977	E_m/O_m	6.0 (0.27)	4.6* (2.21)	-2.6 (1.78)		45	0.23
7.	A	1977	E_m/O_m	-1.2 (0.12)	2.8* (3.13)	-3.0* (4.00)	5.8* (7.70)	60	0.60
8.	B	1977	E_m/O_m	12.0 (0.80)	0.8 (0.54)	-3.6* (3.71)	7.2* (7.17)	45	0.66

and is highly significant in all equations where it is included. Moreover, the inclusion of D results in a marked improvement of the total level of explanation of the regressions. The results with respect to the effect of the overall level of development, income *per capita*, on the manufactured export performance are not unambiguous. In five out of eight regressions this variable is statistically significant. However, it is striking that this variable performs very well in all regressions that relate to all countries while it ceases to be significant in three out of four regressions that relate to developing countries only. Especially in equations 4 and 8, which include three independent variables, the impact of income *per capita* is clearly not significant. This confirms Balassa's findings, mentioned earlier, that there is no clear evidence of a significant impact of income *per capita* on the manufactured export performance if in the sample a distinction is made between countries at low and high income levels.

The contribution of the variable income *per capita* to the total level of explanation is only marginal in regressions 3-4 and 7-8. This becomes evident from a comparison of R^2-values of regressions that include and exclude income *per capita* as an independent variable. Regressions 3-4 and 7-8 have been run again without the variable income *per capita*, the results of which are presented in Table 3.4. For country group A (all countries) the total level of explanation decreases by six percentage points in both the 1973 and 1977

TABLE 3.4
THE EXPORT ORIENTATION OF THE
MANUFACTURING SECTOR — ANALYSIS 3, 1973 AND 1977

No.	Country group	Year	Dependent variable	Constant term	P	D	n	R^2
1.	A	1973	E_m/O_m	17.5* (2.23)	-2.8* (3.48)	5.3* (6.87)	70	0.47
2.	B	1973	E_m/O_m	11.9 (1.42)	-2.8* (3.37)	6.4* (7.67)	56	0.59
3.	A	1977	E_m/O_m	21.2* (2.75)	-3.3* (4.12)	6.0* (7.47)	60	0.54
4.	B	1977	E_m/O_m	18.5* (2.07)	-3.8* (4.30)	7.4* (7.93)	45	0.66

regressions. However, in the regressions that relate to developing countries only the total level of explanation remains virtually the same in both the 1973 and 1977 regressions, whether or not income *per capita* is included. For these regressions, the R^2-values adjusted for degrees of freedom ($\bar{R}^2$) show even a slight increase if income *per capita* is excluded.

What just has been said concerning the variable income *per capita* also holds for the variable size of the manufacturing sector. This variable is assumed to have an impact similar to the level of income *per capita*. In the above regressions, we substituted the share of manufacturing value added in gross domestic production for income *per capita* as an alternative indicator of the level of economic development. This does not yield better statistical results. Apparently, a low level of economic or industrial development does not necessarily impede an outward-oriented industrial development. In other words, a relatively high income level or level of industrial development is — as was hypothesized before — not a necessary precondition for successful manufactured export performance. Consequently, variables that refer to the level of development are excluded from further analyses of manufactured export performance of developing countries.

3.5.4 Analysis 4: The Role of Population Density Once Again

In previous paragraphs we argued that the variable population density has a twofold meaning. First, the variable is a measure for the pressure of population on land. Second, the variable is a proxy for the *per capita* availability of all sorts of natural resources. High population pressure on land may result in an elastic supply of labour for manufacturing industry in developing countries, which may favour the growth of labour-intensive (export) sectors. So far, the variable population density referred to the ratio between total population and total land area. To get a better insight into the impact of population pressure on export performance, the variable population density is defined more strictly as being the ratio between total population and arable land area.[30] Thus, it is implicitly assumed that the arable land area cannot be expanded for physical or financial reasons. In regression analysis 4 we use the new variable population density (Da) and population size as explanatory variables. The results are presented in Table 3.5.

Comparison of the regressions presented in Tables 3.4 and 3.5 shows that the results have improved now that Da instead of D has been introduced. Without exception the values of the t-statistics for the coefficients of Da are higher than those of D. The total level of explanation has also increased in all four regressions. The two variables P and Da explain 75 per cent of the variation among developing countries in their manufactured export performance in 1977. It is of some interest to compare the regression results in Table 3.5 for the two years analyzed. The absolute values of the estimated parameters of variables P and Da are higher in the regressions for 1977 than in the corresponding regressions for 1973. Moreover, all 1977 coefficients are more significant than the corresponding 1973 coefficients. The explanatory power of the 1977 regressions is higher than that of the 1973 regressions.

Figure 3.1 shows the interaction among the three variables. Four curves are presented corresponding to four pre-assigned values of the variable population size. The figure is based on the coefficients in regression 4 in Table 3.5. The shape of the curves shows that the higher the density of population, the higher — though decreasingly — the share of exports in manufacturing production. The different positions of the curves show that the smaller the domestic market, the more production will be outward-oriented, other things being equal.

TABLE 3.5
THE EXPORT ORIENTATION OF THE
MANUFACTURING SECTOR — ANALYSIS 4, 1973 AND 1977

No.	Country group	Year	Dependent variable	Constant term	P	Da	n	R^2
1.	A	1973	E_m/O_m	12.6 (1.63)	−2.4* (3.18)	5.2* (7.58)	70	0.51
2.	B	1973	E_m/O_m	8.6 (1.05)	−2.5* (3.14)	5.9* (8.25)	56	0.62
3.	A	1977	E_m/O_m	10.9 (1.50)	−2.5* (3.54)	6.2* (9.01)	60	0.62
4.	B	1977	E_m/O_m	8.1 (1.02)	−3.0* (3.88)	7.2* (10.10)	45	0.75

Figure 3.1
Relationship between E_m/O_m and D_a at Four Pre-Assigned Values of P

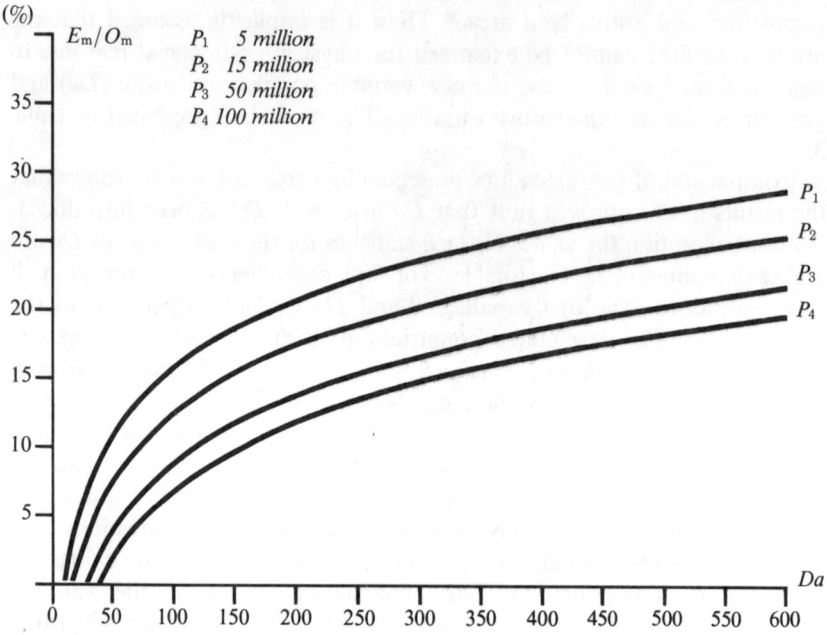

3.5.5 Analysis 5: Introducing Trade Policy

In this section we shall analyze the impact of trade policy on the export orientation of the manufacturing sector within the framework presented earlier. The impact of government intervention on the market orientation of production and the ways in which government may stimulate export production will be studied in more detail in the next chapter. It will be shown there that government intervention in the trade regime is much more predominant in developing countries than it is in developed countries. The core of the system of trade intervention in most developing countries is a large set of import barriers comprising tariffs, quotas, import licenses and import bans. These forms of protection bring about a discrimination between domestic producers, between domestic and foreign products, and between exports and domestic sales. The latter effect is at stake here. Barriers to imports of manufactures favour import-competing industries over export industries and the non-industrial sectors of the economy. Consequently, such barriers tend to have a negative impact on the export orientation of the manufacturing sector and hence on the contribution of this sector to foreign-exchange earnings. When the effective protection for producers of import

EXPORT ORIENTATION OF THE MANUFACTURING SECTOR

substitutes is not compensated by export subsidies, import barriers create a bias against exports.

No adequate set of data is available on the bias against exports that results from government intervention. First of all, there is no comprehensive overview for all countries of all government measures that have an impact on the market orientation of domestic production. Moreover, the price (and income) effects of many forms of government intervention such as licenses, quotas and import bans are hard to estimate. The only relevant data available for a large number of developed and developing countries are the amounts of government revenue from taxes on international trade, published in the IMF *Government Finance Statistics Yearbooks*. These yearbooks have entries for taxes on imports and exports. Since export taxes are predominantly levied on primary products, they are not immediately relevant to our analysis. Two alternative proxies for the bias against manufactured exports are constructed by dividing the value of import duty revenue by the value of total imports and by the value of imports of manufactures. These are only rough indicators for the bias against exports that results from the total system of government intervention in international trade.

In Table 3.6 we present the two ratios for the 50 countries included in our sample for the regressions with base year 1980. To the extent that import duties are predominantly raised on manufactured imports, the latter variable is more accurate. With respect to these two ratios, three points should be kept in mind. First, import duties are only one of the many trade-impeding instruments applied in developing and developed countries. Second, in calculating the ratios, no distinction could be made between competing and non-competing manufactured imports. Third, effective protection for manufacturing activities may exceed by far nominal protection, depending on the output-value added ratio in each manufacturing industry. These are three reasons why the ratios presented here underestimate, probably to a substantial degree, the effective rate of protection of import-substituting activities. Since we do not know to what extent protection for import-substituting industries is compensated by export subsidies, the implicit assumption here is that the higher duties on imports, the greater the bias against exports.

Table 3.7 shows the results of our analysis of the impact of structural and policy-related variables on the export orientation of the manufacturing sector. In comparison with previous analyses, the sample for 1977 had to be reduced slightly as data on import duties were not available for all original sample countries. We added a similar analysis for 1980, based on a sample which is more limited due to a lack of more recent data on the value of manufacturing production. As is indicated in the appendix to the chapter, data on 1979 had to be used for quite a few developing countries. Inclusion of a variable related to trade policy tends to improve the overall level of explanation of the

TABLE 3.6
DUTIES ON IMPORTS IN DEVELOPED AND DEVELOPING COUNTRIES, 1980

Country	Ratio of import duties to total imports (percentage)	Ratio of import duties to imports of manufactures (percentage)	Country	Ratio of import duties to total imports (percentage)	Ratio of import duties to imports of manufactures (percentage)
Australia	10.31	14.24	Jordan	14.13	25.41
Austria	1.54	2.34	South Korea	7.51	19.42
Barbados*	8.79	14.84	Malaysia*	8.83	14.44
Bolivia*	12.97	17.76	Malta	11.07	17.76
Brazil*	6.90	16.44	Mauritius	13.45	27.01
Canada	4.74	6.83	Mexico	10.79	21.86
Chile	7.47	12.93	Netherlands	0.01	0.01
Colombia*	12.25	19.27	Nicaragua	10.86	18.30
Costa Rica	5.97	9.46	Niger	18.97	36.72
Cyprus	7.76	13.08	Norway	0.85	1.38
Dominican Rep.	15.93	31.76	Panama*	6.01	10.63
Ecuador	16.54	20.70	Peru	21.33	31.77
El Salvador	4.04	7.00	Philippines	12.51	29.54
Fiji	11.48	22.32	Portugal	4.06	8.60
Finland	1.78	3.39	Singapore	0.85	1.68
France	0.07	0.14	Sri Lanka	8.69	17.79
Germany (Fed. Rep.)	0.02	0.05	Sweden	1.51	2.64
Ghana	11.64	20.69	Syrian Arab Rep.	11.25	30.41
Greece	5.79	10.53	Tunisia	18.54	35.83
Guatemala	7.18	12.11	Turkey	8.87	23.00
Hong Kong[1]	0.85	1.68	United States	2.97	6.35
India*	37.99	97.88	Uruguay	19.29	37.01
Indonesia	6.59	11.78	Venezuela*	9.18	12.29
Italy	0.26	0.63	Yugoslavia	12.85	25.60
Japan	2.04	11.33	Zimbabwe*	3.38	6.45

Notes : ratios for countries marked by an asterisk (*) refer to 1979.
[1] In the case of Hong Kong we apply the ratios for Singapore as no data on import duties in Hong Kong are available.
Sources : see Appendix to Chapter 3.

variation in the export-output ratio. However, neither proxy for trade policy appears to be significant in the samples that include developing countries only. There is hardly any difference in the overall level of explanation between the regressions in which the first and the second policy-related variable is used. It is noteworthy, though, that the second ratio, in which import duties are

TABLE 3.7
THE EXPORT ORIENTATION OF THE MANUFACTURING SECTOR — ANALYSIS 5, 1977 AND 1980

No.	Country group	Year	Dependent variable	Constant term	P	Da	T^m/M	T^m/M_m	n	R^2
1.	A	1977	E_m/O_m	14.7 (2.00)	−2.6* (3.74)	6.0* (8.81)	−1.8* (2.57)		57	0.69
2.	B	1977	E_m/O_m	12.6 (1.36)	−2.7* (3.42)	7.0* (8.31)	−2.9 (1.23)		41	0.81
3.	A	1977	E_m/O_m	14.6 (2.01)	−2.5* (3.61)	6.1* (9.12)		−1.9* (2.76)	57	0.69
4.	B	1977	E_m/O_m	12.4 (1.38)	−2.6* (3.28)	7.2* (9.31)		−2.7 (1.33)	41	0.81
5.	A	1980	E_m/O_m	16.7* (8.70)	−2.7* (4.56)	6.1* (9.81)	−3.2 (1.85)		50	0.73
6.	B	1980	E_m/O_m	10.8 (1.03)	−2.4* (3.07)	6.5* (7.65)	−2.5 (1.24)		34	0.81
7.	A	1980	E_m/O_m	16.7* (8.75)	−2.5* (3.95)	6.3* (10.24)		−3.3 (1.98)	50	0.73
8.	B	1980	E_m/O_m	11.4 (1.12)	−2.3* (2.88)	6.5* (8.23)		−2.7 (1.42)	34	0.81

related to imports of manufactures only, shows higher values for its *t*-statistics, indicating that it is a somewhat more accurate proxy for protection of the manufacturing sector and the bias against exports of manufactures. Nevertheless, it seems likely that the proxies applied here do not reflect this bias in an adequate way for the reasons mentioned earlier. In many developing countries a dual incentive system is applied, protection being given to industries producing for the domestic market while export industries operate under a free-trade regime in a separate zone. Under such circumstances the manufacturing export performance is almost independent of the trade regime applied to the larger part of the manufacturing sector.

3.6 SUMMARY AND CONCLUSIONS

In this chapter we have studied the impact of structural characteristics of economies and of policy-related variables on the export orientation of the manufacturing sector. We may summarize the findings of our investigation as follows:

(1) The level of income *per capita* and the share of manufacturing production in total production have no significant impact on the export orientation of the manufacturing sector in regressions based on samples of developing countries only. A low level of economic or

industrial development does not necessarily impede an outward-oriented industrial development strategy.

(2) The variable population size as a proxy for the size of the domestic market is significantly negatively associated with a country's export performance: small countries are more export-oriented than large countries. This does not imply that economies of scale are of no importance; it does imply that countries with small domestic markets may be successful in the export of products where economies of scale are not of predominant importance or are, in fact, realized through the export market.

(3) The variable density of population has a twofold meaning: population pressure and relative availability of natural resources. High population pressure on (arable) land may be conceived of as a situation of surplus labour, which may be favourable for the expansion of labour-intensive (export) industries. Alternatively, low availability of natural resources may "force" a country to export non-primary products in order to finance imports. Density of population, as a twofold proxy, has a positive impact on manufactured export performance.

(4) Apart from structural characteristics of the economy, policies do influence the market orientation of the manufacturing sector. The impact of trade policy is investigated by applying variables that reflect protection against imports. Protection has a negative impact on the export orientation of the manufacturing sector, although the impact is not in all samples significant.

The conclusions derived from the analysis provide a framework for understanding the structural characteristics of export-oriented economies, for identifying the driving forces behind the outward orientation of the manufacturing sector in developing countries, and for assessing the effect that trade policy may have on the export performance of the manufacturing sector. The way trade policies limit or stimulate the export orientation of the manufacturing sector is the subject of the next chapter.

APPENDIX

Sources of Data Used in Chapter 3:

Data on import and export values taken from United Nations, *Yearbook of International Trade Statistics*, Volume I, New York, various issues, and UNCTAD, *Handbook of International Trade and Development Statistics*, United Nations, New York, various issues.

Data on values of manufacturing output taken from United Nations, *Yearbook of Industrial Statistics*, Volume I, New York, various issues.

Data on size of population and area of (arable) land taken from FAO, *Production Yearbook*, Rome, various issues.

Data on import duty revenue taken from IMF, *Government Finance Statistics Yearbook*, Washington DC, various issues.

Data on Gross National Production taken from a World Bank tape, The World Bank, *Atlas 1976 Base (1975-1977)*, IBRD-EAPD, 1978, and from The World Bank, *World Tables, The Third Edition*, Volume I, The Johns Hopkins University Press, Baltimore and London, 1984.

Exchange rates taken from IMF, *International Financial Statistics*, Washington DC, various issues; The World Bank, *World Tables, The Second Edition (1980)*, The Johns Hopkins University Press, Baltimore and London, 1980, and United Nations, *Yearbook of International Trade Statistics*, Volume I, New York, 1976 (conversion factors in the country notes).

Samples

The following countries are included in the samples with base years 1973 ($n = 70$), 1977 ($n = 60$) and 1980 ($n = 50$).

	1973	1977	1980		1973	1977	1980
Afghanistan	*	*		Japan	*	*	*
Australia	*	1976	*	Jordan	1974	*	*
Austria	*	*	*	Kenya	*	1976	
Bangladesh		1976		South Korea	*	*	*
Barbados	*	1975	1979	Kuwait	*	1976	
Bolivia	*		1979	Madagascar	*	1975	
Brazil	*		1979	Malawi	*	1975	
UR of of Cameroon	*			Malaysia	*		1979
Canada	*	*	*	Malta	*	*	*
Central African Rep.	*	1976		Mauritius			*
Chile	*	1976	*	Mexico		1976	*
Colombia	*	1976	1979	Netherlands	*	1976	*
Costa Rica			*	New Zealand	*	*	
Cyprus	*	*	*	Nicaragua	*	1976	*
Denmark	*	*		Niger			*
Dominican Rep.	*	*	*	Nigeria	*	1976	
Ecuador	*	1976	*	Norway	*	*	*
Egypt	*			Panama	*	1976	1979
El Salvador	1974	*	*	Papua New Guinea	*	1976	
Ethiopia	*	1976		Peru	*	*	*
Fiji	*	*	*	Philippines	*	*	*
Finland	*	*	*	Portugal	*	*	*
France	*	*	*	Senegal	1974	1975	
Germany (Fed. Rep.)	*	*	*	Singapore	*	*	*
Ghana	1972		*	Somalia	*	1976	
Greece	*	1975	*	Spain	*	1976	
Guatemala	1972	1975	*	Sri Lanka	1974		*
Honduras	*			Sweden	*	*	*
Hong Kong	*	*	*	Syrian Arab Rep.	*	*	*
Iceland		1976		UR of Tanzania	1972		
India	*	1976	1979	Tunisia	*	*	*
Indonesia	*	*	*	Turkey	*	*	
Iran	*			United Kingdom	*	*	
Iraq	*			United States	*	*	*
Ireland	*	1975		Uruguay		*	*
Israel	*	*		Venezuela	*	*	1979
Italy	*	*	*	Yugoslavia		*	
Ivory Coast	*	1976		Zambia	*		
Jamaica	*			Zimbabwe			1979

4
Export Strategies

4.1 INTRODUCTION

In the previous chapter we identified structural variables that have a significant impact on the market orientation of manufacturing industry. It was found that structural characteristics of economies explain to a great extent the export orientation of the manufacturing sector. Given these structural factors, governments have nonetheless some freedom in choosing between different trade and industrialization strategies, thus hampering or stimulating the full exploitation of a country's comparative advantages in the world market. These government policies are the subject of this chapter.

An industry that has outgrown the infant stage in which it needed protection and that has become competitive in world markets, may be considered "mature". It is tempting to go one step further and say that the realization of manufactured exports as such is an indicator of maturity and competitiveness of a country's domestic industries, as is done in fact in some studies. According to Reynolds, for instance "(a) key indicator of successful development is the ability to compete in the world market for at least some types of manufactures, evidenced by a rising share of manufactures in the country's export total. . . . A country that has reached this stage, whatever its *per capita* income level, is well under way to mature-economy status".[1] However, a statement along these lines overlooks the fact that, irrespective of the competitiveness and stage of development of domestic industry, manufactured exports may be generated by TNCs and international trading houses. Exports may be generated in enclaves that can hardly be considered part of the domestic economy. Therefore, a more careful and detailed analysis is needed.

In this chapter we distinguish three avenues that may be pursued to stimulate exports of manufactures:

(1) export stimulation through a transformation of an initially inward-

oriented trade and industrialization regime or through a further extension of trade-stimulating policies;
(2) fostering of domestic processing of primary exports;
(3) creation of export enclaves that operate independently of the rest of the manufacturing sector.

These strategies should not be seen as mutually exclusive in all respects. Rather, the different strategies relate (at least in part) to different sub-sectors of the manufacturing sector at large that require different incentive schemes and also differ in their impact on the exporting economy in terms of employment creation and foreign-exchange earnings. Hence, they can be applied simultaneously with varying emphasis on either. As we already noted in the first chapter of this study, such a distinction between strategies is often bypassed in the literature on trade, industrialization and development. Our differentiation between export strategies is based on studies by Helleiner, Stewart, Lall and Streeten, and Dunning.[2] Making this distinction may help to bridge the gap between the conflicting views regarding optimal industrialization strategies for developing countries.

Before discussing the three strategies distinguished here, we shall study the extent and characteristics of government intervention in Section 4.2. Economic and non-economic arguments for intervention will briefly be reviewed in Section 4.3 while the effects of protection will be studied in Section 4.4. After that, the essential features of the different policies aiming at stimulating exports of manufactures will be reviewed in Sections 4.5 to 4.7. The role of foreign firms such as TNCs and international trading houses in manufactured export performance of developing countries will be the subject of Section 4.8. A summary of our findings will be presented in Section 4.9.

4.2 GOVERNMENT INTERVENTION AND THE TRADE REGIME

The process of industrialization in developing countries has been accompanied by a varying number of policy measures with an impact on the sector's size, structure and market orientation. These policy measures have not necessarily been part of a consistent and deliberately designed industrialization strategy but have often been prompted by *ad hoc* economic or political necessities.

The issue at stake here is not government intervention as such. As will be substantiated below, it is the type of government intervention rather than the extent of it which is typical of developing countries. *Laissez-faire*, or government abstinence from intervention, is a rare phenomenon in both developed and developing countries. The distinction between the two groups of countries is in the way the government sector is financed and domestic activities are stimulated. Intervention in the foreign-trade sector is much more predominant in developing countries than in developed countries. This is not to say that there is no scope for trade liberalization in developed countries. On the contrary, developed countries stimulate domestic production and hamper imports in a number of sectors, that are often of special interest to developing countries, through many different devices among which are tariff and non-tariff barriers.[3] Protection of agriculture and of labour- and capital-intensive decaying industries is a case in point. Nevertheless, the dependence of manufacturing industry on protection against imports, and of government revenue on taxes on international trade is substantially higher in developing countries than in developed countries.

To differentiate between the type and extent of government intervention in the economy, we shall schematically distinguish three types of regimes: *laissez-faire* regimes, free-trade interventionist regimes and protectionist regimes.

Laissez-faire regimes are characterized by the near-absence of government intervention in the economy. Free-trade interventionist regimes are characterized by a more substantial government involvement in the economy without, however, considerable direct government intervention in foreign trade. Protectionist regimes are, above all, characterized by high barriers to imports and by substantial government intervention in the economy. These are typically countries where industry is dependent for its survival on protection against imports and government is financially strongly dependent on taxes on trade. The factors underlying the choice of such an intervention system will be discussed in the next section.

The variables that are used to distinguish the three regimes are presented in Table 4.1. Column two shows the share of taxes in GDP, which is used here as a proxy for the extent of government intervention in the economy. Column three shows the ratio of government revenue from import duties to the total value of imports, which is used as a proxy for the degree of intervention in foreign trade. To be sure, it is not really possible to capture the effects of the entire system of trade barriers in a single variable, for the reasons mentioned already in the previous chapter. However, the only trade-policy-related data available for a large number of developed and developing countries are data on government revenue from taxes on trade. Therefore, when analyzing the role of trade intervention in developing and developed countries in this section, we have to use revenue from import duties as a proxy for the entire system of tariff and non-tariff barriers to imports. Further attention will be paid to other import barriers in Section 4.5 where we discuss the major elements of policy packages that aim at reducing the anti-trade bias in actually pursued government policies. The last two columns of Table 4.1 show the contribution of taxes on foreign-trade-related activities to government revenue to indicate the financial dependence of governments on the actual

TABLE 4.1
INDICATORS OF GOVERNMENT INTERVENTION, 1980

Country	GDP/P (US $)	Ratio of government taxes to GDP	Ratio of import duties to total imports	Ratio of taxes on international trade and transactions to total tax revenue	Ratio of import duties to total government revenue
Nepal	137	0.07	0.20	0.40	0.21
India	230	0.11	0.30	0.26	0.20
Malawi	248	0.13	0.12	0.25	0.17
UR of Tanzania	275	0.17	0.08	0.19	0.09
Sri Lanka	281	0.18	0.09	0.53	0.18
Togo	409	0.28	0.14	0.36	0.23
Kenya	426	0.20	0.11	0.21	0.17
Indonesia	460	0.23	0.07	0.08	0.04
Niger	474	0.12	0.19	0.43	0.31
Sudan	493	0.10	0.30	0.51	0.34
Liberia	507	0.20	0.12	0.36	0.29
Senegal	513	0.22	0.23	0.40	0.29
Honduras	674	0.14	0.07	0.40	0.20
Philippines	696	0.11	0.13	0.27	0.23
Thailand	702	0.12	0.10	0.26	0.20
El Salvador	706	0.12	0.04	0.38	0.10
Nicaragua	722	0.21	0.11	0.29	0.19
UR of Cameroon	851	0.14	0.20	0.42	0.28
Congo	854	0.35	0.18	0.17	0.10
Morocco	876	0.22	0.20	0.24	0.19

TABLE 4.1 (cont'd)

Country	GDP/P (US $)	Ratio of government taxes to GDP	Ratio of import duties to total imports	Ratio of taxes on international trade and transactions to total tax revenue	Ratio of import duties to total government revenue
Jordan	911	0.19	0.14	0.61	0.24
Guatemala	1 081	0.10	0.07	0.34	0.13
Peru	1 082	0.17	0.21	0.30	0.16
Dominican Rep.	1 106	0.11	0.16	0.40	0.24
Colombia	1 245	0.10	0.11	0.24	0.13
Turkey	1 254	0.17	0.09	0.08	0.05
Tunisia	1 372	0.24	0.19	0.32	0.23
Ecuador	1 417	0.12	0.17	0.30	0.24
Paraguay	1 450	0.10	0.18	0.27	0.18
South Korea	1 534	0.17	0.08	0.17	0.15
Malaysia	1 724	0.25	0.09	0.37	0.15
Panama	1 788	0.22	0.06	0.13	0.09
Brazil	1 967	0.17	0.07	0.07	0.03
Fiji	1 974	0.18	0.11	0.32	0.23
Costa Rica	2 190	0.17	0.06	0.20	0.11
Portugal	2 493	0.27	0.04	0.06	0.06
Chile	2 528	0.25	0.07	0.05	0.04
Yugoslavia	2 623	0.09	0.13	0.36	0.35
Mexico	2 662	0.15	0.11	0.29	0.07
Cyprus	3 230	0.17	0.08	0.25	0.19

(cont'd overleaf)

TABLE 4.1 *(cont'd)*

Country	GDP/P (US $)	Ratio of government taxes to GDP	Ratio of import duties to total imports	Ratio of taxes on international trade and transactions to total tax revenue	Ratio of import duties to total government revenue
Barbados	3 261	0.26	0.09	0.21	0.19
Malta	3 341	0.28	0.11	0.33	0.25
Uruguay	3 512	0.21	0.19	0.15	0.14
Venezuela	4 024	0.22	0.10	0.08	0.07
Greece	4 302	0.27	0.06	0.06	0.05
Singapore	4 525	0.19	0.01	0.10	0.07
Trinidad and Tobago	5 251	0.38	0.06	0.08	0.07
Ireland	5 390	0.35	0.08	0.15	0.13
Spain	5 625	0.23	0.09	0.06	0.06
Argentina	5 667	0.15	0.20	0.13	0.08
Oman	5 932	0.12	0.01	0.05	0.01
Italy	6 916	0.33	0.00	0.00	0.00
New Zealand	7 189	0.29	0.04	0.04	0.03
Bahrain	9 159	0.05	0.02	0.50	0.06
Austria	10 290	0.32	0.02	0.02	0.02
Australia	10 303	0.21	0.09	0.06	0.06
Finland	10 358	0.26	0.02	0.02	0.02
Canada	10 527	0.17	0.05	0.08	0.06
USA	11 699	0.19	0.03	0.02	0.01
Netherlands	11 904	0.45	0.00	0.00	0.00

TABLE 4.1 (cont'd)

Country	GDP/P (US $)	Ratio of government taxes to GDP	Ratio of import duties to total imports	Ratio of taxes on international trade and transactions to total tax revenue	Ratio of import duties to total government revenue
France	12 196	0.38	0.00	0.00	0.00
Iceland	12 359	0.26	0.14	0.21	0.17
Denmark	13 002	0.32	0.01	0.01	0.01
Germany (Fed. Rep.)	13 447	0.27	0.00	0.00	0.00
Norway	14 087	0.38	0.01	0.01	0.01
Sweden	14 968	0.31	0.02	0.01	0.01
Switzerland	16 080	0.18	0.05	0.10	0.09
Kuwait	20 114	0.03	0.03	0.26	0.01

Sources: data on GDP, population, and GDP *per capita* taken from UNCTAD, *Handbook of International Trade and Development Statistics, Supplement 1983*, United Nations, New York, 1983, Table 6.1, and United Nations, *Yearbook of National Accounts Statistics 1981*, Volume I, New York, 1983.
Data on government revenue and import duty revenue taken from IMF, *Government Finance Statistics Yearbook*, Volume VIII, Washington DC, 1984.
Exchange rates taken from IMF, *International Financial Statistics*, Volume XXXVII, Number 11, Washington DC, 1984.

system of trade intervention. Column four shows the share of taxes on international trade and transactions in total tax revenue. In almost all developing countries, duties on imports are the most important trade-related source of government revenue, but in some countries export duties on primary products are also of great importance. Other taxes related to international transactions are exchange taxes, taxes on tourism and taxes on travel fares abroad. Finally, column five shows more specifically the contribution of import duties to total government revenue (tax revenue and other revenue such as grants).

The data show that the significant difference between developed and developing countries is not so much in the extent of government intervention as in the characteristics of intervention: developing countries have, in general, a more protectionist regime and show a relatively high financial government dependence on taxes on foreign trade. In developed countries, the average tariff rates, as defined above, are low and taxes on imports and other international transactions do not contribute in a substantial way to government revenue. The characteristics of the three regimes are depicted in Figure 4.1. In the diagram, developed countries are indicated by Δ and developing countries by *.

Only in some small oil-rich countries such as Bahrain, Kuwait and Oman, a *laissez-faire* regime would seem to prevail: government involvement in the economy, as measured by the share of taxes in GDP, and government intervention in international trade, as measured by the ratio of import duty revenue to total imports, are very limited. The group of countries with substantial government involvement and low taxes on trade — the free-trade interventionist regime — consists of developed countries and only a few developing countries. All countries with a protectionist regime — characterized by substantial government involvement in the economy cum protection against imports — are developing countries.

The role of import duties in government finance and in the stimulation of domestic activities in countries at different levels of development and with different opportunities for domestic-market-oriented policies is studied in a cross-section analysis. We expect that countries at higher levels of development have a bureaucratic and financial infrastructure that facilitates alternative ways of tax collection and subsidy of domestic activities. The application of such alternative instruments is often not feasible for countries at low levels of development. The capability of building up an efficient tax and subsidy system is interrelated with the overall level of development of a country. The options for government to manage the economy cannot be seen in isolation from the overall financial and bureaucratic infrastructure of the country, its system of communications, the literacy rate, to mention only a few variables. Additionally, we expect that, especially in the early stages of

Figure 4.1
Duties on Imports and Taxes in GDP, 1980

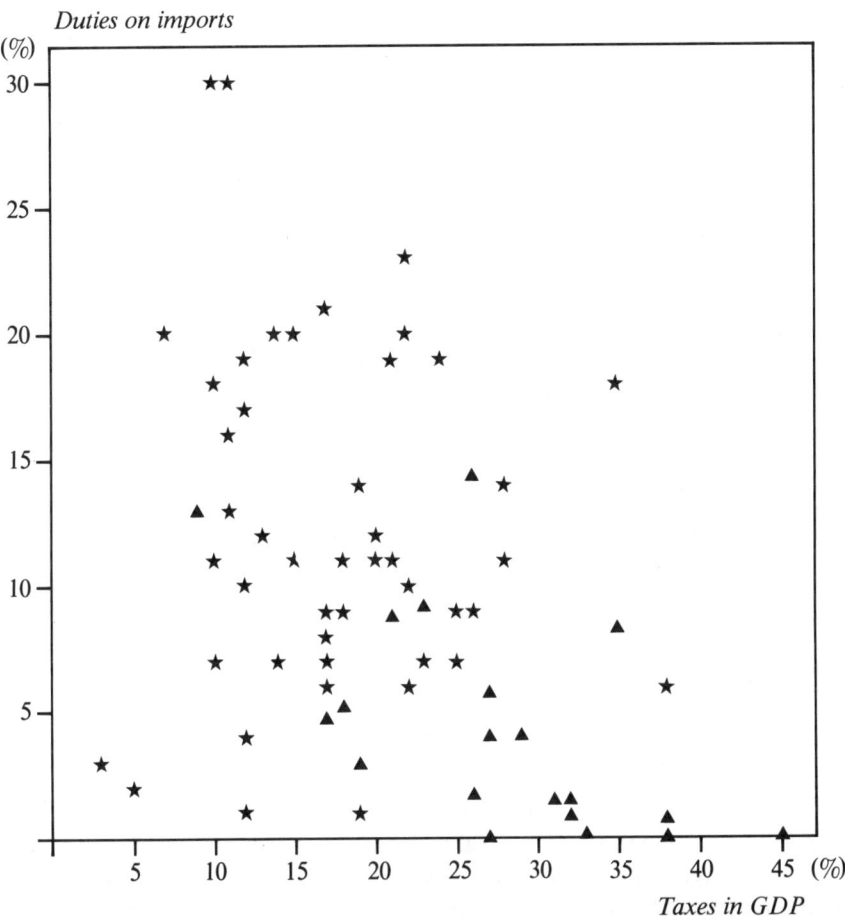

Symbols: developed countries indicated by Δ, developing countries indicated by *.
Sources: as of Table 4.1.

development, manufacturing industry suffers from inadequacies in the general environment, lacks knowledge derived from experience and consequently needs more support to survive foreign competition. The results of the regression analyses, presented in Table 4.2, indicate that the lower the level of development of a country, the higher import duties, the larger the contribution of taxes on international trade and other international transactions to total tax revenue, and the more government is dependent on import duties for its total revenue.

TABLE 4.2
TAXES ON INTERNATIONAL TRANSACTIONS, PROTECTION AND GOVERNMENT REVENUE, 1980

Dependent variables	Constant term	GDP/P	P	n	R^2
T^m/M	3.75*	-.67*	-.15	68	.42
	(3.32)	(6.79)	(1.94)		
T^t/T	7.95*	-.86*	-.39*	68	.57
	(6.90)	(8.56)	(4.85)		
T^m/GR	6.66*	-.82*	-.33*	68	.57
	(6.21)	(8.75)	(4.42)		

Symbols:
- GDP/P = Gross Domestic Production *per capita* in US dollars
- P = size of population in thousands of inhabitants
- T^m/M = ratio of the value of import duty revenue (T^m) to the value of total imports (M)
- T^t/T = contribution of taxes on international trade and transactions (T^t) to total tax revenue (T)
- T^m/GR = contribution of import duty revenue (T^m) to total government revenue (GR)

Notes : equations are in double *In*-form The *t*-statistics are in parentheses. An asterisk (*) indicates that the variable is statistically significant at a 95 per cent confidence interval.

Sources : as of Table 4.1.

4.3 FIRST-BEST AND NEXT-BEST SYSTEMS OF INTERVENTION

There are strong arguments in favour of a situation characterized by free trade rather than a situation characterized by protection against imports. This, however, is merely a comparison of states of being. Rather than highlighting the disadvantages of protection against imports, we shall discuss here the causes of protection and its effects on the economic performance of developing countries. Underlying the existing system of protection are a number of arguments for the extent of intervention as well as for the specific way intervention is organized. Governments and groups in society are dependent on the actually existing system of government intervention for the realization of their goals. Changing the trade regime, therefore, may have significant economic and political consequences. By analyzing the arguments for protection we may gain insight into the problem of trade liberalization. The more a country's trade regime is characterized by import restrictions, the greater the resistance to change towards liberalization is expected to be.

4.3.1 The Infant-Industry Argument

The literature on government intervention and trade policy mentions many arguments for intervention. Presumably the most generally applied argument is the infant-industry argument. According to this argument an industry may temporarily be given support to compensate for a cost disadvantage it has *vis-à-vis* established foreign suppliers as a result of its later start. The early starter is a more efficient producer than late starters as it has learned by doing. Without support, so the argument goes, new suppliers will not be able to enter the market and compete successfully with the early starter, and a situation of imperfect competition may so be perpetuated. This classical argument has been scrutinized by a number of authors. The temporary cost disadvantage to the latecomer as such is not a proper argument for stimulation through subsidy or protection. If losses incurred at the start are later compensated by profits, the investment may be privately sound and will be undertaken by the latecomer. To arrive at a sound argument for protection, the infant industry should create a positive external effect that accrues to society as a free good. In such a case the social rate of return on the investment exceeds the private rate of return. Production may then be stimulated from the level which is optimal from the private investor's point of view up to the level which is optimal from the point of view of society.

Johnson and Baldwin analyze carefully the circumstances which could lead to such cases and conclude that they may be quite exceptional. Both emphasize the case of diffusion of technological knowledge and skills that become available to society as a free good.[4] Westphal finds an empirical justification for infant-industry stimulation on the same grounds. Much of the impact of technological mastery spills over to society and strengthens its technological capacity: "preceding generations of infant industries provide benefits to succeeding generations by augmenting the economy's technological mastery".[5] Corden and Keesing add to the argument the diffusion of commercial knowledge and the more general case of creating the proper atmosphere. As formulated by Corden: "This atmosphere-creating effect may well provide a strong basis — possibly the strongest of all — for an 'infant economy' argument for generalized protection of manufacturing in countries inexperienced in manufacturing production and yet containing the human potentialities for it — the sort of country Friedrich List was writing about".[6]

Selling externalities and the creation of goodwill may also be reasons for stimulating infant industries producing for the domestic and foreign markets. The argument for home-market stimulation rests on the assumption that consumers have an irrational preference for foreign products while the argument for stimulating export industries rests on the assumption that initiating export production may create goodwill for other products from the newly exporting country in the foreign market. More generally, initiating export production may create external economies via the diffusion of export-marketing and production knowledge and the creation of goodwill in foreign markets. According to Corden and Keesing, these effects provide an argument for infant-export-marketing stimulation.[7] The infant-industry argument for stimulation is thus in itself not an argument for the stimulation of domestic-market-oriented industries only.

In brief, the infant-industry argument boils down to the case of an industry which is to be stimulated as it creates a free good. However, it appears difficult to determine when this is the case and, if so, what the rate of subsidy should be so as to stimulate production to the required level. Baldwin and Westphal point out the possibility of a substantial diversion between social and private costs. Consequently, in such cases high effective rates of stimulation may be warranted.[8] However, in view of the lack of evidence on the precise extent of the assumed external effects, Balassa suggests to limit the rate of net effective protection of manufacturing activities to no more than 10–15 per cent.[9]

4.3.2 Correcting for Market Imperfections

The existence of distortions or market imperfections necessitates government intervention to warrant an optimal pattern of allocation. In such circumstances a *laissez-faire* policy would result in a sub-optimal pattern of allocation. A distinction can be made here between distortions in international markets and in the domestic market. Distortions in international markets due to imperfect competition are an argument for intervention in free trade by the imposition of an optimum tariff. Distortions in domestic markets, too, warrant government intervention but in these cases intervention in free trade is not first-best. Here we should distinguish between imperfections in the product market, consumption imperfections and imperfections in the factor market. Imperfections in product markets may be due to imperfect competition or the existence of (static) external economies in production. Imperfections in consumption may be due to externalities in consumption. Imperfections in the capital market may especially create a bias against infant industries. Imperfections in the labour market are reflected by wage rates in particular sectors that deviate from the opportunity costs of labour, or by the inflexibility of wage rates in all or part of the economy.

4.3.3 Non-Economic Arguments for Intervention

In the previous sections we discussed the so-called economic arguments for government intervention. In these cases government intervention is warranted to obtain an allocation in production and consumption that is optimal in the Pareto sense. Apart from these, still other arguments for government intervention have been put forward that are usually referred to as non-economic arguments. In such cases a government is required to intervene in order to contribute to the fulfilment of specific objectives of economic policy. Fulfilling these objectives contributes to the overall level of welfare, be it at the expense of the level of privately appropriable goods and services. The distinction between economic and non-economic arguments has nothing to do with any value judgement about the desirability of the objectives. Moreover, the distinction is not always clear-cut.[10]

Haberler noted in 1933 that the non-economic arguments for intervention and protection are exactly those that have the greatest appeal in discussions of economic policy.[11] Some of these arguments are variations of the infant-industry argument or are in some way related to it. Corden mentions the case of a pseudo-infant-industry argument implying that intervention may take place to support an infant industry when its production is still insufficient to reap the gains from internal economies of scale.[12] Stimulation of specific industrial sectors may be required to diversify the economy and broaden the technological basis of society. In the absence of intervention, production in developing countries, poorly endowed with physical and human capital, will be concentrated in sectors at the lower end of the spectrum of technology. Hirschman, in his classical study on industrialization strategies for development, favours the stimulation of manufacturing industries that have high spread effects through backward and forward linkages.[13] In such a strategy, stimulation of "core" industries could induce investment and production in supplying and using sectors, thus creating a more balanced and diversified manufacturing sector. More general is the case in which a certain level of industrial production as such is aimed at (for a mix of political and economic reasons). Stimulation is required in case the desired level is beyond the level that would be obtained under free-trade conditions.

Reducing dependence on foreign supply for political and strategic purposes is an often-used argument for intervention, particularly in relation to so-called sensitive or strategic industries. A sufficient level of domestic supply of such products as food, military equipment and the like may be in the national interest. Such policies are evidently encouraged in case traditional suppliers threaten boycotts or the application of a kind of "trading with the enemy act".

Finally a number of non-economic arguments for intervention may be mentioned that are not so much related to the stimulation of a specific domestic activity as to other macro-economic objectives. Government intervention may be required for specific purposes related to the balance-of-payments position, employment creation, income distribution or the reduction of specific kinds of consumption (especially luxuries). A system of protection may also be applied to isolate the economy so as to reduce its vulnerability to external shocks.[14]

4.3.4 The Preference for Protection

Above we summarized the major economic and non-economic arguments for governments to intervene in market forces that are traditionally referred to in economic literature. It was postulated, first of all, that governments have a choice between different intervention instruments. Next, it was (implicitly) assumed, as is usually done, that intervention is a costless operation and that consequently the choice of policies is not influenced by differences in costs attached to the application of an instrument. Third, political factors were ignored in our discussion of the selection of systems of government intervention. The main point made above was that, given the validity of a number of assumptions, a hierarchy of policies may be distinguished according to their implications for welfare. First-best policy is to correct for market distortions at the point of divergence. Only in the case of distortions in international markets or in the case of society's non-economic objective to reduce international trade (or increase self-sufficiency) is tariff protection first-best policy. In all other cases first-best policy would be not to apply trade restrictions but to select instruments that offset directly the source of distortion or that aim directly at the pursued (non-) economic objective. Taxes and subsidies on factor use, production and consumption are preferable to trade barriers. This is due to the distortions emanating as a by-product from the application of trade barriers.

Some brief remarks are in place regarding the validity of the above-mentioned assumptions related to the costs and distortions of taxing and the costs of disbursement of subsidies.[15] Like tariffs, taxes on consumption create distortions (the so-called deadweight costs) and have collection costs. It is reasonable to assume that taxes on foreign trade have relatively low collection costs as compared to alternative tax cum subsidy systems because of the high concentration of international trade at only a limited number of economic agents in a few locations. Differences in collection costs may turn a tariff system into a favourable intervention system in spite of the distortions it brings about. Additionally, application of alternative intervention systems may not be feasible for countries at low levels of development, as pointed out earlier. An elaborate system of subsidization presupposes the functioning of a sophisticated network of tax collection and subsidy disbursements. Thus, compared to a system of protection against imports, a system of subsidization may be costly and complex. Restriction of imports by means of tariffs or quotas causes the domestic price level of imported and domestically produced substitutes to rise, so that automatically domestic consumers are taxed and producers subsidized.

Apart from the relatively low costs and the relative simplicity of a system of trade intervention, there may also be political factors that favour a system of protection over alternative forms of government intervention. So far, government was conceived of as a kind of exogenous institution, having perfect insight in the functioning of markets and operating as a benevolent force for the sole purpose of maximizing welfare for society at large. This proposition, however, does not necessarily adequately reflect the actual way in which governments operate. Government has a monopoly position in society in the formulation of policies and the application of instruments which have pecuniary effects on groups in society. This may and will induce groups in society to advocate policies that favour their interests. Such lobbying activities of groups involve the allocation of resources in order to obtain the revenue created by the application of specific instruments such as subsidies, tariffs, quotas, and production and import licenses. Thus, interest groups that demand protection compete in the political market with groups that are interested in other policies. The political market may be imperfect like any other market. Consequently, the outcome of this competition is not simply determined by the relative size of the rival interest groups but also by other factors that determine the persuading power of groups, such as economic power, degree of organization and means to finance lobbying activities.[16]

Specific demands for protection made by interest groups may be supported by other groups that do not have an *ad hoc* interest in the specific case at all. Mutual support in lobbying activities in favour of protection may emerge in circumstances when protection is conceived of as an "insurance policy". The political behaviour of the supporting groups is one of solidarity for the sake of self-interest.[17] When society has come to be characterized by a conservative welfare function in which income stability or job security has become one of society's objectives included in the welfare function, domestic support for specific demands for protection may be widespread.[18] Government, in its turn, is also assumed to pursue its self-interest which may be regarded as an interest in survival. The relationship between government and constituency may take many different forms. In an undistorted democracy, government survival is determined by the outcome of votes. In almost all cases, however, not merely group size but the economic and organizational strength of groups as well determine their impact on the chances of government to survive. As a consequence, for the sake of its own survival, a government may opt to pursue policies that do not purely reflect the preferences of society at large. In case the outcome of this process of policy formulation in a distorted political market is protection, this outcome may not be optimal in terms of national welfare but may be desirable both for the government in terms of political support and for some interest groups that appropriate the revenue created by protection.[19]

A system of trade barriers may have the political advantage for government of taxing its citizens in a less perceptible way while, at the same time, such a system of taxation stimulates specific domestic industries. Such a system of concealed taxation may contribute to a government's popularity and consequently to its chances to survive. As the implicit subsidy to industry is not part of the government budget in the case of trade barriers (as it is in alternative subsidy programmes), it is less likely to be scrutinized frequently, which is an attractive feature to the protected industry.

An unfavourable external position may add to the economic and political attractiveness of protection. To reduce trade deficits in the short term, governments tend to apply quantitative import restrictions rather than increase tariff rates, since the effect of the former type of import control is more predictable. The benefits of import licenses may accrue to rent-seeking firms.[20] Such measures to control imports may further be supported widely by domestic producers of import substitutes in case of an overvalued exchange rate. Such a position of the exchange rate has, in fact, often been the rationale for the imposition of quantitative restrictions. An overvalued exchange rate creates a climate highly conducive to the formation of coalitions of interest groups in support of protection against imports. Under such circumstances all import-competing firms (and also export firms) — not only infant industries and the least efficient firms — seek government assistance.

The point made here is that neither the extent of government intervention nor the way intervention is organized is merely a matter of correcting for market failure in the first-best way or of intervening for the sake of maximizing welfare for society at large. Interest groups invest in the shaping of policies and, once their favoured policies have been adopted, they will obstruct subsequent attempts to implement policies less favourable to them.

4.4 EFFECTS OF PROTECTION

From the point of view of the export performance of the manufacturing sector, the most obvious difference between stimulation through protection against imports and through subsidies is the home-market bias in production which results from the application of import barriers. While a system of across-the-board subsidization of industries would favour industries producing for the domestic and foreign markets over the non-industrial sectors which are taxed to finance the subsidy, a system of barriers to imports of manufactures favours import-competing industries over exporting industries and the non-industrial sector. A system of import barriers may stimulate industrialization and diversification in developing countries and may assist in changing the traditional international division of labour between developed and developing countries. But it discourages production expansion by means of export production and retards change in the structure of exports. This may explain why structural change in exports is a relatively late phenomenon in the pattern of development of developing countries, which can only be brought about after the initial industrial incentive system has been transformed or adapted. Developing countries that have applied a rigorous industrial incentive system by means of import-restrictive policies for a considerable period are thus characterized by a relatively high level of industrialization and a traditional structure of exports. This is especially true of developing countries with a large domestic market.

The expected effects of tariffs and other barriers to imports of manufactures are (1) a reduced share of imports in domestic demand for manufactures; (2) a reduced share of exports in manufacturing production; (3) an increased value of manufacturing production, and diversification of the economic structure; (4) a sub-optimal allocation of resources. Tables 4.3–4.5 show the results of an empirical investigation into the effects of duties on imports. The findings presented in Table 4.3 show that such import barriers have a significant impact on the market orientation of production.

TABLE 4.3
PROTECTION, IMPORT SUBSTITUTION AND THE ANTI-EXPORT BIAS IN MANUFACTURING PRODUCTION, 1977

Dependent variables	Constant term	DD_m	T^m/M_m	n	R^2
M_m/DD_m	1.03*	−0.07*	−0.05*	54	0.57
	(10.66)	(8.27)	(3.53)		
E_m/O_m	0.39*	−0.01	−0.05*	54	0.25
	(4.09)	(1.71)	(4.10)		

Symbols: M_m/DD_m = ratio of the value of manufactured imports (M_m) to the value of domestic demand for manufactures (DD_m)

$DD_m = O_m - E_m + M_m$

E_m/O_m = ratio of the value of manufactured exports (E_m) to the value of manufacturing production (O_m)

T^m/M_m = ratio of the value of total import duty revenue (T^m) to the value of manufactured imports (M_m)

Notes : equations are in semi ℓn-form. The t-statistics are in parentheses. An asterisk (*) indicates that the variable is statistically significant at a 95 per cent confidence interval.

Sources: data on values of manufactured imports and exports taken from UNCTAD, *Handbook of International Trade and Development Statistics, Supplement 1980,* United Nations, New York, 1980. Table 6.1A.
Data on values of manufacturing output taken from United Nations, *Yearbook of Industrial Statistics, 1981 Edition,* Volume I, New York, 1983.
Data on import duty revenue taken from IMF, *Government Finance Statistics Yearbook,* Volume VIII, Washington DC, 1984.
Exchange rates taken from IMF, *International Financial Statistics,* Volume XXXIV, Number 11, Washington DC, 1981.

Additional regression analyses, not presented here, in which the impact of import duties on total and manufactured imports and exports *per capita* is estimated, controlling for GDP *per capita* and population size, also show a significant impact of import duties.[21] The results reconfirm the findings presented in Chapter 3 and above, and indicate that inclusion of a variable related to trade policy in Chenery-like equations may contribute to an explanation of the variation among countries in the level of trade-related activities.

Diversification and broadening the basis of the economy are often used as non-economic arguments for protection. In most developing countries the net effective rate of protection for manufacturing production exceeds by far the net effective rate of protection for non-industrial activities.[22] In this way protection tends to favour the use of domestic and foreign resources in manufacturing sectors over their use in other sectors. We expect this to be reflected in an increased share of the protected manufacturing sector in domestic production.

Table 4.4 shows the impact of duties on manufactured imports on the share of the manufacturing sector in the economy, and on the value of manufacturing production *per capita*. The results are not as expected. There is no significant positive relationship between protection of the manufacturing sector and the sector's size, controlling for GDP *per capita* and population size. The first two regression analyses in Table 4.4, both based on a sample of developed and developing countries, show a negative and insignificant impact of import duties.

Additional estimates for 1980, not presented here, based on a sample of developed and developing countries, also show a negative but insignificant impact of duties on manufactured imports on value added *per capita* in manufacturing production.[23] This may be due to the use of alternative barriers to imports such as quota and import licenses or to the use of subsidies in countries that are less dependent on import duties for the stimulation of domestic industries. As subsidies are predominantly used by developed countries, we made an additional regression analysis based on a reduced sample of developing countries and semi-industrial Mediterranean countries only (n = 40). The results, presented in the last row of Table 4.4, show a positive but insignificant impact of import duties on value added *per capita* in manufacturing production.

Balassa finds that diversification of the manufacturing sector increases significantly as a consequence of protection.[24] His regression analysis shows that, given the level of development and the size of the economy, tariffs tend to reduce the degree of specialization within the manufacturing sector by inducing production in sectors in which the country is not yet efficient enough to compete internationally.

TABLE 4.4
PROTECTION AND THE SIZE OF THE MANUFACTURING SECTOR, 1977

Dependent variables	Constant term	GDP/P	P	T^m/M_m	n	R^2
VA_m/GDP	-0.09 (0.85)	0.03* (2.69)	0.01* (2.37)	-0.01 (1.06)	54	0.35
VA_m/P	-3.72* (5.49)	1.19* (19.03)	0.07* (2.17)	-0.02 (0.35)	54	0.93
VA_m/P	-4.36* (4.26)	1.25* (13.24)	0.07 (1.44)	0.06 (0.49)	40	0.87

Symbols: VA_m/GDP = percentage share of manufacturing value added in GDP
 VA_m/P = manufacturing value added *per capita* in US dollars
 T^m/M_m = ratio of the value of total import duty revenue (T) to the value of manufactured imports (M_m), expressed as a percentage
 GDP = Gross Domestic Production in US dollars
 P = population size in thousands of inhabitants.

Notes : first equation is in semi *ln*-form, second and third equations are in double *ln*-form. The *t*-statistics are in parentheses. An asterisk (*) indicates that the variable is statistically significant at a 95 per cent confidence interval.

Sources : data on GDP *per capita* and population taken from UNCTAD, *Handbook of International Trade and Development Statistics, Supplement 1980*, United Nations, New York, 1980, Table 6.1A.
Percentage share of manufacturing value added in GDP calculated from The World Bank, *World Tables, The Third Edition*, Volume I, The Johns Hopkins University Press, Baltimore and London, 1984.
Sources of data on import duty revenue and exchange rates as of Table 4.3.

The relationship between protection and efficiency is not straightforward. Import duties and other import barriers may be imposed to protect domestic industries at a stage when they are not yet efficient enough to compete with foreign firms. In such cases the rate of protection reflects the margin of inefficiency of domestic firms. However, import duties may also be applied for reasons unrelated to the level of efficiency of domestic industry. As discussed earlier, the objectives of intervention in free trade may be manifold, such as protection of the balance-of-payments position, contribution to government revenue, or reduction of the size of the foreign-trade sector in the economy for strategic or political reasons. These interventions create distortions in the pattern of allocation, so-called policy-imposed distortions. As a consequence of these distortions, induced by taxes on trade, allocation of resources is not optimal and the level of value added generated by available factors of production is not at its maximum when measured in international prices. Indeed, protectionist measures may also have been taken to correct endogenous distortions in product and factor markets but in such cases protection against imports is not first-best policy because of the by-product distortion effect of import duties. Consequently, either protection is used to protect inefficient industries or it creates a sub-optimal allocation.

One way to study the relationship between protection and inefficiency may be to estimate an aggregate production function that includes import duties as a proxy for protection. If it holds that taxes on imports are related to inefficiency in one of the ways described above, we should be able to find a significant negative relationship between import duties and the value of production generated by capital and labour. The production function refers to the manufacturing sector at large. Estimation of the relationship is hampered by the inavailability of data on capital use in manufacturing production. We have applied data on electricity use as a proxy for capital use. Due to the limited availability of such data the sample size is reduced considerably. The results, presented in Table 4.5, indicate that there is a significant relationship between the ratio of import duties to manufactured imports and inefficiency. It has to be noted, however, that the underlying causation is not evident.

TABLE 4.5
PROTECTION AND INEFFICIENCY IN
MANUFACTURING PRODUCTION, 1977

Dependent variable	Constant term	K_m	L_m	T^m/M_m	n	R^2
VA_m	−2.71* (2.76)	0.39* (3.59)	0.62* (4.79)	−0.13* (2.48)	28	0.96

Symbols: VA_m = value added in the manufacturing sector in millions of US dollars
K_m = electricity use in the manufacturing sector in millions of KWH
L_m = number of employees in the manufacturing sector.
T^m/M_m = ratio of the value of total import duty revenue (T^m) to the value of manufactured imports (M_m), expressed as a percentage.

Notes : equation is in double ln-form. The t-statistics are in parentheses. An asterisk (*) indicates that the variable is statistically significant at a 95 per cent confidence interval.

Sources : Data on VA_m, K_m, L_m taken from United Nations, *Yearbook of Industrial Statistics, 1981 Edition,* Volume I, New York, 1983.
Sources of data on import duty revenue and exchange rates as of Table 4.3.

4.5 REGIME TRANSFORMATION: REDUCING THE ANTI-TRADE BIAS

4.5.1 Some General Observations on Regime Transformation

Protectionist countries may want to transform the trade and industrialization regime in order to reduce the anti-trade bias in production and to stimulate manufacturing industries to export. The need of such a transformation or adaptation of the regime does not necessarily follow from the requirements or interests of the manufacturing sector itself but may also emerge from factors outside the sector. Exhaustion of the most obvious import-substitution possibilities may bring about the need of adaptations in trade policy. Unintended side effects, inconsistencies and absurdities, arising from a complex and extensive regime of trade barriers, may necessitate policy reform.[25] Chronic balance-of-payments problems, accumulation of foreign debts and a high debt-service ratio may also force a government to such adaptations. Export-stimulation policies are part of the IMF's conditions for balance-of-payments assistance. However, in spite of compelling reasons to do so, most developing countries with a protectionist history find it difficult to opt wholeheartedly for policy reforms reducing the anti-trade bias.

Applying principal component analysis and discriminant analysis, van Dijck and Hoogteijling attempted to classify developing countries according to their capacity to liberalize.[26] The principal components that are extracted from the original variables in their analysis relate to the trade orientation of the economy, the net trade position, the diversification in production and exports, and the dependence of government on revenue from taxes on international trade. The pattern of scoring of the sample countries indicates that countries at low levels of income *per capita* in particular have a low degree of diversification and a high dependence on taxes on international trade in financing the government budget. Probably, in such countries the government will be reluctant to reduce taxes on trade and there is no strong lobby of exporters in favour of liberalization of the trade regime.

There is no simple change-over from inward-oriented policies towards more open policies, and conceiving this change-over as one decisive step in a one-way development process bypasses the economic and political complexity of policy reforms. Many attempts to alleviate the anti-trade bias in the regime have failed. Case histories show that periods of liberalization may be succeeded by a return to protectionist policies.[27]

The aims of such policy reforms are to bring about (1) a more favourable ratio between the world market price, expressed in the domestic currency, and the domestic market price for tradeables; (2) a more favourable ratio between the supply price of a country's exporters, expressed in foreign currency, and the supply price of foreign competitors. The first element relates to the reduction of the anti-trade bias in the incentive system; the second element relates to increasing the competitiveness of domestic producers in the world market.

In most cases a change in regime is implemented by means of a large nominal devaluation of the overvalued domestic currency, complemented by a set of measures that increases profitability and reduces costs in the export sector, such as tax exemptions, favourable import-licensing schemes, tariff-exemption schemes, rebate schemes for tariffs paid on imported inputs, subsidized export credits and export-insurance programmes. Surveys of the many instruments involved are presented in studies by Donges, Balassa and Krueger.[28] A summary of the evidence is presented by Keesing.[29] A brief overview of export-promotion policies in East and South-East Asian countries is presented in van Dijck and Verbruggen's study and in Part II, Chapters 11–17 of this volume.[30]

To what extent an increase in export orientation takes place depends, apart from the immediate pecuniary effects of the measures, on the expectations of producers with respect to consistency in the future export consciousness of the government. Krueger finds that all developing countries that successfully penetrate world markets with manufactures have in common a realistic exchange rate and a consistent export-stimulation policy.[31] According to Keesing, "... the celebrated success of so-called 'outward-looking' or 'export-promoting' strategies of development is built largely around the use of 'realistically' valued exchange rates.... Use of exchange rates in this way can even be viewed as a development strategy".[32]

4.5.2 An Inventory of World Bank Recommendations on Regime Transformation

Major elements of policy packages that aim at reducing the anti-trade bias in government policies are listed in an inventory of World Bank policy prescription and recommendations in Table 4.6. These recommendations are taken from World Bank country studies based on the findings of World Bank missions. The country studies deal with the country's economic performance in the past and its economic outlook, with the structure and performance of the main economic sectors, and with government policies. It goes without saying that the performance of the manufacturing sector cannot be seen in isolation from the rest of the economy and that the trade and industrialization policies are part and parcel of a much broader package of policies. The inventory presented here does not attempt to list in full all policy recommendations in the country studies but to present, in a stylized fashion, the main policy recommendations that are directly related to the liberalization and export performance of the manufacturing sector.

EXPORT STRATEGIES

The following countries are included in our inventory.

Country	Mission's visit	Report published	Country	Mission's visit	Report published
Argentina	1983	1985	South Korea	1983	1984
Bangladesh	1978	1979	Mauritius	1981	1983
Brazil	1981	1983	Mexico	1976	1979
Chile	1977	1980	Morocco	1978	1981
China	1980	1983	Peru	1980	1981
Colombia	1982	1984	Philippines	1979	1980
Dominican Rep.	1976	1978	Thailand	1982	1984
Ecuador	1983	1984	Uruguay	1978	1979
Kenya	1978	1983			

The list includes 17 developing countries with wide differences in structural characteristics such as level of economic development and industrialization, size of the domestic market, population density and natural-resource endowment, as well as in economic policies and performance at the time of the World Bank mission's visit. At the one extreme we find such countries as Brazil, China and Mexico with a diversified manufacturing sector which is predominantly oriented towards the large domestic market. At the other extreme are small (island) economies such as the Dominican Republic and Mauritius that are highly dependent on the international economy.

Some countries in the sample experimented with a shock-wise opening-up of the economy during the 1970s. This holds in particular for Chile and Argentina. In Chile an essentially *laissez-faire* policy has been pursued since September 1973. The government that took power at that time largely eliminated non-tariff barriers and reduced tariffs drastically to a level which is lower than in any other developing country. In Argentina a "badly designed process of opening the economy" was started in the period 1978–1980.[33] Next are a number of countries that are gradually moving towards an open industrialization regime, albeit not always in a fully consistent fashion over time. Countries characterized by a reduced anti-export bias in the system of incentives are Brazil, Colombia, South Korea, Thailand and Uruguay.

We may also distinguish a number of countries with a typically dual structure of incentives for the manufacturing sector. Manufactured exports in such countries are generated by only a limited number of firms that operate under conditions clearly distinguishable from conditions under which most other firms operate that produce for the domestic market only, apart from some occasional private dumping practices. The most extreme form of such a dual system of incentives is the combination of an EPFZ with a highly protected domestic-market-oriented industry. Cases in point are the

TABLE 4.6
INVENTORY OF WORLD BANK RECOMMENDATIONS TO LIBERALIZE
THE TRADE REGIME AND TO STIMULATE EXPORTS OF MANUFACTURES

Country	Exchange-rate policy	Import policy	Fiscal policy	Factor-market policy	Investment policy	Export-promotion policy
Argentina	Stabilize a realistic exchange rate.	Allow temporarily duty-free imports of inputs for (indirect) exporters.	Give tax rebates and drawbacks for (indirect) exporters.	Give exporters preferential access to credit.		Simplify incentive system. Simplify export administration. Improve government trade-promotion services (market information, trade fairs, promotion of quality standards).
Bangladesh	Facilitate access to foreign exchange for exporters.		Harmonize incentives for non-export and export industries.	Facilitate finance to sustain fledgling export ventures. Stimulate investment in export industries by tax and subsidy incentives.		Strengthen Export Promotion Bureau to supply information on markets and product design. Implement study programmes on export opportunities.
Brazil	Devalue gradually the domestic currency in real terms.	Reduce level of protection during achievement of real devaluation.	Harmonize incentives for non-export and export industries.			

TABLE 4.6 *(cont'd)*

Country	Exchange-rate policy	Import policy	Fiscal policy	Factor-market policy	Investment policy	Export-promotion policy
Chile						
China		Increase import opportunities for exporters.	Cancel indirect taxes and reduce profit mark-ups on domestic inputs used in exports.		Improve design of consumer and capital goods. Update industrial technology.	Decentralize foreign-trade management. Allow exporters to establish sustained and direct contact with (potential) foreign buyers.
Colombia	Accelerate rate of devaluation: speed up crawling peg adjustments.	Dismantle administrative controls: lift import-quota restrictions, relax import licensing. Reduce and equalize tariffs, remove special incentives to import capital goods.		Review labour legislation, especially regarding fringe benefits. Increase availability of capital funds for exporters.	Promote direct foreign investment and joint ventures of domestic and foreign firms.	Promote export marketing. Improve export-related infrastructure (ports and customs).
Dominican Republic	Increase access to parallel market for foreign exchange.	Liberalize imports (of packaging material) for export products.	Reconsider the introduction of export subsidies and its problematic implications.			Create new EPFZs. Improve market information.

(cont'd overleaf)

TABLE 4.6 (cont'd)

Country	Exchange-rate policy	Import policy	Fiscal policy	Factor-market policy	Investment policy	Export-promotion policy
Ecuador	Maintain an appropriate real exchange rate.	Allow duty-free imports for exporters. Reduce dispersion in the tariff structure.	Repay domestic taxes in full to exporters.	Improve access to credits for exporters.		Simplify administrative procedures for exporters. Provide export-support services.
Kenya	Implement system of compensated devaluation.	Replace quantitative restrictions by tariffs. Moderate and harmonize tariffs.	Give temporary export subsidies to equalize tariff incentives.	Introduce programme of export credits and financial guarantees.	Reallocate government investments to contribute to balance of payments.	Establish central export-marketing organization.
South Korea		Reduce non-tariff barriers. Trim tariffs.		Contain wage costs in manufacturing and services.	Automate production methods. Improve productivity and design. Upgrade product mix.	Improve marketing. Collaborate with TNCs and General Trading Companies; stimulate international sub-contracting and joint ventures. Stimulate domestic R and D. Support licensing arrangements.

TABLE 4.6 (cont'd)

Country	Exchange-rate policy	Import policy	Fiscal policy	Factor-market policy	Investment policy	Export-promotion policy
Mauritius		Speed-up administrative issuance of import licenses.	Harmonize incentives for non-export and export industries.	Develop an export-credit-insurance scheme.	Attract foreign export-investment.	Promote sales in import markets.
Mexico	Avoid overvaluation of exchange rate; adjust frequently in case of domestic inflation.	Dismantle or liberalize licensing system.	Consolidate system of CEDIs (sales tax reimbursement).	Limit wage increases to growth of productivity.	Stimulate export-oriented investment and joint ventures.	Increase stability in rules.
		Rationalize tariff system, reduce tariff rates to 10–15 per cent on an average.	Create an effective system of drawbacks on import duties for export firms.	Increase flexibility of labour laws.		Reduce the application of discretionary measures in policies affecting exports.
		Eliminate tariff exemptions for public-sector agencies and for imports of capital goods.				Promote exports by smaller firms by establishing trading companies and by subcontracting arrangements.
		Allow duty-free imports of goods to be re-exported.				

(cont'd overleaf)

TABLE 4.6 (cont'd)

Country	Exchange-rate policy	Import policy	Fiscal policy	Factor-market policy	Investment policy	Export-promotion policy
Morocco		In the short-term, simplify and generalize in-bond system with tariff and tax-free imports for exporters. In the long term, rationalize the system of import quotas, tariffs and export subsidies.	Lengthen period of exemption from business profit tax. Abolish "statistical" export tax. Give direct export subsidies in the case of new products.	Reduce costs of export credits by interest subsidies and favourable maturities.	Stimulate foreign investment.	Strengthen services to exporters (export-training programmes, etc.). Increase provision for losses in manufacturing and shipment.
Peru	Combine rationalization of exchange-rate policy with a reduction of tariffs and export subsidies.	Accelerate tariff reductions. Restrict exceptions for infant industries to a limited number of industries and with clearly defined time with limits.			Attract foreign investment and stimulate joint ventures.	

TABLE 4.6 (cont'd)

Country	Exchange-rate policy	Import policy	Fiscal policy	Factor-market policy	Investment policy	Export-promotion policy
Philippines		Reduce protection by the lowering of peak tariff rates and of tariffs on non-competing imports. Reduce redundancy in tariffs. Lower tariffs to 20–30 per cent on an average. Allow all export firms duty-free imports of raw materials and components. Remove licensing by the Central Bank.	Substitute sales taxes for high tariffs on luxury items.	Improve credit provision of export industries. Create special credit facility for financing raw-material procurement by export firms. Establish an export-credit guarantee and insurance scheme. Reduce rates of short-term export-financing facilities.		Simplify export documentation. Make trading companies help small firms to export.
Thailand		Continue rationalization of the tariff structure by narrowing the tariff band.			Eliminate biases against exporting in investment incentive structure.	Support more explicitly production and marketing of potential exports.

(cont'd overleaf)

TABLE 4.6 *(cont'd)*

Country	Exchange-rate policy	Import policy	Fiscal policy	Factor-market policy	Investment policy	Export-promotion policy
Uruguay	Adjust the exchange rate timely and appropriately.	Accelerate reduction and harmonization of tariffs.	Conditioned on the achievement of an appropriate exchange rate, reduce tax rebates.			Improve institutional co-ordination of export-promotion efforts. Organize labour-training programmes.

Sources : recommendations taken from the following World Bank country studies:

Argentina	:	*Economic Memorandum*, Volumes 1 and 2, 1985.
Bangladesh	:	*Current Trends and Development Issues*, 1979.
Brazil	:	*Industrial Policies and Manufactured Exports*, 1983.
Chile	:	*An Economy in Transition*, 1980.
China	:	*Socialist Economic Development*, Volumes I, II and III, 1983.
Colombia	:	*Economic Development and Policy under Changing Conditions*, 1984.
Dominican Republic	:	*Its Main Economic Development Problems*, 1978.
Ecuador	:	*An Agenda for Recovery and Sustained Growth*, 1984.
Kenya	:	*Growth and Structural Change*, Volumes I and II, 1983.
Korea	:	*Development in a Global Context*, 1984.
Mauritius	:	*Economic Memorandum: Recent Developments and Prospects*, 1983.
Mexico	:	*Manufacturing Sector: Situation, Prospects and Policies*, 1979.
Morocco	:	*Economic and Social Development Report*, 1981.
Peru	:	*Major Development Policy Issues and Recommendations*, 1981.
Philippines	:	*Industrial Development Strategy and Policies*, 1980.
Thailand	:	*Managing Public Resources for Structural Adjustment*, 1984.
Uruguay	:	*Economic Memorandum*, 1979.

Dominican Republic, Mexico, the Philippines, Morocco, Mauritius and China. In the Dominican Republic, the successful export industries were operating in the EPFZ in the period preceding the World Bank mission's visit. In Mexico, manufactured exports expanded "in spite of Mexico's overall policies".[34] About half of the value of manufactured exports was generated in the special zone at the border with the USA. In many ways, export industries in the Philippines are enclave industries even if they do not operate in an EPFZ. The same goes for Morocco. In Mauritius the export performance is entirely dominated by firms operating in the EPFZ. China only recently started a process of liberalization and created special export zones in the vicinity of Hong Kong and Macao. Finally, the list includes some countries where liberalization had barely started by the time of the World Bank mission's visit, as was the case in Bangladesh, Kenya, Ecuador and Peru. Bangladesh is a special case. Textile exports are of great importance to the country's export performance, but apart from the textile sector manufacturing industry hardly contributes to exports.

In the inventory, we distinguish six areas of government intervention: exchange-rate policy, import policy, fiscal policy, factor-market policy, investment policy, and export-promotion policy.

Again, it should be noted that only measures that are recommended in the direct context of trade liberalization and export stimulation for the manufacturing sector are included in the inventory.

The inventory reveals, on the one hand, the many dimensions of the complex process labelled "liberalization of the trade and industrialization regime". It shows, albeit indirectly, the labyrinth of the world of second- and next-best policies. On the other hand, the inventory shows clearly and unequivocally the "hierarchy in policies", ranging from first-best to second- and next-best policies. Reviewing the policy recommendations in the World Bank country studies, we may distinguish the following priorities in the process of liberalization and rationalization of the incentive system. The incentive system should be neutral between domestic-market-oriented industries and export-oriented industries. Management of the balance of payments through exchange-rate adjustment is preferable to the application of specific (and non-automatic) import-control and export-stimulation measures. Across-the-board liberalization is preferable to selective liberalization for export industries only. Tariffs are superior to administrative control of imports. The dispersion in tariff rates should be limited.

From the inventory of World Bank recommendations on regime transformation it follows directly that timely and appropriate adjustment of the exchange rate is seen to be the single most important device to manage the balance-of-payments position of the economy and to provide an unbiased incentive to domestic-market-oriented industry and export industry. In many of the countries under review, the overvalued domestic currency hampers export production and, other things being equal, stimulates imports. Devaluation stimulates export production and enables a reduction in nominal tariff rates without reducing the net effective rate of protection for domestic-market-oriented industry. Compensated devaluation, i.e. the combination of devaluation and tariff reduction, is the most frequently prescribed avenue to liberalization and export stimulation. Changes in effective rates of protection should, preferably, not be implemented shock-wise. Moreover, they should be announced well in advance to allow the process of industrial restructuring to proceed as smoothly as possible. To establish neutrality in the incentive system during the transition towards a more open regime, specific instruments may be applied — temporarily — to stimulate export industries. Export subsidies (preferably not on export values but on domestic value added in exports), tax rebates, and tax- and tariff-exemption schemes for export industries are frequently applied and recommended instruments. Major drawbacks of such instruments are that they do not give an automatic across-the-board incentive to export industries, require administrative control and may turn out to be costly. In a world of second- or next-best policies efficient administrative support is essential for the incentive system to be effective as is stressed time and again in the recommendations.

In view of the precarious balance-of-payments situation of many a developing country, priority is given to straightforward export promotion. Repeatedly, reports call for "aggressive" export-promotion programmes, most clearly so in the country studies on Argentina, the Philippines and Colombia.[35] Improved access to credits and the development of export-credit and insurance schemes are frequently suggested. Export-credit schemes entail a *de facto* subsidy of exports through lowered interest rates and, to a lesser extent, through favourable repayment terms. Export-financing facilities become more and more important in giving a supplier a competitive edge in world markets and are increasingly used by developing countries for export promotion.[36] Development of export-support services, such as marketing and distribution agencies and trading houses, is another frequently suggested tool to stimulate (infant) export industries. Promotion of export-oriented foreign investment is suggested to diversify exports, acquire modern technology, upgrade the product mix, improve product quality and facilitate marketing. Only rarely is the establishment of EPFZs recommended. Such a recommendation for a dual incentive structure is based on the expectation that more favourable policies to expand exports are not feasible in the short term. Cases in point are the Philippines (in the country study of 1976) and the Dominican Republic.[37]

The recommendations are presented here in the quite rigid framework of an inventory. As such, the inventory gives a clear overview of the steps to be

EXPORT STRATEGIES

taken to liberalize the economy and to stimulate manufactured exports. However, to appreciate fully the depth and width of the recommended policy changes and their possible impact, they should be seen against the background of a country's structural characteristics, past economic performance, the characteristics of the trade and industrialization policies actually pursued, and the mission's assessment of the necessity and feasibility of policy change in the future. In some cases, recommended changes in policy are a matter of fine-tuning and are in line with the changes in government policies that are actually taking place. Chile is a case in point. No recommendations on Chile's trade and industrialization regime are included in the inventory since, according to the mission's assessment, the policies actually pursued, which are essentially *laissez-faire* by nature, are to be continued. As stated in the report: "(i)n its broad outlines, the economic policy reforms introduced by the present Government are consistent with advice long offered Chile by the World Bank and other international institutions".[38] In other cases the recommendations imply a strong deviation from actual policies. An extreme example is the set of recommendations on Madagascar, not included in the inventory, where the recommended policy is a scenario for a more open economic development completely different from the actual drive towards a more inward-oriented development.[39]

4.5.3 The Role of Economic Atmosphere in Regime Transformation

Finally, attention should be paid to the implementation of policy reform and to the setting or atmosphere in which export stimulation is to take place since this dimension is not fully dealt with in the inventory itself. To assure an efficient functioning of the instruments listed earlier and an adequate response of the private sector to government policies, a stable and efficient government with a high political commitment to export stimulation, and a synergistic partnership between the public and private sectors are required. These factors may be crucial elements of the "rather special social and political characteristics" that are behind the successful export performance of some East-Asian countries, as was already suggested in the previous chapter.[40] Efficiency, stability and reliability of government policies were stressed by Krueger and Keesing and are sometimes explicitly mentioned in the inventory.

Synergistic partnership as a factor that has an impact on the performance of the manufacturing sector is, as such, not new in the literature. The classical literature on the import-substitution era frequently referred to it, be it in different terms. "Tailor-made protection" and "made-to-measure" intervention can be conceived of as the result of a synergistic partnership between government and the private sector to protect the latter against import competition. In the context of export promotion it implies institutionalized cooperation, indicative planning, the creation of special agencies to stimulate exports and the formulation of export targets in the national agenda. The Japanese and Korean approaches to export-conducive atmosphere creation are by now well documented. Miyohei Shinohara and Toru Yanagihara stress the importance of consensus-making as a variable to explain Japan's industrial development and export drive.[41] In the case of South Korea, Kwang Suk Kim highlights the government's capability of controlling the private sector and of making it contribute to export performance by compulsion.[42]

These so-called non-economic factors are part of the macro-economic management of the economy. Management, then, enters the production function of the economy as a factor separate from capital and labour or, alternatively, as a kind of efficiency parameter. Its impact was shown before, be it in a restricted way, in Table 4.5 where a variable for sub-optimal protectionist policy enters the production function of the manufacturing sector. The role of macro-economic management and synergistic partnership in articulating comparative advantage will be discussed again in the next chapter.

4.6 PROCESSING BEFORE EXPORT OF PRIMARY PRODUCTS

In previous sections we showed the effects of protection on the export performance of the manufacturing sector, and discussed ways to reduce or neutralize the bias against exports in the trade and industrialization regime and the specific instruments to be applied to stimulate industry to export. Stimulation of exports of industrially processed primary products is in itself not so much a strategy entirely distinct from the strategy of export stimulation discussed earlier. It is, rather, a somewhat special option — related to the specific natural-resource endowment of countries — to stimulate industrial development and manufactured exports. As was shown earlier, small, densely populated countries and countries with a poor natural-resource endowment are characterized by an export-oriented pattern of industrialization, and are highly dependent on manufactured exports for foreign-exchange earnings. The availability of abundant natural resources in a country generally results in a development pattern that differs significantly from that in resource-poor countries. Resource-rich countries are characterized by a relatively large contribution of the primary sector to GDP and to total exports, and a relatively high concentration in exports.[43] As long as the primary export sector is capable of earning the foreign exchange required to finance imports, there is no strong inducement to stimulate the manufacturing sector to contribute to foreign-exchange creation. The availability of natural resources, however, may create additional options for industrialization. Natural resources may provide the basis for processing and related heavy industries. They may also create the opportunity to specialize in resource-based manufactured exports. Roemer mentions a series of countries engaged in one or both of these resource-based industrialization strategies such as Brazil, Chile, Jamaica, the Philippines, Venezuela and other oil-exporting countries.[44]

As discussed in Chapter 2, the export performance of many developing countries is still dominated by only a few export crops or mining products that are exported unprocessed or only marginally processed. Some insight into the division of labour between developing and developed countries with respect to processing activities can be obtained from the following data taken from a UNIDO study on processing of natural resources. The data pertain to the exports of primary products of 73 developing countries in 1972.

Not processed in exporting country and not processed in importing country	: 10.4 per cent
Not processed in exporting country and processed in importing country	: 32.7 per cent
Processed in exporting country and not processed in importing country	: 35.9 per cent
Processed in exporting country and processed in importing country	: 21.0 per cent

Thus, nearly 54 per cent of exports of developing countries did undergo further processing in importing countries.[45] However, a trend is discernible of increasing domestic processing before export. A study by Yeats, in which two or more (usually three) processing stages are distinguished, shows that in 16 out of 21 product groups of major interest to developing countries, the percentage contribution of products exported in the first processing stage (unprocessed or marginally processed) decreased between 1964 and 1974 while the percentage contribution of products in the highest processing stage increased in 18 out of 21 products groups.[46] A similar development is shown in an UNCTAD study on the changing composition of developed countries' imports from developing countries during the 1970s, in which imports are distinguished according to the stage of industrial processing. Here again, it appears that in the course of time the percentage share of products from primary sectors that were industrially processed before they were exported increased.[47]

The significant differences between products in the degree of processing before they are exported, as shown in the studies by Yeats and UNCTAD and in the study on mineral processing by Bosson and Varon, may be attributed to a series of distinct factors related to technology, transportation, market structure and government policy in developed countries.[48] A detailed discussion of all barriers to the further development of export-oriented processing industries in developing countries is beyond the scope of this chapter. However, a few remarks are in place with respect to the factors just mentioned.

It is not *a priori* evident that developing countries well endowed with natural resources also have a complementary advantage in industrial processing of primary products. Although there are wide differences in techniques used in processing of different natural resources, most techniques are characterized by high inputs of physical and human capital. In particular processing of minerals and metals is capital-intensive by nature. As will be shown in the next chapter, wood processing is an exceptionally labour-intensive processing industry while food processing, also, is much less capital-intensive than most other processing industries are. Consequently, the availability of unskilled labour is in many cases not a significant locational advantage for developing countries. Of much greater importance are the costs of capital, the availability and costs of skilled labour and of complementary inputs required for processing, and the infrastructural conditions.[49]

Other factors that may tip the balance in the choice of location of processing activities are differentials in transportation costs and taxes. Industrial processing of primary products before export may reduce volume and weight per unit of value and thus reduce the incidence of transportation costs. However, such processing activities may also have the opposite effect, due to a more difficult way of handling processed products compared to bulk transportation of unprocessed products. Much depends on practices of liner conferences that use administered prices, "charging what the traffic can bear".[50] Yeats' calculations show that on an aggregated level, including all commodities, the *ad valorem* freight rate decreases with processing but this does not apply to all commodities.[51]

Negative external economies may be created by certain polluting industrial processing activities. To reduce these negative side effects, taxes may be imposed or specific costs-increasing environmental measures may be dictated by the government. If it is true that concern with environmental quality is positively related to the level of income *per capita* in a country, this may create a differential in production costs that favours the location of polluting activities in developing countries.

Possibilities for developing countries to exploit fully comparative advantages in processing activities are hampered by man-made barriers to enter foreign markets, namely the policies of firms with vested interests in the markets and protectionist policies of governments in developed countries. This, however, is not typical of (processed) primary products and goes for many more products that are potentially of interest to developing countries' exports. Survey studies by UNCTAD and the World Bank indicate a high degree of concentration and vertical integration of production, transportation and marketing in the markets of (processed) primary products.[52] By applying restrictive business practices, oligopolistic firms operating in these markets raise barriers to entry for newcomers. Tariff escalation — i.e. the increase of tariff rates with the stage of processing of the primary product — is another factor, probably of less importance than the former, which inhibits international relocation of processing activities. Not only does this factor add to the other barriers to entry but it also creates another element of uncertainty in the planning of investments in export-oriented processing industries in developing countries, which is of particular importance in view of the high investments in physical capital that are required in many of such industries.

4.7 EXPORT-PROCESSING FREE ZONES

In this section we deal with a third avenue for developing countries to stimulate manufactured exports, viz. by the creation of a new export-oriented enclave. Such enclaves, usually referred to as Export-Processing Free Zones (EPFZs), are a rather recent phenomenon as most of them have come into operation only since the 1970s.

4.7.1 Characteristics of EPFZs

A number of definitions of an EPFZ are in use. For our analysis it is essential to distinguish an EPFZ, in which export-oriented manufacturing activities take place, from a free-trading zone, such as a free port or an entrepôt, in which merely trade-related activities take place but no manufacturing production. EPFZs have a physical infrastructure and a legal framework specifically adapted to export-oriented manufacturing activities to be undertaken by foreign investors. Within the delimited area of the zone, in most cases situated in the vicinity of an air- or seaport, duty-free importation of capital goods and intermediate inputs is allowed, and export of goods is free of tax. Tax-free profit remittances are allowed, at least for the initial period (in most cases five to ten years). In some cases the legislation with respect to the host country's major primary input, unskilled labour, is adapted: wage labourers engaged within the zone are deprived of their rights to unionize and to strike.

The system of incentives and regulations differs from country to country and not all of the characteristics apply to all EPFZs. In some cases not only foreign investors but also joint ventures of foreign and domestic firms operate in the zone; in other cases a limited share of production may be sold in the domestic market; tax incentives differ, and some countries apply incentives for export firms operating outside the zone that are comparable to the incentives applied within the zone; regulations related to labour conditions may not be incorporated in the EPFZ legislation but nevertheless applied in actual fact.[53]

The EPFZ is an enclave and can hardly be considered part of the host country's economy.[54] It is characteristic of an EPFZ that (1) economic activities are almost entirely undertaken by foreign enterprises; (2) management, technology, capital goods (apart from the infrastructure) and intermediate inputs are almost entirely imported; (3) production is destined almost entirely for foreign markets; (4) investment, tax and labour legislation are adapted.

4.7.2 The Spread of EPFZs

Table 4.7 lists the countries in which EPFZs were in operation or were planned or under development in 1980. At that time, 57 zones in 30 developing countries were in operation and 34 zones in 19 countries were planned or under development. The list does not include Singapore and Hong Kong, which can be regarded as enclave-like export economies, Bermuda and the Bahamas, where two EPFZs were in operation, and Puerto Rico, which also can be regarded as an enclave-like export economy. Apart from the four EPFZs in China that were set up in Shenzen, Zhuhai, Shantou (Swatow) and Xiamen (Amoy) in 1980, 14 more Chinese cities on the Pacific border have been opened for foreign investment and trade since 1984.

As follows from the table, the zones are concentrated in two regions: Central America and the Caribbean, and East and South-East Asia. The establishment of EPFZs is apparently not related to any specific structural characteristic of the host country such as level of income *per capita*, size of the domestic market, natural-resource endowment or population density. Neither is there any evident relation to the political structure or the general economic policy of the countries concerned.

4.7.3 The Rationale for Establishing EPFZs

A major "advantage" of this particular export-oriented industrialization strategy is that export production can be initiated without adaptation or transformation of the regime of protection for firms producing for the domestic market. The implementation of a dual system of incentives allows a continuation of protectionist industrialization policies or the retarded implementation of a liberalization and restructuring process required to increase the efficiency and competitiveness of domestic manufacturing industry. Thus, while second- or next-best stimulation policies continue, manufactured exports may start to generate foreign-exchange earnings and employment opportunities. In view of the many economic and political

TABLE 4.7
EXPORT-PROCESSING FREE ZONES IN DEVELOPING COUNTRIES, 1980

Country	EPFZs in operation	EPFZs planned or under development	Country	EPFZs in operation	EPFZs planned or under development
Bangladesh		1	South Korea	2	
Barbados	1		Liberia	1	
Belize	1		Malaysia	10	
Brazil	1		Malta	1	
UR of Cameroon		1	Mauritius	1	
Chile	1		Mexico	2	
China[1]		4	Nicaragua	1	
Colombia	3	1	Pakistan		1
Costa Rica		2	Panama	1	
Dominican Rep.	3		Philippines	3	12
Dubai, United Arab Emirates		1	Saint Lucia		1
El Salvador	1	1	Samoa	1	
Egypt	4		Senegal	1	
Fiji		1	Sierra Leone		1
			Sri Lanka		1
Ghana		1	Sudan		1
Guatemala	1		Syrian Arab Rep.	3	
Haiti	1		Taiwan[2]	3	
Honduras	1		Thailand		1
India	2		Tunisia	2	
Indonesia	2		Venezuela		1
Jamaica	1		Zaire		1
Jordan	1				
Kenya		1			

Notes and sources:
[1] zones (3) in operation in China in 1981 are listed in Basile, A. and D. Germidis, *Investing in Free Export Processing Zones,* OECD, Paris, 1984, Table 1, p. 22. Information on zones (4) set up in China in 1980 taken from *South, The Third World Magazine,* Number 60, October 1985 (South Special Report), pp. 75-83.
[2] Listed in Basile, A. and D. Germidis, Table 1, p. 22.
Unless otherwise indicated, information taken from UNCTAD, *Export Processing Free Zones in Developing Countries: Implications for Trade and Industrialization Policies,* TD/B/C.2/211, 1983, Tables I and II, pp. 32-34.

difficulties involved in regime transformation, this export strategy is an attractive option for governments.

Additionally, countries may resort to an EPFZ policy to remove obstacles that otherwise might obstruct the expansion of non-traditional exports. The obstacles referred to here may be summarized as follows. First, the country may be an efficient and competitive producer of a range of products for which foreign demand is limited or for which the income elasticity of demand in high-income countries is low. Linder and Stewart both stress the differences in the structure of domestic demand and domestic production in countries at different levels of income *per capita*.[55] Developing countries, being competitive in the production and export of products for which there is an extensive market in low-income countries, may be incapable of producing efficiently the range and quality of products in demand in high-income countries, as domestic demand for such products is insufficient to back up an efficient domestic industry. Second, penetration into foreign markets may be hampered by marketing and distribution problems. Extensive market reconnaissance, creation of goodwill and development of marketing and distribution systems are necessary preconditions for successful export performance. Third, foreign-market penetration may be hampered by import restrictions and regulations. The system of protection in developed countries has grown more complex and opaque with the increasing importance of non-tariff barriers and the application of a wide variety of regulations that are (veiled) devices to impede imports. The restrictions may create unsurmountable barriers for industries in developing countries to enter foreign markets.

A country may try to overcome these obstacles to entering foreign markets by encouraging foreign firms to set up export-oriented production lines. These firms possess the production technology, they are familiar with the import markets, they have at their disposal international distribution systems and they may even be in a position to influence trade policies by lobbying in their home countries.[56] In this way, EPFZs may create the opportunity for the host country to expand its exports.

4.7.4 Types of Activity in EPFZs

Two types of industrial activity in the zones may be distinguished. First, old vintages of capital goods that have become marginal or submarginal at the going wage level in developed countries are relocated to countries where such vintages can operate profitably. Such relocation activities take place in labour-intensive and mature production processes. In many cases, such activities are organized by marginally efficient medium-sized firms and not so much by large TNCs from developed countries.[57] Relocation of less efficient vintages is also organized between developing countries by TNCs from developing countries.[58] The second type of export-oriented production activity is undertaken by TNCs in new production processes. In contrast to the sequence in the allocation pattern according to the product-cycle theory of investment and trade, export-oriented labour-intensive production and assembly activities are in this case set up in developing countries right from the beginning of the new production process. As formulated by Sharpton, "(t)he product cycle probably still occurs, but the time-lags have been drastically shortened: if a new process is intensive in the use of low-skilled labour, it may be moved to offshore factories soon after the prototype stage".[59]

4.7.5 The Contribution of EPFZs to Development

A major drawback of export stimulation in enclaves is that its contribution to overall economic growth of the host country's economy is limited, for the following reasons. First, as almost all capital goods and intermediate inputs are imported, production in the enclave does not generate substantial backward-linkage effects to other firms within or outside the zone. This is an outstanding example of what Hirschman called the "antiseptically linkage-free" enclave industry.[60] Second, the domestic value-added component in output that contributes to domestic development is small as profits are allowed to be remitted and taxes are non-existent or only limited, at least in the initial period. The wage component of value added thus appears to be the major contribution to domestic income and foreign exchange. As follows from the analysis to be presented in the next chapter, production in EPFZs is concentrated in a number of sectors that are characterized by relatively low wages per employee. According to UNCTAD, the domestic value-added component in exports in EPFZ is normally below 25 per cent, 70 per cent or more of which is wage income.[61] Third, the contribution to technological development is limited. Production is concentrated in standardized processes within an international intra-sectoral pattern of specialization. As will be shown in the next chapter, the skill intensity of these processes is low. High labour turnover rates, as a result of using young, unmarried female labourers and using apprenticeship contracts, add to this. As formulated by Edgren: "the notion that EPZs could serve as 'nurseries' for the development of industrial skills has not been borne out by experience".[62] Finally, it is likely that in the use of the infrastructure, set up by the government of the host country, a subsidy is involved, which reduces the net benefits of the activities in the zone to the host country. Competition among developing countries to attract foreign investors in export enclaves tends to lower tax revenue and to increase subsidization of production.[63]

Much of the criticism of export-oriented industrialization as summarized in Chapter 1, relates in particular to activities concentrated in EPFZs. It is a fallacy, however, to identify export production with export-enclave production. In some of the major exporting countries the contribution of EPFZs to the manufactured export performance has been limited. In 1978, it was about 4 per cent in South Korea, 7.4 per cent in Taiwan, 0.3 per cent in India, and 7.2 per cent in the Philippines. In Malaysia, however, where ten EPFZs are in operation, 33 per cent of the value of semi-manufactured and manufactured exports was generated in the EPFZs. In Mexico, about 50 per cent of the production of manufactured exports was concentrated in the special zone bordering the USA. Indeed, in some countries where domestic manufacturing industry does not provide a basis for trade, for the reasons mentioned earlier, manufactured export performance is dominated by foreign investors operating within or outside EPFZs. In Mauritius, for instance, about 92 per cent of export production in 1977 was concentrated in the EPFZ.[64] Presumably, the large share of manufactured exports in total exports of goods in a number of Caribbean countries, listed in Chapter 2, is to a high degree.

4.8   FOREIGN FIRMS IN THE EXPORT SECTOR

4.8.1   The Role of TNCs in Export Production

TNCs play a major role in production and trade of manufactured products in the world economy. It has been estimated that in the early 1970s as much as 50 per cent of the total value of manufactured exports of developed countries was handled by firms that may be classified as TNCs. Including the trade of their affiliates, the share could approximate two thirds of total manufactured exports of developed countries.[65] Although by far the larger share of investment and production activities of TNCs is concentrated in developed countries, they play an important role in import substitution, industrial processing of primary products, and export of manufactures in developing countries as well. TNCs, *par excellence*, are in a position to exploit the opportunities created by new systems of communications and transportation, and by new production techniques. They allocate production and assembly activities so as to use to the best advantage international differences in production costs. The major locational advantage of developing countries in export-oriented manufacturing activities is the relatively low wage level in manufacturing industry. However, the changing position of developing countries in the international division of labour, as reflected by their penetration into world markets of manufactures, is not only the result of a changing pattern of allocation of TNCs in search of cheap labour.

As indicated earlier, TNCs may play a predominant role in the export performance of countries where domestic industry does not provide a basis for trade. In general, however, the contribution of TNCs to manufactured export production is considerably less than the contribution of domestic industries, which reflects the maturity of domestic industry and the appropriateness of economic policies to stimulate domestic industry to export. This is substantiated by the data presented in Table 4.8. Most data relate to the early 1970s and possibly underestimate the role played today

TABLE 4.8
CONTRIBUTION OF TRANSNATIONAL CORPORATIONS TO MANUFACTURED EXPORTS

Country	Year	Contribution (percentage)	Country	Year	Contribution (percentage)
Argentina[1]	1969	> 30	Mexico[2]	1970	25-30
			Mexico[1]	1973	35
Brazil[2]	1969	43	Mexico[4]	1974	34
Brazil[1]	1973	40			
			Pakistan[1]	1973	8
Colombia[2]	1970	> 30	Pakistan[4]	1975	< 10
Colombia[3]	1970	> 35			
Colombia[1]	1973	28	Philippines[5]	±1971	20-25
Hong Kong[1]	1973	10	Singapore[3]	1971	> 50
			Singapore[5]	1972	30
India[2]	1970	5	Singapore[1]	1972	75
India[1]	1973	6	Singapore[4]	1978	92
South Korea[1]	1972	15	Taiwan[2]	1971	> 20
South Korea[4]	1978	27	Taiwan[5]	1972	12-15
Malaysia[1]	1971	28	Taiwan[1]	1973	16

Sources: [1] Dunning, J.H., *International Production and the Multinational Enterprise*, George Allen and Unwin, London, 1981, Table 12.1, pp. 330, 331.
[2] Nayyar, D., "Transnational Corporations and Manufactured Exports from Poor Countries", in: *The Economic Journal*, Volume 88, March 1978, Table 1, p. 62.
[3] Cohen, B.I., *Multinational Firms and Asian Exports*, Yale University Press, New Haven and London, 1975, p. 10.
[4] United Nations Centre on Transnational Corporations, *Transnational Corporations in World Development, Third Survey*, New York, 1983, Table IV. 3, p. 137.
[5] Hone, A., "Multinational Corporations and Multinational Buying Groups: Their Impact on the Growth of Asia's Exports of Manufactures — Myths and Realities", in: *World Development*, Volume 2, Number 2, February 1974, pp. 147, 148.

by TNCs. The data are taken from several sources and should be interpreted carefully because of differences in definitions of TNCs that are used in the underlying studies.

It appears from Table 4.8 that TNCs play a major role in the export performance of Latin-American countries. According to Vernon, over 40 per cent of all manufactured exports from Latin America were generated by US-owned subsidiaries in 1968.[66] In addition to this, 58 per cent of trade in manufactures among LAFTA member countries was organized by foreign firms in 1969.[67] The contribution of TNCs is more limited in the Asian countries except Singapore. Apparently, the dynamics of the successful export-led growth strategies of South Korea, Taiwan and Hong Kong do not depend so much on direct investments of TNCs in the export sector. As these Asian countries are the major exporters among the developing countries, the overall share of TNCs in total manufactured exports of developing countries is rather limited. According to Nayyar, around 1974 this share was probably not much greater than 15 per cent and has not show any significant increase since 1966.[68]

The involvement of TNCs in manufactured export performance of developing countries differs between product groups. Dunning distinguishes three degrees of involvement and classifies sectors according to the role TNCs play in exports, as is shown in Table 4.9. Textiles, wearing apparel, food products, wood products, electrical machinery and miscellaneous products are major export categories of developing countries. As follows from the grouping of sectors in the table, TNCs are not strongly involved in exports of textiles, wearing apparel, wood products and miscellaneous products, but they are highly involved in exports of food products and electrical machinery. Activities of TNCs are mainly concentrated in manufacturing sectors characterized by high capital and skill requirements, large research and development efforts, economies of scale and product differentiation. In such sectors the barriers to entering world markets are often unsurmountable for firms from developing countries. By stimulating TNCs to engage in export production, developing countries can reap some gains from trade in sectors that are beyond reach for domestic entrepreneurs. Thus, in sectors with high barriers to entry, we expect manufactured exports to be generated to a great extent by TNCs. As a number of such sectors — particularly electrical machinery and instruments — have favourable demand prospects, we may expect the contribution of TNCs to export performance of developing countries to increase in the course of time.

A recent phenomenon in the sphere of export-oriented foreign direct investment in developing countries is the rise of TNCs from developing countries. In general, TNCs from developing countries apply mature, standardized techniques with small production runs.[69] Most home countries of these corporations are newly industrializing countries such as Hong Kong, Taiwan and South Korea. Most host countries are neighbouring countries. These export-oriented foreign investments are prompted by the following factors: (1) the need to relocate vintages of capital goods that are marginal or submarginal at the going wage level in the home country to countries with lower wage levels; (2) the need to circumvent country-specific import quotas and other import restrictions in developed countries by relocating activities to countries that are less restricted by such protective measures; (3) in the case of densely populated home countries, differences in land costs may be another explanatory factor for this relocation process.[70]

Apart from foreign direct investments there are many other forms of foreign involvement in production and trading of manufactured exports of

TABLE 4.9
CLASSIFICATION OF MANUFACTURING SECTORS ACCORDING TO THE ROLE OF TRANSNATIONAL CORPORATIONS IN EXPORTS[1]

High involvement :	Petroleum processing
	Rubber
	Electrical machinery
	Transportation equipment
	Instruments
	Chemical products
	(pharmaceutical products and petrochemicals)
	Non-electrical machinery
	Food, beverages and tobacco
Medium involvement :	Primary metals
	Fabricated metal products
	Construction materials
	(stone, clay, cement, etc.)
	Printing and publishing
	Textile
	Miscellaneous manufactures
Low involvement :	Wearing apparel
	Wood, wood products and furniture
	Leather and leather products

Note : [1] relates to exports of manufactures from Argentina, Brazil, Hong Kong, India, Mexico, Singapore and Turkey.
Source : Dunning, J.H., *International Production and the Multinational Enterprise,* George Allen and Unwin, London, 1981, Table 12.3, p. 334.

developing countries, such as joint ventures, turnkey projects, loans, technology transfers and international marketing arrangements. International subcontracting arrangements play a vital role in the internationalization of production and the relocation of manufacturing activities from developed to developing countries. Such arrangements may be differentiated according to the contributions of the foreign principal firm and the domestic subcontractor, respectively, as is illustrated in the classification schemes of Watanabe and Michalet.[71] These different kinds of subcontracting arrangements range from a mere commercial relationship — in which the subcontractor is ordered to deliver a product to the principal firm — to a much more comprehensive arrangement in which the principal firm provides the inputs and possibly the machinery and production blueprints, the subcontractor being merely an assembly or processing firm that is wholly dependent on the principal firm for both its inputs and the sale of its output. Such an industrial subcontracting relationship may *de facto* differ only marginally from a vertical intra-firm integration scheme.

4.8.2 The Role of International Trading Houses in the Export Drive

The contribution of international trading houses to the organization of international trade grows rapidly. This is also true of their contribution to the export performance of developing countries. Their role in the expansion of manufactured exports from developing countries is probably more crucial than the role of foreign investment in plant and equipment. International trading houses supply marketing know-how that may be more difficult to acquire than production know-how. International trading houses, particularly the general trading houses, provide for trade-related services such as market research, shipping, warehousing and financing. By means of extensive networks of market-reconnaissance units and the large number of firms that are linked to their operations, these trading houses improve accessibility to international markets. They are able to organize barter-trade arrangements and to settle trade arrangements in local currencies. They render services to small and medium-sized producers and buyers who lack the capacity to operate internationally. By doing so, "trading companies can turn these small-scale manufacturers into multinationals by supplementing all their requirements".[72] To expand trading opportunities, general trading houses make foreign investments and become directly involved in export-oriented manufacturing production. Their main objective, however, is expansion of trade opportunities.[73]

The largest general trading houses are of Japanese origin. *Sogo shosha* have played a critical role in Japan's post-war export drive. By 1975, the ten largest trading houses handled 56 per cent of both total exports and total

EXPORT STRATEGIES

imports of Japan. The total value of their international transactions by that time amounted to over 5 per cent of world exports. Up to 74 per cent of Japan's textile imports were handled by these firms. They have played a particularly important role in Japan's trade with developing countries: 72 per cent of imports from Latin America and 53 per cent of imports from South-East Asia were handled by a dozen or so major Japanese trading houses in 1973.[74] The relocation of labour-intensive manufacturing activities from Japan to its neighbouring countries has typically been brought about by trading houses in co-operation with small and medium-sized manufacturing enterprises.[75]

Since the 1970s and particularly after 1973, Japanese trading houses have become more globally oriented and have increased their participation in trade between third countries. The share of these third-country transactions in their total transactions increased from 5.7 per cent in 1971 to 10.7 per cent in 1974, 11.6 per cent in 1975 and 9.0 per cent in 1977.[76] Japanese trading houses have become increasingly important for the export drive of developing countries in East and South-East Asia.

In some other developed and developing countries also, efforts have been undertaken to establish international trading houses. Barter-trade arrangements, prompted by foreign-exchange shortages in developing countries, have stimulated TNCs from developed countries that are trading with developing countries to set up such trading companies.[77] Trading houses from Western Europe and the USA, however, do not operate on such a vast scale, are not so diversified in their operations, and do not have such extended networks of communications and information at their disposal as the Japanese companies do. Nevertheless, they, too, play an important role in the relocation of industrial activities from their home countries to developing countries in the Caribbean, Northern Africa and Asia.

Some developing countries have set up their own, often state-supported international trading houses. Tsurumi attributes a considerable part of the successful export expansion of Brazil and South Korea since the oil crisis in 1973 to the role of their newly established trading houses. In Brazil, *Interbras* and *Cobec* were created in the 1970s to assist the country's export drive. Although their major activities, up to now, have been the handling of commodities, they have assisted in the export of manufactures as well. In South Korea, trading companies are structured in the Japanese *sogo shosha* style as are the "marketing arms" of the country's leading industrial groups.[78] In some other Asian countries such as Thailand and Indonesia, international trading houses have been created as well, often with assistance from Japanese companies, to facilitate the international marketing of the country's primary and manufactured products.

4.9 SUMMARY AND CONCLUSIONS

In Chapter 3 we showed that, in addition to structural characteristics of an economy, trade policy has a significant impact on the export orientation of the manufacturing sector. The role of trade policy has been the subject of this chapter. Particularly in developing countries, government and industry are dependent on trade intervention. The lower the level of development of a country, the higher duties on imports, the larger the contribution of taxes on trade to tax revenue and total government revenue. Following a review of economic and non-economic arguments for intervention, we have discussed a number of factors that may underly the preference for intervention in international trade over alternative forms of intervention. Next, we have shown the effects of intervention in international trade on the performance of the manufacturing sector. Protection against imports is associated with import substitution, a reduced export orientation and inefficiency. The relationship between protection and the size of the manufacturing sector did not appear to be significant.

To stimulate exports countries have several options. Three broad avenues to generate manufactured exports have been discussed here: regime transformation, fostering of domestic processing of primary exports, and creation of export enclaves.

Export-oriented industrialization may be stimulated by reducing the anti-trade bias in the system of incentives for manufacturing firms. However, many countries with a protectionist history find it difficult to opt for a comprehensive transformation of their trade and industrialization regime. In most cases a change in regime is implemented by means of a large nominal devaluation complemented by a series of measures to increase profitability and reduce costs in the export sector. The complex nature of regime transformation has been revealed by means of an inventory of World Bank recommendations on liberalization and export stimulation. Notwithstanding differences in emphasis between the sets of measures to be implemented in the 17 countries in our sample, the following priorities may be distinguished: incentives should be neutral between industries; exchange-rate adjustment is preferable to specific import controls or export stimuli; liberalization should be across-the-board; tariff protection is superior to quantitative restrictions, and the dispersion in rates of (tariff) protection should be limited. Apart from measures to liberalize and rationalize the trade regime, specific measures are called for to promote exports aggressively in the short term. However, only exceptionally has the creation of EPFZs been recommended in more recent reports of the World Bank.

We have paid special attention to the role of "atmosphere creation" in regime transformation. The interest in this dimension of policy making has increased significantly in the more recent literature on regime transformation. More and more, synergistic partnership between government and the private sector, and a high political commitment to export stimulation are considered to be essential to successful export performance.

It was shown in Chapter 3 that particularly small countries that are densely populated and/or are poorly endowed with natural resources follow an outward-oriented pattern of industrialization. To a high degree, such countries are forced to pursue an industrialization strategy that stimulates exports. As compared to resource-poor countries, resource-rich countries have an additional option to earn foreign exchange by processing natural resources before export. However, it is not self-evident that developing countries have a comparative advantage in the industrial processing of primary products as most such activities are capital-intensive by nature.

Creation of an export enclave that operates separately from the rest of the economy is the third avenue to stimulate manufactured exports. In view of the inefficiency of domestic industry in many countries and the economic and political difficulties involved in transforming the trade and industrialization regime, implementation of a dual industrialization strategy is an attractive option for many governments.

Available evidence suggests that transnational corporations have been of critical importance to the export performance of countries in Latin America but not so much in Asia — Singapore being a striking exception. In the latter region, international trading houses have played a vital role in the export drive since the 1970s.

5
The Composition of the Export Sector

5.1 INTRODUCTION

In previous chapters we dealt with the manufactured export performance of developing countries at an aggregated level and no reference was made to the composition of manufactured exports. We studied the contribution of manufactures, taken as a group of products, to total exports of goods in Chapter 2, the factors underlying the export orientation of the manufacturing sector at large in Chapter 3, and the role of trade policy in bringing about a more open and export-oriented pattern of industrialization in Chapter 4. This chapter will deal with the export performance at a more disaggregated level. We shall study the product composition and factor intensities of manufactured exports in countries at different stages of development. The study is organized along the following lines. First we shall review trade theories and their hypotheses regarding the comparative advantage of developing countries and the structure of their exports to developed countries. Since trade theories aim at establishing a link between characteristics of countries and characteristics of goods, our second step will be to distinguish manufactured goods according to their factor intensities. For that purpose we distinguish 26 groups of manufactured products and study their factor content. The third step will be to link the product composition and factor intensities of exports to the level of development of the exporting economies, as well as to some other variables that we expect to have an impact on the composition of exports. Finally, in order to obtain a more detailed view of the process of upgrading in exports, we shall study the changes in the composition of manufactured exports during the 1970s and early 1980s in a group of eight countries that play a predominant role in the manufactured export performance of developing countries.

5.2 COMPARATIVE ADVANTAGES OF DEVELOPING COUNTRIES: A REVIEW OF TRADE THEORIES

We shall review three theoretical approaches to the comparative advantage of developing countries: the neo-classical theory, Linder's theory and the product-cycle theory. These theories have in common that they link some selected characteristics of economies to some selected characteristics of goods. They differ, however, in their selection of variables and in assumptions on the context in which international trade takes place. As a result, theories differ in their hypotheses regarding the comparative advantage of developing countries and the structure of their exports.

5.2.1 The Neo-Classical Theory of Specialization

In the neo-classical model of specialization, a country has a comparative advantage in the production of goods that require a relatively high input of the production factor that is relatively abundantly available in the country. In Ohlin's classical study, different kinds of capital, labour and natural resources, as well as economies of scale and the economic and political atmosphere are distinguished as factors that determine a country's comparative advantage in production and trade.[1] In the generally applied Heckscher-Ohlin-Samuelson approach, however, only two factors of production, capital and labour, are distinguished and no within-factor differentiations are made. In the later neo-factor proportions approach and the neo-technology approach, human capital, as distinct from physical capital, is incorporated into the model as a determinant of comparative advantage.

In its essentials, the model is built on the assumptions that technologies are universally available, production functions are universally identical, and that there is a universally stable ranking of sectors according to factor use, the so-called strong factor-intensity assumption. We shall deal with this issue in more detail in a subsequent section of this chapter. Other assumptions are absence of transportation costs, fully competitive and undistorted factor and product markets, constant returns to scale and universally identical consumption patterns, reflected by the community-indifference curves.

The basic relationships in the model are depicted in Figures 5.1 and 5.2. Figure 5.1 shows production-possibility curves $P_1 P_1'$ and $P_2 P_2'$ for country 1 and country 2, respectively, which are at successive stages of capital accumulation. The intersections of the production-possibility curves with the y-axes have been constructed at the same point to facilitate intercountry comparisons of production structures. From a comparison of the slopes of the production-possibility curves it follows that the opportunity costs of production of the capital-intensive good, in terms of the labour-intensive

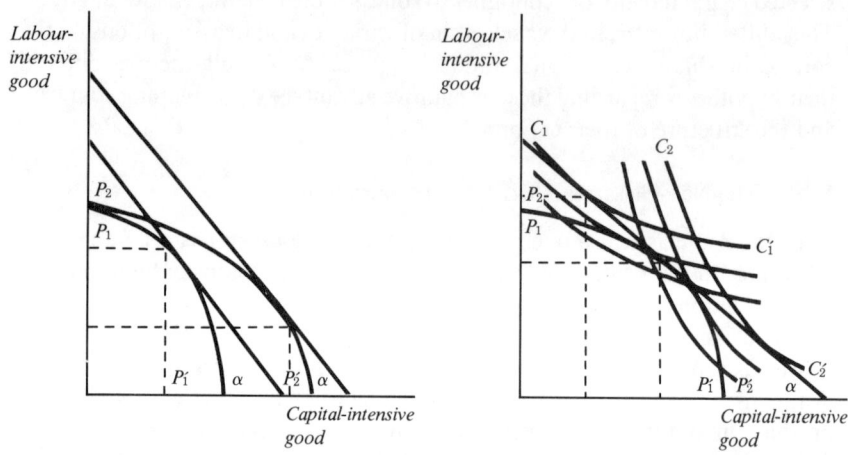

Figure 5.1
Pattern of Specialization in Production

Figure 5.2
Pattern of Specialization in Production and Trade

good, are lower as the level of capital accumulation of a country rises. If price ratios (α) are identical in all countries, i.e. if world market prices prevail, it follows that production in the capital-poor country is more concentrated in the labour-intensive good than in the country at a higher level of capital accumulation. From this it does not necessarily follow that the export structure of the capital-poor country is more labour-intensive than the export structure of the capital-rich country. A country's structure of exports and imports results from the relative position of both its production-possibility curve and its community-indifference curve. As is shown in Figure 5.2, countries with identical factors endowments and production-possibility curves have different structures of trade in the case of non-identical community-indifference curves. While country 1, with community-indifference curve C_1C_1 and with a high preference for the labour-intensive good, exports the capital-intensive good and imports the labour-intensive good, the opposite holds for country 2. Only when countries have identical community-indifference curves and world market prices prevail is it straightforward that the lower the level of capital accumulation in a country, the more predominant the labour-intensive good is its exports.

5.2.2 Linder's Theory

In Linder's approach to the composition of exports the relationship between a country's level of development and the composition of domestic demand is crucial. Linder's theory is based on the assumption that production functions differ between countries and that domestic "representative demand" is a necessary precondition for exports. In other words, a sufficient size of the domestic market is needed to back up efficient production in an industry which in a later stage may turn into an export industry. The lower the level of income *per capita*, the more domestic demand is concentrated in simple, so-called low-income products that differ from their substitutes in high-income countries in quality, design and sophistication. Thus, the lower the level of income *per capita* of a country, the more the basket of potential exports will consist of low-income products. Since such products are mainly in demand in countries at similar levels of development, developing countries have only limited export opportunities to developed countries. Developing countries may be internationally competitive in a range of products for which there is no or only limited demand in developed countries. As formulated by Linder "a labor-abundant country may not be able to achieve a comparative advantage in the kind of labor-intensive products that are demanded in the capital-abundant country".[2]

Linder distinguishes some important exceptions to what he considers the normal conditions for trade. Such exceptions may occur "(1) where it is easy to become aware of the foreign demand in spite of the nonexistence of home demand for the product; (2) where the product as such is available without inventive effort; and (3) where little or no product development work is needed".[3] In such cases production for the domestic market is not a necessary precondition for efficient export production, and footloose export production may take place in developing countries for demand in developed countries.

Some interesting observations regarding the relationship between product characteristics and the structure of demand in countries at different levels of development are made by Stewart. According to Stewart, export to high-income countries require "interlocking" with the technology in developed countries in order to produce products of the quality, design and sophistication that are in demand in high-income countries. For that reason, such high-income products, when exported by developing countries, are produced with inappropriate techniques that are sophisticated and labour-saving.[2] However, this does not necessarily imply that such techniques are more capital-intensive than the techniques already in use for production for the domestic market. Because of the skewed income distribution, a point not referred to so far, part of industrial production in the import-substitution phase is for domestic high-income groups: domestic production is a substitute for high-income products previously imported from high-income countries. Comparing the characteristics of the techniques in use in import-substituting industries and export industries, Stewart concludes that "(t)his type of import-substitution strategy requires continuous adjustments in line with changes in world technology, similar to an export-based strategy, without benefitting from the relative labour-intensity and exploitation of economies of scale that an export-oriented strategy permits. Thus an export-oriented strategy would be likely to lead to a more appropriate technology than this type of import substitution".[5]

5.2.3 The Product-Cycle Theory

The first full presentations of the product-cycle approach to international specialization were presented by Vernon in 1966 and Hirsch in 1967.[6] In 1966, however, Hufbauer formulated a theory of international trade which contains many elements of the product-cycle approach. Therefore we shall start by reviewing briefly the main elements of Hufbauer's theory.

Hufbauer distinguishes two kinds of trade flows: technological-gap trade and low-wage trade.[7] Technological-gap exports stem from the scientific and industrial lead that a country has developed *vis-à-vis* other countries. It is most likely that such a lead in industrial production is taken by producers in developed countries where a sophisticated technological infrastructure facilitates technological breakthroughs. This lead, which results in technological-gap exports, may be undone in the course of time when an imitating country establishes a comparative advantage in this line of production on the basis of low wages. This may result in a reversal of trade flows. Thus, the exports of a country at a lower level of technological development will consist of standardized and mature products for which the country has developed a comparative advantage based on its low wages: "(t)he country with the longest imitation lags must rely almost entirely upon low-wage exports to pay for technological gap imports".[8]

The duration of the imitation lag determines the time it takes to reverse trade flows. According to Hufbauer, the most promising avenues for low-income countries to acquire the technology required to start production are licensing from foreign producers and establishing foreign subsidiaries: "(f)oreign subsidiaries may offer the best hope for less advanced countries to shorten their imitation lags".[9]

The product-cycle theory offers a broader framework to explain reversing trade flows.[10] The theory distinguishes three phases in the life cycle of a product: the introductory phase, the growth phase and the mature phase. In the introductory phase of product development, new technological knowledge and a sophisticated infrastructure of suppliers of intermediate inputs are essential. Production is skill-intensive, production runs are not yet standardized and are short, and consequently production costs are high. During the growth phase, production becomes more standardized, the physical-capital intensity of production increases, production costs decrease and prices will decrease because of increasing competition. In the mature phase, the production process is standardized and characterized by larger inputs of unskilled labour and of physical capital compared to earlier phases in the life cycle.

Mature products give an opportunity for developing countries to become involved in production and trade. The production process may be transferred from a developed country to a developing country where export production is set up with imported capital goods of an early vintage. According to Hirsch, "an industrializing country may be competitive in the manufacture of mature products even when they are capital intensive, because the cost of capital may be less important than that of other factors".[11] However, in an elaboration of the basic model, in which a distinction is made between labour-intensive and capital-intensive mature goods, Hirsch's hypothesis is that labour-intensive mature goods will play a more predominant role in developing countries' exports than capital-intensive goods do.[12]

5.3 CHALLENGES TO THE EXPLANATION OF TRADE FLOWS

Trade theories provide indications for the structure of comparative advantage. The theoretical approaches reviewed above have in common that the level of development of the economy is reflected in its export structure and that a stage-wise change in the export structure will occur in the course of development. The lower the level of development of a country, the more its exports will be dominated by products, the production of which requires small inputs of physical and human capital as compared to inputs of unskilled labour (the neo-classical theory), or by unsophisticated low-income products in case of normal conditions for trade (Linder's theory), or by low-wage products (Hufbauer's theory) or by mature products, more particularly by labour-intensive mature products (the product-cycle theory). Before we pass on to the empirical investigations of the structure of manufactured exports, some remarks are in place with respect to country characteristics and product characteristics, and their possible links.

It is a truism that, as Leontief puts it, "there is a frustrating gap between theory and observation".[13] Many attempts to explain the structure of trade of countries have come up with unsatisfactory or even so-called paradoxical results. Chenery and Hughes, in analyzing trends in industrialization and trade in the 1970s, conclude that "(i)mportant as comparative advantage is as a principle for determining optimal trade patterns, it has been extremely difficult to forecast in practice".[14]

The high growth of export-oriented industry in developing countries, and particularly the rapid world-market penetration by some East-Asian economies in a wide range of products, has drawn attention to some non-economic factors that may underly the successful export performance of these countries and more in particular their competitive edge in some specific kinds of products.

As already noted in Chapter 2, only a few out of many developing countries manage to penetrate world markets of manufactured products. These few countries dominate the export performance of developing countries in almost all manufactured products. Put differently, out of the many countries that are characterized by relatively low levels of physical- and human-capital accumulation and by an abundant availability of unskilled labour, as compared to developed countries, there are only a few countries where the potential for international competitiveness in products characterized by a corresponding intensity of use of these factors of production turns into a *de facto* competitive edge in international trade. The poor export performance of many a country may be partly due to what are usually referred to as market distortions and imponderabilities. In addition to this we mention some other factors that may have an impact on the volume and the product composition of exports of countries.

In his classical study on international trade, Ohlin refers to differences between countries in political and socio-cultural factors that affect the conditions of international trade. Factors mentioned are the stability of the political climate, the reliability and efficiency of government and business morale.[15] More recently, Ohlin re-emphasized the role of such "atmosphere-creating" factors that are beyond the more narrow range of factors that characterize a country's trade and industrialization regime.[16] We have already touched upon these co-called non-economic factors when discussing the impact of institutional factors and of macro-economic management on export performance in the previous chapters.

The significance of these non-economic factors for the creation of comparative advantage is far from clear. Both Keesing and Balassa argue that there is no clear correlation between trade policies and the overall political system of countries.[17] But it is clear from country studies that successful export performance and exploitation of comparative advantage is not merely due to "getting prices right" and even less to a *laissez-faire* attitude of government. The experience of countries successful in exploiting comparative advantage indicates that active government involvement and synergistic partnership between government and the private sector are part and parcel of the export drive. According to Keesing, social congeniality between government officials and entrepreneurs may be an important factor in the creation of a trade-conducive atmosphere.[18]

Active participation and guidance of governments in the shaping of the economy, as is the case in some East-Asian economies with a strong export performance, may have its roots and justification in history and in the socio-cultural values that are prevalent in these countries and that are distinct from those in other countries.[19] As such, differences between countries in political and socio-cultural factors may explain differences in the exploitation of comparative advantage. External factors, such as the near presence of countries with a rival political-economic system, may force governments to implement policies that serve their goals in order to survive politically. South Korea and Taiwan are cases in point.

Socio-cultural factors may have an impact on the efficiency of the available factors of production in a country and consequently on the country's capacity to create a competitive edge in world trade. Differences between countries in inherited skills, social conditions and habits create differences in the efficiency of the (unskilled) labour force, as already noted by Ohlin in his classical study.[20] Consequently, countries do not have the same production function.

Leontief, in explaining the paradoxical structure of US trade in which the country appeared to have a comparative advantage in labour-intensive products, attributes this to the high productivity of the US labour force as compared to labour employed by the same industry abroad. He assumes this differential in productivity to be caused by superior entrepreneurship and organization, education and the general climate of a production-oriented society.[21] The same factors are referred to by Chenery in explaining the competitiveness of industry in a number of newly industrializing countries.[22] Hofheinz and Calder as well as Morawetz embed such factors in a broader approach to the sources of comparative advantage in East-Asian countries by relating them to historical forms of organization of society and its Confucian tradition.[23]

The high efficiency of the female labour force in Asian countries is frequently attributed particularly to traditional values and the historically subordinated position of (young) women in a patriarchal society that made them "ideally suited" for specific labour-intensive activities performed in export industries.[24] Morawetz attributes differences in competitiveness between the East-Asian clothing industry and the industry in Colombia to some degree to cultural factors that affect labour productivity, reliable quality control and punctual delivery. Again, traditional values embedded in Confucianism are put forward as an explanatory variable for the exploitation of a comparative advantage in specific labour-intensive sectors.[25]

The second factor to be mentioned here is related to the impact of new forms of organization of export-oriented production on the product composition of exports. As was shown in the previous chapter, production and assembly of components, concentrated in export enclaves and organized in international subcontracting arrangements with TNCs or international trading houses, is a new and dynamic phenomenon in international trade and in the export performance of developing countries. The increasing importance of these new forms of international production and trade was recognized by Vernon, Helleiner, Sharpton and others in the early 1970s.[26] Whatever the technological characteristics of the end product may be, the production of existing and in particular of more recently developed industrial products has increasingly become an internationally organized process in which component production and assembly are distributed over production sites according to the most appropriate conditions for every separate phase of the production process. The size of the domestic market of the exporting economy and the existence of sufficiently developed industrial infrastructure or of an efficient domestic industry are not necessary preconditions for this type of industrial export since there is no direct link between production for the domestic market and export production. This undermines the relevance of Linder's approach to the normal pattern of exports but fits into his special cases. It also undermines the relevance of distinguishing phases in the life cycle of a product as new production processes are — right from the start — subdivided and subcontracted internationally. Finally, it undermines the concept of a stages approach to the process of industrialization and trade, in which there is a clear sequence in the contribution of industrial sectors — as distinct from the contribution of factors of production — to production and trade. The concepts of early, middle and late export industries become somewhat obsolete and lose their meaning when the division of labour among countries becomes organized on an intra-sectoral basis.[27]

The factors mentioned above do not necessarily contradict the principle of comparative advantage but bear upon turning a potential international cost advantage into a competitive edge in international market, i.e. into a revealed comparative advantage. The empirical analysis of the export performance of developing countries will show that indeed, as Ohlin puts it, "within limits a country may specialize in any one industry as well as in any other".[28] Countries at about the same stage of development happen to have significantly different product compositions of exports. At the same time, there are limits to the variation in the export structure set by relative factor availabilities.

5.4 FACTOR INTENSITIES OF MANUFACTURING SECTORS

5.4.1 Intersectoral Differences in Factor Inputs

The concept of factor intensities of products is crucial to the explanation of

COMPOSITION OF THE EXPORT SECTOR

comparative advantage and the structure of trade. An analysis of the relationship between factor intensities of (export) products and factor availabilities in (exporting) countries requires a characterization of products according to factor content. For the concepts of labour-intensive and capital-intensive products to be meaningful there must be significant differences between products in terms of factor content, and a stable order of ranking of sectors according to factor intensities. In this section we shall study the extent of intersectoral differences in factor content in manufacturing sectors, while in the next section the stability of the order of ranking of sectors according to factor intensities will be analyzed.

In our study on factor inputs per unit of value added 26 manufacturing sectors are distinguished. At this level of disaggregation, statistics on value added, wages and number of employees are given in the UN *Yearbook of Industrial Statistics* for a fairly large number of developed and developing countries. In many cases, however, statistics are incomplete or have not been compiled in a fully standardized way, which hampers accurate intercountry comparisons of factor inputs in manufacturing sectors. Moreover, the factor input coefficients are not strictly "technical" coefficients but are distorted by the impact of trade and industrialization regimes. As discussed in the previous chapter, government policies may create a discrepancy between the value of production measured in world market prices and in domestic market prices. Apart from this distortion in the product market, government intervention may also distort factor use. No data, however, are available revealing the full impact of these distortions on the coefficients.

Table 5.1, column one, shows the ratio of labour inputs per unit of value added in 13 labour-intensive manufacturing sectors to labour inputs per unit of value added in 13 capital-intensive sectors. The two-way division of the 26 manufacturing sectors that are distinguished in the ISIC classification at the three digit level is based on the country-specific order of the ranking of manufacturing sectors. Factor inputs in sectors are compared with the unweighted average factor use in total manufacturing production in each country to eliminate an effect of the composition of manufacturing production on the calculations. The second column shows the between-sector variation in labour inputs in production over all 26 manufacturing sectors. The ratios clearly indicate that changes in the composition of manufacturing production may have considerable consequences for employment creation. A change in industrial policy that would favour the expansion of labour-intensive sectors may result in substantial direct increases in employment opportunities.

Table 5.1, column three, shows the variation among manufacturing sectors in average wage levels. Data on wages, as presented in the UN *Yearbook of Industrial Statistics*, refer to yearly wages. Strictly speaking, any analysis of

TABLE 5.1
FACTOR INPUTS IN MANUFACTURING SECTORS

Country	Ratio of labour inputs in labour-intensive sectors to labour inputs in capital-intensive sectors	Coefficient of variation in labour inputs, all sectors	Coefficient of variation in wage levels, all sectors
Argentina	..	..	0.18
Brazil	1.74	0.48	0.30
Chile	3.95	1.34	0.21
Colombia	2.51	0.66	0.27
Cyprus	1.70	0.32	0.29
Egypt	1.68	0.36	0.20
Hong Kong	2.36	0.64	0.19
India	2.77	0.62	0.36
South Korea	3.40	1.13	0.14
Malaysia	2.29	0.50	0.35
Malta	1.61	0.30	0.21
Mexico	2.35	0.77	0.24
Peru	3.49	1.24	0.25
Philippines	3.67	0.73	0.34
Singapore	2.73	0.56	0.29
Tunisia	2.18	0.41	0.28
Turkey	1.92	0.48	0.23

Symbols: .. = no data available.
Notes : data relate to 1975 except for Brazil (1974), Egypt (1973), Hong Kong (1973), Malaysia (1974), and Peru (1973).
The coefficient of variation of a distribution is defined as the standard deviation divided by the mean.
Source : United Nations, *Yearbooks of Industrial Statistics, 1978 Edition,* Volume I, New York, 1980.

intersectoral differences in factor inputs or factor prices should be based on the effective number of hours worked during a year, as there may be large and systematic intersectoral differences in hours worked per employee per year. For instance, the number of hours worked per employee in some processing industries is presumably low because of seasonal labour. Such data, however, are not available.

Table 5.1 shows that there are wide differences in wage levels between sectors but also that these differences are much smaller than intersectoral

5.4.2 Intersectoral Differences in Wages and Skills

As is often done in empirical studies, intersectoral differences in wage levels are used as proxies for intersectoral differences in inputs of skills of human capital. Consequently, low-wage sectors are considered to be sectors where an above average share of the labour force consists of low-skilled labour. Although there are strong arguments to relate intersectoral differences in wage levels to differences in skill levels, there may also be additional factors at work, as will be seen below.

When all industrial sectors face the same conditions of labour supply on the labour market, differences between sectors in average wage levels originate from differences in the composition of the labour force. The single most important cause of non-homogenity of the labour force is education. Education, from an economic point of view, is investment in human capital and creates skills required in the process of production. Such investment generates a future flow of income, the rent of the investment, to skilled labour. Suppose there are only two kinds of labour in the total sectoral labour force, skilled (L^s) and unskilled (L^u), with two different wage rates, w^s and w^u respectively. The sectoral average wage rate ($\bar{w}_i$) then is:

$$\bar{w}_i = \frac{L^u w^u + L^s w^s}{L^u + L^s}$$

The stock amount of investment in human capital per labourer in the industrial sector (K_i^h) may be calculated by discounting the difference between the average wage rate and the wage rate for unskilled labour, according to:

$$K_i^h = \frac{\bar{w}_i - w^u}{r}$$

where r is the rate of discount. This stock concept of human capital per labourer can be applied to rank sectors according to their skill intensity.[29] If it is assumed that there are no intersectoral wage differences per skill category and that the rate of discount is identical in all sectors of production, the sectoral ranking according to skill intensities can as well be based on intersectoral differences in average wage rates. This flow concept of skill intensity is applied by Lary, Hufbauer, Hirsch, Balassa and others.[30] However, apart from skill levels there are other factors that have a systematic impact on the sectoral wage level, four of which are mentioned below.

(1) Industrial sectors consist of firms that differ in scale of production,

factor use and factor remuneration. In general, large firms are capital-intensive, produce at high levels of labour productivity and pay high wages compared to small firms. This is reflected in large intra-sectoral differences in wage levels between firms, in particular between those operating in the formal and those in the informal sectors of the economy. Consequently, systematic differences between sectors with respect to the contributions of small and large firms to production have a systematic effect on the average wage rate in a sector. It should be noted that the data reported in the UN *Yearbook of Industrial Statistics* do not usually cover firms in the informal sector.

(2) Labour unions may cause wage rates to rise above the equilibrium price of labour; thus, intersectoral differences in the unionization rates of the labour force may result in differences between sectors in wage rates for unskilled and skilled labourers.

(3) There are substantial intra-sectoral differences in wage rates for male and female workers. Not uncommonly, female wage rages are 30 per cent below male wage rates. The forces that bring about relatively low earnings for female workers are not sector-specific but are of a more general character.

(4) Finally we mention the age structure as a variable influencing wage rates systematically. There is a positive relationship between age and the wage rate within all skill categories.

As indicated above, skills are an important but not the only factor affecting wage levels and causing intersectoral differences in wage levels. The role of these additional factors will be re-emphasized in our discussion of wages and labour conditions in export industries. In spite of these complicating factors, differences between sectors in wage levels will have to be used in the present analysis as being indicative of differences in skill levels.

5.4.3 Comparison of Total-, Physical-, and Human-Capital Intensity of Manufacturing Sectors

Total-, physical-, and human-capital intensity of manufacturing sectors are compared in Table 5.2 by calculating Spearman rank correlation coefficients of the order of ranking of sectors according to value added per employee, non-wage value added per employee and wage value added per employee, respectively. The results show that in most cases there is a significant similarity in the three orders of ranking of sectors. This implies that in sectors with a relatively high value of physical capital per employee, the relative wage level is high, which is to a high extent caused by a relatively high ratio of skilled to unskilled employees in these sectors. The relatively high inputs of physical capital and human capital per employee result in a high level of total labour productivity. The results indicate that physical capital and human skills are complementary inputs in production.

TABLE 5.2
COMPARISON OF THE ORDER OF RANKING OF MANUFACTURING SECTORS ACCORDING TO TOTAL-, PHYSICAL-, AND HUMAN-CAPITAL INTENSITY

Country	Total- vs human-capital intensity	Physical- vs human-capital intensity
	Spearman rank correlation coefficients	
Brazil	0.77	0.57
Chile	0.81	0.79
Colombia	0.83	0.77
Cyprus	0.58	0.27
Egypt	0.47	0.30
Hong Kong	0.83	0.75
India	0.82	0.65
South Korea	0.75	0.67
Malaysia	0.76	0.65
Malta	0.51	0.16
Mexico	0.64	0.57
Peru	0.72	0.63
Philippines	0.59	0.60
Singapore	0.92	0.90
Tunisia	0.76	0.61
Turkey	0.57	0.41

Sources: as of Table 5.1.

5.5 CLASSIFICATION OF SECTORS ACCORDING TO FACTOR INTENSITIES

5.5.1 The Strong Factor-Intensity Assumption

In this section we classify manufacturing sectors according to their factor intensities. An analysis of the relationship between the factor intensities of export production and factor availabilities in countries, as will be presented in Sections 5.6 to 5.8, requires a characterization of products according to factor inputs. If products cannot be characterized by their relative factor intensities, generalizations about "what products to produce where" are impossible. A necessary precondition for such a characterization of products is that the order of ranking of sectors according to factor inputs in production is stable, i.e. independent of relative factor availabilities and factor-price ratios. This is the so-called strong factor-intensity assumption. Consequently, when products interchange their positions in the order of ranking, being labour-intensive in one place and capital-intensive in another, generalizations about the (optimal) international division of labour are not possible.

Interest in this aspect of trade theory has revived since the study by Arrow, Chenery, Minhas and Solow on capital-labour substitution in CES production functions.[31] In a world with fixed technical coefficients, as is the case in Leontief-like analyses, or in a world with elasticities of factor substitution with value one, as is the case in the Cobb-Douglas model, the ranking of sectors of production according to factor intensities is identical in all countries, e.g. at all wage-interest ratios. As is illustrated in Figure 5.3, under such conditions interchanges in factor intensities of sectors do not occur: at all wage-interest ratios (w/i), the capital-labour ratio (K/L) of sector i is higher than of sector j. However, in a world in which sectors of production have different (constant) elasticities of substitution, interchanges in factor intensities of sectors, i.e. permutations in the order of ranking by factor inputs, may occur. If this is the case, the ranking of sectors according to the (K/L) ratio is not independent of the (w/i) ratio and sectors cannot be characterized as labour- or capital-intensive. Reversals of factor intensities of sectors may be a cause of the structure of trade being inconsistent with trade-theory hypotheses.

Figure 5.3
The Elasticity of Factor Substitution and the Factor Intensities of Sectors

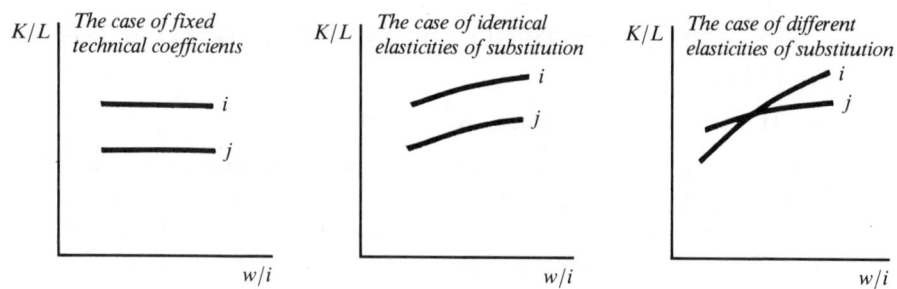

The question of the stability of the order of ranking of sectors according to factor inputs has intrigued many theorists and has provoked firm statements. According to Samuelson: "... the phenomenon of goods that interchange their roles of being more labour intensive is much less important empirically than it is interesting theoretically".[32] Lary compares the ranking of manufacturing sectors according to value added per employee between India and the USA and makes complementary analyses over a number of countries and at different levels of aggregation. He finds a number of major cross-overs but concludes nevertheless that, overall, "there is really nothing that could be regarded as a clear-cut swapping of places between industries. . . ."[33] In his study on the optimal international division of labour, Herman states that "(i)t is the present writer's conviction, . . . that the ranking of industries is substantially the same whatever the definitions adopted for the measurement of factors or whatever the country used as source of data".[34] After a careful examination of concepts and measurements of labour intensity, Bhalla concludes exactly the opposite.[35]

The results of the empirical investigations by Minhas, Fels, Leontief, Teitel, Hillman and Hirsch, and others indicate that one should be reluctant to draw rigid conclusions for or against the correctness of the strong factor-intensity assumption.[36] Fels' findings are particularly illustrative for the problem on hand. Fels shows that the order of ranking of sectors according to physical-, human-, and total-capital intensity is not insensitive to the concept of measurement. The ranking according to the stock concept of capital differs from that according to the flow concept which is used in our study. Next he shows that reversals in the order of ranking occur frequently. Applying the flow concept of total-capital intensity, i.e. value added per employee, for 18 sectors in a sample of 17 developed and developing countries, he finds that no two countries have exactly the same ranking order of sectors and that only four sectors are labour-intensive and two sectors are capital-intensive in all 17 countries.[37] The same two points follow from Teitel's study. In that study, three proxies for capital intensity are applied — value added per employee, electricity consumed per employee, and installed power per employee — to test the stability of the order of ranking of 19 sectors in samples of 26 to 30 countries. Teitel finds values of Kendall's coefficient of concordance in the range of .61 to .69 and corresponding average rank-order correlation coefficients in the range of .59 to .68.[38] Hillman and Hirsch show for 27 countries that significant differences may occur when the physical-capital intensity (non-wage value added per employee) of a country's trade structure is measured by applying US input coefficients rather than the coefficients of the country itself.[39]

5.5.2 The Order of Ranking of Sectors

In this section we show the results of an investigation into the ranking order of sectors according to factor inputs in a group of developing countries. In all subsequent analyses, wages per employee are used as a proxy for skill intensity or human-capital intensity, non-wage value added per employee as a proxy for physical-capital intensity, and total value added per employee as a proxy for total-capital intensity of production. The upper part of Table 5.3 shows the order of ranking of 26 manufacturing sectors according to total-

TABLE 5.3
RANKING OF 26 MANUFACTURING SECTORS ACCORDING TO TOTAL-CAPITAL INTENSITY IN SEVEN DEVELOPING COUNTRIES

ISIC code	Sector	Chile	Colombia	Hong Kong	India	South Korea	Peru	Turkey
				order of ranking				
311/2	Food products	19	19	18	2	16	11	15
313	Beverages	20	26	23	18	25	23	25
314	Tobacco	25	25	26	4	26	25	24
321	Textiles	5	14	19	9	11	10	8
322	Wearing apparel	1	2	3	5	3	1	5
323	Leather and products	16	5	4	10	17	7	6
324	Footwear	6	3	9	7	4	4	2
331	Wood products	3	8	13	3	14	6	9
332	Furniture and fixtures	4	1	14	1	2	2	1
341	Paper and products	24	21	15	22	15	15	21
342	Printing and publishing	14	10	17	11	12	12	20
351	Industrial chemicals	22	24	25	26	24	24	26
352	Other chemical products	23	23	20	25	22	18	23
355	Rubber products	7	20	2	20	7	21	13
356	Plastic products	10	7	8	14	6	9	18
361	Pottery, china	17	4	1	8	1	5	10
362	Glass and products	2	13	5	6	20	3	14
369	Non-metal products	15	18	22	12	23	14	11
371	Iron and steel	21	17	24	21	21	16	22
372	Non-ferrous metals	26	15	21	24	18	22	7
381	Metal products	11	11	11	15	9	8	12
382	Machinery n.e.c.	9	12	6	19	10	20	17
383	Electrical machinery	18	16	7	23	13	17	19
384	Transport equipment	12	22	16	16	19	19	16
385	Professional goods	8	9	10	17	8	13	4
390	Other industries	13	6	12	13	5	26	3

COMPOSITION OF THE EXPORT SECTOR

TABLE 5.3 (cont'd)

	Chile	Colombia	Hong Kong	India	South Korea	Peru	Turkey
	\multicolumn{7}{c}{Spearman rank correlation coefficients}						
Chile	1	.63	.59	.53	.60	.63	.60
Colombia		1	.64	.52	.81	.71	.79
Hong Kong			1	.21	.72	.51	.48
India				1	.32	.64	.49
South Korea					1	.51	.67
Peru						1	.52
Turkey							1

Notes and Sources: as of Table 5.1.

capital intensity in seven developing countries for which a complete set of data on all sectors was available. The lower part of the table shows the degree of similarity in the order of ranking of sectors in the sample countries, as measured by Spearman rank correlation coefficients. The table shows that sectors may take quite different positions in the order of ranking in different countries. Only a few sectors — particularly those at the extremes of the ranking order — do not interchange at all their position of being labour- or capital-intensive. It is not possible to identify the causes of the observed permutations in the order of ranking of sectors among countries. They may be due to substantial differences between sectors in the value of the elasticity of substitution but also to distortions in factor markets and product markets or to imponderabilities and statistical inconsistencies.

Notwithstanding permutations in the ranking orders, there is generally a significant correlation between the order of ranking of sectors in countries, as indicated by the matrix of Spearman rank correlation coefficients. Should no reversals occur, all coefficients in the matrix, of course, would have value one. The results, presented in Table 5.3, show that the choice of any country-specific order of ranking to be applied in a cross-country analysis of patterns of specialization in production and trade is arbitrary. Any selected country-specific set of factor input coefficients yields different results in such cross-country analyses, as shown in Table 5.4.

Table 5.4 shows the percentage share of labour-intensive products in manufactured exports from the seven countries to OECD countries in 1975 measured by relative factor inputs in each of the seven exporting countries. The rows of the table show that the contribution of labour-intensive products to exports in every country differs when measured by factor input coefficients of different countries. The columns show that the positions of countries in the international division of labour according to their specialization in labour-intensive products is not independent of the choice of definition of labour-intensive products.

TABLE 5.4

SPECIALIZATION IN LABOUR-INTENSIVE EXPORTS IN SEVEN COUNTRIES MEASURED BY FACTOR INTENSITIES IN SEVEN COUNTRIES

Exports from	Factor intensities in:						
	Chile	Colombia	Hong Kong	India	South Korea	Peru	Turkey
Chile	*14.83*	14.75	15.70	36.48	14.06	31.48	25.37
Colombia	76.28	*49.88*	47.97	87.66	72.94	80.90	81.24
Hong Kong	86.56	79.82	*89.60*	76.41	97.91	70.09	80.94
India	73.64	54.42	55.34	*81.65*	73.65	82.63	85.40
South Korea	77.04	65.38	77.94	71.51	*82.32*	68.18	73.54
Peru	56.81	40.83	41.84	70.01	50.54	*67.11*	50.67
Turkey	64.60	33.47	34.30	88.03	62.16	88.24	*59.90*

Notes : as of Table 5.1.
Sources: data on manufactured exports to OECD countries taken from OECD, *Trade by Commodities, Market Summaries: Imports, Jan.-Dec. 1975*, Volumes I and II, Series C, Paris. Sources of all other data as of Table 5.1.

5.5.3 A Classification of Manufacturing Sectors

Notwithstanding the questionable value of the strong factor-intensity assumption, almost all cross-country studies of trade structures apply a country-specific set of data on (relative) factor inputs to all countries under investigation. For reasons of data availability these factor inputs relate to industry in a developed country in most cases. The assumption then is that this specific set of data is representative for all countries. However, as theoretically there is no reason why this should be so, and as empirical investigations show intercountry reversals in the order of ranking, we prefer to apply a different approach in this study. In this approach, use is made of coefficients of (relative) factor inputs that are derived from factor input coefficients of 26 manufacturing sectors in 17 developing countries. All major exporting countries for which data are available are included in the analysis.

In constructing the sets of coefficients that represent relative total-, physical-, and human-capital intensity of sectors, the following steps are taken.

First, we calculate the *country-specific* relative factor intensity of sector i ($i = 1...26$) in country j ($j = 1...17$) by dividing the sectoral capital intensity by the country-specific arithmetical average value of the capital intensity in manufacturing. Second, we calculate the sectoral relative factor intensity by taking the arithmetical average of the observations for our sample countries. Third, we rank the 26 sectoral averages according to total-, physical-, and human-capital intensity.

As observed earlier, not all data are of the same quality and uniform definition; hence, "outlying observations" may occur. To obtain insight into the distorting effects of observations that differ significantly from the rest of the observations, rejection tests are applied to the extreme observations per sector. The acceptance region includes the values which have a high probability of being observed, and the rejection region includes the values which are highly unlikely, i.e. which have a probability of less than one per cent. Comparison of the order of ranking of sectors before and after rejection of such "outlying observations" shows that only some minor changes of places of sectors in the ranking order occur. Only in one case (Peru in ISIC sector 390, other industries) does exclusion of an "outlying observation" result in a significant change of the sector's position in the ranking order. In this case —which is by far the most extreme "outlying observation" of all — the relative total-capital intensity of the sector in Peru is 5.95, nine times as high as the sector's average relative total-capital intensity in the rest of the observations. Inclusion of Peru would place the sector among the capital-intensive sectors while exclusion of the extreme observation places it among the labour-intensive sectors. With respect to the physical-capital intensity, the position of this sector in Peru is even more extreme, scoring over twelve times as high as in the rest of the observations. This most extreme observation is due to a statistical inconsistency since value added in Peru's sector of other industries includes the value added in handicraft activities while the data presented on wages and employment are exclusive of such activities. For that reason, this observation is excluded from the samples related to total- and physical intensity.

Table 5.5 shows the positions of the 26 manufacturing sectors in the ranking order, obtained according to the procedure described earlier. Not surprisingly, the similarity in the order of ranking according to total- and physical-capital intensity is large since the larger share — about 70 per cent in most cases — of total value added is non-wage value added. Although, generally speaking, sectors that score high according to their use of physical capital also score high in their use of human capital, this similarity does not hold for all sectors, as is visualized in Figure 5.4.

The representativeness of the three sets of standardized orders of ranking of 26 manufacturing sectors is tested by comparing these standardized orders with the orders of ranking of sectors in the 17 sample countries individually.

TABLE 5.5
TOTAL-, PHYSICAL-, AND HUMAN-CAPITAL INTENSITY OF 26 MANUFACTURING SECTORS

ISIC code	Sector	Total-capital intensity		Physical-capital intensity		Human-capital intensity	
		relative value	order of ranking	relative value	order of ranking	relative value	order of ranking
311/2	Food products	0.92	15	0.95	16	0.84	8
313	Beverages	1.67	24	1.84	24	1.15	21
314	Tobacco	2.58	26	3.05	26	1.06	15
321	Textiles	0.58*	4	0.47*	4	0.85	9
322	Wearing apparel	0.46*	1	0.40*	3	0.65*	1
323	Leather and products	0.66°	9	0.60°	9	0.73*	2
324	Footwear	0.50*	2	0.39*	2	0.79°	5
331	Wood products	0.61*	5	0.54*	6	0.76°	3
332	Furniture and fixtures	0.53*	3	0.37*	1	0.77	4
341	Paper and products	1.08	19	1.10	19	1.04	14
342	Printing and publishing	0.79	13	0.68°	11	1.14	19
351	Industrial chemicals	1.80	25	2.00	25	1.34	26
352	Other chemical products	1.38	22	1.48	22	1.27	24
355	Rubber products	1.08	20	1.10	20	1.14	20
356	Plastic products	0.77	12	0.78	14	0.83	7
361	Pottery, china	0.73	10	0.69	12	0.87	10
362	Glass and products	0.65*	6	0.49*	5	1.03	13
369	Non-metal products	1.03	18	1.02	18	1.07	17
371	Iron and steel	1.33	21	1.35	21	1.31	25
372	Non-ferrous metals	1.67	23	1.71	23	1.21	22
381	Metal products	0.75	11	0.67°	10	0.95	12
382	Machinery n.e.c.	0.86	14	0.77	13	1.06	16
383	Electrical machinery	0.93	16	0.99	17	1.07	18
384	Transport equipment	0.95	17	0.82	15	1.25	23
385	Professional goods	0.65*	7	0.60°	8	0.91	11
390	Other industries	0.66*	8	0.55*	7	0.82	6

Notes : * indicates that the average relative value of capital intensity of the sector in the sample countries is significantly below 1 at a 95 per cent confidence interval.
° indicates that this is the case at a 90 per cent confidence interval.
Sources : as of Table 5.1.

Figure 5.4
Physical- and Human-Capital Intensity of 26 Manufacturing Sectors

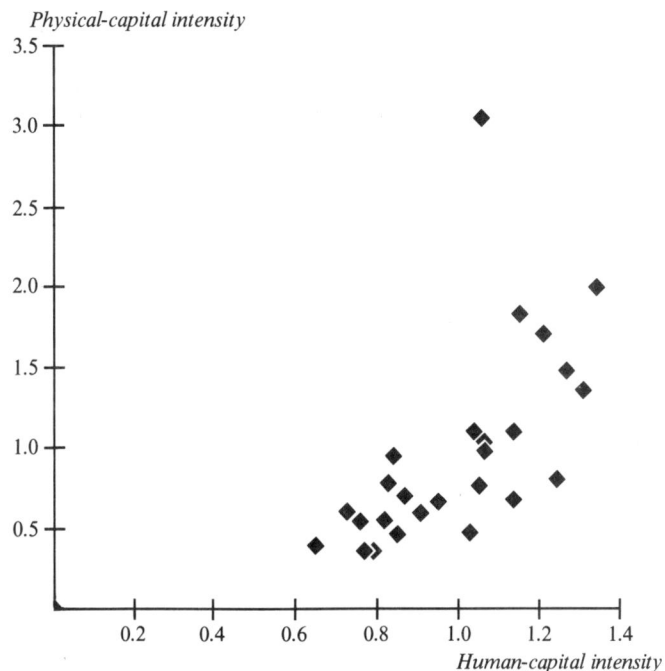

Source : as of Table 5.1.

The representativeness is indicated by the value of the Spearman rank correlation coefficients. All coefficients are statistically significant at a 95 per cent confidence interval.

5.6 SPECIALIZATION IN PRODUCTION AND TRADE

5.6.1 Scope of the Analysis

Having studied the characteristics of manufacturing sectors according to factor use, we shall now focus on the patterns of specialization in manufacturing production and exports. In particular we shall study the contribution of labour-intensive sectors to the manufactured export performance of developing countries. As discussed in the first chapter of this study, an open, trade-oriented pattern of industrial development in developing countries is advocated so as to use the available factors of production in an efficient way and to make an optimal contribution to the

TABLE 5.6
THE REPRESENTATIVENESS OF THE STANDARDIZED ORDERS OF RANKING OF SECTORS

Country	Total-capital intensity	Physical-capital intensity	Human-capital intensity
	Spearman rank correlation coefficients		
Argentina	..	..	.55
Brazil	.74	.94	.85
Chile	.84	.84	.77
Colombia	.87	.83	.90
Cyprus	.83	.64	.78
Egypt	.42	.46	.55
Hong Kong	.60	.58	.49
India	.64	.76	.69
South Korea	.73	.67	.87
Malaysia	.92	.89	.77
Malta	.57	.52	.49
Mexico	.84	.85	.68
Peru	.80	.73	.80
Philippines	.88	.91	.68
Singapore	.84	.81	.87
Tunisia	.78	.78	.78
Turkey	.78	.71	.77

Symbols : . . = no data available.
Note : not for all countries data on all 26 sectors are available.
Sources : as of Table 5.1.

creation of employment opportunities. To bring about such a pattern of industrialization, trade-oriented activities should not be discriminated against and export industry should receive stimulation at a rate equal to that of industry producing for the domestic market. The analysis in the previous sections showed significant differences in factor use between manufacturing sectors. Therefore, full exploitation of comparative advantage in labour-intensive sectors may create substantial employment opportunities. However, there may be some inherent limitations and drawbacks to a general adaptation of such policies in developing countries. Since most developing countries are characterized by an abundant availability of unskilled labour and relatively scarce resources of human and physical capital, so the argument of the critics of such policies goes, these countries will all compete in international markets with a limited range of simple, labour-intensive products. As Hughes and Ohlin indicate, supply of such products may be highly elastic but demand may be less so, a market situation comparable to the situation developing countries face in several commodity markets.[40] Since the wage level of the labour force in the export industry is a critical variable in determining price competitiveness in labour-intensive, standardized products, such a strategy is all about tapping the low-wage sections of the labour force and imposing low-wage regimes: hence, the prevalence of young, unskilled, female workers in export industries, particularly in EPFZs, and the curtailment of labour unions and other labour organizations, as will be discussed later. Additionally, so the critique goes, such policies will lock developing countries in at the lower end of the spectrum of technology since production for markets in developed countries consists merely of simple, fragmented and standardized activities that do not contribute to the upgrading of the labour force. Possibilities of upgrading in world markets are considered limited.[41]

In subsequent sections we shall study the composition and factor intensities of manufactured exports of developing countries along the following lines. First we shall study the variation in the composition of manufacturing production and exports in samples of developing and developed countries. Next we shall compare the contribution of labour-intensive sectors to manufacturing production with their contribution to manufactured exports. The third step will be to discern differences between developing countries in the product composition and factor intensities of their manufactured exports, and to relate the composition of exports to the level of development of the exporting economies as well as to some other variables. Finally, we shall study the changes over time in the composition and labour intensity of manufactured exports of eight countries that have a predominant position in the manufactured export performance of developing countries.

5.6.2 Variation in the Composition of Production and Exports of Manufactures

In this and the next section we shall study the composition of manufactured exports in relation to the structure of manufacturing production in the exporting economy. According to their (potential) contribution to exports, manufacturing sectors may be distinguished as infant industries, mature industries and decaying industries. Infant industries need government protection to survive foreign competition in the domestic market and are not yet capable of competing in the international market. Mature industries have reached a stage of efficiency and price competitiveness in which they potentially contribute to exports. Decaying industries are no longer able to compete internationally, lose their market shares in foreign markets and ultimately need government protection to prolong their life cycle.

As a consequence of government intervention, the manufacturing sector is more diversified than would be the case in the absence of intervention, as already discussed in the previous chapter.

In developing countries net effective rates of protection are, in general, particularly high in rather capital-intensive sectors of durable and non-durable consumer goods and transport equipment. Intermediate products such as industrial chemicals, other chemical products and iron and steel have a lower rate of net effective protection than products for final demand. Capital goods industries generally have low net effective rates of protection.[42] Import of capital goods is governed by licensing systems. In developed countries tariff rates are relatively high, and quantitative restrictions most frequently applied, in labour-intensive sectors of production in which these countries lose comparative advantage. This is particularly true of sectors such as wearing apparel, footwear, textiles, furniture and fixtures, and glass and glass products.[43] Without protection, domestic industries would lose a larger share of the domestic market to foreign competitors.

Because of the protection of capital-intensive infant industries in developing countries and of labour-intensive decaying industries in developed countries, we expect the diversity in the structure of manufacturing production among countries at different levels of development, as measured by the coefficient of variation, to be more limited than the diversity in the structure of manufactured exports. Exports reflect more accurately the structure of comparative advantage and of industrial maturity.

To facilitate a comparison of the structure of manufacturing production with the structure of manufactured exports, a link is constructed between the ISIC classification of manufacturing sectors and the SITC classification of traded goods. This link, covering 26 ISIC sectors at the three digit level, is described in detail in Table A.5.1 in the Appendix to this chapter.

We study the contribution of seven sectors to the total value of production and exports of manufactures in 37 countries. The selected sectors are the following.

Sector	ISIC code	SITC code (SITC Rev. 1)
Textiles	321	65
Wearing apparel	322	84
Chemical products	351 + 352	5
Metal products	381	69
Non-electrical machinery	382	71
Electrical machinery	383	72
Transport equipment	384	73

Note : Only manufactured products in SITC sections 5–8 less 67 and 68 are included.

The sample of 37 countries includes 18 developing and 19 developed countries. All countries in the sample at levels of income *per capita* below US$2000 in 1975 belong to the group of developing countries. The average contribution of the seven manufacturing sectors to total manufacturing production in the sample countries is 46.3 per cent. Table 5.7 shows the share of each of the seven selected sectors in total manufacturing production and in total manufactured exports in developing, developed and in all sample countries, and the variation in these shares, as measured by the coefficient of variation.

As indicated by the coefficients of variation, there is much more variation among countries in the structure of their manufacturing exports than in the structure of their manufacturing production. This is true of the entire sample of all countries as well as of the subsamples of developed and developing countries. The only exception is the sector of wearing apparel in developing countries. To a great extent this exceptional position is due to the case of Malta, where 29.4 per cent of manufacturing is in the sector of wearing apparel, while this share averages only 3.95 per cent in the sample of developing countries.

The sample includes sectors that are at the extremes of the ranking of sectors according to total-, physical-, and human-capital intensity. The sectors of textiles and wearing apparel are labour-intensive; chemical products are extremely capital-intensive by nature; the sector of transport equipment is extremely skill-intensive (see Table 5.5). We expect countries at lower levels of development to have a relatively strong comparative advantage in production and exports of labour-intensive products and countries at higher levels of development to have a relatively strong comparative advantage in production and exports of capital- and skill-intensive products. For that reason we expect the variation in the contribution to manufacturing production and exports in the sample that includes developed and developing countries to be particularly large in sectors that are at the extremes of the order of ranking of sectors according to factor intensities.

As is shown in Table 5.7, the sectors of textiles and wearing apparel are more predominant in production, and particularly in exports in developing countries than in developed countries. Taken together, the average share of the two sectors in manufactured exports in the sample of developing countries is over 33 per cent in the sample of developing countries, while it is less than 10 per cent in the developed countries. Variation in the contribution of these two sectors to production and exports among the sample countries is, indeed, large. The sectors of chemical products — two clustered sectors that are extremely capital-intensive — show, on the contrary, very little variation in their contribution to manufacturing production in countries at widely different levels of development. The average contribution of these sectors to

TABLE 5.7
VARIATION IN THE COMPOSITION OF PRODUCTION AND EXPORTS OF MANUFACTURES

ISIC code	Sector		All countries		Developing countries		Developed countries	
			percentage share	coefficient of variation	percentage share	coefficient of variation	percentage share	coefficient of variation
321	Textiles	Production	9.56	0.87	14.33	0.66	5.05	0.55
		Exports	12.01	1.41	18.84	1.15	5.55	0.88
322	Wearing apparel	Production	3.40	1.39	3.95	1.69	2.88	0.30
		Exports	8.95	1.38	14.41	1.07	3.79	0.98
351/52	Chemical products	Production	9.31	0.35	10.39	0.37	8.28	0.25
		Exports	12.71	0.77	13.26	0.96	12.19	0.48
381	Metal products	Production	5.71	0.41	4.52	0.47	6.84	0.28
		Exports	3.99	0.58	3.31	0.76	4.63	0.42
382	Non-electrical machinery	Production	5.69	0.85	2.31	0.95	8.90	0.49
		Exports	10.80	0.89	4.21	1.21	17.03	0.51
383	Electrical machinery	Production	5.77	0.53	4.01	0.58	7.44	0.36
		Exports	7.62	0.78	5.33	1.01	9.79	0.58
384	Transport equipment	Production	6.88	0.63	3.72	0.69	9.87	0.35
		Exports	10.69	1.07	3.52	1.38	17.49	0.67

Note : data relate to 1975.
Countries included in the sample of developing countries: Bangladesh, Chile, Colombia, Costa Rica, Cyprus, Ecuador, Egypt, El Salvador, India, Indonesia, Kenya, South Korea, Malta, Nigeria, Panama, Portugal, Turkey, Yugoslavia.
Countries included in the sample of developed countries: Australia, Canada, Denmark, Finland, France, Germany (Fed. Rep.), Greece, Ireland, Israel, Italy, Japan, New Zealand, Norway, Singapore, Spain, Sweden, United Kingdom, USA, Venezuela.
Sources : data on manufacturing value added taken from United Nations, *Yearbook of Industrial Statistics*, New York, various issues.
Data on manufactured exports taken from United Nations, *Yearbook of International Trade Statistics, 1978*, Volume I, New York, 1979.

production and exports in developing countries even exceeds their contribution in developed countries. The sector of transport equipment, which is extremely skill-intensive, shows, as expected, a wide variation among countries in its contribution to production and particularly in its contribution to exports. Its role in the manufactured export performance of developing countries is marginal, 3.5 per cent on an average and in most countries much less, while its role in exports of developed countries is predominant, 17.5 per cent on an average.

5.6.3 Labour-intensive Sectors in Production and Exports of Manufactures

In a more aggregated and comprehensive way, the pattern of specialization in production and exports of manufactures in developing countries is studied by comparing the contribution of the sum total of labour-intensive sectors to manufacturing production with their contribution to manufactured exports to OECD countries. This is done for a sample of 22 developing countries. The following are labour-intensive sectors, in order of decreasing labour intensity.

ISIC code	Sector	ISIC code	Sector
322	Wearing apparel	390	Other industries
324	Footwear	323	Leather and products
332	Furniture and fixtures	361	Pottery, china
321	Textiles	381	Metal products
331	Wood products	356	Plastic products
362	Glass and products	342	Printing and publishing
385	Professional goods		

As shown in Table 5.8, the contribution of labour-intensive sectors to total manufacturing production in the sample countries is generally rather limited, on an average 35 per cent only. Capital-intensive sectors such as processing of food, beverages, tobacco and also chemical industries have a predominant position in the manufacturing sector of many a developing country. In most countries in the sample, manufactured exports to OECD countries are strongly concentrated in labour-intensive sectors in comparison with the pattern of specialization in manufacturing production. The average share of labour-intensive products in manufactured exports in the sample countries is 53 per cent. However, in Ethiopia, Chile, Cyprus, Panama, Venezuela and Kuwait, exports are more concentrated in capital-intensive products than overall manufacturing production is. In most of the countries, only a small number of capital-intensive sectors dominate the export performance.

Again, we find the variation in the structure of exports among developing countries to be much larger than the variation in their structure of production. The coefficient of variation of the contribution of labour-intensive sectors to exports and production of manufactures in the sample countries is 0.53 and 0.36, respectively.

TABLE 5.8
SHARE OF LABOUR-INTENSIVE SECTORS IN PRODUCTION AND EXPORTS OF MANUFACTURES, 1975

Country	GDP/P (US $)	Share in production	Share in exports to OECD countries
Ethiopia	93	0.44	0.15
Bangladesh	180	0.39	0.99
India	141	0.27	0.85
Indonesia	234	0.29	0.56
Egypt	309	0.44	0.59
Philippines	377	0.49	0.68
Nigeria	471	0.37	0.65
El Salvador	456	0.45	0.54
Peru	1 043	0.38	0.51
South Korea	583	0.34	0.75
Colombia	568	0.30	0.82
Ecuador	610	0.33	0.80
Chile	708	0.18	0.13
Malaysia	755	0.29[1]	0.51
Turkey	897	0.24	0.62
Costa Rica	998	0.26	0.81
Cyprus	1 117	0.43	0.14
Panama	1 123	0.27	0.23
Hong Kong	1 863	0.76[2]	0.84
Venezuela	2 179	0.25	0.12
Singapore	2 520	0.22	0.37
Kuwait	11 934	0.24	0.03

Notes : [1] relates to 1974.
[2] relates to 1973.

Sources : data on manufacturing value added as of Table 5.7.
Data on GDP *per capita* taken from the World Bank, *World Tables, The Third Edition*, Volume I, The Johns Hopkins University Press, Baltimore and London, 1984.
Data on manufactured exports to OECD countries taken from OECD, *Trade by Commodities, Market Summaries: Imports, Jan.-Dec. 1975*, Volumes I and II, Series C, Paris.

COMPOSITION OF THE EXPORT SECTOR

5.6.4 Specialization in Exports to OECD Countries

The present analysis aims at discerning differences between developing countries in the composition and factor intensities of their exports of manufactures to OECD countries, and at relating factor intensities of exports to the level of development as well as to some other characteristics of the exporting economies. Before we start analyzing the structure of manufactured exports, some general observations are in place regarding the export performance of developing countries to OECD countries during the 1970s and early 1980s.

OECD imports of manufactures (SITC sections 5-8 less 67 and 68) from developing countries expanded from nearly US$6 billion in 1970 to US$65.5 billion in 1980 and US$81.6 billion in 1983. These imports expanded at a much higher rate than overall OECD imports, including intra-OECD trade, as is reflected by the pronounced increase of developing countries' share in total OECD imports of manufactures. While this share was only 5.1 per cent in 1970, it was 9.9 per cent in 1980 and 12.7 per cent in 1983. This indicates a successful exploitation by developing countries of their comparative advantages, notwithstanding clear signs of growing protectionism in OECD countries including the steps that have been taken to slow down the rate of market penetration through voluntary export restraints, orderly marketing agreements and import quotas. The Multi-Fiber Arrangements are clear examples of protective measures specifically implemented to slow down market penetration by developing countries.

The high growth rates of manufactured exports and the successful market penetration by developing countries, taken as a group, are to be attributed largely to the competitiveness of manufacturing industry in only a small group of countries. The share of the major exporters (Brazil, China, Hong Kong, India, South Korea, Mexico, Singapore and Taiwan) in total manufactured imports of OECD countries from developing countries was as much as 72.5 per cent in 1970 and increased further to 76.2 per cent in 1980 and 78.9 per cent in 1983. The changing contribution of each of eight countries mentioned above to these OECD imports from all developing countries is shown in Figure 5.5. While the percentage contribution of India and Hong Kong declined considerably throughout the period, all other countries managed to increase their shares. By the end of the period, 52 per cent of manufactures from developing countries were shipped by only three countries, Taiwan, Hong Kong and South Korea. All this clearly implies that by far most developing countries that export some manufactures or semi-manufactures to OECD markets are only marginal suppliers. In many of the 53 developing countries in our sample, manufactured exports consist of only a very limited range of products exported in small amounts. In such cases the concept of "structure of exports" has hardly any meaning.

Figure 5.5
Share of Eight Countries in Manufactured Exports of Developing Countries to OECD Countries, 1970-1983

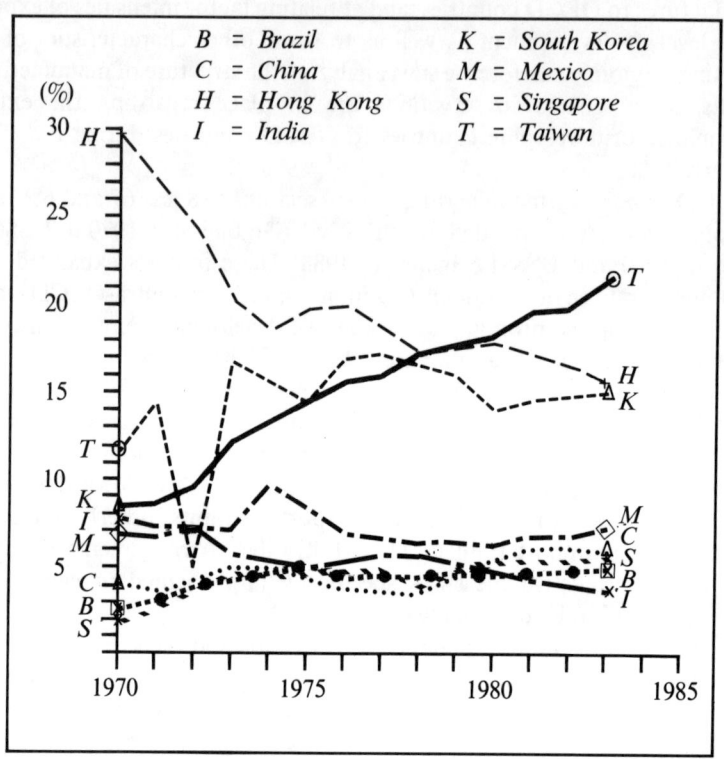

Note : [1] SITC sections 5-8 less 67 and 68.
Source : OECD, *Foreign Trade by Commodities, Imports*, Volume II, Series C, Paris, various issues.

We shall now turn to a discussion of the cross-sectional regression analyses in which factor intensities of manufactured exports are related to factor availabilities in exporting countries. In the initial series of analyses, income *per capita* is used as a proxy for the overall availability of physical and human capital *per capita*. In subsequent analyses, two alternative proxies for the availability of capital in a country are used. Value added per employee in the manufacturing sector is used as a proxy for total capital availability per employee in the manufacturing sector, and non-wage value added per employee is used as a proxy for the availability of physical capital per employee in the manufacturing sector.[44] Due to a lack of data it is not possible to apply alternative variables such as consumption of electricity per employee or the share of skilled workers in the industrial labour force. We assume that there is a negative relationship between the availability of total, physical and human capital *per capita* or per employee and the share in total manufactured exports of products that are characterized by a limited use of such capital. This relationship, however, may be thwarted by government intervention that distorts the pattern of allocation and the market orientation of industries, as well as by many other market imperfections such as monopolization in trade, restrictive business practices, private dumping, i.e. price discrimination, and selective import restrictions in developed countries.

In combination with these variables we use two other variables, population size and population density. Population size is introduced, as we assume that a large domestic market stimulates the growth of industries that need large-scale production to operate efficiently, which is a precondition for export production.[45] Population divided by arable land is the variable used to express population density. We assume that in densely populated countries disguised rural unemployment is high and that people are willing to migrate to urban areas to seek alternative job opportunities. This reserve of unskilled labour will induce firms to engage in labour-intensive lines of operations for foreign markets. Additionally, we assume that governments in such countries are anxious to stimulate labour-intensive productive activities, as employment creation for job seekers may have a stabilizing effect (at least in the short term) on the existing social and political relations in society. Therefore we expect population pressure to have a positive effect on the share of labour-intensive sectors in manufactured exports.

Two concepts of manufactured exports are applied. The first is a broad concept derived from the link between the ISIC classification of manufacturing sectors and the SITC classification to traded goods presented in the Appendix to this chapter. All products in the SITC classification that are linked to the 26 manufacturing sectors in the ISIC classification are conceived of as manufactures. This concept of manufactured exports is broader than the definition usually applied and includes, in addition, manufactured food products (ISIC 311/2), beverages (ISIC 313), tobacco manufactures (ISIC 314), iron and steel (ISIC 371) and non-ferrous metals (ISIC 372). Consequently, this concept includes a number of products in SITC sections 0–4 and SITC divisions 67 and 68 which are not included in the second, narrower concept, which corresponds with the usually applied definition of manufactured exports, SITC sections 5–8 less 67 and 68.

The selection of products, the production of which is characterized by small inputs of total, physical, or human capital, is based on the analysis of factor intensities presented in Section 5.5 (see Table 5.5). Regression analyses are made of the contribution of 13 and of nine labour-intensive sectors to total manufactured exports. In these nine sectors, the relative value of total-capital intensity is significantly below one. Additionally, regression analyses are made of the share of some other clusters of products in total manufactured exports, as will be seen below.

The sample consists of all 53 developing countries in which the value of manufactured exports (according to the broad concept) to developed countries in 1975 amounted to at least US$25 million. The latter amount is slightly over one *pro mille* of the total value of manufactured exports of developing countries to OECD countries as recorded in OECD import statistics, based on c.i.f. values. Below we report the results of the regression analyses made.

Table 5.9 shows that there is a significant negative relationship between the level of development of a developing country and the share of labour-intensive products in its exports of manufactures to developed countries, whether or not manufactured exports are broadly defined. Exclusion of semi-manufactures (items in SITC sections 0–4 and 67 and 68) does not improve the result of the analysis. Controlling for the level of development of a country, population density and population size have a positive impact on the share of labour-intensive products in exports. The impact of these variables ceases to be significant in more disaggregated analyses in which the share of more narrowly defined clusters of products or of individual product groups is related to these variables. However, the results presented indicate also that

TABLE 5.9
SHARE OF LABOUR-INTENSIVE PRODUCTS IN MANUFACTURED EXPORTS TO OECD COUNTRIES, 1975 ($n = 53$)

Dependent variable	Average share	Constant term	GDP/P	P	Da	R^2
	percentage					
$E_{lm,13}/E_m{}^*$	42.19	10.05 (0.26)	−8.49* (2.21)	7.62* (3.69)	4.11* (2.48)	0.46
$E_{lm,9}/E_m{}^*$	40.48	12.83 (0.34)	−8.32* (2.21)	7.18* (3.55)	3.76* (2.31)	0.44
$E_{lm,9}/E_m$	51.22	45.96 (1.05)	−11.00* (2.52)	7.23* (3.08)	2.59 (1.37)	0.41
$E_{pm,11}/E_m{}^*$	41.62	13.46 (0.35)	−8.74* (2.30)	7.43* (3.62)	3.98* (2.42)	0.46

COMPOSITION OF THE EXPORT SECTOR

Symbols :
$E_{lm,13}$ = value of exports of 13 labour-intensive sectors based on a two-way classification of 26 manufacturing sectors according to total-capital intensity (see Table 5.5).
$E_{lm,9}$ = value of exports of nine manufacturing sectors in which the relative value of total-capital intensity is significantly below one (see Table 5.5).
$E_{pm,11}$ = value of exports of 11 manufacturing sectors in which the relative value of physical-capital intensity is significantly below one (see Table 5.5).
$E_m{}^*$ = value of manufactured exports defined according to the broad definition (see text and the Appendix of this chapter).
E_m = value of manufactured exports defined according to the narrow definition (see text and the Appendix of this chapter).
GDP/P = Gross Domestic Production *per capita* in US dollars.
P = size of population in thousands of inhabitants.
Da = density of population on arable land, i.e. the number of inhabitants per km² of arable land area.

Notes : data relate to 1975. As in all regression analyses in this chapter, dependent variables are measured as percentage shares. Equations are in semi *ln*-form. The *t*-statistics are in parentheses. An asterisk (*) indicates that the variable is statistically significant at a 95 per cent confidence interval.

The following 53 countries are included in the sample: Afghanistan, Algeria, Argentina, Bahamas, Bahrain, Bangladesh, Brazil, UR of Cameroon, Chile, China, Colombia, Congo, Cuba, Dominican Rep., Egypt, El Salvador, Ghana, Guyana, Haiti, Honduras, Hong Kong, India, Indonesia, Iran, Ivory Coast, Jamaica, Kenya, South Korea, Kuwait, Lebanon, Liberia, Malaysia, Mexico, Morocco, Netherlands Antilles, Nigeria, Pakistan, Panama, Paraguay, Philippines, Saudi Arabia, Singapore, Surinam, Taiwan, Thailand, Trinidad and Tobago, Tunisia, Turkey, Uruguay, Venezuela, Zaire, Zimbabwe.

Sources : data on imports taken from OECD, *Trade by Commodities, Market Summaries: Imports, Jan.–Dec. 1975*, Volumes I and II, Series C, Paris.

Data on GDP *per capita* taken from The World Bank, *World Tables, The Second Edition (1980)*, The Johns Hopkins University Press, Baltimore and London, 1980; The World Bank, *World Tables, The Third Edition*, Volume I, The Johns Hopkins University Press, Baltimore and London, 1984; UNCTAD, *Handbook of International Trade and Development Statistics, 1977 Supplement*, United Nations, New York, 1977, Table 6.1A.

Data on population taken from FAO, *Production Yearbook 1977*, Volume 31, Rome, 1978, Table 3; UNCTAD, *Handbook of International Trade and Development Statistics, 1977 Supplement*, Table 6.1A. Data on Taiwan taken from *Taiwan Statistical Data Book 1981*, Council for Economic Planning and Development, Executive Yuan, 1981, Table 2-2.

Data on land area taken from FAO, *Production Yearbook 1976*, Volume 30, Rome, 1977, Table 1. Data on Taiwan taken from *Taiwan Statistical Data Book 1981*, Table 2-3.

Exchange rates taken from IMF, *International Financial Statistics*, Yearbook 1984, Volume XXXVII, Washington DC, 1984;[1] The World Bank, *World Tables, The Second Edition (1980)*, and The World Bank, *World Tables, The Third Edition*, Volume I.

there is not a straightforward and smooth relationship between levels of development of countries and their revealed comparative advantage. To obtain a somewhat closer view of the composition of manufactured exports, we show in Figure 5.6 the share of 13 labour-intensive products ($E_{lm,13}$) in total manufactured exports (E_m^*) in the sample countries (Bahrain, Kuwait and Saudi Arabia, with high levels of income *per capita*, are excluded from this presentation). The figure shows that in many countries at low levels of development, labour-intensive products play only a limited role in exports. Additionally, there are some developing countries at relatively high levels of development in which labour-intensive products are still predominant in exports.

Residual analysis shows that in 9 out of the 53 countries in the sample, the actual percentage share of labour-intensive products ($E_{lm,13}$) in manufactured exports (E_m^*) deviates from the fitted share by at least one time the standard

Figure 5.6
Share of Labour-intensive Products ($E_{lm,13}$) in Manufactured Exports (E_m^*) to OECD Countries, 1975

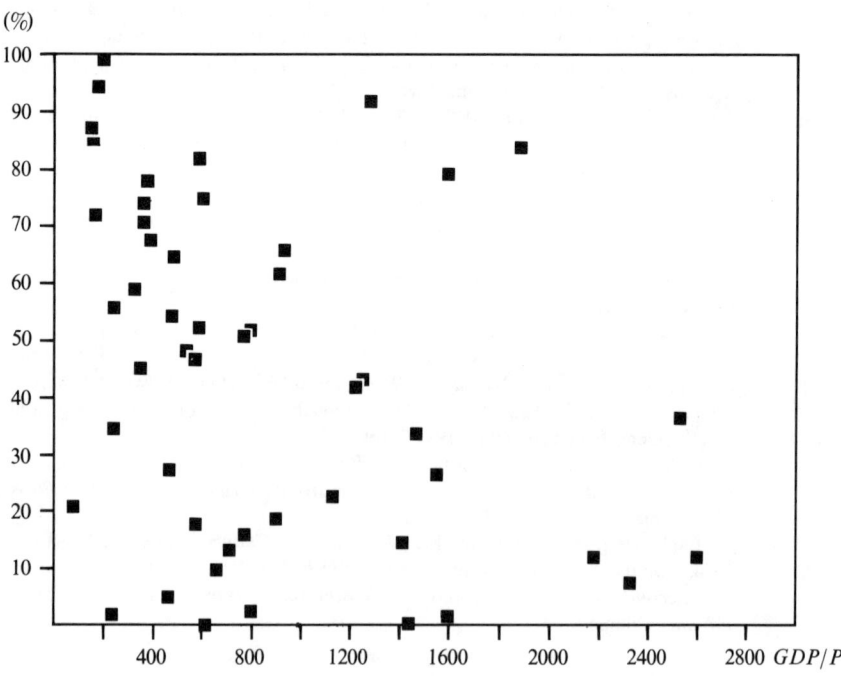

Sources: as of Table 5.9.

deviation (30.5). This is the case in the following countries ($E_{lm,13}/E_m^*$, expressed as a percentage, in parentheses). Zaire (20.8), Guinea (2.0), Honduras (78.2), Colombia (82.1), Zimbabwe (0.1), Cuba (2.5), Uruguay (92.2), Iran (79.7) and Hong Kong (84.3). In low-income Zaire and Guinea, manufactured exports are dominated by chemical products (61.9 and 95.5 per cent respectively) while in Zimbabwe 99.9 per cent of manufactured exports are iron and steel products. Both are extremely capital-intensive product groups. In Cuba, nearly 95 per cent of exports consist of three product groups that are classified as capital-intensive: tobacco manufactures, chemical products and processed food. Apart from these "outlying observations", there are many more countries where manufactured exports are dominated by a few capital-intensive products such as chemicals or non-ferrous metals. Two peculiar cases are Liberia and Panama where exports of transport equipment (ships and boats) are prevalent. The other "outlying countries" show large positive residuals. In Colombia, Iran and Hong Kong, exports are dominated by textile products and/or wearing apparel, in Uruguay by wearing apparel and leather products, and in Honduras by wood products. All these product groups are labour-intensive by nature.

In Table 5.10 we present the results of some alternative specifications with different proxies for the availability of total and physical capital in a country. The sample size is reduced since such data are only available for 27 out of the 53 developing countries in our sample. The results do not provide evidence for the superiority of the two alternative proxies over the commonly used variable, income *per capita*.

Finally, we show in Table 5.11 the results of some of the large number of analyses that have been made of the share of product groups, clustered in many ways, in total manufactured exports. From this series of analyses it follows that the more narrowly defined the product group, the lower the overall level of explanation of the variation in its share in total manufactured exports. Population size and density cease to be significant but the variable income *per capita* is significant and its sign is as expected: the higher the level of development of the economy, the smaller the share of low-wage sectors, textiles and wearing apparel, and the larger the share of transport equipment and electrical machinery in total manufactured exports. These findings tend to confirm Ohlin's point that "within limits a country may specialize in any one industry as well as in any other".[46]

5.6.5 Skills, Wages and Labour Conditions in Export Industries

Skills, wages and labour conditions are much debated issues in the literature on export-oriented industrialization in developing countries. Many case studies focus particularly on these characteristics of the export sectors. As

TABLE 5.10
SHARE OF LABOUR-INTENSIVE PRODUCTS IN MANUFACTURED EXPORTS TO OECD COUNTRIES, 1975 — ALTERNATIVE SPECIFICATIONS ($n = 27$)

Dependent variable	Average share	Constant term	GDP/P	VA_m/L_m	VA_m-W_m/L_m	P	Da	R^2
	percentage							
$E_{lm,13}/E_m^*$	49.77	49.34 (0.84)	−13.14* (2.49)			6.49 (2.04)	5.27* (2.34)	0.53
$E_{lm,13}/E_m^*$	49.77	158.43 (1.66)		−19.53* (2.59)		5.20 (1.52)	2.29 (0.94)	0.54
$E_{pm,11}/E_m^*$	49.12	51.82 (0.89)	−13.26* (2.55)			6.35 (2.02)	5.07* (2.28)	0.54
$E_{pm,11}/E_m^*$	49.12	111.60 (1.32)			−16.01* (2.38)	6.29 (1.93)	2.25 (0.92)	0.52

Symbols:
VA_m = value added in the manufacturing sector in US dollars.
W_m = value of wages of employees in the manufacturing sector in US dollars.
L_m = number of employees in the manufacturing sector.
All other symbols as of Table 5.9.

Notes: unless otherwise indicated, data on value added, wages and employment in the manufacturing sector relate to 1975.
The following 27 countries are included in the sample: Bangladesh, Brazil (1974), Chile, Colombia, Dominican Rep., El Salvador, Egypt (1974), Haiti, Honduras, Hong Kong (1976), India, Indonesia, Iran (1974), Ivory Coast, Jamaica, Kuwait, South Korea, Nigeria, Malaysia (1974), Panama, Philippines, Singapore, Trinidad and Tobago, Tunisia, Turkey, Venezuela, Zimbabwe.
Data on employment refer to the number of employees but in the case of Hong Kong, India, Kenya and Nigeria to the number of operatives.

Sources: data on value added, wages and employment in the manufacturing sector taken from United Nations, *Yearbook of Industrial Statistics*, Volume I, New York, various issues.
Sources of all other data as of Table 5.9.

TABLE 5.11
SHARE OF SELECTED SECTORS IN MANUFACTURED EXPORTS TO OECD COUNTRIES, 1975

Dependent variables	Average share	Constant term	GDP/P	n	R^2
	percentage				
$E_{hm,4}/E_m$*	22.29	67.79* (3.69)	−6.94* (2.50)	53	0.11
$E_{321/2}/E_m$*	21.91	80.48* (3.64)	−8.93* (2.68)	53	0.13
$E_{382/3/4}/E_m$*	15.75	−35.63 (1.86)	7.84* (2.72)	53	0.13
$E_{382/3/4}/E_m$*	13.65	−40.76* (2.59)	8.30* (3.50)	51[1]	0.20

Symbols:
$E_{hm,4}$ = value of exports of four manufacturing sectors in which the relative value of human-capital intensity is significantly below one (see Table 5.5).
$E_{321/2}$ = value of exports of the manufacturing sectors ISIC 321 (textiles) and ISIC 322 (wearing apparel).
$E_{382/3/4}$ = value of exports of manufacturing sectors ISIC 382 (machinery n.e.c.), ISIC 383 (electrical machinery) and ISIC 384 (transport equipment).
All other symbols as of Table 5.9.
Note : [1] Liberia and Panama excluded from the sample.
Sources : as of Table 5.9.

discussed earlier, it is claimed that export production does not contribute to the strengthening of the technological basis of society since the activities are simple and routine. Additionally, the process of international relocation of industry to low-wage economies has been referred to as "super exploitation" and as tapping the low-wage segments of the labour force in developing countries. In view of our previous analyses, some remarks are in place regarding skills, wages and labour conditions in export industries.

Analyses in previous sections showed manufactured exports of developing countries to be concentrated in products, the production of which requires small inputs of physical and human capital. The latter characteristic is measured by the average wage level in a sector relative to the unweighted average wage level in the manufacturing sector at large. In Table 5.5 we showed intersectoral wage differences to be substantial, normally ranging from 0.65 times the average at the low extreme to 1.34 times the average at the upper extreme. However, the actual dispersion in wage rates in the manufacturing sector is larger since our (standardized) range is based on the averages of the wage rates in each sector. Thus, the modal wage rate in low-wage sectors, i.e. the wage rate of unskilled workers in such sectors, is further below the average wage level of the manufacturing sector at large.

To a large extent intersectoral differences in average wage levels are caused by differences in the skill levels of the labour force. However, there may be additional factors at work to explain such wage differences, as mentioned in Section 5.4, such as differences in the gender composition of the labour force, its age structure and the degree of protection of the labour force by labour unions and other organizations. Various detailed studies of the composition of the labour force in export industries show that a relatively large section of the employees are unskilled, young female workers. This is especially true of the labour force in the sectors of textiles, wearing apparel and electrical machinery. These sectors — and the exporting firms within these sectors in particular — tap the low-wage segment of the labour force, as is illustrated by the following cases.

In the Bataan Export Processing Zone in the Philippines, 74 per cent of the labour force in 1980 were female workers and, according to a sample survey, 67 per cent of the labourers were less than 25 years of age.[47] In the Katunayaka Investment Promotion Zone in Sri Lanka, 88 per cent of the labour force in 1981 were females. According to a sample survey, 78 per cent of the labour force were females less than 27 years of age.[48] According to a sample survey in 1980, 83 per cent of the employees in the Malaysian EPFZs were female workers. One third of them were less than 20 years of age and 86 per cent of them were less than 26 years of age.[49] In Singapore, the sectors of electrical machinery and wearing apparel account for nearly 52 per cent of the female labour force in the manufacturing sector at large in 1980. While, on an average, 46 per cent of the total labour force in manufacturing industry are females, these percentages are nearly 76 and 80 in the two sectors mentioned.[50] In the Masan Free Export Zone in South Korea, 75 per cent of the labour force were females and 84 per cent of the total labour force in the zone were younger than 29 years of age in 1975.[51] It is reported that in the three zones in Taiwan, Kaohsiung, Nantze and Taichung, 3 per cent of the labour force in 1975 were females 14–15 years of age, 38 per cent were females 16–19 years of age and 33 per cent were females 20–24 years of age.[52]

These data indicate that the use of young female workers is strongly prevalent in the labour force in export industries in many Asian countries and particularly so in EPFZs.[53] Such employment is temporary and consequently the rate of turnover of the labour force is high. Protracted apprenticeship contracts are frequently applied. The temporary character of the employment — a loop between school enrolment and marriage, as Edgren puts it — may also be due to adverse working conditions.[54] Working times are long and often exceed the number of hours to which the labour legislation limits the

COMPOSITION OF THE EXPORT SECTOR   153

working week. The intensity of the work and the occurrence of health-damaging factors in the production process contribute to the difficulty of the jobs. Many cases are documented of eye ailments, permanent reduction of eyesight and the health-damaging effects of toxic fumes and liquids in the electronics factories, and of textile workers suffering from breathing difficulties, chest pains and skin problems.[55] A UNIDO study concludes that "(i)n the assembly operations there is evidence to suggest that a more stable work force would not maintain the pace of work. That is, to some degree the young workers are 'burnt out' by the inherent monotony and adverse conditions. In the absence of the very rapid turnover and the young age of the labour force, companies would be unable to maintain the very high pace."[56]

These findings tend to confirm that the contribution of this specific form of export-oriented industrialization to the creation of a skilled labour force is limited. This form of production is not likely to create external economies via the diffusion of production knowledge and has hardly any lasting positive effect on the quality of the labour force.

5.7 THE COMPOSITION OF MANUFACTURED EXPORTS TO OECD COUNTRIES: TIME SERIES

Changes over time in the composition in the factor intensities of manufactured exports to OECD countries are analyzed for eight developing countries: Brazil, China, Hong Kong, India, South Korea, Mexico, Singapore and Taiwan. These countries are major exporters of manufactures among developing countries. Some of them have, relatively speaking, a long export tradition, as described in Chapter 2. For these eight countries we study the composition of manufactured exports to OECD countries during the period 1970-1983. The analysis consists of two stages. First we study the variation in the contribution of major product groups to total manufactured exports. Next we study the variation in the share of labour-intensive products in manufactured exports and the process of upgrading in the course of time.

The analysis is based on the narrow definition of manufactured exports (SITC sections 5-8 less 67 and 68). Data are taken from OECD import statistics that record c.i.f. values. The following four clusters of product groups are distinguished.

(1) Traditional labour-intensive products. This cluster includes textiles, wearing apparel, leather products and footwear, four product groups in which developing countries traditionally have a comparative advantage in export to developed countries.

(2) Non-traditional labour-intensive products. This cluster includes a heterogeneous group of products that are classified as professional goods (ISIC 385) and other industries (ISIC 390). Traditionally, these

labour-intensive products do not play such a predominant role in the export performance of developing countries as the former group of products does. The development in the contributions of these two clusters of labour-intensive products to total manufactured exports in most countries under review is strikingly different as will be shown below.

(3) Chemical products (SITC section 5). As noted earlier, these capital intensive products play an important role in the export of many a developing country, particularly in a series of low-income countries.

(4) Machinery and transport equipment (SITC section 7). These products are much more capital-intensive, and particularly more skill-intensive, than the first two clusters of product groups distinguished here. Typically, these products play a predominant role in the production and export structure of developed countries and not so much in developing countries. An increased share of such products in exports of developing countries is, therefore, an indication for upgrading in exports.

The changing contribution of these four clusters of product groups to manufactured exports from the eight selected countries is shown in Figure 5.7. Although the time span of 14 years is short, changes in the composition of manufactured exports are substantial. These changes may be summarized as follows.

First, the share of traditional labour-intensive products decreased significantly in all countries under review except China. The pattern that emerges from the eight country studies is that the notion of developing countries as exporters of merely a limited range of traditional labour-intensive products is rapidly becoming outdated. Such products, indeed, were much more predominant in exports during the 1960s and early 1970s than during the 1980s. Nevertheless, even during the 1980s, over 50 per cent of total manufactured exports consisted of such products in the case of India and China, the two low-income countries in our sample. We may notice that in the case of Brazil, the share of such products tended to rise initially, but after 1973 — when this share was at its peak — the role of such products in exports declined substantially.

Second, the share of non-traditional labour-intensive products in total manufactured exports was more or less constant or increased slightly. Only in Taiwan was this share increasing rapidly. Thus, within the overall group of labour-intensive products, a shift is taking place towards a reduced share of traditional and an increased share of non-traditional labour-intensive products. As detailed import data are only available for the period 1970-1980, the contribution of these products in more recent years cannot be shown.

Chemical products were of relatively great importance in the exports of Brazil, China and Mexico. In the case of Brazil no clear pattern is discernible,

Figure 5.7
Composition of Manufactured Exports of Eight Developing Countries to OECD Countries, 1970–1983

———— = traditional labour-intensive products
—·—·— = non-traditional labour-intensive products
` ` ` ` ` = chemical products
············ = machinery and transport equipment

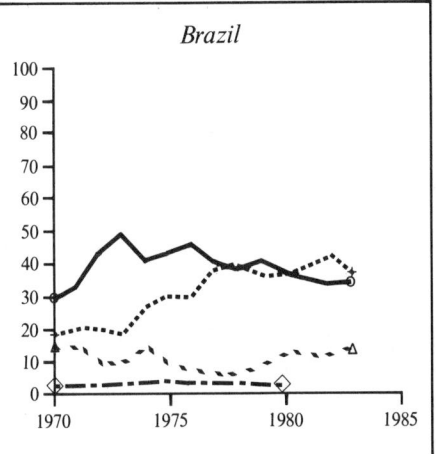

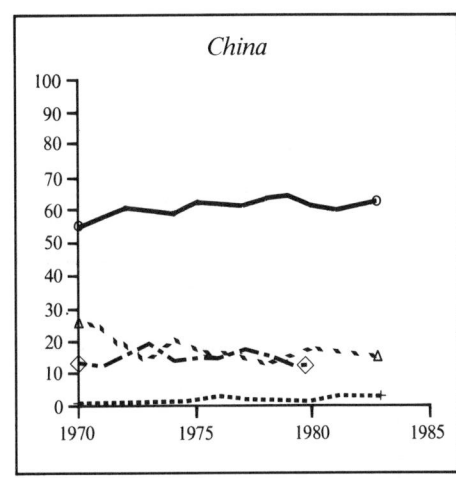

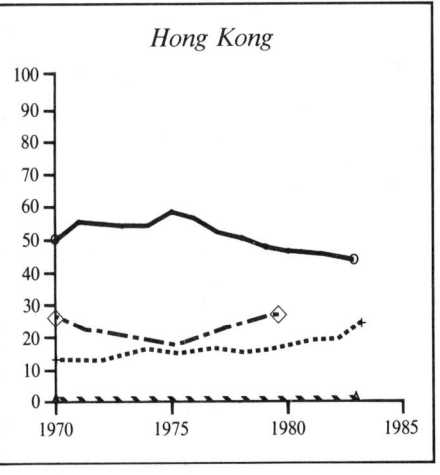

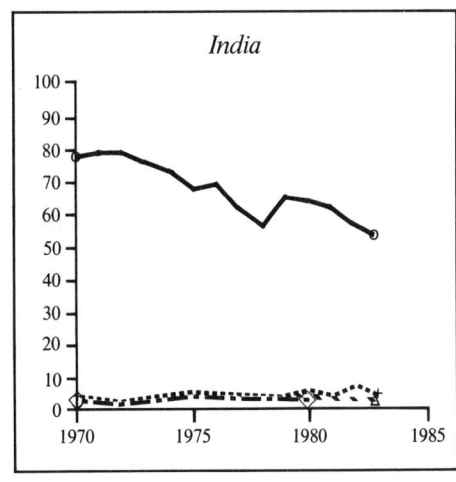

(cont'd overleaf)

Figure 5.7 (cont'd)

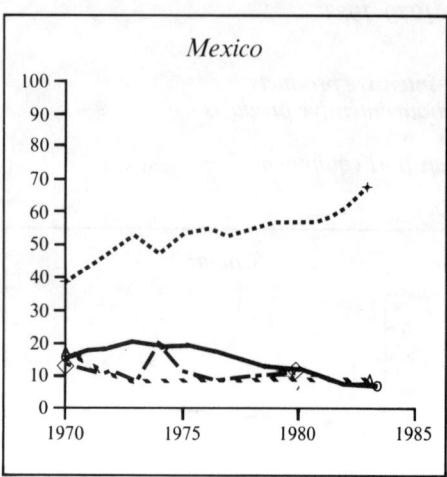
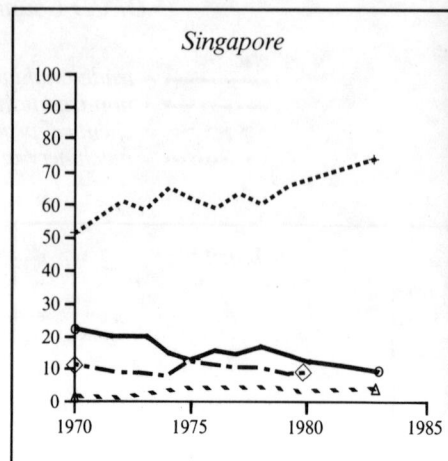
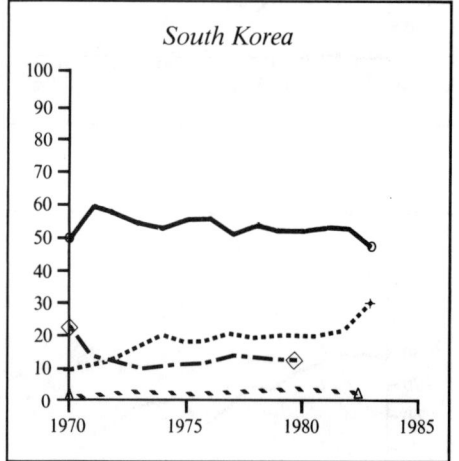
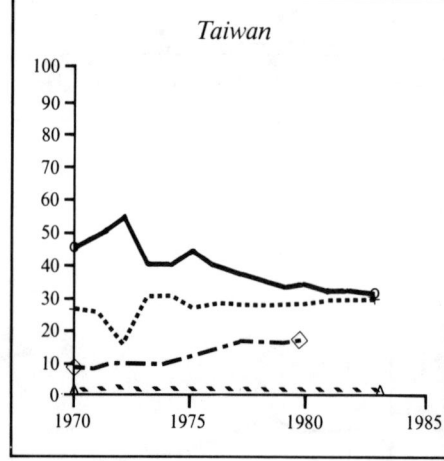

Note   : [1] SITC sections 5-8 less 67 and 68.
Sources : OECD, *Foreign Trade by Commodities, Imports,* Volume II, Series C, Paris, and OECD, *Trade by Commodities, Market Summaries; Imports,* Volumes I and II, Series C, Paris, various issues.

COMPOSITION OF THE EXPORT SECTOR

but in China and Mexico the contribution of these two extremely capital-intensive sectors to total manufactured exports declined substantially.

In all eight countries under review the contribution of machinery and transport equipment (SITC section 7) increased, be it to different degrees. At the end of the period, these products were particularly important in the exports of Singapore and Mexico, where they dominated export performance. Such products contributed about a third to the total value of manufactured exports in Brazil, South Korea and Taiwan and over 20 per cent in Hong Kong. Only in China and India was their contribution of minor importance. To study in some more detail the significance of the changing contribution of this highly aggregated product group, we distinguish some subgroups in Table 5.12 below.

Table 5.12 shows the contribution of the nine divisions in SITC section 7 to total manufactured exports of six developing countries to OECD countries in 1983. It appears that office machines (SITC division 75), telecommunications and sound recording apparatus (SITC division 76) and electrical machinery (SITC division 77), taken together, dominate exports of machinery and transport equipment in the East-Asian economies. The percentage share of these products in the exports of machinery and transport equipment is in Hong Kong 88, in Singapore 87, in Taiwan 74 and in South Korea 71, while it is 66 in Mexico and only 30 in Brazil. Export of such products is stimulated by international subcontracting and an international allocation of production and assembly activities by TNCs so as to use to the best advantage international differences in production costs. These assembly activities are often located in EPFZs. The two Latin-American countries show a somewhat more diverse export structure. Apart from the three sections mentioned above, power generating machinery (SITC division 71) and road vehicles (SITC division 78) are also of major importance in these countries' exports to OECD countries. The strong position of South Korea in the world's shipbuilding industry is reflected in Korea's exports of ships, included in SITC division 79.

As noted earlier, the average total-, physical-, and human-capital intensity of the sectors of machinery, electrical machinery and transport equipment are well above those of the traditional and non-traditional labour-intensive sectors distinguished here. It is likely, however, that developing countries have a competitive edge only in the more standardized and less skill-intensive production and assembly activities in the former three industries. Nevertheless, the patterns in the changing structure of exports of manufactures during the 1970s and early 1980s, discerned here, clearly indicate that a process of diversification is taking place and that the role of traditional labour-intensive products in manufactured exports is declining rapidly.

TABLE 5.12
EXPORTS OF MACHINERY AND TRANSPORT EQUIPMENT (SITC SECTION 7) OF SIX DEVELOPING COUNTRIES TO OECD COUNTRIES, 1983

SITC code	Product	Brazil	Hong Kong	South Korea	Mexico	Singapore	Taiwan
		\multicolumn{6}{c}{percentage share in manufactured exports[1]}					
7	Machinery and transport equipment	36.15	23.87	29.76	67.66	73.77	30.19
71	Power generating machinery	10.05	0.57	0.23	12.08	1.59	0.50
72	Specialized machinery	1.81	0.14	0.26	1.63	0.49	1.18
73	Metal working machinery	0.82	0.03	0.19	0.05	0.34	0.84
74	General industrial machinery and parts	2.01	1.73	0.56	1.62	4.02	2.32
75	Office machines	3.17	5.61	1.48	3.45	18.93	2.94
76	Telecommunications and sound recording apparatus	3.93	7.68	10.80	19.41	19.51	11.30
77	Electrical machinery	3.71	7.62	8.95	21.60	25.85	8.11
78	Road vehicles	8.76	0.08	0.76	7.28	0.37	2.24
79	Other transport equipment	1.89	0.41	6.53	0.54	2.67	0.77

Note : [1] SITC sections 5–8 less 67 and 68.
Source : OECD, *Foreign Trade by Commodities, Imports, 1983*, Volume II, Series C, Paris, 1985.

The final step in our analysis of the changes over time in the composition of manufactured exports of developing countries is an investigation of the pattern of specialization in terms of factor intensities. In Table 5.13 we present the overall share of labour-intensive manufacturing sectors in manufactured exports to OECD countries of the eight countries under review during the period 1970-1980. The category of labour-intensive sectors includes the nine sectors in which the relative value of total-capital intensity is significantly below one (see Table 5.5).

In all countries except China, the share of these labour-intensive product groups in total manufactured exports declined during the 1970s. Singapore, Mexico and Brazil are least of all specialized in exports of such products. Given its level of income *per capita*, Hong Kong's exports are dominated by labour-intensive products to a remarkably high degree. However, a substantial and increasing share of these labour-intensive products are so-called non-traditional labour-intensive products, as noted earlier. Given their large resources of unskilled labour and their low levels of capital accumulation, we expect China and India to be particularly specialized in labour-intensive exports. For that reason, the pattern of upgrading in India, as it appears from our time series, is somewhat unexpected. Closer inspection of India's exports to OECD countries shows that part of this process of apparent upgrading is due to a statistical inconsistency. During the era under investigation the share of pearls and stones (SITC group 677) increased substantially, from 10.2 per cent of total manufactured exports in 1970 to 17.5 per cent in 1980. This product group is included in the definition of manufactured exports that is usually applied in empirical analysis. However, to a large extent, the activities related to the digging and processing of pearls and stones should not be considered manufacturing production but fishing or mining. If this product group is excluded from the analysis, the share of labour-intensive products in India's manufactured exports was 88.2 per cent in 1970 and 81.8 per cent in 1980, which indicates a more pronounced specialization in the labour-intensive range and a less pronounced pattern of upgrading.

One should be careful about drawing rigorous conclusions from the patterns discerned in this section. The evidence presented here suggests that a process of upgrading has taken place in the more advanced developing countries that have a dominant position in overall manufactured export performance of developing countries. However, two factors that may have affected this outcome should be mentioned here. The first factor is purely statistical by nature and related to the level of aggregation applied throughout the analysis. Industrial census and survey data show wide within-sector variations in factor use. Applying average values of factor use at too high a level of aggregation may therefore be somewhat misleading. It has been

TABLE 5.13
SHARE OF LABOUR-INTENSIVE SECTORS IN MANUFACTURED EXPORTS TO OECD COUNTRIES, 1970–1980

percentage

Country	1970	1971	1972	1973	1974	1975	1976	1977	1978	1979	1980
Brazil	48.15	48.69	57.02	61.49	50.43	51.17	53.77	47.30	45.44	47.12	43.00
China	68.59	70.95	77.67	80.31	74.54	78.02	77.38	79.73	81.63	79.16	75.60
Hong Kong	76.83	78.29	76.48	74.76	73.66	75.51	76.18	74.39	75.14	74.38	73.48
India	79.83	80.95	80.94	78.48	76.31	71.70	72.06	63.94	59.28	68.50	67.48
South Korea	88.25	87.20	82.81	77.16	69.64	72.43	72.28	69.64	71.36	68.78	67.00
Mexico	35.44	35.34	34.14	32.20	39.95	32.62	28.63	28.88	26.95	25.93	27.39
Singapore	44.41	39.91	36.07	38.14	28.82	31.81	32.03	29.72	32.20	28.29	25.28
Taiwan	65.76	68.39	76.52	61.73	58.86	63.98	61.54	61.56	61.00	59.11	58.88

Note and Sources : as of Figure 5.7.

COMPOSITION OF THE EXPORT SECTOR   161

argued, for instance, that production of electrical machinery is more labour-intensive than production of other machinery and that, consequently, an increased contribution of such products does not necessarily reflect upgrading.[57] Such questions, however, cannot be settled fully satisfactorily since no internationally standardized data system on factor use is available at a more disaggregated level than the one applied here. Verbruggen's country studies in Part II, Chapters 11-17 of this volume, show that it is hardly possible to give a generally applicable characterization of the nature of technology in narrowly defined sub-sectors.

The second factor is related to economic policies pursued in OECD countries. Tariff and non-tariff barriers in these countries are particularly high for imports of traditional labour-intensive products from developing countries such as textiles, wearing apparel, leather and footwear. Non-traditional labour-intensive products are increasingly affected as well by trade barriers in these countries. These policies may have induced the structure of exports to become less concentrated in such labour-intensive products than would have been the case in their absence.

5.8   SUMMARY AND CONCLUSIONS

In this chapter we have studied patterns of specialization in manufactured exports of developing countries. First we have reviewed hypotheses of trade theories regarding the comparative advantage of developing countries. Trade theories differ in their choice of variables and in their assumptions on the context within which international trade takes place. Consequently, they emphasize different characteristics of the export structure of developing countries: exports are concentrated in labour-intensive products (neo-classical theory), unsophisticated low-income products (Linder), low-wage products (Hufbauer), or mature products (product-cycle theory).

Next we have elaborated two factors that may thwart a systematic relationship between the level of development of the exporting economy and the product composition of exports: socio-cultural and political factors that may shape comparative advantage and international competitiveness, and footloose export-oriented component production and assembly activities that may be undertaken independently of the structure of domestic production and demand and of the competitiveness of domestic industry.

In order to analyze the relationship between factor intensities of manufactured exports and structural characteristics of exporting countries, sectors must be classified according to factor inputs. We have shown that differences between sectors in total-, physical-, and human-capital inputs per unit of value added are significant. This implies that changing the structure of production by changing the trade and industrialization regime potentially has substantial implications for employment creation. Next we have shown the significant differences between countries in the order of ranking of sectors according to their factor intensities. This means that the strong factor-intensity assumption cannot be maintained. Consequently, the choice of any country-specific order of ranking of sectors to be applied in a cross-country analysis is arbitrary. As a way out, we have constructed an order of ranking of sectors that reflects in a representative way the order of ranking in all developing countries in our sample. This order has been applied in the subsequent analysis of the structure of exports.

Comparison of the structure of exports and production in countries at different levels of development has shown that the variation among countries in the structure of exports is much larger than that in the structure of production. The export structure reflects more precisely the structure of comparative advantage of the economy. Developing countries, in general, have a structure of exports that shows a higher concentration in labour-intensive products than their production structure does. Exceptions are mostly those countries that have a (strongly) one-sided export structure in which natural-resource-based products or chemicals dominate.

Differences in the composition of manufactured exports to OECD countries have been studied at different levels of aggregation of product groups. Our results show that there is a significant negative relationship between the level of development of the exporting economy and the share in exports of products, the production of which requires small inputs of physical and human capital. Nevertheless, only a rather small share of the variation among countries in the product composition of their exports is explained by the proxies used for the availability of human and physical capital. Thus, within limits, set by factor availabilities, countries may specialize in any one industry as well as in any other.

Special attention has been paid to skills, wages and labour conditions in export industries. Labour-intensive industries are usually characterized by the prevalence of unskilled workers in the labour force, as is reflected by the relatively low-wage levels in such industries. The predominant role of young female workers in export industries is another reason why wages in such industries are low. Many of these labour-intensive activities are simple and routine. In addition to this, the rate of turnover of the labour force in export industries tends to be high. For these reasons, the contribution of this kind of export-oriented industrialization to the diffusion of industrial skills and the strengthening of the technological basis of society is limited.

The analysis of the changing composition in time of manufactured exports of eight major exporting countries has shown the declining role of traditional labour-intensive products and the increasing importance of sectors characterized by larger inputs of human and physical capital. This finding tends to contradict quite rigorous statements made by theorists opposing export-oriented industrialization for the reason that countries pursuing such strategies remain "locked in" at the lower end of the spectrum of technology, and merely compete in more or less similar product groups in world markets. Products at the lower end of the spectrum of technology, characterized by a high labour intensity, relatively small inputs of skills, and low wages, indeed dominate the export performance of developing countries. However, systematic intercountry differences in the structure of exports, and substantial changes in export specialization in the course of time, suggest that there is room for upgrading manufactured exports to markets of developed countries.

APPENDIX TABLE A.5.1
LINK BETWEEN ISIC AND SITC REV. 1

ISIC code	Sector	SITC code	Product group
311/2	Food products	012	Meat, dried, salted or smoked
		013	Meat in airtight containers, n.e.s., and meat preparations
		032	Fish, in airtight containers, n.e.s., and fish preparations
		046	Meal and flour of wheat or of meslin
		047	Meal and flour of cereals except of wheat and meslin
		048	Cereal preparations and preparations of flour, fruits, vegetables
		052	Dried fruit (including artificially dehydrated)
		053	Fruit, preserved and fruit preparations
		055	Vegetables, roots and tubers, preserved or prepared
		062	Sugar confectionery and other sugar preparations (except chocolate confectionery)
		073	Chocolate and other food preparations containing cocoa or chocolate, n.e.s.
		091	Margarine and shortening
		099	Food preparations, n.e.s.
313	Beverages	111	Non-alcoholic beverages, n.e.s.
		112	Alcoholic beverages
314	Tobacco	122	Tobacco manufactures
321	Textiles	266	Synthetic and regenerated (artificial) fibres
		267	Waste materials from textile fabrics (including rags)
		651	Textile yarn and thread
		652	Cotton fabrics, woven (not including narrow or special fabrics)
		653	Textile fabrics, woven (not including narrow or special fabrics) other than cotton fabrics
		654	Tulle, lace, embroidery, ribbons, trimmings, and other small wares

APPENDIX TABLE A.5.1 (cont'd)

ISIC code	Sector	SITC code	Product group
		655	Special textile fabrics and related products
		656	Made-up articles, wholly or chiefly of textile materials, n.e.s.
		657	Floor covering, tapestries, etc.
322	Wearing apparel	841	Clothing (except fur clothing)
		842	Fur clothing (not including headgear) and other articles made of furskins; artificial fur and articles thereof
323	Leather and products	611	Leather
		612	Manufactures of leather or of artificial or reconstituted leather, n.e.s.
		613	Fur skins, tanned or dressed (including dyed)
324	Footwear	851	Footwear
331	Wood products	243	Wood, shaped or simply worked
		631	Veneers, plywood boards, "improved" or reconstituted wood and other wood, worked, n.e.s.
		632	Wood manufactures, n.e.s.
		633	Cork manufactures
332	Furniture and fixtures	821	Furniture
341	Paper and products	251	Pulp and waste paper
		641	Paper and paperboard
		642	Articles made of paper pulp, of paper or of paperboard
342	Printing and publishing	892	Printed matter
351	Industrial chemicals	431	Animal and vegetable oils and fats, processed, and waxes of animal or vegetable origin
		512	Organic chemicals
		513	Inorganic chemicals, elements, oxides and halogen salts
		514	Other inorganic chemicals
		515	Radioactive and associated materials

(cont'd overleaf)

APPENDIX TABLE A.5.1 (*cont'd*)

ISIC code	Sector	SITC code	Product group
		531	Synthetic organic dyestuffs, natural indigo and colour lakes
		532	Dyeing and tanning extracts, and synthetic tanning materials
		561	Fertilizers, manufactured
		581	Plastic materials, regenerated cellulose and artificial resins
352	Other chemical products	533	Pigments, paints, varnishes and related materials
		541	Medicinal and pharmaceutical products
		551	Essential oils, perfume and flavour materials
		553	Perfumery and cosmetics, dentifrices and other toilet preparations (except soaps)
		554	Soaps, cleansing and polishing preparations
		571	Explosives and pyrotechnic products
		599	Chemical materials and products, n.e.s.
355	Rubber products	621	Materials of rubber
		629	Articles of rubber, n.e.s.
356	Plastic products	893	Articles of artificial plastic materials, n.e.s.
361	Pottery, china	666	Pottery
362	Glass and products	664	Glass
		665	Glassware
369	Non-metal products	661	Lime, cement and fabricated building materials, except glass and clay materials
		662	Clay construction materials and refractory construction materials
		663	Mineral manufactures, n.e.s.
371	Iron and steel	671	Pig iron, spiegeleisen, sponge iron, iron and steel powders and shot and ferro-alloys

APPENDIX TABLE A.5.1 (*cont'd*)

ISIC code	Sector	SITC code	Product group
		672	Ingots and other primary forms (including blanks for tubes and pipes) of iron and steel
		673	Iron and steel bars, rods, angles, shapes and sections (including sheet piling)
		674	Universals, plates and sheets of iron and steel
		675	Hoop and strip of iron and steel
		676	Rails and railway track construction material of iron and steel
		677	Iron and steel (excluding wire rod)
		678	Tubes, pipes and fittings of iron and steel
		679	Iron and steel castings and forgings, unworked, n.e.s.
372	Non-ferrous metals	682–682.1	Copper (682), except copper and alloys, unwrought (682.1)
		684	Aluminium
		688	Uranium depleted in U 235 and thorium and their alloys
381	Metal products	691	Finished structural parts and structures, n.e.s.
		692	Metal containers for storage and transport
		693	Wire products (excluding electric) and fencing grills
		694	Nails, screws, nuts, bolts, rivets and similar articles of iron, steel or of copper
		695	Tools for use in the hand or in machines
		696	Cutlery
		697	Household equipment of base metals
		698	Manufactures of metal, n.e.s.
		812	Sanitary, plumbing, heating and lighting fixtures and fittings
382	Machinery n.e.c.	711	Power generating machinery, other than electric
		712	Agricultural machinery and implements

(*cont'd overleaf*)

APPENDIX TABLE A.5.1 (cont'd)

ISIC code	Sector	SITC code	Product group
		714	Office machines
		715	Metalworking machinery
		717	Textile and leather machinery
		718	Machines for special industries
		719	Machinery and appliances (other than electrical) and machine parts, n.e.s.
		951	Firearms of war and ammunition therefor
383	Electrical machinery	722	Electrical power machinery and switch gear
		723	Equipment for distributing electricity
		724	Telecommunications apparatus
		725	Domestic electrical equipment
		726	Electrical apparatus for medical purposes and radiological apparatus
		729	Other electrical machinery and apparatus
384	Transport equipment	731	Railway vehicles
		732	Road motor vehicles
		733	Road vehicles other than motor vehicles
		734	Aircraft
		735	Ships and boats
385	Professional goods	861	Scientific, medical, optical, measuring and controlling instruments and apparatus
		864	Watches and clocks
390	Other industries	831	Travel goods, handbags and similar articles
		862	Photographic and cinematographic supplies
		891	Musical instruments, sound recorders and reproducers and parts and accessories therefor
		894	Perambulators, toys, games and sporting goods
		895	Office and stationery supplies, n.e.s.

APPENDIX TABLE A.5.1 (cont'd)

ISIC code	Sector	SITC code	Product group
		896	Works of art, collectors' pieces and antiques
		897	Jewellery and goldsmiths' and silversmiths' wares
		899	Manufactured articles, n.e.s.

Source : link is based on United Nations, *Classification of Commodities by Industrial Origin, Links Between the Standard International Trade Classification and the International Standard Industrial Classification,* Statistical Papers, Series M, Number 43, Rev. 1, New York, 1971.

6
Summary and Conclusions

6.1 THE STUDY

This study deals with the factors underlying the increasing export orientation of the manufacturing sector in developing countries and with the economic characteristics of export-oriented industrialization. Export-oriented industrialization in developing countries is a recent phenomenon that reflects a new stage in the process of development and brings about changes in the international division of labour. Whereas during the early stages of industrialization production was almost exclusively oriented towards the domestic market in most developing countries, the manufacturing sector has more recently become a new basis for exports in a growing number of countries, particularly so since the late 1960s and early 1970s.

In economic literature, export-oriented industrialization in developing countries is approached from different angles. On the one hand, a reduction of the anti-trade bias in trade and industrialization regimes is considered a correction of sub-optimal regimes that hamper the full exploitation of comparative advantage. Central to the arguments in favour of liberalization and export stimulation is the creation of foreign-exchange earnings and of employment opportunities. On the other hand, such policies are criticized for their inherent weaknesses and drawbacks. The criticism of liberalization and export stimulation focuses on (1) the economic and political implications of the policies; (2) the technological characteristics of the production processes in the export sector and particularly the quality of employment; (3) the limited effects on the creation of foreign exchange and employment opportunities. The dichotomy that can be observed as regards the way in which regime transformation and export stimulation is assessed may partly be due to the fact that the approach to the subject is often partial, focusing on different forms which liberalization and export stimulation have taken.

SUMMARY AND CONCLUSIONS   171

The ongoing debate on the potential merits and drawbacks of export-oriented industrialization forms the background of this study, in which we attempt to answer the following questions:
(1) What developing countries in particular opt for an export-oriented strategy and what factors underly the export orientation of manufacturing industry?
(2) What policies are pursued to stimulate export production?
(3) What are the characteristics of export production in terms of product composition, factor intensities and technology?

The study is basically a cross-country study. Although — up to now — the manufactured export performance of developing countries has been dominated by a small number of countries, we have attempted to include in the analyses as many countries as possible, irrespective of their contribution to total manufactured exports of developing countries and irrespective of the contribution of manufactures to foreign-exchange earnings in these countries. This approach has been opted for in order to distinguish patterns in export performance and to differentiate more clearly between strategies pursued in stimulating export production.

Up-to-date and comprehensive data systems on exports are available for most countries, but statistics on manufacturing production and on variables related to resource endowments of countries are less up-to-date, incomplete, insufficiently disaggregated, not fully standardized and often inaccurate. Data on policy-related variables are hardly available for many countries. These shortcomings of the data base have presented some limitations for the kind of analysis made here.

6.2   THE CHANGING INTERNATIONAL DIVISION OF LABOUR

In Chapter 2 we show in a stylized fashion the changing position of developing countries in the international division of labour, and the process of transformation of the structure of production and trade since 1960. Manufacturing production has become more diffused in the world economy. Countries in East and South-East Asia have shown the greatest dynamism. While at the beginning of the 1960s the industrial base of most developing countries in this region was still small, they transformed into semi-industrialized countries, and are by now as industrialized as the major economies in Latin America, or even more so. This region is becoming a new industrial centre in the world economy. Including Japan, the second largest producer of manufactures in the world economy, and China, the largest producer of manufactures among developing countries, by 1980 this area produced nearly 20 per cent of the total value of manufacturing production in the world economy excluding the CMEA countries. Also, countries from this region dominate the manufactured export performance of developing countries.

There are wide differences between developing countries in their process of transformation. South Korea and Taiwan are two cases *par excellence* of an early and rapid transformation of the export structure, while exports of manufactures are a rather late phenomenon in most Latin-American countries. However, particularly since the 1970s the contribution of manufactures to exports has been rising sharply in many countries, and the role of developing countries, taken as a group, in world trade in manufactures has been growing substantially, much more than their share in world manufacturing production has done. A large number of developing countries are to a high degree dependent on manufactured exports for their foreign-exchange earnings: by 1980, over 40 per cent of commodity-export earnings were generated by the manufacturing sector in 23 developing countries, but most of these countries were only marginal suppliers in world markets.

6.3 THE EXPORT ORIENTATION OF THE MANUFACTURING SECTOR

Chapter 3 focuses on factors underlying the variation among countries in the export orientation of the manufacturing sector. Structural characteristics of countries determine to a high degree their pattern of development. This, however, does not imply that government policies are irrelevant. Although the options from which government can choose may be limited by the structural characteristics of the economy, there are internal and external factors, independent of these characteristics, that have an impact on the actual choice of policies and on the extent to which comparative advantages in world markets are exploited. Export-oriented industrialization is shown to be the "normal" pattern of development in countries that have specific structural characteristics in common — provided that the trade and industrialization policies pursued do not significantly bias the market orientation of the manufacturing sector. The results of the investigations are the following. A low overall level of economic development or of industrial development does not necessarily impede export-oriented industrial development. Small countries are highly involved in international trade and their manufacturing sector is export-oriented as compared to large countries. Densely populated countries and countries poorly endowed with natural resources are relatively export-oriented. High population pressure on (arable) land may be conceived of as a situation of surplus labour, which may be favourable for the expansion of labour-intensive (export) industries. Also, shortage of natural resources may limit the options in foreign-exchange earnings to the stimulation of the manufacturing sector to export. The export orientation of the manufacturing sector is negatively affected by policies that favour production for the domestic market over export production. Import barriers favour import-substitution and create an anti-trade bias in production. The full impact of policies is likely to be more substantial than is shown in our analysis, in which a variable reflecting tariff protection is included as a proxy for the protection of industries producing for the domestic market. However, the correlation between protection and export orientation in production can be rather weak since governments can apply a wide variety of export-stimulation measures which compensate for the bias against exports created by the protection of the domestic market.

6.4 EXPORT STRATEGIES

Export-oriented industrialization is not simply the outcome of a "normal" process of growth and transformation and does not necessarily reflect industrial maturity. Underlying the rapid expansion of manufactured exports and transformation of the composition of exports in an increasing number of developing countries are significant changes in trade and industrialization strategies. There is a wide variety among countries in trade and industrialization strategies, but in most countries more recently implemented strategies emphasize production for exports. There is no simple change-over from inward-oriented towards more open and export-oriented strategies, and to conceive such a change-over as one decisive step in a one-way process bypasses the complexity of regime transformation. In studying the anatomy of export-stimulation strategies we distinguish three avenues: (1) transformation of an initially inward-oriented regime; (2) fostering of domestic processing of primary exports; (3) creation of export enclaves. The second avenue, however, is not so much a strategy distinct from the first-mentioned avenue but rather a somewhat special option related to the specific natural-resource endowment of countries. The avenues distinguished here are not mutually exclusive but can be applied simultaneously with varying emphasis.

The rationale for emphasizing the role of trade and industrialization regimes in this study is threefold. First, government intervention in the foreign trade sector is more predominant in developing countries than in developed countries, as far as trade in manufactures is concerned. Particularly in developing countries, government is dependent on revenue from taxes on trade, most notably taxes on imports, and industry is dependent on protection against imports. It is the type rather than the extent of government intervention that is typical of developing countries. As noted earlier, this type of intervention creates a bias against exports. As shown, protection is associated with reduced imports and exports, import substitution, and inefficiency in manufacturing production.

Second, the impact of export-oriented industrialization on income, employment, and the balance òf payments is not independent of the export strategy pursued. For that reason, it does not seem fruitful to speak in general terms of "the gains from trade" or, for that matter, of the "drawbacks of export-oriented industrialization".

Third, a distinction between avenues to stimulate manufactured exports, as made here, is often bypassed in the literature on trade, industrialization and development. By making such a distinction, we attempt to bridge the gap between the conflicting views regarding optimal industrialization strategies.

The new models of international competition implemented in an increasing number of developing countries deviate strongly from the *laissez-faire* model and the free-trade model. As compared to developed countries, developing countries have relatively small domestic markets that are heavily protected. Rather than implementing across-the-board liberalization, a dual incentive system is frequently applied, protection being given to industries producing for the domestic market while, at the same time, export industries are stimulated through compensating facilities or by making them operate in an enclave, i.e. in isolation from the rest of the manufacturing sector.

We show the variables involved in regime transformation in an inventory of World Bank recommendations for 17 countries on trade liberalization and export stimulation. Six key areas of government intervention are distinguished: exchange-rate policy, import policy, fiscal policy, factor-market policy, investment policy, and export promotion policy. The following priorities in regime transformation can be distinguished: the system of incentives should be neutral between domestic-market-oriented and export-oriented industries; exchange-rate adjustment is preferable to specific import controls and export stimuli; across-the-board liberalization is preferable to selective liberalization for export industries; tariffs are superior to administrative control of imports; the dispersion in tariff rates should be limited. Compensated devaluation is the most frequently prescribed avenue to liberalization and export stimulation. In order to establish neutrality in the incentive system during the transformation period, specific export-stimulation measures can be applied as shown in the inventory. In view of the precarious balance-of-payments situation of many countries, priority is frequently given to straightforward and "aggressive" export promotion. However, the establishment of EPFZs is rarely recommended.

To assure a successful model of export-oriented industrialization, a stable and efficient government with a high political commitment to export stimulation and a synergistic partnership between the public and private sector are required. Such non-economic factors, related to the "atmosphere" in which firms operate, are increasingly considered vital to the success of such a model.

SUMMARY AND CONCLUSIONS

In view of the inefficiency of domestic industry and its inability to overcome barriers to enter world markets, and because of the economic and political obstacles to a comprehensive transformation of the trade and industrialization regime, implementation of a dual industrialization strategy is an attractive option for many governments. In this context, the most extreme deviation from a free-trade model is the combination of a protected (domestic) sector, producing for the domestic market, and an isolated export sector, dominated by foreign firms that operate in an EPFZ. The contribution of such enclaves to development, however, is small: linkage effects are limited, the share of domestic value added in output is small, and the contribution to the formation of a skilled labour force and the diffusion of technical knowledge is marginal.

In most of the major exporting countries, the contribution of EPFZs to export performance is limited. Exceptions are Mexico, Malaysia and probably China, where more recently such zones have been set up. Hong Kong and Singapore, two other major exporting countries, can be regarded as enclave-like economies. Particularly in countries at low levels of industrial development, such zones allow exploitation of comparative advantages in world markets so as to reap some gains from trade. In many of such countries, export production of manufactures is strongly concentrated in zones.

We mention two new developments in the organization of export-oriented production and international trade, viz. TNCs from developing countries and international trading houses. The role of international trading houses has been growing particularly rapidly since the 1970s, most notably in East and South-East Asia. Through extensive networks of market-reconnaissance units and a wide variety of trade-related services, they improve accessibility to international markets and assist small and medium-sized firms in exporting. International trading houses have been created in a number of developing countries as part of their export strategy.

6.5 THE COMPOSITION OF THE EXPORT SECTOR

Chapter 5 focuses on the characteristics of export production in terms of product composition and factor intensities. Trade theories emphasize different characteristics of products which assumingly developing countries have a comparative advantage in. The lower the level of development of a country, the more its exports will be dominated by products, the production of which requires small inputs of physical and human capital (the neo-classical theory), or by unsophisticated low-income products (Linder's theory), or by low-wage products (Hufbauer's theory), or by (labour-intensive) mature products (the product-cycle theory).

Trade theories link country characteristics such as factor endowments with product characteristics such as factor content. Apart from economic characteristics, socio-cultural factors may also have an impact on comparative advantage by changing the production function. Such factors have frequently been referred to as underlying the high efficiency of the labour force and the comparative advantage in labour-intensive products of some East-Asian countries.

The production of manufactured products has become an internationally organized process in which component production and assembly are distributed over locations according to the most appropriate conditions for every separate phase of the production process. Production and assembly of components is often concentrated in export enclaves and organized in international subcontracting arrangements with TNCs or international trading houses. These new forms of export-oriented manufacturing production tend to loosen the link between the stage of development and other characteristics of an economy, and the product composition of exports. They undermine the concept of a "normal" pattern in the composition of exports, according to which there is a clear sequence in the contribution of manufacturing sectors — as distinct from the contribution of factors of production — to production and trade.

For the concepts of labour-intensive and capital-intensive products to be meaningful there must be significant differences between products in terms of factor content, and a stable order of ranking of sectors according to factor intensities. We show that there are large differences between sectors in labour inputs per unit of value added, and also that differences in wage levels or in inputs of human capital are generally smaller. Comparison of factor inputs in sectors shows that a change in industrial strategy that would favour the expansion of labour-intensive sectors may result in substantial direct increases in employment opportunities.

To enable an analysis of the hierarchy of countries according to their specialization in exports of simple, labour-intensive and/or low-wage exports, products must be classified according to factor content. As shown, this classification of sectors is not stable across countries. Consequently, the choice of any country-specific classification is arbitrary. Reversals of factor intensities of sectors may be a cause of the structure of trade being inconsistent with trade-theory hypotheses. The hierarchy of countries according to their export specialization at the lower end of the spectrum of technology is shown not to be independent of the definition of low-technology products. Our analyses of comparative advantages are based on a sector classification derived from factor-input ratios in 26 manufacturing sectors in 17 developing countries. The order of ranking of sectors according to total-capital intensity is similar to a high degree to the order of ranking according to

SUMMARY AND CONCLUSIONS

physical-capital intensity and, to a somewhat lower degree, to the order of ranking according to human-capital intensity.

A comparison of the composition of manufacturing production with that of manufactured exports in samples of developed and developing countries shows that the variation among countries in the composition of exports is much larger than the variation in that of production. Moreover, exports of developing countries are shown to be generally more concentrated in labour-intensive products than is production.

In addition, we show that there is a clear hierarchy among developing countries in terms of the factor content of their manufactured exports to OECD countries. The lower the level of development of the exporting economy, the larger the share of products, the production of which is characterized by small inputs of physical and human capital. These findings are confirmed in regression analyses in which alternative proxies for factor availabilities in countries are used. However, only a rather small share of the variation among countries in the composition of manufactured exports is explained by the proxies used. Moreover, the more narrowly defined the product group, the lower the level of explanation of the variation in its share in exports. Thus, within limits set by factor availabilities, countries may specialize in any one industry as well as in any other.

Labour-intensive export industries are usually characterized by the prevalence of unskilled workers in the labour force. As shown, young female workers are predominant in export industries, particularly so in assembly activities that are concentrated in EPFZs. These export industries tap the low-wage segment of the labour force. The contribution of such production to the development of a skilled labour force is limited.

Time series of the product composition and factor content of manufactured exports from eight developing countries to OECD countries during the period 1970-1983 show that the notion of developing countries as exporters of merely a limited range of traditional, labour-intensive products is becoming out-dated. Products such as textiles, wearing apparel, leather products and footwear were more predominant in exports during the 1960s and early 1970s than they are in the 1980s. The total share of labour-intensive products decreased in most of the countries under review while the share of more capital-intensive sectors such as (electrical) machinery and transport equipment rose. However, part of the activities in the latter group of sectors is also rather labour-intensive by nature and confined to the assembly of components. Nevertheless, such sectors are generally positioned much higher in the classification of sectors according to factor content in developing countries than former groups of sectors. These findings indicate that there is room for upgrading manufactured exports to OECD markets.

PART II
GAINS FROM EXPORT-ORIENTED INDUSTRIALIZATION — WITH SPECIAL REFERENCE TO SOUTH-EAST ASIA

Harmen Verbruggen

Part II of this volume focuses on the impact of export-oriented industrialization on the development of the national economy. Three different ways of expanding manufactured exports will be distinguished:
(1) industrial processing of products from primary sectors before export;
(2) change-over from import substitution to manufactured export expansion;
(3) establishing new export-oriented industries, whether by means of EPFZs or not.

The effects of these three outward-oriented types of industrialization strategies will be compared with those of a domestic-market-oriented strategy.

In particular, Part II examines four main sets of effects resulting from alternative industrialization strategies:
(1) the extent of production stimuli passed on to other sectors of the economy;
(2) the extent of employment effects, direct as well as indirect through interindustry or linkage effects, and the spending of wage incomes on the domestic market;
(3) the degree to which foreign exchange is earned or saved;
(4) the contribution to the integration of the economy.

Together, these sets of effects are referred to simply as spread effects.

The presentation is as follows. Chapter 7 provides a theoretical assessment of the factors that determine the extent of the various forms of spread effects of manufactured export expansion. These sections seek to examine both the potential spread effects and the constraining factors through which these potentials will not always be fully realized. Chapter 8 deals with the method of investigation that will be employed in this study. To gain insight into the patterns of spread effects associated with manufactured export expansion and production for the domestic market, a number of measures has been developed which can be applied empirically. These measures all fit in with the framework of the input-output analysis. The purpose of Chapter 9 is to explore the uniformities and differences in structures of production among countries. Insight into the factors that govern these uniformities and differences is indispensable, as the spread effects of manufactured export expansion may diverge only as a consequence of differences in production structures among exporting countries. This chapter also provides a brief review of the main findings of other empirical research into the subject matter. Chapter 10 explains the framework of analysis within which the individual country studies will be carried out. Information is provided about the coverage of the country studies and the definition of concepts used in the empirical analysis. Chapters 11 to 17 then present the results of empirical analyses based on the experiences of seven South-East Asian countries: Indonesia, the Philippines, Thailand, South Korea, Taiwan, Malaysia, and Singapore, in this order. Finally, Chapter 18 sums up and attempts to synthesize the findings of these country studies.

7
The Impact of Manufactured Export Expansion on Economic Development

7.1 GAINS FROM TRADE

The relationship between foreign trade and economic growth and development is a continuing theme in economic thinking. Traditionally, studies on the impact of foreign trade are placed within the context of neoclassical theory. According to the static neoclassical theory of trade, an economy engaged in external trade gains in two ways: first, by specializing and reallocating its production according to the principle of comparative advantage, thereby making a more efficient use of its productive resources; second, by exchanging its products at prevailing international price ratios which have become more advantageous as a result of international specialization. Both gains improve welfare.

There are also dynamic gains from trade which extend beyond the static welfare gains suggested by the neoclassical theory. These possible dynamic effects of trade are less concrete. It is, however, commonly agreed that the opening up of trade may give rise to various static and dynamic economies of scale. Clearly, these economies of scale become more important when a country's domestic market is smaller. Thus, instead of small-scale production exclusively for the domestic market, expansion of exports makes possible a realization of static internal economies of scale. This may be due not only to an enlargement of the scale of production in response to a larger market, but also to a tendency to reduce the product variety when an industry operates on a competitive international market. Foreign competition and familiarity with foreign markets will provide incentives to improve the technical and organizational functioning of the production process, which in turn may yield internal economies of scale, such as technological change and learning-by-doing. Technological improvements can be developed autonomously or can be acquired through imports of capital goods, know-how and management. In sum, producing for a larger market than the domestic market can lead to an overall increase in productivity.

An increased level of activity in the export sector may also give rise to dynamic external economies of scale. The broader concept of externalities includes externalities which operate through the market mechanism as well as those elusive externalities which accrue to industries without compensation.[1] In the case of exports, externalities for other industries do not result from the availability of cheaper inputs. But domestic industries that supply exporting sectors with intermediate inputs may profit from an increased demand for their products. In fact, the creation of special service facilities and the establishment of complementary and related industries in response to an expanding export sector can also be conceived as an externality brought about through the signalling function of the market.

Of yet a different nature are externalities accruing to other industries as a consequence of the diffusion of technological knowledge and of the increased availability of trained labour and management. It is frequently assumed that the foreign-trade sector is the channel through which embodied and disembodied technology are introduced and diffused in developing countries.[2] Moreover, among these forms of externalities are also those accruing to domestic industries which now can make use of special facilities in infrastructure, banking and other services, that were initially created in support of the foreign-trade sector. And, finally, an overall increase in the level of economic activity through export expansion provides a stimulating environment for making investment decisions. All these internal and external economies appear separately or in combination in the pleas for an export-oriented strategy of industrialization.

For completeness, in the Keynesian theoretical framework of open economies, an increase in exports gives rise to an increase in national income in exactly the same way as is brought about by an increase in private and public investment or government spending. The expansionary effect of trade on a country's national income is determined by the foreign-trade multiplier.

In the above interpretations of the gains from trade, enlargement of the export sector is a goal in itself. So conceived, export expansion is a final objective of trade policy and export operates as an engine of growth. It is, however, legitimate to broaden the scope of possible gains from trade and attribute to exports also an intermediate objective. Exports are then conceived as an instrument to meet a country's import requirement. Especially developing countries should benefit from trade expansion in case they face an acute shortage of foreign exchange. The capacity to import affects the process of economic development. This process is seriously hampered if those intermediate and capital goods which are necessary to avoid excess capacity and exploit growth potentials cannot be imported. Linder distinguishes three categories or more or less strategic inputs that must be imported if the need for these inputs cannot (yet) be filled by domestic production: (a) operation imports (spare parts and intermediate products); (b) reinvestment imports (to replace former investments); and (c) expansion imports (investments to expand production capacity).[3] An increase in export earnings relaxes the foreign-exchange bottle-neck and facilitates imports of these strategic products. Trade may then even become a "super-engine of growth" for it not only allows fuller utilization of existing capacity but also leads to expansion of productive capacity.[4]

7.2 UNEVEN DISTRIBUTION OF GAINS FROM TRADE

The existence of a smooth relationship between the opening up of foreign trade and subsequent increases in welfare and economic growth has been challenged from different angles during the postwar period. Many theorists have pointed out that the gains from trade are unevenly distributed among developed and developing countries.[5] To begin with, the welfare gains of the neoclassical trade theory are only valid in so far as the simplifying assumptions of this theory are satisfied. Although every theory presents but a simplified picture of reality and for that reason underlying assumptions are never fully met, the neoclassical assumption of perfect competition is too serious a deviation from reality in developing countries. Perfect competition implies flexibility of wages, whereby the real wage rate is determined by the supply and demand curves for labour. In this context the full employment of all productive resources is assured. The existence of large masses of surplus labour in almost all developing countries detracts especially from the relevance of the efficiency gain from trade.

Chenery challenges the relevance of the resource allocation criteria of the static neoclassical trade theory for the formulation of development strategies in developing countries. Specialization according to the principle of comparative advantage ignores a variety of dynamic elements and interdependences among sectors which are considered of great importance for the process of economic development. Moreover, trade theory fails to see that factor prices in developing countries may deviate from opportunity costs and that the quantity and quality of production factors may change over time. This omission also thwarts the possibility of determining where comparative advantage lies. Chenery, therefore, infers that "if, then, the doctrine of comparative advantage is to be useful for development policy, the essential elements of the growth analysis must be combined with it".[6]

Lewis argues that in countries with an unlimited supply of labour, the benefit of increasing productivity in export industries accrues to foreign purchasers in the form of lower prices, as the wage level in the export sector is tied to the minimum level of earnings in the low-productive subsistence sector. Myint's reconstruction of the "vent for surplus" theory of international trade bears a close resemblance to Lewis' model of unlimited labour in an international setting. He argues that the "vent for surplus" theory provides a more effective approach to the problem of international trade of developing countries than the neoclassical trade theory. The latter theory assumes full employment and an internal mobility of production factors, in order that export production can be increased while reducing production for the domestic market. The "vent for surplus" theory assumes, by contrast, that a developing country possesses a surplus productive capacity which implies internal immobility of resources. Given these production conditions, the function of trade then is to create a vent for surplus resources. As these resources would have remained unemployed in the absence of trade, exports can be increased without reducing production for the domestic market and the opening up of trade results in an increase in income. The same assumptions of this theory, however, also indicate the harmful consequences of the development of international trade based on surplus capacity. Once trade is entered, there is no way to absorb external economic disturbances due to the immobility of resources. The established trading country is considered highly vulnerable to the whims of the world market.

Linder also has shown that the welfare effects of trade for countries characterized by a lack of capacity to reallocate productive resources and by labour employed at subsistence wages are highly uncertain. These effects might turn out unfavourable in case participation in international trade leads to unemployment in the import-substitution sector which is, as a consequence of a lack of reallocation capacity, insufficiently compensated by an enlargement of the export sector.

More recently, Fei, Ranis and others have undertaken a number of case studies of the transition process in labour-surplus open dualistic economies. These studies highlight the different impact that international trade can have on the two distinct sectors within this type of economy.

Prebisch and Singer separately argued that the gains from trade for developing countries are eroded by a terms-of-trade squeeze. Production conditions in the developing countries and their specialization in primary commodities, which face a low elasticity of demand, are primarily responsible for this income transfer to the importing developed countries. Singer also indicates the enclave character of export sectors in developing countries, brought about by foreign investment; this enclave character sustains the dualistic tendencies within the developing economy and reduces the gains from trade. Similar ideas to those of Prebisch and Singer were expressed by Myrdal. He argues that the "backwash effects" of international trade on underdeveloped economies dominate the countervailing "spread effects". The latter effects represent the potential gains from trade, but these are "so very much weaker" in underdeveloped than in developed countries, simply because of their low level of development and lack of national economic integration.[7] A fundamental element is their view of the world economy as being composed of unequal trading partners, i.e. the centre or developed countries and the periphery or developing countries. The position and function of the peripheral countries in the international division of labour systematically reduce their gains in trade and impede their development.

The theme of uneven distribution of gains from trade is also a central issue in Marxist-oriented theories on imperialism and unequal exchange. According to Emmanuel's theory of unequal exchange in international economic relations, a permanent transfer of value is taking place from low-wage developing to high-wage developed countries. The existing international inequality of wages causes inequality of exchange in international trade, even under a regime of equilibrium prices.

From the above debate on the generality of neoclassical trade theory, the conclusion can be drawn that if the issue of trade and development is analyzed in the context of duality — both between countries on a world scale and within developing countries — the distribution of gains from trade is likely to be uneven. At the core of this argument lies the view that the production conditions in the trading country as well as country-specific factors must be included in the analysis. Thus, the ability of an economy to benefit from trade is strongly influenced by structural, institutional and social characteristics as well as pursued policies. These factors affect a country's pattern of specialization and play a significant role in the conversion of trade into growth impulses. Therefore, the important aspect of trade not only lies in the development of the export sector itself, but also in the impact of the export sector on the rest of the economy. The spread effects of export expansion determine the extent to which other sectors of the economy may benefit from trade. An analysis of the spread effects of export expansion is an analysis of the link between the export sector and the rest of the economy. And an analysis of this link is a study of the structure of an economy as well. In this way, the export sector is placed in the context of the national economy. In the present study, the gains from trade will be envisaged within this framework of analysis.

Before we deal with this framework in more detail, we have to define the notion of a "gain from trade" more precisely. For a developing economy, gains from trade may materialize on two levels. In the present study these gains are primarily interpreted as the generation of productive employment. This view implies that we assume a developing economy with excess labour capacity which finds expression in unemployment and underemployment at a

IMPACT OF EXPORT EXPANSION ON ECONOMIC DEVELOPMENT 185

given wage rate. Only in this situation is the generation of productive employment a real gain from trade. In addition, it is considered a gain from trade if, per unit of production, the foreign exchange earned in exporting exceeds the foreign exchange saved through import substitution.

Finally, if specialization takes place in those exportables which contribute to a higher level of integration of the often dualistic economic structure of developing countries, this is in itself seen as a gain from trade. The reason for this is obvious: the higher the interrelatedness of the export sector and the rest of the economy, the more the domestic economy will benefit from the above-mentioned different forms of spread effects and externalities.

7.3 THE SPREAD EFFECTS OF MANUFACTURED EXPORT EXPANSION

As explained, the possible gains from trade for production and employment generation are not confined to the export sector itself. It is often stated that a direct increase in production and employment will create a multiple increase in production and employment elsewhere in the economy. In a number of studies, this multiple is assumed to be about 3, on average.[8] The way production and employment-generating effects may spread through the economy is illustrated in Figure 7.1.

Starting at the left side of the figure, additional manufactured exports result in a higher level of output in exporting industries and more people will be employed in these industries. Strictly speaking, this is the direct effect of additional exports on production and employment. Increased activity of export industries may induce growth in other sectors of the economy. These spread effects are commonly known as interindustry or linkage effects. The most important linkage is undoubtedly the increased demand for intermediate inputs that may originate from all sectors of the economy. A manufacturing export sector may purchase inputs from other manufacturing sectors, but also raw materials from agriculture and services from the tertiary sector. Especially the tertiary sector in developing countries can benefit from increased activity, as a manufacturing export sector requires ancillary facilities in order to function, such as infrastructural provisions and professional services. Sabolo has identified this category of services primarily used by intermediate consumers as complementary services. He shows that the share of employment in complementary services relative to total employment is positively and significantly related to the growth of non-tertiary production. The elasticity of the increase in complementary service employment with respect to the growth of non-tertiary production is found to be higher in developing than in developed economies, respectively 0.35 and 0.12.[9] Sabolo attributes this difference to a lower level of labour productivity in service sectors in developing countries.

Figure 7.1
Production and Employment Effects of Manufactured Export Expansion

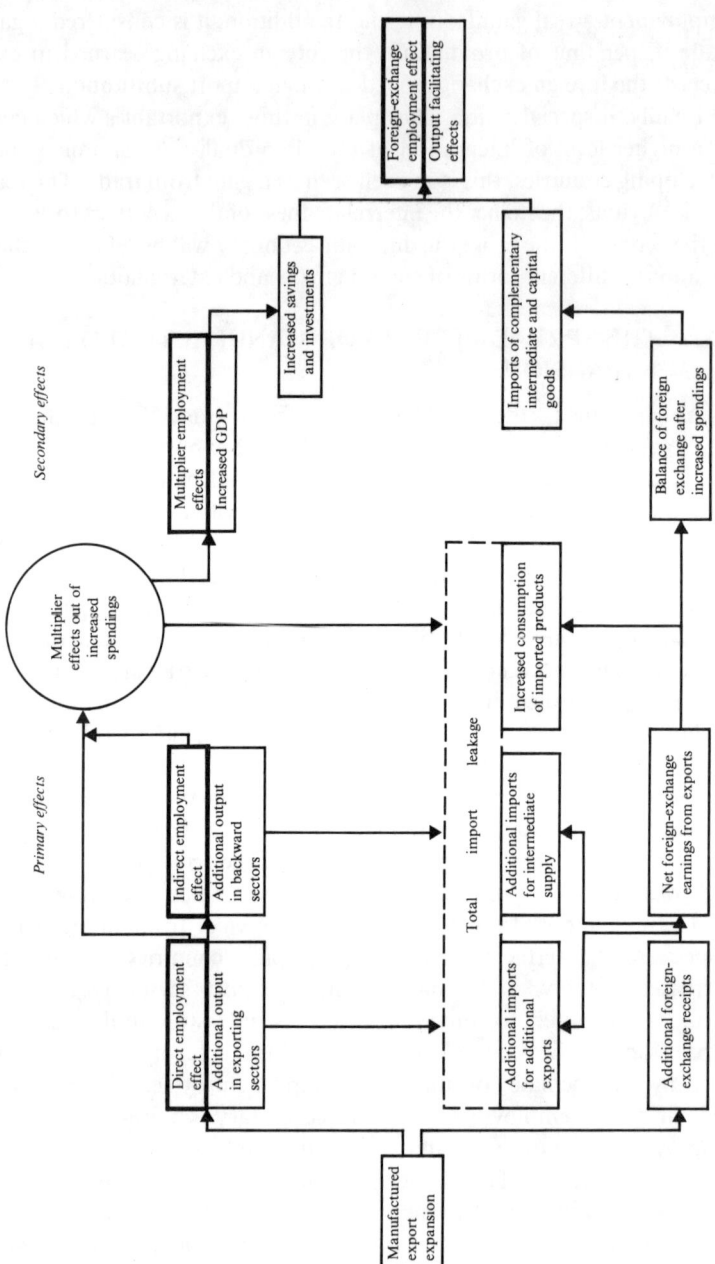

IMPACT OF EXPORT EXPANSION ON ECONOMIC DEVELOPMENT

Both in export industries and linked industries additional profit and wage incomes are realized. These incomes, insofar they are spent on the domestic market, will generate a further increase in production and employment through the working of the Keynesian multiplier (assuming no supply rigidities exist). Clearly, wage goods supplying industries will have to increase production in response to a higher sum of wage incomes earned in export and export-related sectors. But here too, the tertiary sector is expected to benefit from increased disposable incomes.[10] In particular, additional wage employment will be created in so-called new services, as education, health care and restaurants. Sabolo reports an elasticity of 0.55 for the relationship between new service employment in total employment and *per capita* income.[11] The corresponding elasticity for employment in old services (like personal services and petty trade) is equal to –0.32.

As already indicated, manufactured export expansion may also contribute to economic growth in developing countries by providing the foreign exchange to pay for strategic imports. These further rounds of production and employment increases are indicated by the foreign-exchange effect.

In sum, Figure 7.1 shows four types of effects on production and employment that may work their way through the economy:

(1) direct or initial effect;
(2) indirect or linkage effect;
(3) multiplier effect;
(4) foreign-exchange effect.

The direct and indirect effects are conceived as primary effects, the multiplier and foreign-exchange effects as secondary effects. It will be clear that the realization of secondary effects is directly related to the degree to which the primary effects have become effective. The next chapter deals with how and to what extent these effects will be estimated.

7.4 PRODUCTION AND EMPLOYMENT-REDUCING LEAKAGES

The main factor that reduces the production and employment-increasing effects of export expansion is the total import leakage of the economy. The first and often dominating leakage is the value of directly imported inputs to produce the additional exports. The second leakage into imports results from the import content of additional production in supplying industries. Both leakages reduce the domestic value-added component in exports and limit the increase in employment opportunities. The import propensity of the manufacturing sector is one of the structural features of an economy that determines the employment gains from trade. In case manufactured exports are produced in a relatively isolated sector that is highly dependent on imported inputs, as will be the case with EPFZs, the employment gain is largely restricted to direct employment in the exporting sector. If, on the contrary, exports of manufactured products originate from an import-substitution sector that has gone through the second substitution phase successfully, the indirect employment opportunities can be utilized optimally. These extremes show the divergent impact of export expansion as a consequence of differences in the structure of the economy and in pursued industrialization policies.

The import propensity of the manufacturing sector determines the size of increased export incomes and thereby also the potential extent of the multiplier effects. For two reasons this potential will not be fully realized. First, to the extent that increased incomes leak into additional imports of consumption goods, the multiplier effects in the domestic economy are weakened. Second, the working of the multiplier effect can be limited due to supply constraints, including investments, foreign exchange, technology and skilled labour. Unless the domestic supply of consumer goods is adequately adjusted to increased domestic spending, multiplier effects will be seriously eroded in consequence of an increased level of inflation.

The difference between the export earnings and the sum total of import leakages constitutes the net inflow of foreign exchange. At least three conditions must be fulfilled before an additional inflow of foreign exchange will have the desired expansionary effects on domestic production. First of all, there must be a situation of unemployment and excess capacity owing to a shortage of foreign exchange. Second, savings must be, or become, available which are not yet invested for the same reason. Third, the net foreign-exchange earnings should not be used for capital export.

In his study *Trade and Employment*, Lydall takes into account explicitly the leverage effect on capacity use and capacity growth of a relaxation of the foreign-exchange bottleneck through export expansion. Lydall assumes that additional exchange earnings are used to finance additional imports that expand the general level of domestic activity, aggregate demand and hence employment. In his view, the governments of developing countries have to ensure that the net foreign-exchange earnings are fully used to increase either public expenditure or private investment. By setting this task to the governments, Lydall guarantees the existence and working of a foreign-exchange effect, but the size of it remains highly uncertain. The increase in GDP that results from an optimal policy of using all savings and spending all net foreign-exchange earnings might range from 1.7 to 5 times the net foreign-exchange earnings.[12] This example illustrates the impossibility to establish a quantitative relationship between increased foreign-exchange earnings and income and employment-facilitating effects without in-depth studies into the functioning of an economy and the pursued policies.

7.5 LINKAGES TO THE PRIMARY SECTOR

In early stages of industrial development, industries based on raw materials from agriculture perform an important function and are often pioneer industries. These so-called agro-industries link the manufacturing sector with primary activities. The processing of food, beverages and tobacco and the manufacture of non-food products like textiles, wood products, furniture, leather, paper and rubber products absorb huge proportions of primary output.[13] An export-oriented development of these industries could therefore give rise to substantial indirect effects to the benefit of primary sectors. Given the labour-intensive character of most primary production in developing countries, agro-based manufactured export expansion would especially create considerable indirect employment.

Having recognized this, the production and employment-increasing effects on primary sectors can easily be overstated. Three reasons underlie a possible overestimation. First, due to supply constraints it is often questionable whether the agricultural sector is able to expand the supply of raw materials to meet the increased requirements of the manufacturing export sector.

Second, if a developing country already produces primary products required as inputs for export industries in sufficient quantities, another reason for overestimation may become effective, namely the possibility of export substitution. Formerly exported primary products are then diverted to the domestic manufacturing sector to be transformed into (final) export products. In cases of both supply constraints and export substitution, additional manufactured exports would have no extra linkage effects on production and employment in primary sectors.

The above two reasons for overstating the linkage impact on primary sectors refer to the uncertainty of inducing additional primary production. The third reason only has to do with a possible overestimation of induced employment opportunities, due to the actual employment situation in the agricultural sector of many developing countries. The current concept of employment normally refers to a full-time job in a productive activity paying at least a subsistence income. For the agricultural sector of many developing countries this concept should in fact be interpreted rather as a variety of engagements, whether remunerative or not. The subsistence economy and familial nature of agricultural labour still predominate. Most farming is done on limited areas of land, where an increased demand for products and a more profitable conduct of business only diminish underemployment. Hired labour is incidental, unorganized, and occurs under seasonal pressure. In this context, a United Nations' research team remarks with respect to the employment situation in Asian countries that "it is extremely difficult to offer a precise notion of labour requirements, as there is neither a question of retirement in case of loss nor much scope of expansion of the farm in case of profit ... this peculiarity of agriculture makes it truly difficult to project employment requirements".[14]

In sum, because of these three reasons the linkage effects on output and employment in primary sectors cannot easily be established and quantified, and hence must be considered with great caution.

7.6 NEGATIVE EFFECTS ON PRODUCTION AND EMPLOYMENT

Thus far we have examined the spread effects of manufactured export expansion without paying attention to the possibility of negative effects on production and employment in other sectors of the economy. A number of factors has been mentioned which might reduce the potential spread effects, but these effects are still considered to be positive. In a World Bank research publication, written by Squire, the comment is made that "... studies focused on the employment generated by exports without considering the possibility that employment elsewhere was curtailed as a result of switching nonlabor factors of production to exports".[15] In other words, the question arises whether the spread effects of investments in export sectors are larger than those of investments in sectors producing for the domestic market. If not, we may face a situation in which the employment generated by exports is more than offset by forgone employment effects of investment in import-substituting manufacturing sectors.

This issue will be dealt with on an empirical basis in the specific country studies, i.e. the various measures of spread effects of manufactured export production will be compared with those of other manufacturing production. But apart from the subsequent empirical verification there are reasons to expect in general that the net spread effects of manufactured export expansion will remain positive, also after taking into account the forgone effects of alternative investment in manufacturing. Below it will be argued that due to manufactured export expansion, first, the possibility of forgone employment effects is only relevant for larger developing countries, and, second, the occurrence of on balance negative employment effects is most unlikely both in small and in large developing countries. To argue our case, it is useful to make a distinction between the employment impact of investments of domestic and of foreign capital.

In the early stages of inward-looking industrialization in developing countries, the objective of growth and diversification was easily achieved. But after the so-called easy phase of import substitution of light manufactures, a growing number of developing countries experienced difficulties in maintaining the initial high rates of industrial growth. A closer examination of the growth of manufacturing output in terms of light and heavy industry reveals that over the period 1955–1970 the growth rates of light industry slackened most notably: the average annual growth rates dropped from 5.2 per cent during the years 1955–1960 to 4.8 per cent during the years 1960–1965 and dropped further to 4.3 per cent during the years 1965–1970.[16] Average annual growth rates of heavy industry in developing countries for the above-mentioned subperiods were 10.5, 9.0 and 7.7 per cent, respectively. Thus, there was a well pronounced tendency for heavy industry which produces consumer durables, intermediate and capital goods, to grow more rapidly than light industry. In general, heavy industry requires more capital per unit of production and per unit of labour. Moreover, these industries are only able to produce efficiently in a large market, due to economies of scale. For these reasons, only large countries are in a position to establish heavy industry domestically through policies of import substitution.

Evidence with respect to the process of industrial development in individual countries makes it clear that during the 1960s the contribution to the total growth of manufacturing output was realized to a large extent in larger developing countries which deepened their process of import substitution through promotion of heavy industries, most notably the larger developing countries in Latin America.[17] Average annual growth rates of heavy industry in Latin America remained high: during the periods 1955–1960, 1960–1965 and 1965–1970, respectively, 9.4, 8.1 and 9.0 per cent. At the end of the 1960s when many developing countries were completing the first phase of import substitution, these countries were forced to reconsider their industrialization strategy in order to speed up industrial growth. If growth of the domestic market through redistribution of incomes and policy measures to increase the average level of productivity in an economy is not considered, there are only two alternatives to speed up manufacturing growth beyond the level that would be facilitated by a general increase of domestic demand. These alternatives include either the backward integration of industrial development or promotion of manufactured export expansion. As a small domestic market limits a country's ability to develop heavy industry, continuation of import-substitution policies is only feasible for larger developing countries. Smaller developing countries have no choice but to embark on manufactured export expansion. The recovery of growth of manufacturing output in the 1970s can therefore mainly be attributed to continuing high growth levels of heavy manufacturing output in some large countries and an impressive manufactured export performance of a number of South-East Asian countries, primarily based on light manufactures.

As regards the incidence of forgone employment opportunities due to manufactured export expansion, we may now conclude, in general and irrespective of country-specific stages of industrialization, as follows. First, it is unlikely that smaller developing countries will experience substantial forgone employment effects as the domestic market of light manufactures shows signs of saturation and the development of heavy industry producing for the domestic market is not feasible. Second, the occurrence of forgone employment is only possible in larger developing countries. These countries have a real choice between deepening, through backward integration, of the process of import substitution and the promotion of manufactured exports. However, since heavy industry requires more capital investment per unit of production than the predominantly labour-intensive manufactured exports of developing countries, the forgone employment opportunities in domestic-market-oriented industries will probably not outweigh the newly created employment opportunities in export industries. Net negative employment effects in consequence of a re-orientation of domestic investments will therefore not arise.

With respect to foreign direct investment in exporting sectors, the possibility of negative effects on output and employment in domestic-market-oriented industries is not present at all. First, an inflow of foreign capital in exporting sectors does not in fact reduce the availability of domestic investment funds. The latter can still be allocated to domestic industries, except, perhaps, the investment that goes into the development of the physical infrastructure to be used by foreign capital. Second, there are no negative effects because exported products do not enter into competition with the production of industries oriented towards the domestic market. A negative impact of foreign investment on employment can only arise in case of direct competition with local producers on the same market. In developing countries where a protected import-substitution sector and a manufacturing export sector exist abreast in consequence of separate incentive schemes, the products exclusively produced for export are on no account allowed to enter the domestic market. For example, workers employed in EPFZs are often subject to special regulations to prevent smuggling and disruption of the domestic market. Mostly, they have to show special passes to enter a free zone and they have to undergo body checks after finishing their working day.[18]

In view of the arguments elaborated above, it will be clear that it is unlikely that manufactured export expansion will have negative employment effects of any significance.

7.7 BALANCED VERSUS UNBALANCED GROWTH OF MANUFACTURED EXPORTS

In the *Lima Declaration and Plan of Action* and the *Programme of Action on the Establishment of a New International Economic Order* emphasis is given to the need to improve the links between various economic sectors.[19]

The Plan of Action advocates "the promotion of an integrated industrialization process based on the potential of each country, with the object of achieving the highest degree of interaction between industry and the other sectors of the economy, in particular, agriculture...."[20] A broadening economic base is thus widely recognized as a prerequisite for a continued expansion of industrial production. At the same time, export of manufactures is conceived in these declarations as vital to the industrialization process in developing countries. The present study investigates to what extent these two objectives coincide. In other words, do manufactured exports contribute to a higher level of integration of an economy? Opinions differ with respect to this issue and are centered around the developmental impact of manufactured exports produced in so-called footloose industries. Here, we shall briefly explain the arguments.

The recognition of the importance of the interrelatedness of various economic activities was the undisputed starting point of the Balanced *versus* Unbalanced Growth Debate. The important positive contribution of this lively debate to the theory of economic development was the close attention given to various forms of interrelatedness and external economies. The difference of opinion in the debate concerned the appropriate growth strategy to achieve sustainable economic development, taking into account the very existence of sectoral interrelatedness.

The principal exponents of the balanced growth doctrine, Nurkse and Rosenstein-Rodan, stress the need for a balanced and instantaneous expansion of consumer goods industries and intermediate and primary sectors large enough to overcome the bottlenecks of the small size of the domestic market. Their balanced growth version focuses on the creation of effective demand; the production of each newly established industry must be able to find an outlet.[21]

Theorists like Lewis and Scitovsky paid more attention to the supply side of the economy. They not only indicated the need for an expansion of input-supplying industries in balance with an expansion of final-demand industries, but also the need for a balanced development of the various economic sectors. If food shortages, inflation and balance-of-payment problems are to be avoided, "we have to keep balance between imports, exports, manufactures and agriculture, and not just between any two of them".[22] There is, according to Lewis, only one exception to the balanced growth rule. To some degree, manufactured exports can expand out of proportion without being checked by the lagging behind of agricultural and manufacturing production for the home market. Exports themselves provide the foreign exchange which can be used to satisfy increased demand by imports.[23] Thus the balanced growth advocates share the opinion that only a simultaneous and even expansion of industries and sectors is feasible.

The unbalanced growth theorists, on the other hand, regard sectoral unbalances in the process of economic growth as inevitable and even desirable insofar as these unbalances give rise to compensating, i.e. resolving bottlenecks, investment decisions. In their view, as elaborated by Hirschman and Streeten, the simultaneous development of a great number of industries is inconceivable as developing countries are in short supply of exactly those resources which may facilitate the conceptualization and implementation of a consistent and balanced investment programme. Simultaneous growth on many fronts is just too much of a good thing.[24] According to Hirschman, the most important constraint on the economic development of Third World countries is the "insufficient number and speed of development decisions".[25] The lack of decision-making ability is seen to be the only real scarce factor. Economizing on this factor, i.e. the ability to invest, means the creation of inducement mechanisms. Investment decisions are relatively easy to take when, for instance, they are induced by an increased availability of certain goods or services at lower prices, or when a clear and stable demand for certain inputs becomes visible.

Inducement mechanisms can thus work their way forward and backward. They originate in "the specific nature of the investment".[26] Hirschman defined the two mechanisms as follows:[27]

— "The output-utilization or *forward linkage effect*, i.e., every activity that does not by its nature cater exclusively to final demands, will induce attempts to utilize its outputs as inputs in some new activities.
— The input-provision, derived demand, or *backward linkage effects*, i.e., every nonprimary economic activity, will induce attempts to supply through domestic production in inputs needed in that activity."

In the case of forward inducement a "permissive" sequence presents itself as an investment decision is more easily taken when the production of an input is already taking place and is ready for use. In the case of a backward inducement a stronger, more "compulsive" sequence makes itself felt; an investment decision is called forth in reaction to a demand for intermediate inputs, created by a previous investment. The probability that such a compulsive investment decision actually becomes effective will depend on the minimum size on which production of the input demand can take place economically. In the unbalanced growth strategy, that sequence of investment decisions which under given circumstances generates as much induced investment as possible is the most desirable. And that sequence can only be a chain of unbalanced investment decisions.

Conceiving the process of economic growth as necessarily unbalanced does not imply that unbalance is a policy aim in itself. *Ex ante* unbalance is a technique to produce *ex post* balance at a higher level of economic development.[28] Thus, both approaches stress the relevance of functional relationships among economic sectors, but they differ with respect to the policy recommendations to achieve an integrated economy and sustained economic growth.

The balanced *versus* the unbalanced growth debaters argue principally within the context of an inward-looking process of economic growth for larger developing countries. From the start of the 1970s onwards, however, an export-oriented strategy of industrialization is strongly advocated and carried out as a way to accelerate economic growth in developing countries. One of the most dynamic manufactured export activities is assembly and processing operations in footloose industries. These activities, usually subcontracted by transnational corporations and retailing firms, are characterized by a high import content. By their nature, subcontracting activities are of an enclave type. Consequently, integration of subcontracting activities with the rest of the economy is minimal and therefore the contribution to the development of the domestic economy in terms of an induced increase of output and employment will be poor. What then, in light of the above, is the economic rationale for a developing country to embark on this specific type of manufacturing and trade?

Two lines of reasoning may provide this rationale. First, a small densely populated country scarcely endowed with natural resources may have no choice but to go into assembly and processing operations. Processing of primary products before export is not feasible due to a scanty availability of natural resources. Nor can a relatively small and inefficient import-substitution sector be a base for generating manufactured exports. Relatively high costs of domestically supplied inputs would make such exports noncompetitive on the world market. A lack of knowledge of foreign markets and of experience in international trade further hamper the generation of manufactured exports. These obstacles may also apply to larger developing countries with a more developed import-substitution sector. Through a specialization in subcontracting activities these obstacles can be overcome. Subcontracting agents often furnish the subcontractor in developing countries with capital equipment, technological know-how, quality standards and the necessary inputs. Moreover, they save the subcontractor the problem of product design and marketing.[29] A quick start in manufactured exports is therefore possible.

Second, it is tenable that such a highly export-oriented industrialization policy with a heavy reliance on imported inputs can be quite justifiable in terms of the neoclassical factor proportions theory of international trade. Riedel provides the argument for this view.[30] According to Riedel, the Leontief measure of factor intensity of traded products is not appropriate in an open economy which utilizes imported as well as domestically produced inputs. The Leontief measure of factor intensity comprises not only factor requirements at the last stage of production, but also factor requirements at each intermediate stage in producing inputs. However, it is then implicitly assumed that all intermediate products are produced domestically. But if in an open economy these intermediate products are imported in reality, it is appropriate to replace in the Leontief measure the factor requirements of intermediate products as if they were produced domestically by the average weighted factor requirements used up in producing exports; for with foreign-exchange earnings from exports the imported intermediate inputs are purchased. Following Riedel, in case of an open economy one must evaluate the factor intensity of the structure of production not only on the factor intensities of the final stage of production and domestic intermediate supplies, but also on the factor intensity of exports that are used to buy the needed intermediate inputs. Behind this view lies the empirical datum that separate stages of product processing or separate component parts of a final product may differ widely in factor requirements. From the point of view of subcontracting agents, this datum constitutes exactly the economic rationale to subcontract. If the Leontief measure of labour and capital intensity for product j is denoted as L_j and K_j respectively, and the corresponding adjusted Riedel measures as L_j' and K_j', then a labour-abundant developing country acts rationally in opting for subcontracting in case $L_j < L_j'$ and $K_j > K_j'$. The substitution of imported inputs for domestically produced inputs raises the labour and reduces the capital requirements in the economy.

Riedel applied his reasoning to the "footloose" import-dependent industrial structure of Taiwan as presented in the 1969 input-output table. A comparison of $L - L'$ and $K - K'$ reveals that the Taiwan manufacturing sector generated additional employment and saved capital by importing manufactured intermediate inputs rather than, alternatively, producing all manufactured inputs domestically. The economic rationale in terms of neoclassical resource-allocation considerations appears from the net savings, because in the case of Taiwan capital savings well outweighed additional labour costs. Carrying forward this line of reasoning, it could be argued that developing countries, by importing relatively capital-intensive intermediate input with foreign exchange earned by relatively labour-intensive exports, would act rationally with a specialization in footloose manufactured exports. Dealing with South Korea and Taiwan, Little expresses a similar view. He goes as far as to assert that "development·in depth must be declared the enemy of employment and equality. All labour-intensive sectors have their K/L ratios raised by backward linkage, because all the intermediates ... are highly capital intensive. These intermediates are the curse of developing countries."[31]

Does the argument of Riedel and Little weaken the importance of interrelatedness of and balance between economic activities? As Lewis already put forward, an expansion of manufactured exports out of proportion to the development of linked sectors can take place without immediate repercussions. With respect to this point there is no difference of opinion. It should be recognized, though, that the argument of Riedel and Little applies to a static optimum within the context of the neoclassical trade theory. They rightly point to the suboptimal resource allocation when economies at lower levels of development aim at producing intermediates and capital goods domestically. The apparent conflict, however, is overcome by distinguishing between the static and dynamic points of view. As Chenery has argued, static comparative advantage ignores a variety of dynamic elements and interdependences among sectors which are considered conducive to economic development. Without invalidating the static argument, our approach stresses the view that strengthening the economic structure by optimizing — that is to say, not at all costs — the extent of spread effects and externalities is a better guarantee for sustained economic development. Clearly, this view gives more weight to longer term considerations.

8
The Measurement of Spread Effects of Manufactured Export Expansion

8.1 INTRODUCTION

The interrelatedness of economic sectors arises from the fact that each sector delivers output to or demands inputs from one or more other sectors. The input-output method is the standard analytical tool to study this interrelatedness of economic activities. This method not only provides insight into patterns of sectoral interdependence, but also facilitates the measurement of different forms of spread effects.

As "the use of any analytical tool requires an understanding of both its theoretical form and its empirical content",[1] we shall first examine the possibilities and limitations of the input-output method, viewed from the angle of our investigations. Next, a number of measures of sectoral interdependence and spread effects is dealt with, in terms of both production and employment. This chapter provides the methodology to measure empirically the four different forms of spread effects of economic activities, discussed in the preceding chapter.

8.2 THE INPUT-OUTPUT METHOD

In static input-output analysis, an input-output table describes the input and the output of interrelated economic sectors of an economic system by a set of linear equations over a stated period of time.[2] By definition, there holds for an economy disaggregated into n sectors

(8.1) $X_i = \sum_{j=1}^{n} X_{ij} + Y_i$ where
X_i = total output of sector i,
$i = 1, 2 \ldots n$

X_{ij} = output of sector i absorbed as an input in sector j, $j = 1, 2...n$
Y_i = final demand for goods from sector i, $i = 1, 2...n$

Final demand Y consists of various components, such as private consumption expenditures of households, investments in fixed capital formation, government consumption expenditures, exports and changes in inventories. A basic assumption of the input-output model is that the demand of sector j for the output of sector i, that is X_{ij}, is proportional to the output level of sector j. If

(8.2) $\quad a_{ij} = \dfrac{X_{ij}}{X_j}$ $\quad\quad$ where
$\quad\quad\quad\quad\quad\quad\quad\quad\quad\quad\quad a_{ij}$ = direct input coefficient
$\quad\quad\quad\quad\quad\quad\quad\quad\quad\quad\quad X_j$ = total input of sector j

is denoted as the direct input coefficient, which is constant, and substituted into balance equations (8.1), this set of equations can be written in matrix notation

(8.3) $\quad X = AX + Y$ $\quad\quad$ where
$\quad\quad\quad\quad\quad\quad\quad\quad\quad\quad\quad X$ = vector of elements X_i or X_j
$\quad\quad\quad\quad\quad\quad\quad\quad\quad\quad\quad A$ = matrix of elements a_{ij}
$\quad\quad\quad\quad\quad\quad\quad\quad\quad\quad\quad Y$ = vector of elements Y_i

It follows that

(8.4) $\quad X = (I - A)^{-1} Y$ $\quad\quad$ where
$\quad\quad\quad\quad\quad\quad\quad\quad\quad\quad\quad (I - A)^{-1}$ = matrix of elements r_{ij}

The matrix A is called the structural matrix, the matrix $(I - A)$ is the so-called Leontief matrix. The elements r_{ij} of the matrix $(I - A)^{-1}$ give per unit of final demand for sector j's products the total output requirements of sector i. It is clear from (8.4) that each total input coefficient r_{ij} depends on all direct input coefficients a_{ij}. In this way, an economy is described as an interdependent system of inputs and outputs. In an open input-output system, the levels of final demand are exogenous: given the matrix A, vector Y determines vector X.

In input-output analysis, a distinction is made between non-primary inputs represented in the structural matrix A and primary inputs. The former comprise the intersectoral deliveries, the latter usually include wages and salaries and gross profits. These are payments for the primary inputs labour and capital, which together constitute value added in production. When an input-output table is presented in market prices, indirect taxes and subsidies also appear as primary inputs. The total use of primary inputs in sector j is

(8.5) $W_j = \sum_{h=1}^{k} W_{hj}$ where
W_j = value added in sector j
W_{hj} = primary input h in sector j,
$h = 1, 2...k$

while the total output of primary sector h is equal to

(8.6) $W^h = \sum_{j=1}^{n} W_{hj}$ where
W^h = total output of primary sector h.

The primary input component h of sector j can be related to the output of sector j as

(8.7) $w_{hj} = \dfrac{W_{hj}}{X_j}$ where
w_{hj} = primary input coefficient.

If V is the matrix comprising all primary input coefficients w_{hj}, then primary input requirements follow from

(8.8) $W = V(I - A)^{-1} Y$ where
W = vector of primary input requirements
V = matrix of elements w_{hj}.

The production levels X_j in each sector are related to final demand, and the primary input requirements are in turn related to each production level through the primary input coefficients. It is now possible to determine the effects of changes in final demand, or of a component part in it, on the corresponding primary input requirements.

8.3 TREATMENT OF IMPORTS IN INPUT-OUTPUT TABLES

As already pointed out in Section 7.4 of the preceding chapter, the realization of potential spread effects of manufactured export expansion depends mainly on the absence of leakage in the linkages for domestic production activities. The direct and indirect import component in manufactured exports constitutes the most important leakage. The analysis of spread effects must take these import leakages into account explicitly. Only domestic linkages that reflect domestically produced inputs are to be considered. Therefore, intermediate supplies must be freed from linkages that are realized outside the national economy.

Domestic linkages may differ widely from potential linkages, i.e. linkages inclusive of imported inputs. The concept of potential linkages has played an important role in the formulation of alternative development strategies. Among other purposes, analyses of potential sectoral linkages based on input-output tables have been undertaken to identify "key sectors" in the process of development.[3] Especially with respect to the import-substitution strategy of industrialization, potential linkages have been suggested as an investment criterion. In this line of reasoning, sectors with high potential linkages are selected as priority sectors because import leakages in potential linkages offer the possibility of substitution by domestic production, and high-linkage sectors are expected to induce overall growth to a relatively greater extent than low-linkage sectors.

However, our research is not intended to reveal potential linkage effects in the first place, but is directed to an analysis of actual spread effects of manufactured exports in developing countries. For that reason, a distinction between domestically produced and imported inputs is of importance. To be able to make this distinction a specific presentation of input-output tables is required. Distinct treatments of imports in input-output tables are known, not all of which meet our requirements completely. In the following, the various ways in which imports are treated in input-output tables are discussed.

There are two basic methods of treating imports. The first and preferable method requires that a complete matrix of intermediate imports is available as well as a vector of imports which enters final demand directly. In this case the intermediate imports needed for the production of each sector are known, and are subdivided into products groups and allocated according to the corresponding sector classification. The entries along a row of an import matrix represent the sectoral allocation of total intermediate demand for a specific import product, while the entries along the column of this matrix represent the commodity composition of a sector's imported inputs.

If $\overset{*}{M}$ is denoted as the matrix of intermediate imports with elements $\overset{*}{m}_{ij}$, a constant import coefficient can be defined as

(8.9) $\quad m_{ij} = \dfrac{\overset{*}{m}_{ij}}{X_j} \quad$ where
$\qquad\qquad m_{ij}$ = constant import coefficient
$\qquad\qquad \overset{*}{m}_{ij}$ = import of product i absorbed in sector j

and the general solution of the input-output model can now be extended with

(8.10) $\quad \overset{*}{M} = MX \quad$ where
$\qquad\qquad \overset{*}{M}$ = matrix of intermediate imports
$\qquad\qquad M$ = matrix of constant import coefficients m_{ij}.

Total imports M^T are equal to total intermediate demand for imports M^I

plus final demand for imports M^F. Taking into account the two elements of total final demand, (8.4) becomes

(8.11) $X = (I - A^D)^{-1} Y^D$

where
Y^D = final demand for domestically produced products
A^D = domestic structural matrix

and total imports are given by

(8.12) $M^T = M(I - A^D)^{-1} Y^D + M^F$ where
M^T = column vector of total imports
M^F = column vector of final demand for imports.

The symbol D attached to A and Y refers to domestically produced products.

If available data do not allow the compilation of a complete import matrix, the presentation of a row vector of total imports per sector may suffice. In that case, no detailed information is available on the commodity composition of imports per sector. Let $\overset{*}{M}^J$ be the row vector of total intermediate imports per sector $\overset{*}{m}_j$, then again a constant import coefficient can be defined

(8.13) $m_j = \dfrac{\overset{*}{m}_j}{X_j}$

where
m_j = constant total intermediate import coefficient
$\overset{*}{m}_j$ = total intermediate imports absorbed in sector j.

In this case, (8.10) becomes

(8.14) $\overset{*}{M}^J = M^J X$

where
$\overset{*}{M}^J$ = vector of total intermediate imports per sector
M^J = diagonal matrix of constant total intermediate import coefficients m_j.

This first method of treating imports, whether as a complete import matrix or a row vector of total imports, is characterized by the following features. To begin with, the structural matrix A^D only comprises coefficients of domestically produced intermediate inputs. Second, intermediate imports in the above solution are treated endogenously, while imports entering final demand directly are conceived as exogenous variables. Third, this method of treating intermediate imports implies the economic classification of imports in competitive and noncompetitive or complementary imports. Of course, such a classification has to be based on the short-run domestic supply capacity and on the fact whether or not competition in both price and quality really exists between imported and domestically produced products. Implicitly, however, imports presented as an import matrix or as a row vector of imports are, via constant import coefficients, considered to be noncompetitive or complementary imports. This approach leaves no room for alternative assumptions about substitutibility of imports for domestic production, or vice versa. Finally, those imports which are recorded under the heading of final demand are assumed to compete with domestic products.

Due to limitations of available data on imports, a complete import matrix or a row vector of imports is often not available. In this eventuality, information is also usually unavailable about the end-use of imports, so that no distinction can be made between intermediate imports and final demand imports. Then, only the commodity classification of imported products is given, but which sectors are consuming what kind of imported products is unknown. If the available data are of such nature, it is only feasible to enter imported products as a negative component of total final demand. This presentation, where a column vector represents imports as a deduction from total final demand, is the second method of treating imports. The general input-output equation (8.1) now becomes

(8.15) $X_i = \sum_{j=1}^{n} X_{ij} + Y_i - M_i$ where
M_i = imports of product group i.

The solution of X from (8.15) is in matrix notation

(8.16) $X = (I - A)^{-1} (Y - M^T)$ where
M^T = column vector of total imports M_i.

It is important to note that M_i represents imports of product group i which is, of course, not the same as the demand for imports by sector i. Therefore, there are considerable differences between the first and the second methods of handling imports in terms of the computational procedure, and in the quality and applicability of the results.

First, all imported intermediate and final products are included but are concealed in intermediate and final transactions. Deliveries in the structural matrix A represent both domestically produced and imported intermediate inputs. Second, a column vector of negative entries for imports is conceived as an exogenous and given variable. And third, imported products presented in a column vector compete with similar products which are produced domestically. Implicitly, all imports are considered competitive imports.

A consequence of the above features is that an analysis of spread effects based on an input-output table which treats imports as exogenous and competitive may lead to misleading results, because the structural matrix A includes imports and, therefore, linkages realized abroad are unjustly added to linkages realized in the domestic economy. In case of the second method of treating imports, our main concern is to free the structural matrix A from imports, so that an analysis of spread effects can be based on a structural matrix of domestically produced intermediate products. There are several roundabout procedures to free the structural matrix A from imports. These procedures have in common the treatment of imports as derived demand. This leads, in one way or another, to defining a constant import coefficient that relates all or part of the so-called competitive imports to the level of domestic production of, or the level of domestic consumption from, the sector to which these imports are allocated. Two procedures will be dealt with here.

In some cases it is still possible, for instance with the help of additional data sources or separate empirical research, to gain insight into the end-use of imports in such detail that at least the import vector can be divided into two vectors, viz. imports used up in the production process and those entering in final demand. It can now be assumed that competitive imports considered to be for intermediate use, M^I, are proportionate to the level of production of the corresponding sectors. The constant import coefficient m_i is defined as

(8.17) $\quad m_i = \dfrac{m_i^I}{X_i}$ where

$\qquad m_i$ = constant import coefficient
$\qquad m_i^I$ = intermediate imports allocated to sector i.

If $\overset{+}{M}$ is defined as a diagonal matrix with elements m_i, then

(8.18) $\quad M^I = \overset{+}{M}X$ where

$\qquad M^I$ = intermediate demand for imports
$\qquad \overset{+}{M}$ = diagonal matrix of elements m_i.

Parts of the competitive imports are allocated to production sectors and these parts are now considered as endogenous variables; this alters general solution (8.11). Taking into account the subdivision of the total import vector M^T into an intermediate import vector M^I and a final import vector M^F, the balance equation can be rewritten as

(8.19) $\quad X = AX + Y - (M^I + M^F)$.

After substituting $\overset{+}{M}X$ for M^I we obtain

(8.20) $\quad X = (A - \overset{+}{M})X + Y - M^F$

and find the solution

(8.21) $X = (I - A + \overset{+}{M})^{-1} (Y - M^F)$.

The matrices $(A - \overset{+}{M})$ and $(I - A + \overset{+}{M})^{-1}$ no longer contain intermediate imports. However, the matrix $(A - \overset{+}{M})$ is nonetheless not identical to the domestic structural matrix A^D. In fact, two distortions are introduced as a consequence of the procedure followed. First, in the matrices $(A - \overset{+}{M})$ and $(I - A + \overset{+}{M})^{-1}$ intermediate imports are not allocated to consuming sectors, but to competing supplying sectors. In other words, the wrong imports are deducted from the wrong elements of matrix A. Second, total intermediate imports allocated to production sector i are wholly deducted from the diagonal element i of the competing sector.

Thus far we have assumed that it would still be possible to differentiate between intermediate imports and imports for final consumption. However, this extra information is also usually unavailable. We thus have a single negative column vector of imports in the final demand. To "correct" the structural matrix A for imports in this case, one could simply assume that all imports are of an intermediate nature. Via the above approach of constant sectoral import coefficients, the diagonal elements of matrix A would be reduced with all corresponding competitive imports, thus inclusive of imports directly entering final demand. The objections raised against the "correction" of matrix A for imports in (8.21) are equally relevant here. The errors are even larger, because no distinction is made between intermediate and final imports.

In this situation of inadequate information on imports, it is also possible to follow a slightly different procedure to approximate an import-free structural matrix A^D.[4] The starting position is again the availability of a single negative column vector of imports in the final demand block. The steps in this procedure are as follows. To begin with, it is assumed that imports by each sector are proportionate to the level of domestic absorption of that sector's products. Since domestic absorption is equal to total demand for intermediate and final products minus exports, a constant import coefficient for each sector $\hat{m}_i$ is defined as

(8.22) $\hat{m}_i = \dfrac{M_i^T}{\sum_{j=1}^{n} X_{ij} + Y_i^{dc}}$

where
m_i = constant import coefficient for sector i
M_i^T = total imports of sector i products
Y_i^{dc} = domestic final demand for products of sector i.

Total competitive imports are proportionally related to, and accordingly distributed among, intermediate and domestic final demand. This relation is written formally

(8.23) $M^T = \hat{M}(AX + Y^{DC})$ where
M^T = column vector of total imports
$\hat{M}$ = diagonal matrix of constant import coefficients $\hat{m}_i$
Y^{DC} = column vector of domestic final demand.

The input-output balance equation may now be written in the form

(8.24) $X = AX + Y^{DC} + E - M^T$ where
E = column vector of exports.

From (8.23) and (8.24) we obtain, after rearranging,

(8.25) $X = (A - \hat{M}A)X + Y^{DC} + E - \hat{M}Y^{DC}$

and the solution of X becomes

(8.26) $X = [I - (I - \hat{M})A]^{-1} [(I - \hat{M})Y^{DC} + E]$

Solution (8.26) is composed of two parts, namely the level of production required to meet a certain level of final demand minus exports according to $[I - (I - \hat{M})A]^{-1} (I - \hat{M})Y^{DC}$, and the level of production required to meet a certain level of demand for exports which is given by $[I - (I - \hat{M})A]^{-1} E$. The possibility to divide solution (8.26) into two parts is an immediate consequence of the implicit assumption that imports will not directly be re-exported.

The matrix $(A - \hat{M}A)$ in (8.25) can be interpreted as the equivalent of matrix $(A - \overset{+}{\hat{M}})$ in (8.20). Similarly, in matrix $(A - \hat{M}A)$ imports that are allocated to intermediate sectors are subtracted from the deliveries of competing sectors. However, total intermediate imports are not subtracted from the corresponding diagonal elements of the A matrix, but are allocated to the corresponding row element of A in proportion to the weight of an element in the sum of row elements. Thus, in contrast with the corrected structural matrix $(A - \overset{+}{\hat{M}})$ in (8.20) where only the diagonal elements of matrix A have been corrected, the matrix $(A - \hat{M}A)$ differs from matrix A with respect to all elements.

This proportional distribution of intermediate imports among all row elements of the structural matrix A is preferable on *a priori* grounds. This preference can be illustrated by considering the differences in sectoral input structures under the two alternative procedures. The assumed input structure of each sector j after the first procedure has been applied is given by the jth column of the matrix $(A - \overset{+}{\hat{M}})$ and the diagonal element m_j of the import matrix $\overset{+}{M}$, the latter showing imported products that compete with sector jth output. By contrast, under the second procedure, the sector j input structure is expressed by the jth column of the matrix $(A - \hat{M}A)$ completed with the jth column of the import matrix $\hat{M}A$. The element $\hat{m}_i a_{ij}$ $(i=j)$ of the latter column indeed represents competing products, but all other column elements represent noncompeting products which could very well be imported as an intermediate input for the production process of sector j. At any rate, these inputs have actually been used up in sector j; only the proportion in which these inputs are imported or produced domestically is approximated. It should be added, however, that this more balanced allocation of imports under the second procedure does not alter the fact that, just as in the first procedure, it remains incorrect to allocate imports to competing sectors. Furthermore, the proportional allocation of total imports to intermediate and final demand may give rise to an additional distortion of reality. Hence, the two procedures to "correct" the structural matrix A for imports, in case only a negative column vector of imports in final demand is available, have to be considered as provisional solutions.

The two basic methods of treating imports discussed here are both put into practice. Sometimes, a mixture of both methods is applied. As to the input-output tables used, in four of the seven country studies presented in this study imports are dealt with according to the principles of the first method, in three according to those of the second. In the latter case, the last-treated roundabout procedure to arrive at an approximated A^D matrix is applied.

8.4 SOME LIMITATIONS OF THE INPUT-OUTPUT APPROACH

The input-output method facilitates a quantitative analysis of spread effects of manufactured export expansion. However, the application of this method in practice is liable to a number of inherent limitations, some of which need to be explicitly mentioned here. These limitations restrict the scope of the analysis and may affect its reliability.

First of all, one must be well aware of the fact that essentially the structural matrix A has to be conceived as a picture of technology-related ties which arise on account of technological relations among producing sectors. Thus, for analytical purposes, the interpretation of constant input coefficients as ratios of quantities measured in physical units is the only correct one.[5] In practice, however, input-output tables are generally made up in value terms. Hence, the picture of technological relations may be distorted by the prevailing system of relative prices by which physical units are converted into values. This distortion is not serious if intertemporal comparisons could be made in terms of constant prices and if, in the case of international comparisons, a uniform set of relative prices could be used. With respect to intercountry comparisons this condition is satisfied when relatively open economies are compared. Then it can reasonably be assumed that the input-output coefficients are all based on a set of relative prices reflecting free-trade conditions. However, developing economies in particular operate under trade regimes which are far removed from free-trade conditions. In almost all developing countries the manufacturing sector, and more specifically those manufacturing activities that are oriented towards the domestic market, receive preferential treatment while other economic activities are discriminated against. Only recently is the home-market bias of industrialization in developing countries being shifted to or being complemented by a more outward orientation of manufacturing production. The imposition of various price and nonprice measures to protect the manufacturing sector entails a distortion in the domestic system of relative prices. Protective measures also tend to overvalue the domestic currency as compared to a hypothetical free-trade situation. Taken together, the distortion of relative prices of inputs and outputs brought about by protection may create variation between countries in input-output coefficients irrespective of technological factors.

Our empirical research is based on a number of input-output tables of South-East Asian countries which are presented in domestic values. Some of these countries, most notably Indonesia, pursue a policy of domestic-market-oriented industrialization, implemented through a relatively high level of protection. Singapore, by contrast, pursues an export-oriented industrialization strategy and can be characterized as an extremely open economy. Measurements of spread effects of manufactured export expansion in individual countries, which make use of domestic input-output coefficients, may deviate from each other solely on account of differences in the extent or level of domestic protection. It is therefore of importance to examine briefly what kinds of distortions of domestic input coefficients under protection are involved and to determine the direction in which these distortions may operate.

The use of domestic input-output coefficients rather than hypothetical free-trade coefficients may affect the measurement of spread effects on two distinct levels. First, relative prices of intermediate inputs and those of the primary factors — land, labour and capital — change as a result of the imposition of protective measures. Second, in response to changes in relative prices, substitution may take place between and among the various intermediate and primary inputs.

Generally, the purpose of protection is to cover the difference between domestic and foreign costs of production, thereby enabling protected producers to operate with a higher value added than would be realized under free-trade conditions. The nominal rate of protection expresses the extent to which the domestic price of any product exceeds the world market price resulting from the price-raising effects of protective measures. The effective rate of protection gives an estimate of the extent to which the value added measured at domestic prices in a particular sector exceeds the value added at world market prices. The nominal protection concept refers to the product price, while the concept of effective protection indicates the combined impact of different levels of protection of inputs and outputs on the share of value added in production.[6] It will be clear that factors of production tend to move into sectors which benefit from higher protection. The allocation of resources among sectors and the domestic or foreign market orientation of these sectors will therefore depend on the structure of effective protection. The structure of effective protection also affects the remuneration of the factors of production which together make out value added in production.

This being established, we can make the following remarks with respect to the impact of protection on the system of relative prices. Generally, the structure of effective protection in developing countries shows, apart from considerable variation in the extent among countries, a pattern of progression from intermediate inputs to final products. Thus, effective protection is lower for machinery, construction and intermediate products and higher for consumer goods. Starting from the fact that the domestic price-raising effect of protection is closely related to the level of protection, the share of intermediate inputs in production measured at domestic prices is relatively understated. On the other hand, the share of value added in domestic prices is relatively overstated. By using domestic input-output coefficients in the analysis of spread effects the contribution of input-supplying industries is understated as compared to the contribution measured at hypothetical free-trade prices.

The impact of protection on substitution among various inputs is more equivocal. Different substitution processes may take place, for instance, between intermediate and primary inputs, among intermediate inputs and among primary inputs. In studies on the structure of effective protection these substitution possibilities are important. To exclude the substitution effect due to protection, one should ideally estimate effective rates of protection based on input-output coefficients that should prevail under free-trade conditions. However, an analysis of the spread effects of manufactured export expansion clearly differs from an analysis of the structure of effective protection. Our investigations are directed to the actual spread effects of various forms of manufactured exports under alternative trade regimes and the introduction of uniform free-trade conditions would smooth out these differences. This means that the domestic input-output coefficients are the only relevant coefficients, inclusive of possibly occurring substitutions. Apart from this, empirical studies reveal that little substitution takes place between intermediate and primary inputs in response to changes in relative prices. For instance, in a study on the structure of protection in seven countries Balassa et al. estimated two different sets of effective rates of protection per country, one by the use of domestic and one by the use of free-trade coefficients. It appeared that "whatever differences are shown between the two sets of estimates are due largely to considerations unrelated to the substitution issue".[7]

These findings refer to substitution among different intermediate inputs, and between total intermediate inputs and total primary factor inputs. Substitution among primary factors, however, does take place. It is widely recognized that the imposition of protective measures not only affects the remuneration of primary factors of production, but also the choice of techniques within industries. A mechanism frequently at work under a protective trade regime is the encouragement to use relatively capital-intensive techniques which is provided by the relative underpricing of capital goods. This underpricing may, among other things, originate from lower levels of protection for capital-goods industries or from the possibility to import capital goods at overvalued exchange rates without adequate compensating duties. As far as this tendency results in employing relatively less labour-intensive techniques in protected industries, it will be adequately revealed by domestic input-output coefficients which express the relative factor intensity in physical units. If no physical unit of labour utilization is available, as is also the case with some of our empirical country studies, but rather a value unit as the total wage bill per sector, a measurement of factor intensity of industries under protection will certainly involve a bias. However, the direction of this bias cannot be indicated. Labour employed in protected industries may also benefit from the effective protection of value added in the form of relatively higher wage rates. The exact division of the increased returns to labour and capital under protection is *a priori* unknown and will differ from industry to industry. It will depend on the labour legislation in force, the working of the labour and capital market and the extent to which an industry enjoys a monopoly position permitted by protection.

In sum, in the present study domestic input-output coefficients will be used without adjustments for the impact of protection on these coefficients. Although we must be well aware of the extent and direction of this impact, any adjustment would give rise to a distorted picture of actual spread effects of manufactured exports under different trade regimes.

The next problem we should deal with refers to the static character of an input-output analysis, which has everything to do with the fixity of input-output coefficients. This static character may limit the scope of our research findings, depending on the actuality of the input-output coefficients. To illuminate this problem, it must be realized that a change in industrialization strategy from a domestic-market orientation towards a more open orientation implies a fundamental readjustment of the protected economy, completely or in part, and neutralization of the discrimination against exports. In this eventuality, the protective impact of trade regimes is reduced, international competition increases, an overvalued currency loses its rationality and investment promotion schemes favour manufactured export industries above industries producing for the domestic market. These policy changes will affect the structure of relative prices and the remuneration of capital and labour. In turn, the changes will not leave the structure of production unaffected. It is also likely that a change in industrialization strategy will induce a change in the product mix supplied by the various sectors. All this will have consequences for the method of production, the techniques in use and the input structure of industries. A static input-output model cannot take these changes into account, because its basic assumptions are those of proportionality and homogeneity. These two assumptions are closely related.[8]

The inputs of a sector are assumed to bear a fixed proportion to the output of that sector. Homogeneity implies that each sector is assumed to produce a homogeneous product with a single input structure. In practice, however, various industries are aggregated into distinct sectors which have at least a similar input structure and production technique. Input-output coefficients refer then to averages over a range of products and technologies. These assumptions leave no room for substitutions among inputs in response to changes in relative prices. Changes in the product mix of a sector's output are disregarded as well. Furthermore, the fixity of input-output coefficients implies a linear homogeneous production function with constant returns to scale in production. In applying this specific production function, dynamic spread effects due to induced technological change, internal and external economies of scale, and improvements in productivity fall beyond the scope of the analysis.

Finally, a measurement of spread effects based on the input-output approach is sensitive to the level of aggregation at which sectors are specified in an input-output table. The diagonal elements of the structural matrix A, which represent intra-industry deliveries, are especially sensitive to the level of aggregation. Aggregation as such, and the fact that sectors specified in an input-output table represent averages over individual industries, raises the question to what extent these averages can still be representative of export activities. To give an extreme but not unrealistic example, the existence of a dualistic industrial structure where export-oriented industrialization efforts are concentrated in EPFZs, while the rest of the economy continues to produce under import-substitution conditions, is obscured by the average coefficients of a national input-output table if the activities concerned are not recorded as separate sectors. The sectoral input coefficients pertain to all transactions regardless of destination. In general, the higher the share of exports in a sector's output, the greater will be the reliability of the analysis of spread effects for that sector. Special attention should therefore be paid to this condition. A high level of disaggregation facilitates a differentiation between a more domestic or a more outward orientation of sectors.

8.5 MEASURES OF SECTORAL INTERDEPENDENCE AND SPREAD EFFECTS

To gain insight into the pattern of sectoral interdependence in an economy, a number of measures has been developed which can be applied empirically. These measures of sectoral interdependence are all based on the concept of forward and backward linkages within the framework of input-output analysis. First we deal with the linkage measures in value terms, followed by an explanation of the conversion of these measures in terms of employment. Furthermore, we discuss some additional measures that could provide insight into the secondary effects of manufactured export expansion on the domestic economy.

Before we proceed, it must be noted that in principle all measures to be treated are based on the domestic structural matrix A^D. Consequently, only domestically produced intermediate inputs determine the extent of spread effects. It should be emphasized that investments in capital goods are not included in these effects, not even if capital goods are supplied domestically. In the input-output approach, investments in fixed capital formation are a component of final demand.

8.5.1 Measures in Terms of Production

Starting with a simple measure on an aggregated level, the ratio of total intermediate deliveries to total output

$$(8.27) \quad D = \frac{\sum_{i=1}^{n} \sum_{j=1}^{n} X_{ij}}{X} \quad \text{where} \quad X = \sum_{i=1}^{n} X_i$$

expresses the degree of interdependence in the entire economy and hence its degree of internal division of labour.

On a disaggregated level, the direct dependence of a sector on all other sectors which produce its intermediate inputs is given by the ratio of total intermediate input to total production of that sector. Thus, the backward linkage effect of sector j is expressed by

SPREAD EFFECTS OF EXPORT EXPANSION

(8.28) $\quad L_j^B = \dfrac{\sum\limits_{i=1}^{n} X_{ij}}{X_j} = \sum\limits_{i=1}^{n} a_{ij} \quad$ where
$\qquad L_j^B$ = backward linkage effect of sector j.

Similarly, the forward linkage effect of a sector is expressed by the ratio of its intermediate supplies to all other sectors to total supply of that sector

(8.29) $\quad L_i^F = \dfrac{\sum\limits_{j=1}^{n} X_{ij}}{X_i} \quad$ where
$\qquad L_i^F$ = forward linkage effect of sector i.

These two measures constitute the standard notion of forward and backward linkages as developed by Chenery and Watanabe and provided with a theoretical meaning by Hirschman.[9] On a sectoral level these measures give the average intermediate input requirements or average intermediate deliveries per unit of output. From a macroeconomic point of view, a forward linkage of one sector constitutes a backward linkage of another sector. The arithmetic averages of L^B and L^F over all sectors of an economy are by definition identical and equal to D.

As only backward linkages are relevant in the present study — in case of exports, forward linkages are realized outside the national economy — further treatment is restricted to this kind of linkage effect.

The linkage ratio L^B refers to both intrasectoral and intersectoral deliveries. We have already noticed that the level of aggregation adopted in an input-output table affects the sectoral linkage effects. This is mainly caused by the diagonal elements of the structural matrix A which represent intrasectoral deliveries. A measure of intersectoral linkages in the proper sense of the word is obtained if the intrasectoral transactions X_{ij} ($j = i$) are excluded

(8.30) $\quad L_j^{B^*} = \dfrac{\sum\limits_{i=1}^{n} X_{ij} - X_{jj}}{X_j} = \sum\limits_{i=1}^{n} a_{ij} - a_{jj}$

where
$\qquad L_j^{B^*}$ = backward linkage effect of sector j exclusive of intrasectoral deliveries.

The ratio L^{B^*} only comprises intermediate inputs from other sectors. By denoting, as usual, L^B as the *direct* linkage effect a misconception may arise, for the immediate direct effect of a change in the final demand for products of sector j is only noticeable in sector j. Therefore, L^B can better be interpreted as referring to first-round linkage effects.

Several modifications of these linkage measures have been proposed to increase their significance in mutual and international comparisons. A general shortcoming of the standard notion of linkages concerns the fact that they do not tell the whole story of intersectoral relations. Up to now only first-round linkages derived from the structural matrix A were envisaged. A more comprehensive measure can be obtained by using the inverse Leontief matrix. Yotopoulos and Nugent proposed a total linkage index which meets this objection. They define the total linkage for sector j as[10]

$$(8.31) \quad L_j^T = \sum_{i=1}^{n} r_{ij}$$

where
L_j^T = total linkage index of sector j
r_{ij} = elements of the matrix $(I - A)^{-1}$.

The total linkage index captures the finite sum of all backward linkages.[11]

In an early study Rasmussen proposed two pairs of measures, of which the first are measures of dispersion, facilitating a more adequate intersectoral and international comparison of sectors, and the second are measures of variation, supplementing the first pair by reflecting the spread of sectoral inputs and outputs among the economy.[12] Both pairs of measures make use of the elements of the inverse Leontief matrix and refer to total linkage effects. In the case of the backward linkage effect Rasmussen defines the power of dispersion which "describes the relative extent to which an increase in final demand for the products of industry no. j is dispersed throughout the system of industries".[13] The power of dispersion of sector j is composed of the unweighted sum of elements of column j divided by the number of sectors and standardized by the average of all elements of the inverse matrix.

$$(8.32) \quad P_j = \frac{\dfrac{1}{n} \sum_{i=1}^{n} r_{ij}}{\dfrac{1}{n^2} \sum_{i=1}^{n} \sum_{j=1}^{n} r_{ij}}$$

where
P_j = power of dispersion of sector j.

The numerator of the ratio P_j denotes the average increase in output of a sector induced by a unit increase of the final demand for products of sector j. In making international comparisons of sectoral linkage patterns, the average degree of sectoral interdependence must be taken into account. Hence the standardizing of P_j by the average r_{ij} in the denominator. The value of the power of dispersion for an imaginary sector that equals exactly the average value of backward linkages in an economy is 1. Consequently, if $P_j > 1$ it implies that sector j has above-average backward linkage effects, whereas if $P_j < 1$ it can be stated that sector j is operating in relative isolation from other sectors. A dispersion measure based on the sum of row elements r_{ij} gives an index showing the extent of forward linkages and is denoted by Rasmussen as the sensitivity of dispersion.

Analogous to the backward linkage effect exclusive of intrasectoral deliveries, the power of dispersion can be freed from intrasectoral deliveries as follows

$$(8.33) \quad \overset{*}{P}_j = \frac{\dfrac{1}{n-1} \sum_{i=1}^{n} r_{ij} - r_{jj}}{\dfrac{1}{n} \sum_{j=1}^{n} \left[\dfrac{1}{n-1} \left(\sum_{i=1}^{n} r_{ij} - r_{jj} \right) \right]}$$

where
$\overset{*}{P}_j$ = power of dispersion exclusive of intrasectoral deliveries.

Especially when computations are based on the inverse Leontief matrix, the sensitivity of the linkage index to the level of aggregation may be substantial.

According to Rasmussen, to identify key sectors the average measures of dispersion have to be supplemented by a measure of variability characteristics. For the purpose of the present study, however, the computation of such a measure is not necessary.

Furthermore, several weighting schemes have been devised for the linkage measures to take into account the relative importance of a sector in the economy.[14] However, unweighted versions of the linkage measures will be applied in our empirical analysis. The study focuses on a comparison of the linkage performance of individual (groups of) manufactured exports, irrespective of their relative importance. Only in case average figures are presented for aggregated categories of production and exports is an appropriate weighting scheme applied, i.e. either sectoral shares in production or exports.

8.5.2 Measures in Terms of Employment

The measures of sectoral interdependence treated above are all calculated from input and output data. From an employment policy point of view it is more meaningful to investigate the employment-generating effects of economic activities. In that case, the interrelatedness of sectors has to be analyzed in terms of employment associated with these inputs and outputs. Total labour requirements of a sector's production depend on the output-employment ratio of that sector as well as on the dependence of that sector on input-supplying sectors and their output-employment ratios. It will be clear that, depending on the relative factor intensities of final and intermediate production processes, the spread effects in output terms may strongly deviate from those in terms of employment.

To determine the employment effects of particular economic activities, it is necessary to separate labour inputs from other primary factor inputs. If the labour component of primary inputs of sector j is denoted as W_{1j}, the labour input in sector j can be expressed as a fixed proportion of the output of this sector, so that

$$l_j = \frac{W_{1j}}{X_j}$$

is the direct labour coefficient. The vector of these coefficients for all j is denoted as L, and we can write according to solution (8.8)

(8.34) $W_1 = L'(I - A)^{-1} Y$ where
    W_1 = total labour requirements
    L = vector of direct labour coefficients l_j.

The vector $T = L'(I - A)^{-1}$ with total labour coefficients T_j gives the total (direct plus indirect) labour content per unit of final demand. Hence, indirect labour content per unit of final demand is by definition given by the vector $T-L$. The vectors L and T provide us with an approximation for the factor intensity of output. Per sector, these vectors show, respectively, the direct and the total amounts of labour required to produce one unit of final demand.

When the primary input component labour is given in physical units, computations immediately yield the quantity of labour in man-years or any other standard in which labour units may be expressed. Usually, the primary factor labour appears in input-output tables as wages and salaries. It then takes appropriate sectoral wage rates to obtain a physical unit of employment. It is preferable to measure employment in man-hours of labour. Any other unit such as man-weeks or man-years may obscure wide variations in hours worked and thus of employment across industries. However, due to data limitations one has often to make do with yearly average sectoral wage rates with which employment in man-years of labour can be calculated. When no data are available on yearly wage rates per sector, it is inevitable to use a value concept as the wage bill to measure employment. Obviously, in this case no information on the number of persons employed or the number of hours worked is obtained. On the other hand, in case employment is measured in man-hours or man-years, all labour categories are treated alike, irrespective of difference in skill and remuneration.

If data on average sectoral wage rates are available, we may write

(8.35) $\quad N_j = \dfrac{W_{lj}}{s_j}$ 　　where

N_j = primary input of labour into sector j in physical units
s_j = average wage rate in sector j.

Solution (8.34) now becomes

(8.36) $\quad N = (SL)'(I - A)^{-1} Y$ 　　where

N = total employment in physical units
S = diagonal matrix of elements $1/s_j$.

Thus, the direct labour coefficient l_j can either be expressed in value terms (wages and salaries) as

(8.37) $\quad l_j^w = \dfrac{W_{lj}}{X_j}$ 　　where

l_j^w = direct wage coefficient of sector j

or in physical units as

(8.38) $\quad l_j^e = \dfrac{W_{lj}}{s_j X_j} = \dfrac{N_j}{X_j}$ 　　where

l_j^e = direct labour coefficient of sector j in physical units.

In the remainder of this section, the direct labour coefficient may be interpreted in both physical terms and in terms of wages and salaries, i.e. as l_j^e and as l_j^w, respectively. The same goes for the total labour coefficient T_j which may be interpreted as T_j^e and as T_j^w, respectively.

With the help of vector L, all measures of interdependence and spread effects introduced in the preceding section can easily be expressed in terms of employment. For instance, the total linkage index of Yotopoulos and Nugent can be rewritten as

(8.39) $\quad L_j^{TE} = \sum\limits_{i=1}^{n} l_i r_{ij}$ 　　where

L_j^{TE} = total linkage index of sector j in terms of employment.

Averaged and standardized according to Rasmussen's method, this index becomes

$$(8.40) \quad P_j^E = \frac{\dfrac{1}{n} \sum_{i=1}^{n} l_i r_{ij}}{\dfrac{1}{n^2} \sum_{i=1}^{n} \sum_{j=1}^{n} l_i r_{ij}} \quad \text{where} \quad P_j^E = \text{power of dispersion of sector } j \text{ in terms of employment.}$$

Index P^E shows the sector-wise impact on employment throughout the entire economy. Again, this index can be freed from intrasectoral deliveries as follows

$$(8.41) \quad \overset{*}{P}_j^E = \frac{\dfrac{1}{n-1} \sum_{i=1}^{n} l_i r_{ij} - l_j r_{jj}}{\dfrac{1}{n} \sum_{j=1}^{n} \left[\dfrac{1}{n-1} \left(\sum_{i=1}^{n} l_i r_{ij} - l_j r_{jj} \right) \right]}$$

The employment linkage measures can be compared with the corresponding measures in output data. Thus, if for sector j $P_j^E > P_j$, the spread effects of sector j are more extensive in terms of employment than in production impulses. At the same time, one can infer that the total production process of sector j is relatively labour intensive.

In Section 7.5 we discussed several reasons why the linkage effects on output and employment in primary sectors — notably agriculture — have to be considered with great caution. In view of these uncertainties, it is useful to determine also the value of the above-treated measures exclusive of indirect employment opportunities in agriculture. This correction makes only sense if these measures are expressed in fulltime jobs. P^E for sector j then becomes

$$(8.42) \quad P_j^{E-A} = \frac{\dfrac{1}{n-1} \sum_{i=1}^{n} l_i r_{ij} - l_k r_{kj}}{\dfrac{1}{n} \sum_{j=1}^{n} \left[\dfrac{1}{n-1} \left(\sum_{i=1}^{n} l_i r_{ij} - l_k r_{kj} \right) \right]}$$

where subscript k refers to agriculture, and

P_j^{E-A} = power of dispersion of sector j, in terms of employment, exclusive of indirect employment in agriculture.

8.5.3 Measures of Secondary Production and Employment Effects

The measures of sectoral interdependence treated so far all refer to the direct plus indirect spread effects on production and employment due to manufactured export expansion. Although the impact of these effects constitutes the most determining factor in the realization of potential spread effects, a more complete assessment is obtained if the secondary impact of increased domestic incomes and foreign-exchange earnings on the level of output and employment is also taken into consideration. As is illustrated in Figure 7.1, the secondary spread effects comprise the multiplier effect and the foreign-exchange effect. With the help of some additional measures an estimate of the significance of these secondary effects may be made.

The impact on domestic income associated with an expansion of exports will be larger the less dependent a manufacturing sector is on imports and, consequently, the larger the value added generated in the domestic economy. The following measures are therefore closely related or complementary. The vector

(8.43) $\quad M^t = iM(I-A)^{-1} \quad$ where

M^t = (row) vector of total import coefficients per sector, with elements m_j^t

M = matrix of intermediate import coefficients m_{ij}

i = (row) vector with all elements equal to 1 (in order to add up the matrix elements columnwise)

shows total import coefficients per sector. Sector j's total import coefficient indicates the direct and indirect imports which are required to produce one unit of exports of sector j. The value added generated domestically per unit of export of each sector is given by

(8.44) $\quad VA^t = i\hat{VA}(I-A)^{-1} \quad$ where

VA^t = (row) vector of total value-added coefficients per sector, with elements va_j^t

$\hat{VA}$ = diagonal matrix of value-added coefficients va_j;

$$va_j = \frac{\text{value added of sector } j}{\text{output of sector } j}$$

which yields a vector of total value-added coefficients per sector.

To grasp the extent to which different forms of manufactured exports contribute to the relaxation of the foreign-exchange bottleneck, use will be made of an index of net foreign-exchange earnings.[15] The net inflow of foreign exchange is equal to the direct foreign-exchange receipts from exports reduced by the imported inputs which are directly and indirectly required for the production of exportables. Expressed per unit of exports, the index of net foreign-exchange earnings of sector j's exports can be written as

(8.45) $\quad NFEE_j = 1 - m_j^t \quad$ where

$\qquad NFEE_j$ = index of net foreign-exchange earnings from exports of sector j.

This index corresponds to the measure of the total value added generated domestically per unit of final demand, as m_j^t and va_j^t are each other's complement. This can easily be seen from adding their values according to (8.43) and (8.44):

$$M^t + VA^t = i(M + \hat{VA})(I-A)^{-1}$$

As by definition

$$\sum_{i=1}^{n} a_{ij} + \sum_{i=1}^{n} m_{ij} + va_j = 1$$

we have

$$i(M + \hat{VA}) = i(I-A)$$

and therefore

$$M^t + VA^t = i$$

An increase in manufactured exports generates an increase in employment and wage incomes in exporting and input-supplying sectors. Household incomes depend largely upon wage payments. Spending from increased household incomes induces additional demand for consumer goods which in turn stimulates a derived demand for intermediate inputs and for labour. Again, this gives rise to further rounds of income-output-employment effects. In order to be able to include the spending effects from wage incomes due to manufactured exports, both wage incomes and the spending thereof should be made endogenous to the input-output model. This can be done through an augmentation of the structural matrix A by a row of wage incomes and a column of household purchases.[16] The procedure results in a partial closing of the model, where wage payments and household purchases are treated akin to, respectively, purchases of intermediate inputs and deliveries to intermediate sectors. In the new structural matrix $\overset{*}{A}$

$$\overset{*}{A} = \begin{bmatrix} a_{11} \ldots a_{1n} & | & a_{1,n+1} \\ \vdots & | & \\ a_{n1} \ldots a_{nn} & | & \\ \text{-------} & & \\ a_{n+1,1} \ldots & & a_{n+1,n+1} \end{bmatrix}$$

the extra row $(n+1)$ denotes, for each sector j, wage payments per unit of output, and the extra column $(n+1)$ denotes the households' average propensities to consume. The latter column is obtained by dividing household demand for domestically produced products by total household expenditure. To capture the finite sum of all rounds of income effects on output and employment, the new Leontief matrix $(I - \overset{*}{A})$ is inverted. The general solution inclusive of the impact of wage incomes on the level of production becomes

(8.46) $\quad X = (I - \overset{*}{A})^{-1} \overset{*}{Y}$ $\quad$ where
$\overset{*}{Y}$ = vector of final demand components minus endogenous household demand.

The elements of the $(n+1)$th row of the new matrix $(I - \overset{*}{A})^{-1}$ represent sectoral wage-income multipliers

(8.47) $\quad WIM_j = \overset{*}{r}_{n+1,j}$ $\quad$ where
$\quad\quad\quad = \sum_{i=1}^{n} l_i^w \overset{*}{r}_{ij}$ $\quad\quad WIM_j$ = wage-income multiplier of sector j
$\quad\quad\quad\quad\quad\quad\quad\quad\quad\quad\quad \overset{*}{r}_{ij}$ = elements of the matrix $(I - \overset{*}{A})^{-1}$.

The wage-income multiplier can be expressed in employment terms as follows

(8.48) $\quad WIM_j^E = \sum_{i=1}^{n} l_i^e \overset{*}{r}_{ij}$ $\quad$ where
$\quad\quad\quad\quad\quad\quad\quad\quad\quad\quad WIM_j^E$ = wage-income multiplier of sector j in terms of employment.

Generally, the magnitude of the wage-income multiplier depends on the labourers' propensity to consume and their preference for foreign goods. The leakages from imports of consumer goods are taken into account, as the average propensities to consume refer to domestically produced products only. The impact of the wage-income multiplier is, of course, positively affected if the income recipients have a relatively higher preference for domestic products which are characterized by relatively large shares of wages and salaries in value added. In the above procedure, however, no allowance is made for the dampening effect of savings, as the wage incomes appear totally inside the structural matrix $\overset{*}{A}$ and the propensity to consume domestic plus imported products out of wage incomes is assumed to be 1. Sector-wise, the wage-income multiplier of a particular sector will be higher, the larger the share of wages and salaries in value added and the higher the inter-industry demand for products of that sector.

The measures of spread effects based on the new extended matrix $(I-\overset{*}{A})^{-1}$ give an almost complete assessment of the impact of manufactured export expansion on the domestic economy, covering the direct plus indirect effects and some of the secondary effects. With regard to the measure indicating the net foreign-exchange earnings from exports it should be borne in mind that it is defined exclusive of secondary (import) effects resulting from wage-spending behaviour.

9
The Pattern of Interdependence among Economic Sectors

9.1 INTRODUCTION

The uniform changes in the structure of production that normally accompany economic growth are an important issue — and recognized as such at an early stage — in the studies on the process of economic development. Increasingly, however, the generality of the patterns of these structural changes is being questioned. Scholars and policy makers became aware of the necessity to take full account of time and country-specific circumstances, which at least include structural country characteristics as well as the development strategies pursued. Especially since the early 1970s, the developing countries have experienced widely divergent economic performances and it became clear that these countries could not all be treated alike.

If the analyses of the process of economic development should be sensitive to the type of developing country concerned, this has to be equally true of policies and strategies that follow from these analyses. Therefore, the spread effects of the export-oriented strategy of industrialization on the domestic economy will also be examined from this point of view. The spread effects of economic activities reflect the pattern of sectoral interdependence and thus the domestic structure of production. But structures of production differ between countries precisely on account of country-specific circumstances. It may therefore be expected that spread effects of manufactured export production will vary because of mere differences in types of exporting economies.

The purpose of this chapter is to explore both the uniformities and the differences in production structures. This knowledge will facilitate a proper evaluation, i.e. in view of the type of exporting economy, of the impact of manufactured export production on the domestic economy. After a discussion of uniform changes in the structure of production as development proceeds, the attention is shifted to factors that create differences in development patterns and production structures. This is followed by an inquiry into the internal structure of an economy to trace the different functions sectors perform in the successive stages of production. The aim is to gain insight into a hierarchy in the system of interindustry transactions and the accompanying "normal" pattern of sectoral interdependence and spread effects. The latter may act as a frame of reference with which the performance of different export-promotion strategies in different types of exporting economies can be compared. The chapter concludes with a brief review of the main findings of earlier empirical research into the subject matter.

9.2 THE DEVELOPMENT OF THE STRUCTURE OF PRODUCTION

A country's structure of production, as revealed by the pattern of interindustry flows in an input-output table, is the result of the interaction of a number of uniform and country-specific factors.[1] Uniform factors affect all countries in a similar way. These factors can be broken down into:

(1) those factors which are related to the level of economic development;
(2) the size of the domestic market; and
(3) the availability of natural resources.

Factors associated with rising levels of economic development and *per capita* income refer to similar changes in the composition of final demand governed by the law of Engel, accelerated accumulation of both physical and human capital, the availability and use of similar technologies and a greater involvement in international economic relations.[2] These income-induced developments work in the same direction. They are therefore expected to produce both a uniform pattern of development and similarity in the production structure of different countries with rising incomes. Especially access to and use of similar technologies lead to uniformity of production structures. According to Leontief, "each sector or industry ... has its own 'cooking recipe'. The recipe is determined in the main by technology...."[3]

Studies on cross-country comparisons of the pattern of interdependence, some of which will be dealt with in the next sections, demonstrate that there are similarities in production structures at higher levels of economic development. This similarity is the greatest for the pattern of interdependence among manufacturing sectors. To quote Leontief again: "displayed in the input-output table, the pattern of transactions between industries and other major sectors of the system shows that the more developed the economy, the more its internal structure resembles that of other developed economies".[4]

Marx already gave evidence of insight into this uniformity in the process of development when he stated that "the country that is more developed industrially only shows to the less developed the image of its own future".[5]

Continuing the pioneering work of Kuznets, who studied quantitatively the process of structural transformation of economies both country-wise and over time,[6] Chenery, Taylor and Syrquin examined patterns of structural change associated with rising levels of *per capita* income on the basis of a statistical analysis of a large number of countries.[7] The "patterns of development" they derived from a uniform set of regression equations describe the variation in economic structure principally as a function of GNP *per capita* (which served as an overall index of economic development), country size and the level of capital inflow. With this procedure, Chenery *et al.* identified "patterns of principal changes in economic structure that normally accompany economic growth".[8] These "principal changes" focus on accumulation processes, changes in the structure of demand, production and trade, and on demographic and distributional processes. In the Chenery *et al.* studies, changes in economic structures are analyzed in terms of changes in the components of the gross domestic product (GDP). Thus, the dependent variables that represent structural characteristics are taken as ratios to GDP, such as the share of gross domestic saving or primary production in GDP.

This kind of analysis substantially increased the knowledge of the changing composition of production and demand as development proceeds, but not much additional insight was gained into the nature of interdependence among the processes that underlie the patterns of development. Fortunately, with the availability of the input-output tables of the U.N. world model, constructed by Leontief and others for their study on *The Future of the World Economy*,[9] it is possible to shed light on the nature of interdependences among processes that accompany economic development. The interesting feature of the U.N. world model is that not only for the first time is a consistent and comparable set of world-wide input-output accounts available, distinguishing fifteen regional country groupings and thirty industrial sectors, but also that it provides fully articulated interindustry matrices which are differentiated to eight income levels. The U.N. world model produces eight different interindustry structures consistent with eight corresponding levels of *per capita* income.

In their study on employment patterns and income growth in developing countries, Stern and Lewis combined the income-specific interindustry matrices of the U.N. world model with the level and composition of both production and demand in an "average" country at different levels of *per capita* income, derived from Chenery's development patterns. The average country is defined with a population of 20 million. This Stern and Lewis procedure, which integrates two different approaches to identify development patterns, enables us to trace the relationship between the development of the economic structure and rising levels of income. According to the Stern and Lewis study, development from low to higher *per capita* income involves the following main changes in economic structure.[10]

First, the ratio of investment to GDP increases when a country develops from a low to a higher level of *per capita* income. A rising investment ratio is both a cause and an effect of rising income. The share of manufacturing investment in total investment is higher at the lower end of the range of *per capita* income, as the investment shares of construction, transport, services, public utilities and communications services increase at the higher end. At the demand side this structural change is facilitated by a shrinking share of food in total demand, which frees resources for non-food consumption and investments.

Second, the generally known pattern is confirmed that economic development is accompanied by a decreasing share of primary sectors and increasing shares of secondary and tertiary sectors in GDP. In general, the secondary sectors, i.e. manufacturing, take the lead in the process of economic development.

Third, economic development goes along with changes in the output composition of manufacturing. Consistent with this change, the composition of investment and capital stock in manufacturing changes as income rises. In terms of capital stock and production, food processing, textiles and wearing apparel, non-metallic minerals, rubber products and miscellaneous manufactures lose their predominant position in manufacturing, while the relative contributions of printing and wood, cork and furniture show little change. By contrast, manufacturing capital shifts to the production of paper and paper products, chemical products, primary metals, metal products (including transport equipment) and machinery. Generally, the composition of manufacturing production changes in favour of heavy manufacturing sectors employing more technologically advanced methods of production. The relative contributions of the various light manufacturing sectors to total manufacturing production decline. Or, put differently again, the share of producer goods in total production increases at successive levels of *per capita* income.

Fourth, the direct labour coefficients for all industrial sectors decline as development proceeds. This phenomenon reflects the continued substitution of capital for labour associated with technological change, as well as a shift in the product mix whereby relatively capital-intensive products replace relatively labour-intensive products.[11] Declining labour requirements per unit of production would result in a decreasing employment share of a sector, unless this decline is compensated for by an increase in a sector's share in total manufacturing production. Those sectors that experience rising shares in manufacturing production in fact also enlarge their shares in manufacturing employment. Although these sectors have, in general, the lowest direct labour coefficient at higher levels of *per capita* income, the effect of this decline is outweighed by increasing shares in total production — the only exception being the chemical sector, which shows the largest increment in capital stock and production, but nevertheless suffers a set-back in relative employment opportunities.

Fifth, as an economy develops and production activities become more differentiated, interindustry relations become more pronounced. In general, the ratio between the demand for intermediate and final products increases.

Sixth, total labour coefficients also decline as development proceeds. By contrast, total capital coefficients increase. Consequently, there is a general trend of rising capital-labour ratios for each industry. Declining direct labour coefficients and expanding interindustry linkages have opposite effects on the total employment impact of output expansion: a reduction in direct labour coefficients reduces the demand for labour, while increasing interindustry linkages increase that demand. It follows from the finding of declining total labour coefficients in moving to higher *per capita* income levels that the effect of declining direct labour coefficients outweighs the effect of increasing interindustry linkages.

At higher income levels construction and manufacturing tend to have stronger linkages with other sectors than the general service sectors. It was observed that within manufacturing, the technologically most advanced sectors, i.e. those heavy manufacturing sectors producing intermediate and capital goods, show the strongest interindustry linkages, most notably sectors producing chemical products, transport equipment (motor vehicles), and electric and non-electrical machinery. If the reduction of a sectoral total labour coefficient in moving from a *per capita* income of US$200 to US$4,600 (in 1970 prices) is taken as 100 per cent, Stern and Lewis found that the effect of increased interindustry relations offsets this reduction for the construction sector by 6.9 per cent only. Put differently, in case the structure of interindustry relations had remained unchanged, the reduction of the total labour coefficient of the construction sector would have been 6.9 per cent larger. The contribution of increasing interindustry relations to the total labour coefficient of chemical products, motor vehicles, electrical and non-electrical machinery equalled 5.8, 7.6, 4.8 and 4.6 per cent, respectively. Thus, on the whole, the employment-increasing effects of interindustry linkages appear to be relatively weak.

In the Stern and Lewis study, however, the strengthening of interindustry linkages associated with rising *per capita* income levels is caused only by changes in income-specific domestic input-output coefficients that originate in changes in the product mix and the application of more advanced technologies. Changes in the domestic input-output coefficients that may originate in a decline in the ratio of imported to domestic intermediate supply are not taken into account. An increase in domestically supplied intermediate inputs may take place if technologically more advanced industries are established of which the products could replace previously imported inputs. The input-output coefficients of the U.N. world model refer to the total of imported and domestically produced intermediates, and in freeing these coefficients from imports Stern and Lewis used average constant import coefficients irrespective of the level of *per capita* income. Thus, the income-specific interindustry tables neglect changes in the production structure originating in import substitution, and therefore the extent to which domestic interindustry linkages increase with economic development is probably understated.[12]

The findings of recent studies by Chenery and Syrquin suggest a more important role of intermediate demand in the process of economic development.[13] In these studies, an open input-output model is designed to explain the sources of industrialization. The effects of four factors on the growth of output in each sector are identified: (1) expansion of domestic demand; (2) expansion of exports; (3) import substitution; and (4) change in intermediate demand, reflected in changes in input-output relations throughout the economy associated with rising income. This model has been applied to historical data over the post-war period for South Korea, Taiwan, Turkey, Mexico and Japan. In these countries the changes in the first three factors, domestic demand, exports and import substitution, account for about 80 per cent of the rising share of industry, the relative contribution of each of these factors being greatly influenced by the role of international trade in a country. The remainder of about 20 per cent is due to technological change, as measured by an expansion of the demand for intermediate goods. It is notable that the relative contribution of technological change to the expansion of heavy industry is substantially higher than it is to the expansion of light industry.

In sum, many simultaneously operating influences are at work when economic development proceeds. But all these influences work in the same direction, creating a more integrated economy, led by manufacturing activities, and using ever more capital per unit of labour.

In addition to the integrating impact of rising levels of economic development on the economic structure, the size of the domestic market and the natural-resource endowment produce important differences in development patterns and production structures. At the same level of *per capita* income, countries with a larger domestic market are, generally, expected to have a relatively larger and a more developed manufacturing sector than smaller countries. Several studies have established that a large domestic market is a favourable condition to develop a manufacturing sector.[14] The advantages of a large domestic market refer to the economic feasibility of producing a wide range of goods, as the economies of scale that can be realized in a large market favour the introduction of heavy industries even at lower levels of income. For that reason, import-substitution policies can be maintained longer by the larger countries through an extension to branches of heavy industry. Another favourable condition of large countries is their usually more diversified availability of natural resources, which facilitates the establishment of a wide range of processing industries. Finally, in a large domestic market domestic suppliers enjoy a natural protection in the form of relatively high internal transport costs for imports. These factors lead to a lower dependence on international trade and a more diversified and balanced development of the manufacturing sector, with a closer correspondence between domestic supply and demand in each sector.

By contrast, the limited market size of smaller countries reduces the number of industries that could operate efficiently. In these countries, only at high costs the process of import substitution can be extended to industries with an efficient scale of operation beyond the needs of the domestic market. Moreover, smaller countries are usually characterized by less diversified natural resources. This, on the one hand, again reduces the variability of domestic production, while on the other hand, there is a need to import the lacking raw materials. Thus, in smaller countries the degree of industrial specialization is much greater and there will not be a close supply and demand balance among sectors. Consequently, small countries are necessarily more involved in international trade than large countries.[15]

The impact of variations in natural-resource endowment on economic structures is most distinct in small countries, as the availability of natural resources largely determines a country's primary or industrial orientation of production and exports. In the early phases of development an ample resource endowment simply "forces" a small economy to primary exports as a source of foreign exchange. Under these conditions, the process of industrialization is delayed to a later phase. Well-known in this connection is the enclave-type of export economy in which extractive industries and plantations produce and export largely unprocessed primary products in relative isolation from the rest of the economy. However, in a later phase of development when primary products are processed domestically, an ample resource endowment provides the basis for a strong linkage between manufacturing and primary sectors. On the other hand, a lack of exportable natural resources and the resulting foreign-exchange tightness may well "force" a country to develop labour-intensive manufactured exports. As has already been established in Part I of this volume, a small domestic market and a poor natural-resource endowment, measured by the variable population density, appear to have a significant impact on a country's manufactured export performance.[16]

Three important conclusions emerge from above explanation. First, the degree of integration among sectors increases as economic development proceeds. Second, because of the stronger involvement in international trade of small countries, these countries are expected to show a lower degree of integration of their economies than larger countries at the same level of economic development. Leontief found that "the larger and the more advanced an economy is, the more complete and articulated is its structure".[17] Third, an ample resource endowment may contribute to the integration among sectors only in case industrial processing takes place domestically. Export of unprocessed primary products produces the opposite effect. As the industrial processing of primary products often requires large capital investments and a large minimum scale of operation, the impact of the factor natural-resource endowment is not independent from the two other factors.

9.3 THE HIERARCHY OF SECTORS

In the pattern of interdependence among economic sectors a hierarchy can be observed which corresponds to the successive stages of production. The position of a particular sector in this hierarchical order of sectors is based on a sector's destination of output and its proportion and composition of input, thus on its forward and backward linkages. Such a classification of sectors shows the internal structure of an economy.

Figure 9.1 serves to explain the different positions a sector can have in this internal structure. The figure displays a schematized input-output table of a model economy which is broken down into five sectors.[18] Each symbol in the table signifies a flow of goods or services. Intermediate deliveries are subdivided into domestically produced and imported intermediates. To reveal the specific hierarchical pattern of interindustry transactions, the structural matrix is presented in a triangular form. In this presentation, only a one-way relationship among sectors is assumed to exist.

Sector 1 in this table is at one extreme, providing all other sectors with inputs, whereas this sector draws inputs only from itself. Part of the output of sector 1 enters final demand directly. Sector 5, at the other extreme, absorbs inputs from all other sectors and delivers all of its output, except for its own intrasectoral use, directly to final demand. Sector 3 is a typical intermediate sector. It processes the output of two other sectors, whereas, in turn, part of its own output is used as an intermediate input in two other sectors. This pattern of interindustry transactions is representative for an integrated economy, in which each sector is dependent on all other sectors, either as supplier or as customer or both. Sector 1 takes the lowest and sector 5 the

INTERDEPENDENCE AMONG ECONOMIC SECTORS

highest position in this hierarchy of sectors, which corresponds to the successive stages of production, leading from primary via intermediate to final products. Accordingly, these sectors perform distinct functions in the economy.

The structure of real existing economies may and will usually deviate from the one displayed in the model economy. In a small, resource-poor country, for instance, some of the raw materials supplying sectors may be lacking. Moreover, the domestic market of this country may be too small to establish all branches of heavy industry. Countries that have not yet completed the first phase of import substitution largely lack intermediate and capital goods producing industries, a feature of developing economies that is taken up again in the section on the distinct pattern of sectoral interdependence in developing countries. Inputs that are not produced domestically but are nevertheless required to meet final demand have to be imported. Through imports of intermediate and final products, an economy can fill up the gaps in its

Figure 9.1
Schematic Input-Output Table of a Model Economy

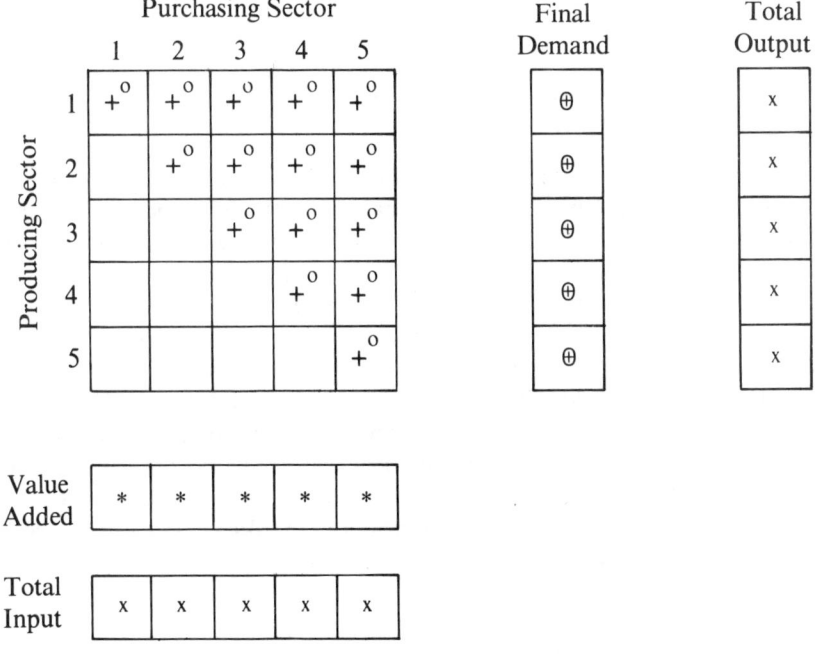

Explanation of symbols:
+ = domestic intermediate delivery; o = imported intermediate input; ⊕ = delivery to final demand; * = value added; x = total input and output.

production structure. This is illustrated in Figure 9.1, where domestic and imported intermediate deliveries are presented as substitutes. In a developed economy with a fully articulated structure, the domestically produced intermediates will outweigh the imported intermediates in nearly all squares of the triangular structural matrix. In the case of a developing economy, imported inputs outweigh domestic inputs in a number of squares, while some squares will contain only imports, indicating that inputs are entirely drawn from imports.

Besides incompleteness, an actual economy may deviate from the strictly triangular structure in Figure 9.1 because of the occurrence of transactions below the main diagonal. These transactions depart from the assumed one-way relationship among sectors as higher-ranked sectors provide lower-ranked sectors with intermediates.

In the next two sections, attention is primarily directed towards earlier empirical research into the pattern of sectoral interdependence in both developed and developing countries. By comparing the "normal" pattern with the pattern actually found in developing countries, a proper frame of reference is obtained with which the performance of different export-promotion strategies in different types of exporting economies can be evaluated.

9.4 THE "NORMAL" PATTERN OF SECTORAL INTERDEPENDENCE

The pattern of sectoral interdependence has been empirically analyzed in a number of studies. Chenery and Watanabe were the first who established a hierarchical ranking of sectors, based on average values of sectoral forward and backward linkage effects for Italy, Japan and the United States. Sectors have been classified according to their combined score of linkage effects.[19] Their approach has subsequently been adopted by other authors. Yotopoulos and Nugent compared the structure of linkages of six developed and five less developed countries.[20] On the basis of 22 input-output tables of 12, mainly Asian, developing countries and two developed countries, Schultz tried to identify high-linkage sectors with the help of various measures of sectoral interdependence.[21] In separate studies, Chakraborty and Laumas analyzed the production structure of the same four South-East Asian countries.[22] These studies suggest a distinction into four categories of sectors, with the following composition.

    I.   *Intermediate Primary Production*

          Sectors appearing in category I have high forward and low backward linkages. They are characterized by the largely unprocessed nature of their production. Hence, category I comprises the real primary sectors of agriculture, forestry, mining and quarrying. The public utility sectors should also fall under this category.

II. *Intermediate Manufacture*
Intermediate manufacturing sectors have both high forward and backward linkages. Sectors appearing in category II process primary inputs into typical intermediate products, such as iron, steel and non-ferrous metals, paper and paper products, petroleum and coal products, chemicals, rubber products, textiles, printing and publishing.

III. *Final Manufacture*
Final manufacturing sectors are characterized by low forward and high backward linkages. Products which are mainly produced for final use are: wearing apparel, leather products, food products, wood products, non-metallic mineral products, shipbuilding, transport equipment, and metal products and machinery.

IV. *Final Primary Production*
Sectors appearing in this category depart from the successive stages of production as both their forward and backward linkages are low. Consequently, these sectors produce in relative isolation from other sectors. This is, for instance, the case with primary products which are directly fit to final use or are processed abroad. The tertiary sectors of transport, trade and services also appear in this category.

This four-way classification of sectors provides a clear picture of the different functions that various sectors perform in the economy. However, the classification of some sectors is equivocal. The public utility sectors of electricity, gas and water should be put on the same footing with manufacturing production in case the utilities are processed or transformed before public distribution. If it is, however, merely a question of distribution, utilities are to be identified as intermediate primary production. In the above classification, transport equipment, machinery and shipbuilding are identified as final manufacturing. This is primarily due to the structure of the input-output model where investment purchases of capital goods are interpreted as final demand transactions. These sectors are better valued at their true linkage impact if they are conceived as intermediate manufacturing.[23] In term of linkages, the construction sector presents the same characteristics as intermediate manufacturing production.

Hirschman incorporated this classification of sectors into his unbalanced growth concept. In this growth concept, as is explained in Section 7.7, the most powerful development stimuli emanate from backward linkages, whereas forward linkages are regarded as a mere reinforcement to the working of backward linkages. Hence, sectors exerting high backward linkages receive a high ranking. Manufacturing production is in this respect superior to primary production. Within manufacturing, the intermediate industries are of special importance. Because of their high score of both forward and backward linkages, these industries constitute the central chain in the hierarchical structure of production. The rise of exactly these intermediate and capital goods producing industries is generally thought to be of crucial importance to the development of a self-sustained industrial sector. Hirschman describes the impact of these sectors on investment decisions as a *pincer cum feedback* movement.[24]

Rasmussen identifies sectors of this type as a "key sector", showing a tight network of intermediate flows which is revealed by a relatively high value of the power of dispersion for these sectors.[25] The core of the argument is that key or strategic sectors maximize linkages and in this way strengthen the structure of industrial development, i.e. these sectors transmit the strongest production stimuli to other sectors and guarantee the widest spread of technological know-how. The findings of Stern and Lewis regarding the high-linkage impact of advanced heavy manufacturing sectors support this argument.

Another important characteristic of manufacturing as compared with primary production and services is its relatively low share of value added in the total value of production, for by its very nature, manufacturing production consists of a relatively large part of the processing of intermediate inputs purchased from other sectors. The extent of backward linkages and the value-added component in production are therefore inversely related.

Given the above considerations concerning the different functions performed by sectors in the economy, it is possible to discern an *a priori* sector-specific pattern of spread effects. Such a pattern is necessarily hypothetical, as it assumes uniformity in production structures. As has been indicated, this uniformity is expected to be the greatest among the larger well developed economies. Using the power of dispersion (P), explained in Section 8.2 of the preceding chapter, as the comparative measure of spread effects, we arrive at the following pattern for the major economic sectors. First, agricultural production will show a P value well below 1, especially if traditional production methods are still prevalent.

Second, the P value for mining and quarrying activities will not be much higher than agriculture. The use of intermediate inputs is scanty, whereas the extensive investments in machinery and buildings usually required in extractive industries show up under final demand.

Third, it can readily be assumed that manufacturing sectors have to show P values well above 1. The highest P values will be realized by manufacturing production destined for final demand, on the understanding that, as available evidence suggests, the technologically most advanced heavy industrial sectors will show the highest P values from 1.

Fourth, the construction sector will rank among the sectors with P values well above 1.

Fifth, the P values for public utilities, trade and other services will be much the same, namely below or close to 1.

Without attaching to it the weight of an immutable law of nature, this sectoral pattern of spread effects closely corresponds to what might be defined as the "normal" pattern of sectoral interdependence. The usefulness of a "normal" pattern of spread effects as defined here, lies in the possibility of ascertaining the extent to which the actual pattern of spread effects of industries, especially manufactured export industries, in developing countries corresponds to or deviates from it. Something like a "normal" pattern of spread effects may act as a frame of reference. Besides, it provides a criterion to examine the contribution of export production in developing countries to a more integrated economy. An integrating impact by way of an above average level of spread effects broadens the industrial base and is therefore in itself conceived as an important strengthening of the process of economic development. As indicated in Chapter 7, this potential contribution of manufactured export expansion is considered just as important as the direct increase in production, employment and foreign-exchange earnings, especially in the longer run.

It should be emphasized that this integration criterion is country-specific. As the structures of production and hence the sectoral patterns of spread effects differ between countries, it is well possible that a particular export production appears to exercise an integrating function in one country, whereas in another country an identical production process could take place in relative isolation from other sectors. The spread effects of export expansion are studied within the context of the exporting economy and, consequently, the assessment of the developmental impact of export-oriented industrialization strategies may differ from country to country.

9.5 THE PATTERN OF SECTORAL INTERDEPENDENCE IN DEVELOPING COUNTRIES

A number of studies attempted to investigate the dissimilarities in production structures, and hence in linkage structures, of developed and developing countries. Some of these studies take up the classical line of economic thinking, whether the Marxist variant or not. A common notion in these studies is that the problems of economic growth in developing countries can only be rightly understood if due account is taken of the specific economic and structural characteristics of these countries, a feature that is largely bypassed in the traditional neoclassical tradition. In the brief review below, emphasis will be placed on these characteristics.

The Lewis-Ranis-Fei concept of the dual economy conceives economies in their early stages of development as basically consisting of two sectors, a modern capitalist and a traditional subsistence sector.[26] Although "tiny islands" of modern production exist throughout the economy and urban centres also accommodate subsistence activities, these sectors are identified as industry and agriculture, respectively. At a low level of development, it is not necessary that there be an interdependence between the modern and the subsistence sector. The interdependence between both sectors only becomes important when the uninterrupted process of industrial expansion reaches its limits and transition has to be made to the stage of self-sustained growth. This is when the labour surplus has disappeared, agricultural productivity and wages start to rise and the terms of trade between the two sectors change. To keep the momentum of growth, it is then inevitable to allocate investment funds to the two sectors in such proportion as to ensure a balance between their respective inputs and outputs.

In one way or another, dualism has become a recurrent concept in theories on economic development of the Third World. In some theories, like the Lewis-Ranis-Fei model and also in the views of Hirschman and Leontief, dualism is a phase in the transition process from stagnation to self-sustained growth. In others, like the theories of Amin and De Janvry ". . . dualism constitutes the analytical centre of theory from which the specific problems and laws of motion of underdevelopment are derived".[27]

In Hirschman's view, "the lack of interdependence and linkage is . . . one of the most typical characteristics of underdeveloped economies".[28] Subsistence agriculture is characterized by the scarcity of linkage effects. The products of plantations and mining are destined directly for export, thereby depriving the exporting economy of any forward linkage. Industrialization in developing countries has principally taken the form of "enclave import industries", which transform imported semi-manufactures into final products. Thus, both the primary and industrial sectors are linkage-free at early stages of development. Hirschman claims, however, that the potential of "enclave import industries" to break out of the enclave situation is promising. By working their way backward from the "final touches" stage to domestic production of intermediate and basic industrial materials, these industries may create an integrated economic structure.[29]

Leontief points out that the production structure of developing economies will be incomplete as a number of sectors are underdeveloped or even absent. The hierarchical system of interindustry transactions, as schematized in Figure 9.1, shows gaps, and some sectors produce in isolation from other sectors. Hence, Leontief defines underdevelopment to the extent that an economy "lacks the working parts of this system".[30]

For Amin, the structural features by which underdevelopment is revealed are threefold: (1) unevenness of productivity as between sectors; (2) disarticulation of the economic system; and (3) economic domination from outside.[31] The determining relationship in a peripheral economic system is that which links the production of luxury goods with the demand emanating from the export sector. Thus, the peripheral economy is distorted toward export activities (is "extroverted"), which limits and distorts the domestic market. These distinctive features of the periphery contrast sharply with those of developed centre economies. These economies display an articulated or autocentric pattern of development, whereby a close relationship exists between sectors producing mass consumer goods and those producing intermediate and capital goods. The economy forms an articulated and organic whole. Consequently, economic progress can spread throughout the economy. Productivity increases are partly translated into increased real wages, thus permitting the domestic market to grow in relation to the development of economic capacity. Centre economies maintain a dynamic, although not interrupted, equilibrium among sectors of production and between production and consumption. While centre economies keep their momentum of growth internally, the periphery transfers its multiplier mechanisms abroad. Export of profits by foreign-owned companies weakens the multiplier effect of investment, whereas, in addition, induced import of intermediate and capital goods sets the accelerator working in the developed country from which imports are drawn. These transfers result in a conspicuous disarticulation of the peripheral economy and a blocking of its growth.

De Janvry's view on the salient features of peripheral economies generally relies upon that of Amin. He distinguishes two broad types of sectorally and socially disarticulated economies in the periphery: (1) export-enclave economies, (2) import-substitution economies.[32] Both purely typified economies are made up of a modern and a traditional sector. The modern sector produces primary exportables and, in the case of the second type of economy, also luxuries. The traditional sector produces wage goods. In these disarticulated economies, the modern sector exerts no forward and backward linkages of any significance. Industry is externally dependent on the import of capital goods and technology. In disarticulated economies, there is no mechanism at work to translate productivity increases into wage increases. The perpetuation of the traditional sector makes it possible to keep wages down, as this sector constitutes a purveyor of cheap labour and cheap food. For De Janvry, this functional dualism between the modern and the traditional sector, whereby the latter sustains the development of the former, is only a transitional phase. Internal dynamism of the peripheral countries can bear on either articulated or disarticulated transformations of the economy, depending on which "fractions of bourgeoisie" have gained control over the state.

In sum, the above studies all stress the distinct features of the dissimilar production structures of developing countries. Apart from the size of the domestic market and the availability of natural resources, which may explain deviations from the model economy in Figure 9.1, underdevelopment as such is characterized by a juxtaposition of economically unequivalent sectors (modern versus traditional), which hardly interact with one another. This phenomenon is recognized by, first, primary export activities, and second, a relatively capital-intensive industrialization process biased toward last-stage assembling activities and the absence of intermediate and capital goods producing industries.

In light of the above, the important question is whether the same function and impact as the long-standing primary export strategy in developing countries can be attributed to the export-oriented strategy of industrialization. According to its opponents, this is definitely the case when they characterize manufactured export expansion as a shallow development facilitated by an ample supply of low-wage labour. The present study addresses this question, whereby the starting position as well as the type of exporting economy constitute an integral part of the analysis.

9.6 THE SPREAD EFFECTS OF MANUFACTURED EXPORTS IN DEVELOPING COUNTRIES — A SURVEY OF EMPIRICAL EVIDENCE

Although export-oriented industrialization and trade policies of developing countries have recently commanded widespread interest, only a few studies are devoted to a systematic cross-country analysis of the spread effects of manufactured export expansion in exporting economies, whether in terms of production or employment generation. Attention is, on the contrary, almost exclusively directed towards two main issues, namely, in the first place, the structure of protection and the anti-trade bias of import-substituting regimes and export-promotion policies to correct the discrimination against manufactured exports, and second, the growth and structure of manufactured exports from developing countries. The structure of manufactured exports is commonly dealt with in the context of the neo-classical model of international trade, whereby a specialization in labour-intensive products is considered to meet the objective of maximum employment generation. Only in those studies where the measure of factor intensity of traded products also comprises factor requirements of intermediate inputs does information become available, as a by-product, on the indirect employment effects of manufactured exports.

There are also many case studies on individual country experiences with export-oriented industrialization and on the functioning of EPFZs. Case studies on EPFZs mainly focus on the generous export and investment incentives eligible for firms in the zone, the role of foreign investment, labour conditions, and the rights to unionize. Sparingly, these studies give quantitative information on the import content of the EPFZ-type of production. Findings from these empirical studies for a variety of countries and EPFZs are of great interest in their own right, but they are, however, not sufficiently uniform and comprehensive to permit cross-country comparisons.

Tyler was the first who tried to assess the total employment generation of export expansion in developing countries on a cross-country basis.[33] For eight developing countries, the direct plus indirect employment effects of manufactured exports were estimated through a straightforward application of the standard input-output procedure. The input-output tables used were all compiled in the 1950s and 1960s. Tyler's employment estimates revealed that the total may exceed the direct employment generation by considerable amounts, depending on the country concerned. The results suggest that diversified and industrialized economies display the greatest indirect, relative to direct, labour requirements per unit of exports. In addition, the share of food products in total manufactured exports is found to be of importance. Due to the highly labour-intensive agricultural inputs which enter food processing, exports of food products show by far the largest indirect labour requirements. Thus, of the countries examined, the large and more industrialized countries, i.e. India, Brazil, Egypt and Mexico, are at one extreme, displaying an average ratio of total to direct employment generated by manufactured exports of 8.7, 8.6, 6.2 and 5.2, respectively. At the other extreme are the Philippines, Yugoslavia, South Korea and Taiwan with values for the same ratio of 2.5, 2.5, 2.2 and 2.0, respectively. It is noteworthy to learn from Tyler's estimates that it makes a large difference whether or not the indirect labour requirements in input-supplying primary sectors are fully included in the total employment impact of manufactured exports. To mention some extreme examples, derived from Tyler's estimates: total employment generated through exports of food products would be 27.3 times the directly generated employment in Brazil and 19.1 times in India. For the export of grain mill products from Egypt, this ratio is as high as 54.5. The total employment effects of processed cotton exports from Egypt would be 17.1 times the direct effects. It is therefore not surprising to find considerably lower values for the average ratios of total to direct employment generation, ranging from as low as 1.1 for the Philippines to 1.6 for Yugoslavia, if the indirect employment generation is confined to the manufacturing sector alone. Interestingly enough, the country that now shows the highest average ratio, i.e. Yugoslavia, is characterized by both an integrated manufacturing sector and a relatively capital-intensive composition of manufactured exports.

In his explorative study already mentioned, Lydall aims at estimating the employment effects in both developed and developing countries of an increased penetration in markets of developed countries of manufactured imports from developing countries.[34] With respect to the employment effects of export expansion in developing countries, Lydall considers in addition to the direct and indirect effects, which are restricted to non-primary sectors only, a broadly working multiplier effect on employment. Lydall assumes that developing countries will fully employ the additional foreign-exchange receipts due to export expansion to support an increase in their domestic production and employment. Increased savings generated by the expansion of GDP have to be fully used to increase public and private investment. The relaxation of the foreign-exchange bottleneck facilitates an increase of additional imports up to the point where all net foreign-exchange earnings are spent. The working of this multiplier also makes allowance for an enlargement of productive capacity.

Lydall's approach to estimating these different types of employment effects explicitly takes account of the relationship between labour productivity, and hence employment effects of output growth, and the level of economic development. Thus, both the direct and indirect employment effects are directly made conditional on the level of GDP *per capita*. In addition, the indirect effects are supposed to vary with the size of the exporting economy. As Lydall is interested in the international re-allocation of employment due to a change in trade pattern, he estimated the direct plus indirect increase in employment opportunities in developing countries at different income levels when trade expansion leads to the displacement of one worker in the developed countries. On average, against one displaced worker in the EG, 4.7 workers would need to be taken on in the same industry in a developing country with a GDP *per capita* of US$100, and 1.4 workers in a developing country with an income level of US$1000 in 1975 (measured in 1963 prices). The corresponding average employment effects *vis-à-vis* a displaced worker in the United States are greater, namely 6.6 and 2.0 in countries of the same income range.[35] Slightly higher indirect employment effects would be realized in developing countries with larger domestic markets. Firm empirical estimates of employment effects due to the working of the multiplier appeared to be impossible. What Lydall's explorations do show is that these effects can be very large, especially in the poorest countries. If, as Lydall assumes, governments of developing countries ensure that the whole of their net foreign-exchange earnings are used to support an increase in domestic production, the increase in GDP is determined by a country's import elasticity for capital and intermediate goods. The total employment effects are then mainly determined by the average labour productivity for the economy as a whole. Depending on the values of these two determining factors, the ratio of total to direct plus indirect employment ranges from a maximum of 9.0 to a minimum of 1.7.[36] Lydall restricts the most plausible range of values of this ratio to 2-5. Clearly, the impact of this multiplier on employment depends very greatly on a country's dependence on imports and level of development.

In a comprehensive research project on alternative trade strategies, Krueger *et al.* have undertaken ten uniform individual country studies.[37] The main objectives of this project have been to investigate under which trade strategy, i.e. import substitution or export promotion, the potential for creating employment will be greater, and to examine the extent of commodity and factor-market imperfections and their possible effect on employment and factor proportions in exportable and import-competing industries. Because of the common framework of the country studies, the use of direct plus indirect labour requirements per unit of value added as a measure of factor intensity and the classification of commodities in distinct categories (natural-resource-based versus so-called Heckscher-Ohlin-Samuelson products and exportables versus importable products), the project yields interesting cross-country findings. First of all, it appeared that, in most cases, export-oriented policies have been far more favourable than import substitution in expanding employment opportunities. The results indicate that exportables make use of much more unskilled labour than importables. Closely related to this conclusion is the finding that industries subject to higher rates of protection were generally less labour intensive than those subject to lower rates of protection. Thus, exportables have a larger employment spread effect per unit of value added than import-substituting activities. The choice of a trade strategy turned out to be of decisive importance, as factor market distortions did not prove to be strong enough to reverse the commodity composition of trade between capital-intensive and labour-intensive products. The separate classification of natural-resource-based products proved to be enlightening indeed. Marked differences in total labour requirements were found in individual cases. In some of these cases, the inclusion of natural-resource-based products strengthened the labour-intensive character of exports; in others, the average factor intensity of exports reversed from labour to capital intensive. These findings suggest that the market orientation of natural-resource-based industries is largely independent of the pursued trade strategy.

Our survey of cross-country and individual country studies[38] reaches the conclusion that the extent of employment spread effects of manufactured export production in developing countries shows notable differences. These differences are found in direct as well as in indirect employment generation. Hence, the impact of export production on the exporting economy differs

from country to country. While care is needed in drawing conclusions, at this stage of our analysis it is already clear that the following three sets of interrelated factors exercise a decisive impact on the extent of spread effects:
(1) the scope and vigour of a country's export-promotion strategy and the structure of manufactured exports;
(2) a country's level of industrial development;
(3) structural country characteristics, particularly domestic market size and natural-resource endowment.

The transition to an outward-looking strategy of industrialization may imply a partial or a total adjustment of policies.[39] A partial policy shift is often observed in larger countries with an already relatively well developed manufacturing sector where vested interests of import-substituting industries prohibit a liberal trade regime. The promotion of manufactured exports is then realized by means of subsidies and/or the establishment of EPFZs. Under these conditions the structure of manufactured exports is more or less balanced between labour and capital-intensive products, especially when these exports are produced by import-substituting industries extending their production to export markets. This is, for instance, illustrated by the export performance of Brazil, Mexico and India. In the latter country, industries with lower labour intensities are in fact the ones that show a higher outward orientation.

By contrast, some smaller countries that embarked on a comprehensive policy of promoting manufactured exports show a more consistent specialization in the most labour-intensive exportables. Their level of industrial development was not particularly high before the policy switch, as they often went through only a relatively short period of moderate import substitution. Hence, the growth of manufactured exports in these countries is largely brought about by a newly established and relatively labour-intensive export sector, whether or not accommodated in EPFZs.

In sum, from the point of view of direct employment generation, an unconditioned outward-looking strategy seems to be preferable. However, country-specific differences in the above-mentioned factors also produce differences in the spread effects of export production. Exportables which are produced in a re-oriented import substitution sector show a greater indirect production and employment effect than exports originating from newly established industries or EPFZs. The case studies on EPFZs suggest that this instrument to promote manufactured exports may lead to an isolated enclave export sector, characterized by relatively high direct labour absorption, but with only a small indirect employment effect.[40] In general, the more export industries are rooted in a diversified manufacturing sector and the more efficient the production of input-supplying industries, the higher potentially the spread effects of export production. Thus, the ultimate impact of differences in these factors on total employment spread effects cannot be judged beforehand.

The availability of natural resources determines a country's performance in exports of processed primary products to a high degree, particularly at lower levels of industrial development, as the processing of primary products, notably foods and wood products, often marks the first strides on the path towards industrialization. Obviously, the spread effects of resource-based manufacturing are mainly realized in primary sectors. The linkages within the manufacturing sector are limited. Notwithstanding the often capital-intensive final stage of processing natural-resource-based products, these exports may still show high employment spread effects. This is only true, of course, if the possibility of export substitution is excluded and if supply by the primary sectors is not inelastic.

As these factors seem to have such distinctive influences on a country's export structure as well as on the impact of export expansion on the domestic economy, it is of major importance to take these factors explicitly into account in our country analyses. The framework of the country studies is presented in the next chapter.

10
Framework of the Individual Country Studies

10.1 INTRODUCTION

The foregoing three chapters gave an outline of both the underlying theoretical framework and the method of investigation that will be employed in the individual country studies. The main purpose of the country studies is to discover the orders of magnitude in developing countries of the spread effects of different forms of manufactured export expansion, as compared with manufacturing production directed towards the domestic market. An empirical assessment is made of primary and secondary effects of both categories of production on production and employment throughout the economy. To enhance the comparability of the findings, the country studies are undertaken within this common analytical framework and will be structured along identical lines, explained in this chapter.

First, information is provided about the selection of countries and the structure and coverage of the country studies. Next, the concepts used in the empirical analysis will be set forth. A description of the data is given thereafter.

10.2 SELECTION OF COUNTRIES

The empirical analysis of this study is based on the experience of seven South-East Asian countries. The country studies cover Indonesia, Malaysia, the Philippines, Singapore, Thailand, together the founders of the Association of South-East Asian Nations (ASEAN), South Korea and Taiwan. The rationale for selecting just these seven countries, apart from the availability of a recent and sufficiently disaggregated input-output table, is two-fold.

First of all, of the developing world the South-East Asian region made the largest gains and accounted for the highest share in world exports of manufactures during the 1970s. Some countries in this region, most notably South Korea, Taiwan, Hong Kong and Singapore, are forerunners of the export-oriented strategy of industrialization in developing countries. Exports of manufactures have become a significant element in their export growth and overall economic development and, accordingly, these countries are considered the newly industrializing countries. The quantitative importance of the seven selected countries in world trade of manufactures is indicated in Table 10.1. The share of developing countries in world manufactured exports averaged 5.17 per cent in 1970 and rose to 9.45 per cent in 1980. The corresponding shares for the selected countries together were 1.40 and 4.57 per cent, respectively. Clearly, the selected countries witnessed in this period a larger increase in their share in world manufactured exports than other developing countries. In 1980, the selected countries accounted for almost 50 per cent of total manufactured exports by developing countries.

TABLE 10.1
SHARES OF REGIONS AND SELECTED DEVELOPING COUNTRIES IN WORLD TRADE OF MANUFACTURES,[1] 1970 AND 1980

Region and country	Percentage shares	
	1970	1980
World	100	100
Developing countries	5.17	9.45
Sample countries	1.40	4.57
ASEAN	0.37	1.42
Indonesia	0.01	0.05
Malaysia	0.06	0.24
Philippines	0.04	0.11
Singapore	0.24	0.87
Thailand	0.02	0.15
South Korea	0.36	1.38
Taiwan	0.67	1.77
Other developing countries	3.77	4.88

Note : [1] Manufactures are defined as SITC 5-8, less 67 and 68.
Sources : UNCTAD, *Handbook of International Trade and Development Statistics*, United Nations, New York, 1983, Tables A.6, A.9 and A.10, *Taiwan Statistical Data Book 1981*, Council for Economic Planning and Development, Executive Yuan, 1981, Table 10.8.

Secondly, although the countries chosen for the study are all situated in one of the most dynamic regions of the developing world, they can certainly not be viewed as a homogeneous country group. The individual countries show marked differences in *per capita* income level and structural country characteristics, such as domestic market size, population density and availability of natural resources. Hence, one can observe differences among these countries in the industrialization and trade strategies pursued and in manufactured export performances. Some of the selected countries are highly successful exporters, others have, as countries of the second tier, a less outstanding record, whereas export-promotion efforts in Indonesia are of very recent date.

This heterogeneity in performance and country characteristics facilitates a comparative analysis of the spread effects of different forms of manufactured exports under different structural economic conditions.

10.3 COVERAGE OF THE COUNTRY STUDIES

Each country study is structured as follows. After the introductory remarks, which characterize the country in question on the basis of *per capita* income level, size and density of population and the availability of natural resources, the country's industrialization and trade strategy is dealt with. Attention is especially directed towards the switch, if any, from import-substitution to export-promotion strategies. Furthermore, it has to be established what kind of export-promotion policies are actually adopted. Thus, do the policy reforms involve a genuine export promotion accompanied by a fairly open and liberal trade regime, or is, by contrast, the incentive system applied characterized by a dissimilar treatment of production for domestic and for export markets? In the former case, both exporters and domestic-market-oriented producers are provided similar incentives. In the latter case, a dualistic strategy is applied, i.e. the import-substitution strategy is still pursued, whether or not by moving to a second stage, whereas the inherent discrimination against exports is reduced by granting various subsidies and tariff and tax exemptions to exporters. Attention will also be paid to the role of EPFZs in a country's manufactured export performance. The aim is to examine the scope and vigour of the export-promotion strategies being pursued, as these are likely to have an impact on the extent of spread effects of manufactured exports that are generated.

The country studies proceed with an analysis of the economic structure, emphasizing the position of the manufacturing sector in the context of the national economy. For this analysis, the different sector classifications of the input-output tables have been aggregated into a standardized five-sector classification, including the major economic sectors agriculture and mining, manufacturing, construction, utilities and services. On this level of aggregation, we consider the manufacturing contribution to total gross output, GDP and exports, the average import content of manufacturing production and the interdependence of the manufacturing sector with other sectors of the economy. If available data permit, we also address the average factor intensity of manufacturing production and the average remuneration of the manufacturing labour force *vis-à-vis* other sectors. Although computations are based on the same input-output table, it should be noted that data in this part of the analysis are not strictly comparable with those presented in the remainder of the country studies because of the difference in aggregation level.

Next, the analysis turns to the development and structure of a country's manufactured exports in the 1970s. First, export performance and changes in the composition of exports are singled out for particular attention. The structure of manufactured exports is then considered in greater detail for the year covered by the input-ouput table employed. For this purpose, manufacturing sectors are subdivided into three separate groups that correspond with the three different ways in which developing countries can seek to expand manufactured exports,[1] i.e.:

(1) industrial processing of products from primary sectors before export;
(2) change-over from import substitution to manufactured export expansion;
(3) establishing new export-oriented industries, whether by means of EPFZs or not.

Thus, the first step is to introduce a distinction between sectors engaged in the processing of primary products and sectors producing products of which the value-added component is largely generated in manufacturing. In the course of the country studies, the former type of sector is denoted as natural-resource-based (NRB sectors) and the latter type as non-natural-resource-based (non-NRB sectors). The second step is a further subdivision of non-NRB sectors into typical export sectors (E sectors) and sectors primarily oriented towards the domestic market (DMO sectors). Accordingly, exports can be classified as NRB exports and exports originating from E sectors or DMO sectors.

Using the input-output table, the structure of manufactured exports is analyzed with the help of various measures of factor intensity. For total manufactured exports and for each of the three subcategories of exports, weighted average values of these measures are presented, in which the weights are proportional to each sector's share in exports. For comparative purposes, the weighted average factor intensities of the corresponding categories of total production are also computed, the weights now being proportional to each sector's share in production. Again, if available data permit, this analysis is supplemented by estimates of the average wage levels in NRB, E and DMO sectors. For three countries, South Korea, Taiwan and Singapore, data could also be obtained on the skill and gender composition of the manufacturing labour force.

Next, matrices of Spearman rank order correlations are estimated in attempting to establish statistical relationships between a sector's export performance, factor intensity and average wage rate. These rank correlations may provide additional insight into a country's specialization pattern.

Finally, in each country study a comparative analysis is made of the spread effects of manufacturing production for export and domestic markets. An assessment is made of direct, indirect and secondary effects on production and employment throughout the economy. The core of this analysis is summarized in weighted average values of various measures of spread effects for different categories of export and production, corresponding to the three-way classification of sectors indicated above. Here again, sectoral shares in export and production are applied as weights.

Finally, by means of a Spearman rank order correlation analysis possible relationships are explored between, on the one hand, sectoral rankings according to export performance and factor intensity, and on the other hand, sectoral rankings according to the various measures of spread effects. Each country study concludes with a summary of the major findings.

10.4   DEFINITION OF CONCEPTS

Definition of Manufactured Exports

The use of input-output tables as the prime source of trade and production data obviates the cumbersome attempts to reconcile trade and production statistics. This, however, implies the broadest of all conceivable definitions of manufactured exports. Exports are simply classified by industrial origin, which, in defining manufactured exports, leads to the inclusion of all products that originate from the major sector manufacturing. The sector classifications of the input-output tables used in the country studies fairly tally with the ISIC classification of economic activities.[2] Thus, manufactured exports defined in this way comprise all products produced in ISIC Major Division 3 *Manufacturing*. The use of this definition of manufactured exports has the disadvantage of including many products that contain so little industrial value added relative to the value derived from primary sectors that they hardly can be conceived as manufactured. Often, a mere preparation for export is the case. Examples include some products from food processing industries, saw-mill products, vegetable and animal oils, mineral products and unwrought ferrous and non-ferrous metals. Yet, for consistency reasons, use is made of this broad definition in the analyses of the structure and spread effects of export production.

As will be seen in some of the country studies, the value of a country's manufactured exports defined according to the broad definition may deviate substantially from the value following from the UNCTAD classification of traded products. Unless otherwise indicated, the so-called Total A definition of UNCTAD is applied in analyzing a country's manufactured export performance in time. Compared to the broad definition, this definition of manufactured exports excludes petroleum and related products, unworked non-ferrous metals and a number of processed primary products which are not far removed from the primary stage. A list of SITC codes for manufactures included in the UNCTAD definition is given in Appendix Table A.10.1.

NRB, E and DMO Sectors

Two criteria are applied in assigning economic activities to NRB, E or DMO sectors. First, the following three-digit industries in the ISIC classification are considered NRB:
— Food manufacturing (ISIC 311/2);
— Beverage industries (ISIC 313);
— Tobacco manufactures (ISIC 314);
— Manufacture of wood and wood and cork products, except furniture (ISIC 341);
— Petroleum refineries and manufacture of miscellaneous products of petroleum and coal (ISIC 353/4);
— Iron and steel basic industries (ISIC 371);
— Non-ferrous metal basic industries (ISIC 372).

This categorization is strictly applied in each country study. Only in some minor cases did arbitrary decisions have to be made, due to identification problems.

Second, non-NRB exports are classified as originating from typical E sectors if these sectors show an above average export orientation. This is the case for a non-NRB sector if its export-output ratio equals or exceeds the average ratio for total non-NRB production. The remaining non-NRB sectors are identified as DMO sectors. These two criteria exclude a double classification of sectors.

The manufactured export performance of a sector, or category of sectors, is indicated by two ratios:
— export-output ratio (E_i/O_i);
— share in total manufactured exports (E_i/E_m);
where E stands for exports, O for output, E_m for total manufactured exports, and the subscript i for a sector.

Measures of Factor Intensity and Spread Effects

In country studies where the input-output table could be supplemented by adequate estimates of either the number of persons engaged per sector or average sectoral wage rates, the measures of factor intensity comprise:
— direct labour coefficient in man-years of labour (l^e);
— total labour coefficient in man-years of labour (T^e);
— value added per employee in national currency units (VA/L);
— gross profit per employee in national currency units (GP/L);
— average annual wage rate in national currency units (s);
— share of wages and salaries in gross value added.

Beside the direct and total coefficient, value added and gross profit per employee are used as alternative measures of factor intensity, whereby gross profit equals the non-wage component of gross value added. As in Part I of this study, value added per employee approximates overall capital intensity of production and gross profit per employee is indicative of physical capital intensity of production. The average wage rate is then conceived as a proxy for the skill or human capital intensity of production.[3] In addition, the share of wages and salaries in gross value added is another measure revealing the proportion in which labour and capital are employed in production. In analyzing the structure of manufactured exports, a distinction is made between labour- and capital-intensive products. The average direct labour coefficient of total manufacturing production is used as the cutoff point for this distinction.

In country studies where no reasonable estimates can be constructed for sectoral data on employment or wages, we have to manage with only three measures of factor intensity:
— direct wage coefficient (l^w);
— total wage coefficient (T^w);
— share of wages and salaries in gross value added.

Here, the wage bill replaces a physical unit as measure of factor intensity of production. As explained in Section 8.5.2, use of the physical measure is not *a priori* superior. Furthermore, rankings of sectors by l^e and l^w and by T^e and T^w turn out very similar for those countries where both pairs of measures could be constructed. For manufacturing sectors in South Korea and Singapore the rank correlation coefficients are all significant at the 1 per cent level, ranging from 0.85 to 0.90.

The measures of spread effects capturing the impact on production include:
— power of dispersion (P);
— power of dispersion exclusive of intrasectoral deliveries ($\overset{*}{P}$);
— net foreign-exchange earnings *c.q.* domestic value-added component per unit of export or production ($NFEE$).

FRAMEWORK OF THE COUNTRY STUDIES

The measures of employment spread effects include:
- power of dispersion in terms of employment (P^E);
- power of dispersion in terms of employment exclusive of indirect employment in agriculture (P^{E-A});
- wage-income multiplier (WIM);
- wage-income multiplier in terms of employment (WIM^E).

If, again, data limitations make the expression in physical units of employment unattainable, the employment spread effects are formulated as the generation of wage incomes. Using wages as the unit of observation, the measures include:
- power of dispersion in terms of wages (P^W);
- wage-income multiplier (WIM).

We refer to Chapter 8 for the explanation and exact definitions of the various measures enumerated here.

10.5 DESCRIPTION OF THE DATA

The greater part of the data incorporated in the country studies is compiled from national sources. These sources are given in appendix tables at the end of each country study. Some comments on the nature of these data are in place.

The national data sources include first of all the input-output tables. For the seven countries that constitute the case studies, at least one input-output table is available for a year around the mid-1970s. Except in the case of Singapore, all tables value transactions at producers' prices. These are defined, in principle, as purchasers' prices less trade and transport margins. The Singapore tables are valued at basic prices which are, above trade and transport margins, also freed from commodity taxes such as import and excise duties. Apart from this passable uniformity of valuation, these tables are far from being uniformly compiled.

The level of aggregation, and hence the number of manufacturing sectors, varies from table to table, ranging from 56 to 180 sectors. No attempts have been made to arrive at a standardized sector classification, which would inevitably result in aggregating sectors up to the number of the most aggregated input-output table. Instead, the highest possible level of disaggregation is preferred in order to increase the reliability of the empirical investigation.

The treatment of imports also varies. The input-output tables of Thailand, South Korea, Malaysia and Singapore provide separate rows or even complete matrices of intermediate imports. We may therefore assume that the structural A matrices for these countries only contain domestically supplied intermediates. In the input-output tables for Indonesia, the Philippines and

Taiwan, on the contrary, no distinction is made between domestic and imported intermediates. All imports are treated on an equal basis by entering a negative column vector of total imports in final demand. Consequently, as only domestically supplied inputs are to be considered, these tables have been adjusted via a roundabout procedure, facilitating a per sector estimate of the intermediate import content of production. This procedure is explained in Section 8.3.

One of the major problems encountered was the reconciliation of employment and wage data with the relevant sector classification of the input-output tables. In fact, only the Indonesian table is accompanied by estimates of the number of persons engaged per sector. For the remaining six country studies, we have attempted to construct reasonable estimates from other sources.

In four cases, i.e. Thailand, the Philippines, South Korea and Singapore, this proved to be possible. But it appeared to be only partly possible for Taiwan and quite impossible for Malaysia. Data on either sectoral wage levels or employment were mainly compiled from industrial censuses covering the same year as the input-output table. Additional data sources of international agencies were used only in cases where no national censuses or surveys of primary and tertiary sectors were available.

The use of different data sources has the inevitable consequence of working with a variety of concepts and definitions of employment and remuneration of

TABLE 10.2
INPUT-OUTPUT TABLES USED IN THE COUNTRY STUDIES

Country	Year	Number of sectors	Number of manufacturing sectors	Treatment of imports[1]	Data on employment[2]
Indonesia	1975	66	24	a	yes
Philippines	1974	121	67	a	no*
Thailand	1975	180	93	b	no*
South Korea	1975	66	43	a and b	no*
Taiwan	1976	99	61	a	no**
Malaysia	1975	56	34	b	no
Singapore	1973	74	51	b	no*
	1978	150	114	b	no*

Notes : [1] a = all imports are treated as competitive; b = intermediate imports are treated as complementary, final demand imports as competitive.
[2] * = the table could be supplemented by sectoral data on either employment or wages; ** = the table could only partly be supplemented by sectoral data on employment and wages.

FRAMEWORK OF THE COUNTRY STUDIES

labour. Coverages vary from country to country and from census to census. However, notwithstanding the arbitrary decisions that sometimes had to be made, we believe that our estimates are probably as good as can be made with the existing data sources.

Finally, Table 10.2 presents a summary of the special features of the input-output tables used in the country studies.

APPENDIX TABLE A.10.1
DEFINITION OF MANUFACTURED EXPORTS IN SITC, REVISED, CODE

SITC, Revised, Code[1]

012	052	072.3
013	053	073
032	055	091
046	062	099
047	071.3	
048	072.2	

111
112
122

231.2	244.02
231.3	251
231.4	266
243	267

331.02	341.2
332	351

431

5 less 513.65

6 less 681, 682.1, 683.1, 685.1, 686.1, 687.1 and 689

7[2]

8

951

Notes : [1] United Nations, *Standard International Trade Classification, Revised*, Statistical Paper Series M, No. 34, New York, 1961.
[2] Contrary to the Total A definition of UNCTAD, exports of SITC, Revised, 711 and 735 from developing countries are included in this definition.

Source : UNCTAD, *The Definition of Primary Commodities, Semi-manufactures and Manufactures*, Trade and Development Board, TD/B/c.2/3, 1965.

11
The Case of Indonesia

11.1 INTRODUCTORY REMARKS

Indonesia is generally thought to have a high development potential. It is, after China and India, the third largest developing country in the world with a population of about 148 million at the start of the 1980s. Indonesia has a huge and diversified endowment of natural resources. The islands of the Indonesian archipelago cover a land area of 2.0 million km². The average population density of about 78 persons per km² is not particularly high. However, Indonesia cannot adequately be described by average figures. The country exhibits a basic dichotomy between Java and the outer islands as regards the distribution of population, natural resources and manufacturing activities.

Java's share in Indonesia's population is close to two thirds, while it covers only 7 per cent of total land area. Population pressure on Java is, therefore, extremely high with a density of approximately 700 persons per km². Although manufacturing activities are almost entirely concentrated on Java, these activities employ only a small part of the workforce. Traditional agriculture and plantation crops still dominate Java's economy. Hence, Java can be characterized as a dualistic, labour-surplus economy. By contrast, the outer islands are sparsely populated economies, largely deprived of manufacturing but amply endowed with natural resources. Indonesia earns its foreign exchange almost exclusively with exports of primary products that originate from these outer islands and from the sea.

Since the late 1960s, there has been a marked acceleration in the growth of the Indonesian economy. Annual average growth rates of real GDP *per capita* amounted to 5.1 per cent from 1970 to 1980, compared to 0.8 per cent during the preceding decade. Much of this growth was due to a recovery from a stagnating economy in the 1960s and to booming world market prices for Indonesia's primary exports, most notably oil, in the first half of the 1970s.

This boom made Indonesia, which is a member of OPEC, move from a low-income to a middle-income economy with a GNP *per capita* of US$530 in 1981. In 1975, the year covered by the input-output tables that will be used for our analysis, Indonesia was still a low-income economy with a GNP *per capita* of US$260.[1]

11.2 INDUSTRIALIZATION AND TRADE STRATEGIES IN INDONESIA

One of the most distinctive features of Indonesian industrialization strategies after independence was its extreme domestic-market orientation, although these strategies have undergone changes over the years. It is only recently that the Government has taken some action to promote exports of manufactures.

Upon examination, Indonesia's process of industrialization seems to be marked off by three different phases.[2] The strategy during the first phase after independence, ending in 1965 with the overthrow of President Sukarno, emphasized reconstruction and expansion of the manufacturing sector. Protection was provided by tariffs and quotas especially in support of consumer goods industries, and a number of priority industries received preferential treatment. In 1957, Sukarno set out to implement his concept of "Guided Economy", which was principally aimed at self-reliance and Indonesianization. Foreign investments were kept down, the Government started to actively intervene in the market and state enterprises were established or expanded, especially in basic industrial sectors. Government-sponsored promotional schemes were developed to stimulate small-scale firms and production co-operatives. However, as all observers of this phase agree, these policies were clearly ineffective. This period is described as one of political instability and hyper-inflation, falling export receipts and scarcity of foreign exchange, resulting in severe shortages of investable capital, intermediate inputs and machinery. The manufacturing sector was operating far below its capacity level. Paauw summarizes the performance of the economy during this period with the statement that "per capita real income was not restored to prewar levels until 1957, and from then until the late 1960s remained essentially stagnant".[3]

The industrialization policy of the second phase, roughly covering the years 1966–1971, showed a marked change. The "New Order" policies proclaimed by Suharto ushered in, by Indonesian standards, a relatively liberal era. Industrial development policies de-emphasized the role of state enterprises and government intervention. Private enterprise, both foreign and domestic, was thought to foster industrial growth along with the state sector. Private domestic investment was stimulated by the enactment of a new Domestic

Investment Law (1968), while foreign investment was attracted by a new Foreign Investment Law (1967). Both laws provided a "remarkable package of fiscal and customs tariff incentives" during the first years of operation.[4] Foreign companies were allowed to remit profits and to withdraw capital. In combination with a simplified and liberalized foreign trade regime, these sets of laws induced a burst of investment which has led to a flood of new technologies into Indonesia. The bulk of both foreign and domestic investment was allocated to the extractive industries petroleum, minerals and lumber. Within manufacturing, foreign investors showed most interest in basic metals, followed by textiles. Domestic investment was mainly undertaken in textiles and chemicals.[5]

The manufacturing sector expanded rapidly during this undoubtedly easy phase of import substitution. Virtually all manufacturing growth took place in nondurable consumer goods industries of medium and large scale. Notwithstanding the relatively liberal trade regime during these years, the incentive system definitely favoured import-substitution industries and did not encourage exports. Moreover, until 1971, most manufactured exports were charged an export tax of 10 per cent on export proceeds.

The strategy that emerged during the third phase, covering the 1970s, gradually moved back toward an ever more controlling and protectionist position. A complicated regime of tariffs, quantitative and other restrictions was recreated, resulting in a highly protected manufacturing sector. The Rupiah became increasingly overvalued. During the first half of the decade, the manufacturing sector continued to grow at a relatively high rate of annually 14.5 per cent.[6] This growth was mainly achieved through further import substitution of consumer goods and an increased domestic demand for those goods due to the acceleration in the growth of the Indonesian economy.[7] However, from 1975 the scope for further import substitution of light manufactures narrowed. Output growth in, for instance, textiles slowed down. In parts of the manufacturing sector excess capacity became a severe problem. This, in turn, strengthened the call for still higher levels of protection and the Government switched to a policy of limiting entry of new companies in stagnating subsectors. During the second half of the 1970s, manufacturing growth therefore slowed down to a still relatively high rate of 11.0 per cent per year. That this growth rate remained at this level can mainly be attributed to the accelerated growth of a number of intermediate input-supplying industries. The rise of these industries is of recent date in Indonesia. The Government actively takes part in the promotion of steel, cement, fertilizer, paper and agro-chemical industries.[8]

The tariff system and the numerous non-tariff barriers to import are generally in accordance with an import-substitution regime. Pitt estimated effective protection rates on the basis of the 1971 input-output table and found that effective protection levels substantially exceeded nominal protection levels, and were benefitting consumer goods industries more than intermediate and capital goods industries. Pitt also distinguished between exportable sectors and import-competing sectors and it was found that the former group of sectors had a negative protection of −11 per cent, whereas the latter group enjoyed an effective protection of 66 per cent.[9] This trade regime was unmistakenly inward-looking. In 1973 and 1977 major reforms in the system of tariffs took place, but their impact was certainly not one of declining effective protection.[10] In fact, since 1973, the trade regime has become increasingly protectionist. Apart from an already complicated tariff and quota system, ever more complementary measures took effect, such as limited entry into sectors, production ceilings, licensing of investments, credit arrangements to discourage imports and subsidy of intermediate imports.

Not until the third Five-Year Plan (1979–1984) did the Indonesian Government explicitly recognize the need to promote the development of export industries. This gradual change in the industrialization strategy is obviously dictated by the need to reduce dependence on primary exports, most notably petroleum, as the almost exclusive source of foreign-exchange revenue. Exports of manufactures are expected to be conducive to maintaining manufacturing growth rates in the face of the narrowing scope for further import replacement and to contribute to the generation of employment opportunities. Recently, a package of policy measures was adopted to increase the international competitiveness of Indonesian manufactures, including cheaper export credits and insurance, relaxation of some foreign-exchange controls, lower port charges and an improvement of transport facilities.[11] Furthermore, potential exporters will be assisted in selling their products in foreign markets.

The competitiveness of Indonesian manufactures certainly improved as a result of the large devaluations in recent years, which were at least partly dictated by the interests of potential exporters. First, the nominal exchange rate, constant since 1971, was devalued from Rp. 415 to Rp. 625 per U.S. dollar in 1978. Thereafter, the Rupiah slightly depreciated against the U.S. dollar and, once more, a large devaluation took place to Rp. 980 per U.S. dollar in mid-1983.

Two product categories are considered to be promising exportables: first, natural-resource-based products like food products such as shrimps and tapioca chips, wood products, and mineral-based products such as tin, aluminium and nickel products; second, labour-intensive products like textiles, batik garments and leather products.[12]

Finally, for years there have been plans for the establishment of an EPFZ on Batam, an island near Singapore. It is thought that Batam could be a promising site to capture the labour-intensive industries that Singapore might push off due to increasing labour costs. Up to the time of writing, however, no EPFZ is yet in operation.

11.3 STRUCTURAL FEATURES OF THE INDONESIAN ECONOMY

As Table 11.1 shows, primary activities dominate the Indonesian economy, accounting for almost half of GDP and two thirds of total employment in 1975. The manufacturing sector contributes 22.7 per cent to total gross

TABLE 11.1
BASIC DATA ON THE STRUCTURE OF THE INDONESIAN ECONOMY, 1975

Indicators	Agriculture & Mining	Manufacturing	Construction	Utilities	Services
1. Share in total gross output (%)	37.9	22.7	9.2	.8	29.4
2. Share in GDP (%)	47.8	11.2	5.2	.6	35.1
3. Share in total employment (%)	62.1	9.3	2.8	.1	25.7
4. Export-output ratio (%)	33.3	5.2	.0	.0	6.0
5. Share in total exports (%)	81.0	7.6	.0	.0	11.4
6. Share in intermediate imports (%)	9.3	42.1	26.9	2.3	19.4
7. Input structure					
— Domestic intermediate inputs	.18	.57	.45	.30	.20
— Imported intermediate inputs	.02	.12	.19	.19	.04
— Gross value added	.80	.31	.36	.51	.76
Total inputs	1.00	1.00	1.00	1.00	1.00
8. $NFEE$	.98	.84	.78	.77	.94
9. P	.83	1.20	1.11	.99	.87
10. P^E	1.68	1.14	.79	.42	.96
11. P^{E-A}	.09	1.17	1.15	.69	1.91
12. WIM^E (per 10^9 Rps. output)	4,987	3,833	3,265	2,057	3,769
13. I^e (per 10^9 Rps. output)	3,752	933	695	354	1,984
14. VA/L (10^3 Rps.)	214.0	334.8	522.7	1,431.1	383.6
15. T^e (per 10^9 Rps. output)	4,475	3,035	2,105	1,142	2,552
16. s (10^3 Rps.)	27.2	107.5	276.3	454.0	133.8

For explanation of symbols, see Section 10.4.
Source : see Appendix to Chapter 11.

output, but only 11.2 per cent to GDP and 9.3 per cent to total employment. Primary products also dominate Indonesian exports with a share of 81.0 per cent of total earnings from exports of goods and services. The primary sectors show the highest average export-output ratio of 33.3 per cent, whereas the manufacturing sector exports only 5.2 per cent of its output. In fact, Indonesia's export sector is based on petroleum. While the contribution of the manufacturing sector to export receipts is small, its 42.1 per cent share in the use of intermediate imports is relatively high.

The share of total domestic value added in total manufacturing production equals 0.84. This is certainly not low, but account has to be taken of the fact that, in 1975, NRB products constituted the largest part, i.e. 57.7 per cent, of manufacturing production. This results in a close link between primary sectors and manufacturing. It is therefore especially the non-NRB production that shows a relatively high dependence on imported intermediates, due to the underdevelopment of intermediate and capital goods industries. Chemicals, non-metallic mineral products, cement, metal products and machinery together accounted for only 12.9 per cent of total manufacturing production by 1975. The contribution of transport equipment was 15.2 per cent, but this figure includes an extensive repair sector. As is shown by the input structure of the manufacturing sector, the ratio of domestic intermediate input to total production equals 0.57. More than half of these intermediates originate in the agricultural and mining sector. As could be expected from the close interrelatedness of the manufacturing and primary sectors, the P value for manufacturing is well above 1.

To gain proper insight into the employment spread effects of manufacturing, account has to be taken of two features, namely the already established close link between manufacturing and primary sectors and the duality of the Indonesian manufacturing sector. The outstanding labour-intensive character of agricultural production explains both the high P^E value for the primary sectors and, through its large share in intermediate inputs entering manufacturing production, the relatively high P^E value for manufacturing. The second feature relates to the fact that small scale, household and cottage activities contributed 20 per cent to total manufacturing value added, but employed 87 per cent of the manufacturing work force by the mid-1970s.[13] Food processing, wood products and textiles dominate the cottage sector. These activities are mainly undertaken in rural areas where especially females carry out the work, often part-time, to supplement family income. Some authors maintain that the industrialization strategy of the 1970s aggravated the already existing duality of the manufacturing sector.[14] Foreign and domestic manufacturing investments were mainly allocated to modern large-scale capital-intensive enterprises. Government investments in manufacturing have shown a similar allocation pattern. These investments have led to significant increases in capital intensity, most notably in chemical industries. Modern large-scale firms increased their production mainly by increasing their productivity, thereby diminishing their employment-creating capacity per Rupiah invested. By contrast, household, cottage and small-scale industries have suffered from increased competition from the modern sector in the domestic market, which held back substantial increases in production. However, ever more job seekers became engaged in small-scale industries due to a lack of alternative employment opportunities. Consequently, productivity in the traditional sector declined during the 1970s. In one and the same sector traditional and modern technologies are in use which show huge differences in physical productivity. The textile sector may serve as an illustration. In the weaving industry, productivity per man-day varies from 1 metre of fabric for backstrap looms, to about 7 metres on handlooms, to perhaps 1,000 metres in the modern, capital-intensive, integrated textile mills.[15] In general, the various programmes to assist small-scale manufacturing turned out to be ineffective.

Considering these two features of Indonesia's manufacturing sector, it is explicable that both the P^E and P^{E-A} values for manufacturing are well above 1, i.e. 1.14 and 1.17, respectively. For the same reasons, primary sectors and manufacturing show the highest WIM^E values. Obviously, the employment spread effects do not refer to full-time jobs. In Indonesia, underemployment is a regular phenomenon in primary sectors, manufacturing and services. This is reflected by the wage structure of the economy and the sectoral factor requirements. The average wage level in manufacturing is four times that in primary sectors, but lags behind the average wage levels in construction, utilities and services.

It is true that measured by the direct labour coefficient, manufacturing production uses relatively little labour. But more significant is the rather low value added per employee in manufacturing, indicating a relatively low average level of capital intensity and labour productivity of manufacturing production in total. Only the value added per employee in agriculture is lower than in manufacturing. As one would expect on account of the above, manufacturing shows the highest total labour coefficient next to the primary sectors.

11.4 DEVELOPMENT AND STRUCTURE OF INDONESIAN MANUFACTURED EXPORTS

Indonesia's exports are almost exclusively composed of primary products. In the 1970s, petroleum became the most important source of export revenue, as a result of dramatically higher production and prices. By the mid-1970s, petroleum and petroleum products accounted for almost three quarters of export proceeds. In subsequent years, the relative importance of petroleum slightly decreased. Minerals, non-ferrous metals and, increasingly, lumber are the remaining major primary exports.

The extreme domestic-market orientation of manufacturing production is evident from Figure 11.1, which shows the development of the share of manufactures in total merchandise exports. This share fluctuated around 2 per cent during the 1970s; inclusive of petroleum products, it ranged from about 6 to 9 per cent. Figure 11.1 also shows that the export-output ratio of the manufacturing sector, exclusive of petroleum refining, did not change appreciable until 1979. Only in recent years have both shares seemed to increase.

Figure 11.2 shows the changing composition of manufactured exports in the 1970s. The leading position of chemicals has been overtaken by rapidly growing exports of wood products. Exports of electrical machinery, mainly transistors and valves, and clothing have become important exportable manufactures in recent years.

For the analysis of the structure and the spread effects of Indonesia's manufactured exports, the 24 manufacturing sectors distinguished in the 1975 input-output table are classified according to the procedure described in

Figure 11.1
Manufactured Export Performance of Indonesia, 1970–1981

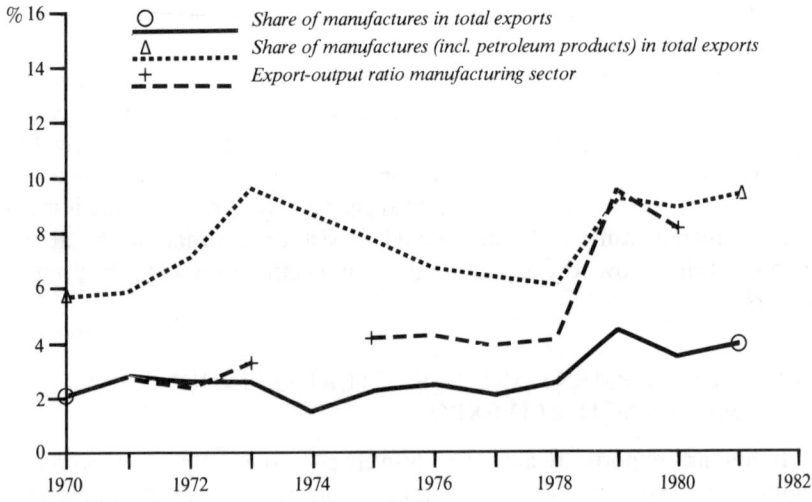

Figure 11.2
Composition of Indonesian Manufactured Exports, 1970–1981
(percentage shares)

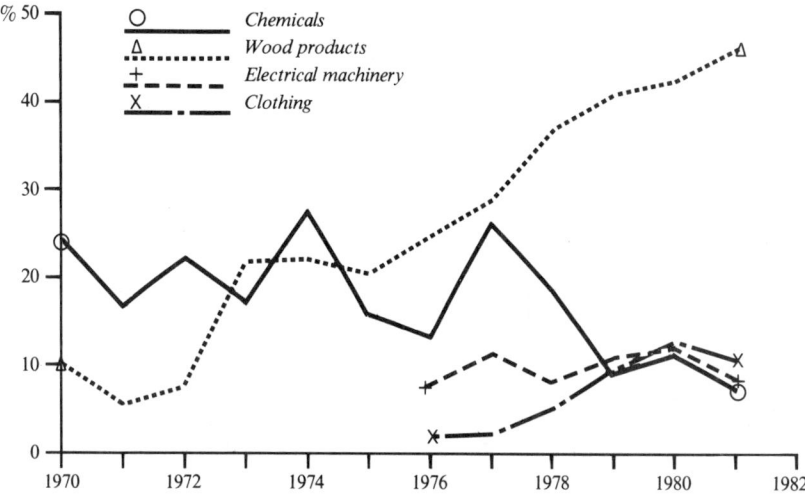

Sources: United Nations, *Yearbook of International Trade Statistics*, Volume I, New York, various issues; United Nations, *Yearbook of Industrial Statistics*, Volume I, New York, various issues.

Chapter 10. Table 11.2 follows this classification and provides data on the structure of manufactured exports.

In 1975, no less than 90.3 per cent of total manufactured export earnings was contributed by NRB sectors, among which petroleum refining was the dominant sector, followed by food-processing industries and non-ferrous basic industries. NRB sectors exported 8.2 per cent of their production on average. The export-output ratio of non-NRB production appears to be as low as 1.2 per cent. Only three non-NRB sectors show a higher export orientation, i.e. chemicals, machinery and electrical appliances, and other manufacturing. Due to the predominance of exports of petroleum products, total manufactured exports are produced with substantially less labour than average manufacturing production, in terms of both the direct and the total labour coefficient. The share of labour-intensive products in total manufactured exports is only 3.3 per cent. In comparing the direct and total labour coefficients for total exports exclusive of petroleum products, one sees

TABLE 11.2
CHARACTERISTICS OF MAJOR PRODUCTION AND EXPORT CATEGORIES, INDONESIAN MANUFACTURING SECTOR, 1975

Category	E/O	E/E_m	l^e	T^e	Share of labour-intensive products	VA/L	GP/L	s	Share of wages & salaries in gross value added
	(%)	(%)	(per 10⁹ Rps. output)		(%)	(10³ Rps.)	(10³ Rps.)	(10³ Rps.)	(%)
Total manufactured exports[1]	—	100	241	871	3.3	—	—	—	—
		(32.1)	(655)	(2,359)	(10.3)				
Total manufacturing production	5.2	—	933	3,218	—	334.8	227.3	107.5	32.1
NRB manufactured exports[1]	—	90.3	179	788	.2	—	—	—	—
		(22.4)	(587)	(2,672)	(1.1)				
NRB manufacturing production	8.2	—	629	3,894	—	434.1	326.5	107.6	24.8
Exports from E sectors	—	6.8	592	1,366	3.2	—	—	—	—
Production in E sectors	4.8	—	906	1,722	—	373.1	235.0	138.1	37.0
Exports from DMO sectors	—	2.9	1,331	2,269	97.9	—	—	—	—
Production in DMO sectors	.4	—	1,443	2,416	—	257.9	154.6	103.3	40.1

For explanation of symbols, see Section 10.4.

Note : [1] Figures in parentheses refer to exports exclusive of petroleum products.

Source : see Appendix to Chapter 11.

that the average labour requirements of exports are still lower than for manufacturing in total. Thus we find that Indonesia's manufactured exports are relatively capital intensive.

As to the three different export categories, a systematic pattern is discernible; according to both the direct and total labour coefficients, exports are less labour intensive than the corresponding total production categories. NRB exports have the lowest labour requirements, also if petroleum products are excluded. However, it is striking to note that exports from E sectors require less labour than exports from DMO sectors. Moreover, exports from E sectors consist for only 3.2 per cent of labour-intensive products. These results clearly indicate that Indonesia's specialization pattern has been inconsistent with the comparative advantage doctrine. In conformity with this finding, value added and gross profit per employee in E sectors is higher, and the share of wages and salaries in total value added is lower than in DMO sectors. Given the fact that the average wage rate in E sectors is about one third higher than in DMO sectors, Indonesia's manufactured exports are certainly not concentrated in low-wage sectors. Contrary to the current specialization pattern in South-East Asian countries, it is typical for the Indonesian case that the labour-intensive textile and clothing sectors could not be classified as E sectors, at least not in 1975, displaying an average export-output ratio of 0.3 per cent. It is to be expected that the recent changes in the composition of manufactured exports, i.e. the rise of clothing and wood products and the relative fall of chemicals, have increased the average labour intensity of Indonesia's manufactured exports. The manufacture of wood products, classified as a NRB activity, is extremely labour intensive (see Table A.11.1).

The set of rank correlations between seven sector characteristics, presented in Table 11.3, supports our findings. First, we observe that no inconsistencies are found in the ranking of sectors according to different measures of factor intensity and average wage level; all correlation coefficients are statistically significant at the 1 per cent level. Second, it is found that the most export-oriented sectors largely coincide with the most dominant sectors in total manufactured exports. Third, there appear to be no significant relationships between, on the one hand, sectoral rankings according to export orientation, and on the other hand, sectoral rankings according to measures of factor intensity and average wage rates. Moreover, from the angle of the comparative advantage doctrine, the correlation coefficients bear the wrong sign, indicating that a higher export-output ratio tends to be associated with a lower labour intensity and a higher wage level. Finally, it is remarkable to find almost identical sets of relationships, irrespective of whether NRB sectors are excluded or not.

TABLE 11.3
MATRIX OF SPEARMAN RANK CORRELATION COEFFICIENTS FOR SECTOR CHARACTERISTICS, INDONESIA, 1975[1,2]

Variable	E_i/O_i	E_i/E_m	l_i^e	VA_i/L_i	GP_i/L_i	T_i^e	s_i
E_i/O_i	1	.88**	−.22	.28	.24	−.24	.28
		.93**	−.27	.24	.25	−.31	.31
E_i/E_m		1	−.25	.22	.17	−.07	.28
			−.35	.28	.32	−.39	.37
l_i^e			1	−.86**	−.87**	.62**	−.76**
				−.95**	−.93**	.98**	−.92**
VA_i/L_i				1	.99**	−.81**	.81**
					.98**	−.95**	.90**
GP_i/L_i					1	−.81**	.75**
						−.95**	.85**
T_i^e						1	−.73**
							−.87**
s_i							1

For explanation of symbols, see Section 10.4.

Notes : [1] The upper coefficients in a row refer to rankings of all manufacturing sectors (n = 24), the lower coefficients refer to rankings of non-NRB sectors only (n = 11).
[2] Correlation coefficients that are significant at the 5 per cent level are denoted by one asterisk (*), those significant at the 1 per cent level by two asterisks (**).

Source : see Appendix to Chapter 11.

11.5 SPREAD EFFECTS OF INDONESIAN MANUFACTURED EXPORTS

Table 11.4 shows the spread effects of manufactured exports in the Indonesian economy. The production stimuli generated by total manufactured exports have about the same relative extent as manufacturing in total, as is indicated by the P values of 1.20 for both total manufactured exports and total manufacturing production. This holds, both inclusive and exclusive of petroleum exportables. It will be clear that NRB exports show the highest P value. Although the P values for non-NRB exports are well above 1, it is striking that exports from E sectors perform a less integrating function than those from DMO sectors.

As expected, the net foreign-exchange earnings per unit of NRB exports are high, namely 0.92. The values of the index $NFEE$ for non-NRB exports are substantially lower: 0.66 for exports from E sectors and 0.70 for exports from DMO sectors. It is already established that non-NRB production is still rather dependent on imports of intermediates. Now it appears that this is all the more so for production in E sectors. Thus, Indonesia's non-NRB specialization pattern is not only biased towards capital-intensive exportables, it also results in relatively limited production spread effects as manufacturing activities go.

The production stimuli generated by export production are still above the economy's average, but the employment spread effects are extremely meagre. The P^E value for total manufactured exports is as low as 0.28. If the capital-intensive petroleum products are excluded, these employment spread effects become relatively more extensive. Still, the employment generation per unit of exports lags behind that of total manufacturing production.

It is striking that non-oil NRB exports show such a poor performance in employment generation. In general, the processing of primary products requires relatively little labour. In the case of Indonesia, moreover, non-ferrous basic metal products occupy more than half of the non-oil NRB exports and the processing of these metals takes place with highly capital-intensive methods.

Non-NRB exports, most notably exports from E sectors, display P^E values far below 1. The capital-intensive specialization pattern of Indonesia's manufactured exports is herewith clearly reflected. Add to this the relatively high import dependence of E sectors, and it is clear that exports from exactly these sectors generate the fewest employment opportunities. Accordingly, E sectors also show the lowest spending effects of wage income on production and employment in the rest of the economy. As Table A.11.2 indicates, the export of machinery and electrical appliances is especially responsible for the poor performance in terms of spread effects. Exclusion of employment linkages to

TABLE 11.4
WEIGHTED AVERAGE MEASURES OF SPREAD EFFECTS FOR MAJOR CATEGORIES OF EXPORTS AND PRODUCTION, INDONESIAN MANUFACTURING SECTOR, 1975

Category	P	$NFEE$	P^E	P^{E-A}	WIM	WIM^E (per 10^9 Rps. output)
Total manufactured exports[1]	1.20 (1.20)	.90 (.82)	.28 (.76)	.49 (1.27)	.12 (.23)	1,438 (3,416)
NRB exports[1]	1.21 (1.24)	.92 (.88)	.25 (.86)	.42 (1.30)	.11 (.22)	1,296 (3,700)
Exports from E sectors	1.09	.66	.44	.97	.23	2,401
Exports from DMO sectors	1.14	.70	.73	1.78	.29	3,599
Total manufacturing production	1.20	.83	1.04	1.20	.26	4,393
NRB production	1.25	.92	1.26	.78	.23	4,954
Non-NRB production	1.14	.70	.74	1.76	.29	3,627

For explanation of symbols, see Section 10.4.
Note : [1] Figures in parentheses refer to exports exclusive of petroleum products.
Source : see Appendix to Chapter 11.

the agricultural sector results in a better performance in employment generation of non-NRB sectors. However, the P^{E-A} value for exports from E sectors is still below 1, again an indication of the relatively capital-intensive character of Indonesia's export production. Surprisingly enough, NRB exports exclusive of petroleum products display the rather high P^{E-A} value of 1.30. This high value can also be explained by the predominance of non-ferrous metal products in non-oil NRB exports, as the mining of these metals is a labour-intensive activity in Indonesia.

The rank order correlations between sectoral export-output ratios, direct labour coefficients, average wage rates and six measures of spread effects, which are summarized in the first row of Table 11.5, reveal no significant relationships, irrespective of whether NRB sectors are excluded or not. The following relationships could indeed be established. First, a higher labour intensity and a lower average wage rate are strongly associated with higher employment spread effects. Second, there is a weaker, but still significant at the 1 per cent level, positive relationship between the spread effects in terms of production and employment. This relationship has much to do with the employment linkages to the agricultural sector. If these are excluded, or if the ranking is restricted to non-NRB sectors only, this relationship is still positive but ceases to be statistically significant. Removing NRB sectors does improve the relationship between P and WIM. This implies that the supposed close relationship between a high level of backward linkages and a high indirect wage component in production is not automatically translated into a high level of employment generation. In the case of non-NRB sectors, this automatism is invalidated by the highly capital-intensive nature of some production processes, most notably chemicals and rubber processing. Note, finally, that the positive correlation coefficients for the rankings of non-NRB sectors by l^e versus P and l^e versus $NFEE$ indeed suggest a positive relationship between labour intensity and production spread effects, although this correlation is not strong enough to be statistically significant.

It is of interest to look for alternative exportables that would show a better record of spread effects. In the first place, exports of wood products would best meet the objective of maximum spread effects. The processing of wood is an extremely labour-intensive activity, the domestic value-added component is close to 90 per cent and the P value is as high as 1.22 (see Table A.11.1). Of the non-NRB products, textiles, leather products, wearing apparel and non-metallic mineral products show the most favourable record of spread effects (see Table A.11.3).

11.6 SUMMARY

The analysis in this country study indicates that Indonesia's pronounced

TABLE 11.5

MATRIX OF SPEARMAN RANK CORRELATION COEFFICIENTS FOR SECTOR CHARACTERISTICS AND VARIOUS MEASURES OF SPREAD EFFECTS, INDONESIA, 1975[1,2]

Variable	E_i/O_i	l_i^e	s_i	P_i	$NFEE_i$	P_i^E	P_i^{E-A}	WIM_i	WIM_i^E
E_i/O_i	1	−.22	.28	.15	−.02	−.24	−.24	−.15	−.26
		−.27	.31	.05	−.40	−.31	−.25	−.03	−.29
l_i^e		1	−.76**	−.08	−.27	.62**	.88**	.59**	.62**
			−.92**	.34	.31	.98**	.99**	.67*	.95**
s_i			1	−.29	.12	−.73**	−.77**	−.26	−.70**
				−.25	−.12	−.87**	−.88**	−.45	−.83**
P_i				1	.27	.55**	.13	.25	.54**
					−.05	.34	.33	.71*	.45
$NFEE$					1	.21	−.30	−.06	.19
						.35	.33	.33	.38
P_i^E						1	.68**	.65**	.99**
							.99**	.75*	.98**
P_i^{E-A}							1	.61**	.69**
								.73*	.96**
WIM_i								1	.72**
									.84**

For explanation of symbols, see Section 10.4.

Notes: [1] The upper coefficients in a row refer to rankings of all manufacturing sectors (n = 24), the lower coefficients refer to rankings of non-NRB sectors only (n = 11).
[2] Correlation coefficients that are significant at the 5 per cent level are denoted by one asterisk (*), those significant at the 1 per cent level by two asterisks (**).

Source: see Appendix to Chapter 11.

inward-looking industrialization strategy, facilitated by a large domestic market and an ample endowment of natural resources, has been biased against the export of labour-intensive manufactures. Clearly, the rationale for exporting processed natural resources is found in the increase in domestic value added and hence higher receipts of foreign exchange. Except for wood products, however, this strategy contributes little to employment generation. But no rationale can be found in Indonesia's specialization pattern of non-NRB exports. On average, non-NRB export production generates substantially less employment than production for the domestic market. This holds true whether only direct employment or indirect and secondary employment effects are considered.

Moreover, the analysis reveals that, on average, the capital-intensive exports from E sectors show a higher dependency on imported inputs and contribute less to the integration of the economy than the labour-intensive production of DMO sectors. These findings clearly illustrate that, by 1975, Indonesia was still in an early stage of industrialization. For that stage, the specialization pattern of non-NRB manufactured exports is perverse.

APPENDIX TABLE A.11.1
CHARACTERISTICS OF MANUFACTURING SECTORS CLASSIFIED AS NRB SECTORS, INDONESIA, 1975

I-O Code	Sector	E_i/O_i (%)	E_i/E_m (%)	f_i^e (per 10⁹ Rps. output)	T_i^e (per 10⁹ Rps. output)	VA_i/L_i	GP_i/L_i (10³ Rps.)	s_i	P_i	$NFEE_i$	P_i^E	P_i^{E-A}	WIM_i	WIM_i^E (per 10⁹ Rps. output)
27	Processing and preserving of foods	.9	.2	451	1,884	594	530	63	1.38	.85	.61	.93	.17	2,670
28	Oil and fats	16.1	4.3	431	2,873	341	290	131	1.38	.88	.93	.76	.26	4,051
29	Rice milling and polishing	.3	1.2	431	5,931	382	226	156	1.31	.97	1.92	.46	.28	7,223
30	Wheat flour and other grain mill products	.1	.1	431	3,963	577	473	104	1.41	.90	1.28	1.06	.20	4,854
31	Sugar refinery	2.5	1.3	431	1,266	1,342	1,088	253	1.05	.91	.41	.59	.24	2,356
32	Food products n.e.c.	1.7	1.7	756	5,803	378	289	89	1.26	.90	1.88	.91	.22	6,790
33	Beverage industries	.2	.0	494	1,013	1,327	1,141	187	.96	.90	.33	.75	.19	1,868
34	Cigarettes	.1	.1	149	1,133	2,690	2,488	202	1.12	.83	.37	.43	.18	1,962
37	Wood and wood products	.5	.2	6,342	7,560	57	28	29	1.22	.89	2.45	5.97	.38	9,300
38	Paper and paper products and printing	2.4	1.1	458	1,161	1,053	685	369	1.08	.82	.38	.84	.32	2,609
41	Petroleum refinery	50.9	67.9	44	166	6,107	5,402	705	1.20	.94	.05	.12	.07	502
45	Iron and steel basic industries	.8	.0	558	1,025	523	413	110	.98	.56	.33	.82	.14	1,677
46	Non-ferrous basic metal industries	6.3	12.1	558	2,081	632	515	117	1.22	.87	.67	1.68	.20	2,982

APPENDIX TABLE A.11.2
CHARACTERISTICS OF MANUFACTURING SECTORS CLASSIFIED AS E SECTORS, INDONESIA, 1975

I-O Code	Sector	E_i/O_i (%)	E_i/E_m (%)	t_i^e (per 10^9 Rps. output)	T_i^e (per 10^9 Rps. output)	VA_i/L_i	GP_i/L_i (10^3 Rps.)	s_i	P_i	$NFEE_i$	P_i^E	$P_i^{E\cdot A}$	WIM_i	WIM_i^E (per 10^9 Rps. output)
40	Chemical industries	4.6	3.8	499	1,408	598	379	220	1.18	.67	.46	.92	.25	2,550
48	Machinery and electrical appliances	6.1	2.8	397	968	315	197	118	.97	.64	.31	.76	.17	1,760
50	Other manufacturing	1.5	.2	4,794	5,869	84	14	70	1.12	.79	1.90	4.62	.52	8,236

APPENDIX TABLE A.11.3
CHARACTERISTICS OF MANUFACTURING SECTORS CLASSIFIED AS DMO SECTORS, INDONESIA, 1975

I-O Code	Sector	E_i/O_i (%)	E_i/E_m (%)	t_i^e (per 10^9 Rps. output)	T_i^e (per 10^9 Rps. output)	VA_i/L_i	GP_i/L_i (10^3 Rps.)	s_i	P_i	$NFEE_i$	P_i^E	$P_i^{E\cdot A}$	WIM_i	WIM_i^E (per 10^9 Rps. output)
35	Spinning industries	.0	.0	1,078	1,981	257	159	98	1.06	.63	.64	1.31	.24	3,084
36	Textile, leather and wearing apparel	.3	.7	1,801	3,005	186	102	84	1.27	.71	.99	2.35	.34	4,589
39	Fertilizer industries	.3	.0	123	458	5,712	4,946	766	.89	.89	.15	.36	.17	1,214
42	Rubber products	.1	.0	414	1,442	964	693	271	1.26	.79	.47	.88	.30	2,796
43	Non-metallic mineral product industries	.0	.0	2,712	3,827	197	84	113	1.04	.90	1.24	2.92	.48	6,009
44	Cement	.0	.0	2,712	3,408	202	164	38	1.04	.87	1.10	2.73	.22	4,424
47	Prefabricated metal products	.5	.4	1,001	1,624	315	197	118	1.00	.59	.53	1.30	.22	2,614
49	Manufacture and repair of transport equipment	.6	1.8	1,240	2,128	304	186	118	1.12	.71	.69	1.69	.29	3,452

For explanation of symbols, see Section 10.4.
Source: computations are based on data from *Tabel Input-Output Indonesia 1975*, Volumes IIA and IIB, Biro Pusat Statistik, Jakarta, 1980.

12
The Case of the Philippines

12.1 INTRODUCTORY REMARKS

The Philippine archipelago covers 300,000 km² of land area. With a population of 48.4 million in 1980, the average density of population equals 161 persons per km². Thus, the Philippines is a not very densely populated middle-large country. Moreover, the country is amply endowed with natural wealth. It has vast resources of forest and large amounts of deposits in various kinds of metallic and non-metallic mineral ores.

The postwar growth of the Philippine economy has been moderate. From 1950 to 1960, the average annual growth rate of real GDP *per capita* was 3.3 per cent, from 1960 to 1970 1.9 per cent and from 1970 to 1980 3.2 per cent. Available evidence suggests that this performance can mainly be attributed to industrialization policies adopted during the period. The 1950s represent the heyday of import substitution, whereas the slowdown of growth in the 1960s can be imputed to the exhaustion of the domestic market. The shift to a more export-oriented strategy of industrialization in the early 1970s marked again the beginning of a decade of better growth performance.

The base year of our analysis is 1974. By that year the Philippines ranked among the middle-income economies with a GNP *per capita* of US$340.[1]

12.2 INDUSTRIALIZATION AND TRADE STRATEGIES IN THE PHILIPPINES

From 1950 onwards, import substitution has been the principal policy instrument to promote industrialization in the Philippines.[2] Initially, this strategy relied on a strict regime of controls on imports and foreign exchange to relieve the pressure on the balance of payments. The import regime was aimed at a sharp import reduction of so-called non-essential products, which were identified as nondurable consumer goods. Hence, the high average annual growth rate of manufacturing production of 12.1 per cent from 1950 to 1955 was mainly realized by the domestic production of substitutes for consumer goods.[3] The domestic production of intermediate and capital goods was not stimulated. Imports of these essential products were in fact subsidized, as they could be obtained at an overvalued exchange rate. By the late 1950s, the domestic market started to impose serious limitations on further expansion. As a result, the manufacturing growth rate slowed down to 7.7 per cent per annum from 1955 to 1960. Moreover, the balance-of-payment problems persisted due to the heavy import dependency of the new industries. This state of affairs prompted the authorities to carry through a number of policy reforms in the early 1960s, the most important of which were a gradual replacement of the strict import regime by a tariff system and the imposition of a more realistic exchange rate. However, these reforms did not bring about a different incentive structure. The tariff protection that took the place of import controls was characterized by a clear cascading structure whereby higher tariff rates were imposed on imports of products with higher degrees of processing. Thus, final, mainly nondurable consumer goods industries enjoyed the highest protection rates, those producing intermediate and capital goods the lowest. Consequences of this incentive structure were the inability to foster the growth of intermediate industries and to produce for export markets.[4] These two outlets for continued manufacturing growth largely being shut off, there was, as a result, a further reduction of the average annual manufacturing growth rate to 5.3 per cent during the decade of the 1960s.

In addition to the sluggish manufacturing growth, once again the Philippines was faced with severe balance-of-payments problems in the late 1960s. These developments induced a number of policy devices to intensify industrial promotion efforts and, moreover, to actively promote exports of manufactures. The Industrial Incentives Act of 1967 provided a new package of incentives, mainly in the form of tax privileges, for industrial investments. Together with this Act, the Board of Investment (BOI) was created. The BOI formulates investment priority plans and administers the granting of incentives. So-called pioneer projects are eligible for additional benefits. For the first time, the 1967 Act provided some assistance to export production. Manufactured export products were allowed tax credits on duties on imported materials and supplies, which eased their importation and reduced the cost for exporting firms. In addition, shipping costs and promotional expenses for exports were made doubly deductible from taxable income.

It was, however, both the floating of the exchange rate in 1970 and the enactment of the Export Incentives Act in 1971 which truly signalled the shift in official policy towards export of manufactures. The floating of the domestic currency meant a *de facto* devaluation of more than 60 per cent in 1970. The Export Incentives Act extends the various tax incentives to all exports of manufactures that are registered with the BOI and exempts manufactured exports from export taxes. Moreover, extra fiscal benefits of export-oriented firms were introduced. These involve mainly the possibility of tax and duty-free importation of capital equipment and spare parts and the duty-free importation of intermediates used in the production of exports. Duty-free importation of inputs is effected through a drawback scheme that refunds the tariffs paid or through the permission for BOI-registered firms to operate under bonded warehouse arrangements. The purpose of these facilities is, of course, to reduce the cost of inputs and increase the competitiveness of exports. Some measures have also come into force to reduce the cost of domestically produced inputs. The Export Incentives Act provided tax credits for taxes paid on domestic capital equipment and intermediate inputs. In 1973, the cost of local raw materials was made deductible up to a maximum of 25 per cent of export revenue.

In line with and in addition to the export promotion programme, an EPFZ was established at the tip of Bataan province in 1972, and others have been planned. Companies located in the Bataan EPFZ enjoy a clear advantage over exporting companies outside the zone.[5] Apart from better infrastructural provisions, the main incentives to companies in the zone are: net operating loss carry-over, accelerated depreciation, exemption from local taxes and licences and a simplified import-export procedure. The latter assures, among others, releases of all imports of capital equipment, spare parts and intermediates within 48 hours, duty and tax free. Moreover, the zone has no restrictions on foreign ownership. Labour disputes affecting any industry located inside the zone are to be settled immediately through application of compulsory arbitration.

During the 1970s, several amendments to this export-incentive programme were made. Some of these reduced or eliminated incentives granted earlier, such as the abolishment of the double deduction of shipping costs and export-promotion expenses, others meant a further liberalizing of the above-mentioned incentives. Basically, the export-incentive programme remained intact. Meanwhile, the import-substitution regime was carried through with the same vigour. The 1970 devaluation was not accompanied by a marked trade liberalization. In 1973, a new and simplified tariff code took effect, but this also did not usher in a more liberal trade era. In fact, the balance-of-payment position determined the strictness of the import regime throughout the 1970s. Consequently, the level of protection for the domestic market is high and has remained so since the mid-1960s. The pattern of effective protection in 1974 favoured manufacturing over agriculture and mining. Within manufacturing, consumer goods enjoyed, on average, effective protection rates of 77 per cent. The cascading structure is evident by the lower effective protection afforded to the intermediate goods and capital goods sectors, namely 23 and 18 per cent, respectively. By contrast, exportables frequently receive negative protection. If, however, exporting firms benefit from the free-trade regime, the price-raising effect of protection on intermediate inputs is bypassed and these firms receive in effect a zero protection.[6]

It is important to note that the new export-promotion policies of the early 1970s did not lead to a full turn-around towards an export-oriented industrialization strategy. In fact, a dualistic industrialization and trade regime is pursued: Philippine manufacturing is still an import-substitution activity, with, in addition, a subsidy regime to neutralize the penalty that tariff protection imposes on exports. During the 1970s, the manufacturing sector showed again a stronger performance with an average annual growth rate of production of 7.0 per cent. Until the early 1980s, the industrialization and trade strategy remained essentially intact. From that time, however, some major policy reforms are being implemented to improve Philippine manufacturing capability. These reforms mainly refer to a gradual reduction and rationalization of tariff rates and improvements in export incentives. Moreover, a number of new EPFZs will be established.[7]

12.3 STRUCTURAL FEATURES OF THE PHILIPPINE ECONOMY

The Philippines have a relatively long history of industrialization. Therefore, by 1974, the manufacturing sector had already assumed an important place in the economy with shares in total gross output and GDP of 41.0 and 25.2 per cent, respectively (see Table 12.1). By contrast, in the same year only 9.7 per cent of the total labour force was employed in the manufacturing sector, indicating that this sector is relatively capital intensive in the context of the national economy. This is also evident from the direct labour coefficient for the manufacturing sector, which is considerably lower than for the primary sector, construction and services. Only the direct labour requirements per unit of production in utilities are lower. Consequently, value added per employee in manufacturing is roughly 5 times higher than in primary sectors and twice that in construction and services.

It is true that underemployment is a dominant phenomenon in primary and tertiary sectors, resulting in an overestimation of the labour intensiveness of these sectors. But in the Philippines this is equally true of the manufacturing sector which exhibits a dualism. According to our estimates, manufacturing establishments employing 5 or more workers produced nearly two thirds of total value added in manufacturing in 1974, whereas this organized sector employed only about 44 per cent of the manufacturing labour force. Our

TABLE 12.1
BASIC DATA ON THE STRUCTURE OF
THE PHILIPPINE ECONOMY, 1974

Indicators	Agriculture & Mining	Manufacturing	Construction	Utilities	Services
1. Share in total gross output (%)	22.9	41.0	4.9	1.2	30.0
2. Share in GDP (%)	32.1	25.2	4.3	1.1	37.3
3. Share in total employment (%)	58.9	9.7	3.4	.2	27.8
4. Export-output ratio (%)	18.0	14.3	.1	.0	11.8
5. Share in total exports (%)	30.5	43.2	.2	.0	26.1
6. Share in intermediate imports (%)	8.0	76.4	7.5	.8	7.3
7. Input structure					
— Domestic intermediate inputs	.14	.49	.35	.41	.18
— Imported intermediate inputs	.03	.15	.12	.05	.02
— Gross value added	.83	.36	.53	.54	.80
Total inputs	1.00	1.00	1.00	1.00	1.00
8. $NFEE$	.96	.81	.83	.89	.96
9. P	.82	1.14	1.05	1.12	.86
10. P^E	2.05	.86	.81	.45	.83
11. P^{E-A}	.10	.75	1.58	.70	1.86
12. WIM^E (per 10^6 Pesos output)	264.9	124.2	128.2	80.2	136.7
13. I^e (per 10^6 Pesos output)	193.9	17.7	53.0	12.3	69.8
14. VA/L (Pesos)	4,287	20,568	10,005	43,555	11,443
15. T^e (per 10^6 Pesos output)	212.7	88.8	84.4	47.1	86.1
16. s (Pesos)	1,648	4,999	3,961	9,658	4,258

For explanation of symbols, see Section 10.4.
Sources: see Appendix to Chapter 12.

estimate most likely understates employment in cottage industries. Some estimates arrive at a share of these industries in manufacturing employment of more than two thirds.[8] It will be clear that the organized manufacturing sector employs relatively capital-intensive methods of production. The average manufacturing wage rate is therefore one of the highest in the economy.

Available evidence suggests that the bias towards large-scale and capital-intensive manufacturing is a consequence of the postwar industrial incentive structure.[9] The import control policies of the 1950s created, through a sudden opening of a protected market, profitable opportunities for relatively large investments of capital. And being established, large-scale firms have found it easier to argue their interests with the authorities, which improved their growth record. Moreover, the BOI incentives as such make capital-intensive techniques artificially more attractive by lowering the cost of capital relative to that of labour.

The primary sectors show a higher outward orientation than the manufacturing sector. Copper, ore and logs constitute the bulk of primary exports. Yet, manufactures accounted for a larger share in total exports of goods and services, i.e. 43.2 per cent in 1974. However, in 1974 more than 70 per cent of these manufactured exports consisted of only two processed primary products: sugar and coconut oil.

Philippine manufacturing production is dominated by NRB products, accounting for 73.7 per cent in 1974. Of that, the mere share of food manufactures, beverages and tobacco products was close to two thirds. Consequently, there is a strong linkage between the primary sector and manufacturing. Nearly half of the domestic intermediates entering manufacturing production originates in primary sectors. The average production linkages emanating from the manufacturing sector, measured by the value of P, are clearly above the economy's average, i.e. 1.14. Contrarily, the 26.5 percentage share of manufacturing production that is not natural-resource based shows a relatively high dependence on imported inputs. The manufacturing sector accounts for more than three quarters of the economy's total import of intermediates.

On average, the manufacturing sector has the lowest domestic value-added component in production. This reflects the limited capacity of Philippine manufacturing to produce intermediates for non-NRB industries. Again, the postwar protection system is held responsible for this structural feature. The prevailing incentive system is biased towards the production of substitutes for consumer goods at the finishing stages, whilst imports of intermediates are in fact subsidized. This impaired the development of intermediate industries and stimulated the growth of an import-dependent non-NRB manufacturing sector.

Given its relatively capital-intensive character, it is explicable that the employment spread effects of manufacturing production are relatively small, as follows from the low P^E value of 0.86. The WIM^E value for manufacturing production is less than half that of primary production, and slightly less than the WIM^E values for construction and services. Considering that these measures include the employment spread effects to the labour-intensive agricultural sector, it is not surprising to find a P^{E-A} value for manufacturing of 0.75. The P^{E-A} values for construction and services, of 1.58 and 1.86 respectively, contrast favourably with that of manufacturing.

12.4 DEVELOPMENT AND STRUCTURE OF PHILIPPINE MANUFACTURED EXPORTS

In the second half of the 1970s, Philippine exports of manufactures expanded markedly. As is shown in Figure 12.1, the share of manufactures in total exports increased from about 10 to almost 30 per cent. The increasing significance of exports for the manufacturing sector is also seen in the gradually enlarging share of products exported. Figure 12.2 reveals that there has been a substantial shift in manufactured exports towards electronic equipment and components. The rapid expansion of these exports has led to a share in total manufactured exports of nearly one third by 1980. The export growth of clothing, handicrafts and food products and beverages slightly lagged behind the impressive performance of electronics exports. The concentration of manufactured exports in only the four mentioned products is also evident, contributing almost three quarters of total manufactured exports.

One reason for the much improved performance of Philippine manufactured exports has been the reduced discrimination against export production due to the policy package adopted in the early 1970s, most notably the establishment of the Bataan EPFZ. From 1974, the year in which exports from the zone got well under way, to 1979, exports doubled

Figure 12.1
Manufactured Export Performance of the Philippines, 1970-1980

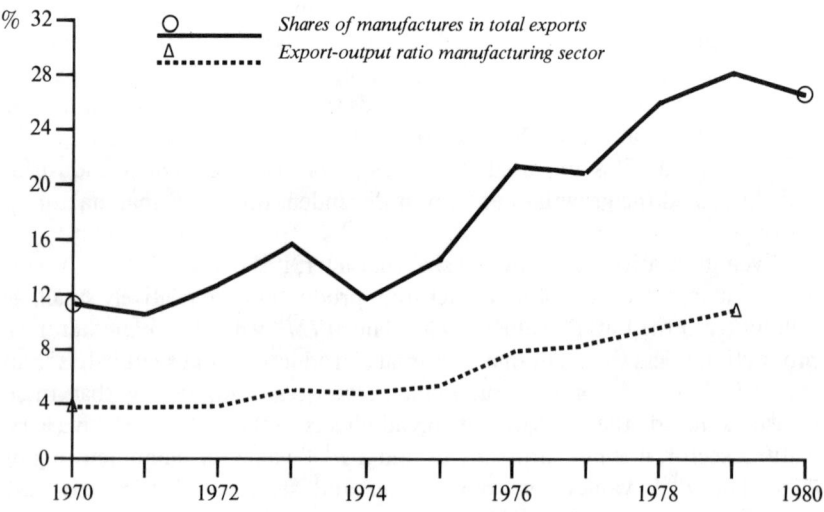

Figure 12.2
Composition of Philippine Manufactured Exports, 1970-1980
(percentage shares)

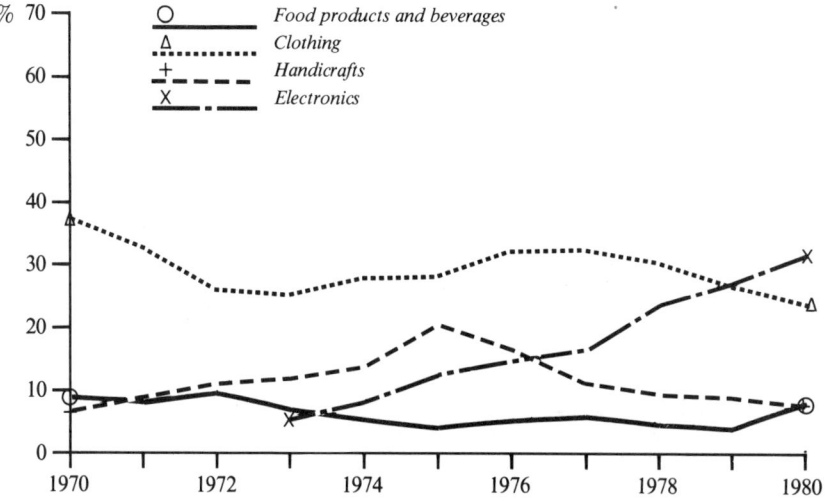

Sources: United Nations, *Yearbook of International Trade Statistics*, Volume I, New York, various issues; NEDA, *1981 Philippine Statistical Yearbook*, Manila; United Nations, *Yearbook of Industrial Statistics*, Volume I, New York, various issues.

every year on average. By 1979, it is reported that US$277 million worth of exports were produced at the Bataan location, accounting then for 18.2 per cent of total manufactured exports.[10] Clothing and electronics constitute the bulk of exports from Bataan EPFZ. As of the base year of our analysis, 1974, exports from Bataan EPFZ were still negligible.

Before we turn to the structure of Philippine manufactured exports, it should be noted that the classification of tradables by industrial origin, as results from the application of the 1974 input-output table, implies a much broader definition of manufactured exports than the one used for Figures 12.1 and 12.2. The most notable difference is the inclusion of sugar refining as a manufacturing activity. Traditionally, refined sugar is an important exportable for the Philippines, accounting for 44.2 per cent of total manufactured exports, broadly defined, in 1974.

As Table 12.2 indicates, according to the 1974 input-output table, Philippine manufactured exports consisted for 90.7 per cent of NRB products. On average, primary product processing industries also show a

TABLE 12.2
CHARACTERISTICS OF MAJOR PRODUCTION AND EXPORT CATEGORIES, THE PHILIPPINE MANUFACTURING SECTOR, 1974

Category	E/O (%)	E/E_m (%)	l^e	T^e	Share of labour-intensive products (%)	VA/L (Pesos)	GP/L (Pesos)	s (Pesos)	Share of wages & salaries in gross value added (%)
			(per 10⁶ Pesos output)						
Total manufactured exports	—	100	19.9	114.1	46.6	—	—	—	—
Total manufacturing production	14.3	—	17.7	90.8	—	20,568	15,569	4,999	24.3
NRB manufactured exports	—	91.7	19.0	119.8	43.9	—	—	—	—
NRB manufacturing production	17.7	—	15.2	107.6	—	22,880	17,764	5,122	22.4
Exports from E sectors	—	7.4	31.1	52.4	76.0	—	—	—	—
Production in E sectors	8.8	—	30.2	52.0	—	12,184	8,673	3,511	28.8
Exports from DMO sectors	—	0.9	20.0	40.8	70.5	—	—	—	—
Production in DMO sectors	0.9	—	20.6	37.3	—	21,982	15,637	6,346	28.9

For explanation of symbols, see Section 10.4.
Sources: see Appendix to Chapter 12.

higher export orientation than non-NRB industries, displaying export-output ratios of 17.7 and 4.5 per cent, respectively. This clearly reflects the Philippine's ample endowment of natural resources.

Total manufactured exports require per unit slightly more direct labour than manufacturing in total. This is due to the more labour-intensive composition of exports from NRB and E sectors compared with the average production of these sectors. This does not alter the fact that the average labour requirements per unit of E sector exports are almost two thirds higher than those of NRB exports. The production of many of the NRB exports is extremely capital intensive, sugar refining being the prime example.

Non-NRB exports are almost exclusively produced in E sectors. Footwear and wearing apparel rank among the most labour-intensive items, whereas the production of textiles, basic industrial chemicals, plastic materials, hydraulic cement and glass products requires per unit substantially less labour, as is shown in Table A.12.2. The figures in Table 12.2 also show a marked difference in factor intensity of production between E and DMO sectors. Production in E sectors requires not only half as much direct labour as DMO production, it also generates substantially less value added and gross profit per employee. In conformity herewith, E sectors display the lowest average wage level. Thus, manufactured exports of the Philippines are either resource based and relatively capital intensive, or non-resource based and, on average, relatively labour intensive. This is in line with the country's factor endowments. Of course, this pattern is clearly different in case the total labour requirements are used as a measure of factor intensity. Then, due to the high labour intensity of raw material input, the labour requirements of NRB exports amount to more than twice those of E sector exports.

The results of the rank order correlation analysis, summarized in Table 12.3, provide only weak support for the finding that the Philippines' specialization pattern tallies with its factor endowments. First, we observe that the most export-oriented sectors largely coincide with sectors that account for higher shares in total manufactured exports. Second, correlation coefficients between the rankings according to the different measures of factor intensity show the right signs and are all highly significant. But, third, the rank order relationships between sectoral export-output ratios, direct labour coefficients and value added and gross profit per employee have the expected signs but are statistically insignificant. Removing NRB sectors only improves the relationships between export-output ratios and the variables value added and gross profit per employee beyond the 5 per cent level of significance. By contrast, the rank order relationship between sectoral export-output ratios and total labour coefficients is positive and significant at the 1 per cent level. This is easily accounted for if the highly labour-intensive primary inputs in the more export-oriented NRB production are taken into account. This

TABLE 12.3
MATRIX OF SPEARMAN RANK CORRELATION COEFFICIENTS FOR SECTOR CHARACTERISTICS, THE PHILIPPINES, 1974[1,2]

Variable	E_i/O_i	E_i/E_m	I_i^e	VA_i/L_i	GP_i/L_i	T_i^e	s_i
E_i/O_i	1	.82**	.22	−.24	−.22	.38**	−.26*
		.84**	.28	−.35*	−.34*	.38*	−.41**
E_i/E_m		1	.05	−.18	−.16	.42**	−.21
			−.13	−.29	−.30	.34*	−.31*
I_i^e			1	−.77**	−.76**	.41**	−.67**
				−.83**	−.83**	.85**	−.74**
VA_i/L_i				1	.99**	−.66**	.89**
					.99**	−.86**	.92**
GP_i/L_i					1	−.66**	.83**
						−.85**	.85**
T_i^e						1	−.60**
							−.73**
s_i							1

For explanation of symbols, see Section 10.4.

Notes : [1] The upper coefficients in a row refer to rankings of all manufacturing sectors (n = 67), the lower coefficients refer to rankings of non-NRB sectors only (n = 42).
[2] Correlation coefficients that are significant at the 5 per cent level are denoted by one asterisk (*), those significant at the 1 per cent level by two asterisks (**).

Sources : see Appendix to Chapter 12.

relationship is, noteworthy enough, still significant at the 5 per cent level in case NRB sectors are excluded, implying that the domestically produced intermediates that enter E sectors tend to be relatively labour intensive. This finding is taken up in the next section.

Although a higher export-output ratio is not significantly related to a higher labour intensity, a relationship between sectoral export-output ratios and average wage levels proves to be significant at the 5 per cent level, and even at the 1 per cent level if NRB sectors are excluded. This is not as contradictory as it seems, for some relatively capital-intensive sectors which show relatively high export-output ratios nonetheless pay below average wages. A notable example is the preserving and canning of fruits and vegetables (see Table A.12.1). The stronger negative rank order relationship between sectoral export-output ratios and average wage level is the only firm indication of the Philippine effort to promote exports of manufactures by taking advantage of its surplus labour.

In sum, it emerges from our analysis of the structure of Philippine manufactured exports that, whilst, on average, non-NRB exports can be characterized as labour intensive, there has been no profound specialization in the most labour-intensive exportables, at least not by 1974. Most likely, this is due to the dualistic industrialization and trade strategies pursued by the Philippines during the 1970s, whereby the discrimination against exports is neutralized via subsidies. Under these conditions, the structure of exports will reflect the structure of import-substituting production. For that reason, sectors like textiles and hydraulic cement appear to be important E sectors, whereas these sectors definitely do not rank among the most labour-intensive ones of Philippine manufacturing (see Table A.12.2).

12.5 SPREAD EFFECTS OF PHILIPPINE MANUFACTURED EXPORTS

Table 12.4 sets out the relevant data on the spread effects of Philippine export production. As the share of NRB products in manufactured exports is higher than in total manufacturing production, the spread effects according to the measures P and $NFEE$ for total exports are higher than for manufacturing in total. Especially the net foreign-exchange earnings of NRB exports are impressive, amounting to 93 per cent of export receipts.

The P and $NFEE$ values of exports from E and DMO sectors display a disturbing picture at first sight. The production stimuli emanating from E sector exports are more extensive than those from DMO sectors, 1.15 versus 1.09, respectively, whilst, by contrast, the $NFEE$ value for E sector exports is lower than for DMO sectors, namely 0.72 versus 0.76, respectively. Thus, exports from E sectors show a higher import dependency as well as a higher

TABLE 12.4
WEIGHTED AVERAGE MEASURES OF SPREAD EFFECTS FOR MAJOR CATEGORIES OF EXPORT AND PRODUCTION, THE PHILIPPINES MANUFACTURING SECTOR, 1974

Category	P	NFEE	P^E	P^{E-A}	WIM	WIM^E (per 10^6 Pesos output)
Total manufactured exports	1.15	.91	1.25	.72	.39	159.4
NRB exports	1.15	.93	1.31	.68	.40	166.3
Exports from E sectors	1.15	.72	.57	1.20	.28	84.6
Exports from DMO sectors	1.09	.76	.45	.91	.29	75.1
Total manufacturing production	1.14	.80	.99	.74	.33	129.4
NRB production	1.16	.82	1.17	.64	.35	148.4
Non-NRB production	1.09	.72	.48	1.02	.28	76.1

For explanation of symbols, see Section 10.4.
Sources : see Appendix to Chapter 12.

level of spread effects in terms of production. This phenomenon can be attributed to a substantially lower share of value added in the value of production in E sectors compared to DMO sectors, viz. 36.8 versus 45.3 per cent, respectively. This feature is also reflected in the *WIM* value, which is slightly lower for exports from E sectors than for DMO sectors. The *NFEE* value for E sector exports is, however, certainly not exceptionally low, as it exactly equals the corresponding value for non-NRB production in general.

NRB exports exhibit the most extensive employment spread effects, as measured by their average P^E and WIM^E values of 1.31 and 166.3, respectively. Compared therewith, the record of employment generation by non-NRB exports is rather weak, displaying P^E values far below 1 and WIM^E values not half so high. If, however, the indirect employment in the agricultural sector is excluded from the employment effects, this picture reverses entirely. Now we see NRB exports displaying the lowest P^{E-A} value of 0.68 and it is once again confirmed that the processing of primary products generates relatively little employment opportunities. Again, the refining of sugar may serve as an example. As Table A.12.1 demonstrates, sugar milling and refining ranks among the sectors with the lowest direct labour coefficients, whereas the growing of sugar cane requires twenty times as much labour per unit of production. A special case is the export production of furniture and fixtures, and other wood, cane and cork products. These manufactures which partly belong to the category of handicrafts, are natural-resource based and yet require many hands in their manufacture.

As appeared, exports from E sectors are not only relatively labour intensive on average, but also show a stronger interrelatedness with other sectors of the economy. The employment spread effects of exports from E sectors are, therefore, on average more extensive than of DMO production. The P^{E-A} value for exports from E sectors is even 1.20. As Table A.12.2 reveals, from an employment policy point of view, exports of footwear, wearing apparel and leather products are optimal. These exportables show the best record for employment generation, production stimuli and foreign-exchange earnings. However, the import dependency of some E sectors is relatively high. The direct and indirect import content is the highest in textile, plastic materials, hydraulic cement and miscellaneous manufactures. Clearly, these products rank among the more capital-intensive exportables. As already mentioned, the production of intermediate goods was still underdeveloped in the mid-1970s, but the lower *NFEE* value for E sectors than for DMO sectors is most likely also associated with the 1970 export-promotion measure which facilitates duty-free import of inputs.

There is every reason to expect that the specific characteristics of the Philippines' export sector, viz. a high import dependency and a relatively low proportion of value added in the value of production, have aggravated as a result of the coming into operation of the Bataan EPFZ since 1974. An ILO-ARTEP study on the operation of this zone presents some supporting evidence. For five out of 56 firms operating in the zone by 1980, some reliable data could be obtained on operating accounts.[11] These data reveal extremely low shares of less than 8 per cent of value added in the value of production in three firms, and corresponding shares of 21 and 36 per cent in the remaining two firms. Value-added generation in all these EPFZ firms is lower than the average record for exports from E sectors. The direct import dependence of these firms is extremely high, averaging 54 per cent of the value of exports and ranging from 32 to 77 per cent. For comparison, intermediate imports entering E sectors directly accounted for 16 per cent of the export value in 1974. This case study provides a rather clear indication of the isolated character of the EPFZ-type of export production. In the Philippines, this production is heavily concentrated in low-skill assembly activities in garment industries, miscellaneous light manufactures and electronics. In terms of spread effects, garment exports from the Bataan EPFZ contrast particularly unfavourably with garments produced outside the zone. The record of spread effects of the latter is presented in Table A.12.2.

Finally, rank order correlations have been made, attempting to establish relationships between sectoral export-output ratios, measures of factor intensity and spread effects. The results, which are presented in Table 12.5, are on a par with our earlier findings. A higher export orientation is not significantly related to a higher labour intensity of production, but indeed a positive and significant relationship does exist between the export orientation of production and the employment spread effects that go along with that production. The latter relationship, measured by P^E and WIM^E is statistically significant at the 1 per cent level in case all sectors are included in the rankings, and still at the 5 per cent level for non-NRB sectors only. In other words, the indirect inputs entering export production are produced relatively labour intensive, clearly so with NRB exports, but also in the case of non-NRB exportables. It also appears that a higher export orientation is significantly associated with a higher level of production spread effects, measured by P. This relationship still holds at the 5 per cent level of significance for the rankings of non-NRB sectors only, reinforcing our finding as to the higher level of production spread effects of E sectors. As expected, the rank correlations between sectoral wage rates, on the one hand, and measures of employment spread effects on the other, are negative and significant at the 1 per cent level.

It is further interesting to note that labour-intensive products are less dependent on imported inputs. The rank order relationship between sectoral direct labour coefficients and *NFEE* values is positive and significant. Exclusion of NRB sectors even raises this correlation to a 1 per cent level of

TABLE 12.5
MATRIX OF SPEARMAN RANK CORRELATION COEFFICIENTS FOR SECTOR CHARACTERISTICS AND VARIOUS MEASURES OF SPREAD EFFECTS, THE PHILIPPINES, 1974[1,2]

Variable	E_i/O_i	l_i^e	s_i	P_i	$NFEE_i$	P_i^E	P_i^{E-A}	WIM_i	WIM_i^E
E_i/O_i	1	.22	−.26*	.33**	.29*	.38**	.16	.26*	.34**
		.28	−.41**	.37*	.09	.38*	.28	.18	.31*
l_i^e		1	−.67**	−.10	.28*	.41**	.95**	.35**	.41**
			−.74**	−.10	.50**	.85**	.96**	.59**	.81**
s_i			1	−.37**	−.23	−.60**	−.63**	−.24*	−.50**
				−.24	−.02	−.73**	−.75**	−.09	−.52**
P_i				1	.39**	.58**	−.03	.46**	.56**
					−.09	.25	.09	.11	.20
$NFEE_i$					1	.72**	.20	.78**	.76**
						.47**	.49**	.80**	.62**
P_i^E						1	.36**	.83**	.98**
							.92**	.65**	.95**
P_i^{E-A}							1	.31*	.36**
								.64**	.89**
WIM_i								1	.91**
									.83**
WIM_i^E									1

For explanation of symbols, see Section 10.4.

Notes : [1] The upper coefficients in a row refer to rankings of all manufacturing sectors (n = 67), the lower coefficients refer to rankings of non-NRB sectors only (n = 42).
[2] Correlation coefficients that are significant at the 5 per cent level are denoted by one asterisk (*), those significant at the 1 per cent level by two asterisks (**).

Sources : see Appendix to Chapter 12.

significance. At the same time, there appears to be a highly significant and positive rank order relationship between sectoral *NFEE* values and employment spread effects, implying that a higher domestic value-added component in production will benefit the creation of employment opportunities.

Unfortunately, there appears to be no similarity whatsoever between the rankings of non-NRB sectors according to export-output ratios and *NFEE* values. In interpreting these findings, it should be recalled that the Philippines' composition of non-NRB exports is labour intensive on average, but comprises relatively capital-intensive products as well. This explains the absence of any relationship between the rankings according to export-output ratios and *NFEE* values, for the more capital-intensive exportables are characterized by a higher import dependency. Thus, if the Philippines had gone through a more consistent shift towards labour-intensive exports, both the contribution to employment generation and foreign-exchange earnings would have been higher.

12.6 SUMMARY

From 1970 onwards, the Philippines have pursued a dualistic industrialization and trade strategy. Import-substitution industries receive protection, whereas the discrimination against exports is neutralized via subsidies, a free-trade regime and the possibility to produce in EPFZs. In the context of the economy, manufacturing production has been biased in a capital-intensive direction, and especially the non-NRB component depends heavily on imports of intermediates and producer goods. These features are explained by the prevailing cascading system of incentives, biased in favour of the finishing stages of producing consumer goods. The empirical analysis shows that the structure of non-NRB manufactured exports under such an industrialization strategy does not deviate substantially from the structure of DMO production, although, on average, non-NRB exports are produced relatively labour intensive at, for manufacturing, a relatively low average wage level. Hence, the most export-oriented sectors do not systematically coincide with sectors producing the most labour-intensive exportables.

Due to the dominance of NRB products in Philippine manufactured exports, total manufactured exports show an excellent record of spread effects. Disregarding, however, the employment linkages in the labour-intensive input-supplying agricultural sector reveals that, in fact, the most important gain from NRB exports is the high net foreign-exchange receipts. The NRB exports of various wood products and other handicrafts are an exception to this finding, because their manufacture requires relatively much labour.

Two important findings emerge from the analysis of spread effects of non-NRB exports. First, exports from E sectors show a better record of spread effects in terms of production and employment than DMO production. By contrast, the *NFEE* values for exports from E sectors appear to be lower than for exports from DMO sectors. This is explained by the relatively low proportion of value added in the value of E sector production. The high import dependency can mainly be imputed to the more capital-intensive exportables; from rank order correlations it turns out that a higher labour intensity is significantly associated with a lower dependency on imported inputs. Second, it is interesting to find that the inputs used in export production are relatively labour intensive. Relative to this good performance of labour-intensive exportables, the EPFZ-type of export contrasts unfavourably. In the Philippine context, the establishment of an EPFZ exercises a disintegrating influence upon the economy.

APPENDIX TABLE A.12.1
CHARACTERISTICS OF MANUFACTURING SECTORS CLASSIFIED AS NRB SECTORS, THE PHILIPPINES, 1974

I-O Code	Sector	E_i/O_i (%)	E_i/E_m (%)	l_i^e (per 10⁶ Pesos output)	T_i^e	VA_i/L_i (Pesos)	GP_{ij}/L_i (Pesos)	s_i (Pesos)	P_i	$NFEE_i$	P_i^E	P_i^{E-A}	WIM_i	WIM_i^E (per 10⁶ Pesos output)
26	Meat products	1.3	.6	13.5	181.8	17,940	12,860	5,080	1.42	.97	1.98	.65	.51	241.2
27	Dairy products	6.7	.6	8.9	49.4	44,810	34,770	10,040	1.21	.82	.54	.57	.28	82.3
28	Rice milling	.0	.0	13.0	232.6	10,920	8,000	2,920	1.37	.95	2.54	.52	.56	297.4
29	Sugar milling and refining	75.2	44.2	12.9	140.1	32,500	26,340	6,160	1.17	.94	1.53	.52	.42	188.6
30	Processed fruits and vegetables	43.1	2.4	16.0	113.6	17,080	12,430	4,650	1.32	.90	1.24	.68	.37	156.2
31	Processed fish and other seafoods	11.2	1.4	30.3	122.0	14,950	11,030	3,920	1.13	.94	1.33	.94	.39	167.2
32	Other grain mill products	.1	.0	9.9	158.2	16,570	11,650	4,920	1.18	.74	1.73	.44	.42	207.0
33	Bakery products	1.9	.3	37.1	123.9	7,230	4,890	2,340	1.47	.82	1.35	1.41	.39	168.7
34	Cocoa, chocolate and sugar confectionery	6.9	.3	24.8	96.3	12,240	9,100	3,140	1.30	.87	1.05	1.02	.33	134.7
35	Desicated coconut products	77.2	3.4	28.4	123.9	15,180	12,330	2,850	1.20	.95	1.35	.96	.36	165.3
36	Other manufactured foods	3.1	.9	13.6	93.9	22,790	17,180	5,610	1.32	.88	1.02	.76	.36	135.9
37	Liquors, wines, brewery and malt products	1.9	.2	20.9	35.5	29,830	24,620	5,210	1.03	.91	.39	.87	.24	63.8
38	Soft drinks and carbonated water	.3	.0	17.7	43.4	31,970	24,540	7,430	1.10	.89	.47	.81	.31	79.0
39	Tobacco products	1.0	.3	18.6	47.7	28,760	24,990	3,770	1.06	.87	.52	.79	.21	72.0
45	Lumber	19.9	1.9	19.1	99.5	12,560	8,490	4,070	1.29	.88	1.09	.72	.32	137.2
46	Plywood and veneer plants	37.3	2.7	26.0	96.6	12,580	8,910	3,670	1.24	.89	1.05	.89	.33	134.6
47	Furniture and fixtures	22.1	.6	56.7	83.8	9,090	5,520	3,570	1.14	.85	.91	1.83	.40	130.5
48	Other wood, cane and cork products	42.6	1.6	49.9	101.1	8,610	5,340	3,280	1.32	.92	1.10	1.70	.40	147.8
49	Pulp, paper and paperboard manufacturing	8.2	.5	21.6	35.1	23,210	16,490	6,720	1.00	.75	.38	.83	.29	68.8
50	Articles of pulp, paper and paperboard	.5	.1	34.4	45.7	15,380	10,220	5,160	1.00	.77	.50	1.16	.33	84.1
58	Coconut oil	71.7	27.1	25.4	106.4	21,250	14,880	6,360	1.09	.96	1.16	.79	.42	155.3
59	Other oils and fats	50.1	.2	12.1	117.2	29,810	21,650	8,160	1.14	.85	1.28	.54	.40	164.1
66	Petroleum refineries	1.2	1.0	2.4	11.3	149,260	129,280	19,980	.84	.52	.12	.29	.12	25.6
71	Basic ferrous metal industries	.1	.0	8.4	20.7	36,800	31,380	5,420	1.14	.60	.23	.52	.15	38.3
72	Basic non-ferrous metal industries	46.1	1.4	8.2	18.2	38,850	31,560	7,280	1.00	.55	.20	.45	.16	36.7

APPENDIX TABLE A.12.2
CHARACTERISTICS OF MANUFACTURING SECTORS CLASSIFIED AS E SECTORS, THE PHILIPPINES, 1975

I-O Code	Sector	E_i/O_i (%)	E_i/E_m (%)	f_i^e (per 10⁶ Pesos output)	T_i^e	VA_i/L_i (Pesos)	GP_i/L_i (Pesos)	s_i (Pesos)	P_i	$NFEE_i$	P_i^E	$P_i^{E,A}$	WIM_i	WIM_i^E (per 10⁶ Pesos output)
40	Textile and knitting mill products	4.4	1.4	16.9	43.1	15,910	12,160	3,750	1.21	.64	.47	.89	.22	68.9
41	Cordage, twine and other textile products	23.2	.7	24.1	60.9	16,420	12,100	4,310	1.09	.74	.66	.94	.28	93.3
42	Footwear	7.3	.3	108.7	138.7	5,130	3,000	2,130	1.13	.89	1.51	3.41	.46	191.8
43	Other wearing apparel	10.1	.8	69.1	91.5	6,130	3,270	2,860	1.23	.79	1.00	2.30	.40	138.2
44	Other made-up textile goods	9.6	.5	31.7	58.6	8,800	5,590	3,210	1.33	.69	.64	1.38	.29	92.0
53	Leather and leather products	11.1	.1	45.5	97.4	9,880	6,860	3,020	1.25	.86	1.06	1.62	.37	140.9
56	Other rubber products	6.7	.1	40.6	53.8	12,200	9,450	2,760	.96	.71	.59	1.33	.23	80.7
57	Basic industrial chemicals	6.1	.3	14.5	26.7	34,060	27,520	6,540	.98	.73	.29	.63	.21	51.4
62	Plastic materials	7.2	.2	19.1	30.3	21,890	17,530	4,360	.92	.62	.33	.70	.18	51.5
67	Hydraulic cement	21.2	1.9	19.5	34.4	16,870	11,820	5,050	1.18	.70	.38	.88	.26	64.2
68	Structural clay and concrete products	9.8	.2	28.6	43.7	17,560	12,900	4,650	1.10	.80	.48	1.11	.29	77.4
69	Glass and glass products	4.5	.2	14.8	28.0	30,750	24,120	6,630	1.05	.74	.31	.69	.23	54.5
70	Other non-metallic mineral products	10.3	.2	33.1	45.9	18,500	13,560	4,940	.93	.81	.50	1.17	.30	81.1
78	Special industry machinery	24.2	.1	23.1	35.9	24,620	18,380	6,240	1.00	.81	.39	.89	.29	69.1
82	Communication equipment, excl. radio, TV	12.8	.1	24.4	38.3	19,290	14,170	5,120	1.02	.74	.42	.98	.27	70.0
92	Miscellaneous manufactures	7.6	.6	37.0	48.9	12,170	8,810	3,360	.97	.67	.53	1.24	.25	78.0

APPENDIX TABLE A.12.3
CHARACTERISTICS OF MANUFACTURING SECTORS CLASSIFIED AS DMO SECTORS, THE PHILIPPINES, 1974

I-O Code	Sector	E_i/O_i (%)	E_i/E_m (%)	f_i^c (per 10⁶ Pesos output)	T_i^e	VA_i/L_i (Pesos)	GP_i/L_i (Pesos)	s_i (Pesos)	P_i	$NFEE_i$	P_i^E	P_i^{E-A}	WIM_i	WIM_i^E (per 10⁶ Pesos output)
51	Newspaper, periodicals, books and pamphlets	1.1	.0	28.1	42.6	17,370	11,170	6,200	1.02	.76	.46	1.07	.35	82.6
52	Printing and bookbinding	.3	.0	47.1	60.4	13,650	8,580	5,080	.98	.88	.66	1.54	.42	109.4
54	Rubber footwear	.6	.0	28.0	42.5	13,510	10,030	3,480	1.03	.64	.46	1.08	.23	69.0
55	Tires, tires vulcanizing and recapping	.3	.0	13.1	30.0	27,330	19,150	8,180	1.01	.62	.33	.66	.24	58.4
60	Fertilizer and lime	.0	.0	8.1	17.7	41,840	30,900	10,940	.92	.54	.19	.45	.19	39.9
61	Paints and varnishes	1.0	.0	14.8	26.3	25,340	17,650	7,690	.95	.59	.29	.65	.23	53.3
63	Medical and pharmaceutical preparations	1.7	.2	9.9	32.2	38,090	27,470	10,630	1.21	.79	.35	.77	.31	68.1
64	Soap and other cleaning compounds	.6	.0	5.1	30.8	64,410	49,690	14,720	1.13	.72	.34	.61	.27	61.8
65	Other chemical products	1.8	.2	18.1	54.6	21,070	14,580	6,480	1.18	.82	.60	.96	.34	94.5
73	Cutlery, handtools and general hardware	3.7	.0	17.5	32.1	16,340	12,610	3,730	1.17	.61	.35	.81	.20	55.0
74	Fabricated structural metal products	1.6	.0	18.7	30.9	22,740	17,340	5,400	1.07	.68	.34	.78	.22	56.8
75	Heating apparatus, lighting and plumbing fixtures	.5	.0	27.8	39.1	14,850	11,490	3,360	1.02	.65	.43	1.01	.21	63.5
76	Other fabricated metal products	.3	.0	19.1	32.1	18,940	14,110	4,830	1.10	.64	.35	.81	.22	57.5
77	Tractors and other agricultural machinery	.4	.0	14.5	27.7	34,130	26,500	7,630	1.01	.76	.30	.70	.25	56.6
79	General industry machinery (excl. electrical)	3.4	.1	25.7	37.7	19,730	14,740	4,990	1.01	.74	.41	.93	.25	67.2
80	Office, computing and accounting machines (excl. electrical)	.6	.0	29.1	37.6	24,570	19,590	4,990	.87	.87	.41	.96	.26	67.8
81	Electrical industrial machinery	1.9	.0	23.0	32.4	27,390	20,250	7,140	.91	.82	.35	.83	.30	66.7
83	Batteries	.9	.0	15.3	28.8	30,650	22,680	7,970	1.00	.73	.31	.73	.26	59.3
84	Electric lamps, fixtures, wires and wiring devices	1.5	.0	24.2	39.3	16,860	11,940	4,920	1.08	.71	.43	.99	.27	70.7

APPENDIX TABLE A.12.3 (cont'd)

I-O Code	Sector	E_i/O_i (%)	E_i/E_m (%)	l_i^e (per 10⁶ Pesos output)	T_i^e	VA_i/L_i (Pesos)	GP_i/L_i (Pesos)	s_i (Pesos)	P_i	$NFEE_i$	P_i^E	P_i^{E-A}	WIM_i	WIM_i^E (per 10⁶ Pesos output)
85	Household radio, TV, phonos	1.5	.1	22.5	38.2	24,510	19,390	5,120	1.03	.85	.42	.98	.27	69.5
86	Refrigeration and air-conditioning equipment	.2	.0	24.2	37.0	24,290	18,530	5,760	.97	.83	.40	.95	.28	69.7
87	Other household electrical appliances and wares	.4	.0	16.4	29.1	29,760	23,550	6,220	1.01	.75	.32	.74	.23	56.2
88	Motor vehicles, engines, bodies and parts	.1	.0	28.6	38.1	22,650	15,140	7,520	.89	.81	.42	.98	.36	79.6
89	Repair of motor vehicles	.8	.0	43.7	53.1	13,880	9,610	4,270	.95	.80	.58	1.37	.33	91.1
90	Shipbuilding and repairing	3.9	.0	40.1	50.6	15,410	10,900	4,510	.97	.82	.55	1.27	.32	88.1
91	Other transport equipment	.0	.0	36.8	46.3	15,730	11,470	4,270	.91	.76	.51	1.19	.28	79.0

For explanation of symbols, see Section 10.4.

Sources : Computations are based on data from: *1974 Interindustry (Input-Output) Accounts of the Philippines*, National Economic and Development Authority (National Census and Statistics Office), Manila, 1979; *1974 Annual Survey of Establishments: Manufacturing, Construction, Mining and Quarrying, Private Services, Transportation, Communication and Storage, Wholesale and Retailing, Electricity, Gas and Water*, National Economic and Development Authority (National Census and Statistics Office), Manila, 1979; The World Bank, *Industrial Development Strategy and Policies in the Philippines*, Volume III: The Statistical Appendix and Annexes, 1979, Table 1.26; ILO, *Year Book of Labour Statistics*, Geneva, various issues, Table 2A.

13
The Case of Thailand

13.1 INTRODUCTORY REMARKS

Thailand's total land area amounts to 514,000 km^2. At the start of the 1980s, it was inhabited by 47.2 million people, resulting in an average population density of 92 persons per km^2. Hence, like the Philippines, Thailand is a middle-large country in terms of both population and territory. The country, however, is not so abundantly endowed with natural resources as Indonesia and the Philippines. Natural wealth consists largely of the produce of agriculture and forestry, like rice, maize, sugar, tapioca, rubber and teak. Tin is the most important mineral ore.

Thailand remained predominantly an agricultural economy till the early 1960s. From that date onwards, manufacturing growth gained momentum and the economy witnessed rapid structural change. The growth of manufacturing production can, in the first instance, be attributed to import-substitution activities almost exclusively. In addition, since 1970, a policy of export promotion has been implemented, which provided new outlets for manufacturing growth. *Per capita* real GDP experienced an average annual growth rate of 3.3 per cent during the 1950s, and 5.1 per cent during the 1960s. This growth rate slowed down to 4.2 per cent per annum during the 1970 decade.

Thailand has a middle-income economy. In 1975, the year on which our empirical analysis is based, GNP *per capita* amounted to US$350.[1]

13.2 INDUSTRIALIZATION AND TRADE STRATEGIES IN THAILAND

It was not until 1961, the initial year of Thailand's First National Economic and Social Development Plan, that the process of industrialization was taken in hand seriously. Not much industrial progress had actually been made during the 1950s, due in part to the absence of a consistent framework of industrial policy. On the one hand, the Industrial Promotion Act of 1954 provided the tariff protection and tax incentives for potential import-substitution industries. On the other hand, the second half of the 1950s experienced a gradual relaxation of the existing restrictive control system. Besides, the Government sought to accelerate industrialization by direct participation in production activities through state enterprises. These policies largely failed in their intended effect to enlarge and diversify the small base of manufacturing production, the bulk of which consisted of the processing of primary products. Therefore, this period cannot be characterized as one of import substitution.

By contrast, the First and Second Economic Plans, covering the period 1961-1971, set out a clear import-substitution strategy, based on the private sector. Domestic industries that faced competitive imports were protected by tariff rates. Additionally, these industries were encouraged through various incentive measures. These took the form of tax exemptions and other privileges under the completely revised Investment Promotion Law of 1962, administered by the newly established Board of Investment (BOI). Industries, for instance, promoted by the BOI were granted exemption from import duties on intermediates and capital goods fully or in part, depending on their promotional status. In the early 1960s, tariff protection was rather moderate.[2] The most powerful incentives to domestic production were, therefore, found in the various tax exemptions and other privileges meant to stimulate investments. During the 1960s, these instruments gradually changed in importance. There was a number of upward adjustments in tariff rates during the period, and two major revisions were carried through in 1964 and 1970. These changes resulted in a more cascading structure of tariff protection. In addition to increased tariff protection, several other protective devices were implemented, particularly to support existing firms. These included direct interventions through controls and prices, imports and exports and through restrictions on expansion of firms and new entry. Meanwhile, tax incentives to promote investments were reduced. Throughout the period, no attention was paid to the export of manufactures.

The importance of the manufacturing sector increased rapidly, with average annual growth rates of value added reaching 11 per cent from 1960 to 1970. In 1960, the contribution of manufacturing to GDP was 11.7 per cent, but rose to 15.5 per cent in 1970.[3] At the start of the import-substitution process, manufacturing activities were concentrated heavily in the processing of primary products, of which the production of food, beverages and tobacco accounted for almost 60 per cent of manufacturing value added in 1960. By the early 1970s, the share of processed agricultural products had declined markedly to about 40 per cent in favour of other consumer goods and even some producer goods. The establishment of a petroleum industry in this period especially contributed to the broadening of the manufacturing sector.

However, there were signs that the first stage of import substitution in Thailand attained its completion. For one, the call for direct industrial controls to regulate the market became ever stronger. For another, manufacturing was, as a matter of course, concentrated in activities producing finished products, largely based on imported intermediates and capital goods. These signals led to a policy reform which basically aimed at providing similar incentives to production for domestic and for export markets. In other words, after 1970, Thailand pursued a dualistic industrialization and trade strategy. Import-substitution industries were further encouraged through increased tariff protection resulting from the tariff revisions in 1970 and 1974. Other instruments were increasingly applied to provide protection, such as, for instance, a business tax that is imposed on imported products only.

At the same time, more emphasis is placed upon promoting exports. The Third Economic Plan (1972-1976) explicitly emphasized the need to promote the export of manufactures. To include additional incentives for exports, the Investment Promotion Act was again revised in 1972. Privileges for officially promoted export-oriented firms include since then full exemption from import duties and business taxes on intermediates and machinery, exemption from export duties, tax advantages, and a rediscount facility at subsidized interest rates. Firms not promoted by the BOI are entitled to a refund of import duties and all other taxes incurred in the production of exportables. Exporters can also claim a reduction in the cost of electricity. Technical and marketing assistance for exporters is provided by the Export Service Centre. This export-promotion policy is continued in the Fourth Economic Plan (1977-1981).[4] At present, the establishment of an EPFZ near Bangkok Harbour, the first in Thailand, is complete and operation can start.

The combined impact of these export-promotion measures has been to reduce the significant negative protection of exportables during the 1970s. It is estimated that the negative effective protection rates on exports increased from 24 per cent in 1971 to about 40 per cent at the end of the 1970s. By contrast, effective protection rates on manufactured products directed towards the domestic market, exclusive of food, beverages and tobacco, increased during the same period from 44 per cent to about 90 per cent. Also in Thailand, the familiar cascading protection structure is found, whereby consumer goods enjoy a higher level of protection than intermediate products and machinery. Notably, the transport equipment sector in Thailand ranks among the most protected sectors.[5] Although it is believed that the rates of protection in Thailand have generally been lower than in many other developing countries, and notwithstanding the existence of an export-incentive programme, a quantitative evaluation of these incentives reveals that they are still inadequate to compensate completely for the discrimination against exports.[6]

Manufacturing production continued to grow rapidly during the 1970s, with an average annual percentage of about 10. The share of manufacturing in GDP has risen steadily, to more than 20 per cent in 1980.[7] A significant factor in this rapid expansion has been the upsurge in export production. Accordingly, the composition of production has undergone some change. The share of food, beverages and tobacco further decreased to about one third of manufacturing value added. The major exportables, like clothing and electrical machinery, gained in importance. Also some producer goods industries developed well, particularly textiles, chemicals and transport equipment.

Recent adjustments in the industrialization strategy aim at reducing effective protection for import-substituting industries by means of comprehensive tariff reductions. At the same time, it is tried to further reduce the existing biases against manufactured exports.

13.3 STRUCTURAL FEATURES OF THE THAI ECONOMY

As indicated above, the importance of the manufacturing sector has increased rapidly since 1960. Table 13.1 shows that the share of manufacturing in total gross output reached 38.7 per cent by 1975, followed by the primary sector and services with corresponding shares of 18.2 and 35.2 per cent, respectively. The manufacturing contribution to GDP is, however, markedly lower, viz. 22.7 per cent. Despite the rapid growth of the manufacturing sector, Thailand is still largely an agricultural economy as is seen from the sectoral distribution of employment. The primary sectors employed 72.8 per cent of the labour force in 1975, as compared to a 7.9 per cent employment share of the manufacturing sector. The very discrepancies between the contributions of the primary sectors to total gross output, GDP and total employment already reveal a severe dualism between agriculture and the rest of the economy, a feature to which we shall refer repeatedly.

In the exports of goods and services, manufactures already accounted for the largest share of 59.1 per cent by 1975. It should be remembered that this share is based on a classification of exportables by industrial origin and includes, as we shall see in the next section, substantial exports of processed primary products. The manufacturing sector has also become the most export-oriented sector of the Thai economy with an average export-output ratio of 13.5 per cent in 1975.

At the same time, manufacturing appears to be the sector that shows the highest dependency on imports. The share of imported inputs in total

TABLE 13.1
BASIC DATA ON THE STRUCTURE OF THE THAI ECONOMY, 1975

Indicators	Agriculture & Mining	Manufacturing	Construction	Utilities	Services
1. Share in total gross output (%)	18.2	38.7	6.7	1.2	35.2
2. Share in GDP (%)	25.7	22.7	4.4	.9	46.3
3. Share in total employment (%)	72.8	7.9	1.2	.2	17.9
4. Export-output ratio (%)	6.4	13.5	—	1.3	6.9
5. Share in total exports (%)	13.2	59.1	—	.2	27.5
6. Share in intermediate imports (%)	4.7	78.5	8.9	.6	7.3
7. Input structure					
— Domestic intermediate inputs	.19	.52	.53	.53	.25
— Imported intermediate inputs	.02	.15	.10	.04	.01
— Gross value added	.79	.33	.37	.43	.72
Total inputs	1.00	1.00	1.00	1.00	1.00
8. $NFEE$	.96	.80	.83	.88	.95
9. P	.79	1.08	1.13	1.16	.85
10. P^E	2.5	.93	.60	.52	.48
11. P^{E-A}	.17	.96	1.06	1.08	1.73
12. WIM^E (per 10^6 Baht output)	201.5	82.3	59.6	50.9	57.3
13. I^e (per 10^6 Baht output)	121.0	6.2	5.0	5.2	15.4
14. VA/L (Baht)	6,545	52,945	73,032	81,893	47,997
15. T^e (per 10^6 Baht output)	133.5	50.1	32.3	28.2	25.7
16. s (Baht)	5,930[1]	13,214	19,575	13,668	18,158

For explanation of symbols, see Section 10.4.
Note : [1] Refers to wage and gross profit incomes.
Sources : see Appendix to Chapter 13.

manufacturing production was 15 per cent in 1975, which equals 78.5 per cent of the economy's total imports of intermediate products. In this connection, it should be realized that by the mid-1970s, NRB industries still accounted for almost 60 per cent of total manufacturing value added. About half of the domestic intermediates entering the manufacturing sector originates in primary sectors. NRB industries show, therefore, only a small dependency on imported inputs, petroleum refineries and iron and steel being the only clear exceptions. Consequently, the bulk of imported intermediates is used in non-NRB industries. Textiles, chemicals, metal products and machinery are

THE CASE OF THAILAND 301

among the largest importers of foreign inputs. This illustrates that intermediate and engineering goods industries, notwithstanding their relatively small weight in manufacturing production, absorb a disproportionally large share of imported inputs. These industries are also responsible for manufacturing showing the lowest average $NFEE$ value, although a value of 0.80 for this index is not particularly low.

Given the predominance of NRB industries, it is explicable that the P value for manufacturing production is well above 1. The spread effects in terms of employment provide a different picture. Compared with other sectors, primary production generates per unit of output the largest direct plus indirect employment opportunities, due to the extremely labour-intensive character of primary production itself. According to both the direct labour coefficient and the value added per employee, there appears to be a huge productivity gap between agriculture and the rest of the economy. It is noteworthy to see that this is the basic dichotomy in the economy and not, as in the Philippines, a manufacturing sector standing high in capital intensity above all other sectors of the economy. In fact, manufacturing production requires more labour per unit than construction and utilities. Value added per employee in manufacturing is therefore lower than in these two sectors, and it does not differ much from that in services. Put differently, the factor intensity of Thai manufacturing production is in line with that of other non-agricultural sectors. An additional indication for this feature is provided by the sectoral wage structure. The manufacturing work force is paid the lowest average wage rate of all non-agricultural workers. The wage differential between manufacturing on the one hand, and construction and services on the other, is even more than one third at the expense of manufacturing. The wage structure also illustrates the income aspect of the dichotomy in the economy. For a correct assessment of the income gap between agriculture and the rest of the economy, it should be noted that the number of 121 employees to produce one million Baht of primary output refers to man-years of both wage labour and self-employed and conceals substantial underemployment. Hence, the average earnings per employee in primary sectors refer to the sum of wage and gross profit income per person at work. Notwithstanding this broader income concept, income per head in agriculture and mining is less than half of the average wage income per employee in manufacturing.

Thus, notable features of Thai manufacturing by the mid-1970s seem to be the strong linkage between a large part of production and agriculture, and the fact that, on average, manufacturing is not too seriously biased in favour of large-scale capital-intensive production. These features are reflected in the different measures of employment spread effects. The P^E value and total labour coefficient for manufacturing are the highest, next to primary sectors.

Spending of wage incomes earned in manufacturing has the greatest impact on employment generation throughout the economy. If the employment linkages to the agricultural sector are excluded from the P^E measure, it appears, of course, that not only do the employment spread effects of primary production drop drastically but that also the P^E value for manufacturing of 0.93 increases to 0.96 P^{E-A} value. This indicates that the labour intensity of manufacturing is only slightly less than the economy's average. Postwar inward-looking industrialization policies in Thailand, which have been relatively mild in general, and the subsequent shift to export promotion, certainly did not produce an unfavourable effect hereon.

13.4 DEVELOPMENT AND STRUCTURE OF THAI MANUFACTURED EXPORTS

During the 1970s, Thailand's manufactured export performance has been impressive. This emerges with clarity from Figure 13.1. The share of manufactures in total exports underwent a steady increase from about 6 per cent in 1970 to almost 30 per cent in 1980. The same figure shows that manufacturing production is increasingly being sold on foreign markets. At the same time the composition of exports has been undergoing marked changes, as can be seen in Figure 13.2. It is evident that exports of clothing

Figure 13.1
Manufactured Export Performance of Thailand, 1970–1980

Figure 13.2
Composition of Thai Manufactured Exports, 1970-1980
(percentage shares)

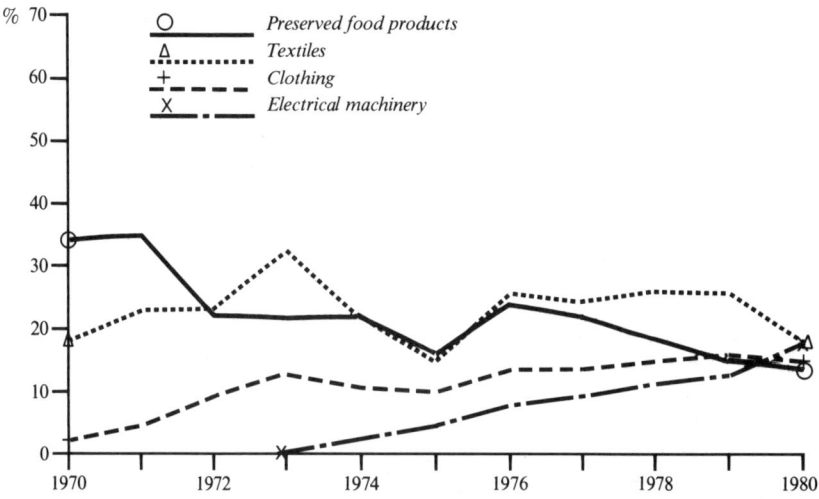

Sources: United Nations, *Yearbook of International Trade Statistics*, Volume I, New York, various issues; United Nations, *Statistical Yearbook for Asia and the Pacific*, ESCAP, Bangkok, various issues.

and electrical machinery occupy an increasingly important position among Thai manufactured exports. Starting from very low values in 1970, these exportables accounted for, respectively, about 15 and 18 per cent of total exports in 1980. Exports in the category of electrical machinery almost exclusively refer to switchgears. The share of textiles in total manufactured exports fluctuated around a constant level of 25 per cent. By contrast, exports of processed food products lagged behind the general growth performance of manufactured exports, resulting in a declining share from about one third in 1970 to less than 14 per cent in 1980. Consequently, Thai manufactured exports have become more industrialized during the period under consideration.

Table 13.2 sets out the relevant data to analyze the structure of Thai manufactured exports. It shows that when exportables are classified by industrial origin according to the 1975 input-output table, 78.3 per cent of total manufactured exports were still produced in NRB sectors in 1975. Processed primary exportables almost completely consisted of only six

TABLE 13.2
CHARACTERISTICS OF MAJOR PRODUCTION AND EXPORT CATEGORIES, THAI MANUFACTURING SECTOR, 1975

Category	E/O	E/E$_m$	l^e	T^e	Share of labour-intensive products	VA/L	GP/L	s	Share of wages & salaries in gross value added
	(%)	(%)	(per 10^6 Baht output)		(%)	(Baht)	(Baht)	(Baht)	(%)
Total manufactured exports[1]	—	100	6.5 (6.1)	70.7 (68.4)	35.1 (27.6)	—	—	—	—
Total manufacturing production	13.5	—	6.2	45.8	—	52,945	39,730	13,214	25.0
NRB manufactured exports[1]	—	78.3	6.3 (5.9)	85.2 (83.7)	25.6 (16.0)	—	—	—	—
NRB manufacturing production	17.4	—	5.6	64.4	—	55,484	42,820	12,664	22.8
Exports from E sectors	—	17.0	6.9	19.0	66.9	—	—	—	—
Production in E sectors	15.1	—	7.0	17.9	—	54,604	41,412	13,192	24.2
Exports from DMO sectors	—	4.7	7.7	16.6	77.1	—	—	—	—
Production in DMO sectors	2.8	—	7.3	16.1	—	46,974	32,669	14,305	30.5

For explanation of symbols, see Section 10.4.
Note : [1] Figures in parentheses refer to exports exclusive of rubber sheet and block rubber.
Sources : see Appendix to Chapter 13.

products: canned sea food, processed rice, tapioca, sugar, rubber and non-ferrous metals. The NRB sectors also show a markedly higher export orientation than non-NRB sectors, namely 17.4 against 7.5 per cent, respectively. Thus, manufactured exports are more strongly dominated by NRB products than total manufacturing production, which is for about 60 per cent accounted for by NRB products.

The data on direct labour coefficients in Table 13.2 shows that total manufactured exports are produced with, on average, 6.5 man-years of direct labour per one million Baht of exports. This figure for total manufacturing production equals 6.2, indicating that Thai manufactured exports are slightly more labour intensive than average manufacturing output. According to the direct labour coefficient, NRB exports are less labour intensive than other manufactured exports. However, total manufactured exports, and most notably NRB exports, appear to be relatively capital intensive if the exports of rubber sheets and block rubber are excluded. Exports of this NRB product make up 7.5 per cent of total manufactured exports and the processing stage before export is one of the most labour-intensive activities in the Thai manufacturing sector. Apart from this rubber product, NRB exports, and consequently total manufactured exports, are dominated by processed primary products which are relatively capital intensive. The share of products defined as relatively labour intensive in NRB exports is only 16 per cent in case rubber sheets and blocks are excluded.

Measured by the direct labour coefficient, the remaining exports are predominantly but not one-sidedly concentrated in labour-intensive manufactures. Wearing apparel, jute mill products and other manufactures are among the most important labour-intensive exportables, whereas cement, motor vehicles, and radio, television and communication equipment and apparatus constitute the relatively capital-intensive component in non-NRB exports (see Table A.13.2). It is striking that exports from E sectors are, on average, less labour intensive than those from DMO sectors. Moreover, the composition of E sector exports is slightly less labour intensive than the composition of total production in these sectors. Apart from this finding, it is remarkable how little the values of the average direct labour coefficient for different production and export categories deviate from each other. Consequently, it turns out that Thai manufactured exports are not systematically concentrated in the most labour-intensive products.

This picture changes drastically if the total factor intensity of export production is examined. The NRB exports now appear to be relatively labour intensive. This, of course, is due to purchases of raw materials from highly labour-intensive primary sectors. The weighted average total labour coefficient for non-NRB exports is considerably lower, about 4.5 times. It is important to note that exports from E sectors have a larger indirect labour content than the remaining non-NRB production categories, resulting in the highest T^e value of 19.0.

Table 13.2 also provides information on value added and wages per employee for the three sector categories distinguished. From the data on value added and gross profit per employee it is apparent that NRB production shows the highest capital intensity. Also according to these two measures, production in E sectors appears to be clearly less labour intensive than DMO production. Against expectation, the average wage level is the lowest in the capital-intensive NRB sectors and the highest in the labour-intensive DMO sectors. The wage level in E sectors lies in between and is very close to, but yet below, the average of the whole manufacturing sector. The wage shares in value added of the different sector categories correspond again to what might be expected, with a lower wage share in the capital-intensive NRB sectors and a higher in the labour-intensive DMO sectors. The differentials between these average wage levels are probably too small to speak of a truly paradoxical finding. But it cannot be denied that some export-oriented sectors, perhaps due to the pressure of international competition, pay relatively low wages. As we observed in the case of the Philippines, this is clearly true for some food-processing industries, like canned sea foods, and tapioca and rice milling (see Table A.13.1). And the export-oriented wearing apparel production, for instance, is almost the least remunerative for labour out of all manufacturing activities (see Table A.13.2).

Next we have estimated a matrix of rank correlation coefficients for pairs of sector characteristics in two samples, one comprising all manufacturing sectors and one comprising non-NRB sectors only. The correlation coefficients presented in Table 13.3 lead to the following observations. First, there is a high degree of correspondence in the ranking of sectors by export orientation and the share in total manufactured exports. Thus, the most export-oriented sectors are the same sectors that dominate exports. Second, the rankings of sectors by the various measures of factor intensity are very similar. All pairs of measures show the expected sign and are significant at the 1 per cent level. The third observation refers to the close correspondence between the various measures of factor intensity and the average wage level per sector, indicating that a lower wage level if significantly associated with a more labour-intensive production process. Finally, and most important, we observe that there is no correlation at all between, on the one hand, sectoral rankings according to export orientation, and on the other hand, sectoral rankings according to the various measures of factor intensity and average wage rates. This holds irrespective of whether NRB sectors are included or not. If there is a difference between these two sets of rankings, one can point at the positive and stronger correlation between the rankings by export orientation and value added or gross profit per employee for non-NRB

TABLE 13.3
MATRIX OF SPEARMAN RANK CORRELATION COEFFICIENTS FOR SECTOR CHARACTERISTICS, THAILAND, 1975[1,2]

Variable	E_i/O_i	E_i/E_m	I_i^e	VA_i/L_i	GP_i/L_i	T_i^e	s_i
E_i/O_i	1	.81**	−.03	.00	.02	.21	−.07
		.76**	−.12	.25	.30*	.11	.06
E_i/E_m		1	−.14	.02	.03	.20	.03
			−.12	.23	.25	.02	.18
I_i^e			1	−.62**	−.56**	.49**	−.72**
				−.75**	−.68**	.63**	−.71**
VA_i/L_i				1	.98**	−.47**	.69**
					.98**	−.44**	.73**
GP_i/L_i					1	−.41**	.58**
						−.37**	.60**
T_i^e						1	−.63**
							−.53**
s_i							1

For explanation of symbols, see Section 10.4.

Notes : [1] The upper coefficients in a row refer to rankings of all manufacturing sectors (n = 93), the lower coefficients refer to rankings of non-NRB sectors only (n = 57).
[2] Correlation coefficients that are significant at the 5 per cent level are denoted by one asterisk (*), those significant at the 1 per cent level by two asterisks (**).

Sources : see Appendix to Chapter 13.

sectors, suggesting that sectors showing a higher export to output ratio tend to produce with a higher capital intensity.

These findings reinforce our earlier impression that there is no question of a systematic concentration in the most labour-intensive exportables. One can interpret this finding to mean that, in Thailand, there is no marked difference between producing for the domestic market and for the export market.

13.5 SPREAD EFFECTS OF THAI MANUFACTURED EXPORTS

It has already been noted that NRB products occupy a larger share in manufactured exports than in total manufacturing production. Hence, as is evident from Table 13.4, manufactured export production displays a relatively high level of spread effects in the economy, especially realized in primary sectors. Five out of six measures of spread effects show higher values for total manufactured exports than for total manufacturing production, the measure P^{E-A} being the only exception. Both these higher values and the exception are explained by the dominance of NRB products in manufactured exports.

As expected, the P value of NRB exports is the highest, but it is important to note that the values of this measure for non-NRB exports are also above 1. Strikingly, total backward linkages generated by exports from E sectors are more extensive than those of DMO sectors, which is apparent from their P values of 1.09 and 1.02, respectively. The $NFEE$ values for the different export categories provide a similar picture, with the highest value of 0.92 for NRB exports, followed by values of 0.75 and 0.64 for exports from E and DMO sectors, respectively.

The employment spread effects of NRB and non-NRB exports differ widely, with, of course, NRB exports paramounting. Disregarding the indirect employment connected with labour-intensive intermediates from the agricultural sector, we observe non-NRB exports to generate above average employment spread effects. It is noteworthy that the employment linkages of exports produced in E sectors are also more extensive than those of exports from DMO sectors. The values of P^E, P^{E-A}, WIM and WIM^E are systematically higher for the former. Thus, the stronger intersectoral relations of E sectors also find expression in higher employment spread effects. Moreover, the results in Table 13.4 clearly show that exports from NRB and E sectors generate more extensive spread effects than the average production of the sectors. The conclusion seems to be that, on average, Thai manufactured exports exhibit a bias in favour of the more integrated production processes.

Table A.13.2 summarizes the characteristics for the 19 sectors that are classified as E sectors. The good performance of Thai manufactured exports

TABLE 13.4
WEIGHTED AVERAGE MEASURES OF SPREAD EFFECTS FOR MAJOR CATEGORIES
OF EXPORT AND PRODUCTION, THAI MANUFACTURING SECTOR, 1975

Category	P	$NFEE$	P^E	P^{E-A}	WIM	WIM^E (per 10^6 Baht output)
Total manufactured exports	1.15	.87	1.59	.83	.82	111.0
NRB exports	1.17	.92	1.92	.77	.95	131.7
Exports from E sectors	1.09	.75	.43	1.07	.36	36.8
Exports from DMO sectors	1.02	.64	.37	1.06	.35	33.6
Total manufacturing production	1.11	.77	1.03	.87	.59	74.7
NRB production	1.14	.83	1.45	.74	.74	100.9
Non-NRB production	1.07	.68	.38	1.08	.35	33.8

For explanation of symbols, see Section 10.4.
Sources: see Appendix to Chapter 13.

in terms of spread effects is mainly due to weaving, wearing apparel, jute mill products and other manufactures (stationery, toys, umbrellas, zippers, buttons and so on). Other exportables like motor vehicles and engines and turbines show, besides being relatively capital intensive, low P and $NFEE$ values and generate therefore little employment. In this respect, electrical apparatus and the like, which exports witnessed a steady increase in recent years, take a middle position.

In turn, there appears to be an interesting set of significant relationships between sectoral rankings by factor intensity and various measures of spread effects. Table 13.5 presents the rank order correlation coefficients for pairs of relevant sector characteristics. The results indicate that a higher labour intensity and a lower average wage rate are significantly associated with higher levels of intersectoral integration, both in terms of production and employment. It is, of course, not very surprising to find a strong correlation between factor intensity and employment spread effects. All correlation coefficients for these sectoral rankings have the right sign and are highly significant. But there is also a positive correlation between labour intensity and spread effects in terms of production stimuli to other sectors, measured by P and $NFEE$. This implies that labour-intensive, low-wage sectors in Thailand transmit stronger production and employment stimuli to other sectors than capital-intensive, high-wage sectors. Put differently, labour-intensive products are characterized by a larger domestic value-added component, and, consequently, export of such products generates the highest foreign-exchange earnings. By and large, these relationships still hold in case NRB sectors are excluded from the rankings, although the positive relationship between the direct labour coefficient and the power of dispersion just ceases to be statistically significant at the 5 per cent level. The similarity in the ranking of non-NRB sectors by labour intensity and the index $NFEE$ remains positive and statistically significant.

These results carry our previous finding a step further. It now appears that the relatively high level of production spread effects displayed by E sector export production is no coincidence, but is mainly due to the labour-intensive exportables already referred to in the above. Clearly, the spread effects of Thai non-NRB exports might further increase if a more careful specialization should take place in the most labour-intensive exportables. As we have observed, this was not yet the case by the mid-1970s. That is why, as the coefficients of the first row of Table 13.5 demonstrate, no distinct pattern emerges from the sectoral rankings by export-output ratio, factor intensity and the various measures of spread effects.

TABLE 13.5
MATRIX OF SPEARMAN RANK CORRELATION COEFFICIENTS FOR SECTOR CHARACTERISTICS AND VARIOUS MEASURES OF SPREAD EFFECTS, THAILAND, 1975[1,2]

Variable	E_i/O_i	l_i^e	s_i	P_i	$NFEE_i$	P_i^E	P_i^{E-A}	WIM_i	WIM_i^E
E_i/O_i	1	−.03	−.07	.20	.20	.21*	−.01	.24*	.22*
		−.12	.06	.15	.28*	.10	−.04	.10	.10
l_i^e		1	−.72**	.24*	.34**	.49**	.77**	.49**	.49**
			−.71**	.23	.34*	.63**	.84**	.59**	.62**
s_i			1	−.47**	−.49**	−.63**	−.55**	−.58**	−.61**
				−.40**	−.25	−.53**	−.69**	−.38**	−.47**
P_i				1	.55**	.62**	.53**	.68**	.65**
					.63**	.62**	.64**	.65**	.65**
$NFEE_i$					1	.84**	.25*	.80**	.83**
						.72**	.59**	.74**	.75**
P_i^E						1	.37**	.96**	.99**
							.80**	.94**	.99**
P_i^{E-A}							1	.42**	.40**
								.82**	.82**
WIM_i								1	.99**
									.98**
WIM_i^E									1

For explanation of symbols, see Section 10.4.

Notes: [1] The upper coefficients in a row refer to rankings of all manufacturing sectors (n = 93), the lower coefficients refer to rankings of non-NRB sectors only (n = 57).
[2] Correlation coefficients that are significant at the 5 per cent level are denoted by one asterisk (*), those significant at the 1 per cent level by two asterisks (**).

Sources: see Appendix to Chapter 13.

13.6 SUMMARY

Although Thailand went through different phases of restriction and liberalization of trade, postwar inward-looking industrialization policies have in general been relatively mild. Since 1970, a smooth transition from import substitution to export promotion has taken place. Discrimination against exports was gradually reduced without, however, neglecting the interests of import-substitution industries. Hence, Thailand pursues a dualistic industrialization and trade strategy.

In the mid-1970s, Thai manufacturing was still dominated by NRB production activities. This brings about a strong production linkage between a large part of manufacturing production and agriculture. Non-NRB-production, however, is highly dependent on imported inputs. Another notable feature of manufacturing seems to be that its capital intensity of production stands, on average, on the same level as in other non-agricultural sectors. During the 1970s, manufactured exports grew rapidly, especially the non-NRB exports of textiles, wearing apparel and electrical machinery. But in 1975, manufactured exports were still dominated by processed products which are relatively capital intensive. The remaining non-NRB exports are predominantly but not one-sidedly concentrated in labour-intensive manufactures.

Thai manufactured exports appear to have an above average impact on the economy, both in terms of production stimuli and employment generation. This is not only caused by the dominance of NRB products. The non-NRB exportables show a relatively favourable record of spread effects as well. Our analysis reaches the conclusion that the more labour-intensive products show a higher level of spread effects, also in terms of domestic production linkages.

APPENDIX TABLE A.13.1
CHARACTERISTICS OF MANUFACTURING SECTORS CLASSIFIED AS NRB SECTORS, THAILAND, 1975

I-O Code	Sector	E_i/O_i (%)	E_i/E_m (%)	l_i^e (per 10⁶ Baht output)	T_i^e	VA_i/L_i (Baht)	GP_i/L_i (Baht)	s_i (Baht)	P_i	$NFEE_i$	P_i^E	P_i^{E-A}	WIM_i	WIM_i^E (per 10⁶ Baht output)
042	Slaughtering	1.1	.4	4.1	92.3	32,170	20,830	11,350	1.64	.96	2.08	.88	1.03	143.0
043	Canning and preservation of meat	3.7	.1	8.7	46.2	51,610	40,260	11,350	1.39	.94	1.04	1.27	.62	76.5
044	Dairy products	3.2	.2	8.5	28.7	53,050	41,700	11,350	1.10	.84	.65	1.20	.43	50.0
045	Canning and preservation of fruits and vegetables	39.6	1.2	5.9	56.8	49,030	33,300	15,730	1.15	.86	1.28	1.00	.75	93.6
046	Canning and preservation of fish and other sea foods	25.1	5.1	8.3	51.7	56,000	44,650	11,350	1.07	.94	1.17	1.03	.64	83.2
047	Coconut and palm oil	6.3	.1	8.9	51.1	70,970	59,620	11,350	.90	.96	1.15	.88	.61	81.0
048	Animal oil, animal fat, vegetable oil and by-products	6.9	.2	7.3	68.3	42,730	30,130	12,600	1.27	.94	1.54	1.14	.84	109.6
049	Rice milling	15.8	18.0	6.1	115.0	31,920	20,580	11,350	1.23	.96	2.59	.65	1.21	174.7
050	Tapioca milling	92.2	12.1	4.8	122.1	42,920	31,570	11,350	1.22	.97	2.75	.48	1.26	184.2
051	Grinding of Maize	.0	.0	8.5	90.5	34,970	23,630	11,350	1.22	.94	2.04	.95	1.01	140.3
052	Flour and other grain milling	14.3	.4	6.8	54.5	40,630	29,280	11,350	1.15	.75	1.23	.94	.66	86.9
053	Bakery products	1.0	.0	7.9	45.8	47,610	36,270	11,350	1.30	.90	1.03	1.29	.62	76.2
054	Noodles and similar products	1.8	.1	10.2	57.7	31,080	19,740	11,350	1.36	.93	1.30	1.59	.77	95.8
055	Sugar	60.4	16.1	5.0	86.3	63,320	46,300	17,020	1.17	.95	1.94	.65	.99	134.8
056	Confectionery	1.2	.0	10.0	39.8	45,870	34,520	11,350	1.15	.89	.90	1.32	.56	67.6
057	Ice	.0	.0	10.0	14.0	73,260	61,290	11,350	.89	.91	.32	1.06	.27	27.3
058	Monosodium glutamate	1.8	.1	8.8	32.3	60,300	47,700	12,600	1.08	.91	.73	1.12	.49	56.3
059	Coffee and tea processing	.5	.0	8.4	80.8	35,440	22,840	12,600	1.14	.93	1.82	1.05	.95	127.6
060	Other food products	5.0	.3	6.3	48.4	59,500	48,150	11,350	1.09	.93	1.09	1.06	.61	78.6
061	Animal feed	.1	.0	6.0	65.6	52,770	41,420	11,350	1.34	.93	1.48	1.02	.78	103.9
062	Distilling and spirits blending	.8	.2	5.3	18.6	40,840	22,840	18,000	.88	.95	.42	.65	.33	34.7
063	Breweries	.8	.0	4.1	11.1	136,090	114,490	21,600	.92	.78	.25	.63	.27	24.5
064	Soft drinks and carbonated water	.7	.0	6.9	21.1	72,700	58,980	13,720	1.02	.81	.48	.96	.37	39.5
065	Tobacco processing	18.5	1.6	9.3	96.1	28,510	18,110	10,410	1.21	.93	2.17	1.03	1.06	148.2
066	Tobacco products	.4	.1	2.9	16.8	203,380	182,560	20,820	.85	.76	.38	.45	.27	29.9
078	Saw mills	19.8	3.0	9.2	70.3	44,540	33,940	10,590	1.09	.94	1.59	.96	.80	109.7

(cont'd overleaf)

APPENDIX TABLE A.13.1 (cont'd)

I-O Code	Sector	E_i/O_i (%)	E_i/E_m (%)	I_i^e (per 10^6 Baht output)	T_i^e	VA_i/L_i (Baht)	GP_i/L_i (Baht)	s_i (Baht)	P_i (Baht)	$NFEE_i$	P_i^E	P_i^{E-A}	WIM_i	WIM_i^E (per 10^6 Baht output)
079	Wood and cork products	27.7	.9	9.3	48.2	47,470	36,870	10,590	1.13	.93	1.09	1.23	.61	78.4
080	Wooden furniture and fixtures	4.5	.4	9.3	37.6	41,910	31,310	10,590	1.18	.87	.85	1.36	.53	63.8
081	Pulp, paper and paperboard	5.4	.4	6.2	16.3	62,060	47,080	14,980	1.00	.67	.37	.89	.32	32.1
082	Paper and paperboard products	1.1	.1	7.6	15.0	47,810	36,200	11,600	1.07	.69	.34	1.12	.30	29.9
093	Petroleum refineries	4.7	2.3	.1	1.2	1,715,620	1,610,020	105,600	.71	.29	.03	.07	.05	3.5
094	Other petroleum products	3.5	.1	6.9	15.6	56,520	42,470	14,060	1.17	.78	.35	1.11	.34	32.5
095	Rubber sheet and block rubber	85.7	7.5	10.5	99.3	25,550	15,580	9,970	1.16	.93	2.24	1.06	1.08	152.5
105	Iron and steel	.1	.0	3.3	6.0	92,940	74,940	18,000	.83	.46	.14	.47	.16	14.0
106	Secondary steel products	2.0	.3	3.4	7.5	97,780	79,780	18,000	1.07	.60	.17	.59	.20	17.6
107	Non-ferrous metal	56.6	7.2	5.9	15.6	38,040	24,120	13,920	1.20	.85	.35	1.25	.32	31.1

APPENDIX TABLE A.13.2
CHARACTERISTICS OF MANUFACTURING SECTORS CLASSIFIED AS E SECTORS, THAILAND, 1975

I-O Code	Sector	E_i/O_i (%)	E_i/E_m (%)	L_i^E (per 10⁶ Baht output)	T_i^E	VA_i/L_i (Baht)	GP_i/L_i (Baht)	s_i (Baht)	P_i	$NFEE_i$	P_i^E	$P_i^{E,A}$	WIM_i	WIM_i^E (per 10⁶ Baht output)
068	Weaving	10.9	2.6	6.6	16.9	46,530	32,130	14,400	1.20	.67	.38	1.21	.37	35.0
072	Wearing apparel	10.5	2.8	11.8	22.0	28,850	18,970	9,880	1.30	.75	.50	1.73	.42	42.7
073	Carpets and rugs	7.5	.0	8.8	19.7	34,970	23,500	11,470	1.27	.74	.44	1.43	.40	39.5
074	Jute mill products	31.3	1.4	11.1	53.3	40,380	28,910	11,470	1.06	.90	1.20	1.26	.69	87.4
075	Tanneries and leather finishing	17.1	.2	5.8	53.3	49,150	35,020	14,130	1.53	.87	1.20	1.08	.70	87.6
076	Leather products	14.4	.3	6.2	25.9	70,610	56,480	14,130	1.27	.85	.58	1.08	.43	47.2
101	Structural clay products	17.4	.2	11.6	33.3	38,590	28,360	10,230	1.08	.86	.75	1.46	.49	57.3
102	Cement	19.0	1.2	3.0	9.9	32,800	8,800	24,000	1.14	.76	.22	.71	.27	23.2
111	Other fabricated metal products	9.1	.3	7.2	11.4	53,430	41,720	11,710	.86	.56	.26	.87	.23	22.5
112	Engine and turbines	24.9	.6	3.9	8.6	97,290	73,290	24,000	.90	.63	.19	.69	.27	21.9
118	Radio, television and communication equipment and apparatus	43.7	1.5	4.4	12.2	78,090	61,290	16,800	1.03	.66	.27	.85	.28	26.1
122	Other electrical apparatus and supplies	7.4	.2	6.2	13.8	50,480	37,310	13,170	1.11	.67	.31	1.07	.31	29.0
125	Motor vehicles	7.3	1.2	1.9	7.4	192,580	167,470	25,120	.93	.61	.17	.49	.20	17.0
126	Motor cycles and bicycles	12.4	.4	2.9	9.0	134,060	116,060	18,000	.98	.67	.20	.64	.22	19.9
130	Photographic and optical goods	61.4	.2	6.5	14.7	53,300	38,900	14,400	1.14	.73	.33	1.12	.35	31.7
131	Watches and clocks	32.1	.1	4.7	13.6	65,770	48,970	16,800	1.24	.75	.31	1.05	.35	30.5
132	Jewellery and related articles	31.5	2.8	6.5	9.5	11,720	93,720	18,000	.78	.87	.22	.75	.26	22.2
133	Recreation and athletic equipment	25.1	.1	7.0	30.0	48,470	36,500	11,970	1.27	.83	.68	1.29	.48	53.6
134	Other manufactured goods	17.0	1.1	7.3	31.1	48,520	36,550	11,970	1.26	.81	.70	1.22	.48	54.6

APPENDIX TABLE A.13.3
CHARACTERISTICS OF MANUFACTURING SECTORS CLASSIFIED AS DMO SECTORS, THAILAND, 1975

I-O Code	Sector	E_i/O_i (%)	E_i/E_m (%)	l_i^* (per 10⁶ Baht output)	T_i^* (per 10⁶ Baht output)	VA_i/L_i (Baht)	GP_i/L_i (Baht)	s_i (Baht)	P_i	$NFEE_i$	P_i^E	P_i^{EA}	WIM_i	WIM_i^E (per 10⁶ Baht output)
067	Spinning	4.3	.9	7.4	15.2	38,560	24,160	14,400	.87	.45	.34	.85	.30	29.8
069	Textile bleaching and finishing													
070	Made-up textile goods	.0	.0	12.2	18.3	34,290	22,830	11,460	1.05	.73	.41	1.46	.38	37.1
071	Knitting	4.1	.3	7.7	27.7	42,260	30,810	11,460	1.25	.76	.62	1.29	.46	50.1
077	Footwear, except of rubber	1.6	.3	7.8	16.4	51,050	36,650	14,400	1.11	.70	.37	1.20	.36	34.3
083	Printing and publishing	.5	.0	10.6	26.9	36,490	25,180	11,310	1.33	.83	.61	1.58	.48	50.4
084	Basic industrial chemicals	1.7	.1	9.1	15.6	42,420	29,670	12,750	.96	.65	.35	1.15	.33	31.8
085	Fertilizer and pesticides	1.0	.1	6.5	13.2	53,640	35,660	17,980	1.03	.70	.30	1.00	.33	29.7
086	Synthetic resins, plastic and artificial fibre materials	.6	.0	5.7	12.2	49,970	35,700	14,270	1.02	.60	.27	.96	.28	26.2
087	Paints, varnishes and lacquers	2.7	.0	6.2	16.7	59,000	44,740	14,270	1.18	.78	.38	1.15	.39	35.7
088	Drugs and medicines	2.0	.1	5.5	12.4	56,200	38,220	17,980	1.03	.64	.28	.95	.33	28.4
089	Soap and cleaning preparations	3.6	.3	6.7	17.6	58,890	44,630	14,270	.97	.69	.40	.96	.35	34.7
090	Cosmetics	5.1	.2	7.0	15.7	56,040	41,780	14,270	1.04	.71	.35	1.05	.35	32.7
091	Matches	2.0	.0	6.9	17.1	60,820	46,560	14,270	1.13	.81	.38	1.20	.40	36.7
092	Other chemical products	4.9	.0	10.1	22.7	35,200	26,520	8,670	1.21	.84	.51	1.54	.38	41.5
096	Tyres and tubes	5.6	.1	6.9	17.4	57,590	43,320	14,270	1.10	.78	.39	1.10	.36	35.3
097	Other rubber products	1.2	.1	2.8	17.8	191,920	162,020	29,900	.98	.82	.40	.63	.35	34.9
098	Plastic ware	4.0	.1	11.8	31.6	29,600	19,630	9,970	1.13	.76	.71	1.58	.48	55.4
099	Ceramic and earthen ware	5.5	.4	14.1	17.5	37,100	19,120	17,980	.81	.67	.39	1.41	.50	41.9
100	Glass and glass products	4.0	.1	13.6	23.3	38,790	29,590	9,210	1.06	.88	.53	1.63	.39	42.5
103	Concrete and cement products	2.3	.1	6.9	14.6	65,530	47,560	17,980	1.10	.81	.33	1.07	.37	33.1
104	Other non-metallic products	.0	.0	7.9	17.3	45,590	33,590	12,000	1.24	.85	.39	1.32	.37	35.5
108	Cutlery and hand tools	3.0	.0	6.6	12.3	31,400	21,170	10,230	1.03	.53	.28	.98	.25	24.5
109	Metal furniture and fixture	5.7	.3	6.1	13.3	54,500	42,790	11,710	1.12	.69	.30	1.02	.27	26.6
110	Structural metal products	.1	.0	8.8	16.1	38,430	26,720	11,710	1.15	.69	.36	1.26	.33	32.4
113	Agricultural machinery and equipment	5.7	.2	7.4	13.5	48,720	37,010	11,710	1.02	.65	.30	1.05	.27	27.1
		.5	.0	7.3	13.8	47,640	34,050	13,590	1.04	.67	.31	1.11	.32	29.5

APPENDIX TABLE A.13.3 (cont'd)

I-O Code	Sector	E_i/O_i (%)	E_i/E_m (%)	I_i^e (per 10⁶ Baht output)	T_i^e (per 10⁶ Baht output)	VA_i/L_i (Baht)	GP_i/L_i (Baht)	s_i (Baht)	P_i	$NFEE_i$	P_i^E	$P_i^{E \cdot A}$	WIM_i	WIM_i^E (per 10⁶ Baht output)
114	Wood and metal working machines	4.3	.0	6.9	13.7	51,240	37,650	13,590	1.09	.68	.31	1.08	.31	29.1
115	Special industrial machinery	1.7	.1	6.7	12.0	47,380	33,790	13,590	.91	.57	.27	.96	.27	25.5
116	Office and household machinery and appliances	3.6	.1	6.2	12.9	55,230	38,430	16,800	1.00	.64	.29	.98	.32	28.7
117	Electrical industrial machinery and appliances	1.1	.0	5.7	11.8	57,580	43,990	13,590	1.03	.62	.27	.94	.27	25.0
119	Household electrical appliances	1.0	.0	5.8	14.6	59,810	43,010	16,800	1.16	.75	.33	1.12	.37	32.6
120	Insulated wire and cable	2.0	.0	7.7	16.3	42,300	29,140	13,170	1.16	.73	.37	1.28	.36	34.3
121	Electric accumulators and batteries	.0	.0	8.2	15.6	38,970	25,800	13,170	1.09	.67	.35	1.23	.35	32.7
123	Ship building and repairing	2.8	.1	5.6	18.8	62,540	45,740	16,800	1.07	.72	.42	.99	.38	37.3
124	Railroad equipment	.0	.0	5.1	10.2	52,930	39,050	13,880	.87	.46	.23	.71	.22	20.9
127	Repair of vehicles	2.4	.6	5.6	13.1	36,270	22,390	13,880	1.11	.58	.29	.90	.29	27.5
128	Aircraft	.4	.0	3.2	8.4	43,380	13,380	30,000	.94	.38	.19	.62	.27	21.8
129	Scientific equipment	1.0	.0	6.9	12.4	45,990	31,590	14,400	.97	.59	.28	1.01	.30	26.9

For explanation of symbols, see Section 10.4.

Sources : computations are based on data from: *Basic Input-Output Table of Thailand 1975*, NESDB, NSO, IDE, Bangkok and Tokyo, 1980; Direk Patmasiriwat, *Industrial Growth and Employment*, Thai University Research Association, Research Report No. 7, Bangkok, 1980, Table 2.7 (modified); NSO, Office of the Prime Minister, *Report of the 1976 Industrial Census — Whole Kingdom*, Statistical Tables, Part I, Table 3.

14
The Case of South Korea

14.1 INTRODUCTORY REMARKS

South Korea is a middle-large developing country with a population of 38 million and a total land area of 98,500 km^2, implying a rather high population density of 387 persons per km^2. It was created in 1948 by the partition of the Korean peninsula. From its independence, South Korea has been seriously handicapped by a lack of natural resources. Partition left the South with the majority of population, the minority of land, and some light industry. The North could dispose of heavy industry, large mineral deposits and almost all hydroelectric power facilities. After independence, South Korea started an extensive land reform programme which increased agricultural efficiency and production markedly. However, the prospects for agricultural development were unfavourable, due to the limited availability of cultivable land. Consequently, South Korea is dependent on imports for most raw materials.

These structural country characteristics led South Korea to industrialize. At first, after the Korean War, industrial expansion was largely oriented towards the domestic market. In the early 1960s, Korea recognized the need to promote exports of manufactures in order to be able to meet its increasing import requirements. The switch to an export-promotion policy was followed by an unprecedented rapid development of a modern manufacturing export sector. During this development GDP rose sharply. From 1960 to 1970 GDP *per capita* grew at 6.4 per cent a year on average, as against 2.0 per cent during the 1953–1960 period. This growth rate even accelerated to 7.5 per cent in the 1970s.

By 1975, the base year of our analysis, the export-oriented industrialization strategy had been in effect for over 10 years. GNP *per capita* in that year amounted to US$590, with which South Korea ranked among the middle-income countries.[1]

14.2 INDUSTRIALIZATION AND TRADE STRATEGIES IN SOUTH KOREA

During the second half of the 1950s, when South Korea had largely recovered from its wartime destruction, an import-substitution strategy of industrialization was carried out behind protective barriers in the form of both tariffs and quantitative restrictions.[2] The latter form of import control was increasingly being relied upon to offset the disturbing effect of a highly overvalued domestic currency, the Won, on the balance of payments. In addition, recurrent balance-of-payments problems led to a complex system of multiple exchange rates, of which the rates varied depending upon the type of import. In general, high levels of protection were granted to finished consumer goods industries. No, or low, tariffs were imposed on imports of food grains, intermediates and machinery. The promotion of manufactured export production was not given serious consideration, although some export incentives did exist. Hence, the second half of the 1950s was a period of major import substitution for consumer nondurables and other light industry, during which exports played a minor role in Korea's industrialization. Manufacturing activity expanded rapidly during this period, albeit from a small base and with much of the impetus coming from the sizeable foreign economic assistance, mainly from the United States.

During the next few years, South Korea came to experience sweeping upheavals politically as well as economically. Severe social instabilities came to a head and led to several changes in the Government during the 1960–1964 period. At the same time, manufacturing growth began to falter and it became apparent that further opportunities for first-stage import substitution were limited. Moreover, balance-of-payments problems persisted and came to a crisis in 1963, when grant aid from the United States was reduced substantially. Accordingly, new policies had to be devised to attain again high rates of manufacturing growth, to mobilize new financial resources and to improve the balance of payments. Korean authorities came to the view that these objectives could only be attained through an export-oriented industrialization strategy and an opening up of the economy. In the early 1960s, a number of attempts were made at economic liberalization and export promotion. Some policy reforms, however, had to be withdrawn, such as the establishment of a unified exchange rate in 1961 that had to be undone in 1963, but gradually an incentive system was created that generally favoured manufactured exports over import substitution.

The most important elements of this incentive system are the following. As early as 1959, exporters obtained tariff exemptions on imported intermediate inputs used in export production. In 1962, exporters were granted exemption from indirect taxes on both imported and domestically purchased intermediate inputs. In addition, indirect taxes no longer had to be paid on export sales. In the same year, a 50 per cent income tax reduction on foreign-exchange earnings from exporting became operative. The major and lasting policy reforms were implemented in the 1964-1967 period. The exchange rate was again unified and the Won devalued against the U.S. dollar by almost 100 per cent in 1964. A notable policy change was carried through in 1965, when all export incentives were extended to producers supplying intermediate inputs to exporters. This extension aimed at neutralizing the bias against domestically produced intermediates which resulted from the duty-free availability of imported intermediates to exporters. From 1966 onwards, imports of capital goods and equipment used in export production, both directly and indirectly through input supplies, were exempted from tariffs. Moreover, it was permitted to apply accelerated depreciation schemes, thus reducing taxable income substantially. Furthermore, exporters were afforded credits at preferential interest rates and reduced prices for electricity and railroad transport. Finally, mention has to be made of the so-called wastage allowance subsidy. Exporters are entitled to duty-free imports of intermediate inputs up to stated limits, including a generous allowance to cover defective inputs and wastage in the production process. The allowances granted seem to have significantly exceeded actual wastages. The fraction of imported inputs not used up in the production of exportables can be legally and profitably sold in the domestic market. This package of export incentives comprises measures to subject exporters to world market prices for their inputs and outputs as well as genuine subsidies.

Meanwhile, the tariff structure that had been created to protect import-substituting industries remained essentially unchanged, albeit import controls have been liberalized and partial or complete tariff exemptions have been increasingly granted since the mid-1960s. In fact, tariff exemptions far outweighed tariff collections on imports as early as 1968. All this did not mean that further import-substitution attempts were given up. On the contrary, the Korean Government continued to promote import substitution, but only in selected areas and no sooner than an efficient scale of operation could be realized. Some intermediate industries, especially synthetic fibre yarns and thread, petroleum products and metal products receive strong government support. More recently, attention has been shifted to machinery, ship building and transport equipment as new areas of support. These priority industries are also selected for their long-term possibilities of penetrating export markets. No dualistic policy goals are therefore found in the Korean industrialization and trade regime, because, in fact, no strategic differentiation is made between import substitution and export promotion.[3]

The net result of these policy reforms can be assessed from the effective protection afforded to different categories of production. Westphal and Kim got through a detailed analysis of the impact of Korean incentive policies for the year 1968.[4] They found that Korea's pattern of protection is virtually unique among developing countries for the following reasons. To begin with, the average nominal protection rate in South Korea appeared to be quite low, namely 14 per cent in 1968. Furthermore, it was found that primary production received a higher effective protection and subsidy rate than manufacturing. Effective protection afforded to manufacturing in total was slightly negative. Differentiating between manufacturing production for export and for the domestic market, Westphal and Kim found domestic sales to be penalized. In 1968, the effective protection and subsidy rate on manufactured exports was 12.4 per cent as against –8.9 per cent for sales on the domestic market. If account is taken of the slight overvaluation of the Won in 1968, Westphal concludes that in South Korea, ". . . the average net effective subsidy rate on manufactured exports was virtually zero . . .", thus amounting to free-trade conditions for exporters.[5]

The principal instruments of the export-promotion policy remained unchanged throughout the 1970s, although the accents were gradually shifted. In general, subsidies were abolished or lowered and greater efforts were undertaken in the organizational sphere. Subsidies, which were required to offset the periodic overvaluation of the Won, were reduced in 1973 for instance, following an exchange rate devaluation of over 20 per cent against the U.S. dollar. Major exchange rate adjustments took place in the early 1980s as well. Some new instruments were developed, such as the launching of an EPFZ programme, leading to the establishment of the Masan (1970) and Iri (1973) EPFZs. These zones were explicitly designed to attract direct foreign investments in export industries. This policy meant a break with the 1960s, as during these years Korea's manufactured exports have been produced almost exclusively by domestic firms. Wholly or partly foreign-owned firms were responsible for only 6 per cent of Korea's total merchandise exports in 1971. Thereafter, the inflows of direct foreign investments in the export sector, both inside and outside EPFZs, accelerated. In 1975, wholly or partly foreign-owned foreign firms accounted for 18 per cent of merchandise exports. Direct foreign investments in the export sector have been disproportionally directed to electronics, followed by textiles and clothing. In 1978, foreign firms were responsible for three quarters of the exports of electronics and a tenth of those of textiles and clothing.[6] The export electronics industry is concentrated in EPFZs, which are particularly suited to the offshore assembly activities of multinational electronics firms. Clearly, electronics presents an atypical case in regard to the overall modest contribution of foreign firms to Korea's export expansion. A new development in the field of marketing exports has been the establishment of indigenous general trading houses after the Japanese model. The Government promoted the grouping of companies with their own trading houses which could function as purchasing and sales agent for their aggregate production. At the start of the 1980s, 13 of such trading companies were already established.[7] Mention should also be made of the deliberate policy to upgrade the country's composition of manufacturing and exports by shifting to more skill- and technology-intensive lines of production. Since the mid-1970s, the Korean Government has started to project future patterns of production and exports and tries at the same time to direct investments accordingly.[8] New production activities may temporarily enjoy import-substitution protection, but exporting is always the ultimate aim, as has already been noted.

In sum, under the incentive system prevailing in South Korea, manufactured exports are vigorously and continually being promoted. From 1965, the resulting expansion of manufactured exports has been unprecedented. In terms of dollar value, in the period 1965–1980, manufactured exports grew from US$110 million to US$15,900 million, an average growth rate of about 40 per cent per year. In turn, the growth of exports substantially contributed to the growth of manufacturing output, leading almost to a redoubling of the manufacturing share in GDP from 17.9 per cent in 1965 to 33.2 per cent in 1980.[9]

Finally, as most observers mention in explaining Korea's export performance, one should not fail to note the importance of other factors that are not directly related to the trade regime. These factors all refer to the strong commitment of the government to economic development and export-oriented industrialization, a commitment that might also be interpreted as a direct and indirect government control of large and essential parts of the economy. The government, for instance, largely owns the organized banking sector and the shares of public ownership in utilities, transport, communication, mining and manufacturing are substantial. In the mid-1960s, a number of reforms were carried through in the field of monetary and fiscal policy in order to mobilize additional financial sources to meet the rapid decline in grant aid from the United States. Through its control over the banking sector, the government could raise the interest rates to increase private savings. Tax reforms were introduced to increase government savings. Along with measures to encourage an inflow of foreign loans, which required official approval, the government was placed in control of more than two thirds of the investable resources of the economy.[10] In addition to direct control, the government succeeded in regulating the private sector through an ingenious system of close collaboration. Confining ourselves to export promotion, the government-subsidized Korean Trade Promotion Corporation was founded to promote exports and explore new markets, and was also assigned to special diplomatic trade missions abroad by the government. The already mentioned government support for Korean trading

THE CASE OF SOUTH KOREA 323

houses and guided government intervention in moving into higher quality exports may also serve as illustrations. But perhaps most important has been the institution of full-scale annual export targets, formulated and administered by the Ministry of Commerce and Industry. These export targets are broken down quarterly and in detail by exporter, product and market destination. At monthly sessions of officials and exporters at the Ministry, the realization of export targets is monitored and possible difficulties in meeting targets are identified. If necessary, coordinated action is undertaken, both by exporters and officials at the highest levels. Furthermore, successful exporters are officially honoured and thereby receive strong encouragement.

Korea's experience with export-oriented growth is often presented as a typical case of successful capitalist development. Be that as it may, it is certainly not one of the classical *laissez-faire* type. The economy operates under a highly centralized guidance. Some authors understand this guidance as ". . . an unusual degree of acceptance of the identity between the interest of groups and national economic advancement".[11] This social environment is characterized by a well- educated, industrious, mobile and non-militant labour force, and an entrepreneurial class that associates individual objectives with national economic aspirations. Others speak of ". . . a highy interventionist regime, where the nature of intervention was a mixture of direct and indirect controls as well as a combination of formal and informal mechanisms of coercion and compliance".[12]

14.3 STRUCTURAL FEATURES OF THE KOREAN ECONOMY

In a relatively short time, South Korea has been transformed from a largely agricultural society into a semi-industrialized economy. It emerges from Table 14.1 that, by 1975, almost half of the economy's total gross output and over one third of total employment originated in the manufacturing sector — even though its contribution of GDP substantially lagged behind that of services. Korea's successful export-oriented industrialization is reflected in the 74.5 per cent share of manufactures in total export of goods and services. Unlike most developing countries, exports of primary products are of only minor importance.

Two phenomena of the Korean economy may deserve special attention. The first is the relatively isolated character of the manufacturing sector in the context of the Korean economy. This becomes evident in observing the 87.5 per cent share of manufacturing in total intermediate imports and its rather low *NFEE* value of 0.61 in 1975. The high import content of Korea's total manufacturing production stems in the first instance from the country's poor endowment of natural resources. Characteristic of manufacturing production

TABLE 14.1
BASIC DATA ON THE STRUCTURE OF THE KOREAN ECONOMY, 1975

Indicators	Agriculture & Mining	Manufacturing	Construction	Utilities	Services
1. Share in total gross output (%)	15.3	47.7	6.7	1.6	28.7
2. Share in GDP (%)	24.2	27.1	5.2	1.2	42.3
3. Share in total employment (%)	17.0	35.2	9.8	.7	37.3
4. Export-output ratio (%)	6.1	21.0	.4	.3	8.6
5. Share in total exports (%)	6.9	74.5	.2	.0	18.4
6. Share in intermediate imports (%)	2.7	87.5	3.0	.7	6.1
7. Input structure					
— Domestic intermediate inputs	.24	.49	.58	.60	.29
— Imported intermediate inputs	.02	.25	.06	.06	.03
— Gross value added	.74	.26	.36	.34	.68
Total inputs	1.00	1.00	1.00	1.00	1.00
8. $NFEE$	.92	.61	.76	.76	.90
9. P	.79	1.05	1.15	1.17	.85
10. $\overset{*}{P}$	.48	.54	1.74	1.74	.50
11. P^E	.88	.88	1.39	.80	1.05
12. P^{E-A}	.17	.99	1.65	.92	1.26
13. WIM^E (per 10^9 Won output)	425.3	440.0	728.2	425.5	578.7
14. l^e (per 10^9 Won output)	264.4	174.8	344.0	102.2	307.6
15. VA/L (10^3 Won)	2,786	1,506	1,035	3,349	2,216
16. T^e (per 10^9 Won output)	350.6	351.3	558.7	321.4	421.5
17. s (10^3 Won)	422.8	481.3	672.1	865.3	836.7

For explanation of symbols, see Section 10.4.
Sources: see Appendix to Chapter 14.

in the three countries treated in the preceding chapters is the prevalence of NRB activities, based on an ample local and diversified supply of primary products. As established, it facilitates a strong production linkage between manufacturing and primary sectors in those countries, and, consequently, the import content of NRB production is very low. This is, however, certainly not representative for manufacturing production in South Korea. In 1975, about 40 per cent of manufacturing consisted of NRB production, but a large majority of the required raw materials had to be imported. In fact, the share of raw materials from domestic agriculture and mining constituted only 5 per cent of the total value of manufacturing production. The remainder of the 49 per cent share of domestic inputs entering manufacturing originated largely in the manufacturing sector itself. Thus, the linkages between the manufacturing sector and the rest of the economy are weak. Manufacturing production is, on the contrary, linked with the world economy and shows a relatively high level of internal interdependence. This specific input structure is clearly illustrated if two dispersion measures are compared, viz. the common P measure and the P^* measure that excludes intrasectoral deliveries. As Table 14.1 shows, the P value for manufacturing drops sharply from 1.05 to 0.54 in case the intrasectoral deliveries are not taken into account. The high P value for manufacturing, however, cannot solely be ascribed to the intensity of intrasectoral deliveries. As is revealed by the sectoral input structures presented in Table 14.1, value added in manufacturing accounted for only 26 per cent of total output. This low value-added component as such raises the share of intermediate inputs in the value of production, and therewith, the relative importance of backward linkages.

The second specific phenomenon relates to the relatively low labour intensity of Korean manufacturing. The direct labour coefficient of manufacturing production is, next to utilities, the lowest of the entire economy. Yet, manufacturing may not be characterized as a capital-intensive activity, as value added per employee in manufacturing is relatively low as well. Not only is in manufacturing the value-added component the lowest of the economy, manufacturing workers also generate the least value added, next to construction. Value added per employee in manufacturing is roughly half and two thirds of that in primary sectors and services, respectively. This picture contrasts sharply with the experience of the countries treated earlier where always a reverse pattern of productivity differences between primary sectors and manufacturing was observed. Apparently, Korean manufacturing production largely consists of the further processing or assembly of semi-manufactured intermediates. In conformity herewith, a relatively low average remuneration per employee is paid for these activities. The manufacturing wage rate is by far the lowest among the non-agricultural sectors. The wage differential compared to the primary sector was not more than 12 per cent in favour of manufacturing in 1975. Consequently, the Korean manufacturing sector is a low-wage sector which generates little value added.

Finally, the employment spread effects of manufacturing, measured by P^E, are below the economy's average. The P^{E-A} value for manufacturing is, by contrast, very close to 1, again an indication of the weak interdependence with the primary sector.

14.4 DEVELOPMENT AND STRUCTURE OF KOREAN MANUFACTURED EXPORTS

As is seen in Figure 14.1, manufactures already accounted for over three quarters of total merchandise exports in 1970, and witnessed even a further increase to more than 90 per cent in 1980. During the same period, the share of exports in total manufacturing output rose from 15 to over 25 per cent. The growth of manufactured exports faltered only in 1975 and 1980, due to depressed world economic conditions. The increasing diversification of Korea's exports over time may be seen in Figure 14.2. In the early 1970s, almost 50 per cent of manufactured exports was accounted for by textiles and clothing. This share dropped to about 32 per cent in 1980. Other exportables gained in importance, most notably telecommunication products, sound equipment and electrical machinery. The latter product group mainly consists of transistors, valves and micro-circuits, which are increasingly being produced in EPFZs. The contribution of EPFZs to Korea's export performance has been rather unimportant otherwise. The share of exports from Masan EPFZ, by far the largest of the two zones in South Korea, in total manufactured exports did not amount to more than 4.5 per cent in 1979.[13]

Figure 14.1
Manufactured Export Performance of South Korea, 1970-1980

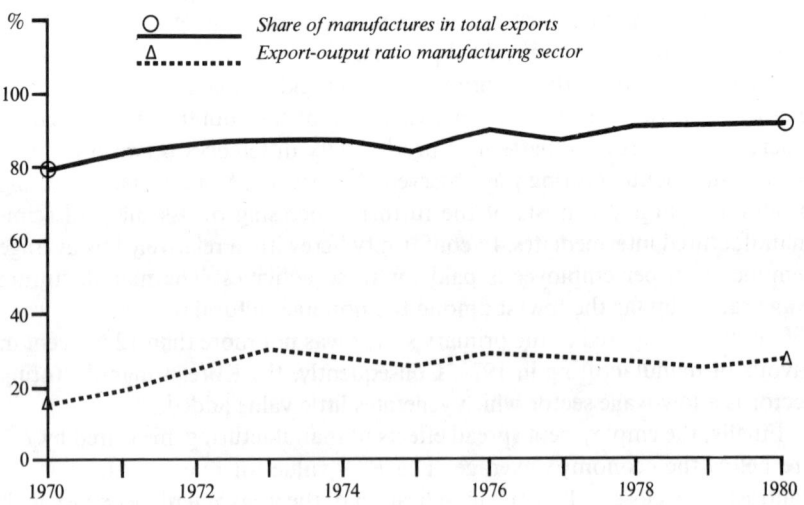

Figure 14.2
Composition of Korean Manufactured Exports, 1970-1980
(percentage shares)

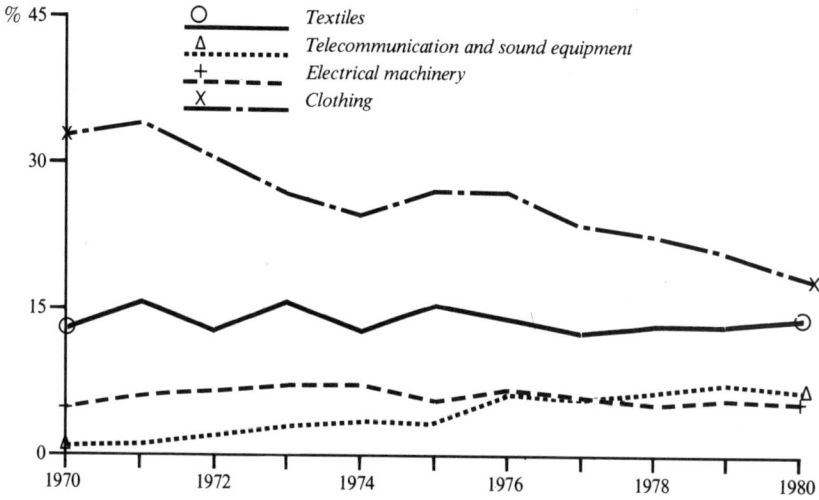

Sources: United Nations, *Yearbook of International Trade Statistics*, Volume I, New York, various issues; United Nations, *Yearbook of Industrial Statistics*, Volume I, New York, various issues.

The data presented in Table 14.2 provide insight into the structure and characteristics of Korean manufactured exports by 1975. First of all we observe that manufactured exports are dominated by non-NRB products. The export orientation of non-NRB sectors, as well as the share of these sectors in total exports, is markedly higher than for NRB sectors. Next, it appears that the structure of Korean manufactured exports is an outstanding example of a consistent pattern of specialization in labour-intensive manufactures. As the average values of the direct and total labour coefficients in Table 14.2 indicate, total manufactured exports as well as the distinguished sub-categories of exports are more labour intensive than corresponding categories of total production. Among the different export categories, exports from E sectors show the highest labour requirements per unit of exports. The mutual differences between the production and export categories are substantial. The average direct labour coefficient for exports from E sectors is almost twice and three times as high as production in DMO and NRB sectors, respectively. The data on value added and gross profit per employee

TABLE 14.2
CHARACTERISTICS OF MAJOR PRODUCTION AND EXPORT CATEGORIES, KOREAN MANUFACTURING SECTOR, 1975

Category	E/O (%)	E/E_m (%)	I^e	T^e (per 10^9 Won output)	Share of labour-intensive products (%)	VA/L (10^3 Won)	GP/L (10^3 Won)	O^1 (%)	F^2 (%)	s (10^3 Won)	Share of wages & salaries in gross value added (%)
Total manufactured exports	—	100	242.9	394.7	71.5	—	—	—	—	—	—
Total manufacturing production	21.0	—	174.8	310.3	—	1,506	1,025	85.4	48.0	481.3	32.0
NRB manufactured exports	—	21.0	140.8	289.4	16.2	—	—	—	—	—	—
NRB manufacturing production	10.8	—	107.0	232.1	—	2,432	1,904	79.3	29.2	528.6	21.7
Exports from E sectors	—	63.4	296.6	453.6	93.7	—	—	—	—	—	—
Production in E sectors	47.3	—	292.8	451.3	—	920	544	90.2	61.9	376.3	40.9
Exports from DMO sectors	—	15.6	162.4	297.2	55.9	—	—	—	—	—	—
Production in DMO sectors	10.6	—	156.9	285.4	—	1,666	1,049	81.0	42.8	616.6	37.0

For explanation of symbols, see Section 10.4.
Notes : ^{1} O = share of operatives in employment.
 ^{2} F = share of females in employment.
Sources : see Appendix to Chapter 14.

provide the same picture, with the highest average values for NRB sectors, followed by DMO sectors and clearly the lowest for E sectors. Consistent with this specialization pattern, E sectors pay, on average, the lowest wages, while the share of labour's remuneration in gross value added in these sectors is higher than in the remaining sectors.

Fortunately, for 1975, information could be gathered on the skill and gender composition of the labour force, broken down in considerable detail by sector so that a sector classification could be obtained identical to the one used in our application of the 1975 input-output table. From these data, also presented in Table 14.2, it emerges with clarity that E sectors employ both the highest share of operatives and females. A notable feature is the fact that, in South Korea, females are for 93.6 per cent employed as operatives.

The relationships between export orientation, factor intensity and the composition and remuneration of labour can be gauged from the matrix of rank order correlation coefficients presented in Table 14.3. The percentage share of females in sectoral employment is added as a variable in the rankings. In the case of South Korea, two inevitable conclusions emerge from this analysis. To begin with, the extent of correlation between the rankings by the four measures of factor intensity is very strong and they show the expected signs. The same is true of the rankings by these measures of factor intensity and sectoral wage rates, implying that a higher labour intensity is significantly associated with a lower wage rate. Moreover, there appears to be a high degree of negative correspondence in the sectoral rankings according to wage level and the female share in the labour force. The existence of this correlation, which is significant at the 1 per cent level, clearly illustrates that female participation in the labour force depresses the average wage level. Thus we find a consistent set of relationships, indicating that a higher labour intensity of production is significantly associated with a lower average wage rate and a higher employment share of females.

The second conclusion refers to the highly significant rank order relationship between sectoral export-output ratios on the one hand, and measures of factor intensity, sectoral wage rates and the share of females in sectoral employment on the other. The signs of the correlation coefficients reveal that the higher a sector's export orientation, the higher will be its labour intensity of production, and, in turn, the lower the average sectoral wage level, brought about by a relatively high employment of female workers. From this analysis it turns out that Korean export specialization is consistently directed towards labour-intensive and low-wage products, which are primarily being produced by female operatives. Both these conclusions hold as well when NRB sectors are excluded from the analysis.

Among the E sectors, which are presented in Table A.14.2, the various textile and clothing products, electronic components and miscellaneous

TABLE 14.3
MATRIX OF SPEARMAN RANK CORRELATION COEFFICIENTS FOR SECTOR CHARACTERISTICS, SOUTH KOREA, 1975[2,3]

Variable	E_i/O_i	E_i/E_m	I_i^e	VA_i/L_i	GP_i/L_i	T_i^e	s_i	F_i^l
E_i/O_i	1	.80**	.49**	−.47**	−.43**	.40**	−.71**	.57**
		.75**	.45*	−.54**	−.44**	.45*	−.77**	.50**
E_i/E_m		1	.21	−.18	−.14	.16	−.46**	.45**
			.32	−.32	−.24	.38*	−.67**	.47*
I_i^e			1	−.63**	−.63**	.86**	−.71**	.52**
				−.64**	−.66**	.92**	−.66**	.49**
VA_i/L_i				1	.98**	−.63**	.64**	−.42**
					.97**	−.65**	.57**	−.44**
GP_i/L_i					1	−.63**	.57**	−.37*
						−.67**	.47**	−.36
T_i^e						1	−.67**	.44**
							−.68**	.50**
s_i							1	−.69**
								−.70**
F_i^l								1

For explanation of symbols, see Section 10.4.
Notes : [1] F_i = share of females in sectoral employment.
[2] The upper coefficients in a row refer to rankings of all manufacturing sectors (n = 43), the lower coefficients refer to rankings of non-NRB sectors only (n = 28).
[3] Correlation coefficients that are significant at the 5 per cent level are denoted by one asterisk (*), those significant at the 1 per cent level by two asterisks (**).
Sources : see Appendix to Chapter 14.

manufactures fit distinctly into this specialization pattern. These products have a relatively high labour intensity and the remuneration of labour in their manufacture is relatively low. In conformity herewith, the share of female workers in the labour force of sectors producing these exportables is high, ranging from about two thirds in electronic components and miscellaneous manufacturing to three quarters in wearing apparel.

14.5 SPREAD EFFECTS OF KOREAN MANUFACTURED EXPORTS

Although Korean manufactured exports are highly dependent on intermediate imports, these exports nevertheless perform a relatively integrating function, especially between industries within the manufacturing sector. This at first glance conflicting finding with respect to the spread effects of Korean manufactured exports emerges from the evidence in Table 14.4. Total manufactured exports show a $NFEE$ value as low as 0.58, whereas the production linkages emanating from these exports are clearly above the economy's average as well as above the average for total manufacturing production, namely 1.10. These findings are explained if we consider, first, the fact that the entire manufacturing sector is highly import dependent and, second, the relatively limited amount of value added that is directly generated in the production of manufactured exports. The domestic value-added component of total manufactured exports is a little higher than that of total manufacturing production, as indicated by their $NFEE$ values of 0.58 and 0.56, respectively. Strikingly, the extremely low $NFEE$ value of 0.49 for NRB exports contrasts unfavourably with that of total manufactured exports. Exports from E sectors show in this respect a better record, with a slightly higher $NFEE$ value than that for non-NRB production. The extremely high import dependence of NRB export and production illustrates again the decisive impact of the availability of natural resources on the level of integration of the economy. A lack of natural wealth leads inevitably to an import dependent economy. If, against this background, due account is taken of the already established relatively low direct value-added component in Korean manufacturing production, which for all three different categories of sectors lies in the vicinity of 26 per cent, it is explicable that the different categories of exports and production nonetheless show P values above 1. The somewhat higher $NFEE$ value for exports from E sectors is therefore also immediately reflected in the highest P value of 1.13.

Likewise, the employment spread effects are more extensive for total manufactured exports than for total manufacturing production. This difference stems from the higher level of sectoral integration of non-NRB sectors, but above all, from the avowed labour-intensive nature of non-NRB

TABLE 14.4
WEIGHTED AVERAGE MEASURES OF SPREAD EFFECTS FOR MAJOR CATEGORIES OF EXPORT AND PRODUCTION, SOUTH KOREA, 1975

Category	P	$NFEE$	P^E	$P^{E\text{-}A}$	WIM	WIM^E (per 10^9 Won output)
Total manufactured exports	1.10	.58	.98	1.06	.23	467.7
NRB exports	1.01	.49	.72	.64	.18	346.4
Exports from E sectors	1.13	.60	1.12	1.26	.25	532.2
Exports from DMO sectors	1.07	.58	.74	.81	.23	369.2
Total manufacturing production	1.04	.56	.77	.83	.21	375.2
NRB production	.94	.52	.57	.56	.16	283.1
Non-NRB production	1.10	.59	.90	1.01	.24	438.8

For explanation of symbols, see Section 10.4.
Sources: see Appendix to Chapter 14.

exports. Both these mutually reinforcing effects appear to be most notably at work in the case of exports from E sectors. Whereas the employment spread measures P^E and P^{E-A} for NRB and DMO categories of export and production lie below 1, these measures for exports from E sectors are 1.12 and 1.26, respectively. Accordingly, the secondary employment effects through the spending of wage incomes are far more extensive for E sectors, about 50 per cent, than those for other production categories. Thus, given the structural features of the Korean economy, the export-oriented strategy pursued optimally contributes to employment growth in manufacturing.

A closer examination of individual manufactured exports, presented in Table A.14.2, reveals that the record of spread effects varies substantially between different product groups. The strongest spread effects are most clearly found in the production and exports of textiles and wearing apparel. In the case of these production processes, a clear hierarchy of sectors can be established leading from intermediate to finished products. For example, the proportion of domestic intermediate purchases by knit goods industries equals 69.3 per cent of total value of production. These inputs consist again for 66.6 per cent of fibre yarn. In turn, industries producing fibre yarn purchase domestically produced synthetic resins, which constitute almost half of their total input requirement. Finally, industries producing synthetic resins are highly dependent on imports of basic petrochemical products. The relatively extensive backward linkages of textiles and clothing production contribute to a broadening of the industrial base and are the result of the government's selective efforts to support the import substitution of some intermediate products.

By contrast, production and export of electrical appliances and electronic components, which constitute the main activities in Korea's EPFZs, equally cannot be typified as integrating production activities. As can be seen from Table A.14.2, the spread effects of this type of export production are substantially below the economy's average. Exports of electronic components, which are channelled as internal transfers of mainly Japanese multinational corporations, show the poorest record of spread effects among all major exportables, the *NFEE* value of these exports being as low as 0.42.

Turning now to the correlation analysis of sectoral rankings by export orientation, direct labour coefficient and different measures of spread effects, the following observations can be made. First, from the matrix of correlation coefficients given in Table 14.5, we find no significant correlation between sectoral export-output ratios on the one hand, and sectoral spread effects in terms of production linkages, measured by *P* and *NFEE*, on the other. The absence of any significant relationship indicates that Korean manufacturing industries show a high import dependency irrespective of their market orientation. Second, there is a strong positive relationship, significant at the 1

TABLE 14.5
MATRIX OF SPEARMAN RANK CORRELATION COEFFICIENTS FOR SECTOR CHARACTERISTICS AND VARIOUS MEASURES OF SPREAD EFFECTS, SOUTH KOREA[1,2]

Variable	E_i/O_i	l_i^e	s_i	P_i	$NFEE_i$	P_i^E	P_i^{E-A}	WIM_i	WIM_i^E
E_i/O_i	1	.49**	−.71**	.22	−.05	.40**	.41**	.18	.37*
		.45*	−.77**	.03	−.04	.45*	.44*	.04	.40*
l_i^e		1	−.71**	.14	.48**	.86**	.89**	.72**	.85**
			−.66**	.13	.48*	.92**	.93**	.63**	.91**
s_i			1	−.20	−.32*	−.67**	−.65**	−.34*	−.63**
				−.19	−.29	−.68**	−.66**	−.19	−.63**
P_i				1	.40**	.48**	.41**	.53**	.50**
					.45*	.41*	.39*	.49*	.43*
$NFEE_i$					1	.67**	.59**	.69**	.68**
						.66**	.66**	.75**	.69**
P_i^E						1	.97**	.90**	1.00**
							1.00**	.77**	.99**
P_i^{E-A}							1	.88**	.97**
								.78**	.99**
WIM_i								1	.92**
									.82**
WIM_i^E									1

For explanation of symbols, see Section 10.4.

Notes :   [1] The upper coefficients in a row refer to rankings of all manufacturing sectors (n = 43), the lower coefficients refer to rankings of non-NRB sectors only (n = 28).
[2] Correlation coefficients that are significant at the 5 per cent level are denoted by one asterisk (*), those significant at the 1 per cent level by two asterisks (**).

Sources : see Appendix to Chapter 14.

per cent level in case all sectors are included and at the 5 per cent level for non-NRB sectors only, between a sector's direct labour coefficient and its *NFEE* value. Thus, the more labour-intensive sectors have a lower import content in production. Notwithstanding this relationship, labour-intensive sectors, however, do not show a significantly higher level of production linkages. Indeed, there is a positive correlation between the rankings by direct labour coefficient and *P* value, but this relationship ceases to be statistically significant. As expected, the correlations between the direct labour coefficient on the one hand, and the various measures of employment spread effects on the other, are positive and highly significant. Third, we observe highly significant rank order correlations between the various measures of spread effects. It is, finally, remarkable to find no changes, or only minor ones, in the level of significance of the correlations if NRB sectors are excluded from the sample. This implies that Korean manufacturing industries all produce under comparable economic conditions, whether their production is based on the processing of natural resources or not.

Thus, our analysis reaches the conclusion that differences in market orientation have no significant impact on the extent of production spread effects. What indeed became clear is the generally lower import content in labour-intensive products and this reinforces our earlier finding as to the higher level, on average, of both production and employment spread effects of the more export-oriented E sectors.

14.6 SUMMARY

South Korea is one of the few countries that stands out as a successful case of transition from import substitution to an export-oriented strategy of industrialization. The shifts in the trade and industrialization regime were carried through from the early 1960s onwards, and created free-trade conditions for exporters. Export promotion was accompanied by moderate import substitution of intermediate and producer goods on the understanding, however, that this development in depth may not conflict with the interests of exporters. In fact, secondary import-substitution industries have to generate the future exports. The Korean government has assumed a dominant role in indicating the course of economic development.

The Korean case suggests that a developing country deprived of natural resources and geared towards the export of manufactures brings about a specific economic structure, characterized by a relatively labour-intensive manufacturing sector with a relatively low wage level *vis-à-vis* other sectors. In addition, manufacturing is a highly import-dependent production activity that generates little domestic value added per unit of output.

By 1975, Korean manufactured exports were consistently directed towards labour-intensive and low-wage products. The participation of female operatives appears to be higher along with a higher labour intensity and a lower wage rate. Apparently, export production largely consists of labour-value-added processing.

The spread effects of Korean manufactured exports do not compare unfavourably with the average record of manufacturing production. Quite the contrary, both the production and employment spread effects are actually the most extensive for manufactured exports. Moreover, exports show a slightly higher domestic value-added component. It emerges with clarity that especially the more labour-intensive sectors have a lower import content in production. This finding does not hold for the export production of electronics in EPFZs.

APPENDIX TABLE A.14.1
CHARACTERISTICS OF MANUFACTURING SECTORS CLASSIFIED AS NRB SECTORS, SOUTH KOREA, 1975

I-O Code	Sector	E_i/O_i (%)	E_i/E_m (%)	f_i^e (per 10^9 Won Output)	T_i^e	VA_i/L_i	GP_i/L_i (10^3 Won)	s_i	O_i^1 (%)	F_i^2 (%)	P_i	$NFEE_i$	P_i^E	P_i^{E-A}	WIM_i	WIM_i^E (per 10^9 Won Output)
10	Slaughtering, dairy products and fruits processing	10.5	1.4	127.4	450.8	1,060	590	470	79.9	48.1	1.44	.85	1.12	.68	.27	533.8
11	Sea food processing	58.1	2.4	360.8	816.9	590	280	310	86.8	64.3	1.21	.79	2.02	1.33	.39	940.0
12	Grain polishing	.0	.0	490.7	569.8	1,430	920	510	82.9	9.4	.86	.89	1.41	1.61	.38	688.1
13	Cereal flours	.0	.0	94.8	131.1	−150	−670	510	82.9	9.4	.67	.08	.32	.37	.09	160.7
14	Other food preparations	11.1	3.1	140.3	251.3	1,620	1,110	510	77.3	46.3	.95	.51	.62	.63	.17	303.5
15	Beverages	2.7	.5	81.9	207.7	5,510	4,880	630	63.4	19.6	1.02	.78	.51	.54	.16	257.9
16	Tobacco	.1	.0	122.8	232.3	5,670	5,210	460	79.8	36.2	.80	.90	.58	.49	.13	274.0
21	Lumber and plywood	43.2	4.6	167.0	233.9	1,080	630	450	84.7	28.6	.79	.36	.58	.64	.15	281.1
22	Wood products and furniture	21.7	.4	522.9	699.7	590	250	330	89.3	26.9	1.08	.66	1.73	1.93	.35	808.6
23	Pulp and paper	5.6	.6	199.6	332.2	1,340	810	530	82.4	29.4	.98	.60	.82	.90	.23	405.1
31	Petroleum products	6.3	2.7	13.4	24.8	18,650	17,080	1,570	54.9	8.3	.63	.29	.06	.07	.04	36.4
32	Coal products	.2	.0	122.5	758.7	1,320	850	470	69.2	3.7	1.26	.84	1.88	2.10	.62	952.9
35	Pig iron and raw steel	1.3	.2	56.0	175.5	1,830	1,150	680	82.1	4.5	1.06	.36	.43	.49	.15	222.6
36	Primary iron and steel products	23.8	4.9	52.5	177.0	2,390	1,710	680	82.1	4.5	1.24	.41	.44	.50	.15	224.9
37	Non-ferrous metal ingots and primary products	6.2	.3	131.0	277.2	1,780	1,200	580	79.5	10.7	.96	.53	.69	.78	.22	345.8

APPENDIX TABLE A.14.2
CHARACTERISTICS OF MANUFACTURING SECTORS CLASSIFIED AS E SECTORS, SOUTH KOREA, 1975

I-O Code	Sector	E_i/O_i (%)	E_i/E_m (%)	l_i^e	T_i^e (per 10⁹ Won Output)	VA_i/L_i	GP_i/L_i (10³ Won)	s_i	O_i^1 (%)	F_i^2 (%)	P_i	$NFEE_i$	P_i^E	P_i^{EA}	WIM_i	WIM_i^E (per 10⁹ Won Output)
18a	Textile fabrics	36.8	7.6	216.9	419.9	960	560	400	92.7	73.0	1.37	.64	1.04	1.15	.26	499.9
19a	Knit goods	60.6	10.1	293.8	471.8	940	570	370	91.2	73.7	1.29	.67	1.17	1.29	.26	554.1
19b	Ropes and fishing nets	55.0	.7	201.5	368.4	1,080	670	410	88.3	59.4	1.25	.61	.91	1.01	.23	441.1
19c	Wearing apparel and apparel accessories	47.9	11.2	450.0	639.8	640	320	320	92.2	75.9	1.22	.66	1.58	1.79	.31	736.0
19d	Other fabricated textile products	46.1	2.6	483.0	641.9	670	340	330	90.0	67.5	1.17	.70	1.59	1.76	.31	739.1
20	Leather and leather products	44.1	3.8	297.8	456.2	950	540	400	88.0	43.3	.97	.56	1.13	1.27	.25	534.9
29b	Plastic products	34.5	2.9	249.5	372.5	1,100	730	370	87.8	45.4	1.09	.61	.92	1.05	.22	439.6
33	Rubber products	53.4	4.7	278.0	431.2	790	370	420	92.3	53.6	1.05	.54	1.07	1.21	.26	511.7
38	Fabricated metal products	29.1	2.7	227.2	359.4	1,050	580	470	86.2	15.4	1.19	.56	.89	1.01	.25	436.0
41a	Household electronic appliances	43.1	4.0	174.7	294.1	2,000	1,600	400	83.3	30.9	.91	.57	.73	.83	.17	346.7
41c	Electronic appliances	74.3	.9	214.3	319.0	860	440	420	84.8	44.2	.86	.38	.79	.90	.19	377.0
41d	Electronic components	61.3	6.0	246.0	320.6	1,060	620	440	87.4	69.3	.80	.42	.79	.90	.19	379.6
43	Measuring, medical and optical instruments	52.0	1.4	265.7	368.8	900	460	430	85.8	36.0	.91	.47	.91	1.04	.23	439.6
44	Miscellaneous manufacturing	58.2	4.8	260.3	419.5	1,300	920	380	90.9	62.5	1.10	.69	1.04	1.17	.25	496.1

APPENDIX TABLE A.14.3
CHARACTERISTICS OF MANUFACTURING SECTORS CLASSIFIED AS DMO SECTORS, SOUTH KOREA, 1975

I-O Code	Sector	E_i/O_i (%)	E_i/E_m (%)	I_i^e	T_i^e (per 10⁹ Won Output)	VA_i/L_i	GP_i/L_i (10⁶ Won)	s_i	O_i^1 (%)	F_i^2 (%)	P_i	$NFEE_i$	P_i^E	$P_i^{E\cdot A}$	WIM_i	WIM_i^E (per 10⁹ Won Output)
17	Fibre yarn	16.2	4.9	113.4	239.8	1,530	1,060	470	89.6	73.0	1.13	.50	.59	.60	.16	290.7
18b	Fibre bleaching and dyeing	.0	.0	265.1	340.7	1,330	850	480	89.2	58.5	.90	.59	.84	.96	.23	412.2
24	Printing and publishing	6.3	.3	322.5	518.3	1,120	460	650	73.7	26.7	1.15	.75	1.28	1.45	.41	646.7
25	Basic organic chemicals	9.3	.6	55.4	130.2	3,910	3,070	850	74.3	12.9	1.08	.52	.32	.37	.13	172.2
26	Basic inorganic chemicals	3.9	.2	81.7	164.8	3,290	2,440	850	74.3	12.9	.99	.53	.41	.46	.16	215.8
27	Chemical fertilizers	.0	.0	76.2	240.5	−880	−1,830	950	77.8	15.1	1.46	.42	.60	.68	.25	319.1
28	Drugs and cosmetics	1.9	.2	172.7	314.8	2,040	1,310	730	58.4	46.5	1.01	.69	.78	.87	.28	402.7
29a	Synthetic resins, synthetic rubber and chemical fibres	4.4	.7	82.1	149.0	2,880	2,230	660	78.3	19.9	.94	.47	.37	.42	.13	190.1
30	Other chemical products	2.9	.2	121.7	224.4	1,910	1,220	690	63.2	42.7	.96	.52	.56	.63	.19	285.1
34	Non-metallic mineral products	13.3	2.1	206.2	397.0	1,780	1,200	590	83.5	21.8	1.06	.74	.98	1.12	.29	488.1
39	General machinery	9.8	.8	263.0	410.1	1,270	730	540	84.6	12.1	1.13	.65	1.02	1.15	.30	503.1
40	Electrical machinery	11.8	1.2	204.4	356.8	1,510	1,050	460	83.1	33.5	1.11	.64	.88	1.00	.24	430.7
41b	Communication equipment	12.4	.2	331.6	469.9	1,050	620	440	87.4	69.3	1.03	.64	1.16	1.32	.28	558.2
42	Transportation equipment	19.7	4.0	180.2	307.4	1,690	890	800	77.6	6.6	1.03	.58	.76	.87	.28	396.3

For explanation of symbols, see Section 10.4.

Notes: [1] O_i = share of operatives in sectoral employment.
[2] F_i = share of females in sectoral employment.

Sources: computations are based on data from *1975 Input-Output Tables (II)*, The Bank of Korea, 1978; *Report on Mining and Manufacturing Survey 1975*, Economic Planning Board, 1977; *Year Book of Labour Statistics 1976*, Geneva, 1976, Table 2A.

15
The Case of Taiwan

15.1 INTRODUCTORY REMARKS

The islands of Taiwan Province or the Republic of China, hereafter simply referred to as Taiwan, cover 36,000 km^2. By 1980, 17.8 million people populated the limited area of the island republic, which implies a high population density of almost 500 persons per km^2.[1] Due to the mountainous and inhospitable character of Taiwan island, only a fourth of the total land area has been brought under cultivation. The population density per km^2 of cultivated land is therefore almost 2,000. Taiwan is poorly endowed with natural resources. From 1970, the contribution of mining activities, mainly the extraction of coal, gas and some non-metallic minerals, to net domestic product (NDP) has not been higher than 1.4 per cent.

During the 1950s, Taiwan embarked on a standard policy of import substitution which was, however, relatively mild and flexible. Due to the satisfactory performance of the manufacturing sector, domestic markets for non-durable consumer goods became more and more saturated. About 1960, Taiwan responded to these signs with a rather systematic package of policy changes to facilitate a shift from an inward-looking to an outward-looking strategy of industrialization. The growth performance since then has been impressive.

During the 1960s, the annual increases in real GNP *per capita* averaged 6.7 per cent. From 1970 to 1980, the real growth rate of GNP *per capita* rose to an average of 7.5 per cent per year. With an estimated GNP *per capita* of US$2,100 in 1980, Taiwan ranks among the middle-income developing countries. In 1976, the year covered by the input-output tables that will be used for our analyses, GNP *per capita* was estimated at US$1,040.

15.2 INDUSTRIALIZATION AND TRADE STRATEGIES IN TAIWAN

The impressive economic development of Taiwan is often directly attributed to its successful implementation of an export-oriented industrial expansion policy. However, there are several factors that might explain Taiwan's development as a major success story. First of all, during the period of Japanese colonial rule from 1895 to 1945, the island was transformed into a productive agricultural colony that provided Japan with foodstuffs, mainly sugar and rice. The Japanese spared no pains or expense to modernize agricultural production. They introduced better seeds, chemical fertilizers and new cultivating techniques and constructed an extensive irrigation system. New rural institutions ensured that innovations were widely disseminated. Large parts of the island were opened up through the construction of a network of railroads and feeder roads. But, second, unlike the common practice in a colonial situation, the Japanese also laid the base for industrialization of the economy.[2] The early industrial activities were closely linked to agriculture, either by using its output for further processing, like sugar refining, or providing the inputs to that sector, as was the case with the fertilizer-producing chemical industries. To support industrialization, the electrification of the economy was vigorously taken in hand. Later on, the Japanese were actively engaged in broadening the industrial structure through investments in intermediate and producer goods industries. In fact, the Japanese almost completely controlled Taiwan's modern industrial sector, both in terms of ownership, management and skilled labourers. By the outbreak of World War II, Taiwan possessed a modern agricultural sector and an excellent infrastructure. The substantial industrialization that already had taken place was rooted in agriculture.

The war, and the subsequent repatriation of the Japanese in 1945, followed thereafter by civil war and the evacuation of more than one million mainland refugees to Taiwan, necessitated a radical re-orientation of the economy. The postwar Taiwanese development strategies equally stressed the growth of agriculture and industry. Even prior to 1953, a comprehensive rural reconstruction and land reform programme was carried out which made agriculture increasingly more productive. The expropriated landlords were compensated in the form of government bonds and shares in large public-sector enterprises.

Industrial development could start on the basis of the industrial capital and infrastructure that passed into government control when the Japanese residents left Taiwan. Experienced managers and entrepreneurs from mainland China took over the Japanese positions and facilitated a quick recovery of the economy from its wartime destruction. By 1952, the public sector accounted for 56.2 per cent of total manufacturing production and accommodated food-processing industries and large-scale production of chemicals, fertilizers, cement, petroleum products and metal products.

In the early 1950s, a standard policy of import substitution gradually took shape. Primarily in response to inflation and balance-of-payments crises, the government imposed the usual package of import controls, tariffs and multiple exchange rates, while maintaining an overvalued domestic currency. Nondurable consumer goods industries enjoyed a higher level of protection than industries producing either intermediate or capital goods.[3] Thus, contrary to prewar industrialization which moved into secondary import substitution, the postwar process of import substitution emphasized the replacement of nondurable consumer goods imports. This primary import substitution proceeded at a rapid pace. Over the period 1952-1960, manufacturing production displayed an average annual growth rate of 13.0 per cent, resulting in an increasing share in NDP from 10.9 to 16.8 per cent during this period. The highest growth rates were realized in textiles, clothing, wood and leather products, and bicycles. Lower growth rates were recorded for food processing and intermediate goods industries that were accommodated in the public sector.[4] In this process, private enterprise has increasingly outgrown the public sector. Simultaneously, the already satisfactory infrastructure was further extended, and electric power became available throughout the island at uniform prices. The inflows of aid and loans from the United States during this period strongly supported economic development in Taiwan. It stabilized the economy, relaxed the foreign-exchange constraint and permitted a substantially higher level of capital formation, especially in the infrastructure. A notable share of aid was also allocated to education and skill creation.[5]

Two features of the Taiwanese process of import substitution distinguish it from many other developing countries.[6] First, import substitution was characterized by a relative mildness and flexibility of its regime. Second, thanks to the continued government support of the agricultural sector, agriculture was not severely discriminated against, as is usually the case during this phase. However, the shift in the direction of manufacturing growth away from food processing and intermediate goods resulted in a delinking of manufacturing from agriculture. By decreasing the import of nondurable consumer goods and favouring the import of intermediate and capital goods, the balance-of-payments pressures persisted. When during the second half of the 1950s, the growth of some nondurable consumer goods industries slowed down, private-sector investments stagnated and competition on the domestic market intensified, it became increasingly clear that the first stage of import substitution was already completed. The government responded to these signs with a rather systematic package of policy changes to facilitate a shift from an inward-looking to an outward-looking strategy of industrialization.

Policy reforms to liberalize trade and promote export of manufactures were initiated in 1958, and were extended in subsequent years.[7] The following major reforms may be recorded. First, the multiple exchange rate system was gradually transformed into a devalued unitary rate. For exporters, the effective devaluation of the domestic currency amounted to about 60 per cent. Second, quantitative restrictions on imports of intermediate and capital goods for exporting manufacturers were practically removed. Third, the procedure for rebate of import duty, commodity and other taxes on export products, already introduced in 1955, was simplified. Fourth, the effective protection for products on the domestic market was gradually reduced. Ever more products were scratched from the list of prohibited or controlled imports, until only a few remained by the end of the 1970s. A marked reduction in the general level of tariffs was effectuated in 1973. Fifth, a broad package of fiscal incentives, subsidies and other measures was put in place to promote exports. This package includes, for instance, cheap credit for exporters, income tax exemptions, cheap export insurance and marketing support. Finally, in view of filling the gap that was caused by the termination of aid from the United States in 1965, foreign direct investors were stimulated to participate in export production. Apart from a duty and tax-free trade regime, foreign investors were granted, among other things, a five-year corporate income tax holiday and a maximum of 25 per cent tax upon termination of this period. The investment climate was further improved by the establishment of EPFZs, bonded factories and warehouses. Investors in the zones enjoy all the aforementioned privileges and tax incentives provided to exporters, but, most importantly, without the red tape involved. The two larger EPFZs of Kaohsing and Nantze, established in 1965 and 1969, respectively, accommodate mainly electronics, garments and plastics industries. The smaller Taichung zone is especially designed for precision instruments.

Although there are very few studies available on the impact of the post-1958 reforms on the structure of protection, there can be little doubt that export production has become substantially more profitable than producing for the domestic market.[8] It is also clear that manufactured exports have grown very rapidly since then, and industrialization has gained its momentum. The manufacturing share in NDP further increased from 16.8 per cent in 1960 to 26.4 and 34.3 per cent in 1970 and 1980, respectively.

Direct foreign investors responded equally well to the shift in trade strategy. Foreign investment was negligible during the 1950s, but grew in importance to over 11 per cent of gross capital formation in Taiwan in 1971. After this peak year the relative importance of foreign investment ebbed.[9] Thus, on average, the contribution of foreign investment to capital accumulation has not been impressive in Taiwan. This is, however, not true of all sectors to the same degree. The bulk of foreign investment was directed to export industries, most notably to those producing electronics and electrical appliances in EPFZs. Judging by approvals, 52 per cent of cumulative private foreign investment in manufacturing from 1952 to 1980 has gone into electronics industries, followed by chemicals with a share of 21 per cent. By the mid-1970s, foreign firms accounted for over 80 per cent of the exports of electronics and electrical appliances.[10] In this respect, however, this sector is clearly exceptional.

The industries that grew fastest during the period of export-oriented industrialization, were, as will be shown hereafter, relatively intensive in unskilled labour. As a consequence of this and the rapid growth of exports, surplus labour in Taiwan was virtually exhausted at the start of the 1970s.[11] The scarcity of unskilled labour made it increasingly clear that future growth should be directed towards more capital- and skill-intensive industries. Since that time, the government has encouraged technology-intensive industries. Concomitantly, labour-intensive investments can count on less support; tax holidays, for instance, were periodically abandoned for such investments, whereas higher quality lines of production, intermediate industries and machinery are given extra attention. This new industrialization phase is oriented to both the export and the domestic market.

15.3 STRUCTURAL FEATURES OF THE TAIWANESE ECONOMY

Table 15.1 summarizes some salient features of the Taiwanese economy, derived from the aggregated five-sector input-output table for 1976. The rapid structural changes that have occurred in the economy during the past two decades have resulted in a 57.2 per cent share of manufacturing in total gross output. The share of agriculture and mining has fallen to 10.5 per cent. The contribution of manufacturing to GDP is less dominant, but still three times that of primary sectors and only slightly less than that of services. Employment is more or less equally distributed among primary, secondary and tertiary sectors. This economic structure approximates the structure of a developed country.

By 1976, manufactures occupied 92.1 per cent of total exports of goods and services. Exports of primary products accounted for only 3.0 per cent of total exports and consisted mainly of horticultural crops and fisheries. Exports of extractive primary products are insignificant. With an export-output ratio of 29.2 per cent, the manufacturing sector is definitely the most export-oriented sector. These data indicate the explicit orientation of the Taiwanese economy towards an export-oriented strategy of industrialization.

TABLE 15.1
BASIC DATA ON THE STRUCTURE OF THE TAIWANESE ECONOMY, 1976

Indicators	Agriculture & Mining	Manufacturing	Construction	Utilities	Services
1. Share in total gross output (%)	10.5	57.2	6.3	2.2	23.8
2. Share in GDP (%)	13.6	37.6	5.7	2.0	41.1
3. Share in total employment (%)	30.4	28.4	6.2	0.5	34.5
4. Export-output ratio (%)	5.2	29.2	—	—	3.8
5. Share in total exports (%)	3.0	92.1	—	—	4.9
6. Share in intermediate imports (%)	4.2	77.1	4.3	1.8	12.6
7. Input structure					
— Domestic intermediate inputs	.39	.53	.52	.49	.19
— Imported intermediate inputs	.06	.19	.10	.12	.08
— Gross value added	.55	.28	.38	.39	.73
Total inputs	1.00	1.00	1.00	1.00	1.00
8. $NFEE$	.84	.66	.76	.74	.88
9. P	.97	1.11	1.10	1.09	.74
10. $\overset{*}{P}$	.91	.63	1.66	1.45	.34
11. P^W	1.24	.81	1.11	.59	1.24
12. WIM	.73	.48	.66	.35	.73
13. I^w (per 10^3 NT$ output)	319.9	118.9	238.4	69.4	393.4
14. T^w (per 10^3 NT$ output)	469.4	307.7	423.3	224.5	468.5
15. Average monthly earnings of employees (NT$)	6,302[1]	4,707	4,911	7,238	6,371

For explanation of symbols, see Section 10.4.
Note : [1] Refers to mining only.
Sources : see Appendix to Chapter 15. Lines 3 and 15 are calculated from *Taiwan Statistical Data Book 1981*, Council for Economic Planning and Development, Executive Yuan, Republic of China, 1981, Tables 2.10 and 2.13.

About three quarters of Taiwan's total imports are made up of intermediate products. The vast majority of these intermediates, 77.1 per cent in 1976, enters the manufacturing sector. This sector shows the highest dependency on imported inputs, the ratio of intermediate imports to total production being 0.19 on average. Considering the input structure of the manufacturing sector more closely, it appears that this sector consumes, moreover, relatively the largest share of domestically produced intermediate inputs. The overall ratio of intermediate inputs to total production of 0.72, composed of the sum of the ratios for domestic and imported intermediates of 0.53 and 0.19, respectively, is particularly high. Besides, it appears that the largest part of domestic intermediates that enter manufacturing are produced within the manufacturing sector itself. Only a minor part originates from the primary sectors. The ratio of domestic intermediates to total manufacturing production of 0.53 can be subdivided into three components: 0.10 for intermediates from primary sectors, 0.34 for intrasectoral deliveries and 0.09 for deliveries from construction, utilities and services. Reflecting upon the relatively large share of intermediates in total production, the Taiwanese manufacturing sector apparently assembles or further processes mainly industrial intermediates without adding much value added; the ratio of gross value added to total production is only 0.28.

In terms of spread effects, this specific input structure of the manufacturing sector has two important consequences. First, the manufacturing sector generates extensive production impulses due to its relatively large share of domestic intermediates in total production. Consequently, manufacturing shows the highest P value of 1.11. The interrelatedness of the manufacturing sector with other sectors of the economy is not so high as appears at first sight. The largest part of the domestically produced intermediates consists of intrasectoral deliveries. The dispersion measure $\overset{*}{P}$ is therefore markedly lower, only 0.63. Second, notwithstanding the high P value, the total domestic value-added component of manufacturing production is relatively low. This is indicated by a value of 0.66 of the index *NFEE* for manufacturing. The low domestic value-added component in manufacturing is explained by the relatively high import content of production as well as, although it seems a contradiction, the relatively strong interrelatedness of manufacturing sectors, whereby the former feature is reinforced by the latter. These features of the Taiwanese manufacturing sector by the mid-1970s reveal an ongoing process of de-linking of manufacturing production from agriculture. Postwar import substitution started this development and it was strengthened by the subsequent strategy of export-oriented industrialization. Both strategies emphasized the production of light nondurable consumer goods, based on imported intermediates.[12]

For lack of employment data that could be reconciled with the sector classification of the 1976 input-output table, the employment impact of the different sectors is approximated by the wages and salaries component in value added. The employment spread effects in terms of the total wage bill are most extensive for the primary sector and services, both displaying a P^W value of 1.24. By contrast, those for manufacturing, indicated by a P^W value of 0.81, are clearly below the average of the economy. The sectoral values of the WIM measure reveal a similar picture. Concomitantly, the direct and total wage coefficients for manufacturing production are low compared to those of the primary sector, construction and services.

From this finding it may not be inferred that manufacturing production is characterized by a relatively high level of productivity and capital intensity. The only correct conclusion is that manufacturing generates little value added in production, thus employing less labour as well as capital per unit of production than other sectors. There is, by contrast, every reason to characterize manufacturing as a labour-intensive and low-productive activity in the context of the economy. One of these reasons is the relatively low wage level in manufacturing. As Table 15.1 demonstrates, the average wage rate in manufacturing is lower than in other sectors of the economy. It should be noted, however, that the average wage rate for agriculture and mining refers to mining only. But, in fact, there was little difference between the agricultural and manufacturing wage rate by the mid-1970s. Thorbecke provides evidence that in 1975, the wage rate in agriculture had surpassed that in manufacturing at the level of operatives. Taiwan's agricultural sector relies on modernized production methods and is highly productive. The very rapid rate of industrial development since the early 1960s provided alternative employment for job-seeking members of the rural population. Increasingly, rural family income was complemented by non-farm receipts. At the beginning of the 1970s, it became apparent that no more agricultural labour could be released without affecting the level of agricultural production. Thorbecke argues that as a result of an increasing labour shortage in agriculture, the ratio of the wage rate of farm workers to that of factory workers rose from a level of about 0.75 in 1966–1968 to about 1.04 in 1975.[13] Thus, within the context of the Taiwanese economy, manufacturing is a low-wage sector.

That agricultural and manufacturing wages approach each other so closely is explicable from the phenomenon that, in Taiwan, manufacturing activities are carried out throughout the island and are not concentrated in urban areas. EPFZs are located in port cities, but thanks to the excellent infrastructure many branches of industry prefer to be located near the main sources of rural labour supply.

15.4 DEVELOPMENT AND STRUCTURE OF TAIWANESE MANUFACTURED EXPORTS

Very soon after the policy reforms, manufactured exports from Taiwan started to accelerate from an initially very low level. Expressed in current U.S. dollars, manufactured exports grew annually on the average by 25 per cent during the period 1960-1970 and by 30 per cent from 1970 to 1980. Figure 15.1 illustrates the drastic compositional changes in total exports since 1960. The share of manufactures in total exports steadily increased till, by 1980, no less than over 90 per cent of exports was accounted for by manufactured products. As Figure 15.2 indicates, from the very beginning, Taiwan's export boom was led by textiles and clothing. Until the early 1970s, the share of these exportables in total manufactured exports centred around 40 per cent. In addition, exports of wood products (including plywood) played an important role in the 1960s. In the 1970s, new export products emerged, most notably electronics and plastic products, resulting in a contribution of these products to total manufactured exports of 20 and 8 per cent, respectively, in 1980. The export of metal products and machinery gained in importance as well. The shift towards electronics, plastic products, metal manufactures and machinery and the resultant diversification in the structure of exports indicate an upgrading process of Taiwan's manufacturing production.

The contribution of EPFZs to Taiwan's export performance is not impressive. Exports from all three zones, for about 60 per cent made up of

Figure 15.1
Manufactured Export Performance of Taiwan, 1960-1980

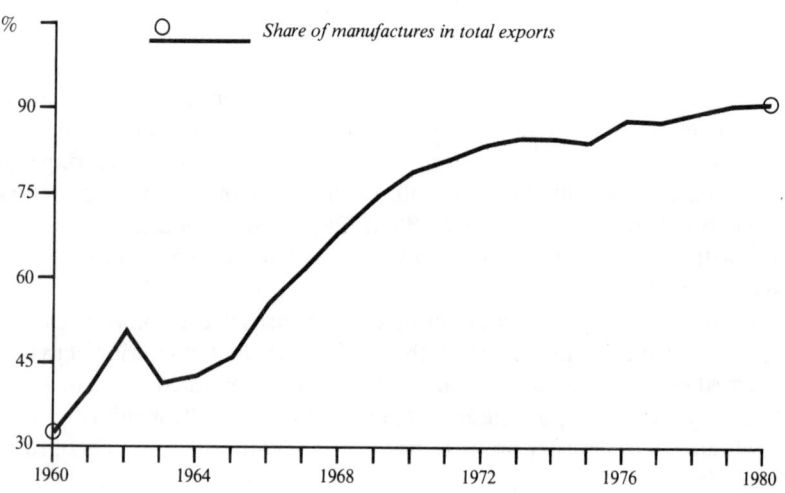

Figure 15.2
Composition of Taiwanese Manufactured Exports, 1960–1980
(percentage shares)

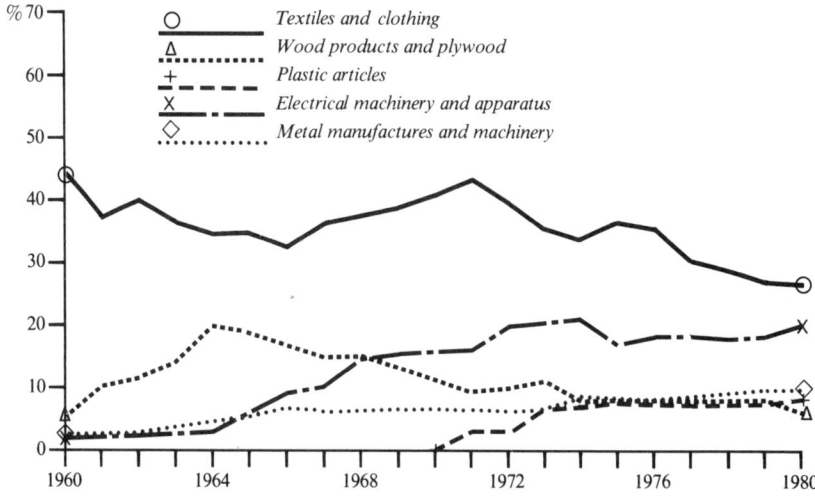

Sources: *Taiwan Statistical Data Book 1981*, Council for Economic Planning and Development, Executive Yuan, Republic of China, Tables 10.8 and 10.13.

electronics, amounted to some 8 to 9 per cent of total manufactured exports by the mid-1970s.[14] Moreover, the attractiveness of EPFZs has diminished in recent years, especially as a result of the establishment of bonded factories and warehouses. These give the investor a wider choice of location which can be a real advantage, given Taiwan's excellent infrastructure.[15]

Table 15.2 provides insight into the specialization pattern of Taiwanese manufactured exports, whereby, due to data limitations, wage coefficients might be assumed to approximate labour coefficients as an index of labour intensity of production. Processed NRB manufactures did not even generate 20 per cent of export receipts in 1976. This reflects Taiwan's poor natural resource endowment and, consequently, its emphasis upon encouraging non-NRB manufactured exportables. Table 15.2 reveals that total manufactured exports are considerably more labour intensive than manufacturing in total, and, in turn, manufactured exports originating from E sectors are far more labour intensive than those produced in DMO sectors. Measured by the direct wage coefficient, exports from E sectors are on average about one and a half times as labour intensive as the composition of total manufacturing production. Only the category of NRB exports shows a slightly lower average wage coefficient. Taiwan's avowed specialization in labour-intensive exports

TABLE 15.2
CHARACTERISTICS OF MAJOR PRODUCTION AND EXPORT CATEGORIES,
TAIWANESE MANUFACTURING SECTOR, 1976

Category	E/O (%)	E/E_m (%)	l^w	T^w	Share of wage-intensive products (%)	Share of wages in gross value added (%)
			(per 10^3 NT$ output)			
Total manufactured exports	—	100	156.1	311.7	77.6	—
Total manufacturing production	29.2	—	118.9	269.9	—	42.7
NRB manufactured exports	—	19.1	112.6	310.1	49.8	—
NRB manufacturing production	14.9	—	65.5	235.4	—	28.0
Exports from E sectors	—	57.1	179.9	327.7	100.0	—
Production in E sectors	64.8	—	179.6	326.7	—	59.2
Exports from DMO sectors	—	23.8	134.0	274.7	46.4	—
Production in DMO sectors	19.0	—	130.8	265.4	—	42.7

For explanation of symbols, see Section 10.4.
Sources: see Appendix to Chapter 15.

emerges most clearly from the finding that the production of all ten export sectors, which are presented in Table A.15.2, can be classified as labour intensive. Four of the dominant E sectors, i.e. garments, fabrics, plastic products and other manufactures, are among the most labour intensive. The direct wage coefficient of electronics, the most important E sector, is only a little above the manufacturing average. Also according to the total labour coefficient, Taiwan's composition of manufactured exports is substantially more labour intensive than manufacturing in total. It is striking to note that the total wage coefficients for NRB production and exports are lower than for total manufacturing and total exports, respectively. Apparently, the volume and labour intensity of domestically produced primary inputs entering NRB production are insufficient to compensate for the generally low labour intensity of their processing. On average, non-NRB exports still appear to be the most labour intensive in terms of the total wage coefficient. This is particularly true of exports produced in E sectors. We shall return to this finding, which contrasts with the experience in the average developing country, in the next section.

Finally, Table 15.2 shows that for all three export categories both the direct and the total wage coefficients are, on average, higher than for corresponding production totals. This finding illustrates once more that, within each category of sectors, careful export specialization has taken place in the, relatively, most labour-intensive products. In conformity with the labour-intensive character of production in E sectors, these sectors show the highest average share of wages in gross value added.

Data on the composition and remuneration of the manufacturing labour force are only available for an aggregated 20-sector level. Table 15.3 assembles the data for 1976. Of the 1.9 million manufacturing workers in that year, 41.6 per cent could be considered skilled. On average, skilled workers earn over 60 per cent more than unskilled workers. For the greater part, almost 60 per cent, unskilled work is carried out by females, while over 70 per cent of the skilled jobs are occupied by males. The manufacturing labour force is almost equally distributed among males and females, their shares being 52.9 and 47.1 per cent, respectively. The male labour force was for 55.5 per cent employed in skilled occupation. By contrast, unskilled categories of work absorbed 74.0 per cent of female workers.

As shown in Table 15.3, those sectors which employ a majority of unskilled workers largely coincide with sectors where females are prevalent, namely textiles, garments, leather products, electronics, plastic products, precision instruments and other manufactures. Except for electronics, these sectors have the lowest average annual wage bill per worker. Although 68.9 per cent of all workers in electronic industries are unskilled, three fourth of them being females who earn even less than the average wage for unskilled work, the

TABLE 15.3
COMPOSITION AND REMUNERATION OF THE MANUFACTURING LABOUR FORCE, TAIWAN, 1976

Sector	E_i/O_i (%)	E_i/E_m (%)	Total number of employees per sector (10³)	Share of females (%)	Share of skilled employees in sectoral employment (%)	of which females (%)	Share of unskilled employees in sectoral employment (%)	of which females (%)	Average annual wage rate (NT $)	Annual wage rate for skilled workers (NT $)	Annual wage rate for unskilled workers (NT $)
Total manufacturing	29.2	100.0	1,893.7	47.1	41.6	29.4	58.4	59.6	51,610	59,850	36,740
1 Food products	15.5	9.3	131.1	42.0	41.7	21.1	58.3	56.9	58,670	63,800	31,680
2 Beverages and tobacco	3.5	.3	14.7	35.6	49.8	21.4	50.2	49.8	90,510	92,570	58,510
3 Textiles	30.5	9.0	339.5	69.7	34.7	54.2	65.3	77.9	48,440	58,120	38,410
4 Garments	68.9	17.7	104.0	80.6	42.4	72.8	57.6	86.2	40,200	45,190	31,750
5 Leather products	50.1	1.9	32.5	60.5	39.7	52.0	60.3	66.5	43,580	47,790	33,700
6 Wood products	49.0	5.8	112.4	27.3	37.1	19.1	62.9	44.7	45,390	49,210	35,740
7 Paper and printing	5.7	.7	71.5	28.7	53.6	19.4	46.4	36.3	53,060	56,510	37,190
8 Industrial chemicals	14.7	3.0	39.8	28.7	51.3	14.6	48.7	43.5	85,240	92,420	64,480
9 Other chemical products	6.5	.7	41.9	40.3	54.4	30.2	45.6	52.3	60,480	70,960	37,290
10 Petroleum refining products	9.0	1.7	10.1	11.1	74.9	6.6	25.1	24.4	179,540	188,940	69,650
11 Rubber products	51.7	2.2	37.1	47.4	31.9	28.7	68.1	56.2	52,010	58,140	42,420
12 Plastic products	41.4	9.3	166.3	54.5	34.0	37.0	66.0	63.5	47,080	55,080	36,670
13 Non-metallic mineral products	9.8	1.1	85.8	34.6	38.8	25.7	61.2	40.2	51,710	62,530	36,390
14 Primary metal products	14.7	3.5	50.6	10.6	53.2	9.0	46.8	12.4	66,690	68,250	52,730
15 Metal products	16.6	1.3	129.7	21.0	49.9	13.9	50.1	28.1	45,250	45,410	32,240
16 Machinery	30.2	2.8	88.0	10.9	64.0	9.8	36.0	12.8	55,560	56,540	37,980
17 Electrical and electronic apparatus and parts	51.9	18.3	238.1	61.9	31.1	32.2	68.9	75.4	53,150	76,420	35,600
18 Transport equipment	19.6	2.6	96.1	12.2	70.6	8.5	29.4	21.1	49,520	49,030	35,510
19 Precision instruments	92.4	1.6	19.8	55.3	35.0	34.5	65.0	66.4	46,930	59,350	34,960
20 Other manufactures	65.4	7.2	84.5	61.7	26.7	38.6	73.3	70.1	39,530	51,960	30,750

For explanation of symbols, see Section 10.4.

Source: calculated from *Report of 1976 Industrial and Commercial Censuses of Taiwan-Fukien District of the Republic of China*, Volume I, General Report, Committee on Industrial and Commercial Censuses of Taiwan-Fukien District of the Republic of China, Executive Yuan, 1978, Tables 6 and 8.

average annual wage per worker in electronics is relatively high. This is explained by the relatively high wages that are obtained by skilled employees, a phenomenon originating in the standardized production process that is characteristic for export-oriented electronic industries in developing countries. The organization, supervision and maintenance of standardized processes that make use of standardized inputs demand highly qualified organizational and technical skills. The activities still to be carried out in such production processes largely consist of routine assembly work, which explains the prevalence of relatively low-paid unskilled workers.

It is striking to find the average wage level in garment industries the lowest but one, whereas 9 out of 20 sectors show a higher employment share of unskilled workers. This is most likely explained by the high female participation rates in both skilled and unskilled employment in garment industries, namely 72.8 and 86.2 per cent, respectively. In Taiwan, wage discrimination against women is substantial. Fei, Ranis and Kuo established that for all educational levels the female wage rate was less than half that for males in 1966.[16] According to Galenson this wage differential does not appear to have diminished during the course of development. Women in manufacturing were still reported as earning only 50 per cent of the male level in January 1976.[17]

The above-mentioned sectors which employ a larger proportion of unskilled and female workers and pay relatively low wages per worker correspond to the sectors which are classified as E sectors. Consequently, these sectors are generally labour intensive. From a set of rank correlations presented in Table 15.4, the following pattern of relationships among sectoral

TABLE 15.4
MATRIX OF SPEARMAN RANK CORRELATION COEFFICIENTS FOR SECTOR CHARACTERISTICS IN THE 20-SECTOR SAMPLE[3]

Variable	E_i/O_i	s_i	U_i^1	F_i^2
E_i/O_i	1	−.72**	.66**	.60**
s_i		1	−.52*	−.50*
U_i^1			1	.74**
F_i^2				1

For explanation of symbols, see Section 10.4.

Notes : [1] U_i = share of unskilled workers in sectoral employment.
          [2] F_i = share of female workers in sectoral employment.
          [3] Correlation coefficients that are significant at the 5 per cent level are denoted by one asterisk (*), those significant at the 1 per cent level by two asterisks (**).

Sources : see Appendix to Chapter 15 and Table 15.3.

outward orientation, wage level and employment of unskilled and female workers is discernible. The rank correlations between export orientation, on the one hand, and average wage level and the shares of unskilled and female workers in sectoral employment, on the other hand, are significant at the 1 per cent level and have the expected sign. The negative relationship between average wage level and the shares of unskilled and female workers is weaker, but still significant at the 5 per cent level. Rankings by the shares of unskilled and female workers in sectoral employment are positively correlated and this correlation is, not surprisingly, highly significant. All this implies that Taiwanese manufacturing sectors show a higher export-output ratio if the average wage they have to pay is lower and, in turn, a relatively low wage level can be realized by employing a larger proportion of unskilled, female workers.

Women have played a major part in the export drive of Taiwan. Their contribution is evidenced by the large-scale entrance of women into manufacturing occupations since the mid-1960s. The number of women in manufacturing rose by a factor of three from 1965 to 1975.[18] As Table 15.3 shows, their share of the manufacturing labour force reached 47.1 per cent in 1971. The new female recruits were predominantly unskilled and in the 15 to 24-year age group.[19] They found employment especially in the typical export industries, like textiles, garments, plastic products and electronics. In 1976, 63 per cent of all women employed in manufacturing were in only these four industries, as is shown in Table 15.3. Even more noteworthy is the fact that, in 1976, 82.5 per cent of the 78,000 employees at the three EPFZs were women.[20]

Next we have estimated a matrix of correlation coefficients for rankings by export orientation and direct and total wage coefficients. From Table 15.5 it is apparent that the correlation between export-output ratios and the two proxies of factor intensity I^w and T^w are positive and significant at the 1 per cent level. These relationships appear to be weaker in case NRB sectors are removed from the sample, although the correlation between the export orientation of a sector and its direct wage coefficient is still significant at the 5 per cent level. Thus, our earlier finding is confirmed that Taiwan's manufactured exports are systematically concentrated in labour-intensive products. We may also safely conclude that these exportables are predominantly produced by unskilled, female workers who are paid relatively low wages.

15.5 SPREAD EFFECTS OF TAIWANESE MANUFACTURED EXPORTS

It has been noted above that, in spite of the heavy reliance of manufacturing on imported inputs, this sector showed an above-average level of

TABLE 15.5
MATRIX OF SPEARMAN RANK CORRELATION COEFFICIENTS FOR SECTOR CHARACTERISTICS, TAIWAN, 1976[1, 2]

Variable	E_i/O_i	E_i/E_m	l_i^w	T_i^w
E_i/O_i	1	.88**	.54**	.48**
		.86**	.38*	.30
E_i/E_m		1	.39**	.33*
			.18	.15
l_i^w			1	.74**
				.85**
T_i^w				1

For explanation of symbols, see Section 10.4.

Notes : [1] The upper coefficients in a row refer to rankings of all manufacturing sectors (n = 61), the lower coefficients refer to rankings of non-NRB sectors only (n = 37).
[2] Correlation coefficients that are significant at the 5 per cent level are denoted by one asterisk (*), those significant at the 1 per cent level by two asterisks (**).

Source : see Appendix to Chapter 15.

intersectoral dependence in terms of production linkages, most notably consisting of intrasectoral deliveries. The employment spread effects of manufacturing were below the economy's average. Table 15.6 gives the record of spread effects for the different categories of manufactured exports. The calculations indicate that, first of all, the spread effects of manufactured exports are, all along the line, more extensive than for manufacturing in total. Additionally, the differences between the average values of the spread effects for exports from NRB, E and DMO sectors are rather small, except for the values of P^W.

Considering the measures of spread effects more closely, we find the highest value of P for exports originating in E sectors and the lowest for NRB exports, viz. 1.15 and 1.10, respectively. This point should be stressed, as in contrast to the general pattern, NRB manufactured exports from Taiwan are less integrated with other sectors of the economy than non-NRB exports. The lack of available domestic resources is most apparent for petroleum, various metals, wood, and for some food products like wheat and vegetable oils. Although NRB exports are concentrated in sugar products and canned foods for which inputs are domestically available, the production linkages of these exports are, on average, very limited compared to other categories of manufactured exports. This finding also explains the rather low average value for NRB exports of the total wage coefficient, dealt with in the preceding

TABLE 15.6
WEIGHTED AVERAGE MEASURES OF SPREAD EFFECTS FOR MAJOR CATEGORIES OF EXPORT AND PRODUCTION, TAIWAN, 1976

Category	P	NFEE	P^W	WIM
Total manufactured exports	1.14	.64	.95	.45
NRB exports	1.10	.66	.95	.45
Exports from E sectors	1.15	.64	1.00	.47
Exports from DMO sectors	1.14	.62	.84	.40
Total manufacturing production	1.11	.63	.82	.39
NRB production	1.11	.60	.72	.34
Non-NRB production	1.12	.64	.89	.42

For explanation of symbols, see Section 10.4.
Source : see Appendix to Chapter 15.

section. The *NFEE* values for different categories of export and production deviate only a little from one another, or, put differently, all manufacturing production appears to be highly import dependent. Yet, a minor difference may not be overlooked: the average import content of total manufactured exports is slightly less than that of total manufacturing production, i.e. 0.64 against 0.63, respectively. The composition of NRB exports appears to be less import dependent than NRB production in general. Strikingly enough, the *NFEE* value for exports from E sectors also compares favourably in this connection.

Due to the outstanding labour-intensive export specialization, E sector exports show the highest dispersion of employment with a P^W value of 1.00. The relatively high level of production spread effects is, of course, an additional favourable factor for this good record. In fact, the contribution of all three export categories to employment is greater than that of average manufacturing production. This picture appears again in the values of the *WIM* measures.

Table A.15.2 summarizes the record of spread effects for ten individual E sectors. It shows substantial differences in performance. Garment production, for instance, is relatively well integrated with the domestic economy. Since the mid-1960s, Taiwan has succeeded in increasing the use of domestically produced synthetic fibre in the production of clothing. It is estimated that by 1976, almost 90 per cent of the inputs entering the production of garments were produced domestically, one third composed of artificial fibres and about a quarter of cotton fabrics. Fabrics and fabric products showed a similar input structure: 87 per cent of total intermediate inputs were of Taiwanese origin. Cotton fabrics for about a quarter, and artificial fabrics and synthetic fibres for another quarter, were the main domestic intermediates. By contrast, the sectors producing electronics and precision instruments operate in relative isolation. For both sectors, the P and P^W values are below 1, whereas their values of the WIM and the index $NFEE$ are the lowest of all E sectors. Considering the direct backward linkages of electronics production in more detail, it appears that intermediate inputs constitute 73 per cent of the production value. Of these intermediates, 40 per cent is imported, 25 per cent is produced within the electronic sector itself and 35 per cent is obtained from domestic supplies. The import component of intermediates that enter the production of precision instruments is even 62 per cent. It will be clear that clothing products substantially contribute towards the backward integration of the Taiwanese economy, whereas electronics and precision instruments are outstanding examples of footloose export production in EPFZs.

Finally, we may turn to examine the relationships between a sector's export orientation and the extent of its spread effects. Table 15.7 gives the

TABLE 15.7
MATRIX OF SPEARMAN RANK CORRELATION COEFFICIENTS
FOR SECTOR CHARACTERISTICS AND VARIOUS MEASURES
OF SPREAD EFFECTS, TAIWAN, 1976[1,2]

Variable	E_i/O_i	l_i^w	P_i	$NFEE_i$	P_i^W	WIM_i
E_i/O_i	1	.54**	.11	.03	.48**	.48**
		.38*	.21	−.25	.30	.30
l_i^w		1	.01	.29*	.74**	.74**
			.05	.30	.85**	.85**
P_i			1	.12	.37**	.37**
				.07	.39*	.39*
$NFEE_i$				1	.52**	.52**
					.43**	.43**
P_i^W					1	1.00**
						1.00**
WIM_i						1

For explanation of symbols, see Section 10.4.

Notes : [1] The upper coefficients in a row refer to rankings of all manufacturing sectors (n = 61), the lower coefficients refer to rankings of non-NRB sectors only (n = 37).
[2] Correlation coefficients that are significant at the 5 per cent level are denoted by one asterisk (*), those significant at the 1 per cent level by two asterisks (**).

Source : see Appendix to Chapter 15.

relevant rank correlation coefficients. From these coefficients it is apparent that a sector's market orientation does not have any impact upon the extent of its production linkages and the domestic value-added component in its production. The correlation coefficient for rankings by export-output ratio and the two dispersion measures P and $NFEE$ are clearly insignificant. As expected, given Taiwan's specialization in labour-intensive exports, there is a positive and significant correlation between rankings by export-output ratio on the one hand, and the two measures of employment spread effects P^W and WIM on the other. These relationships just cease to be statistically significant at the 5 per cent level if the less labour-intensive and less export-oriented NRB sectors are excluded from the rankings.

Furthermore, it is of interest to establish that a higher labour intensity of production is significantly associated with a higher domestic value-added component in production. Evidence for this relationship is provided by, first, the positive and significant correlation between the rankings by direct wage coefficient and the index $NFEE$ in case all sectors are included in the sample, and, second, the positive and highly significant correlation between the rankings by P^W and the index $NFEE$ in both samples. The second relationship provides additional evidence, as correlation between the ranking by P and the index $NFEE$ is virtually absent. It would appear, then, that a specialization in labour-intensive exportables has a favourable effect on the foreign-exchange receipt per unit of export.

15.6 SUMMARY

After an agricultural-based industrialization in the 1930s and a relatively mild import-substitution process in the 1950s, Taiwan embarked on a vigorous export-oriented strategy of industrialization. Taiwan's manufactured export performance has been impressive since then. Both the import-substitution and export-oriented industrialization emphasized the production of light nondurable consumer goods, and consequently, manufacturing lost the roots it had in agriculture. From the very beginning, a careful export specialization has taken place in the relatively most labour-intensive products. The analysis reveals that the sectors producing these labour-intensive products show a higher export orientation and lower average wage level. In turn, a low wage level can be realized by employing a larger proportion of unskilled, female workers. The production processes that come up to these characteristics mainly consist of labour-value-added processing activities, which make relatively much use of imported intermediates. Hence, in the context of the national economy, manufacturing is a low-wage sector that generates relatively little value added.

THE CASE OF TAIWAN 359

Notwithstanding the relatively high import content in production, manufacturing shows an above average level of production spread effects. To a considerable extent, however, these spread effects are accounted for by intra-sectoral deliveries. The production and employment spread effects that are associated with manufactured exports are more extensive than those for manufacturing production on average. Especially exports originating in E sectors perform relatively well in this respect. The mutual differences, however, are not substantial. This implies that a sector's market orientation has no significant effect on the extent of its spread effects. By contrast, it indeed became clear that the more labour-intensive products are slightly less dependent on imported intermediates. These general conclusions do not hold for all export products to the same extent. The record of spread effects of electronics and precision instruments is at variance herewith. These products are outstanding examples of footloose export production in EPFZs.

Taiwan is now adjusting to a situation of relative labour scarcity by moving to the second stage of both import substitution and export promotion.

APPENDIX TABLE A.15.1
CHARACTERISTICS OF MANUFACTURING SECTORS CLASSIFIED AS NRB SECTORS, TAIWAN, 1976

I-O Code	Sector	E_i/O_i (%)	E_i/E_m (%)	I_i^a	T_i^a (per 10³ NT$ output)	W_i/VA_i^1 (%)	P	$NFEE_i$	P_i^n	WIM_i
16	Slaughtering and by-products	1.3	.2	6.1	233.8	4.5	1.68	.62	.71	.34
17	Rice	.0	.0	35.4	469.9	48.0	1.30	.91	1.43	.68
18	Wheat flour	.0	.0	29.3	134.3	15.3	.75	.37	.41	.19
19	Sugar	43.6	2.0	154.7	412.1	35.2	1.07	.90	1.26	.60
20	Canned foods	87.9	3.4	104.5	436.5	58.0	1.23	.76	1.33	.63
21	Edible vegetable oil and by-products	.9	.0	25.2	140.4	15.5	.82	.37	.43	.20
22	Monosodium glutamate	10.2	.1	92.2	264.4	28.8	1.20	.77	.81	.38
23	Frozen food	69.5	2.0	60.1	316.3	40.8	1.54	.68	.97	.46
24	Miscellaneous food products	15.0	1.6	121.9	309.6	43.0	1.15	.67	.94	.45
25	Animal feeds	.1	.0	24.8	169.8	23.8	1.05	.41	.52	.25
26	Non-alcoholic beverages	16.5	.2	101.8	287.1	28.1	1.11	.75	.88	.42
27	Alcoholic beverages	.3	.0	59.0	122.0	7.6	.77	.91	.37	.18
28	Tobacco	2.2	.1	36.5	85.7	4.8	.71	.89	.26	.12
36	Lumber	19.9	.5	132.4	276.3	44.6	.83	.58	.84	.40
37	Plywood	61.3	2.4	130.0	287.0	51.6	.90	.58	.88	.42
38	Wood, bamboo and rattan products	56.9	1.9	194.3	353.2	53.6	1.01	.70	1.08	.51
39	Non-metallic furniture	49.7	1.0	197.5	337.4	44.9	.99	.74	1.03	.49
40	Pulp and paper	8.7	.5	103.7	279.4	43.2	1.20	.65	.85	.40
41	Paper products	3.0	.1	144.6	306.2	46.3	1.21	.69	.93	.44
53	Petroleum refining products	9.0	1.7	19.6	38.0	10.2	.67	.30	.12	.05
58	Pig iron and crude steel	4.7	.4	34.9	185.3	35.8	1.39	.46	.57	.27
59	Primary iron and steel products	8.9	.8	72.3	202.7	43.7	1.30	.49	.62	.29
61	Aluminium	2.6	.0	90.1	222.5	55.2	1.23	.51	.68	.32
63	Miscellaneous metals	15.9	.2	77.3	179.4	30.6	1.00	.48	.55	.26

APPENDIX TABLE A.15.2
CHARACTERISTICS OF MANUFACTURING SECTORS CLASSIFIED AS E SECTORS, TAIWAN, 1976

I-O Code	Sector	E_i/O_i (%)	E_i/E_m (%)	I_i^w (per 10³ NT$ output)	T_i^w	W_i/VA_i^1 (%)	P_i	$NFEE_i$	P_i^w	W/M_i
32	Garments	78.7	15.2	202.9	388.1	73.0	1.35	.70	1.18	.56
33	Other fabrics and fabric products	54.4	2.5	216.8	384.7	71.7	1.24	.69	1.17	.56
35	Leather and leather products	50.1	1.9	194.2	380.5	63.7	1.30	.72	1.16	.55
43	Rubber and rubber products	51.7	2.2	196.6	316.2	50.5	1.07	.67	.97	.46
50	Plastic products	50.0	8.7	170.6	305.3	55.1	1.16	.69	.93	.44
67	Other machinery	43.8	.7	162.7	281.4	52.5	1.06	.57	.86	.41
70	Electronic products	71.0	16.0	134.1	253.9	49.2	.99	.53	.77	.37
74	Other transport equipment	59.6	1.1	195.1	328.9	61.7	1.06	.61	1.00	.48
75	Precision instruments and apparatus	92.4	1.6	190.4	265.3	62.0	.82	.48	.81	.38
76	Other manufactures	65.4	7.2	227.7	379.7	58.9	1.09	.73	1.16	.55

APPENDIX TABLE A.15.3
CHARACTERISTICS OF MANUFACTURING SECTORS CLASSIFIED AS DMO SECTORS, TAIWAN, 1976

I-O Code	Sector	E_i/O_i (%)	E_i/E_m (%)	I_i^w	T_i^w (per 10^3 NT$ output)	W_i/VA_i^1 (%)	P_i	$NFEE_i$	P_i^w	W/M_i
29	Cotton and cotton fabrics	31.5	5.3	105.5	302.8	52.7	1.24	.61	.92	.44
30	Wool and worsted fabrics	13.9	.4	98.0	306.0	52.9	1.62	.66	.93	.44
31	Artificial fabrics	33.6	3.3	110.8	260.9	49.6	1.30	.65	.80	.38
34	Dyeing of textiles	.0	.0	173.2	282.2	43.7	1.01	.69	.86	.41
42	Printing, publishing and bookbinding	3.1	.1	252.8	411.3	67.8	1.13	.72	1.26	.59
44	Petrochemical raw materials	5.6	.3	34.0	98.4	11.1	.94	.57	.30	.14
45	Other industrial chemicals	7.3	.3	105.4	231.4	33.0	1.00	.65	.71	.33
46	Chemical fertilizers	.0	.0	93.1	285.3	94.9	1.19	.53	.87	.41
47	Synthetic fibres	26.4	2.3	73.9	168.7	32.1	1.11	.57	.52	.24
48	Other artificial fibres	14.0	.2	81.6	232.2	20.7	.91	.70	.71	.34
49	Synthetic resins	11.5	.6	45.2	102.6	12.2	.94	.61	.31	.15
51	Medicines	5.3	.1	130.8	277.0	43.1	1.06	.64	.85	.40
52	Miscellaneous chemical manufactures	7.0	.5	121.3	250.2	40.0	1.06	.64	.76	.36
54	Cement	3.4	.1	66.5	198.8	13.7	.93	.77	.61	.29
55	Cement products	.4	.0	148.4	325.9	52.7	1.15	.74	.99	.47
56	Glass	23.0	.3	208.3	321.9	51.9	.94	.67	.98	.47
57	Miscellaneous non-metallic mineral products	15.2	.6	258.8	419.5	58.4	.95	.76	1.28	.61
60	Iron and steel products	31.6	2.4	177.5	301.5	59.2	1.12	.58	.92	.44
62	Aluminium products	26.0	.3	164.6	291.0	50.1	1.12	.63	.89	.42
64	Miscellaneous metallic products	19.2	.7	222.0	318.0	54.2	.95	.63	.97	.46
65	General industrial machinery	23.3	.3	205.0	306.7	50.8	.99	.64	.94	.44
66	Industrial machinery	35.4	1.5	197.2	314.5	65.2	1.13	.58	.96	.45
68	Machinery parts, repair and maintenance	11.5	.2	246.6	353.3	50.1	.96	.73	1.08	.51
69	Household electric appliances	12.0	.6	153.6	278.9	42.8	1.03	.64	.85	.40
71	Electrical machinery and apparatus	22.3	1.8	148.6	269.6	44.1	1.03	.62	.82	.39
72	Shipbuilding	36.1	.8	175.4	313.2	73.4	1.07	.56	.96	.45
73	Motor vehicles	7.8	.7	123.8	260.8	34.7	1.07	.69	.80	.38

For explanation of symbols, see Section 10.4.

Note : ^{1} W_i/VA_i = share of wages in gross value added.

Source : computations are based on data from *Taiwan Input-Output Tables — Republic of China 1976*, Council for Economic Planning and Development, Executive Yuan, 1980.

16
The Case of Malaysia

16.1 INTRODUCTORY REMARKS

Malaysia is comprised of Peninsular Malaysia, Sabah and Sarawak and covers a land area of 330,000 km^2. Its total population was about 13.6 million people at the start of the 1980s, resulting in a rather low population density of 41 persons per km^2. Malaysia combines this low population pressure with a rich natural-resource base. It is the world's leading producer of both natural rubber and tin. In addition, petroleum, palm oil and timber are among the major commodity exports. As a small and amply endowed economy, Malaysia has always been trade oriented. This was the case in the colonial period, but it is equally true of the present. After vigorous attempts to replace imports of both agricultural and industrial products by domestic production during the 1960s, Malaysia again resorted to a more outward-looking strategy. With respect to industrialization, this policy shift led to the creation of a new export sector, mainly accommodated in EPFZs.

GDP *per capita* rose by a moderate 3.0 per cent per annum in the 1960s, followed by a much stronger performance during the 1970s with an average annual growth rate of 5.7 per cent. In 1975, the base year of our analysis, Malaysia already ranked among the middle-income countries with a GNP *per capita* of US$750.

It should be noted that the present case study is limited to Peninsular Malaysia, simply because the 1975 input-output table is restricted to this territory only. This is not a serious omission, as population and economic activity are highly concentrated in Peninsular Malaysia. Although the peninsula accounts for 40 per cent of the total land area, 83 per cent of the population resides there. The population density in Peninsular Malaysia is therefore twice as high as the country's average. But, most importantly, no less than 95 per cent of all manufacturing production originates from Peninsular Malaysia.[1]

16.2 INDUSTRIALIZATION AND TRADE STRATEGIES IN MALAYSIA

Before independence in 1957, the Malaysian economy was mainly geared towards the production and export of the primary commodities rubber and tin. Therefore, diversification of the economy and industrialization were placed at the centre of development plans after independence. Thus, serious efforts towards the industrialization of Malaysia did not start sooner than 1958, when the Pioneer Industries Ordinance was enacted.[2] This set the familiar stage for the import-substitution type of industrialization. The 1958 Ordinance was revised and broadened by the Investment Incentives Act of 1968. At first, fiscal incentives constituted the major policy instrument to stimulate investments. The most important of these was, and still is, the award of "pioneer status". A company granted this status is entitled to an exemption from company tax for a period of at least two years. This period can be extended up to eight years depending upon the amount of capital invested, and some additional conditions, such as location in a development area, production of priority products and the use of domestically produced intermediates. Additional fiscal concessions for pioneer firms include carrying forward capital expenditures and losses in the post-pioneer period. Fiscal incentives are also provided to non-pioneer firms, such as the investment tax credit and the tax relief on labour utilization. These, however, are clearly of less importance than pioneer status.

Up to independence tariff protection was virtually absent in Malaysia. The import duties that existed served mainly revenue purposes. This state of affairs remained essentially unchanged until 1963. In that year, a start was made with a made-to-measure system of tariff protection, supplemented by quantitative import restrictions and quotas. Initially, tariffs were rather low by international standards. But in subsequent years, both tariff and non-tariff protection increased steadily. Several studies on the pattern of nominal and effective protection, covering the years 1965, 1970 and 1974, confirm this rising trend in the protection of domestic manufacturing.[3] These studies also reveal that the effective rates of protection considerably exceed the nominal rates. This indicates the familiar tariff escalation with the stage of production: tariffs on intermediate and capital goods are generally lower than those on finished manufactures. Another general feature appears to be a strong bias against exporting, especially against manufactured exports. The existing structure of protection fostered the growth of the manufacturing sector, especially pioneer industries, as is clearly evidenced by the increased contribution of manufacturing to GDP from 8.1 per cent in 1961 to 13.4 per cent in 1970.[4]

Diversification of manufacturing production found its expression in the relative fall in primary processing activities and food products and the relative rise in the production of consumer nondurables and some intermediate and capital goods. This compositional change meant a relative reduction in the use of locally available raw materials and, consequently, a higher import dependency of manufacturing production.

In a small country such as Malaysia, the domestic market began to show signs of saturation after a decade of rapid industrialization. Import-substitution possibilities were exhausted in food manufacturing, rubber products, chemicals and non-metallic mineral products. Moreover, towards the end of the 1960s, it became apparent that this type of industrialization provided insufficient employment opportunities for the growing labour force. The pioneer incentive system especially had generally encouraged more capital-intensive industries which tended to use more skilled labour,[5] whereas the employment situation for unskilled workers worsened over the 1960s.

The New Economic Policy, introduced in 1970, placed much more weight on employment creation and distributional goals. Although the foundation of an export-incentive policy was already laid down in the 1968 Investment Incentives Act, export expansion became a central element in Malaysia's industrial development from 1970 onwards. In Malaysia, the promotion of manufactured exports takes place along two distinct lines. On the one hand, various incentive measures were introduced to stimulate domestic manufacturers to export part of their production, whereas, on the other hand, EPFZs were established to speed up exports more directly.

The principal export incentives facing domestic industries, first enacted in 1968 and amended several times in later years, are of four categories. First, an export allowance is granted that provides a deduction from taxable income. The amount of this subsidy is related to export performance and the domestic content in exports. Second, an accelerated depreciation allowance is available to modernizing industries which export at least 20 per cent of their production. Third, promotional expenses for exports are deductible from taxable income. Fourth, various export financing facilities are in operation which provide domestic exporters with credit facilities at preferential rates of interest. The income tax reductions are of no value for firms enjoying a tax holiday. Therefore, pioneer companies have a special privilege, as they are permitted to carry forward those deductions to the post-pioneer period. Apart from these financial incentives, the government also provides other forms of assistance to exporters. These include, among others, marketing support, trade missions and an export insurance scheme.

Starting in 1972, EPFZs were set up for industries producing exclusively for the export market, and, most notably, to attract foreign investments. In the early 1980s, ten of these zones were in operation. Apart from low-cost infrastructural facilities, industries located within an EPFZ enjoy, in addition to the afore-mentioned export incentives, minimum customs formalities and a complete free-trade regime. Thus, imports of intermediates and machinery required directly in the manufacturing of exportables are free from any duty. The latter privilege gives firms located inside the zone an especially clear advantage over non-EPFZ firms. For non-EPFZ firms that produce for export, regulations do exist to facilitate exemptions from or drawbacks of surtaxes and import duties on imported intermediates and machinery. The conditions applied, however, are rather stringent, the procedures are cumbersome and the applicant always has to bear the cost of advancement and waiting. In sum, the most favourable combination of incentives for an exporting firm is pioneer status together with location in an EPFZ; the former provides many years' tax holiday and the latter offers a free-trade regime.

To assess the impact of Malaysia's export-promotion policies, one must realize that the process of import substitution is pushed with the same vigour. In fact, the shift in industrialization policies was partially to the effect that, in addition to and yet apart from the import-substitution sector, a new export sector was created. The subsidies entailed by the export incentives aim, therefore, at a lowering of the inherent anti-export bias. Ariff, Lim and Lee cautiously conclude that the export incentives substantially reduce discrimination against exports. In this respect they add that EPFZ firms are placed in the most favourable position.[6]

Manufacturing growth was rapid in the 1970s. From 1970 to 1980, the average annual real growth rate amounted to 13.5 per cent, and the manufacturing contribution to GDP rose from 13.4 to 22.4 per cent over this period. Export expansion was the principal source of growth, which, in turn, was fostered by export production in EPFZs. From 1972 to 1979, approximately 80,000 employment opportunities were created in Malaysia's EPFZs, equalling almost one eighth of the total manufacturing labour force. This development points to the important role of foreign investment in the export-oriented industrialization strategy of Malaysia. A census of firms located in EPFZs in 1978 reveals that about 94 per cent of the firms are either fully foreign-owned or owned and managed by foreign companies on a majority basis.[7]

In fact, foreign ownership has dominated Malaysia's industrial development throughout, irrespective of the industrialization policies pursued. The magnitude of foreign involvement in manufacturing can be gauged from the fact that, in 1972, 52 per cent of total assets accumulated in the manufacturing sector were owned by foreign companies. The share of foreign ownership fell to 40 per cent in 1978, notwithstanding a 140 per cent increase in the value of foreign-owned assets in intervening years. This relative fall has to be attributed to deliberate government efforts to increase local ownership under the New Economic Policy, which is principally realized through the establishment of public enterprises.[8]

Recent policy changes in Malaysia indicate, besides a continued emphasis on export promotion, efforts to evolve into a more capital-intensive agro-based and other resource-based industries. This growth pattern should make better use of the advantage of ample local resources.

16.3 STRUCTURAL FEATURES OF THE MALAYSIAN ECONOMY

The sectoral compositions of total gross output and GDP in Malaysia, presented in Table 16.1, give a distorted picture of the importance of manufacturing production. In 1975, manufacturing already outweighed agriculture and mining with a share in total production of 45.4 against 15.9 per cent and a share in GDP of 27.9 against 23.3 per cent, respectively. By the same year, exports were made up almost exclusively of manufactures. However, 66.9 per cent of manufacturing value added was generated in raw material processing industries. In the 1975 input-output table, all of these activities are included in manufacturing output, whereas some of the most important NRB products are not far removed from a primary stage, most notably crude rubber, unwrought tin, palm oil and lumber. In 1975, the shares of these products in manufacturing value added and in total exports equalled 40 and 60 per cent, respectively. Thus, in 1975, the manufacturing contribution to GDP was in fact less than one fifth, while about a quarter of total exports was accounted for by "real" manufactures.

Given the predominance of NRB products in manufacturing output, it is striking that more than two thirds of the economy's imports of intermediates enter the manufacturing sector. The input structure of the manufacturing sector reveals that 20 per cent of the total value of production is composed of imported intermediate inputs as against 46 per cent of domestically produced inputs. The lion's share of NRB manufacturing production is based on local raw materials. Consequently, non-NRB industries are highly import dependent. The same is true of construction and utilities. These three sectors also show the lowest values for the index *NFEE*.

Because data on employment and wage levels in manufacturing industries are not available for 1975, only a tentative conclusion can be drawn with respect to the relative labour intensity of manufacturing production. We may infer from an intersectoral comparison of average direct wage coefficients that the manufacturing sector requires markedly less labour in production compared to primary and tertiary sectors. In comparing these direct wage

TABLE 16.1
BASIC DATA ON THE STRUCTURE OF THE ECONOMY, PENINSULAR MALAYSIA, 1975

Indicators	Agriculture & Mining	Manufacturing	Construction	Utilities	Services
1. Share in total gross output (%)	15.9	45.4	4.5	1.0	33.2
2. Share in GDP (%)	23.3	27.9	2.1	.8	45.9
3. Export-output ratio (%)	4.8	46.7	—	1.7	7.3
4. Share in total exports (%)	3.1	86.9	—	.1	9.9
5. Share in intermediate imports (%)	6.5	69.4	7.0	1.6	15.5
6. Input structure					
— Domestic intermediate inputs	.13	.46	.54	.35	.17
— Imported intermediate inputs	.06	.20	.20	.20	.06
— Gross value added	.81	.34	.26	.45	.77
Total inputs	1.00	1.00	1.00	1.00	1.00
7. $NFEE$	.92	.74	.68	.71	.91
8. P	.81	1.09	1.23	1.04	.84
9. P^W	1.82	.86	.70	.46	1.16
10. WIM	1.31	.62	.50	.34	.84
11. I^w (per 10^3 M$ output)	678.0[1]	84.3	78.2	66.4	391.9
12. T^w (per 10^3 M$ output)	731.7[1]	347.9	281.3	187.4	467.3
			1970		
13. VA/L (M$)	5,760	13,930	8,210	11,170	7,510
14. s (M$)	1,750	2,180	4,790	2,750	3,510

For explanation of symbols, see Section 10.4.

Note : [1] For agriculture, inclusive of both the compensation of employees and the operating surplus.

Sources: see Appendix to Chapter 16. Lines 13 and 14 are calculated from *Input-Output Tables Peninsular Malaysia 1970*, Department of Statistics, Kuala Lumpur; *Survey of Manufacturing Industries 1971*, Volume I, Department of Statistics, Kuala Lumpur, 1974, Table 2; ILO, *Year Book of Labour Statistics*, Geneva, various issues, Table 2A.

coefficients, it should be noted that the direct wage coefficient for agriculture includes both the compensation of employees and the operating surplus per unit of production. These two value-added components are taken together to provide a more realistic picture of employment in agriculture, as the 1975 input-output table gives an extremely low wage component in agricultural value added. Sectoral data on value added per employee according to the 1970 input-output table, which indeed could be supplemented with data on sectoral wages and employment, confirm the relatively capital-intensive nature of manufacturing production. In that year, as is also shown in Table 16.1, value added per employee in manufacturing was 2.4 and 1.9 times that in primary sectors and services, respectively. The relatively high average productivity of a manufacturing worker was entirely due to the NRB component of manufacturing production: value added per employee in these production activities amounted to M$20,440 as against M$7,240 in non-NRB industries in 1970.

Notwithstanding this productivity gap between manufacturing and the rest of the economy, the average manufacturing wage level was relatively low in the context of the national economy. In 1970, manufacturing wages were about a third higher than wages in agriculture, but compared to all other sectors, manufacturing wages lagged behind considerably. The combination of a low population pressure and a rich resource base certainly exerts an influence on this wage structure.

The spread effects of manufacturing are above the economy's average according to the P measure. The large share of NRB production in total manufacturing results in a strong production linkage with primary sectors. It is, therefore, striking to note that the dispersion of employment, measured by P^W, is relatively thin. This contrast is explained by two salient features of the Malaysian manufacturing sector. First, NRB production requires relatively little labour. Second, non-NRB production is highly dependent on imports of intermediates.

16.4 DEVELOPMENT AND STRUCTURE OF MALAYSIAN MANUFACTURED EXPORTS

The growth of manufactured exports from Malaysia was remarkable in the decade of the 1970s. The current U.S. dollar value of these export rose, on average, by 28.8 per cent per year from 1970 to 1980. As Figure 16.1 illustrates, both the export share of manufacturing production and the share of manufactures in total exports underwent a steady increase. Figure 16.2 shows that the sharp increase in exports of manufactures was accounted for basically by only two clusters of products: first and foremost electrical machinery (almost exclusively consisting of component parts, circuit fittings, transistors and valves) and precision equipment, and second, textiles, clothing and footwear. The former cluster of products increased its share in total manufactured exports from about 2 per cent in the early 1970s to over 42 per cent in 1980. Exports of textiles, clothing and footwear increased at a slightly faster pace than total manufactured exports. By contrast, after 1973, exports

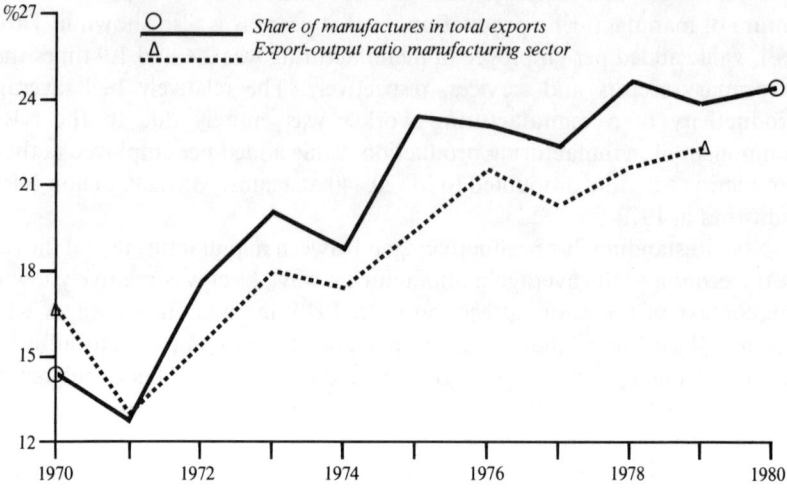

Figure 16.1
Manufactured Export Performance of Malaysia, 1970–1980

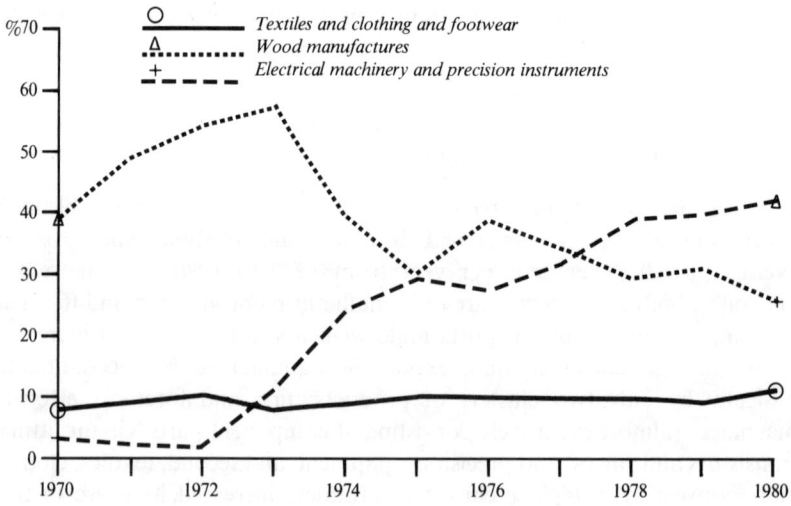

Figure 16.2
Composition of Malaysian Manufactured Exports, 1970–1980
(percentage shares)

Sources : United Nations, *Yearbook of International Trade Statistics*, Volume I, New York, various issues; United Nations, *Yearbook of Industrial Statistics*, Volume I, New York, various issues.

of wood manufactures clearly lagged behind. EPFZs have been instrumental in Malaysia's export drive. Exports of EPFZ industries reached a level of about M$1,380 million in 1978.[9] According to our definition of manufactured exports, this equalled 33 per cent of total manufactured exports in that year. It is estimated that, in 1978, about 85 per cent of EPFZ exports consisted of electrical machinery, thereby accounting for at least three quarters of the country's total export of this product group. Textiles, garments and precision instruments are the major remaining exports from EPFZs.

Table 16.2 provides insight into the structure of Malaysian manufactured exports, based on the 1975 input-output table. According to the classification of exportables by industrial origin used in this input-output table, the share of NRB manufactures in total manufactured exports was 80.4 per cent. NRB industries also showed the highest export orientation. The average weighted direct wage coefficient, which here approximates labour intensity of production, for total manufactured exports is only slightly higher than for manufacturing in total, 89.1 versus 84.3, respectively. The relatively labour-intensive character of total manufactured exports is solely explained by the high labour intensity of exports from E sectors. This category of exports, largely consisting of textiles, wearing apparel, electrical machinery and precision instruments, requires on average about 100 per cent more direct labour inputs per unit of output than NRB exports. As shown in Table A.16.2, precision instruments perform very well in this respect, with a direct wage coefficient of 277.1. For comparison, the direct wage coefficient in the production of wearing apparel, after precision instruments requiring the highest labour input of non-NRB exports, equals 134.3. The weight of precision instruments in exports from E sectors is so substantial that the direct wage coefficient of exports exclusive of this product group is reduced from 158.0 to 110.3 on average. It then appears that the average labour requirements of exports from E sectors hardly deviate from those of total production in E sectors, which equals 109.3 exclusive of precision instruments. Strikingly, the remaining non-NRB exports, which are produced outside the EPFZs, show a lower average direct wage coefficient than total DMO production. As Table 16.2 illustrates, less than half of DMO sector exports consist of relatively labour-intensive manufactures.

In other words, Malaysia does not consistently specialize in the most labour-intensive exportables. In fact, we are dealing here with a very narrow range of manufactures which dominate non-NRB exports. Of these, textiles and wearing apparel are relatively labour intensive, and the EPFZ exports of precision instruments are extremely labour intensive. By contrast, electronics exports from EPFZs definitely do not belong to the most labour-intensive exportables. Hence, the rank order relationship between sectoral export-output ratios and direct wage coefficients is positive but not statistically

TABLE 16.2
CHARACTERISTICS OF MAJOR PRODUCTION AND EXPORT CATEGORIES, MANUFACTURING SECTOR OF PENINSULAR MALAYSIA, 1975

	E/O (%)	E/E_m (%)	l^w (per 10³ M$ output)	T^w (per 10³ M$ output)	Share of wage-intensive products (%)	Share of wages in gross value added (%)
Total manufactured exports	—	100.0	89.1	364.7	70.7	—
Total manufacturing production	46.7	—	84.3	347.9	—	24.7
NRB manufactured exports	—	80.4	77.0	402.1	67.3	—
NRB manufacturing production	53.8	—	71.1	378.7	—	21.8
Exports from E sectors	—	14.0	158.0	219.3	100.0	—
Production in E sectors	47.2	—	134.2	202.6	—	32.9
Exports from DMO sectors	—	5.6	91.3	191.7	46.4	—
Production in DMO sectors	16.0	—	98.1	189.6	—	28.5

For explanation of symbols, see Section 10.4.
Source : see Appendix to Chapter 16.

significant, as is shown in Table 16.3. Removing the NRB sector does not improve the relationship.

Obviously, the findings on the labour intensity of NRB and non-NRB exports are reversed if the total wage coefficient is used as a measure. The heavy reliance of NRB exports on local supplies results in an average total wage coefficient about twice as high as for non-NRB exports. It is interesting to note that the total wage coefficients for exports and production in both E and DMO sectors deviate but little from each other. Here again, rank order correlations reveal no significant relationship between a sector's export orientation and the total wage coefficient. It seems, therefore, that export expansion in Malaysia is a concern for only a few industries, mainly located in EPFZs, leaving the rest of the manufacturing sector unaffected, on the understanding that no systematic specialization is brought about in the most labour-intensive exportables.

TABLE 16.3
MATRIX OF SPEARMAN RANK CORRELATION COEFFICIENTS FOR SECTOR CHARACTERISTICS,
PENINSULAR MALAYSIA, 1975[1], [2]

Variable	E_i/O_i	E_i/E_m	l_i^w	T_i^w
E_i/O_i	1	.71**	.26	.25
		.80**	.15	.25
E_i/E_m		1	−.00	.29
			.18	.16
l_i^w			1	.20
				.48*
T_i^w				1

For explanation of symbols, see Section 10.4.

Notes : [1] The upper coefficients in a row refer to rankings of all manufacturing sectors (n = 33), the lower coefficients refer to rankings of non-NRB sectors only (n = 21).
[2] Correlation coefficients that are significant at the 5 per cent level are denoted by one asterisk (*), those significant at the 1 per cent level by two asterisks (**).

Source : see Appendix to Chapter 16.

16.5 SPREAD EFFECTS OF MALAYSIAN MANUFACTURED EXPORTS

Dealing at first with the spread effects of the different categories of exports, it can be observed from Table 16.4 that NRB exports generate the most

TABLE 16.4
WEIGHTED AVERAGE MEASURES OF SPREAD EFFECTS FOR DIFFERENT CATEGORIES OF EXPORT AND PRODUCTION, MANUFACTURING SECTOR OF PENINSULAR MALAYSIA, 1975

	P	$NFEE$	P^W	WIM
Total manufactured exports	1.13	.79	1.03	.62
NRB exports	1.16	.83	1.14	.69
Exports from E sectors	.96	.62	.62	.37
Exports from DMO sectors	1.08	.57	.54	.33
Total manufacturing production	1.13	.71	.92	.55
NRB production	1.18	.77	1.07	.65
Non-NRB production	1.03	.58	.55	.33

For explanation of symbols, see Section 10.4.
Source : see Appendix to Chapter 16.

extensive spread effects, both in terms of production and employment. The average P and P^W values for NRB exports are substantially above 1, and this export production contains the largest domestic value-added component of all production and export categories. By contrast, the spread effects of exports from E sectors are the lowest according to all four measures. This line of export expansion, which has so vigorously been promoted since the early 1970, takes place in relative isolation as is indicated by an average P value of 0.96.

Exports from E sectors show a better performance as a vehicle for employment creation, the P^W value being 0.62 which is markedly higher than for exports from DMO sectors as well as for non-NRB production in general. This, however, has to be solely attributed to the heavy weight of direct employment effects of export production originating in E sectors. The indirect component in the total employment effect of these exports is relatively small. A caveat has, however, to be added immediately. Our findings are strongly affected by the rather deviating record of spread effects of the EPFZ-type exports of precision instruments. Compared to non-NRB production in general, the P value of 0.80 for precision instruments, shown in Table A.16.2, is relatively low, whereas its $NFEE$ value of 0.79 is rather high. This puzzling combination of P and $NFEE$ values is due to the specific input structure of precision instrument production, which was already conspicuous in the preceding section. The production value of precision instruments is composed of 10 per cent domestic inputs, 18 per cent imported inputs and 72 per cent value added. The high value-added component is exceptional for a manufacturing activity. Apparently, the processing and assembling of imported components and parts into precision instruments requires much labour. The domestic value-added component in precision instruments is therefore high, even though this export production is clearly an enclave-type activity.

This also explains why the average P value for exports from E sectors is below 1, whereas the domestic value-added component in these exports is higher than in other categories of non-NRB production. Consequently, removing precision instruments results in a higher P and a lower $NFEE$ value for exports from E sectors, namely 1.02 and 0.55, respectively. Both measures of spread effects now clearly lie below the averages for non-NRB production in general. Indeed, the contrast between this still above-average P value for exports from E sectors and the high import content of these exports confirms the already established overall high import dependency of non-NRB production. E sectors are only slightly more import dependent than DMO sectors.

An ILO-ARTEP study, based on survey data, reveals an even higher level of isolation of export sectors than is apparent from the application of the 1975 input-output table. According to this table, the input of the electrical machinery sector, for instance, is composed of domestic intermediates, imported intermediates and domestic services for 24, 32 and 9 per cent of the total value of production, respectively. Value added in this sector accounts for 35 per cent of the production value. Thus, about 57 per cent of the material inputs used in electrical machinery is imported. It emerges from the above-mentioned study that the typical electronics assembly plant located in one of the EPFZs imports about 60 per cent of its total intermediate input requirement. The remaining 40 per cent is mainly spent on electricity purchases and some other domestic inputs of negligible value.[10] Put differently, almost all of the tradable material inputs entering electronics are purchased from abroad. In our analysis, electronics is included in input-output sector electrical machinery and, consequently, the specific characteristics of this EPFZ production are partly smoothed out. As regards the textile and garments industries located in EPFZs, the ILO-ARTEP study mentions yet another remarkable feature, namely the phenomenon of intra-EPFZ deliveries. Textile industries in Penang EPFZs sold, in 1978, about a quarter of their production of yarn and fabric to other textile and garment industries in the free zone to be processed further before exporting.[11] Such a development begins to look like a process of import substitution within an EPFZ.

The pursuit of a dualistic industrial strategy in Malaysia, leading to an export sector largely situated in EPFZs and standing apart from the usual import-substitution sector, not only thwarts a systematic specialization in labour-intensive manufactures for export production. This strategy also produces a relationship between factor intensity of production and extensiveness of production linkages that we have thus far not come across. As the correlation coefficients of the sectoral rankings by direct wage coefficient and P value in Table 16.5 indicate, there is a strongly negative relationship between these two variables. The correlation is significant at the 1 per cent level for the sample of all manufacturing sectors, and just significant at the 5 per cent level for the sample of non-NRB sectors only. This implies that labour-intensive production processes show a systematically lower level of spread effects, measured by their P values. It is, of course, not unexpected to find a negative rank correlation between labour intensity and P values in case of the full sample. The relatively capital-intensive primary processing industries in Malaysia are based on domestic raw materials, whereas the more

TABLE 16.5
MATRIX OF SPEARMAN RANK CORRELATION COEFFICIENTS FOR SECTOR CHARACTERISTICS AND VARIOUS MEASURES OF SPREAD EFFECTS, PENINSULAR MALAYSIA, 1975[1, 2]

Variable	E_i/O_i	l_i^w	P_i	$NFEE_i$	P_i^w	WIM_i
E_i/O_i	1	.26	-.06	.27	.25	.25
		.15	-.28	.06	.25	.25
l_i^w		1	-.46**	.01	.21	.21
			-.44*	.15	.48*	.48*
P_i			1	.32	.55**	.55**
				-.07	.29	.29
$NFEE_i$				1	.63**	.63**
					.40	.40
P_i^w					1	1.00**
						1.00**
WIM_i						1

For explanation of symbols, see Section 10.4.
Notes : [1] The upper coefficients in a raw refer to rankings of all manufacturing sectors (n = 33), the lower coefficients refer to rankings of non-NRB sectors only (n = 21).
[2] Correlation coefficients that are significant at the 5 per cent level are denoted by one asterisk (*), those significant at the 1 per cent level by two asterisks (**).
Source : see Appendix to Chapter 16.

labour-intensive non-NRB production shows a heavy import dependence. However, the finding that the conditions of non-NRB production in Malaysia result in fewer production linkages of the more labour-intensive industries may deserve special attention.

16.6 SUMMARY

Before independence, the Malaysian economy was geared towards the production and export of primary commodities in line with the country's wealth in natural resources. Since independence, however, development strategies have been concentrated on a diversification of the economy. From the late 1950s onwards, the familiar stage was set for the import-substitution type of industrialization. This strategy continued in force, even though towards the end of the 1960s Malaysia resorted to a vigorous promotion of manufactured exports. Malaysia thus appears to be evolving a dualistic industrialization strategy since then, which has led to the creation of a new export sector, mainly accommodated in EPFZs. Exports from these zones contributed substantially to the rapid growth of Malaysian manufactured exports in the 1970s.

The results show no consistent specialization pattern of non-NRB industries in the most labour-intensive exportables. It is true that non-NRB exports are on average relatively labour intensive, but, in fact, these exports are dominated by a very narrow range of manufactures which strongly differ in labour intensity. The direct wage coefficient of the EPFZ export of precision instruments is, for instance, almost three times as high as that for electrical machinery. The spread effects of non-NRB exports are meagre and the import dependency of these exports is high. Apart from precision instruments, these exports show a heavier reliance on imported inputs than non-NRB production in general. The results further show fewer production spread effects as the labour intensity of production increases. These findings are most likely explained by the dualistic industrialization strategy of Malaysia, which facilitates the creation of an enclave export sector.

APPENDIX TABLE A.16.1
CHARACTERISTICS OF MANUFACTURING SECTORS CLASSIFIED AS NRB SECTORS, PENINSULAR MALAYSIA, 1975

I-O Code	Sector	E_i/O_i (%)	E_i/E_m (%)	I_i^w (per 10³ M$ output)	T_i^w	W_i/VA_i (%)	P_i	$NFEE_i$	P_i^w	WIM_i
17	Oil and fats	70.9	18.0	20.2	482.2	5.0	1.17	.93	1.36	.82
18	Rice milling	6.8	.6	67.0	627.5	34.0	1.41	.89	1.78	1.07
19	Other grain and flour products	10.1	.6	57.7	411.2	27.2	1.39	.71	1.16	.70
20	Sugar	20.3	1.0	7.5	192.8	32.8	1.40	.33	.55	.33
21	Other food products	15.6	3.0	70.6	447.8	24.6	1.41	.80	1.27	.77
22	Beverage and tobacco	13.5	1.1	50.0	164.1	9.7	1.05	.77	.46	.28
29	Lumber	60.0	4.6	159.5	494.1	31.0	1.06	.90	1.40	.84
30	Wooden products	46.4	2.2	125.7	387.6	28.8	1.15	.83	1.10	.66
36	Petroleum and its products	12.6	1.5	70.6	79.4	32.2	.74	.24	.22	.14
38	Other rubber products	96.2	25.5	95.9	570.0	28.8	1.20	.89	1.61	.97
42	Iron and steel	15.5	.5	56.6	155.5	18.6	1.07	.56	.44	.27
43	Non-ferrous metal	92.1	21.9	86.7	159.9	26.9	1.11	.75	.45	.27

APPENDIX TABLE A.16.2
CHARACTERISTICS OF MANUFACTURING SECTORS CLASSIFIED AS E SECTORS, PENINSULAR MALAYSIA, 1975

I-O Code	Sector	E_i/O_i (%)	E_i/E_m (%)	I_i^w (per 10^3 M$ output)	T_i^w	W_i/VA_i (%)	P_i	$NFEE_i$	P_i^w	WIM_i
24	Weaving and dyeing	42.6	.8	107.9	215.1	44.1	1.27	.53	.61	.37
25	Knitting	45.3	.6	114.1	221.8	41.9	1.26	.56	.63	.38
26	Wearing apparel	31.1	1.1	134.3	198.0	32.2	1.00	.58	.56	.34
45	Industrial machinery and equipments	50.0	2.2	129.1	181.7	35.4	.90	.51	.51	.31
46	Other electrical machinery and apparatus	34.8	4.3	95.4	176.0	27.4	1.04	.57	.50	.30
49	Precision instruments	91.2	4.0	277.1	305.3	38.6	.80	.79	.86	.52
50	Other manufacturing products	53.5	1.1	106.7	173.4	26.4	.95	.58	.49	.30

APPENDIX TABLE A.16.3
CHARACTERISTICS OF MANUFACTURING SECTORS CLASSIFIED AS DMO SECTORS, PENINSULAR MALAYSIA, 1975

I-O Code	Sector	E_i/O_i (%)	E_i/E_m (%)	l_i^w (per 10³ M$ output)	T_i^w	W_i/VA_i^1 (%)	P_i	$NFEE_i$	P_i^w	WIM_i
23	Spinning	15.0	.4	93.7	154.0	35.8	.93	.41	.44	.26
27	Other made-up textile goods	12.2	.3	130.7	204.5	41.2	1.04	.51	.58	.35
28	Leather and fur, and their products	14.6	.1	74.7	209.7	28.6	1.27	.57	.59	.36
32	Paper and printing	8.4	.4	118.1	214.3	30.6	1.10	.65	.61	.37
33	Basic industrial chemicals	25.2	.3	109.7	184.2	32.0	.99	.54	.52	.31
34	Chemical fertilizers and pesticides	13.0	.3	82.4	154.3	22.0	1.02	.59	.44	.26
35	Other chemical products	26.5	1.0	61.7	277.3	28.4	1.28	.65	.79	.47
37	Tyre and tubes	28.5	.4	82.1	171.5	20.1	1.01	.60	.49	.29
39	Cement	4.0	.1	65.1	141.2	21.7	1.10	.52	.40	.24
40	Glass and glass products	21.9	.1	96.8	173.3	30.2	1.02	.52	.49	.30
41	Non-metallic mineral products	7.7	.3	141.9	208.5	26.3	.95	.71	.59	.36
44	Other metal products	14.3	.7	102.7	166.8	26.9	1.04	.59	.47	.29
47	Automobile, motorcycles and bicycles	27.0	1.1	79.1	148.3	27.4	1.06	.50	.42	.25
48	Other transport equipment	13.5	.1	117.8	209.7	42.9	1.08	.51	.59	.36

For explanation of symbols, see Section 10.4.

Note : ¹ W_i/VA_i = share of wages in gross value added.

Source : computations are based on data from *Input-Output Table Peninsular Malaysia 1975*, IDE Statistical Data Series No. 37, Institute of Developing Economies, Tokyo, 1982.

17
The Case of Singapore

17.1 INTRODUCTORY REMARKS

Singapore, a city-state, covers slightly more than 600 km^2 with scarcely any natural resources. The population of this small island republic amounted to 2.5 million at the start of the 1980s, resulting in an extremely high population density of over 4000 persons per km^2. In the past two decades, Singapore's economic performance has been impressive. In the 1960s and 1970s, real GDP *per capita* grew at an average annual rate of 6.8 per cent. From the mid-1960s onwards, when Singapore embarked on an export-oriented strategy of industrialization, growth has been largely led by export of manufactures.

It is often stated that Singapore's industrial development is unique and non-transferable to other countries.[1] This uniqueness refers to the special features of the Singapore economy which, on the one hand, should lead perforce to an export-oriented strategy of industrialization, while, on the other hand, the same features constitute the ingredients for the success of this strategy. Mention is then made of Singapore as a city-state with a small domestic market and a high population density. Concomitantly, a relatively well-educated industrious labour force and a strategic geographical location at international shipping and aviation cross-roads are considered as "resources". Admittedly, Singapore's policy alternatives are limited, but by holding only these conditions responsible for its economic success attaches too little weight to deliberate and comprehensive policy initiatives of the Singapore government. Some advantages have been developed. Conceived in this way, the case of Singapore loses its uniqueness and can indeed be an instructive experience for other industrializing developing countries. The more so, as the export-promotion policies adopted transformed, more or less, the whole of Singapore into an EPFZ, characterized by an extremely liberal trade regime, a minimum of restrictions and regulations and a high degree of dependence on direct foreign investment.[2] Singapore's experience approaches laboratory conditions and is, therefore, of direct relevance to a broader evaluation of the role of EPFZs in export-oriented industrialization efforts of developing countries.

During the 1970s, the structures of production and exports in Singapore were subject to considerable change. Fortunately, two input-output tables, covering the years 1973 and 1978, are available which enable an investigation of the nature of structural change that may be brought about through an EPFZ-type of export production. In the 1970s, Singapore already ranked high in the country group of middle-income economies, with a *per capita* GNP of US$1,940 and US$3,290 in 1973 and 1978, respectively.[3]

17.2 INDUSTRIALIZATION AND TRADE STRATEGIES IN SINGAPORE

As an entrepôt trade economy, Singapore has a long-standing policy of free trade. It channelled to Europe the primary commodity exports of South-East Asia and served as a transit point for manufactures to this region. Singapore was a financial, administrative and service centre for Western colonial enterprise. On the eve of self-government in 1959, the economic outlook of entrepôt trade was not promising and it was realized that the only future source of economic growth and employment was industrialization. In particular, the employment situation became critical.

The switch from entrepôt trade to manufacturing started with the establishment of the Economic Development Board (EDB) in 1961.[4] The expectation that Singapore would join in a common market with Malaysia was the basis for an import-substitution strategy. Until that time, relatively little industrialization had taken place and a local industrial entrepreneurial class was virtually absent. Hence, industrial policy strongly leaned towards attracting foreign investors by providing a favourable investment climate. Efforts were directed towards improvement of the physical and institutional infrastructure and ensuring industrial peace. Protective tariffs were first introduced in 1960, complemented by quantitative imports restrictions in 1963. In addition, fiscal incentives were liberally applied to promote investments.

The Malaysian common market effectively came into being in 1963, but did not last long. The Malaysian federation and common market collapsed in 1965, which at the same time terminated Singapore's import-substitution efforts. Thus, Singapore passed through an inward-looking industrialization phase of very short duration. Domestic industry, moreover, was offered but a low level of tariff and quota protection. Yet, manufacturing growth during this period could mainly be attributed to import substitution and expansion of domestic demand.[5] Real average annual growth of manufacturing value added amounted to 9.5 per cent, leading to an increase in the manufacturing contribution to GDP from 12.7 per cent in 1960 to 15.2 per cent in 1965.[6]

Singapore's political independence and the consequent reduction in domestic market size necessitated a reconsideration of industrialization strategy. The first two years after independence were characterized by excess capacity in the manufacturing sector, growing unemployment and indistinctness regarding a strategy choice. Protection, for instance, was extended, whereas at the same time the first export-promotional measures were introduced. By 1967, however, export-oriented industrialization was being vigorously pursued. During a very brief space of time a consistent set of policy measures was implemented to promote industrialization. Promotion policies in Singapore aim at a direct stimulation of private investments in manufacturing rather than export-promotion schemes. Specific export incentives are of minor importance. But, given the limited size of the domestic market, industrialization inevitably involves export-oriented industrialization. To stimulate investments, most notably by foreign enterprise, earlier efforts to improve the overall investment climate were strenuously and more comprehensively carried through. Simultaneously, the protection of domestic industry was removed. After another round of tariff escalation in 1969, tariffs were either reduced or removed at a rapid pace till no tariffs of any significance were left. In addition, all quota restrictions were removed. Thus, export manufacturing — but in fact the whole of Singapore — enjoys a free-trade regime, with hardly any import restriction and the absence of any export tax. The government's approach to making Singapore attractive to foreign investors encompassed from the outset three major fields: (1) creation of industrial institutions and the development of industrial estates; (2) provision of tax incentives, financial assistance schemes and specific export incentives; and (3) accelerated manpower development and enforcement of labour discipline.

As already indicated, the EDB has been the main executor of Singapore's industrialization strategy. Prior to 1968, the EDB disposed of a wide range of instruments to promote and guide industrial investments. It was authorized to invest, give and guarantee loans, underwrite issues of stocks and bonds, develop industrial estates and give technical consultancy services. With the switch from import substitution to export promotion in 1967–1968, a number of EDB responsibilities was taken over by separate bodies. The Development Bank of Singapore was established and took over the industrial financing function of the EDB. The development and management of industrial estates became the responsibility of the Jurong Town Corporation (JTC). Other institutions that arose from the EDB are the Singapore Institute for Standards and Industrial Research, the Engineering Industries Development Agency and the National Productivity Board. Finally, an International

Trading Company was established to facilitate the marketing of Singapore's manufactures abroad, a function that was again taken over by the Trade Development Board in 1983. In a few years, the EDB, set up under the regime of import substitution, was transformed into a promotion agency of export-oriented foreign investors, surrounded by specialized independent institutions. The EDB retained its main responsibility as the general promotor and coordinator of industrial investments. And most importantly, the EDB guides the process of industrialization by preparing a list of industries which are feasible for Singapore and by processing and evaluating applications for pioneer status, a requirement for eligibility for various tax reliefs.

The development of industrial estates and infrastructural provisions has been instrumental in attracting foreign investment into Singapore. The largest industrial estate, Jurong Town, was developed at the south-west corner of Singapore and placed under the direction of the JTC in 1968. This industrial town is subdivided into various zones, each of which accommodates different activities, i.e. heavy industry, light industry, business and housing and recreation. The Jurong labour force is housed in low-cost flats and does not have to leave the estate for shopping and recreation. Apart from managing Jurong Town and providing the housing-cum-recreational services for industrial workers, the JTC accomplishes a broader task, especially the development and management of new industrial estates, provision of port facilities and services and provision of technical consultancy services for firms in the estates. By 1980, 19 industrial estates were in operation. Prepared sites in these estates are leased to investors who can, in addition, lease or purchase a standard factory building from the JTC. The so-called outer ring estates, located at the outer fringes of the island, mainly accommodate the heavier and more environmentally detrimental industries. The other, inner ring, estates are spread over the island, and mainly consist of "flatted" factories which are located close to or within public flat buildings in densely-populated residential areas. Labour-intensive, clean light industries take advantage of these sites as their production processes are relatively space intensive and workers, especially females, are more readily available close to their homes.

Tax incentives, most notably tax holidays, form the second cornerstone of Singapore's industrial investment promotion. The switch in strategy can clearly be dated from the enactment of the Economic Expansion Incentives Act of 1967. This Act replaced ordinances of 1959 which allowed income tax concessions to designated pioneer industries. The pioneer status was granted to industries and products that were considered essential to Singapore's economic development. The five-year holiday from the corporate income tax of 40 per cent was the most important tax exemption to be enjoyed by pioneer firms. The tax concessions were basically retained in the 1967 Act and later amendments in 1970, on the understanding that two new eligibility criteria were introduced. First, tax holidays were only allowed in case of new capital investments in pioneer industries of at least S$1 million, whereas in case of expansion investments the qualifying level for tax concessions was raised to S$10 million. Large-scale investments were purposefully encouraged. Second, the qualification of export firm was introduced. Those firms which export more than 20 per cent of their production, amounting to at least S$100 thousand, may apply for 90 per cent tax relief on export profits during a five-year period. Extension of this tax relief period is possible up to 15 years. Pioneer firms may enjoy this tax relief for three years after the five-year tax holiday. Tax concessions attached to the pioneer and export status were granted in addition to other tax incentives offered by Singapore's tax legislation, such as carry-forward of losses, accelerated depreciation allowances, double deduction for export-promotion expenses and special tax incentives to encourage foreign borrowing and the inflow of foreign technology. Foreign and national investors are treated alike and can equally take advantage of these, in general, liberally applied incentives. Foreign investors, however, take an additional interest in the free import of any amount of capital and the absence of any restriction on the remittance of profit and repatriation of capital.

The switch in strategy was also extended to the functioning of the labour market. The government started to intervene actively in skill development and industrial relations. The educational system was re-oriented and technical courses were introduced at various levels, while, at the same time, technical education was made attractive for students. Concomitantly, several new technical training institutes, some in close co-operation with foreign companies, were established. To produce a disciplined work force and guarantee peaceful industrial relations, the labour unions were brought under political control. Industrial disputes were already subject to compulsory arbitration. The Employment Act and the Industrial Relations (Amendment) Act of 1968 curtailed further the unions' freedom to negotiate working conditions. These Acts, *inter alia*, regulated working hours, controlled fringe benefits and overtime payments and stipulated that the sole responsibility and competence to decide on such matters as the recruitment, promotion, transfer and dismissal of workers belonged to the firm management. Since 1972, the National Wage Council (NWC), in which government, employers and trade unions are equally represented, formulates general guidelines on wage increases in view of the state and needs of the national economy.

This broad set of policy initiatives did not fail to produce its effect on industrial growth. The 1965-1973 period witnessed an unprecedented high average annual growth in real manufacturing value added of 18.8 per cent. The share of manufacturing in GDP approached one quarter in 1973. Strikingly enough, this growth record was largely brought about by the inflow of direct foreign investment, especially into export-oriented manufacturing industries. Singapore owes its major source of foreign investment to international oil companies which have chosen the island as regional location of their petroleum refineries. From 1970 to 1981, the petroleum share in the total inflow of foreign investment in fixed assets amounted to 41.2 per cent. The next largest concentration of foreign assets was in the electrical and electronic industry, with a share of 16.6 per cent. The remaining foreign investments in the manufacturing sector have gone into machinery, transport equipment, chemicals, and textiles and clothing.[7] To put the role of foreign capital in manufacturing production and exports in perspective, majority-owned foreign affiliates accounted for more than two thirds of manufacturing value added and no less than 85 per cent of manufactured exports in 1979. Foreign firms appear to be larger and show a distinctly higher export orientation than local firms.[8] It can, therefore, safely be established that the policy measures introduced in the late 1960s and the subsequent large inflow of direct foreign investment transformed Singapore, in fact, into an EPFZ.

From 1973 onwards, Singapore was confronted with a hesitant world economy, with an erratic impact on its export performance and manufacturing growth. The years 1975 and 1982 even showed a negative real growth rate of manufacturing value added. Yet, on average, manufacturing value added increased annually by 6.8 per cent in real terms, from 1973 to 1982. At first, a strict wage restraint policy was followed for fear of loss of international competitiveness. The NWC set guidelines for annual wage increases that lagged behind productivity increases in order to stabilize wage costs. The increasingly tight labour market was eased by an inflow of foreign labour and the active encouragement of females to enter the labour market. This conservative policy, however, was abandoned in 1979, when the government forcefully embarked on a second-stage export-oriented process of industrialization. A slowdown in productivity growth, increasing dependence on foreign unskilled labour and increasing competition from newly industrializing exporters were the grounds for this switch in strategy. Productivity increase became the new goal. For that purpose, the manufacturing sector needed to be restructured away from labour-intensive, low-wage export-processing industries towards more sophisticated, skill-intensive and higher value-added production activities. Noteworthy is the concurrent policy option to deepen the industrial structure through assisting local entrepreneurs in meeting the input and services requirements of foreign companies operating in Singapore.

Once again, the industrial-promotion strategy was changed so as to initiate a process of upgrading and, once again, the government took the lead by directing the flow of resources through an adjusted set of policy measures. In 1975, the pioneer tax holiday period was extended up to 10 years and the minimum investment requirement abolished to meet the specific requirements of smaller scale and technology-intensive industries. Since then, pioneer awards have been increasingly used to direct the upgrading process. In addition, new tax incentives were introduced in 1979-1980 to encourage new investments and research and development activities. Skill development efforts were further intensified through the establishment of a Skill Development Fund, which finances training schemes and provides incentives to invest in labour-saving technology. Labour market policies too changed accordingly. First, the inflow of unskilled foreign labour was kept under restraint. Second, the tightness of the labour market was countered with accelerated wage increases in the period from 1979 to 1982. These wage adjustments were also deliberately aimed at increasing the wage costs for employers, averaging nearly 20 per cent per year, to induce them to adopt labour-saving technologies and upgrade their activities. In line with this process of economic restructuring, the government supports those manufacturers who cannot keep pace with the upgrading process and, consequently, are threatened in their economic feasibility, in reallocating their production activities to surrounding countries with lower wage levels. As appears from the above, the government of Singapore plays a heavily interventionist role in industrial development. Singapore's export manufacturing has essentially been led by a close alliance of the government and foreign investors.

17.3 STRUCTURAL FEATURES OF THE SINGAPORE ECONOMY

The specific structural features of Singapore as an outward-looking city-state are clearly revealed by Tables 17.1 and 17.2. As one of the busiest ports in the world and because of its function as a financial and business centre for the region, the service sector is evidently the prominent sector of the Singapore economy for income and employment generation. Despite the recently renewed emphasis on communication and banking, this traditional function is increasingly being challenged by manufacturing. In terms of gross output, manufacturing had superseded the service sector as the largest sector of the economy by 1978.

The shares in GDP and total employment accounted for by manufacturing are clearly much less, 26.9 and 32.7 per cent in 1978, respectively, but still rising. The corresponding shares of services fell to 62.9 and 59.8 per cent in 1978. Agricultural and mining activities are almost absent in Singapore. The importance of manufacturing in Singapore's foreign-trade sector is paramount. Manufacturers managed to raise the share of their products in total exports of goods and services from the already high level of 71.7 per cent in 1973 to almost three quarters in 1978. The proportion of total manufacturing sales exported increased from 65.0 to 73.1 per cent during this period.

TABLE 17.1
BASIC DATA ON THE STRUCTURE OF THE SINGAPORE ECONOMY, 1973

Indicators	Agriculture & Mining	Manufacturing	Construction	Utilities	Services
1. Share in total gross output (%)	2.3	43.0	6.4	1.4	46.9
2. Share in GDP (%)	2.4	23.0	6.6	2.2	65.8
3. Share in total employment (%)	1.0	30.7	6.6	1.3	60.4
4. Export-output ratio (%)	9.0	65.0	—	3.7	22.9
5. Share in total exports (%)	.5	71.7	—	.2	27.6
6. Share in intermediate imports (%)	.4	77.6	6.2	.0	15.8
7. Input structure					
— Domestic intermediate inputs	.45	.16	.21	.21	.22
— Imported intermediate inputs	.06	.59	.31	.06	.11
— Gross value added	.49	.25	.48	.73	.67
Total inputs	1.00	1.00	1.00	1.00	1.00
8. *NFEE*	.69	.34	.58	.85	.83
9. P	1.18	.92	.96	.96	.97
10. $\overset{*}{P}$	2.20	.42	1.02	.98	.37
11. P^E	.76	.77	1.06	1.04	1.36
12. P^{E-A}	.43	.84	1.14	1.13	1.47
13. WIM^E (per 10^6 S\$ output)	37.6	37.7	56.5	50.0	69.3
14. l^e (per 10^6 S\$ output)	14.5	24.5	35.2	33.3	44.2
15. VA/L (S\$)	33,720	10,130	13,560	21,990	15,210
16. T^e (per 10^6 S\$ output)	30.6	31.1	42.7	41.7	54.6
17. s (S\$)	4,820	4,210	7,000	3,880	5,610

For explanation of symbols, see Section 10.4.
Sources: see Appendix to Chapter 17.

Manufacturing is also the largest importer in the economy, accounting for over three quarters of intermediate imports.

It is striking to find the openness of the economy to have been increased so markedly during only a five-year period. Not only did the export-output ratios increase for the economy as a whole and for each sector separately, but the already high import content of domestic production also increased further all along the line. This development is clearly revealed by comparing the input structures and indexes of *NFEE* of the distinguished sectors for 1973 and 1978. All sectors have increased the proportion of directly imported interme-

TABLE 17.2
BASIC DATA ON THE STRUCTURE OF THE SINGAPORE ECONOMY, 1978

Indicators	Agriculture & Mining	Manufacturing	Construction	Utilities	Services
1. Share in total gross output (%)	1.3	49.3	5.6	1.4	42.4
2. Share in GDP (%)	1.7	26.9	6.4	2.1	62.9
3. Share in total employment (%)	.6	32.7	5.7	1.2	59.8
4. Export-output ratio (%)	10.0	73.1	—	6.2	29.2
5. Share in total exports (%)	.3	74.1	—	.2	25.4
6. Share in intermediate imports (%)	.6	78.2	4.1	.8	16.3
7. Input structure					
— Domestic intermediate inputs	.34	.15	.28	.25	.25
— Imported intermediate inputs	.19	.65	.29	.23	.16
— Gross value added	.47	.20	.43	.52	.59
Total inputs	1.00	1.00	1.00	1.00	1.00
8. $NFEE$	.62	.27	.52	.61	.75
9. P	1.08	.90	1.02	.99	1.01
10. $\overset{*}{P}$	1.68	.31	1.40	1.18	.43
11. P^E	.69	.72	1.10	.95	1.55
12. P^{E-A}	.33	.77	1.19	1.03	1.68
13. WIM^E (per 10^6 S$ output)	16.6	16.9	28.8	22.5	38.4
14. I^e (per 10^6 S$ output)	7.4	11.2	17.3	14.5	23.9
15. VA/L (S$)	64,630	17,970	24,540	36,040	24,530
16. T^e (per 10^6 S$ output)	13.6	14.2	21.8	18.8	30.7
17. s (S$)	8,580	7,010	13,560	7,550	9,720

For explanation of symbols, see Section 10.4.
Sources: see Appendix to Chapter 17.

diate inputs in total production and, consequently, all sectors witnessed a substantial reduction in the total domestic value-added component per unit of production. Focusing on manufacturing, in 1973, total production was for three quarters composed of intermediate products and for a quarter of value added. These intermediate input requirements were for 78.9 per cent met from imports. Compared to 1973, manufacturing production became even more import dependent. The proportion of imported intermediate inputs in total production rose from 59.0 per cent in 1973 to 65.0 per cent in 1978, now accounting for 80.7 per cent of total intermediate input requirements. This increased import dependency was at the expense of the value-added component in production, which fell from 25.0 per cent in 1973 to 20.0 per cent in 1978. Consequently, in an economy that on the whole showed a stronger dependence on imports, the total domestic value-added component in manufacturing production witnessed a still sharper fall, namely from an average of 34.0 per cent in 1973 to the extremely low average percentage of 27.0.

Given this specific input structure, it is obvious to find manufacturing exerting the lowest spread effects, in terms of both production and employment. Manufacturing showed the lowest P values in 1973 as well as in 1978. Compared to 1973, the value of this measure even decreased by two percentage points to 0.90 in 1978. The isolated character of manufacturing in Singapore is most apparent from its low $\overset{*}{P}$ values, which exclude intrasectoral deliveries. In 1978, the $\overset{*}{P}$ value for manufacturing activities fell to 0.31.

The relatively low level of employment spread effects of manufacturing, indicated by P^E values of 0.77 and 0.72 in 1973 and 1978, respectively, is, of course, a reflection of the high and increasing import content in production but is also explained by the specific nature of manufacturing activities in Singapore. According to the average direct and total labour coefficients, the labour requirements per S$1 million of manufacturing production were substantially lower than in construction, utilities and services. This pattern is found in 1973 and 1978. In the context of the national economy, manufacturing is, however, anything but a relatively capital-intensive production activity. On average, employees in manufacturing generate the lowest amount of value added of the entire economy. Both in 1973 and 1978, manufacturing value added stood at roughly 0.3, 0.7, 0.5 and 0.7 of the value added per employee in the primary sector, construction, utilities and services, respectively. Accordingly, in these years, workers in manufacturing received the lowest average wages among workers in different sectors of the economy. Moreover, the intersectoral wage differentials developed unfavourably for manufacturing over this five-year period. At least till 1978, export-oriented manufacturing in Singapore was a labour-intensive and low value-added generating activity, characterized by a relatively low average wage level. Thus, per unit of value added, manufacturing makes the largest contribution to employment, whereas, per unit of production, its contribution is the smallest, due to the low value-added component in manufacturing production. Add to this the already established extremely high import content of manufacturing production, and it is logical to find relatively low values for the employment spread effects measures P^E and WIM^E.

It may be inferred from the foregoing analysis that the attainment of virtually full employment in Singapore in 1974 and then from 1976 onwards — with unemployment rates below 4 per cent[9] — is primarily due to the tremendous increase in absolute value of manufactured exports and hence employment opportunities. Domestic value-added generation and indirect employment opportunities have clearly been of less significance.

It should be recalled that the period bridged by the two input-output tables was characterized by a strict wage restraint policy to keep the existing package of exports competitive. Yet, as can be inferred from Tables 17.1 and 17.2, value added per employee and the average wage rate in manufacturing rose by an annual average rate of 12.1 and 10.7 per cent, respectively, between 1973 and 1978. In real terms, however, after deflating by the GDP deflator for manufacturing,[10] value added per employee grew annually by 4.9 per cent and the average manufacturing wage level by 3.6 per cent during this period. Thus, the low-wage policy proved to be effective in reducing employers' labour cost. As already indicated, this policy was abandoned in 1979.

17.4 DEVELOPMENT AND STRUCTURE OF SINGAPORE'S MANUFACTURED EXPORTS

In the case of Singapore, different definitions of manufactured exports also give quite different pictures of manufactured export performance. This is largely explained by Singapore's extensive exports of petroleum products, which constituted roughly 25 to 30 per cent of total merchandise exports throughout the 1970s. Nevertheless, the trend towards an increasing share of manufactures in total exports and an increasing outward orientation of the manufacturing sector are undeniable. As Figure 17.1 illustrates, exports of manufactures rose from nearly a third of total exports in 1970 to over 50 per cent in the early 1980s. Inclusive of petroleum products, these shares rose from 56.0 to almost 78.0 per cent, respectively. The share of export sales in manufacturing production went up to over 90 per cent at the start of the 1980s. It is, among other characteristics, particularly also this extremely high export share that makes manufacturing production in Singapore resemble EPFZ conditions. The compositional changes that occurred in Singapore's manufactured exports during the 1970s are evident from Figure 17.2. At the outset of the export-oriented industrialization programme, textiles and clothing were the leading exportables. Exports of wood and wood products were also of importance at that time, but these clearly labour-intensive manufactures lost ground rapidly. Electrical products and electronics, which also in Singapore are characterized by assembly-type (semi-) manufactures, quickly emerged to become by far the most important exportables, with a share in manufactured exports of about a third at the end of the 1970s. Chemicals became the next major category of exportables. Exporters of non-electrical machinery and transport equipment (mainly ships and boats, and oil rigs) succeeded in keeping their export shares. Thus, the compositional shifts in Singapore's manufactured exports during the 1970s were away from

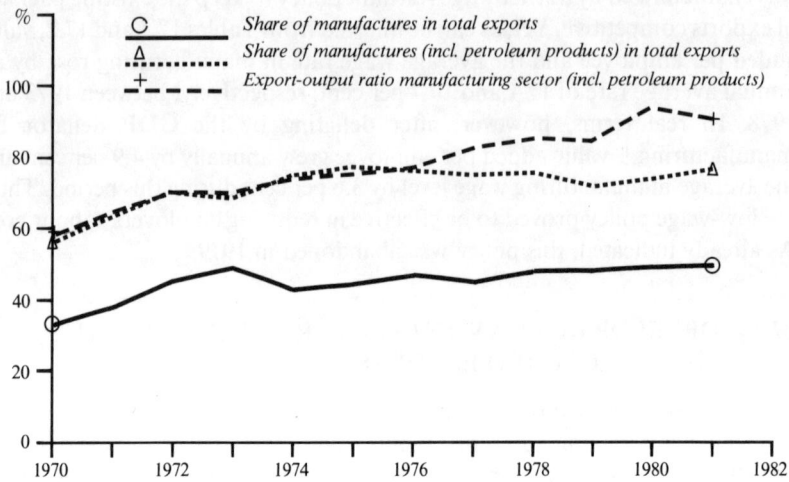

Figure 17.1
Manufactured Export Performance of Singapore,
1970-1981

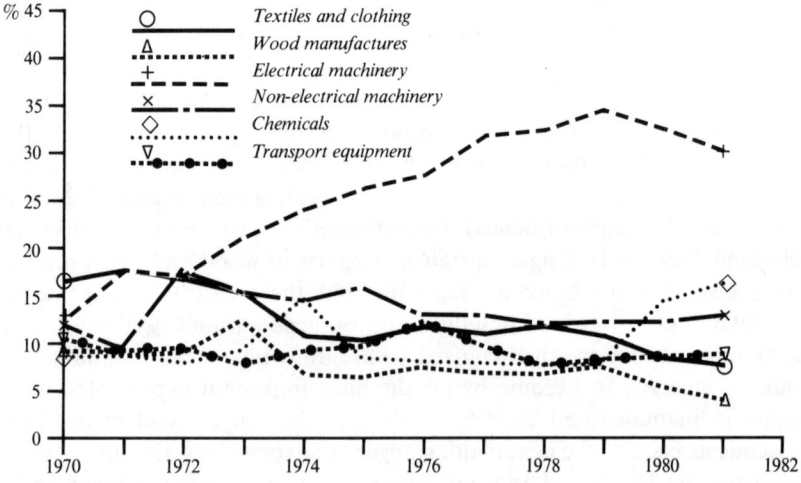

Figure 17.2
Composition of Singapore Manufactured Exports,
1970-1981, (percentage shares)

Sources: United Nations, *Yearbook of International Trade Statistics*, Volume I, New York, various issues; United Nations, *Yearbook of Industrial Statistics*, Volume I, New York, various issues.

labour-intensive products towards a more diversified package of more capital-intensive products.

This diversification-cum-upgrading process is also evident in comparing the structural features of Singapore's manufactured exports in 1973 and 1978, which are presented in Table 17.3. We have deviated in this table from the standard procedure of distinguishing between E and DMO sectors. The average percentages of exports in output of non-NRB sectors were as high as 56.4 and 63.3 per cent in 1973 and 1978, respectively. It is misleading to classify sectors showing a lower export-output ratio as predominantly oriented towards the domestic market. Besides, as already indicated, nearly all manufacturing production in Singapore takes place under EPFZ conditions.

Highlighting the similarities in both years first, it appears that, although Singapore is deprived of natural resources, the greater part of manufactured exports is accounted for by NRB products: 55.7 per cent in 1973 and 61.4 per cent in 1978. The bulk of NRB exports consists of petroleum products and rubber. Petroleum products alone accounted for 56.0 per cent of NRB exports in 1973, a share that rose to 85.5 per cent in 1978. Rubber processing in Singapore is mainly a transit activity whereby little value is added, about 4 per cent, to the value of raw material imports. In a way, the same is true for oil refining. All crude oil is imported, whereas the direct value-added component in oil refineries averaged 15 per cent in 1973 and only 7 per cent in 1978, a fall that is undoubtedly due to the oil price increases. Consequently, both oil refining and rubber processing show very low direct labour coefficients: 1.6 and 4.6 per S$1 million production, respectively, in 1973 and 0.3 and 2.6 per S$1 million production, respectively, in 1978. Unlike rubber processing, however, oil refining is a highly capital-intensive production process, generating by far the highest amount of value added per employee of the economy. Tables A.17.1 and A.17.3 present the relevant data on NRB sectors individually.

The predominance of these two products in NRB exports strongly affects the average values of the various characteristics denoting the factor use of this export category, and produces a great contrast *vis-à-vis* non-NRB exports. Thus, the following picture emerges with clarity from the evidence in Table 17.3, relevant to both 1973 and 1978. Measured by average direct and total labour coefficients, non-NRB exports are many times more labour intensive than NRB exports. The share of labour-intensive products in non-NRB exports is about 95 per cent. Value added and gross profit per employee are, on average, in non-NRB sectors also substantially lower than in NRB sectors. Accordingly, the average wage rate in non-NRB sectors is lower, and the wage component in value added higher, than in NRB sectors.

The data on the sectoral composition of the labour force easily fit in with the findings so far. Census data on Singapore's manufacturing production

TABLE 17.3
CHARACTERISTICS OF MAJOR PRODUCTION AND EXPORT CATEGORIES, SINGAPORE MANUFACTURING SECTOR, 1973 AND 1978

Category	E/O (%)	E/E$_m$ (%)	l^e (per 10^6 S$ output)	T^e	Share of labour-intensive products (%)	VA/L S$	GP/L S$	W^1 (%)	F^2 (%)	s S$	Share of wages and salaries in gross value added (%)
						1973					
Total manufactured exports	—	100.0	21.1	25.8	46.2	—	—	—	—	—	—
Total manufacturing production	65.0	—	24.5	30.7	—	10,130	5,920	82.9	51.2	4,210	41.6
NRB manufactured exports	—	55.7	6.7	9.4	7.8	—	—	—	—	—	—
NRB manufacturing production	73.9	—	9.7	14.0	—	16,150	11,020	78.1	34.1	5,130	31.8
Non-NRB manufactured exports	—	44.3	39.2	46.3	94.5	—	—	—	—	—	—
Non-NRB manufacturing production	56.4	—	38.7	46.7	—	8,690	4,700	84.3	56.3	3,990	46.0
						1978					
Total manufactured exports	—	100.0	9.4	12.2	39.4	—	—	—	—	—	—
Total manufacturing production	73.0	—	11.2	14.8	—	17,970	10,960	80.2	52.6	7,010	39.0
NRB manufactured exports	—	61.4	1.7	2.8	4.9	—	—	—	—	—	—
NRB manufacturing production	80.7	—	3.3	5.1	—	31,970	23,880	75.0	36.6	8,090	25.3
Non-NRB manufactured exports	—	38.6	21.7	27.1	94.2	—	—	—	—	—	—
Non-NRB manufacturing production	63.3	—	21.2	26.9	—	15,270	8,470	81.2	55.7	6,810	44.6

For explanation of symbols, see Section 10.4.
Notes : [1] W = share of workmen in employment.
 [2] F = share of females in employment.
Sources : see Appendix to Chapter 17.

subdivide paid employees into workmen and other employees. The former category of employees refers to persons employed directly in the process of production and includes skilled, semi-skilled and unskilled workmen. The latter category comprises staff personnel, like managers, supervisors, engineers, technicians, and clerical staff. Although inappropriate as a distinct measure of skill intensity of production, the higher share of employed workmen in non-NRB sectors suggests, in connection with the other results, a lower skill intensity of these sectors' production. In addition, increasing female labour force participation during the 1970s mainly took effect in lower-skilled jobs. In 1973 and 1978, 90.1 and 87.2 per cent, respectively, of all working women were employed as "workmen". Consequently, given female manufacturing labour force participation rates of 51.2 per cent in 1973 and 52.6 per cent in 1978, women are over-represented relative to men in the category of workmen, accounting for shares of 55.7 per cent in 1973 and 57.3 per cent in 1978.[11] It appears, then, that females account for clearly more than half of all employees in non-NRB manufacturing sectors. In Singapore, female workers systematically belong to the lowest-paid workers on all occupational levels. In 1980, they earned on average 63.5 per cent of male income. This income disparity is even greater among production and related workers; consequently, in manufacturing females receive only 44.8 per cent of the mean income of their male colleagues.[12] As already noticed in the preceding section, manufacturing workers already receive the lowest average remuneration among all workers of the economy.

From these findings we may conclude that, with respect to non-NRB exports, Singapore has sought to specialize in labour-intensive, low-wage exportables, which, to a disproportionately large extent, are produced by relatively cheap female labour.

Turning now to the differences in the structure of manufactured exports between 1973 and 1978, we find some threads of evidence for a gradual shift towards producing more capital-intensive products. For this, the increase of gross profit per employee in manufacturing is the most significant indication. As shown in Table 17.3, average gross profit per employee almost doubled in current prices between 1973 and 1978. After deflating by the GDP deflator for manufacturing from the preceding section, gross profit per employee grew by 5.7 per cent a year during this period. For NRB and non-NRB production, this growth rate was 9.2 and 5.2 per cent, respectively. This trend towards increasing capital intensiveness of manufacturing production is also reflected by the other measures of factor intensity, which all show changes in the appropriate directions.

Additional insight into Singapore's pattern of export specialization in the 1970s, and changes therein, emerges from rank correlation tests between the values of the various sector characteristics for 1973 and 1978. Tables 17.4 and

TABLE 17.4
MATRIX OF SPEARMAN RANK CORRELATION COEFFICIENTS FOR SECTOR CHARACTERISTICS SINGAPORE, 1973[2], [3]

Variable	E_i/O_i	E_i/E_m	k_i^e	VA_i/L_i	GP_i/L_i	T_i^e	s_i	F_i^1
E_i/O_i	1	.70**	.17*	−.22	−.20	.10	−.24	−.43**
		.65**	.40*	−.32	−.28	.32	−.35*	.70**
E_i/E_m		1	−.12	.07	.05	−.22	.06	.19
			.14	.02	.03	.03	−.04	.41*
k_i^e			1	−.75**	−.74**	.97**	−.61**	.46**
				−.75**	−.74**	.94**	−.57**	.48**
VA_i/L_i				1	.96**	−.71**	.79**	−.55**
					.94**	−.74**	.77**	−.56**
GP_i/L_i					1	−.71**	.60**	−.42**
						−.76**	.54**	−.39**
T_i^e						1	−.58**	.40**
							−.54**	.37*
s_i							1	.75**
								.77**
F_i								1

For explanation of symbols, see Section 10.4.
Notes: [1] F = share of females in sectoral employment.
[2] The upper coefficients in a row refer to rankings of all manufacturing sectors (n = 51), the lower coefficients refer to rankings of non-NRB sectors only (n = 32).
[3] Correlation coefficients that are significant at the 5 per cent level are denoted by one asterisk (*), those significant at the 1 per cent level by two asterisks (**).

Sources: see Appendix to Chapter 17.

17.5 present the results. For 1973, it is apparent that a higher export orientation of production is associated with the following characteristics: higher direct and total labour coefficients, a lower level of productivity, a lower average wage level and a higher female participation rate in sectoral employment. These relationships are particularly relevant for the sample of non-NRB sectors only. The correlation coefficients for the rankings from this sample by export-output ratio on the one hand, and direct labour coefficient and average wage level on the other, are significant at the 5 per cent level, whereby the coefficient for the latter variable is just on the verge of the critical value. The relationship between export-output ratios and the female share in sectoral employment even shows a significance at the 1 per cent level in both samples. In turn, the rank correlations between the various measures of factor intensity, average wage level and female employment share show the expected signs and are highly significant. This implies that the female-intensive industries are generally low productive, labour intensive and low labour remunerative. By 1973, non-NRB industries of this nature were the typical export industries in Singapore.

The same set of relationships also applies to 1978, on the understanding, however, that the extent of correlation is generally weaker. Rank correlations between export-output ratios and the measures of factor intensity are now clearly insignificant. The absence of these correlations in 1978 may be seen as an indication of an ongoing upgrading process of export industries. In contrast, the low-wage and female-intensive nature of export industries, however, still held in 1978, although the ranking by export-output ratios and average wage level again appears to be on the verge of statistical significance. Nevertheless, the existence of this relationship in 1978 is most likely explained by the wage-restraint policy still in force during that year.

In fact, by the end of the 1970s, Singapore's export industries showed a mixture of both labour-intensive, low-productivity industries and relatively more capital-intensive industries. Table A.17.4 sets out the relevant data. Confining the illustrations to non-NRB export production, textiles and clothing are, as one of the earliest export industries in Singapore, an example of the former category of industry. The largest and most export-oriented subsector, i.e. other outer garments (I-O code 035), shows both the highest direct labour coefficient and the lowest value added per employee of any manufacturing sector, with the exception of only one minor clothing subsector. Workers in garment industries earned only 58.2 per cent of the manufacturing average in 1978. A large majority of over 90 per cent of these workers are women, who, strikingly enough, dominate both the employment categories "workmen" and "other employees". As one of the lowest-productive industries in Singapore, clothing, and to a lesser extent textiles, have faced severe competition from other newly industrializing countries in

TABLE 17.5
MATRIX OF SPEARMAN RANK CORRELATION COEFFICIENTS FOR SECTOR CHARACTERISTICS SINGAPORE, 1982, [3]

Variable	E_i/O_i	E_i/E_m	f_i^e	VA_i/L_i	GP_i/L_i	T_i^e	s_i	F_i^1
E_i/O_i	1	.75**	−.01	.02	.07	−.03	−.07	.33**
		.71**	.12	−.12	−.01	.08	−.23*	.45**
E_i/E_m		1	−.11	.14	.17	−.13	.08	.21*
			−.04	.06	.12	−.07	.04	.25*
f_i^e			1	−.78**	−.74**	.97**	−.64**	−.47**
				−.77**	−.71**	.97**	−.67**	−.56**
VA_i/L_i				1	.96**	−.75**	.78**	−.55**
					.95**	−.75**	.79**	−.65**
GP_i/L_i					1	−.73**	.61**	−.43**
						−.69**	.61**	−.51**
T_i^e						1	−.58**	.45**
							−.63**	.55**
s_i							1	−.73**
								−.80**
F_i								1

For explanation of symbols, see Section 10.4.

Notes : [1] F = share of females in sectoral employment.
[2] The upper coefficients in a row refer to rankings of all manufacturing sectors (n = 114), the lower coefficients refer to rankings of non-NRB sectors only (n = 72).
[3] Correlation coefficients that are significant at the 5 per cent level are denoted by one asterisk (*), those significant at the 1 per cent level by two asterisks (**).

Sources : see Appendix to Chapter 17.

recent years. A restructuring process, however, has already begun, partly by upgrading existing activities through higher quality products and productivity increases, partly by farming out the most labour-intensive operations to neighbouring countries.

Next in labour intensity and the major non-NRB export industry is the category of electrical and electronics industries. These industries show markedly lower direct labour coefficients and generate somewhat more value added per employee than clothing industries. The largest subsector comprises firms manufacturing semi-conductors and other electronic components and communication equipment and apparatus (I-O code 098). The second largest subsector produces radios and television sets (I-O code 097). Among electronics industries, both subsectors have the lowest average wage rate and the highest female participation in employment: the wage rate amounted to about three quarters of the manufacturing average, while women accounted for over 80 per cent of total employment in these subsectors. Unlike the clothing industry, females are almost exclusively employed directly in the process of production. These mainly young female workers carry out the low-skilled electronic assembly operations, which still characterized the main production processes in Singapore's electronics industry by the end of the 1970s. Yet, electronics is viewed as a priority industry that should facilitate Singapore's industrial restructuring process in the 1980s. Electronics is one of the world's most technologically dynamic industries and Singapore is actively attracting more skill- and capital-intensive stages of electronic production. Both foreign and local firms should contribute to deepening and upgrading electronics production. Some change in this direction already occurred in the 1970s. As Table A.17.4 shows, a few subsectors within the electronical and electronics industry (I-O sectors 095–103) could already be considered higher value-added industries. In real terms, gross profit per employee in the largest subsector of communication equipment production grew at 4.8 per cent a year on average between 1973 and 1978. Electronics, textiles and clothing make the largest contribution to employment in Singapore's manufacturing sector. By 1978, these sectors employed 60,500 and 40,400 persons, respectively, together accounting for nearly 40 per cent of the manufacturing labour force.

The office equipment sector (I-O code 091), which manufactures data processing equipment and office machinery, should be mentioned as a final example of labour-intensive export manufacturing in Singapore. The production of this sector is almost exclusively destined for export and shares many of the characteristics of the electronics industry.

Examples of relatively more capital-intensive industries which also feature among the main exporters comprise chemicals, industrial machinery, shipbuilding and oil rigs. Apart from relatively low direct labour coefficients and a relatively high value-added generation per employee, these sectors have an above average wage level and employ relatively few females. Among these higher-productive industries, the shipbuilding and oil rig sector is the largest, employing about 24,000 workers in 1978.

17.5 SPREAD EFFECTS OF SINGAPORE'S MANUFACTURED EXPORTS

Section 17.3 already revealed the high and even increasing import dependency of manufacturing production in Singapore. We now address this finding in more detail with the help of average measures of spread effects for different categories of exports and production, summarized in Table 17.6.

Focusing on 1973 first, we observe all measures of spread effects to be lower for total manufactured exports than for total manufacturing production. The same is true for both NRB and non-NRB exports *vis-à-vis* their corresponding total production categories. If, in addition, due account is taken of the, by any standard, low values of these measures of spread effects, the conclusion emerges that export production takes place in relative isolation. Virtually all of Singapore's manufactured export production is footloose, the measures P and $NFEE$ for total manufactured exports being only 0.87 and 0.31, respectively, in 1973. NRB exports show the poorest record, which is mainly due to the export of processed rubber and petroleum products. As Table A.17.1 shows, in 1973 these exportables showed P values of 0.76 and 0.79, respectively, and $NFEE$ values of 0.05 and 0.19, respectively. The employment spread effects of NRB exports are equally meagre, again mainly due to the same dominant NRB exportables. In terms of spread effects, the performance of non-NRB exports is better than that of NRB exports. The employment effects, measured by P^E and P^{E-A}, were above the economy's average in 1973, although the average P value for non-NRB exports was 0.92 and the domestically generated value-added component in the value of these exports was on average clearly less than half. From this, it can be inferred that the above-average employment spread effects of non-NRB exports are for the greatest part explained by the relatively extensive direct labour requirements of this export production. Of the major export sectors in 1973, only the shipbuilding sector shows both P and P^E values above 1, as is apparent from Table A.17.2. This sector falls more or less outside the EPFZ-type of export production. Two smaller export sectors, electrical machinery and other manufactures, also show a reasonably good record of spread effects. The remaining major export sectors have P values below 1 and generate less than half of their export value as net foreign-exchange receipts.

Even the clothing sector, which is normally one of the most integrated

TABLE 17.6
WEIGHTED AVERAGE MEASURES OF SPREAD EFFECTS FOR MAJOR CATEGORIES OF EXPORT AND PRODUCTION, SINGAPORE 1973 AND 1978

Category	P	NFEE	P^E	P^{E-A}	WIM	WIM^E (per 10^6 S$ output)
1973						
Total manufactured exports	.87	.31	.57	.58	.14	31.3
NRB exports	.83	.19	.21	.21	.07	12.1
Non-NRB exports	.92	.47	1.02	1.04	.24	55.5
Total manufacturing production	.92	.37	.68	.69	.17	37.3
NRB production	.89	.25	.31	.31	.09	17.5
Non-NRB production	.95	.48	1.03	1.05	.25	56.2
1978						
Total manufactured exports	.86	.24	.42	.42	.11	15.0
NRB exports	.81	.11	.10	.10	.03	3.7
Non-NRB exports	.94	.43	.93	.94	.24	33.0
Total manufacturing production	.89	.28	.51	.51	.14	18.2
NRB production	.84	.15	.17	.17	.05	6.4
Non-NRB production	.95	.45	.92	.93	.24	33.0

For explanation of symbols, see Section 10.4.
Sources: see Appendix to Chapter 17.

sectors, produces in relative isolation. In 1973, 81 per cent of the intermediate input requirements of the clothing sector was met from imports, whereas only less than 5 percentage points of the 19 per cent domestic intermediate deliveries originated from the most obvious input-supplying industries, namely the textile sector. The relatively extensive employment spread effects are almost entirely due to the highly labour-intensive nature of clothing manufacturing as such: of the 74 man-years of labour both directly and indirectly required in the manufacture of S$1 million of clothing in 1973, 69 man-years were involved directly.

Electronics is yet another example of footloose export manufacturing in Singapore. As regards intermediate input requirements, 84 per cent was directly imported from abroad and 16 per cent purchased locally. The domestic intermediate deliveries were largely accounted for by non-material inputs like electricity, trade, and various financial services. Due to a lower direct labour intensity of production and the insignificance of indirect labour requirements, the P^E value for electronics industries is well below 1.

A similar pattern of spread effects is found for 1978, but then on a generally lower level. Thus, all measures of spread effect, but one, for total and for both NRB and non-NRB exports declined from 1973 to 1978. During this period, the P value for total manufactured exports declined from 0.87 to 0.86, the *NFEE* value from 0.31 to 0.24 and the P^E value from 0.57 to 0.42. The lower level of spread effects emanating from NRB exports can be readily explained with reference to the oil price increases since 1973, which resulted in a relative reduction of the domestic value-added component in the value of petroleum products. Hence, the *NFEE* value for the petroleum-refining sector witnessed a fall of 10 percentage points from 1973 down to 0.09 in 1978. Largely for the same reason, the other measures for NRB exports fell accordingly.

It is, therefore, particularly striking to observe a reduction in the level of spread effects of non-NRB exports which almost equals that of NRB exports. The net foreign-exchange earnings per unit of non-NRB exports fell from 47 per cent in 1973 to 43 per cent in 1978. Measured by P^E, the employment effects of these exports even showed a reduction from 1.02 in 1973 to 0.93 in 1978, implying employment spread effects significantly below the economy's average. At first sight, export industries seem indeed to have developed more production linkages with domestic supporting firms, judging by the small increase in the P value for non-NRB exports from 0.92 in 1973 to 0.94 in 1978. This development would be the only exception to the general reduction in the level of spread effects already referred to above. However, this inference would be quite misleading, as an increased level of intersectoral linkages is at complete variance with a simultaneously reduced domestic value-added component in non-NRB exports. What in fact occurred was a reduction in the direct value-added component of non-NRB production from 34 to 32 per cent between 1973 and 1978, thereby attributing relatively more weight to the already existing domestic linkages.

Our evaluation of the spread effects in 1973 and 1978 reaches the remarkable conclusion that, along with a significant increase in productivity and a trend of upgrading, there has been a definite increase in the overall import dependency of export manufacturing in Singapore. Apart from some minor exceptions, this phenomenon has taken place all along the line. Confining ourselves again to the major non-NRB export industries (compare Tables A.17.2 and A.17.4), the *NFEE* value of the largest clothing exporter, for instance, declined from 0.39 to 0.37 in the period under scrutiny. This measure for the priority export sector electronics and telecommunication averaged 0.41 in 1973, whereas the three subsectors that are included in this sector, radios and television sets, other communication equipment and records, tapes and musical instruments, showed *NFEE* values of 0.24, 0.36 and 0.37, respectively, in 1978. The same development is even found in the shipbuilding sector. One of the few changes in the opposite direction has taken place in medical and pharmaceutical industries, the most important exporters of chemical products. Their average *NFEE* value rose from 0.59 to 0.66.

Turning finally to the rank order correlation tests between sector characteristics and various measures of spread effects, the results of which are presented in Tables 17.7 and 17.8, the observed relationships are expected in the light of our earlier findings. Moreover, there are no major differences to be noted when comparing the results for 1973 and 1978. Thus, what these rank correlations show is, first of all, a negative relationship between a sector's export-output ratio and both its *P* and *NFEE* values. These rank correlations are at least significant at the 5 per cent level for the full sample in 1973. In 1978, only the rankings by export-output ratio and *P* value appear to be significantly correlated at the 5 per cent level, but then in both samples. This implies that, in Singapore, sectors with higher export-output ratios generate fewer production linkages and show an overall higher dependence on imported inputs. This feature of export industries also thwarts a significant correlation between rankings by export-output ratio and rankings by any of the employment spread effect measures. The insignificance of this relationship is the more striking in 1973, as in that year a strong rank correlation between a direct labour intensity of production and a higher export-output ratio was still apparent. Second, it is noteworthy to find a positive and significant correlation between the rankings by direct labour coefficient and *NFEE* value in case of the full sample in both years. This means that relatively labour-intensive sectors have a higher domestic value-added component in production than the more capital-intensive ones. If, however, the highly capital-intensive and import-dependent NRB sectors are excluded from the sample,

TABLE 17.7

MATRIX OF SPEARMAN RANK CORRELATION COEFFICIENTS FOR SECTOR CHARACTERISTICS AND VARIOUS MEASURES OF SPREAD EFFECTS, SINGAPORE, 1973[1],[2]

Variable	E_i/O_i	l_i^e	s_i	P_i	$NFEE_i$	P_i^E	P_i^{E-A}	WIM_i	WIM_i^E
E_i/O_i	1	.17	−.24	−.39**	−.28*	.10	.10	−.05	.08
		.40*	−.35*	−.29	−.12	.32	.32	.03	.27
l_i^e		1	−.61**	.12	.36**	.97**	.97**	.79**	.95**
			−.57**	−.22	.10	.94**	.94**	.67**	.92**
s_i			1	.01	.11	−.58**	−.58**	−.12	−.52**
				.29	.33	−.54**	−.53**	.06	−.47**
P_i				1	.55**	.31*	.31*	.43**	.34*
					.63**	.06	.06	.31	.11
$NFEE_i$					1	.46**	.47**	.67**	.51**
						.26	.27	.61**	.32
P_i^E						1	1.00**	.85**	.99**
							1.00**	.77**	.99**
P_i^{E-A}							1	.85**	.99**
								.78**	.99**
WIM_i								1	.89**
									.83**
WIM_i^E									1

For explanation of symbols, see Section 10.4.

Notes : [1] The upper coefficients in a row refer to rankings of all manufacturing sectors (n = 51), the lower coefficients refer to rankings of non-NRB sectors only (n = 32).
[2] Correlation coefficients that are significant at the 5 per cent level are denoted by one asterisk (*), those significant at the 1 per cent level by two asterisks (**).

Sources : see Appendix to Chapter 17.

TABLE 17.8
MATRIX OF SPEARMAN RANK CORRELATION COEFFICIENTS FOR SECTOR CHARACTERISTICS AND VARIOUS MEASURES OF SPREAD EFFECTS, SINGAPORE, 1978[1,2]

Variable	E_i/O_i	l_i^e	s_i	P_i	$NFEE_i$	P_i^E	P_i^{E-A}	WIM_i	WIM_i^E
E_i/O_i	1	-.01 .12	-.07 -.23*	-.20* -.29*	-.10 -.11	-.03 .08	-.03 .08	-.11 -.17	-.06 .02
l_i^e		1	-.64** -.67**	.07 .02	.36** .15	.97** .97**	.96** .97**	.70** .62**	.95** .95**
s_i			1	.07 .17	.12 .24*	-.58** -.63**	-.58** -.63**	-.03 .05	-.51** -.55**
P_i				1	.40** .33**	.26** .20	.26** .20	.44** .44**	.31** .27*
$NFEE_i$					1	.44** .21	.44** .21	.69** .57**	.49** .28*
P_i^E						1	1.00** 1.00**	.78** .68**	.99** .99**
P_i^{E-A}							1	.78** .68**	.99** .99**
WIM_i								1	.83** .76**
WIM_i^E									1

For explanation of symbols, see Section 10.4.

Notes : [1] The upper coefficients in a row refer to rankings of all manufacturing sectors (n = 114), the lower coefficients refer to rankings of non-NRB sectors only (n = 72).
[2] Correlation coefficients that are significant at the 5 per cent level are denoted by one asterisk (*), those significant at the 1 per cent level by two asterisks (**).

Sources : see Appendix to Chapter 17.

this relationship ceases to be statistically significant. Unfortunately, no additional significant relationships are observed that could reinforce our finding as to the higher domestic value-added component in labour-intensive production processes. Yet, the above established relationships provide a clearer insight into the simultaneous developments towards higher value-added production along with an increased import dependence of that production.

17.6 SUMMARY

Unlike South Korea and Taiwan, Singapore's rapid emergence as a newly industrializing country is based on the EPFZ-type of export manufacturing with a concomitant dominant role of foreign direct investment. In explaining Singapore's success one cannot fail to recognize the heavily interventionist role of the Singapore government in the process of economic development. From the top, an export-oriented industrialization strategy was shaped and effectively implemented. At first, the objective was to attract foreign investment especially in labour-intensive export manufacturing to create employment. The analysis has shown that, by 1973, the typical export industries were characterized by a low productivity, a high labour intensity, a low wage level and high concentration of female workers. Hence, in the context of the national economy, manufacturing was a labour-intensive and little value-added generating activity and manufacturing workers drew the lowest average wages among all workers.

During the first half of the 1970s, Singapore transformed from a labour-surplus into a labour-shortage economy, with an upward pressure on wages and a consequent threat to her comparative advantage in labour-intensive exportables. This in particular, but also such unfavourable demand-side prospects as slow growth of the international economy and increasing protectionism, necessitated the government's reconsidering its industrialization policies. Since 1978, policies aim at restructuring manufacturing production towards more capital, technology and skill-intensive activities. Again, foreign capital and technology are given a place in this process. The analysis of the structure of manufactured exports in 1978 shows that the first steps in this direction were already undertaken during the 1970s. Exports in 1978 were more diversified and, most importantly, showed a mixture of both relatively labour- and more capital-intensive manufactures. Consequently, a consistent specialization pattern in the most labour-intensive exports could no longer be established in 1978. It still appeared, however, that the most export-oriented sectors could be typified by a low average wage level and an over-representation of women in sectoral employment. It may be concluded, therefore, that the first stage of export-oriented industrialization in Singapore was completed in part by the end of the 1970s. As regards spread effects, our analysis provides an unambiguous indication of the isolated character of the EPFZ-type of production. Virtually all of Singapore's manufactured export production is footloose. Due to a complete lack of natural resources, the import dependency of NRB exports is even higher than that of non-NRB exports. Only the employment effects generated by non-NRB exports in 1973 were above the economy's average, which is almost entirely explained by the relatively extensive direct labour requirements of these exports. This, however, was no longer true in 1978. When comparing 1973 and 1978, the measures applied clearly indicate a generally increasing import dependency of export production and a lower level of both production and employment spread effects. To the extent, therefore, that economic restructuring in Singapore should also meet the objective of deepening the economic structure, the developments in the 1970s are not promising. The experience of Singapore indeed shows that the EPFZ-type of export production can be upgraded and diversified in the course of time, but not that domestic linkages can easily be developed.

APPENDIX TABLE A.17.1
CHARACTERISTICS OF MANUFACTURING SECTORS CLASSIFIED AS NRB SECTORS, SINGAPORE, 1973

I-O Code	Sector	E_i/O_i (%)	E_i/E_m (%)	I_i^e (per 10⁶ S$ output)	T_i^e	VA_i/L_i S$	GP_i/L_i S$	s_i S$	W_i^1 (%)	F_i^2 (%)	P_i	$NFEE_i$	P_i^E	P_i^{EA}	WIM_i	WIM_i^E (per 10⁶ S$ output)
5	Rubber processing	100.0	12.8	4.6	5.2	8,200	3,810	4,390	84.9	53.8	.76	.05	.11	.12	.03	6.3
6	Meat and meat preparations	12.8	.1	41.7	57.6	4,280	1,600	2,690	90.5	68.1	1.29	.55	1.27	1.19	.25	67.1
7	Dairy products	16.1	.1	7.5	19.6	21,380	15,460	5,920	56.2	25.9	1.06	.34	.43	.44	.13	24.7
8	Milled cereal and cereal preparations	29.8	.8	20.2	29.6	9,700	6,430	3,270	83.0	42.2	1.03	.35	.65	.66	.14	35.1
9	Sugar and sugar confectionery	29.5	.5	17.2	25.6	8,890	4,570	4,320	78.2	59.0	.98	.29	.57	.57	.15	31.4
10	Oils and fats	46.7	1.2	7.2	13.0	17,260	12,820	4,430	71.4	31.3	.93	.22	.29	.29	.08	16.1
11	Other food	42.8	.9	15.5	23.7	13,310	8,300	5,010	72.7	28.7	.96	.35	.52	.53	.16	29.7
12	Animal feed	23.5	.7	5.1	10.6	12,290	6,620	5,670	58.7	26.3	.87	.17	.23	.24	.08	13.5
13	Beverages	19.0	.3	34.1	52.5	11,210	5,840	5,370	74.2	27.5	1.21	.66	1.16	1.18	.36	66.5
14	Tobacco products	5.6	.1	9.2	14.3	78,510	72,450	6,060	66.2	48.6	.86	.80	.32	.32	.10	18.2
21	Sawmilling	87.4	2.8	20.7	24.3	7,810	3,440	4,370	82.5	6.2	.83	.24	.54	.55	.14	29.7
22	Wood products except furniture	75.5	3.4	33.1	39.2	8,910	5,040	3,870	87.6	38.9	.90	.42	.86	.87	.20	47.0
23	Rattan processing	47.2	.1	36.9	66.5	9,890	7,090	2,800	91.5	57.8	1.36	.73	1.47	1.49	.26	76.4
24	Furniture and fixtures	18.1	.2	53.4	68.8	5,460	1,790	3,670	82.9	22.7	1.12	.52	1.52	1.54	.34	81.9
25	Paper and paper boards	34.7	.1	59.6	68.6	6,320	3,420	2,900	85.0	56.8	.97	.58	1.51	1.54	.28	79.4
26	Products of paper and paper boards	15.9	.2	37.1	52.5	7,740	4,840	2,900	85.0	56.8	1.09	.51	1.16	1.18	.22	61.1
33	Petroleum and petroleum products	94.0	31.2	1.6	3.5	98,600	81,000	17,600	40.4	11.9	.79	.19	.08	.08	.05	5.4
42	Basic iron and steel	12.0	.2	13.0	23.5	34,000	27,420	6,580	76.3	4.2	1.05	.67	.52	.53	.18	30.5
43	Non-ferrous basic metals	32.8	.2	15.9	33.5	17,570	12,790	4,780	77.1	15.5	1.18	.55	.74	.75	.21	41.7

APPENDIX TABLE A.17.2
CHARACTERISTICS OF MANUFACTURING SECTORS CLASSIFIED AS NON-NRB SECTORS, SINGAPORE, 1973

I-O Code	Sector	E_i/O_i (%)	E_i/E_m (%)	I_i^e (per 10⁶ S$ output)	T_i^e (per 10⁶ S$ output)	VA_i/L_i S$	GP_i/L_i S$	s_i S$	W_i^1 (%)	F_i^2 (%)	P_i	$NFEE_i$	P_i^E	P_i^{E-A}	WIM_i	WIM_i^E (per 10⁶ S$ output)
15	Textile yarn and thread	65.7	2.0	31.5	37.1	11,580	7,960	3,620	86.0	66.5	.88	.48	.82	.83	.18	44.0
16	Textile fabrics	61.4	.4	26.1	34.8	7,650	4,870	2,770	87.1	84.7	.94	.33	.77	.78	.14	40.2
17	Textile articles	50.7	.3	74.6	80.2	3,690	890	2,800	88.7	62.2	.89	.39	1.77	1.80	.29	91.5
18	Clothing	46.8	5.0	68.7	74.3	4,310	1,870	2,440	89.8	88.9	.87	.39	1.64	1.67	.24	83.5
19	Footwear	37.6	.2	71.9	84.3	5,520	2,640	2,880	89.7	59.1	1.05	.57	1.86	1.89	.33	97.0
20	Leather and leather products	40.0	.2	24.5	45.5	6,480	3,370	3,120	89.9	50.8	1.31	.44	1.00	1.00	.21	53.4
27	Printing and publishing	23.1	.7	44.1	51.5	10,640	5,750	4,890	80.8	34.0	.92	.60	1.14	1.16	.32	63.9
28	Paints and dyeing materials	21.6	.2	19.8	30.4	14,510	7,630	6,880	54.0	18.7	1.01	.45	.67	.68	.23	39.5
29	Medicinal and pharmaceutical products	82.8	1.1	13.4	24.1	30,810	26,040	4,770	56.4	57.9	.99	.59	.53	.54	.16	30.3
30	Toilet preparations	30.7	.3	21.7	36.4	15,260	10,520	4,740	66.2	53.3	1.13	.57	.80	.82	.23	45.3
31	Plastic and plastic products	39.7	1.1	38.2	41.9	8,030	4,890	3,150	84.5	52.5	.84	.38	.92	.94	.17	48.6
32	Other chemicals	44.2	.5	16.5	24.6	25,740	18,520	7,220	64.1	15.9	.96	.59	.54	.55	.21	32.7
34	Rubber products except footwear	28.8	.2	32.5	39.5	13,120	7,860	5,260	78.1	21.8	.93	.57	.87	.87	.26	49.6
35	Pottery, china and earthen ware	15.8	.0	85.7	100.2	5,690	2,530	3,160	90.8	27.0	1.12	.80	2.21	2.25	.44	117.1
36	Glass and glassware	33.8	.1	38.2	52.0	7,930	1,080	6,850	66.7	23.8	1.08	.56	1.15	1.17	.44	68.8
37	Bricks, tiles and other structural clay products	21.1	.1	56.4	66.8	10,370	6,120	4,250	88.9	19.9	1.01	.80	1.47	1.50	.37	81.3
38	Cement	5.1	.1	6.0	15.4	41,570	35,480	6,090	71.2	19.7	1.15	.49	.34	.34	.11	19.8
39	Structural cement and concrete products	2.4	.0	30.3	51.9	9,340	4,870	4,470	85.9	11.1	1.48	.76	1.14	1.16	.33	64.8
40	Non-metallic minerals	33.3	.3	22.5	39.2	19,490	13,380	6,110	76.7	7.7	1.21	.75	.86	.88	.29	50.2
41	Metal ores and scrap	12.5	.0	13.3	28.7	20,270	13,510	6,760	92.1	3.6	1.12	.53	.63	.64	.24	37.8
44	Fabricated metal products	28.3	1.6	30.7	42.5	10,000	5,520	4,480	81.4	30.0	1.06	.52	.94	.95	.25	52.2
45	Non-electrical machinery	65.1	2.5	36.6	46.6	8,800	3,780	5,020	80.6	31.4	.98	.49	1.03	1.05	.29	57.9
46	Electrical goods and machinery	64.8	1.5	34.8	45.5	9,130	3,860	5,270	80.7	55.5	1.01	.51	1.00	1.02	.30	57.2
47	Insulated wires and cables	14.0	.1	25.0	32.8	9,940	5,290	4,650	81.8	40.8	.92	.38	.72	.74	.19	40.3
48	Electronics and telecommunication	93.7	17.3	35.7	39.7	9,660	6,330	3,330	86.4	86.0	.85	.41	.88	.89	.17	46.5
49	Musical instruments	83.1	.1	91.9	107.0	4,920	2,460	2,460	89.2	76.5	1.09	.68	2.36	2.40	.37	121.4
50	Vehicles	21.0	.3	27.1	34.8	8,670	3,280	5,380	77.3	12.1	.93	.38	.77	.78	.24	44.0

(cont'd overleaf)

APPENDIX TABLE A.17.2 (cont'd)

I-O Code	Sector	E_i/O_i (%)	E_i/E_m (%)	I_i^e (per 10⁶ S$ output)	T_i^e (per 10⁶ S$ output)	VA_i/L_i S$	GP_i/L_i S$	s_i S$	W_i^1 (%)	F_i^2 (%)	P_i	$NFEE_i$	P_i^E	P_i^{E-A}	WIM_i	WIM_i^E (per 10⁶ S$ output)
51	Ships and aircraft	50.3	5.8	33.9	46.3	12,100	5,240	6,860	83.5	4.3	1.05	.62	1.02	1.04	.39	61.4
52	Watches and clocks	77.0	.2	62.9	70.7	5,380	1,280	4,100	86.5	49.2	.94	.49	1.56	1.59	.38	85.2
53	Scientific and precision equipment	80.5	1.6	49.4	55.9	6,050	1,810	4,240	76.1	63.4	.91	.42	1.23	1.25	.30	67.6
54	Jewellery	3.1	.1	15.8	18.6	7,360	3,870	3,490	89.3	22.2	.81	.18	.41	.42	.09	22.1
55	Other manufactures	76.0	.7	57.4	67.6	4,140	1,680	2,460	89.2	76.5	1.01	.41	1.49	1.52	.24	76.8

For explanation of symbols, see Section 10.4.

Notes: ¹ W_i = share of workmen is sectoral employment.
² F_i = share of females in sectoral employment.

Sources: computations are based on data from *Singapore Input-Output Tables 1973*, Department of Statistics, Singapore, 1978; *Report on the Census of Industrial Production 1973*, Department of Statistics, Singapore, 1975; Wong Yew Kwan, *Report on the Agricultural Census of Singapore 1973*, Ministry of National Development — National Statistical Commission, Singapore, 1975; *Report on the Census of Wholesale and Retail Trades, Restaurants and Hotels 1973*, Department of Statistics, Singapore, 1976; ILO, *Yearbook of Labour Statistics 1975*, Geneva, 1975, Table 2A; United Nations, *1978 Statistical Year Book*, New York, 1979, Table 138.

APPENDIX TABLE A.17.3
CHARACTERISTICS OF MANUFACTURING SECTORS CLASSIFIED AS NRB SECTORS, SINGAPORE, 1978

I-O Code	Sector	E_i/O_i (%)	E_i/E_m (%)	l_i^e (per 10⁶ S$ output)	T_i^e	VA_i/L_i S$	GP_i/L_i S$	s_i S$	W_i^1 (%)	F_i^2 (%)	P_i	$NFEE_i^3$	P_i^E	$P_i^{E,A}$	WIM_i	WIM_i^E (per 10⁶ S$ output)
005	Meat preparations	32.6	.1	20.6	29.3	17,930	11,690	6,240	84.0	63.1	1.12	.60	1.01	1.00	.26	36.2
006	Milk	21.0	.1	6.9	17.8	18,540	9,980	8,550	67.6	33.2	1.19	.35	.61	.61	.18	22.2
007	Other dairy products	12.3	.0	16.6	27.1	11,690	3,140	8,550	67.6	33.2	1.11	.43	.93	.94	.29	33.8
008	Fruit and vegetable preparations	37.1	.0	7.1	22.3	29,580	20,810	8,770	68.0	30.9	1.33	.48	.77	.77	.22	27.8
009	Seafood preparations	67.8	.1	17.0	23.4	17,880	13,410	4,470	82.6	72.2	1.08	.55	.80	.74	.17	28.6
010	Coconut oil	70.4	.2	4.4	9.2	15,750	9,770	5,980	77.0	32.2	.97	.19	.32	.32	.09	11.6
011	Other oils and fats	70.1	.9	4.0	8.5	26,140	18,450	7,690	62.9	35.7	.91	.20	.29	.29	.09	10.6
012	Wheat milling	57.0	.4	4.3	6.3	35,600	26,830	8,770	68.0	30.9	.82	.20	.22	.22	.07	7.9
013	Other milled products	22.0	.0	4.3	9.2	40,860	32,010	8,770	68.0	30.9	.93	.29	.32	.32	.10	12.0
014	Biscuits	27.1	.0	43.7	52.1	6,790	1,900	4,890	81.6	60.5	1.15	.49	1.79	1.80	.35	60.5
015	Bread and confectionery	1.6	.0	30.5	39.6	7,230	2,920	4,310	84.8	28.8	1.26	.49	1.36	1.36	.27	46.7
016	Noodles and related products	24.0	.0	29.3	38.7	7,770	3,020	4,750	81.7	45.8	1.22	.47	1.33	1.34	.28	45.9
017	Sugar and sugar products	11.3	.1	12.8	19.1	12,190	7,820	4,380	76.6	54.9	.97	.33	.66	.66	.14	22.4
018	Chocolate and chocolate products	62.5	.2	10.0	16.6	20,420	12,860	7,560	68.5	57.1	1.00	.35	.57	.57	.17	20.7
019	Coffee powder	3.0	.0	12.6	15.7	15,030	8,700	6,330	48.0	28.6	.86	.27	.54	.54	.13	18.9
020	Spices	24.2	.0	8.5	15.8	16,200	7,510	8,700	56.6	26.4	1.10	.32	.54	.55	.19	21.4
021	Soya bean products	29.5	.0	30.6	38.6	10,790	4,920	5,870	69.5	32.2	1.05	.49	1.33	1.33	.30	46.1
022	Other food preparations	47.7	.1	11.3	20.3	28,810	20,260	8,550	68.1	33.1	1.09	.52	.70	.70	.22	26.3
023	Animal feeds	35.7	.4	4.9	7.4	28,620	18,950	9,670	61.7	22.4	.83	.20	.25	.26	.09	9.4
024	Ice	1.9	.0	26.3	35.2	12,730	4,950	7,780	75.2	2.9	1.22	.63	1.21	1.22	.35	43.3
025	Soft drinks	36.4	.3	15.4	30.0	13,460	3,580	9,870	64.9	30.8	1.33	.49	1.03	1.04	.34	39.2
026	Alcoholic drinks	39.8	.2	8.5	21.4	33,750	23,040	10,710	80.2	32.9	1.21	.53	.74	.74	.26	27.7
027	Tobacco products	7.3	.1	7.2	10.6	28,340	19,190	9,160	72.3	52.3	.84	.27	.36	.37	.12	13.3
041	Sawmilling	1.5	.0	13.9	16.2	14,430	8,010	6,430	70.3	6.2	.82	.26	.56	.56	.14	19.4
042	Preserving of wood	6.6	.0	10.3	15.7	25,220	16,150	9,080	71.8	24.0	.97	.38	.54	.54	.17	20.1
043	Plywood and veneer	69.8	1.4	19.2	25.8	14,850	7,890	6,960	87.6	48.1	1.01	.42	.89	.89	.23	31.7
044	Rattan processing	89.8	.2	14.4	16.2	13,970	8,260	5,710	88.3	47.3	.80	.25	.56	.56	.12	19.0
045	Wooden products for buildings	20.3	.1	20.1	26.3	16,120	10,080	6,040	82.8	41.6	.80	.46	.90	.91	.22	31.7
046	Other wood and cork products	35.0	.1	26.8	34.8	9,950	4,910	5,040	86.6	22.4	1.04	.43	1.20	1.20	.25	41.1
047	Wooden furniture and fixtures	38.2	.4	34.5	44.7	8,250	3,020	5,230	84.5	36.9	1.11	.47	1.54	1.55	.32	53.0

(cont'd overleaf)

APPENDIX TABLE A.17.3 (cont'd)

I-O Code	Sector	E_i/O_i (%)	E_i/E_m (%)	I_i^e (per 10⁶ S$ output)	T_i^e	VA_i/L_i S$	GP_i/L_i S$	s_i S$	W_i^1 (%)	F_i^2 (%)	P_i	$NFEE_i^3$	P_i^E	$P_i^{E,A}$	WIM_i	WIM_i^E (per 10⁶ S$ output)
048	Paper and paperboard	44.9	.1	21.2	25.9	14,950	8,740	6,210	76.3	43.5	.98	.47	.89	.90	.21	30.8
049	Paper containers	9.0	.0	22.7	27.1	10,270	3,980	6,280	81.5	48.2	.89	.35	.93	.94	.23	32.4
050	Joss paper	5.6	.0	38.9	46.3	3,850	1,750	2,100	93.4	74.3	.94	.26	1.59	1.60	.15	50.2
051	Sanitary towels and toilet paper	16.2	.0	18.4	24.7	14,240	8,840	5,400	81.5	54.1	.96	.40	.85	.85	.19	29.2
052	Other paper articles	21.3	.0	20.1	24.7	14,380	8,170	6,210	76.3	43.5	.90	.41	.85	.86	.20	29.5
064	Petroleum refining	94.6	52.5	.3	.8	225,000	201,230	23,760	37.4	7.7	.76	.09	.03	.03	.01	1.1
065	Bitumen and asphalt premix	78.0	.0	3.3	11.9	44,110	20,340	23,760	37.4	7.7	1.08	.35	.41	.41	.21	18.5
066	Rubber processing	56.4	2.7	2.6	5.1	15,430	8,930	6,500	81.8	45.7	1.30	.09	.18	.17	.05	6.6
067	Processing of natural gums	61.9	.1	6.7	12.8	10,980	3,670	7,320	57.8	35.6	1.23	.19	.44	.44	.14	17.4
080	Iron and steel rolling mills	24.5	.3	6.2	11.9	67,770	56,380	11,400	71.1	7.5	1.04	.59	.41	.41	.16	15.9
081	Iron foundries	23.0	.0	19.0	25.8	21,640	10,240	11,400	71.1	7.5	1.03	.60	.89	.89	.35	34.4
082	Non-ferrous basic metals	81.8	.3	10.9	15.3	17,710	8,630	9,080	70.7	34.2	.92	.31	.52	.53	.17	19.5

APPENDIX TABLE A.17.4
CHARACTERISTICS OF MANUFACTURING SECTORS CLASSIFIED AS NON-NRB SECTORS, SINGAPORE, 1978

I-O Code	Sector	E_i/O_i (%)	E_i/E_m (%)	l_i^e (per 10⁶ S$ output)	T_i^e	VA_i/L_i S$	GP_i/L_i S$	s_i S$	W_i^1 (%)	F_i^2 (%)	P_i	$NFEE_i^3$	P_i^E	P_i^{E-A}	WIM_i	WIM_i^E (per 10⁶ S$ output)
28	Yarn	95.1	.5	25.6	28.9	13,500	7,780	5,730	85.5	67.9	.88	.43	.99	1.00	.21	33.8
29	Fabrics	77.6	.5	28.7	32.5	8,870	3,140	5,730	85.5	67.9	.89	.35	1.12	1.13	.24	38.2
30	Textile articles	80.0	.1	15.9	21.8	9,040	2,930	6,110	75.3	63.9	.95	.27	.75	.75	.18	26.2
31	Knitted fabrics	35.0	.2	21.5	26.3	10,050	4,290	5,760	78.6	50.9	.92	.33	.90	.91	.20	31.1
32	Other knitted products	83.2	.3	40.5	50.8	7,050	2,260	4,800	85.3	83.9	1.01	.43	1.75	1.76	.32	58.6
33	Carpets, rope and nets	35.7	.0	33.6	44.9	3,850	-2,260	6,110	75.3	63.9	1.08	.32	1.54	1.55	.37	54.3
34	Shirts	59.5	.3	43.3	49.5	6,580	2,150	4,430	88.9	89.5	.92	.39	1.70	1.71	.29	56.4
35	Other outer garments	81.2	2.6	44.0	50.9	5,930	1,850	4,080	88.5	90.6	.94	.37	1.75	1.76	.28	57.7
36	Tailoring and dressmaking	.2	.0	10.6	13.1	60,770	55,780	4,980	86.2	57.4	.84	.72	.45	.45	.09	15.4
37	Undergarments	48.8	.0	42.8	49.0	6,790	3,020	3,770	84.2	87.8	.95	.41	1.69	1.70	.26	55.3
38	Other wearing apparel	30.2	.0	45.6	57.1	5,610	2,040	3,570	86.1	77.9	1.12	.47	1.96	1.98	.31	64.8
39	Footwear	45.4	.2	30.6	39.4	12,890	8,380	4,520	83.5	51.9	1.03	.55	1.36	1.36	.25	45.4
40	Leather and leather products	39.2	.1	24.7	34.2	9,110	4,450	4,660	82.0	54.0	1.07	.42	1.18	1.18	.24	40.7
53	Printing of newspapers	4.6	.3	20.2	25.9	27,390	15,590	11,800	50.3	30.8	.94	.70	.89	.90	.37	34.8
54	Other printing and publishing	26.7	.5	34.1	41.4	10,725	4,390	6,330	79.2	45.4	.96	.52	1.42	1.43	.34	49.7
55	Industrial gases	11.7	.0	18.1	25.3	25,710	15,710	10,390	56.6	16.8	1.05	.67	.87	.87	.31	32.7
56	Basic industrial chemicals	96.2	.3	9.6	17.0	22,920	12,530	10,390	56.6	16.8	1.08	.42	.58	.59	.21	22.2
57	Paints	24.8	.1	11.0	17.5	21,070	10,880	10,190	48.6	22.4	1.00	.37	.60	.61	.21	23.0
58	Medicinal and pharmaceutical products	81.7	1.1	4.9	11.6	103,660	93,150	10,510	58.0	49.0	.97	.66	.40	.40	.14	15.3
59	Toiletries	50.0	.2	12.4	22.8	27,170	17,660	9,510	48.0	60.6	1.10	.55	.78	.79	.27	30.1
60	Soap, detergent and related products	42.8	.1	13.4	19.7	27,160	18,220	8,940	63.3	36.4	.96	.50	.68	.68	.22	24.9
61	Incense, joss sticks and matches	8.3	.0	19.8	31.4	17,930	10,240	7,690	63.0	32.2	1.13	.57	1.08	1.09	.31	39.7
62	Inks and carbon black	26.8	.1	13.6	20.3	20,120	6,100	14,020	42.9	18.6	1.01	.43	.70	.70	.32	28.1
63	Other chemical products	61.7	.1	21.1	27.6	12,610	4,920	7,690	63.0	32.2	.98	.42	.95	.95	.27	34.2
68	Tyres and tubes	43.3	.1	20.6	23.6	17,520	9,000	8,520	79.7	14.3	.86	.45	.81	.82	.25	29.4
69	Rubber products	67.9	.1	23.0	26.2	13,870	6,930	6,930	79.2	27.8	.87	.40	.90	.91	.23	31.5
70	Plastic materials	71.3	.4	4.2	8.3	55,260	43,670	11,600	51.9	13.9	.89	.33	.29	.29	.11	10.9
71	Plastic bags	34.8	.3	20.0	24.5	10,010	5,020	4,980	83.5	53.4	.94	.31	.84	.85	.17	28.9

(cont'd overleaf)

APPENDIX TABLE A.17.4 (cont'd)

I-O Code	Sector	E_i/O_i (%)	E_i/E_m (%)	l_i^e (per 10⁶ S$ output)	T_i^e (per 10⁶ S$ output)	VA_i/L_i S$	GP_i/L_i S$	s_i S$	W_i^1 (%)	F_i^2 (%)	P_i	$NFEE_i^3$	P_i^E	P_i^{E-A}	WIM_i	WIM_i^E (per 10⁶ S$ output)
72	Plastic parts for radios and television sets	10.6	.0	41.5	48.6	7,960	3,290	4,670	87.8	65.3	.97	.46	1.67	1.68	.31	56.0
73	Other plastic products	56.8	.5	26.0	30.5	11,350	5,920	5,430	81.2	49.7	.93	.41	1.05	1.05	.22	36.0
74	Pottery and earthenware	.0	.0	26.7	34.7	11,620	1,660	9,960	77.4	20.9	1.12	.53	1.19	1.20	.41	44.4
75	Glass and glass products	46.9	.1	15.3	23.3	18,910	8,950	9,960	77.4	20.9	1.06	.47	.80	.81	.29	30.8
76	Cement	28.3	.3	3.1	6.6	51,520	40,730	10,790	64.6	14.2	.96	.26	.23	.23	.09	9.1
77	Concrete products	7.9	.0	18.1	25.3	16,270	8,720	7,550	79.1	11.0	1.06	.48	.87	.88	.27	33.3
78	Bricks and earth-baked products	4.8	.0	24.9	29.0	17,370	8,680	8,680	83.9	15.7	.96	.54	1.00	1.00	.31	36.3
79	Non-metallic mineral products	34.5	.2	13.4	19.9	24,020	14,920	9,100	79.1	11.2	1.01	.48	.68	.69	.23	25.8
83	Cutlery and tools	32.9	.0	35.9	42.5	12,700	5,190	7,510	74.3	50.3	.98	.62	1.46	1.47	.41	52.3
84	Metal furniture	40.5	.1	27.4	33.2	9,510	3,470	6,040	79.6	33.8	.98	.40	1.14	1.15	.27	40.0
85	Fabricated metal products	52.7	.8	17.3	21.8	13,920	6,400	7,520	75.7	19.1	.94	.37	.75	.75	.22	27.3
86	Non-insulated wire and cable products	30.5	.1	11.6	15.9	13,100	4,510	8,590	73.4	19.9	.96	.28	.55	.55	.18	20.7
87	Tin-plate cans	17.2	.1	17.4	24.2	10,610	3,360	7,260	79.8	54.6	1.01	.35	.83	.84	.24	30.5
88	Other metal containers	19.9	.1	8.6	13.3	31,250	20,190	11,060	80.2	1.7	.96	.40	.46	.46	.18	18.1
89	Electroplating	77.5	.1	26.4	32.0	15,940	9,260	6,680	82.1	30.4	.97	.56	1.10	1.11	.28	38.5
90	Other metal products	51.5	.7	21.8	28.2	14,190	5,020	9,170	84.0	39.0	1.00	.47	.97	.97	.32	36.2
91	Office equipment	93.6	1.2	24.4	28.3	15,150	8,600	6,550	80.8	75.1	.86	.46	.97	.98	.24	33.9
92	Lifting and hoisting machines	10.7	.0	34.1	42.0	13,930	5,290	8,640	75.5	9.1	.97	.63	1.44	1.45	.46	53.0
93	Air-conditioners and refrigerators	56.4	.6	15.4	21.1	23,910	16,910	7,000	83.3	35.1	.96	.51	.73	.73	.20	26.2
94	Industrial machinery and equipment	45.5	1.3	20.9	28.2	18,090	9,120	8,970	71.4	24.8	1.01	.55	.97	.97	.32	36.3
95	Electric motors and generators	66.9	.2	29.6	37.1	14,230	8,820	5,420	83.3	59.8	1.00	.58	1.27	1.28	.28	44.1
96	Electrical industrial apparatus	48.0	.4	20.2	26.7	13,940	6,880	7,070	79.1	55.0	.99	.43	.92	.92	.25	33.0
97	Radios and television sets	86.1	4.1	19.7	24.2	8,910	3,770	5,150	84.3	81.3	.86	.24	.83	.84	.17	28.3
98	Other communication equipment	91.8	9.9	18.3	20.7	16,630	11,200	5,430	87.0	83.0	.82	.36	.71	.71	.15	24.1
99	Records, tapes and musical instruments	71.1	.2	23.7	29.2	10,620	4,470	6,160	78.8	73.7	.93	.37	1.00	1.01	.24	35.1
100	Household appliances	67.5	.5	23.7	35.0	13,280	6,380	6,900	86.7	76.8	1.12	.51	1.20	1.21	.32	43.4

APPENDIX TABLE A.17.4 (cont'd)

I-O Code	Sector	E_i/O_i (%)	E_i/E_m (%)	I_i^e (per 10⁶ S$ output)	T_i^e (per 10⁶ S$ output)	VA_i/L_i S$	GP_i/L_i S$	s_i S$	W_i^1 (%)	F_i^2 (%)	P_i	$NFEE_i^3$	P_i^E	P_i^{E-A}	WIM_i	WIM_i^E (per 10⁶ S$ output)
101	Storage and primary batteries	85.0	.5	17.2	22.1	23,790	13,770	10,020	77.2	43.9	.94	.53	.76	.76	.27	28.6
102	Electrical wires and cables	39.7	.1	18.6	22.0	14,300	6,910	7,380	78.9	45.8	.88	.35	.76	.76	.21	27.1
103	Lamp and lighting fixtures	70.0	.1	38.9	44.5	8,430	2,940	5,490	81.6	62.9	.96	.47	1.53	1.54	.33	52.6
104	Motor vehicles	8.9	.1	12.7	16.1	19,840	10,760	9,080	74.5	11.6	.88	.34	.55	.56	.18	20.6
105	Motor vehicle bodies and parts	22.5	.0	31.0	38.2	10,680	4,810	5,880	72.1	26.9	1.00	.49	1.31	1.32	.31	46.0
106	Motor cycles and non-motorized vehicles	62.9	.1	11.8	16.3	28,100	19,030	9,080	74.5	11.6	.91	.43	.56	.56	.18	20.8
107	Ships and boats	73.0	4.9	19.8	29.8	19,240	8,320	10,920	77.0	5.7	1.11	.60	1.02	1.03	.40	40.3
108	Oil rigs	70.6	.9	13.4	19.0	33,290	22,370	10,920	76.6	5.3	.96	.58	.65	.66	.25	25.5
109	Ship breaking	26.1	.0	6.1	17.2	18,150	9,080	9,080	74.5	11.6	1.29	.45	.59	.59	.22	23.5
110	Aircraft	42.7	.3	14.1	20.2	47,100	33,480	13,620	65.1	13.9	1.02	.90	.70	.70	.34	28.5
111	Scientific and precision equipment	69.8	.1	21.5	28.0	17,540	11,380	6,160	87.6	67.9	.98	.53	.96	.97	.23	33.9
112	Photographic and optical goods	80.0	.6	41.7	46.6	12,590	6,870	5,710	85.9	70.3	.89	.64	1.60	1.61	.34	54.6
113	Watches and clocks	77.3	.3	27.3	35.8	12,920	7,080	5,840	88.2	69.3	1.02	.53	1.23	1.24	.28	42.9
114	Toys and recreational goods	84.6	.3	38.1	46.9	10,960	6,260	4,700	84.3	81.9	1.02	.57	1.61	1.62	.30	54.5
115	Jewellery	27.3	.2	13.5	23.2	14,210	7,660	6,550	71.0	39.2	1.20	.38	.80	.80	.22	29.6
116	Umbrellas	55.6	.1	18.4	25.3	9,470	5,960	3,510	78.0	70.6	.99	.29	.87	.88	.14	29.1
117	Signs and displays	15.6	.0	25.7	33.3	13,230	6,610	6,610	64.0	26.0	1.01	.52	1.15	1.15	.29	40.7
118	Other manufactures	40.7	.2	21.0	28.1	11,720	5,860	5,860	81.4	52.4	1.01	.39	.97	.97	.23	34.1

For explanation of symbols, see Section 10.4.

Notes: [1] W_i = share of workmen in sectoral employment.
[2] F_i = share of females in sectoral employment.
[3] The values of the index $NFEE$ presented in this table are slightly lower than those presented in *Singapore Input-Output Tables 1978*, Department of Statistics, Singapore, 1978, Table 17, because the definition of value added used in our calculations excludes import duties and other commodity taxes.

Sources: *Singapore Input-Output Tables 1978*, Department of Statistics, Singapore, 1978; *Report on the Census of Industrial Production 1978*, Department of Statistics, Singapore, 1979, Tables 40 and 43; *Report on the Survey of Services 1978*, Department of Statistics, Singapore, 1981; ILO, *Year Book of Labour Statistics 1979*, Geneva, 1979, Table 2A.

18
Cross-Country Summary of Findings and Conclusions

18.1 INTRODUCTION

In evaluating the results of the country studies, it first of all becomes clear that any general statement on the developmental impact of the export-oriented strategy of industrialization in developing countries violates reality: the structures and spread effects of manufactured exports differ too widely among countries and products.

Chapter 9 explained that the spread effects of economic activities are a reflection of the pattern of sectoral interdependence in any economy and hence of the structure of production. In turn, a country's production structure is the result of the interaction of three major factors: the level of economic development, domestic market size and the availability of natural resources. It was therefore first of all expected that the spread effects of export expansion would diverge in consequence of mere differences in overall production structures among exporting economies. In addition, it was hypothesized that the scope and vigour of a country's export-promotion strategy and the structure of manufactured exports itself would bear an impact upon the extent of spread effects. Trade strategy and export pattern appear to be closely related and are, of course, also affected by the major factors governing a country's economic structure. Yet, although trade strategies are formulated in and tied to the content of structural country characteristics, they entail policy choices and hence are a differentiating factor themselves. Through a differentiation among trade and industrialization strategies, we have attempted to associate alternative strategies with the gains from manufactured export expansion. It is this angle of incidence which might also result in useful implications for economic policy.

Evidence in the country studies shows, however, that trade regimes exhibit a varying mixture of import substitution and export promotion. And of the

SUMMARY OF FINDINGS AND CONCLUSIONS

three distinguished avenues to promote manufactured exports, viz. processing of primary products before export, change-over from import substitution to export expansion, and the establishment of new export-oriented industries, whether or not by means of EPFZs, the latter two are especially difficult to trace back in reality separately. A combination of both avenues is almost always found in practice. Nonetheless, the findings of the country studies point to the significance of the strategy choice and the different policy instruments that are employed to promote manufactured exports.

The relationships among country characteristics, alternative trade strategies and the extent of spread effects of export production are the central questions addressed in this final chapter. The study ends with an attempt at drawing some lessons from the experience of the seven South-East Asian countries under study.

18.2 TRADE STRATEGY AND THE STRUCTURE OF THE ECONOMY

In order to depict the impact of alternative trade and industrialization strategies the first step consists of identifying the major characteristics of the trade strategies followed in the case-study countries during the mid-1970s. This identification cannot be more than a ranking of the biases in trade regimes within the spectrum that ranges from heavy import substitution towards comprehensive export promotion.

At one end of this spectrum we find Indonesia which meets all the salient features of an import-substitution regime. At the other end are the generally known newly industrializing countries, South Korea, Taiwan and Singapore. Their export-promotion policy is accompanied by a fairly open and liberal trade regime, although South Korea and Taiwan still use the instrument of protection to encourage some branches of industry. EPFZs contribute relatively little to the export performance of these two countries. By contrast, the EPFZ-type of export production plays a crucial role in Singapore's export drive. In between these extremes, we find the Philippines, Thailand and Malaysia. These countries pursue a combined or dualistic strategy: domestic production is protected, whereas the discrimination against exports is reduced via subsidies or EPFZs. The intercountry differences within this group, however, may not be disregarded. Protection given to domestic industry in Thailand is moderate and no EPFZs were in operation during the 1970s. As in Thailand, domestic industry in Malaysia is protected moderately, but export manufacturing, on the contrary, has from the outset taken place in EPFZs. The Philippines, in turn, combines a heavily protected manufacturing sector with a policy of export promotion based on both subsidies and EPFZs.

Thus, three fairly distinct groups can be identified. Indonesia alone belongs in the first group and represents the pure strategy of import substitution. The second group consists of the Philippines, Thailand and Malaysia which achieved a remarkable upsurge in manufactured exports through pursuing a dualistic trade strategy. The third group, comprising South Korea, Taiwan and Singapore, stands out as the prime example of a genuine, comprehensive export-oriented industrialization strategy.

In one respect, this grouping is in need of modification. During the 1970s, in five out of the seven countries under study EPFZs have been set up and were actually in operation. In the remaining two countries, EPFZs were being planned or under development. But only in two countries does the EPFZ-type of export manufacturing undeniably prevail, namely in Malaysia and Singapore. In the remaining countries, free-zone activities dominate at most the export of one or two product groups, electronics in particular. To evaluate the usefulness of the EPFZs as an instrument of trade and industrialization policy for developing countries, we have to rely mainly on the experience of Malaysia and Singapore, and on that of some major sectors of production in EPFZs in the other countries.

One of the remarkable findings of the country studies is that the economic structures of the countries included in the third group are so clearly different from those found in the countries of the first and second groups. It is evident that a comprehensive outward-looking strategy in line with comparative advantage entails a radical restructuring of the economy. In the context of the national economy, manufacturing has to be transformed from a protected, relatively capital-intensive and high-wage activity under import substitution into a competitive and relatively labour-intensive export sector. Thus, the manufacturing sectors in South Korea, Taiwan and Singapore share the following salient characteristics:

(1) relatively high export-output ratio of production, especially of non-NRB production;
(2) relatively small contribution of NRB sectors to total production and exports;
(3) relatively low share of the direct value-added component in the total value of production;
(4) relatively high labour intensity of production in comparison with other sectors of the economy;
(5) the lowest average wage level among all sectors of the economy.

Due to the dominant contribution, in value terms, of petroleum refining to Singapore's manufacturing production, the first two characteristics only partly hold for Singapore. If, however, this specific refining activity is disregarded, all the above characteristics equally apply to Singapore's manufacturing sector.

SUMMARY OF FINDINGS AND CONCLUSIONS 419

The low labour productivity in terms of value added that characterizes manufacturing operations under a comprehensive export-oriented strategy reflects the exposure of manufacturing production to international competition and a resource allocation according to comparative advantage. The free-trade regime applied to exporters in these countries enables them to choose between domestic and imported inputs. Not only do exporters not have to bear the excess cost of using domestic inputs produced under protection, a free-trade regime also results in a more complete specialization in labour-intensive production processes. For labour-intensive export production can be expanded to supply-side limits, whereas capital-intensive intermediate inputs and capital equipment can be obtained at internationally competitive prices. Of course, the specific place manufacturing occupies in these countries is also due to their poor natural-resource endowment. It is true that this does not necessarily block the possibility of establishing extensive NRB production activities, as the case of Singapore clearly shows, but it commonly results in a generally minor contribution of NRB production to total manufacturing. This, in turn, reduces the average capital intensity of manufacturing production. Without exception, the industrial processing of primary products appears, on average, to be a more capital-intensive activity than the manufacture of non-NRB products in the countries studied.

18.3 TRADE STRATEGY AND THE STRUCTURE OF MANUFACTURED EXPORTS

The three country groups also differ from one another as regards the pattern of export specialization in manufactures. The specialization patterns per country are summarized in the first sub-columns of every country column in Table 18.1. These sub-columns show ratios representing weighted average labour intensities of different categories of export and production relative to the labour intensity of total manufacturing production, measured by direct labour (or wage) coefficients.

Considering first the NRB component of manufactured exports, it turns out that, on average, NRB exports systematically show a substantially lower direct labour input than non-NRB exports. The country studies showed that there are large differences among individual NRB products in terms of factor intensity. Petroleum products, at the one extreme, are found to be the most capital intensive. At the labour-intensive extreme, and this is true in all countries studied, we find various wood manufactures as important exportables, like plywood, veneers, rattan products, and wooden furniture and fixtures. Some of these manufactures are the produce of pure handicraft. Intercountry differences in the relative importance and factor intensity of NRB exports are in large part explained by differences in natural-resource

TABLE 18.1
RELATIVE DIRECT, INDIRECT AND SECONDARY EMPLOYMENT EFFECTS OF DIFFERENT CATEGORIES OF EXPORT AND PRODUCTION, CASE-STUDY COUNTRIES, VARIOUS YEARS

	Indonesia 1975			Philippines 1974			Thailand 1975			South Korea 1975		
	(1)	(2)	(3)	(1)	(2)	(3)	(1)	(2)	(3)	(1)	(2)	(3)
Total manufactured exports	.26	.28	.48	1.12	1.29	1.17	1.04	1.62	1.39	1.39	1.12	1.13
NRB manufactured exports	.19	.27	.43	1.07	1.38	1.20	1.01	1.99	1.61	.81	1.10	.88
Non-NRB manufactured exports	.87	.36	.96	1.68	.29	.84	1.14	.29	.61	1.55	1.13	1.19
Total manufacturing production	1.00	1.00	1.00	1.00	1.00	1.00	1.00	1.00	1.00	1.00	1.00	1.00
NRB manufacturing production	.67	1.43	.90	.85	1.26	1.06	.90	1.47	1.26	.62	.92	.79
Non-NRB manufacturing production	1.44	.41	1.13	1.41	.26	.83	1.16	.27	.59	1.27	1.05	1.15

For explanation of symbols, see Section 10.4.
Explanation of the columns:
(1) relative direct employment effect, defined as l_i^e/l_m^e or l_i^w/l_m^w;
(2) relative indirect employment effect, defined as $(T_i^e-l_i^e)/(T_m^e-l_m^e)$ or $(T_i^w-l_i^w)/(T_m^w-l_m^w)$;
(3) relative secondary employment effect, defined as $(WIM_i^E-T_i^e)/(WIM_m^E-T_m^e)$ or $(WIM_i-T_i^w)/(WIM_m-T_m^w)$;

where
l_i^e or l_i^w = weighted average direct labour (wage) coefficient production category i;
l_m^e or l_m^w = weighted average direct labour (wage) coefficient total manufacturing production;
T_i^e or T_i^w = weighted average total labour (wage) coefficient production category i;
T_m^e or T_m^w = weighted average total labour (wage) coefficient total manufacturing production;
WIM_i^E or WIM_i = weighted average WIM^E or WIM coefficient production category i;
WIM_m^E or WIM_m = weighted average WIM^E or WIM coefficient total manufacturing production.

Sources: see Appendices to Chapters 11–17.

TABLE 18.1 (cont'd)

	Taiwan 1976			Malaysia 1975			Singapore 1973			Singapore 1978		
	(1)	(2)	(3)	(1)	(2)	(3)	(1)	(2)	(3)	(1)	(2)	(3)
Total manufactured exports	1.31	1.03	1.15	1.06	1.15	1.13	.86	.76	.83	.84	.79	.81
NRB manufactured exports	.95	1.31	1.15	.91	1.36	1.24	.27	.44	.41	.15	.31	.24
Non-NRB manufactured exports	1.40	.96	1.16	1.65	.30	.65	1.60	1.16	1.39	1.93	1.55	1.71
Total manufacturing production	1.00	1.00	1.00	1.00	1.00	1.00	1.00	1.00	1.00	1.00	1.00	1.00
NRB manufacturing production	.55	1.12	.87	.84	1.29	1.17	.39	.70	.53	.29	.51	.38
Non-NRB manufacturing production	1.27	.93	1.08	1.36	.34	.60	1.58	1.29	1.44	1.88	1.62	1.77

For explanation of symbols, see Section 10.4.
Explanation of the columns:
(1) relative direct employment effect, defined as l_i^e/l_m^e or l_i^w/l_m^w;
(2) relative indirect employment effect, defined as $(T_i^e - l_i^e)/(T_m^e - l_m^e)$ or $(T_i^w - l_i^w)/(T_m^w - l_m^w)$;
(3) relative secondary employment effect, defined as $(WIM_i^E - T_i^e)/(WIM_m^E - T_m^e)$ or $(WIM_i - T_i^w)/(WIM_m - T_m^w)$;

where
l_i^e or l_i^w = weighted average direct labour (wage) coefficient production category i;
l_m^e or l_m^w = weighted average direct labour (wage) coefficient total manufacturing production;
T_i^e or T_i^w = weighted average total labour (wage) coefficient production category i;
T_m^e or T_m^w = weighted average total labour (wage) coefficient total manufacturing production;
WIM_i^E or WIM_i = weighted average WIM^E or WIM coefficient production category i;
WIM_m^E or WIM_m = weighted average WIM^E or WIM coefficient total manufacturing production.

Sources: see Appendices to Chapters 11-17.

endowments. Yet, it is striking to observe that the composition of NRB exports in five countries is less capital intensive than that of NRB production in total. The two exceptions, Indonesia and Singapore, are explained by the dominant role played by petroleum products in these countries' exports.

The effect of trade strategy on a country's pattern of specialization in non-NRB products is clearly less ambiguous. The country of the first group, Indonesia, pursues an inward-looking strategy and shows a specialization pattern in sharp contrast with the notion of comparative advantage. The system of incentives is clearly biased in favour of import substitution in capital-intensive products and against labour-intensive exportables. Exports that are nonetheless realized show a structure that reflects this bias. Thus, average direct labour requirements are lower for non-NRB exports than for total non-NRB production, and even lower than for total manufacturing. Correspondingly, the major non-NRB exports originate from relatively high-wage and high value-added sectors.

An entirely opposite pattern of specialization is found for countries included in the third group. Not only do these countries show on average a highly labour-intensive product composition of non-NRB exports, as appears from Table 18.1, but the country studies also revealed a high degree of consistency in their export specialization. The evidence is quite conclusive that a comprehensive export-promotion policy leads especially to superior export performance of these industries in which developing countries are thought to have a comparative advantage. It could be established that industries in these three countries with a higher export-output ratio show, accordingly, a higher labour intensity of production, generate less value added per unit of production and per employee, and pay lower wages. Furthermore, and in line herewith, unskilled occupational classes are relatively strongly represented in the labour force of these industries. Another striking feature of export industries in these countries is that they provide disproportionately large employment opportunities to women. The rationale for active policies to increase female labour force participation is found in reducing the wage-cost component for exporters. In all three countries, female, and especially young female, workers earn substantially less than their male colleagues in comparable functions. The role of female workers in the export drive of these countries is hard to overestimate. Some observers even wonder whether the pattern of industrialization as found in the third country group would have been possible without the deployment of the female labour reserves.[1]

The specialization pattern of countries of the second group that follow a dualistic strategy is less straightforward. As is to be expected for an in-between group, their pattern of export specialization shares elements from both other country groups. On the one hand, non-NRB exports are on average relatively labour intensive. On the other hand, however, no consistent specialization in the most labour-intensive exportables has been carried through in these countries. Non-NRB exports also include a substantial share of relatively capital-intensive products that are produced in relatively high-wage industries. Consequently, for the second group of countries no significant correspondence could be found among a sector's export orientation, factor intensity and average wage level.

18.4 PRODUCTION SPREAD EFFECTS OF MANUFACTURED EXPORTS

It will be immediately clear that the industrial processing of primary raw materials before they are exported results in a strong production linkage between manufacturing and primary sectors, and a strengthening of a country's economic structure. The domestic value-added component in NRB exports and, hence, the net foreign-exchange earnings are high. Integration of the economy and high exchange receipts are to be considered as the most important gains from the export of NRB manufactures. These gains can, of course, only be realized if the raw materials are produced or extracted domestically. In case many of the raw material inputs have to be imported, the economic rationale of NRB-processing activities has to be derived from other criteria.

Table 18.2 provides summary data pertaining to the production spread effects of NRB exports in the seven case-study countries. The *NFEE* values allow an intercountry comparison in absolute terms, the *P* values are country-tied relative measures of production linkages. The substantial intercountry variation of average *NFEE* values for NRB exports introduces an unmistakeable differentiation between resource-rich and resource-poor countries. Indonesia, the Philippines, Thailand and Malaysia generate NRB exports on the basis of their ample resource endowment, which yields them a net foreign-exchange receipt of 83 to 93 per cent per unit of exports. Taiwan and to a greater extent South Korea process and export primary products largely obtained through imports. Consequently, the domestic value-added component of NRB exports from these countries is markedly lower, namely 66 and 49 per cent respectively. Singapore's NRB exports are almost exclusively based on imported inputs, i.e. crude oil and unprocessed rubber. In 1978, only 11 per cent of the total export value of NRB manufactures could be considered as net foreign-exchange receipts. The integrating effect of NRB exports in resource-rich countries emerges with clarity from the relatively high *P* values in Indonesia, the Philippines, Thailand and Malaysia, ranging from 1.15 to 1.21. Moreover, *P* values are higher for NRB than for non-NRB exports in these four countries. The opposite appears to be the case in the resource-poor countries. First, NRB exports show relatively fewer

TABLE 18.2
WEIGHTED AVERAGE *P* AND *NFEE* VALUES FOR DIFFERENT CATEGORIES OF EXPORT AND PRODUCTION, CASE-STUDY COUNTRIES, VARIOUS YEARS

Category	Indonesia 1975		Philippines 1974		Thailand 1975		South Korea 1975		Taiwan 1976		Malaysia 1975		Singapore 1973		Singapore 1978	
	P	NFEE	P	NFEE	P	NFEE	P	NFEE	P	NFEE	P	NFEE	P	NFEE	P	NFEE
Total manufactured exports	1.20	.90	1.15	.91	1.15	.87	1.10	.58	1.14	.64	1.13	.79	.87	.31	.86	.24
NRB manufactured exports	1.21	.92	1.15	.93	1.17	.92	1.01	.49	1.10	.66	1.16	.83	.83	.19	.81	.11
Non-NRB manufactured exports	1.10	.67	1.14	.72	1.07	.73	1.12	.60	1.14	.64	.99	.61	.92	.47	.94	.43
Total manufacturing production	1.20	.83	1.14	.80	1.11	.77	1.04	.56	1.11	.63	1.13	.71	.92	.37	.89	.28
NRB manufacturing production	1.25	.92	1.16	.82	1.14	.83	.94	.52	1.11	.60	1.18	.77	.89	.25	.84	.15
Non-NRB manufacturing production	1.14	.70	1.09	.72	1.07	.68	1.10	.59	1.12	.64	1.03	.58	.95	.48	.95	.45

For explanation of symbols, see Section 10.4.
Sources: see Appendices to Chapters 11–17.

SUMMARY OF FINDINGS AND CONCLUSIONS

production linkages, in Singapore even susbtantially below the economy's average. Second, P value are, on average, lower for NRB than for non-NRB exports. The economic rationale of NRB export production in these countries must be sought in their efforts to diversify, upgrade and deepen their manufacturing production, a question that is taken up in the final section.

The production spread effects of non-NRB exports, also summarized in Table 18.2, show markedly less intercountry variation. In explaining this variation, natural-resource endowments are not longer thought to play a role of importance. This leaves us with domestic market size, level of industrial development and trade policy as the remaining factors which may shed light on the differences observed. However, generalizations are difficult in depicting the influence of each of these three factors on the level of production spread effects on the basis of only a seven country sample. Yet, at least three observations may be made.

The first is that, as expected, the $NFEE$ values for non-NRB exports are generally higher in the three largest countries, ranging from 0.67 to 0.73, as compared to the four smaller countries which show $NFEE$ values from 0.43 to 0.64. Evidently, the four smaller economies showing the highest export orientation of non-NRB production also show the highest dependency on imported inputs. From this, however, the conclusion may not be drawn that a higher export dependency is closely associated with, or even results in, a higher import dependency and hence a lower level of production spread effects. Before this question is addressed, it shoud be recalled that the domestic value-added component of non-NRB production in the three larger countries is overvalued in consequence of their relatively more highly protected and larger import substitution sector. The domestic value added of non-NRB production in the smaller and more open economies is likely to approach international values. Thus, the $NFEE$ values of non-NRB production in the individual countries probably differ less in fact than the figures in Table 18.2 suggest.

The second observation refers to the impossibility of establishing whether the economically and industrially more developed countries also show a better record of production spread effects, given the size of the domestic market. In fact, during the mid-1970s, industries producing intermediate and capital goods were still underdeveloped in all seven countries. South Korea, Taiwan, Singapore, and to a lesser extent also Malaysia, are respresentative of a group of forerunners which embarked on an export-oriented industrialization strategy after completing a first-stage import substitution mainly in nondurable consumer goods. These countries did not move into a secondary or backward-linkage type of import substitution, but extended the first stage to export markets. The larger countries — Indonesia, the Philippines and Thailand — reached the limits of the domestic market roughly ten years later and were then confronted with the choice of turning to exportation of manufactures or moving to second-stage import substitution. In other words, all countries studied were still in a first-stage industrialization process during the mid-1970s, directed either towards domestic or export markets, or both. Hence, the underdeveloped state of intermediate and capital goods industries. At this stage of industrialization, production of nondurable consumer goods is highly import dependent, whatever its market orientation.

Thus, and we now arrive at the third observation, export-oriented manufacturing production as such cannot be held responsible for the relatively high import dependency of non-NRB production in general. On the contrary, the results of the country studies indicate that a consistent export specialization in labour-intensive manufactures has or should have had a predominantly positive effect on the level of integration within the economy. This finding has been demonstrated on two different levels of analysis that will be discussed now.

The first piece of evidence emerges from Table 18.2. It shows that in four countries — the Philippines, Thailand, South Korea and Taiwan — the production spread effects of non-NRB exports, measured by *P* and *NFEE* values, are higher than or at least equal to non-NRB production in total. Opposite results have been obtained for Indonesia and Singapore, where non-NRB exports have fewer production spread effects than non-NRB production in total. Malaysia's non-NRB exports take an intermediate position: the *P* value is lower and the *NFEE* value is higher than for total non-NRB production. To explain these different records of production spread effects of non-NRB exports, use is again made of the three-way classification of countries according to alternative trade strategies. It then appears that the country group characterized by an inward-looking strategy has a relatively capital-intensive structure of non-NRB exports and shows a relatively low level of production spread effects generated by these exports. The second country groups pursues a dualistic strategy, their exports being on average labour-intensive non-NRB manufactures. The production spread effects of these exports in the Philippines and Thailand are relatively extensive, with an intermediate position for Malaysia. The third country group of comprehensive exporters shows a consistent specialization pattern in the most labour-intensive exportables, which, as far as South Korea and Taiwan are concerned, have relatively extensive production spread effects. By contrast, Singapore's export production takes place in relative isolation. The partial exception in the second country group, Malaysia, and the clear exception in the third country group, Singapore, are undoubtedly due to the predominance of the EPFZ-type of export production in these countries. The conclusion emerges that labour-intensive non-NRB export production shows a higher level of production spread effects than capital-intensive production

SUMMARY OF FINDINGS AND CONCLUSIONS 427

activities, on the understanding, however, that this general conditoin does not apply to labour-intensive manufactures produced under EPFZ conditions.

Second, similar evidence was obtained in further analysis on a disaggregated level. This analysis, carried out in the country studies, revealed noteworthy rank order relationships between measures of factor intensity and measures of production spread effects in a number of cases. The following pattern of non-NRB sectors could be discerned in all countries, except Malaysia and Singapore. The relationship between sectoral direct labour (wage) coefficients and P values is weak but positive, except in the Philippines. The relationship between sectoral direct labour (wage) coefficients and $NFEE$ values is stronger, positive as well and statistically significant in the Philippines, Thailand and South Korea. In turn, the correspondence between sectoral rankings by wage level on the one hand, and P and $NFEE$ values on the other hand, is negative in all cases. Except in Thailand, where the negative correlation coefficient between sectoral wage levels and P values is highly significant, these correspondences are generally weak. An almost completely reverse pattern of relationships is found for non-NRB sectors in Malaysia and Singapore. In Malaysia, a higher labour intensity of production appears to be significantly associated with a lower level of production linkages, whereas low-wage sectors in Singapore show a significantly lower domestic value-added component.

In sum, the results of the analyses on two different levels suggest that labour-intensive, low-wage sectors show a higher level of backward integration than capital-intensive sectors. This finding contradicts the general phenomenon that at higher levels of economic development intersectoral linkages are stronger for technologically more advanced and relatively capital-intensive sectors. Apparently, at lower levels of economic development it is easier to supply labour-intensive production processes with domestically produced intermediates than capital-intensive processes. This also explains why labour-intensive export production performs so well as regards production spread effects. The above-mentioned restriction must be recalled here: the established relationships are completely thwarted in case EPFZs occupy an important place in a country's manufacturing sector.

We may now also infer that the high import dependency of countries vigorously promoting manufactured exports may generally not be attributed to an export-oriented strategy as such. Only the EPFZ variant of export promotion has this effect. Apart from this case, the proper reasoning would seem to be that it is the smallness of the domestic market that causes both a high export and import dependency of manufacturing production. Given this fact, a comprehensive export-promotion policy generally reduces import dependency: first, by the very act of exporting labour-intensive manufactures, and second, by overcoming the limitations of a narrow domestic market. The latter may have its full effect in the longer run only. In smaller countries, the efficient plant size of intermediates and producer's goods can only be obtained through enlargement of the market. In the course of first-stage export production, the establishment of these second-stage industries may become economically feasible as input suppliers to export industries when the latter reach higher production volumes. Consequently, the opponents of the export-oriented model of industrialization are generally wrong in their criticism that this model only results in the creation of a highly import-dependent and footloose export sector, thereby aggravating the dualistic nature of developing economies. They unjustly consider the features of one, often minor, avenue of export-oriented industrialization strategies, namely the operation of EPFZs, to be representative for the whole of it.

These findings may have important policy implications for the developing countries. They reveal that the potential gains a country can realize from manufactured export expansion are a function of its pattern of specialization, which in turn is related to its pursued trade strategy and the policy instruments applied to implement this trade strategy. At lower levels of economic development, a consistent specialization in labour-intensive exportables yields the maximum level of production spread effects from exports. Consequently, a policy package that systematically stimulates the exports of these manufactures, without, however, having recourse to the instant solution of EPFZs, contributes to the integration and hence strengthening of the economy and improves a country's balance-of-payments position.

18.5 EMPLOYMENT SPREAD EFFECTS OF MANUFACTURED EXPORTS

The employment implications for developing countries of their manufactured exports are now to be evaluated. The starting point of our investigations has been the view that the direct employment effect constitutes but a part of the total employment opportunities potentially to be created by manufactured export expansion. The indirect or linkage employment effect as well as the secondary employment effect from spending of increased wage incomes on domestically produced products are therefore explicitly taken into account. The relevance of this approach is stressed by Table 18.3, which presents three types of employment ratios for manufactured exports of the case-study countries, subdivided into twenty product categories. The first ratio denotes the primary employment ratio, defined as T_i^e/I_i^e (or T_i^w/I_i^w), the second ratio equals the first, except that indirect employment opportunities in agriculture are excluded. The third ratio denotes the overall (primary plus

TABLE 18.3
PRIMARY AND OVERALL (PRIMARY PLUS SECONDARY) EMPLOYMENT RATIOS FOR DIFFERENT PRODUCT CATEGORIES OF MANUFACTURED EXPORTS, CASE-STUDY COUNTRIES, VARIOUS YEARS

Product Category	Indonesia 1975			Philippines 1974			Thailand 1975			South Korea 1975		
	(1)	(2)	(3)	(1)	(2)	(3)	(1)	(2)	(3)	(1)	(2)	(3)
1 Food products, beverages and tobacco	7.22	1.89	9.69	7.96	1.42	10.93	17.80	1.38	27.42	2.32	1.60	2.75
2 Textiles	1.84	1.50	2.86	2.54	1.84	4.01	2.43	1.96	4.96	2.01	1.87	2.40
3 Wearing apparel	1.70	1.61	2.55	1.54	1.44	2.36	2.83	1.65	5.07	1.50	1.47	1.75
4 Leather products and footwear	1.70	1.61	2.55	1.56	1.26	2.20	6.54	2.14	11.06	1.53	1.51	1.80
5 Wood products and furniture	1.19	1.16	1.47	3.53	1.34	4.96	6.81	1.34	10.74	1.40	1.35	1.67
6 Paper and paper products	2.54	2.25	5.70	1.59	1.45	3.10	2.55	1.71	5.03	1.66	1.59	2.03
7 Printing and publishing	2.54	2.25	5.70	1.45	1.40	2.77	1.70	1.49	3.49	1.61	1.59	2.01
8 Chemicals	2.83	2.30	5.15	2.61	2.12	4.98	2.41	1.83	4.99	2.01	1.99	2.61
9 Petroleum refineries	3.74	3.45	11.41	4.67	4.52	10.67	8.02	6.12	24.61	1.87	1.85	2.74
10 Rubber products	3.48	2.63	6.75	1.53	1.41	2.50	9.31	1.22	14.34	1.55	1.54	1.84
11 Plastic products n.e.c.	2.82	2.28	5.11	1.58	1.41	2.70	1.24	1.19	2.97	1.49	1.48	1.76
12 Non-metallic mineral products	1.41	1.33	2.22	1.73	1.69	3.20	3.12	2.56	6.99	1.93	1.91	2.37
13 Iron and steel basic industries	1.84	1.81	3.01	2.48	2.39	4.56	2.22	2.07	5.17	3.36	3.34	4.27
14 Non-ferrous metal basic industries	3.73	3.71	5.34	2.22	2.13	4.48	2.65	2.51	5.27	2.12	2.10	2.64
15 Metal products	1.62	1.60	2.61	1.68	1.63	2.99	1.86	1.68	3.71	1.58	1.58	1.92
16 Non-electrical machinery	2.44	2.37	4.43	1.52	1.45	2.85	2.10	1.98	5.18	1.56	1.55	1.91
17 Electrical machinery	2.44	2.37	4.43	1.63	1.59	3.07	2.69	2.25	5.75	1.49	1.48	1.76
18 Transport equipment	1.72	1.68	2.78	1.26	1.23	2.26	3.31	2.64	7.43	1.71	1.70	2.20
19 Professional goods	1.22	1.19	1.72	1.32	1.29	2.11	2.44	2.22	5.37	1.39	1.38	1.65
20 Other manufactures	1.22	1.19	1.72	1.32	1.29	2.11	2.31	1.55	4.63	1.61	1.59	1.91
Total manufactured exports	3.89	3.19	9.73	7.01	1.48	9.75	11.99	1.68	19.15	1.76	1.67	2.13
NRB manufactured exports	4.06	3.31	10.32	7.47	1.47	10.34	14.56	1.61	22.94	2.28	2.00	2.84
Non-NRB manufactured exports	2.35	2.10	4.15	1.92	1.65	3.26	2.71	1.93	5.49	1.63	1.59	1.94

(cont'd overleaf)

TABLE 18.3 (cont'd)

Product Category	Taiwan 1976			Malaysia 1975			Singapore 1973			Singapore 1978		
	(1)		(3)	(1)		(3)	(1)	(2)	(3)	(1)	(2)	(3)
1 Food products, beverages and tobacco	4.31		6.23	20.19		34.50	1.69	1.69	2.11	1.87	1.86	2.35
2 Textiles	2.69		3.90	1.90		3.25	1.19	1.19	1.40	1.18	1.18	1.39
3 Wearing apparel	1.89		2.74	1.49		2.55	1.08	1.08	1.22	1.16	1.16	1.31
4 Leather products and footwear	1.96		2.83	2.81		4.80	1.55	1.54	1.81	1.33	1.33	1.55
5 Wood products and furniture	1.98		2.87	3.09		5.29	1.20	1.19	1.44	1.32	1.32	1.60
6 Paper and paper products	2.59		3.75	1.81		3.10	1.36	1.36	1.58	1.23	1.23	1.46
7 Printing and publishing	1.63		2.35	1.81		3.10	1.17	1.17	1.45	1.22	1.22	1.48
8 Chemicals	2.32		3.35	3.39		5.80	1.69	1.69	2.14	2.08	2.08	2.71
9 Petroleum refineries	1.94		2.80	1.12		1.92	2.26	2.25	3.46	2.28	2.28	3.34
10 Rubber products	1.86		2.70	5.88		10.05	1.13	1.12	1.37	1.89	1.89	2.42
11 Plastic products n.e.c.	1.82		2.63	1.63		2.78	1.10	1.10	1.27	1.46	1.46	1.80
12 Non-metallic mineral products	1.78		2.58	1.67		2.86	1.67	1.67	2.13	1.78	1.78	2.41
13 Iron and steel basic industries	3.60		5.21	2.75		4.70	1.82	1.82	2.37	1.85	1.85	2.47
14 Non-ferrous metal basic industries	1.69		2.44	1.84		3.15	2.10	2.10	2.62	1.40	1.40	1.79
15 Metal products	1.70		2.46	1.62		2.78	1.39	1.39	1.70	1.29	1.29	1.64
16 Non-electrical machinery	1.61		2.32	1.41		2.41	1.28	1.28	1.58	1.28	1.28	1.60
17 Electrical machinery	1.88		2.73	1.85		3.16	1.13	1.13	1.33	1.18	1.18	1.39
18 Transport equipment	1.83		2.65	1.87		3.19	1.36	1.36	1.80	1.48	1.48	2.00
19 Professional goods	1.39		2.02	1.10		1.88	1.13	1.13	1.37	1.20	1.20	1.42
20 Other manufactures	1.67		2.41	1.63		2.78	1.18	1.18	1.34	1.40	1.40	1.69
Total manufactured exports	2.19		3.17	7.39		12.63	1.55	1.55	2.11	1.85	1.85	2.57
NRB manufactured exports	3.28		4.74	8.76		14.98	1.82	1.81	2.62	2.20	2.20	3.18
Non-NRB manufactured exports	1.94		2.80	1.75		2.99	1.22	1.21	1.47	1.31	1.31	1.62

Explanation of the columns:
(1) weighted average primary employment ratio product category i, defined as T_i^e/l_i^e or T_i^w/l_i^w;
(2) as primary employment ratio, exclusive of indirect employment in agriculture;
(3) weighted average overall (primary plus secondary) employment ratio product category i, defined as WIM_i^E/l_i^e or WIM_i/l_i^w.

For explanation of symbols, see Section 10.4.
Sources: see Appendices to Chapters 11–17

SUMMARY OF FINDINGS AND CONCLUSIONS

secondary) employment ratio, defined as WIM_i^E/l_i^e (or WIM_i/l_i^w). These ratios are averaged per product category, using exports as weights. The direct employment effect from exports of a particular product category has to be multiplied by the relevant ratio to arrive at the associated total primary or total primary plus secondary employment effect.

Indeed, as the values of the employment ratios reveal, indirect and secondary employment effects can raise the employment impact from exports considerably. Consider, for instance, exports of food products, beverages and tobacco which show overall employment ratios rising, respectively, to almost or over a multiple of thirty in Thailand and Malaysia. On average, the primary and overall employment ratios for NRB exports from the four resource-rich countries range from 4.06 to 14.56 and from 10.32 to 22.94, respectively. Obviously, these ratios are much lower for the resource-poor countries. The corresponding ratios for non-NRB exports are markedly lower, ranging from 1.22 to 2.71 for the primary employment ratio and from 1.47 to 5.49 for the overall employment ratio.

The higher ratios for NRB exports are of course explained by the relatively high labour intensity of input-supplying sectors relative to the low labour intensity of NRB-processing industries. If it is assumed that export expansion will not create new jobs in agriculture but only lead to fuller employment, the employment ratios turn out substantially lower. The effect is particularly strong in the resource-rich countries. As Table 18.3 shows, the primary employment ratio for NRB exports drops from 4.06 to 3.31 in Indonesia, from 7.47 to 1.47 in the Philippines and from 14.56 to 1.61 in Thailand if indirect employment opportunities in agriculture are disregarded.

The employment ratios are useful in gauging the orders of magnitude of employment spread effects associated with manufactured export expansion in developing countries. For illustrative purposes only, the primary and overall employment ratios for non-NRB manufactured exports of the case-study countries have been averaged, using 1980 export shares as weights. This rather conservative estimate results in average primary and overall employment ratios of 1.7 and 2.4, respectively. It has been estimated that in the seven case-study countries almost 2.1 million direct employment opportunities were generated by manufactured export production destined for the markets of the OECD countries in 1980.[2] These 2.1 million jobs increase to 3.6 million if the indirect, and to 5.1 million if also the secondary effects on employment are included. Extending this rough procedure, the total primary and secondary employment effect of all developing countries' manufactured exports to OECD countries is then estimated at 10.5 million jobs in 1980, given the 48.4 per cent share of the case-study countries in total manufactured exports of developing countries in that year.

Analytically, however, the employment ratios are hardly informative. For, like all ratios, the outcome is determined by the size of both the numerator and the denominator. Petroleum refining, for instance, has low primary and secondary employment effects per unit of export, but compared to its extremely low direct labour coefficient the employment ratios suggest an excellent record of employment spread effect. In evaluating the total employment impact per unit of export, one should therefore look at the three constituting effects separately. Furthermore, the employment ratios not only differ widely product-wise, they also show a substantial variation among the countries. These intercountry differences reflect differences in the level of production spread effects among countries, which in turn are governed by differences in structural country characteristics and trade strategies pursued. Relationships among these factors have been identified in the preceding sections.

The analysis may be carried a step further by separating the employment effects. For this purpose, Table 18.1 has been constructed, presenting separately the direct, indirect and secondary employment effects of various categories of manufactured exports, relative to the corresponding average effects for manufacturing in total. This form of presentation permits a closer examination of each of the three employment effects and might permit us to discover the specific influence of alternative trade strategies, without the results being distorted by the general degree of interdependence within an economy.

It has already been established that the three country groups each show a distinct pattern of export specialization in manufactures. As far as direct employment creation is concerned, the third country group yields optimal results through its consistent specialization in the most labour-intensive exportables. The export pattern of the second country group is less optimal in this regard, whereas the capital-intensive export pattern of Indonesia creates the fewest direct employment opportunities. In turn, a labour-intensive pattern of export specialization also appears to have favourable effects on indirect and secondary employment generation.

Considering first the indirect or linkage employment effects of NRB exports, it is apparent that the relative extent of this effect is larger in those cases where the composition of exports is more labour intensive than that of production in general. Thus, as Table 18.1 shows, if the direct employment effect is higher per unit of NRB exports than per unit of NRB production, this is equally true for the indirect employment effects. In the two countries, Indonesia and Singapore, where NRB exports show both a relatively low direct and indirect employment effect, these exports are dominated by petroleum products.

Similar results are obtained for the relative indirect employment effects of non-NRB exports, except in Malaysia and Singapore. These two exceptions may be taken to reflect the small extent of production spread effects associated with export production in EPFZs. In both countries, the direct employment effect per unit of non-NRB exports exceeds that of total non-NRB production, whereas the indirect employment impact of these exports falls behind the manufacturing average.

The same pattern emerges if the secondary employment implications of NRB and non-NRB manufactured exports are considered, with only one modification. The direct employment effect of non-NRB manufactured exports in Malaysia is sufficiently large to compensate for the low indirect effect, resulting in a secondary employment effect just exceeding the average for non-NRB production. This compensation does not occur in Singapore.

In sum, the conclusion appears justified that a consistent specialization in labour-intensive exports not only generates, by definition, the maximum number of direct employment opportunities in export industries, it also provides the best guarantee that the employment spread effects are maximized throughout the economy. Again, the caveat must be added that labour-intensive exports from EPFZs constitute an exception to this general conclusion. The employment impact of the EPFZ-type of export production is largely confined to direct employment alone.

In explaining the overall higher employment creating capacity of labour-intensive export production, we should consider the following four salient features of labour-intensive *vis-à-vis* capital-intensive production processes in developing countries. First, labour-intensive production processes generate per unit of output more direct employment and have a larger wage component in value added. Second, in developing countries, labour-intensive production processes show more extensive production spread effects. Third, labour-intensive production processes generate more indirect employment effects. That the higher level of production spread effects of labour-intensive manufactures does not fail in its effect on the extent of indirect employment creation is a finding that may deserve special attention. It implies that the labour intensity of inputs entering labour-intensive production processes is, on average, about equal to, and certainly not much below, the average for the entire economy. With the exception of oil refining and some other mining-based manufacturing, this is definitely the case with NRB processing activities. But, strikingly enough, it appears to be equally true for labour-intensive non-NRB manufacturing. Fourth, as can be inferred from the three preceding features and as indeed has been established in the country studies, labour-intensive production processes show the largest wage share in total, direct plus indirect, value added. This is specially conducive to the creation of secondary employment effects, induced by the spending on domestic products from wage incomes.

The above considerations incontestably indicate the advantages of a consistent export specialization in labour-intensive manufactures for productive employment creation in developing countries.

18.6 LESSONS FROM SOUTH-EAST ASIA'S EXPERIENCE

We come finally to four lessons to be learned from the experiences of the seven countries under consideration. The first lesson offered is the proven effectiveness of a comprehensive as compared to a dualistic export-promotion strategy in generating labour-intensive manufactured exports, and, consequently, its superiority in both production and employment spread effects. It is true that one unit of foreign exchange earned in exporting is equivalent to one unit of foreign exchange saved through import substitution. But, for one thing, the net foreign-exchange earnings per unit of output from labour-intensive exports are generally higher than, or at least equal to, the net foreign-exchange savings from capital-intensive production oriented towards the domestic market. For another, direct, indirect and secondary employment effects associated with one unit of foreign exchange in exporting labour-intensive exports are each clearly more extensive than corresponding employment effects associated with one unit of foreign exchange saved through capital-intensive domestic-market-oriented production.

These observations are pertinent to early stages of export and import-substituting industrialization. Apart from the processing of domestically available primary products, manufacturing production at this stage is generally import dependent as intermediate and capital goods producing industries are still undeveloped. The economic feasibility of establishing intermediate and capital goods sectors comes in sight once the first stage of industrialization, either as import substitution or export promotion, is completed. One can argue that for smaller countries, export production after a first phase of import substitution constitutes an essential interim phase before second-stage industrialization becomes economically feasible. Only then can the efficient scale of production of intermediate and capital goods industries, being larger than the domestic needs in most of the medium-sized and smaller developing countries, be realized. It follows that the manufacture of intermediate and capital goods in these countries has to be undertaken for both the domestic and export markets, in order to fully exploit economies of scale. Production for export market can take the form of direct exports or indirect exports through input supplies to exporting industries.

The question is whether or not the development of these direct or indirect exports again has to be preceded by a second-stage import substitution phase. Interestingly enough, examples of both developments can be provided. Among the case-study countries, South Korea, Taiwan and Singapore increasingly upgraded their first-stage export production and began exporting durable consumer goods, intermediates and machinery. Several of these exports, including petroleum refineries and oil rigs in Singapore, ships and boats in Singapore and South Korea, and electrical machinery and electronics in all three countries, were hardly or not preceded by an import-substitution phase. Some new second-stage production activities in South Korea and Taiwan, on the contrary, enjoy forms of import-substitution protection, like (petro)chemicals, synthetic fibres, metal products, automobiles and machinery. In these instances, protection is supposed to be selective and temporary. Production for the domestic market as well as exporting, directly and indirectly, are simultaneously pursued.

In this connection, it is of great interest to realize that a comprehensive export-promotion strategy provides more favourable conditions to increase the backward integration of export production than dualistic export strategies. For the system of incentives that goes with a comprehensive strategy does not discriminate between the use of imported and domestically produced intermediate inputs, whereas dualistic policies discriminate against, rather then encourage, domestic input supplies from a protected import-substitution sector.

This leads us to the second lesson, namely the poor record of spread effects associated with the EPFZ-type of export promotion. This fact emerges with clarity from the experiences in Singapore and Malaysia and from the EPFZ production especially of electronics in South Korea and Taiwan. The direct employment effects are the only substantial gain to be reaped from this specific export-promotion device. Moreover, the experience of Singapore shows that, although the EPFZ-type of export production as such can be upgraded and diversified in the course of time, a backward integration with the domestic economy cannot easily be developed. Consequently, the employment implications of exports from EPFZs will necessarily remain limited. This strategy can therefore only be advocated for those countries which have no policy alternative, most notably small countries that are poorly endowed with natural resources and, in absolute terms, a small labour force. In all other cases, EPFZs are less optimal, especially where these zones are grafted on to a protected import-substitution sector.

The third lesson refers to a salient feature of textile and clothing exports. Without exception, textiles and clothing are among the exportables exerting the highest level of spread effects, both in terms of production and employment. By contrast, as noted above, the EPFZ production of electronics generates the poorest spread effects. It is therefore highly regrettable that the rising tide of protectionism in developed countries is specially directed against the exports of exactly those products which appear to be the most favourable for production and employment growth in developing countries — the "voluntary" export restraints under the Multi

Fibre Arrangement being the evidence. Restrictive trade practices against offshore electronics asssembly are less severe and sometimes even completely absent.

The fourth lesson to be learned from the South-East Asian experience is that the first or easy phase of export-oriented industrialization is based on specialization in a rather narrow range of labour-intensive exportables. From the point of view of employment creation, this specialization pattern proved to be optimal. However, as every light has its shadow, there are several drawbacks to be noted. To begin with, the quality of the employment created is low. Workers in export industries are the lowest paid among workers within manufacturing, and in the most export-oriented countries even in the entire economy. Unskilled or low-skilled occupations strongly predominate in employment in export industries, which require either unsophisticated technologies or rest upon standardized assembly operations. The diffusion of technological know-how and the acquisition of technical skills are therefore meagre.

This being established, it is none the less unjust, as do the opponents of an export-oriented industrialization indeed, to designate these trade flows from developing to developed countries as a mechanism of economic exploitation at the cost of workers in export industries. In evaluating the appropriate wage level in export industries in developing countries one should not consider the general wage level pertaining in the importing countries, but rather the alternatives open to workers in these export industries. Thus, the relevant criteria are the prevailing domestic wage rate and labour productivity, together with the social opportunity cost of labour.[3]

Another drawback, as already indicated in the first lesson, refers to the finding that these exports, like non-NRB production in general, are highly import dependent. Furthermore, a narrow range of exportables tends to make the growth process very vulnerable to changes in external demand.

In the face of these features of the easy phase of export-oriented industrialization as well as the slackening demand in the developed countries, either because of conjunctural reasons or growing protectionism, there is a need to diversify and upgrade export production and to increase the use of domestically produced inputs in order to preserve the momentum of growth for production and employment. This involves a transition to a subsequent industrialization phase that may be characterized as secondary import substitution cum export promotion.[4] In order to facilitate this transition, policy initiatives are required over a broad field. It will, first of all, entail an identification of industries, products and technologies to be promoted. Next, the system of incentives has to be modified accordingly. In addition, manpower training and wage and labour market policies will be needed to produce skilled manpower in appropriate quantity and composition.

SUMMARY OF FINDINGS AND CONCLUSIONS

The current attempts of South Korea, Taiwan and Singapore to enter into second-stage import substitution cum export promotion make clear that this transition may indeed become the real *tour de force*.[5] On the one hand, future comparative advantages are uncertain and an appropriate policy package to serve both export and import-substituting industries is not readily available, whereas, on the other hand, large capital investments are required in physical and human capital, and in the adaptation of imported or the development of indigenous technology. However, without diversification, upgrading and increasing the backward integration of export production, the easy phase of export-oriented industrialization is a dead end in the longer run. Moreover, this transition is also the obvious way to improve the quality and remuneration of labour.

Notes

CHAPTER 1

1. For critical studies on export-oriented policies see, for instance, J. Friedmann, 1979; F. Fröbel, J. Heinrichs and O. Kreye, 1980; J. Heinrichs, 1980; A.G. Frank, 1981. For critical studies on EPFZs see, for instance, AMPO, 1977 and G. Edgren, 1982.
2. For four of these individual countries, the national context and in particular the national policies regarding industrialization and manufactured exports are discussed in considerable detail in the companion volume of the present study; see Chia Siow Yue (ed.), 1987 (forthcoming).
3. In 1984, Brunei joined the ASEAN as the sixth member country.

PART I

CHAPTER 2

1. Unless otherwise indicated the term manufacturing production refers to activities that are included in major division 3 of the International Standard Industrial Classification (ISIC). The term manufactured exports refers to products that are included in sections 5-8 less divisions 67 and 68 of the Standard International Trade Classification (SITC).
2. UNIDO, 1981, Figure 1, p. 29.
3. UNIDO, 1981, pp. 60-62.
4. World Bank, 1983a, Volume I, Appendix Table A.10, p. 290; Volume II, pp. 115-119.
5. World Bank, 1982, Table 3, p. 114. Low-income countries were at a level of GNP *per capita* of US$410 and below in 1980. All other developing countries are in the group of middle-income countries.
6. World Bank, 1982, Tables 2 and 3, pp. 112-115.
7. World Bank, 1983a, Volume II, pp. 423, 424.
8. World Bank, 1983a, Volume II, Table 3.1, p. 152 and Table 1.7, p. 424.
9. Estimates are based on data presented in World Bank, 1983a, Volume II, Table 3.1, p. 152; Table 1.7, p. 424 and Table 1.8, p. 425.

CHAPTER 3

1. See S. Kuznets, 1965; A. Maizels, 1970; H.B. Chenery and H. Hughes, 1973; H. Chenery and M. Syrquin, 1975; H. Chenery, 1979, Chapter 3; UNIDO, 1979, Chapter III; R.A. Batchelor, 1980a.

2. H. Chenery, 1979, p. 6.
3. See B. Balassa and Associates, 1971 and 1982.
4. M. Lipton, 1977.
5. H.B. Chenery and H. Hughes, 1973, pp. 6, 7.
6. H.B. Chenery and H. Hughes, 1973, p. 4.
7. H. Chenery, 1979, p. 44.
8. R. Hofheinz, Jr. and K.E. Calder, 1982, pp. 42-52 and pp. 110-118.
9. UNCTAD, 1969, pp. 28-41.
10. Four countries were excluded among which Hong Kong and Israel. The values of manufactured exports *per cápita* in these countries were exceptionally high and distorted the analysis.
11. Manufactured exports defined according to the so-called Total B defintion of UNCTAD.
12. A.H.M. Mahfuzur Rahman, 1973, pp. 78-106.
13. A.H.M. Mahfuzur Rahman, 1973, p. 100.
14. UNIDO, 1974, Annex "Determinants of Manufactured Exports", pp. 296-299.
15. T.K. Morrison, 1976a.
16. Hong Kong was excluded from the sample as it distorted the analysis.
17. T.K. Morrison, 1976a, Table 7, p. 64.
18. T.K. Morrison, 1976b, p. 327.
19. T.K. Morrison, 1976a, pp. 67, 68.
20. B. Balassa, 1969, pp. 201-204.
21. D.B. Keesing, 1968, p. 451.
22. D.B. Keesing, 1968, pp. 454, 455.
23. D.B. Keesing and D.R. Sherk, 1971, p. 957.
24. D.B. Keesing and D.R. Sherk, 1971, p. 961.
25. B. Balassa, 1969, p. 203.
26. D.B. Keesing and D.R. Sherk, 1971, p. 957.
27. J.B. Donges and J. Riedel, 1977, p. 62.
28. UNIDO, 1979, Annex I, pp. 331-339 and pp. 358-364.
29. D.B. Keesing and D.R. Sherk, 1971.
30. On the basis of FAO statistics on land use we define arable land as land area less other land. Other land includes unused but potentially productive land, built-on areas, wasteland, parks, ornamental gardens, roads, lanes, barren land, etc. See FAO, *Production Yearbook*, Rome, "Notes on the Tables".

CHAPTER 4

1. L.G. Reynolds, 1977, pp. 186, 187.
2. G.K. Helleiner, 1973; F. Stewart, 1978; S. Lall and P.P. Streeten, 1977; S. Lall, 1978; J.H. Dunning, 1981.
3. See World Bank, 1985a, pp. 38-42; UNCTAD, 1985, Annex Table A.9, pp. 208-212.
4. H.G. Johnson, 1981, pp. 162-165; R.E. Baldwin, 1969, p. 297.
5. L.E. Westphal, 1981, p. 10.
6. W.M. Corden, 1974, p. 264.
7. W.M. Corden, 1974, pp. 268, 269; D.B. Keesing, 1979, pp. 47, 48.
8. R.E. Baldwin, 1969, p. 297; L.E. Westphal, 1981, p. 16.
9. B. Balassa, 1975, p. 28.
10. J.N. Bhagwati and T.N. Srinivasan, 1983, pp. 233-248.
11. G. Haberler, 1950, p. 237. The original German edition was published in 1933.
12. W.M. Corden, 1974, pp. 272-275.

13. A.O. Hirschman, 1958.
14. For a classification of non-economic arguments for government intervention see J.N. Bhagwati and T.N. Srinivasan, 1983, p. 234.
15. W.M. Corden, 1974, pp. 42–57.
16. For a classical study on this issue see M. Olsen, 1971. See also K. Anderson and R.E. Baldwin, 1981; R.E. Baldwin, 1982; J.J. Pincus, 1975.
17. R.E. Baldwin, 1982.
18. W.M. Corden, 1974, pp. 107–109.
19. R.F. Feenstra and J.N. Bhagwati, 1982.
20. For reviews of rent-seeking activities see A.O. Krueger, 1974; J.N. Bhagwati and T.N. Srinivasan, 1983, pp. 313–334.
21. P. van Dijck and E. Hoogteijling, 1985, p. 23.
22. See B. Balassa and Associates, 1971 and 1982.
23. P. van Dijck and E. Hoogteijling, 1985, p. 24.
24. B. Balassa, 1976, p. 15.
25. A.O. Krueger, 1978, p. 48.
26. P. van Dijck and E. Hoogteijling, 1985.
27. A.O. Krueger, 1978, pp. 12–41.
28. J.B. Donges, 1976; B. Balassa, 1978; 1981, Essays 1–3 and Part II; 1982a and 1982b; A.O. Krueger, 1978; A.O. Krueger, H.B. Lary, T. Manson and N. Akrasanee (eds.), Volume I, 1981.
29. D.B. Keesing, 1979.
30. P. van Dijck and H. Verbruggen (eds.), 1984.
31. A.O. Krueger, 1978, pp. 211, 212.
32. D.B. Keesing, 1979, pp. 24, 25.
33. World Bank, 1985b, Volume I, p. 158.
34. World Bank, 1979a, p. 2.
35. On Argentina see World Bank, 1985b, Volume I, p. 193; on the Philippines see World Bank, 1976, p. 452 (in the inventory in Table 4.6 we included recommendations from the report of 1980a); on Colombia see World Bank, 1984a, p. 124.
36. A.C. Cizauskas, 1980, pp. 23–28.
37. On the Philippines see World Bank, 1976, p. 225. On the Dominican Republic see World Bank, 1978, p. 61.
38. World Bank, 1980b, p. 257.
39. World Bank, 1980c.
40. Yung Whee Rhee, 1985, pp. 177–200; Yung Whee Rhee, B. Ross-Larson and G. Pursell, 1984, pp. 9–38.
41. Miyohei Shinohara and Toru Yanagihara, 1983, p. 21.
42. Kwang Suk Kim, 1983, p. 68.
43. H. Chenery and M. Syrquin, 1975, pp. 89–101.
44. M. Roemer, 1979, p. 165.
45. UNIDO, 1979, p. 178.
46. A.J. Yeats, 1979, pp. 51–53.
47. UNCTAD, 1981, Appendix Table 1, pp. 26–28.
48. A.J. Yeats, 1979; R. Bosson and B. Varon, 1977.
49. M. Roemer, 1979; UNIDO, 1979, pp. 175–222.
50. A.J. Yeats, 1979, pp. 173–201.
51. A.J. Yeats, 1979, p. 197.
52. UNCTAD, 1982, Table A, pp. 19–60; World Bank, 1983e.
53. UNCTAD, 1983; A. Basile and D. Germidis, 1984.

NOTES   441

54. This point can be illustrated by referring to the IMF concept of an economy. As formulated by the IMF, "an economy is conceived as being comprised of the economic entities that have a closer association with a given territory than with any other territory". See IMF, *Balance of Payments Statistics*, Washington, Annex I, "Conceptual Framework of the Balance of Payments and Its Relationship to National Accounts".
55. S.B. Linder, 1961; F. Stewart, 1978.
56. With respect to the latter point see G.K. Helleiner, 1977; E. Verreydt and J. Waelbroeck, 1982.
57. For examples of this type of export-oriented foreign investments from Japan see T. Ozawa, 1979, pp. 73–78 and p. 81; S. Sekiguchi, 1979, pp. 12, 13; K. Kojima, 1978. For examples of European firms see F. Fröbel, J. Heinrichs and O. Kreye, 1980, p. 129.
58. K. Kumar and M.G. McLeod (eds.), 1981.
59. M. Sharpton, 1975, p. 110.
60. A.O. Hirschman, 1958, p. 112.
61. UNCTAD, 1983, p. 5.
62. G. Edgren, 1982, p. 11.
63. A. Basile and D. Germidis, 1984, pp. 57, 58.
64. Data on South Korea, India, the Philippines and Taiwan taken from A. Basile and D. Germidis, 1984, p. 50. Data on Malaysia taken from M. Ariff, Chee Peng Lim and D. Lee, 1984, Section 3.3. Data on Mauritius taken from UNCTAD, 1983, p. 40. On Mexico see A. Basile and D. Germidis, 1984, p. 44 and World Bank, 1979a, p. 2.
65. A.D. Morgan, 1980, p. 91.
66. R. Vernon, 1971, p. 102.
67. B.I. Cohen, 1975, p. 10.
68. D. Nayyar, 1978, p. 78.
69. L.T. Wells, Jr., 1981.
70. D.J. Lecraw, 1981; Sung-Hwan Jo, 1981; Wen-Lee Ting and Chi Schive, 1981; E.K.Y. Chen, 1981.
71. S. Watanabe, 1971 and 1972; C.A. Michalet, 1980; see also D. Germidis, 1980.
72. K. Kojima and T. Ozawa, 1984, p. 29.
73. A.K. Young, 1979, pp. 11–13; Y. Tsurumi and R.R. Tsurumi, 1980, pp. 41–57.
74. A.K. Young, 1979, pp. 4–9.
75. A.K. Young, 1979; Y. Tsurumi and R.R. Tsurumi, 1980; K. Kojima and T. Ozawa, 1984.
76. A.K. Young, 1979, p. 197.
77. K. Kojima and T. Ozawa, 1984, p. 13.
78. Y. Tsurumi and R.R. Tsurumi, 1980, pp. 59–72.

CHAPTER 5

1. B. Ohlin, 1967.
2. S.B. Linder, 1961, p. 129.
3. S.B. Linder, 1961, p. 188.
4. F. Stewart, 1978, Chapters 1 and 7.
5. F. Stewart, 1978, p. 171.
6. R. Vernon, 1966; S. Hirsch, 1967.
7. G.C. Hufbauer, 1966.
8. G.C. Hufbauer, 1966, p. 32.
9. G.C. Hufbauer, 1966, p. 91.
10. See S. Hirsch, 1967; R. Vernon, 1971, pp. 60–112.
11. S. Hirsch, 1967, p. 28.

12. S. Hirsch, 1974a, pp. 68-71.
13. W. Leontief, 1966, p. 70.
14. H.B. Chenery and H. Hughes, 1973, p. 10.
15. B. Ohlin, 1967, pp. 61, 62.
16. B. Ohlin, 1979.
17. D.B. Keesing, 1979, p. 151; B. Balassa, 1981, p. 4.
18. D.B. Keesing, 1979, p. 146.
19. R. Hofheinz, Jr. and K.E. Calder, 1982.
20. B. Ohlin, 1967, p. 92.
21. W. Leontief, 1966, p. 90.
22. H. Chenery, 1979, p. 44.
23. R. Hofheinz, Jr. and K.E. Calder, 1982; D. Morawetz, 1981, pp. 132-142.
24. G. Edgren, 1982, p. 19.
25. D. Morawetz, 1981, pp. 132-142.
26. R. Vernon, 1971; G.K. Helleiner, 1973; M. Sharpton, 1975.
27. For an application of these concepts see H.B. Chenery and H. Hughes, 1973; H. Chenery, 1979, Chapter 3. For a somewhat different approach see R.A. Batchelor, 1980b.
28. B. Ohlin, 1967, p. 92.
29. G. Fels, 1972, p. 77.
30. H.B. Lary, 1968; G.C. Hufbauer, 1970; S. Hirsch, 1974b and 1977; B. Balassa, 1977.
31. K.J. Arrow, H.B. Chenery, B.S. Minhas and R.M. Solow, 1961.
32. P. Samuelson, 1951-52, pp. 121, 122.
33. H.B. Lary, 1968, p. 72.
34. B. Herman, 1975, p. 17.
35. A.S. Bhalla, 1981, pp. 35-39.
36. B.S. Minhas, 1962; G. Fels, 1972; W. Leontief, 1977; S. Teitel, 1978; A.L. Hillman and S. Hirsch, 1979.
37. G. Fels, 1972, pp. 77-90.
38. S. Teitel, 1978, p. 330.
39. A.L. Hillman and S. Hirsch, 1979, p. 276.
40. H. Hughes and G. Ohlin, 1980, p. 283.
41. See J. Friedmann, 1979.
42. B. Balassa and Associates, 1971 and 1982.
43. A.V. Deardorff and R.M. Stern, 1983, Table 20.1, pp. 674, 675. The study presents tariff rates that will be applicable after completion of the annually phased reductions in the Tokyo Round in 1987.
44. See S. Hirsch, 1974b, pp. 538-542.
45. For a discussion of the effect of population size on the volume and composition of manufactured exports, see Chapter 3.
46. B. Ohlin, 1967, pp. 61, 62.
47. J.S. Castro, 1982, pp. 28, 29.
48. D. Ramanayake, 1982, pp. 47, 48.
49. M. Datta-Chaudhuri, 1982, p. 20.
50. Chia Siow Yue, 1982, Table 7, p. 35.
51. M. Kei, 1977, p. 71.
52. J.P. Zenger, 1977, p. 85.
53. For additional evidence on the role of female workers and on wage levels in export industries in some Asian countries, see Chapters 11-17.
54. G. Edgren, 1982, p. 34.
55. For a summary of case studies see G. Edgren, 1982, pp. 17-19.

NOTES

56. Cited in G. Edgren, 1982, p. 19.
57. J. Nugent, 1985, p. 105.

CHAPTER 7

1. T. Scitovsky, 1954.
2. R. Hsia, 1981, p. 120.
3. S.B. Linder, 1967, p. 11.
4. S.B. Linder, 1967, p. 50; C. Hsieh, 1973, pp. 2–4.
5. H.W. Singer, 1950; W.A. Lewis, 1954; H. Myint, 1954/55; G. Myrdal, 1957; H. Myint, 1958; H.B. Chenery, 1961; S.B. Linder, 1961; R. Prebisch, 1962; A. Emmanuel, 1972; J.C.H. Fei and G. Ranis, 1975; T. Szentes, 1976, Chapter VI; H. Singer and J. Ansari, 1982, pp. 35–42 and 63–65.
6. H.B. Chenery, 1961, p. 22.
7. G. Myrdal, 1957, pp. 54–55.
8. W.G. Tyler, 1974, p. 370; H.F. Lydall, 1975, Chapter 6; H.W. Singer, 1975, pp. 8–9; H.W. Singer, 1978, pp. 97–98.
9. Y. Sabolo, 1975, pp. 58–59 and Appendix 2.
10. W. Galenson, 1963; A.S. Bhalla, 1973.
11. Y. Sabolo, 1975, p. 49 and Appendix 2.
12. H.F. Lydall, 1975, pp. 97–100.
13. UNIDO, 1974, pp. 222–231.
14. ECAFE, 1970, p. 32. This study is devoted to sectoral output and employment projections 1970–1980 for nine Far East and Asian developing countries.
15. L. Squire, 1981, p. 149.
16. These growth rates and the ones that follow in this section are defined as average annual growth rates which are based on index numbers indicating trends in value added at constant prices. They are calculated from United Nations, *The Growth of World Industry, 1969 Edition*, Vol. I; *The Growth of World Industry, 1972 Edition*, Vol I; United Nations, *Yearbook of Industrial Statistics, 1977 Edition*, Vol. I; and United Nations, *Monthly Bulletin of Statistics*, Vol. XXXVI, May 1982, No. 5, Special Table A. Developing market economies include Caribbean, Central and South America, Africa (other then South Africa) and Asian Middle East and East and South East Asia (other than Israel and Japan).
17. UNIDO, 1973, p. 19 and Table 13; UNIDO, 1974, pp. 16–19; UNIDO, 1979, pp. 76–79.
18. T. Tsuchiya, 1977, p. 1.
19. UNIDO, *Lima Declaration and Plan of Action on Industrial Development and Cooperation*. UNIDO public information pamphlet P1/38, 1975; United Nations, *Programme of Action on the Establishment of a New International Economic Order*, General Assembly resolution 3202 (S. VI), 1 May 1974.
20. UNIDO, 1975, Plan of Action, Chapter I.
21. R.B. Sutcliffe, 1964, p. 623.
22. W.A. Lewis, 1955, p. 278.
23. W.A. Lewis, 1955, p. 278–281.
24. A.O. Hirschman, 1958, pp. 50–54.
25. A.O. Hirschman, 1958, p. 25.
26. A.O. Hirschman, 1958, p. 74.
27. A.O. Hirschman, 1958, p. 100.
28. B. Higgins, 1968, p. 342; R.B. Sutcliffe, 1964, pp. 625–626.
29. T.K. Morrison, 1976b; M. Sharpston, 1975.

30. J. Riedel, 1975.
31. I.M.D. Little, 1981, p. 41.

CHAPTER 8

1. H.B. Chenery and P.G. Clark, 1962, p. 7.
2. W. Leontief, 1966, p. 134.
3. K.N. Raj, 1975.
4. *Input-Output Table Indonesia 1971*, Volume I, Central Bureau of Statistics, Bank Indonesia, Institute of Developing Economies, Center for South-East Asian Studies, Kyoday and Tokyo, 1977, Section 3.7, pp. 23-25.
5. W. Leontief, 1966, p. 138.
6. B. Balassa and Associates, 1971, Chapter 1 and Appendix A; W.M. Corden, 1971, Chapter 3.
7. B. Balassa and Associates, 1971, p. 53. This study includes the six developing countries of Brazil, Chile, Mexico, West Malaysia, Pakistan and the Philippines, and the developed country Norway. The free-trade input-output coefficients are primarily based on the input-output tables of Belgium and the Netherlands.
8. H.B. Chenery and P.G. Clark, 1962, pp. 33-42 and 157-158.
9. H.B. Chenery and T. Watanabe, 1958; A.O. Hirschman, 1958, in particular Chapter 6. See also Section 7.7 of this study.
10. P.A. Yotopoulos and J.B. Nugent, 1973, p. 161.
11. L.P. Jones, 1976, p. 325.
12. P.N. Rasmussen, 1956, pp. 133-140.
13. P.N. Rasmussen, 1956, p. 135.
14. S. Schultz, 1977.
15. This index of net foreign-exchange earnings is also presented in *Input-Output Table Indonesia 1971*, Volume I, Central Bureau of Statistics, Bank Indonesia, Institute of Developing Economies, Center for South-East Asian Studies, Kyoday and Tokyo, 1977, pp. 28-29; and *Input-Output Table of Thailand for Analytical Uses 1975*, NESDB, IDE and NSO, Bangkok and Tokyo, 1980, p. 10.
16. H.B. Chenery and P.G. Clark, 1962, pp. 63-65. See also P.A. Yotopoulos and J.B. Nugent, 1976, p. 268; J.J. Stern, 1977, pp. 22-23.

CHAPTER 9

1. Some selected studies on the subject of economic growth and the development of production structures are: W.A. Lewis, 1955; S. Kuznets, 1966; W. Leontief, 1966, Chapter 4; H.B. Chenery and T. Watanabe, 1958; H.B. Chenery and L.J. Taylor, 1968; H.B. Chenery and M. Syrquin, 1975; H.B. Chenery, 1979.
2. H.B. Chenery and M. Syrquin, 1975, p. 5.
3. W. Leontief, 1966, p. 44.
4. W. Leontief, 1966, p. 42.
5. K. Marx, 1889, p. xvii (author's preface to the first edition of *Capital*, 1867).
6. S. Kuznets, 1966, Chapters 3, 4, 5 and 8.
7. H.B. Chenery and L.J. Taylor, 1968; H.B. Chenery and M. Syrquin, 1975.
8. H.B. Chenery and M. Syrquin, 1975, p. 3.
9. W. Leontief, A.P. Carter and P.A. Petri, 1977.
10. J.J. Stern and J.D. Lewis, 1980.
11. P. van Dijck, 1986, Chapter 6.
12. J.J. Stern and J.D. Lewis, 1980, Section II, pp. 7-9 and p. 37, note 1.

NOTES

13. H.B. Chenery and M. Syrquin, 1980; H.B. Chenery, 1982.
14. See, for instance, UNIDO, 1979, pp. 43–51 and Annex I; H.B. Chenery and M. Syrquin, 1975, pp. 74–89.
15. See Sections 3.4.3 and 3.5.
16. See Section 3.6.
17. W. Leontief, 1966, p. 49.
18. W. Leontief, 1966, pp. 44–48.
19. H.B. Chenery and T. Watanabe, 1958.
20. P.A. Yotopoulos and J.B. Nugent, 1973. The countries included are Canada, Israel, Japan, Sweden, the United Kingdom, the United States, Chile, Greece, South Korea, Mexico and Spain.
21. S. Schultz, 1977. The countries included are India, Indonesia, Iran, South Korea, Malaysia, Pakistan, the Philippines, Sri Lanka, Taiwan, Turkey, Israel, Yugoslavia, West Germany and Japan.
22. D. Chakraborty, 1975; P.S. Laumas, 1975. In both studies the countries included are Taiwan, South Korea, Malaysia and Sri Lanka. The authors arrive at different findings, as Laumas' measures of sectoral interdependence are weighted by the importance of each sector in final demand.
23. See also A.O. Hirschman, 1958, p. 107.
24. A.O. Hirschman, 1958, p. 117.
25. P.N. Rasmussen, 1956, pp. 140–141.
26. W.A. Lewis, 1954; G. Ranis and J.C.H. Fei, 1961.
27. T. Szentes, 1976, p. 74.
28. A.O. Hirschman, 1958, p. 109.
29. A.O. Hirschman, 1958, p. 112.
30. W. Leontief, 1966, p. 49.
31. S. Amin, 1974, pp. 261–302.
32. A. de Janvry, 1981, pp. 32–60.
33. W.G. Tyler, 1974.
34. H.F. Lydall, 1975.
35. H.F. Lydall, 1975, Tables 22–23, pp. 88–89.
36. H.F. Lydall, 1975, Table 25, p. 102.
37. A.O. Krueger et al., 1981. The country studies include Brazil, Chile, Colombia, Indonesia, Ivory Coast, Pakistan, South Korea, Thailand, Tunisia and Uruguay.
38. This evaluation is based on the aforementioned cross-country studies and S. Watanabe, 1972b; S. Watanabe, 1974; W.G. Tyler, 1976; Tzong-biau Lin and Victor Mok, 1978; Kuo-shu Liang and Ching-ing Hou Liang, 1975; Kuo-shu Liang and Ching-ing Hou Liang, 1978; R.M. Bautista, 1975; R.G. Nambiar, 1979.
39. See Chapter 4, in particular Section 4.5.
40. See special issue of AMPO: *Japan-Asia Quarterly Review*, 1977; F. Fröbel, J. Heinrichs and O. Kreye, 1980, Part III; J.S. Castro, 1982, Chapter IV; M.K. Datta-Chaudhuri, 1982, Chapter III; A. Basile and D. Germidis, 1984, pp. 46–50.

CHAPTER 10

1. See Section 4.1.
2. United Nations, *Indexes to the International Standard Industrial Classification of All Economic Activities*, Statistical Papers, Series M, No. 4, Rev. 2, Add. 1, New York, 1971.
3. See Section 5.4.

CHAPTER 11

1. Data in this section are derived from UNCTAD, *Handbook of International Trade and Development Statistics 1981 — Supplement*, United Nations, New York, 1982, Table 6.2; World Bank, *World Development Report*, Oxford University Press, New York, various issues, Table 1.
2. M.M. Pitt, 1981, pp. 182-186.
3. D.S. Paauw, 1981, p. 151.
4. J.B. Donges, B. Stecher, F. Wolter, 1974, p. 25.
5. H. Poot, 1981, Table 3.8, p. 93.
6. United Nations, *Statistical Yearbook for Asia and the Pacific*, 1980, ESCAP, Bangkok, Table 10, p. 197.
7. H. Poot, 1981, Table 3.2, p. 81.
8. P. McCawley, 1981, p. 67.
9. M.M. Pitt, 1981, Section 5.3, pp. 204-211, and Table 5A.1, pp. 226-229.
10. H. Poot, 1981, Table 3.9, p. 96; P. McCawley, 1981, p. 80.
11. R.M. Bautista, 1982, pp. 45-49.
12. R.M. Bautista, 1982, p. 46.
13. P. McCawley, 1981, Table 3.4, p. 68.
14. H. Poot, 1981, pp. 103-105 and Section 3.5, pp. 108-124.
15. This example is mentioned by P. McCawley, 1981, p. 77.

CHAPTER 12

1. Data in this section are derived from UNCTAD, *Handbook of International Trade and Development Statistics*, United Nations, New York, various issues, Table 6.2; World Bank, *World Development Report*, Oxford University Press, New York, various issues, Table 1.
2. R.M. Bautista, J.H. Power and Associates, 1979, Chapter 2.
3. The average annual growth rates of real manufacturing production given in this section are calculated from G.M. Jurado, R.D. Ferrer and E.F. Esguerra, 1983, Table 9, p. 40.
4. R.M. Bautista, J.H. Power and Associates, 1979, p. 40.
5. J.S. Castro, 1982, pp. 18-23.
6. N.A. Tan, 1979, Table 1, pp. 139-143 and Table 5, p. 148.
7. See for more details R.M. Bautista, 1982, pp. 35-39.
8. ILO, 1974, Table 23, p. 142.
9. See, for instance, ILO, 1974, pp. 140-148; R.M. Bautista, J.H. Power and Associates, 1979, pp. 32-34.
10. J.S. Castro, 1982, Table 6, p. 17. According to Basile and Germidis, exports from the Bataan EPFZ accounted for only 6.8 per cent of total manufactured exports in 1979, see A. Basile and D. Germidis, 1984, Table 15.
11. J.S. Castro, 1982, pp. 26-27.

CHAPTER 13

1. Data in this section are derived from UNCTAD, *Handbook of International Trade and Development Statistics*, United Nations, New York, various issues, Table 6.2; World Bank, *World Development Report*, Oxford University Press, New York, various issues, Table 1.
2. For a detailed review of Thailand's postwar industrialization and trade strategies, see N. Akrasanee, 1975; and N. Akrasanee, 1981.

NOTES

3. NESDB, *National Income of Thailand*, Bangkok, various issues.
4. See for more details on Thailand's export-promotion policy S. Tambunlertchai, 1984.
5. N. Akrasanee, 1980.
6. S. Tambunlertchai, 1984, p. 112.
7. NESDB, *National Income of Thailand*, Bangkok, various issues.

CHAPTER 14

1. Data in this section are derived from UNCTAD, *Handbook of International Trade and Development Statistics*, United Nations, New York, various issues, Table 6.2; World Bank, *World Development Report*, Oxford University Press, New York, various issues, Table 1.
2. This section draws especially on L.E. Westphal and Kwang Suk Kim, 1977; L.E. Westphal, 1978; P. Hasan, 1976.
3. M.K. Datta-Chaudhuri, 1981, p. 60.
4. L.E. Westphal, 1978.
5. L.E. Westphal, 1978, p. 359.
6. L.E. Westphal, Y.W. Rhee and G. Pursell, 1981, pp. 53–58.
7. E. Lee, 1981, p. 195.
8. R. Hsia, 1981, p. 141.
9. United Nations, *Statistical Yearbook for Asia and the Far East*, ESCAP, Bangkok, 1981.
10. M.K. Datta-Chaudhuri, 1981, p. 56.
11. P. Hasan, 1976, p. 29.
12. M.K. Datta-Chaudhuri, 1981, p. 62.
13. UNCTAD, 1983, Table VIII, p. 40.

CHAPTER 15

1. Unless otherwise indicated, data in this chapter are derived from *Taiwan Statistical Data Book 1981*, Council for Economic Planning and Development, Executive Yuan, Republic of China, 1981.
2. S.P.S. Ho, 1978, Chapter 5.
3. S.P.S. Ho, 1978, p. 191.
4. G. Ranis, 1979, pp. 211–221.
5. S.P.S. Ho, 1978, pp. 111–120.
6. G. Ranis, 1979, pp. 214–215.
7. For a detailed review of policy reforms, see M. Scott, 1979, pp. 321–345.
8. S.P.S. Ho, 1978, p. 198; G. Ranis, 1979, p. 220; T.H. Lee and Kou-Shu Liang, 1982, pp. 310–332.
9. G. Ranis, 1979, Table 3.28, p. 250.
10. G. Ranis, 1979, p. 241.
11. J.C.H. Fei, G. Ranis, S.W.Y. Kuo, 1979, p. 34.
12. G. Ranis, 1979, pp. 221–222.
13. E. Thorbecke, 1979, pp. 184–187.
14. A. Basile and D. Germidis, 1984, Table 15, p. 50.
15. M. Scott, 1979, p. 338.
16. J.C.H. Fei, G. Ranis, S.W.Y. Kuo, 1979, Table 4.3, p. 136.

17. W. Galenson, 1979, pp. 416–419.
18. W. Galenson, 1979, pp. 391–395.
19. W. Galenson, 1979, pp. 391–395.
20. W. Galenson, 1979, p. 393, note 16; M. Scott, 1979, Table 5.7, p. 337.

CHAPTER 16

1. Data in this section are derived from UNCTAD, *Handbook of International Trade and Development Statistics*, United Nations, New York, various issues, Table 6.2; World Bank, *World Development Report*, Oxford University Press, New York, various issues, Table 1.
2. See for a more detailed treatment of industrialization and trade strategies in Malaysia, M. Ariff, Chee Peng Lim and D. Lee, 1984, Chapters 2 and 3.
3. J.H. Power, 1971; L. Hoffman and Tan Siew Ee, 1980, Chapter III; M. Ariff, Chee Peng Lim and D. Lee, 1984, Chapter 2.
4. Data on manufacturing growth given in this section are derived from United Nations, *Statistical Yearbook for Asia and the Far East*, ESCAP, Bangkok, various issues.
5. Chee Peng Lim, D. Lee and Foo Kok Thye, 1981, pp. 264–265.
6. M. Ariff, Chee Peng Lim and D. Lee, 1984, Chapter 3.
7. M.K. Datta-Chaudhuri, 1982, pp. 15–17.
8. Khor Kok Peng, 1983, Table 7.3, p. 78.
9. M. Ariff, Chee Peng Lim and D. Lee, 1984, Section 3.3.
10. M.K. Datta-Chaudhuri, 1982, p. 28.
11. M.K. Datta-Chaudhuri, 1982, Table A-1, p. 36.

CHAPTER 17

1. J. Wong, 1979, pp. 71–72.
2. Chia Siow Yue, 1982, pp. 1–6.
3. Data in this section are derived from UNCTAD, *Handbook of International Trade and Development Statistics*, United Nations, New York, various issues, Table 6.2; World Bank, *World Development Report*, Oxford University Press, New York, various issues, Table 1.
4. See for a more detailed treatment of industrialization and trade strategies in Singapore, K. Yoshihara, 1976; Chia Siow Yue, 1982; Chia Siow Yue, 1984; L. Lim and Pang Eng Fong, 1982.
5. Nyaw Mee-Kau, 1979.
6. The real growth rates of manufacturing value added given in this section are based on United Nations, *Yearbook of National Account Statistics*, Volume I, New York, various issues.
7. F. von Kirchbach, 1982, Table 4.
8. Chia Siow Yue, 1982, pp. 54–61.
9. *Yearbook of Statistics Singapore, 1982/83*, Department of Statistics, Singapore, Table 31.
10. If 1973 is the base year, the GDP deflator for manufacturing production reached 139.7 in 1978, *Yearbook of Statistics Singapore, 1982/83*, Department of Statistics, Singapore, Table 4.5.

11. *Report on the Census of Industrial Production 1973*, Department of Statistics, Singapore, 1975, Table 17; *Report on the Census of Industrial Production 1978*, Department of Statistics, Singapore, 1979, Table 40.
12. L. Lim and Pang Eng Fong, 1982, pp. 103–112.

CHAPTER 18

1. W.Galenson, 1979, p. 395.
2. P. van Dijck and H. Verbruggen (eds.), 1984, Table 7, p. 32.
3. Chia Siow Yue, 1982, p. 72.
4. B. Balassa, 1981, pp. 1–24; Y.C. Park, 1981, pp. 111–114.
5. Y.C. Park, 1981, pp. 111–114; I.M.D. Little, 1979, pp. 501–507.

Bibliography

Akrasanee, N. *The Structure of Effective Protection in Thailand: A Study of Industrial and Trade Policies in the Early 1970s*. Report prepared for the Ministry of Finance, the National Economic and Social Development Board of the Government of Thailand, and the International Bank for Reconstruction and Development (Washington, 1975), mimeographed.

_____. *Industrial Sector in the Thai Economy*. Thai University Research Association, Research Report No. 1 (Bangkok, 1980), mimeographed.

_____. "Trade Strategy for Employment Growth in Thailand", in A.O. Krueger, H.B. Lary, T. Monson and N. Akrasanee (eds.), 1981.

Amin, S. *Accumulation on a World Scale — A Critique of the Theory of Underdevelopment* (New York and London, 1974).

Amjad, R. (ed.), *The Development of Labour Intensive Industry in ASEAN Countries*. Asian Employment Programme (Geneva and Bangkok, 1981).

AMPO, "Free Trade Zones and Industrialization of Asia", Special Issue of AMPO: *Japan-Asia Quarterly Review*, Vol. 8, No. 4 and Vol. 9, Nos. 1–2, 1977.

Anderson, K. and R.E. Baldwin. *The Political Market for Protection in Industrial Countries: Empirical Evidence*. World Bank Staff Working Paper No. 492 (Washington, 1981).

Ariff, M., Chee Peng Lim and D. Lee. "Export Incentives, Manufactured Exports and Employment: Malaysia", Discussion Paper Series No. 84E09, Council for Asian Manpower Studies (Quezon City, 1984), mimeographed.

Arrow, K.J., H.B. Chenery, B.S. Minhas and R.M. Solow. "Capital-Labor Substitution and Economic Efficiency", *The Review of Economics and Statistics*, Vol. 43, No. 3, 1961.

Balassa, B. "Country Size and Trade Patterns: Comment", *The American Economic Review*, Vol. 59, No. 1, 1969.

_____. *Reforming the System of Incentives in Developing Countries*. World Bank Staff Working Paper No. 203 (Washington, 1975).

———. *Some Effects of Commercial Policy on International Trade, the Location of Production, and Factor Movement.* World Bank Staff Working Paper No. 236 (Washington, 1976).

———. *A "Stages" Approach to Comparative Advantage.* World Bank Staff Working Paper No. 256 (Washington, 1977).

———. "Export Incentives and Export Performance in Developing Countries: a Comparative Analysis", *Weltwirtschaftliches Archiv*, Vol. 114, 1978.

———. *The Newly Industrializing Countries in the World Economy* (New York, 1981).

———. "Structural Adjustment Policies in Developing Economies", *World Development*, Vol. 10, No. 1, 1982a.

———. "The Structure of Incentives in Six Semi-Industrial Economies", in B. Balassa and Associates, 1982b.

——— and Associates. *The Structure of Protection in Developing Countries* (Baltimore and London, 1971).

———. *Development Strategies in Semi-Industrial Economies* (Baltimore and London, 1982).

Baldwin, R.E. "The Case against Infant-Industry Tariff Protection", *The Journal of Political Economy*, Vol. 77, 1969.

———. "The Political Economy of Protectionism", in J.N. Bhagwati (ed.), 1982.

Basile, A. and D. Germidis. *Investing in Free Export Processing Zones* (Paris, 1984).

Batchelor, R.A. "The Process of Industrialisation", in R.A. Batchelor, R.L. Major and A.D. Morgan, 1980a.

———. "Development Patterns and the Basis for Trade", in R.A. Batchelor, R.L. Major and A.D. Morgan, 1980b.

———, R.L. Major and A.D. Morgan. *Industrialisation and the Basis for Trade* (Cambridge, 1980).

Bautista, R.M. "Employment Effects of Export Expansion in the Philippines", *The Malayan Economic Review*, Vol. 20, No. 1, 1975.

———. "ASEAN New Industrial Development Strategy". Paper presented at a conference on *ASEAN-EEC Economic Relations*, Brussels, organized by the Institute of Southeast Asian Studies (Singapore, 1982).

———, J.H. Power and Associates. *Industrial Promotion Policies in the Philippines*. Philippine Institute for Development Studies (Manila, 1979).

———, H. Hughes, D. Lim, D. Morawetz and F.E. Thoumi. *Capital Utilization in Manufacturing — Colombia, Israel, Malaysia, and the Philippines* (New York, 1981).

Bhagwati, J.N. (ed.). *Import Competition and Response* (Chicago and London, 1982).

―――― and T.N. Srinivasan. *Lectures on International Trade* (Cambridge and London, 1983).

Bhalla, A.S. "The Role of Services in Employment Expansion", in R. Jolly, E. de Kadt, H. Singer and F. Wilson (eds.). *Third World Employment —Problems and Strategy* (Baltimore, 1973).

――――. "The Concept and Measurement of Labour Intensity", in A.S. Bhalla (ed.), *Technology and Employment in Industry — A Case Study Approach* (Geneva, 1981).

Booth, A. and P. McCawley (eds.). *The Indonesian Economy During the Soeharto Era* (Kuala Lumpur, 1981).

Bosson, R. and B. Varon. *The Mining Industry and the Developing Countries* (New York, 1977).

Castro, J.S. *The Bataan Export Processing Zone.* Asian Employment Programme Working Papers, ILO-ARTEP (Bangkok, 1982).

Chakraborty, D. "A Study of the Production Structure of ECAFE Countries: An International Comparison", *The Asian Economic Review*, Vol. 17, Nos. 1–3, 1975.

Chee Peng Lim, D. Lee and Foo Kok Thye. "The Case for Labour Intensive Industries in Malaysia", in R. Amjad (ed.), 1981.

Chen, E.K.Y. "Hong Kong Multinationals in Asia: Characteristics and Objectives", in K. Kumar and M.G. McLeod (eds.), 1981.

Chenery, H.B. "Comparative Advantage and Development Policy", *The American Economic Review*, Vol. 51, No. 1, 1961.

――――. *Structural Change and Development Policy* (New York, 1979).

――――. *Industrialization and Growth — The Experience of Large Countries.* World Bank Staff Working Paper No. 539 (Washington, 1982).

―――― and P.G. Clark. *Interindustry Economies* (New York, 1962).

―――― and H. Hughes. "Industrialization and Trade Trends: Some Issues for the 1970s", in H. Hughes (ed.), *Prospects for Partnership, Industrialization and Trade Policies in the 1970s* (Baltimore and London, 1973).

―――― and M. Syrquin. *Patterns of Development, 1950–1970* (Oxford, 1975).

―――― and M. Syrquin. "A Comparative Analysis of Industrial Growth", in R.C.O. Matthews (ed.), *Economic Growth and Resources*, Volume 2: *Trends and Factors* (London and Basingstoke, 1980).

―――― and L.J. Taylor. "Development Patterns: Among Countries and Over Time", *The Review of Economics and Statistics*, Vol. 50, No. 4, 1968.

―――― and T. Watanabe. "International Comparisons of the Structure of Production", *Econometrica*, Vol. 26, No. 4, 1958.

Chia Siow Yue. *Export Processing and Industrialisation: The Case of Singapore.* Asian Employment Programme Working Papers, ILO-ARTEP (Bangkok, 1982).

――――. "Export Incentives, Manufactured Export and Employment in

Singapore", in P. van Dijck and H. Verbruggen (eds.), 1984.
Cizauskas, A.C. *The Changing Nature of Export Credit Finance and Its Implications for Developing Countries.* World Bank Staff Working Paper No. 409 (Washington, 1980).
Cohen, B.I. *Multinational Firms and Asian Exports* (New Haven and London, 1975).
Corden, W.M. *The Theory of Protection* (Oxford, 1971).
_____. *Trade Policy and Economic Welfare* (Oxford, 1974).
Datta-Chaudhuri, M.K. "Industrialisation and Foreign Trade: The Development Experiences of South Korea and The Philippines", in E. Lee (ed.), 1981.
_____. *The Role of Free Trade Zones in the Creation of Employment and Industrial Growth in Malaysia.* Asian Employment Programme Working Papers, ILO-ARTEP (Bangkok, 1982).
Deardorff, A.V. and R.M. Stern. "The Economic Effects of Complete Elimination of Post-Tokyo Round Tariffs", in W.R. Cline (ed.), *Trade Policy in the 1980s* (Washington, 1983).
Dijck, P. van. *Causes and Characteristics of Export-Oriented Industrialization in Developing Countries* (Amsterdam, 1986).
_____ and E. Hoogteijling. *Causes and Effects of Protectionism in Developing Countries.* Economic and Social Institute, Free University (Amsterdam, 1985), mimeographed.
_____ and H. Verbruggen (eds.), *Export-Oriented Industrialization and Employment: Policies and Responses — With Special Reference to ASEAN Countries.* Council for Asian Manpower Studies (Manila, 1984).
Donges, J.B. "A Comparative Survey of Industrialization Policies in Fifteen Semi-Industrial Countries", *Weltwirtschaftliches Archiv*, Vol. 112, 1976.
_____ and J. Riedel. "The Expansion of Manufactured Exports in Developing Countries: An Empirical Assessment of Supply and Demand Issues", *Weltwirtschaftliches Archiv*, Vol. 113, 1977.
_____ , B. Stecher and F. Wolter. *Industrial Development Policies for Indonesia*, Kieler Studien 126 (Tübingen, 1974).
Dunning, J.H. *International Production and the Multinational Enterprise* (London, 1981).
ECAFE. *Sectoral Output and Employment Projects for the Second Development Decade.* Development Programming Techniques Series No. 8 (Bangkok, 1970).
Edgren, G. *Spearheads of Industrialisation or Sweatshops in the Sun?: A Critical Appraisal of Labour Conditions in Asian Export Processing Zones.* Asian Employment Programme Working Papers, ILO-ARTEP (Bangkok, 1982).

Emmanuel, A. *Unequal Exchange: A Study of the Imperialism of Trade* (New York and London, 1972).
Feenstra, R.C. and J.N. Bhagwati. "Tariff Seeking and the Efficient Tariff", in J.N. Bhagwati (ed.), 1982.
Fei, J.C.H. and G. Ranis. "A Model of Growth and Employment in the Open Dualistic Economy: The Cases of Korea and Taiwan", *The Journal of Development Studies*, Vol. 11, No. 2, 1975.
_____, G. Ranis and S.W.Y. Kuo. *Growth with Equity — The Taiwan Case* (New York, 1979).
Fels, G. "The Choice of Industry Mix in the Division of Labour between Developed and Developing Countries", *Weltwirtschaftliches Archiv*, Vol. 108, 1972.
Frank, A.G. *Crisis: In the Third World* (London, 1981).
Friedman, J. "The Crisis of Transition: A Critique of Strategies of Crisis Management", *Development and Change*, Vol. 10, No. 1, 1979.
Fröbel, F., J. Heinrichs and O. Kreye. *The New International Division of Labour — Structural Unemployment in Industrialised Countries and Industrialisation in Developing Countries* (Cambridge, 1980).
Galenson, W. "Economic Development and the Sectoral Expansion of Employment", *International Labour Review*, Vol. 87, No. 6, 1963.
_____. "The Labor Force, Wages, and Living Standards", in W. Galenson (ed.), 1979.
_____(ed.), *Economic Growth and Structural Change in Taiwan — The Postwar Experience of the Republic of China* (Ithaca and London, 1979).
Germidis, D. "International Subcontracting and Industrialisation of the Third World: Problems and Perspectives", in D. Germidis (ed.), 1980.
_____(ed.), *International Subcontracting — A New Form of Investment* (Paris, 1980).
Giersch, H. (ed.). *The International Division of Labour — Problems and Perspectives* (Tübingen, 1974).
Haberler, G. *The Theory of International Trade — With Its Applications to Commercial Policy* (London, 1950).
Hasan, P. *Korea — Problems and Issues in a Rapidly Growing Economy* (Baltimore and London, 1976).
Heinrichs, J. "The Impact of the New International Division of Labour on the Patterns of Transfer of Technology and the Related Social Costs", in D. Ernst (ed.), *The New International Division of Labour, Technology, and Underdevelopment — Consequences for the Third World* (Frankfurt, 1980).
Helleiner, G.K. "Manufactured Exports from Less-Developed Countries and Multinational Firms", *The Economic Journal*, Vol. 83, 1973.
_____. "Transnational Enterprises and the New Political Economy of U.S.

Trade Policy", *Oxford Economic Papers*, Vol. 29, No. 1, 1977.
Herman, B. *The Optimal International Division of Labour* (Geneva, 1975).
Higgins, B. *Economic Development — Principles, Problems and Policies* (London, 1968).
Hillman, A.L. and S. Hirsch. "Factor Intensity Reversals: Conceptual Experiments with Traded Goods Aggregates", *Weltwirtschaftliches Archiv*, Vol. 115, 1979.
Hirsch, S. *Location of Industry and International Competitiveness* (Oxford, 1967).
_____. "Hypotheses regarding Trade between Developing and Industrial Countries", in H. Giersch (ed.), 1974a.
_____. "Capital or Technology? Confronting the Neo-Factor Proportions and Neo-Technology Accounts of International Trade", *Weltwirtschaftliches Archiv*, Vol. 110, 1974b.
_____. *Rich Man's, Poor Man's, and Every Man's Goods — Aspects of Industrialization* (Tübingen, 1977).
Hirschman, A.O. *The Strategy of Economic Development* (New Haven, 1958).
Ho, S.P.S. *Economic Development of Taiwan, 1860–1970* (New Haven and London, 1978).
Hoffman, L. and Tan Siew Ee. *Industrial Growth, Employment and Foreign Investment in Peninsular Malaysia* (Kuala Lumpur, 1980).
Hofheinz, Jr., R. and K.E. Calder. *The Eastasia Edge* (New York, 1982).
Hone, A. "Multinational Corporations and Multinational Buying Groups: Their Impact on the Growth of Asia's Exports of Manufactures — Myths and Realities", *World Development*, Vol. 2, No. 2, 1974.
Hsia, R. "Technological Change, Trade Promotion and Export-Led Industrialisation in Hong Kong and South Korea", in E. Lee (ed.), 1981.
Hsieh, C. "Measuring the Effects of Trade Expansion on Employment: A Review of Some Research", *International Labour Review*, Vol. 107, No. 1, 1973.
Hufbauer, G.C. *Synthetic Materials and the Theory of International Trade* (London, 1966).
_____. "The Impact of National Characteristics and Technology on the Commodity Composition of Trade in Manufactured Goods", in R. Vernon (ed.), *The Technology Factor in International Trade* (New York, 1970).
Hughes, H. and G. Ohlin. "The International Environment", in J. Cody, H. Hughes and D. Wall (eds.), *Policies for Industrial Progress in Developing Countries* (New York, 1980).
ILO. *Sharing in Development — A Programme of Employment, Equity and Growth for the Philippines*. A WEP Study (Geneva, 1974).

Janvry, A. de. *The Agrarian Question and Reformism in Latin America* (Baltimore and London, 1981).

Johnson, H.G. "Optimal Trade Intervention in the Presence of Domestic Distortion", in J.N. Bhagwati (ed.), *International Trade: Selected Readings* (Cambridge and London, 1981).

Jones, L.P. "The Measurement of Hirschmanian Linkages", *The Quarterly Journal of Economics*, Vol. 90, No. 2, 1976.

Jurado, G.M., R.D. Ferrer and E.F. Esquerra. *Trade Policy, Growth and Employment: A Study of the Philippines*. WEP Research Working Paper, ILO (Geneva, 1983).

Keesing, D.B. "Population and Industrial Development: Some Evidence from Trade Patterns", *The American Economic Review*, Vol. 58, No. 3, 1968.

――――. *Trade Policy for Developing Countries*. World Bank Staff Working Paper, No. 353 (Washington, 1979).

―――― and D.R. Sherk. "Population Density in Patterns of Trade and Development", *The American Economic Review*, Vol. 61, No. 5, 1971.

Khor Kok Peng. *The Malaysian Economy — Structures and Dependence* (Kuala Lumpur and Singapore, 1983).

Kirchbach, F. von. "Transnational Corporations in the ASEAN Region: A Survey of Major Issues", *Economic Bulletin for Asia and the Pacific*, Vol. 33, No. 1, 1982.

Kojima, K. *Direct Foreign Investment — A Japanese Model of Multinational Business Operations* (London, 1978).

―――― and T. Ozawa. *Japan's General Trading Companies — Merchants of Economic Development* (Paris, 1984).

Krueger, A.O. "The Political Economy of the Rent-Seeking Society", *The American Economic Review*, Vol. 64, No. 3, 1974.

――――. *Foreign Trade Regimes and Economic Development: Liberalization Attempts and Consequences* (Cambridge, 1978).

――――, H.B. Lary, T. Monson and N. Akrasanee (eds.). *Trade and Employment in Developing Countries*, Volume I: *Individual Studies* (Chicago and London, 1981).

Kumar, K. and M.G. McLeod (eds.). *Multinationals from Developing Countries* (Lexington, 1981).

Kuo-shu Liang and Ching-ing Hou Liang. *Exports and Employment in Taiwan*. Discussion Paper Series No. 75-06, Council for Asian Manpower Studies (Quezon City, 1975), mimeographed.

――――. *Employment and Distribution Implications of Export Expansion in Taiwan*. Discussion Paper Series No. 78-14, Council for Asian Manpower Studies (Quezon City, 1978), mimeographed.

Kuznets, S. *Economic Growth and Structure — Selected Essays* (London, 1965).

_____. *Modern Economic Growth — Rate, Structure and Spread* (New Haven and London, 1966).

Kwang Suk Kim. "Korea's Experience in Managing Development through Planning, Policymaking, and Budgeting", in Miyohei Shinohara, Toru Yanagihara, Kwam Suk Tim and Ramgopal Agarwala (eds.), 1983.

Lall, S. "Transnationals, Domestic Enterprises and Industrial Structure in Host LDCs: A Survey", *Oxford Economic Papers*, Vol. 30, No. 2, 1978.

_____ and P.P. Streeten. *Foreign Investment, Transnationals and Developing Countries* (London and Basingstoke, 1977).

Laumas, P.M. "Key Sectors in Some Underdeveloped Countries", *Kyklos* Vol. 28, No. 1, 1975.

Lary, H.B. *Imports on Manufactures from Less Developed Countries* (New York, 1968).

Lecraw, D.J. "Internationalization of Firms from LDCs: Evidence from the ASEAN Region", in K. Kumar and M.G. McLeod (eds.), 1981.

Lee, E. (ed.). *Export-Led Industrialization & Development*. Asian Employment Programme (Geneva, 1981).

Lee, T.H. and Kuo-Shu Liang. "Taiwan", in B. Belassa and Associates, 1982.

Leontief, W. *Input-Output Economics* (New York, 1966).

_____. "Domestic Production and Foreign Trade: The American Capital Position Re-examined" (1953), in W. Leontief, 1966.

_____. "An International Comparison of Factor Costs and Factor Use", in W. Leontief, *Essays in Economics — Theories, Facts and Policies*, Volume 2 (Oxford, 1977).

_____, A.P. Carter and P.A. Petri. *The Future of the World Economy* (New York, 1977).

Lewis, W.A. "Economic Development with Unlimited Supplies of Labour", *Manchester School of Economic and Social Studies*, Vol. 22, No. 2, 1954.

_____. *The Theory of Economic Growth* (London, 1955).

Lim, L. and Pang Eng Fong. *Trade, Employment and Industrialisation in Singapore*. WEP Research Working Paper, ILO (Geneva, 1982).

Linder, S.B. *An Essay on Trade and Transformation* (New York, 1961).

_____. *Trade and Trade Policy for Development* (London, 1967).

Lipton, M. *Why Poor People Stay Poor — A Study of Urban Bias in World Development* (London, 1977).

Little, I.M.D. "An Economic Reconnaissance", in W. Galenson (ed.), 1979.

_____. "The Experience and Causes of Rapid Labour-Intensive Development in Korea, Taiwan Province, Hong Kong, and Singapore and the Possibilities of Emulation", in E. Lee (ed.), 1981.

Lydall, H.F. *Trade and Employment — A Study of the Effects of Trade Expansion on Employment in Developing and Developed Countries* (Geneva, 1975).

Mahfuzur Rahman, A.H.M. *Exports of Manufactures from Developing Countries — A Study in Comparative Advantage* (Rotterdam, 1973).

Maizels, A. *Growth and Trade* (Cambridge, 1970).

Matsuo Kei. "South Korea: The Working Class in the Masan Free Export Zone". AMPO: *Japan-Asia Quarterly Review*, Vol. 8, No. 4 and Vol. 9, Nos. 1-2 (Special Issue), 1977.

Marx, K. *Capital — A Critical Analysis of Capitalist Production*. Translated from the third German edition by S. Moore and E. Aveling (London, 1889).

McCawley, P. "The Growth of the Industrial Sector", in A. Booth and P. McCawley (eds.), 1981.

Michalet, C.A. "International Sub-Contracting: A State-of-the-Art", in D. Germidis (ed.) (Paris, 1980).

Minhas, B.S. "The Homohypallagic Production Function, Factor-Intensity Reversals, and the Heckscher-Ohlin Theorem", *The Journal of Political Economy*, Vol. 70, No. 1, 1962.

Miyohei Shinohara and Toru Yanagihara. "Japan's Experience in Managing Development", in Miyohei Shinohara, Toru Yanagihara, Kwang Suk Kim and Ramgopal Agarwala (eds.), 1983.

_____, Kwan Suk Kim and Ramgopal Agarwala (eds.). *The Japanese and Korean Experiences in Managing Development*. World Bank Staff Working Paper No. 574 (Washington, 1983).

Morawetz, D. *Why the Emperor's New Clothes Are Not Made in Colombia — A Case Study in Latin American and East Asian Manufactured Exports* (New York, 1981).

Morgan, A.D. "Export Competition and Import Substitution: The Industrial Countries 1963 to 1971", in R.A. Batchelor, R.L. Major and A.D. Morgan, 1980.

Morrison, T.K. *Manufactured Exports from Developing Countries* (New York, 1976a).

_____. "International Subcontracting: Improved Prospects in Manufactured Exports for Small and Very Poor LDC's", *World Development*, Vol. 4, No. 4, 1976b.

Myint, H. "The Gains from International Trade and the Backward Countries", *The Review of Economic Studies*, Vol. 22, 1954-1955.

_____. "The 'Classical Theory' of International Trade and the Underdeveloped Countries", *The Economic Journal*, Vol. 63, 1958.

Myrdal, G. *Economic Theory and Under-Developed Regions* (London, 1957).

Nambiar, R.G. "Employment Through Exports: A Study of India", *Indian Journal of Industrial Relation*, Vol. 15, No. 1, 1979.

Nayyar, D. "Transnational Corporations and Manufactured Exports from

Poor Countries", *The Economic Journal*, Vol. 88, 1978.

Nugent, J. "The Potential for South-South Trade in Capital Goods Industries", *Industry and Development*, No. 14, 1985.

Nyaw Mee-Kau. "A Shift-Share Analysis of the Growth and Structural Change of Manufacturing Industries in Singapore", *International Quarterly for Asian Studies*, Vol. 10, Nos. 3-4, 1979.

Ohlin, B. *Interregional and International Trade* (Cambridge, 1967).

_____. *Some Insufficiencies in the Theories of International Economic Relations*. Essays in International Finance No. 134 (Princeton, 1979).

Olson, M. *The Logic of Collective Action — Public Goods and the Theory of Groups* (Cambridge and London, 1971).

Ozawa, T. *Multinationalism, Japanese Style — The Political Economy of Outward Dependency* (Princeton, 1979).

Park, Y.C. "Export-Led Development: The Korean Experience 1960-78", in E. Lee (ed.), 1981.

Pauw, D.S. "Frustrated Labour-Intensive Development: The Case of Indonesia", in E. Lee (ed.), 1981.

Pincus, J.J. "Pressure Groups and the Pattern of Tariffs", in *The Journal of Political Economy*, Vol. 83, No. 4, 1975.

Pitt, M.M. "Alternative Trade Strategies and Employment in Indonesia", in A.O. Krueger, H.B. Lary, T. Monson and N. Akrasanee (eds.), 1981.

Poot, H. "The Development of Labour-Intensive Industries in Indonesia", in R. Amjad, 1981.

Power, H.J. "The Structure of Protection in West-Malaysia", in B. Balassa and Associates, 1971.

Prebisch, R. "The Economic Development of Latin America and its Principal Problems", *Economic Bulletin for Latin America*, Vol. 7, No. 1, 1962.

Ramanayake, D. *The Katunayake Investment Promotion Zone: A Case Study*. Asian Employment Programme Working Papers, ILO-ARTEP (Bangkok, 1982).

Raj, K.N. "Linkages in Industrialization and Development Strategy: Some Basic Issues", *Journal of Development Planning*, No. 8 (New York, 1975).

Ranis, G. "Industrial Development", in W. Galenson (ed.), 1979.

_____ and J.C.H. Fei. "A Theory of Economic Development", *The American Economic Review*, Vol. 51, No. 4, 1961.

Rasmussen, P.N. *Studies in Inter-Sectoral Relations* (Copenhagen and Amsterdam, 1956).

Reynolds, L.G. *Image and Reality in Economic Development* (New Haven and London, 1977).

Riedel, J. "Factor Proportions, Linkages and the Open Developing Economy", *The Review of Economics and Statistics*, Vol. 57, No. 4,

1975.

Roemer, M. "Resource-Based Industrialization in the Developing Countries — A Survey", *The Journal of Development Economics*, Vol. 6, 1979.

Sabolo, Y. *The Service Industry*. A WEP Study (Geneva, 1975).

Samuelson, P. "A Comment on Factor Price Equalisation", *The Review of Economic Studies*, Vol. 19, 1951-1952.

Schultz, S. "Approaches to Identifying Key Sectors Empirically by Means of Input-Output Analysis", *The Journal of Development Studies*, Vol. 14, No. 1, 1977.

Scitovsky, T. "Two Concepts of External Economies", *The Journal of Political Economy*, Vol. 62, No. 2, 1954.

Scott, M. "Foreign Trade", in W. Galenson (ed.), 1979.

Sekiguchi, S. *Japanese Direct Foreign Investment* (London and Basingstoke, 1979).

Sharpton, M. "International Sub-Contracting", *Oxford Economic Papers*, Vol. 27, No. 1, 1975.

Singer, H.W. "U.S. Foreign Investment in Underdeveloped Areas — The Distribution of Gains Between Investing and Borrowing Countries", *The American Economic Review*, Vol. 40, No. 3, 1950.

──── . "Trade Expansion, Employment and Income Distribution", *Institute of Development Studies Bulletin*, Vol. 6, No. 4, 1975.

──── . "Trade Liberalization and Economic Development", in Sir Alec Cairncross and Mohinder Puri (eds.), *The Strategy of International Development* (London, 1978).

──── and J. Ansari. *Rich and Poor Countries* (London, 1982).

Squire, L. *Employment Policy in Developing Countries — A Survey of Issues and Evidence*. A World Bank Research Publication (New York, 1981).

Stern, J.J. *The Employment Impact of Industrial Investment: A Preliminary Report*. World Bank Staff Working Paper No. 255 (Washington, 1977).

──── and J.D. Lewis, *Employment Patterns and Income Growth*. World Bank Staff Working Paper No. 419 (Washington, 1980).

Stewart, F. "Technology and Employment in LDCs", *World Development*, Vol. 2, No. 3, 1974.

──── . *Technology and Underdevelopment* (London and Basingstoke, 1978).

Sung-Hwan Jo. "Overseas Direct Investment by South Korean Firms: Direction and Pattern", in K. Kumar and M.G. McLeod (eds.), 1981.

Sutcliffe, R.B. "Balanced and Unbalanced Growth", *The Quarterly Journal of Economics*, Vol. 78, No. 4, 1964.

Szentes, T. *The Political Economy of Underdevelopment* (Budapest, 1976).

Tambunlertchai, S. "Manufactured Exports and Employment in Thailand",

in P. van Dijck and H. Verbruggen (eds.), 1984.
Tan, N.A. "The Structure of Protection and Resource Flows in the Philippines", in R.M. Bautista, J.H. Power and Associates, 1979.
Teitel, S. "The Strong Factor-Intensity Assumption: Some Empirical Evidence", *Economic Development and Cultural Change*, Vol. 26, No. 2, 1978.
Thorbecke, E. "Agricultural Development", in W. Galenson (ed.), 1979.
Tsuchiya, T. "Introduction". AMPO: *Japan-Asia Quarterly Review*, Vol. 8, No. 4 and Vol. 9, Nos. 1–2 (Special Issue), 1977.
Tsurumi, Y. and R.R. Tsurumi. *Sogoshosha — Engines of Export-Based Growth* (Montreal, 1980).
Tyler, W.G. "Employment Generation and the Promotion of Manufactured Exports in Less Developed Countries: Some Suggestive Evidence", in H. Giersch (ed.), 1974.
_____. *Manufactured Export Expansion and Industrialization in Brazil* (Tübingen, 1976).
Tzong-biau Lin and V. Mok. *Employment Implications of Exports: A Case Study of Hong Kong*. Discussion Paper Series No. 78–12, Council for Asian Manpower Studies (Quezon City, 1978), mimeographed.
UNCTAD. *Study on World Demand for and Supply of Manufactures and Semi-Manufactures of Export Interest to the Developing Countries*, TD/B/C.2/91 (Geneva, 1969).
_____. *The Processing and Marketing of Primary Commodities: Approach to a Framework of International Co-operation*, TD/B/C.1/PSC/23 (Geneva, 1981).
_____. *Approach to Frameworks of International Co-operation on Processing and Marketing of Primary Commodities*, TD/B/C.1/PSC/27 (Geneva, 1982).
_____. *Export Processing Free Zones in Developing Countries: Implications for Trade and Industrialization Policies*, TD/B/C.2/211 (Geneva, 1983).
_____. *Trade and Development Report, 1985* (New York, 1985).
UNIDO, *Industrial Development Survey*, Vol. 5 (New York, 1973).
_____. *Industrial Development Survey — Special Issue for the Second General Conference of UNIDO* (New York, 1974).
_____. *World Industry since 1960: Progress and Prospects — Special Issue of the Industrial Development Survey for the Third General Conference of UNIDO* (New York, 1979).
_____. *World Industry in 1980 — Regular Issue of the Biennial Industrial Development Survey* (New York, 1981).
United Nations Centre on Transnational Corporations. *Transnational Corporations in World Development, Third Survey* (New York, 1983).
Verbruggen, H. *Gains from Export-Oriented Industrialization in Developing*

Countries — With Special Reference to South-East Asia (Amsterdam, 1985).

Vernon, R. "International Investment and International Trade in the Product Cycle", *The Quarterly Journal of Economics*, Vol. 80, No. 2, 1966.

_____. *Sovereignty at Bay — The Multinational Spread of U.S. Enterprises* (London, 1971).

Verreydt, E. and J. Waelbroeck. "European Community Protection against Manufactured Imports from Developing Countries: A Case Study in the Political Economy of Protection", in J.N. Bhagwati (ed.), 1982.

Watanabe, S. "Subcontracting, Industrialisation and Employment Creation", *International Labour Review*, Vol. 104, Nos. 1–2, 1971.

_____. "International Subcontracting, Employment and Skill Promotion", *International Labour Review*, Vol. 105, No. 5, 1972a.

_____. "Exports and Employment: The Case of the Republic of Korea", *International Labour Review*, Vol. 106, No. 6, 1972b.

_____. "Constraints on Labour-Intensive Export Industries in Mexico", *International Labour Review*, Vol. 109, No. 1, 1974.

Wells Jr., L.T. "Foreign Investors from the Third World", in K. Kumar and M.G. McLeod (eds.), 1981.

Wel-Lee Ting and Chi Schive. "Direct Investment and Technology Transfer from Taiwan", in K. Kumar and M.G. McLeod (eds.), 1981.

Westphal, L.E. "The Republic of Korea's Experience with Export-Led Industrial Development", *World Development*, Vol. 6, No. 3, 1978.

_____. *Empirical Justification for Infant Industry Protection*. World Bank Staff Working Paper No. 445 (Washington, 1981).

_____ and Kwang Suk Kim. *Industrial Policy and Development in Korea*. World Bank Staff Working Paper No. 263 (Washington, 1977).

_____, Y.W. Rhee and G. Pursell. *Korean Industrial Competence: Where It Came From*. World Bank Staff Working Paper No. 469 (Washington, 1981).

Wong, J. *ASEAN Economies in Perspective — A Comparative Study of Indonesia, Malaysia, The Philippines, Singapore and Thailand* (London and Basingstoke, 1979).

World Bank. *The Philippines, Priorities and Prospects for Development*. A World Bank Country Economic Report (Washington, 1976).

_____. *Dominican Republic: Its Main Economic Development Problems*. A World Bank Country Study (Washington, 1978).

_____. *Mexico: Manufacturing Sector: Situation, Prospects and Policies*. A World Bank Country Study (Washington, 1979a).

_____. *Bangladesh: Current Trends and Development Issues*. A World Bank Country Study (Washington, 1979b).

_____. *Uruguay: Economic Memorandum*. A World Bank Country Study

(Washington, 1979c).
_____. *Philippines: Industrial Development Strategy and Policies*. A World Bank Country Study (Washington, 1980a).
_____. *Chile: An Economy in Transition*. A World Bank Country Study (Washington, 1980b).
_____. *Madagascar: Recent Economic Developments and Future Prospects*. A World Bank Country Study (Washington, 1980c).
_____. *Morocco: Economic and Social Development Report*. A World Bank Country Study (Washington, 1981a).
_____. *Peru: Major Development Policy Issues and Recommendations*. A World Bank Country Study (Washington, 1981b).
_____. *World Development Report 1982* (New York, 1982).
_____. *China: Socialist Economic Development*, Volumes I, II and III. A World Bank Country Study (Washington, 1983a).
_____. *Brazil: Industrial Policies and Manufactured Exports*. A World Bank Country Study (Washington, 1983b).
_____. *Kenya: Growth and Structural Change*, Volumes I and II. A World Bank Country Study (Washington, 1983c).
_____. *Mauritius: Economic Memorandum: Recent Developments and Prospects*. A World Bank Country Study (Washington, 1983d).
_____ (in co-operation with The Commonwealth Secretariat). *Case Studies on Industrial Processing of Primary Products*, Volumes I and II (Washington, 1983e).
_____. *Colombia: Economic Development and Policy under Changing Conditions*. A World Bank Country Study (Washington, 1984a).
_____. *Korea: Development in a Global Context*. A World Bank Country Study (Washington, 1984b).
_____. *Ecuador: An Agenda for Recovery and Sustained Growth*. A World Bank Country Study (Washington, 1984c).
_____. *Thailand, Managing Public Resources for Structural Adjustment*. A World Bank Country Study (Washington, 1984d).
_____. *World Development Report 1985* (New York, 1985e).
_____. *Argentina: Economic Memorandum*, Volumes 1 and 2. A World Bank Country Study (Washington, 1985f).

Yeats, A.J. *Trade Barriers Facing Developing Countries — Commercial Policy Measures and Shipping* (London, 1979).

Yoshihara, K. *Foreign Investment and Domestic Response — A Study of Singapore's Industrialization* (Singapore, Kuala Lumpur and Hong Kong, 1976).

Yotopoulos, P.A. and J.B. Nugent. "A Balanced-Growth Version of the Linkage Hypothesis: A Test", *The Quarterly Journal of Economics*, Vol. 87, No. 2, 1973.

───── and J.B. Nugent. *Economics of Development — Empirical Investigations* (New York, 1976).

Young, A.K. *The Sogo Shosha: Japan's Multinational Trading Companies* (Boulder, 1979).

Yung Whee Rhee, B. Ross-Larson and G. Pursell. *Korea's Competitive Edge, Managing the Entry into World Markets* (Baltimore and London, 1984).

─────. *Instruments for Export Policy and Administration — Lessons from the East Asian Experience.* World Bank Staff Working Paper No. 725 (Washington, 1985).

Zenger, J.P. "Taiwan: Behind the Economic Miracle". AMPO: *Japan-Asia Quarterly Review*, Vol. 8, No. 4 and Vol. 9, Nos. 1–2 (Special Issue), 1977.

Subject Index

Aggregation level, 211-212, 246-247, 251
Arable land *per capita*, 37, 39-40, 48, 57-58, 61-62
Atmosphere creation, 75, 97-98, 112-113, 120, 174

Balanced versus unbalanced growth, 192-197

Capacity to liberalize, 85
Capital intensity
 see factor intensity
Comparative advantage, 4, 36-37, 100, 113, 115-122, 182, 197
Country studies
 framework of, 244-254
 Indonesia, 255-273
 Malaysia, 363-380
 the Philippines, 274-295
 Singapore, 381-415
 South Korea, 318-339
 Taiwan, 340-362
 Thailand, 296-317
 compared, 416-437

Distortion
 in domestic markets, 76, 78-79, 83-84
 in international markets, 76, 78
Domestic market size, 36-38, 42-44, 47-48, 122, 228-229
Dual economy, 37, 183-185, 236-238, 428
Dualistic trade strategy, 87, 96, 102, 113, 175, 417-418, 422

Economies of scale, 47-48, 62, 77, 180-181

Exchange rate, 80, 86, 95-96, 112
Export enclave, 4, 38, 50, 65-66, 95, 101-106, 113, 122, 236
 see also export-processing free zone
Export-output ratio, 51-62, 81, 249
Export-processing free zone (EPFZ), 3-4, 38, 50, 87, 95-96, 101-106, 112, 152, 157, 174-175, 192, 242
 in Indonesia, 258-259
 in Malaysia, 365-366, 371, 373, 375, 377
 in the Philippines, 276-277, 291
 in Singapore, 381-382, 386, 407
 in South Korea, 321, 326, 333
 in Taiwan, 343-344, 347-349, 357
 in Thailand, 298
 compared and assessed, 417-418, 427-428, 433, 435
Export strategy, 65-113, 173-175, 241-243
 see also trade and industrialization regime

Factor intensity, 122-163, 195-196, 247-248
 measures of, 250
Footloose industry, 4, 38, 117, 193, 196, 357, 407
Foreign capital, 36-37, 39-40, 96, 106-111, 113, 183, 192

Government intervention, 66-80
 see also trade and industrialization regime
Government revenue from foreign trade, 67-74, 85

Import duty revenue as proxy for protection level, 59-62, 81-84
Import leakages, 187-188, 200-207
Import substitution, 10, 18, 38, 85, 190-192, 241
    as compared to export promotion, 434-437
Income *per capita*
    in regression analysis, 44, 53-56, 144-149
    and structural change, 36-38, 45-46, 61, 102, 117, 225-228
Industrial transformation and manufactured exports, 18-26, 36-64, 171-172
Infant industry, 75-77
Input-output method
    basic features, 6, 198-200
    treatment of imports, 200-207
    some limitations, 207-212
    tables used, 251-253
International trading houses, 4, 65, 110-111, 113, 122, 175
    in South Korea, 321-322

Labour coefficient, 216-217, 250
Labour intensity
    see factor intensity
Labour-intensive products, 145-150, 153-161, 176-177
Labour-intensive sectors, 123-124, 141-142, 159-161, 176-177
Level of industrialization
    see manufacturing production — share in GDP
Linder hypothesis, 47, 104, 117, 122
Linkages, 4, 5-6, 77, 105, 184
    to primary sector, 189-190
    forward and backward, 194, 212-215, 232-234
    actual versus potential, 200-201
    lacking or weak, 236-238
    see also spread effects
Locational factors, 3, 37, 100, 106, 109

Manufactured exports
    ways to promote them, 5, 65-66, 85-113, 247
    data on performance of developing countries, 26-31
    earlier cross-country analyses, 39-45
    hypotheses regarding explanatory variables, 45-50
    results of cross-country analysis, 50-62, 172-173
    definition of, 50-51, 145, 248-249, 254
    sectoral composition, 114-169
    impact on development, 178-197
    of Indonesia, 261-266
    of Malaysia, 369-373
    of the Philippines, 280-285
    of Singapore, 391-400
    of South Korea, 326-331
    of Taiwan, 348-354
    of Thailand, 302-308
    and trade strategy, 419-423
    and production spread effects, 423-428
    and employment spread effects, 428-434
Manufacturing production
    changing shares in world production, 9-15
    growth in developed countries, 10-11, 13, 15-16
    growth in developing countries, 10-15, 16-18
    three causes of growth, 18
    value of output in developing countries, 33-35
    share in GDP, 36-38, 40, 42, 46, 56
Manufacturing sectors and their characteristics
    subdivision into NRB, E, and DMO sectors, 247, 249
    in Indonesia, 272-273
    in Malaysia, 378-380
    in the Philippines, 292-295
    in Singapore, 408-415
    in South Korea, 337-339
    in Taiwan, 360-362
    in Thailand, 313-317
    compared, 419-428

Natural-resource endowment, 36-39, 43-45, 48-49, 53-58, 61-62, 98-100, 102, 113, 229-230, 243
Neo-classical theory, 115-116
Net foreign exchange earnings, index, 220, 250
Non-economic factors, 39, 98, 120-121

SUBJECT INDEX

Population density
　see natural-resource endowment
　see population pressure
Population pressure, 39, 56–58, 62, 145–150
Population size, 36, 44, 47–48, 53–58, 61–62, 145–150
Power of dispersion, 214–215, 218, 234–235, 250–251
Product-cycle theory, 105, 118–119, 122
Production structure
　see sectoral interdependence
　see dual economy
Protection
　effective rate of, 37, 76, 82, 96, 138
　level of, 43–44, 50, 58–62
　arguments for, 74–80, 112
　effects of, 80–84, 209–210
　nominal versus effective, 208–209
　in developed countries, 435–436

Ranking of sectors, 5, 126–127, 130–136, 162, 176–177

Sectoral independence
　and level of development, 223–228
　impact of size of domestic market, 228–229
　impact of natural-resource endowment, 229–230
　hierarchy of sectors, 230–232
　patterns of, 232–238
　effect on spread effects, 238–243
　see also spread effects
Skills, skill intensity, 125–126, 149–153, 162, 177, 436
Spread effects, 5–6, 178–179, 184–187
　possibility of negative effects, 190–192
　measurement of:
　　production spread effect, 212–215
　　employment spread effect, 215–218
　　foreign exchange effect, 219–220
　　multiplier effect, 220–222
　sector-specific pattern, 234–235
　survey of empirical evidence, 238–243

comparative analysis of, 248
measures of, 250–251
in Indonesia, 267–269
in Malaysia, 373–377
in the Philippines, 285–290
in Singapore, 400–406
in South Korea, 331–335
in Taiwan, 354–358
in Thailand, 308–311
compared, 416, 423–436

Trade and industrialization regime, 36–39, 41–42, 49–50, 58–62, 65–98, 112, 120
　in Indonesia, 256–259
　in Malaysia, 364–367
　in the Philippines, 274–277
　in Singapore, 382–387
　in South Korea, 319–323
　in Taiwan, 341–344
　in Thailand, 296–299
　compared, 416–423, 434–437
Trade liberalization, 74, 85–97
Trade strategy
　see export strategy
　see trade and industrialization regime
Trade theory
　review of theories, 115–122
　strong factor-intensity assumption, 127–129
　gains from trade, 180–185
Transnational corporation (TNC), 3, 4, 65, 100–101, 105–111, 113, 122, 157

Upgrading, 4, 114, 159, 177, 322, 344, 386–387, 399, 436–437

Wage coefficient
　see labour coefficient
Wage-income multiplier, 221–222, 251
Wages, wage levels, 123–126, 137, 149–152, 162, 177, 436
Welfare, welfare function, 77, 79–80, 180, 182–183
World Bank recommendations, 86–97, 112, 174